Counsel for Kings: Wisdom and Politics in Tenth-Century Iran

VOLUME II

Edinburgh Studies in Classical Arabic Literature
Series Editors: Wen-chin Ouyang and Julia Bray

This series departs from conventional writing on Classical Arabic Literature. It integrates into its terms of enquiry both cultural and literary theory and the historical contexts and conceptual categories that shaped individual writers or works of literature. Its approach provides a forum for path-breaking research which has yet to exert an impact on the scholarship. The purpose of the series is to open up new vistas on an intellectual and imaginative tradition that has repeatedly contributed to world cultures and has the continued capacity to stimulate new thinking.

Books in the series include:

The Reader in al-Jāḥiẓ
Thomas Hefter

Recognition in the Arabic Narrative Tradition: Deliverance and Delusion
Philip F. Kennedy

Counsel for Kings: Wisdom and Politics in Tenth-Century Iran
Volume I: *The* Naṣīḥat al-mulūk *of Pseudo-Māwardī: Contexts and Themes*
L. Marlow

Counsel for Kings: Wisdom and Politics in Tenth-Century Iran
Volume II: *The* Naṣīḥat al-mulūk *of Pseudo-Māwardī: Texts, Sources and Authorities*
L. Marlow

Al- Jāḥiẓ: In Praise of Books
James E. Montgomery

Al- Jāḥiẓ: In Censure of Books
James E. Montgomery

Hikayat Abi al-Qasim*: A Literary Banquet*
Emily Selove

The Literary Qur'an
Shawkat M. Toorawa

www.edinburghuniversitypress.com

Counsel for Kings: Wisdom and Politics in Tenth-Century Iran

Volume II

The *Naṣīḥat al-mulūk* of Pseudo-Māwardī: Texts, Sources and Authorities

L. Marlow

EDINBURGH
University Press

to

SAM and DJL

Edinburgh University Press is one of the leading university presses in the UK. We publish academic books and journals in our selected subject areas across the humanities and social sciences, combining cutting-edge scholarship with high editorial and production values to produce academic works of lasting importance. For more information visit our website: www.edinburghuniversitypress.com

Edinburgh University Press Ltd
The Tun – Holyrood Road
12 (2f) Jackson's Entry
Edinburgh EH8 8PJ

Typeset in 11/15 Adobe Garamond by
Servis Filmsetting Ltd, Stockport, Cheshire

A CIP record for this book is available from the British Library

ISBN 978 0 7486 9698 7 (hardback)
ISBN 978 0 7486 9699 4 (webready PDF)
ISBN 978 1 4744 0651 2 (epub)
Volumes I and II available as a two-volume set: ISBN 978 0 7486 9756 4

Contents

Preface vi

Part I The Cultural Landscape

1 The Presentation of Counsel 3

2 Sources and Authorities: The Living Meaning of Ancient Wisdom 35

Part II The Three Governances: Translations and Commentary

3 The King's Self-governance 73

4 The Governance of the Élites 139

5 The Governance of the Common People 197

Conclusion 246

Notes 253

Bibliography 315

Index 369

Preface

Wisdom and Politics in Tenth-Century Iran attempts a contextualised reading of a tenth-century mirror for princes. Stated in the broadest terms, Volume I concentrated on the environment that produced the mirror and to which it responded; Volume II focuses on the structure, logic, characteristics and techniques displayed in the text. The distinction is imprecise; it is assumed that the text and its many contexts are, for most purposes, inseparably linked. The emphasis in Volume II is placed upon the mirror's construction of meaning for its tenth-century audience. The notes to this volume provide several cross-references, which, it is hoped, will facilitate the reader's movement from one volume to the other.

This second volume of *Wisdom and Politics in Tenth-Century Iran* explores parts of Pseudo-Māwardī's text. Part I, in two chapters, addresses the cultural–literary context for *Naṣīḥat al-mulūk*. Chapter 1 discusses Pseudo-Māwardī's preface and first chapter, both of which deal with counsel (*naṣīḥa*). Chapter 2 situates the mirror in the context of the cultural and literary activities of tenth-century eastern Iran, and studies Pseudo-Māwardī's use of an extensive and diverse set of authorities. Part II discusses Pseudo-Māwardī's three central chapters, devoted to the three 'governances' of practical philosophy. Chapter 3 explores Pseudo-Māwardī's fifth chapter, 'On the governance and discipline of the self'; Chapter 4 concentrates on his sixth chapter, 'On the governance of the élites'; and Chapter 5 discusses his seventh chapter, 'On the governance of the common people'. In order to portray the sequence of Pseudo-Māwardī's exposition, each chapter in Part II of this volume follows the corresponding chapter in *Naṣīḥat al-mulūk*.

Of particular importance in Volume II are Pseudo-Māwardī's numerous and diverse citations, paraphrases and allusions. By these devices Pseudo-

Māwardī integrates into his text several additional voices, among them the Qurʾānic voice, and the voices of prophetic, historical, narrative and poetic utterance. The materials that he cites and to which he alludes did not carry single or fixed meanings. Volume II studies Pseudo-Māwardī's methods of instilling meanings into these materials, the significance of which he thereby expanded and renewed for contemporaneous audiences.

The three chapters that comprise Part II of this volume attempt to convey Pseudo-Māwardī's general arguments and specific points, and the techniques and materials that he employed in order to communicate them in a persuasive manner. Accordingly, Part II presents large sections of the text in translation. For reasons of length it has not been possible to reproduce all Pseudo-Māwardī's quotations and narratives in the translated passages. As Chapter 2 seeks to demonstrate, Pseudo-Māwardī adduced a copious number of materials, of particularly diverse provenance, in order to present, develop and win his audience's assent for his points. Although in its arrangement the text often presents a statement followed by supporting examples and quotations, these materials, invoked by citation or allusion, are not separable from but are rather integral parts of Pseudo-Māwardī's text. I have aimed in the chapters of Part II to include at least some examples of each type of material that Pseudo-Māwardī uses to formulate, illustrate, support and illuminate the arguments of his exposition. The translated passages therefore include Qurʾānic verses, Prophetic ḥadīth, *āthār* passed down from the Prophet's Companions and individuals of the early Islamic period; quotations from texts of Middle Persian provenance; quotations from Arabic authors; narrative accounts (*akhbār*); and verses of Arabic poetry (*ashʿār*). I hope to provide some indication of how these varied materials contributed to Pseudo-Māwardī's conception and articulation of his points, and how his use of them encouraged his audience to draw specific inferences. The notes include some references to earlier and near-contemporary occurrences of Pseudo-Māwardī's citations; the invaluable editions of al-Ḥadīthī and Aḥmad, in particular, provide further references, including to occurrences in texts written later than *Naṣīḥat al-mulūk*.

In order to provide the non-linguist with independent access to the text, and to convey the interconnections among different parts of Pseudo-Māwardī's presentation, I have included key terms in Arabic and Persian in parentheses. I have also used parentheses to indicate terms or phrases that represent my interpretation of a passage, but that do not appear in the Arabic. Where an English rendering clarifies a sense already implicit in the Arabic, I have not usually felt it necessary to indicate the clarification in the translation. Square brackets denote information designed to illuminate the significance of a reference or allusion in the text.

Some passages of *Naṣīḥat al-mulūk* that were adduced for discussion in Volume I were drawn from the fifth, sixth and seventh chapters of the mirror, and consequently they are mentioned again in Part II. For the most part, I have not reproduced these passages in this volume. Instead, I have indicated where the extracts fall in the context of the complete literary work, and referred the reader to the earlier discussion. I have made some comparisons with earlier and near-contemporary writers' treatments of Pseudo-Māwardī's topics. Among other examples, the advisory and moralising writings of the eighth-century Ibn al-Muqaffa^{c} and the later tenth-century Abū l-Layth al-Samarqandī, both of whom addressed several of the subjects treated in *Naṣīḥat al-mulūk*, provide instructive points of reference. I have also indicated *Naṣīḥat al-mulūk*'s anticipation of later Arabic and Persian mirrors for princes, especially those composed in or linked to the eastern Iranian regions. A reading of Pseudo-Māwardī's three central chapters compels attention to his theological and philosophical as well as his literary context. The methods and doctrines of the Baghdadi Mu^{c}tazila, especially the distinctive thought of Abū l-Qāsim al-Ka^{c}bī, have left a deep imprint in these chapters, and several examples have been noted as they occur in the text. Mu^{c}tazilite concepts and language appear in a particularly marked fashion in Pseudo-Māwardī's fifth and longest chapter, discussed in Chapter 3 of the present volume. The index to this volume includes several topics also listed in the index to Volume I, to which the interested reader is also referred.

PART I

THE CULTURAL LANDSCAPE

1

The Presentation of Counsel

Mirrors for princes, an ancient and ubiquitous genre of literature, perform many functions for their authors and for their recipients. Authors addressed predictable themes and availed themselves of familiar materials, and the very durability of these elements across vast expanses of time and space lends an abstract and timeless appearance to their compositions.[1] With reference to a significant example, this book seeks to demonstrate that mirrors nevertheless responded to specific historical moments and to the character and exigencies of specific relationships. In the context of the limits imposed by the inequality in power of author and recipient, it was, indeed, the appeal to perennial and universal wisdom that facilitated commentary in the present. Read within the context that Volume I attempted to establish, *Naṣīḥat al-mulūk* displays the highly particularised kind of communication that the mirror for princes made possible.

Structure and Literary Characteristics

Naṣīḥat al-mulūk is among the earliest book-length mirrors in Arabic. Its principal predecessor, the ninth-century *Kitāb al-Tāj*, approaches it in scale but differs from it in scope and complexity; extant tenth-century examples appear in smaller forms.[2] Pseudo-Māwardī conceived of his composition as a 'book'; he refers repeatedly to 'this book of ours' (*kitābunā hādhā*), and displays his presiding presence in the text by means of ample internal cross-references.[3] The mirror consists of ten thematic chapters. Pseudo-Māwardī's contemporary al-Yaᶜqūbī (d. after 292/905) reported having seen a version of *Kalīla wa-Dimna* in ten chapters, a form also evident in the later tenth-century 'Long Form' of the Pseudo-Aristotelian *Sirr al-asrār* ('Secret of Secrets'), the advisory text that, addressed to Alexander, includes political counsels and treats an eclectic set of topics deemed relevant to kings and the ruling élites, later known in Europe as *Secretum secretorum*.[4] These two texts, the Arabic versions of which circulated across Eurasia and provided the basis for translations into numerous languages, including Persian, Turkish, Hebrew, Latin, Castilian, Provençal, French, English and German, were, with *Bilawhar wa-Būdhāṣaf*, the most widely disseminated wisdom-related texts of the period. Ibn Qutayba (213–76/828–89) had adopted a subject-based ten-part form for his anthology *ᶜUyūn al-akhbār* ('Choice Accounts'), the first 'book' of which is entitled the 'Book of Authority' (*Kitāb al-Sulṭān*).[5] *Naṣīḥat al-mulūk* recapitulates the ten-chapter format and shares in the extensive cultural repertoires that shaped these diverse texts.

In its form, Pseudo-Māwardī's *Naṣīḥat al-mulūk* suggests the convergence of several literary vehicles, among them the 'testament' (*waṣiyya* or *ᶜahd*), the *adab* encyclopaedia (or anthology) and the philosophical treatise. In a work that combines the distinctive qualities and characteristic techniques of these genres, Pseudo-Māwardī seeks to persuade his audience by means of sequenced argument; he develops each point through the reasoned extrapolation of copious and varied exemplary texts.

First among the genres that contributed to the formation of the book-length mirror is the *waṣiyya* or *ᶜahd*, the 'testament' or 'charge'. The *waṣiyya*, usually in continuous prose and of variable length, had flourished in Arabic well before the rise of Islam. In the early Islamic period the genre enjoyed a prolific production, in part stimulated by interaction with the substantial repertoire of Middle Persian *andarz*, 'advice', rendered into Arabic, usually under the rubric of *ᶜahd*.[6] Testaments, often composed in the voice of a king or a father, characteristically addressed a particular individual, often the writer's son, for a specific purpose or to mark a particular occasion. Frequently, testaments convey the elderly author's last instructions to his heirs or mark the transfer of power from a king to his successor. Sometimes the speaker addresses a larger but still identified constituency, such as the king's officials at the time of their appointment or even, on the occasion of a ruler's accession, the generality of the subjects.

The author of the *waṣiyya* or *ᶜahd*, regardless of its subject matter and occasion, invariably addressed his recipient(s) directly.[7] Direct address, by a variety of formal means, remained an abiding feature of the genre, in accordance with Ibn Qutayba's prescriptions.[8] In the moralising and exhortative variant of the testament, authors frequently began their address with the distinctive formulation, 'I commend you to godliness' (*ūṣīkum bi-taqwā Allāh*), a Prophetic utterance that shaped the genre's development, and became an established feature of the *khuṭba* delivered in conjunction with the Friday noon-time prayer. The *khuṭba*, marked by the extensive use of parallelism, also came to include, from Umayyad times, public prayer on behalf of the ruler, and provided the occasion for the community's acknowledgement of the ruler's authority; this responsibility complemented the subjects' duty to offer prayers on the ruler's behalf.[9]

The commendation *ūṣīkum bi-taqwā Allāh* marks the opening of numerous testaments in which men of learning and piety addressed their students and followers; the (*Kitāb*) *al-ʿĀlim wa-l-mutaʿallim* ('Book of the Learned and the Learner') transmitted from Abū Ḥanīfa, to provide a single example, illustrates the pattern.[10] The widely disseminated *waṣiyya* or *ʿahd* of Ṭāhir b. al-Ḥusayn (r. 205–7/821–2), leader of al-Maʾmūn's forces in his war against his brother al-Amīn (r. 193–8/809–13) and founding figure of the Tahirid dynasty in Khurasan, similarly begins with the direct injunction: 'It is incumbent upon you that you commit yourself to godliness . . . cling to the well-being with which God has enveloped you by remaining mindful of your final return (in the afterlife) and that towards which you are proceeding' (*ʿalayka bi-taqwā llāh . . . wa-lzam mā albasaka Allāh min al-ʿāfiya bi-l-dhikr li-maʿādika wa-mā anta ṣāʾir ilayhi*).[11] The occasion for Ṭāhir's composition of his testament was his son ʿAbdallāh's appointment to the governorship of Diyar Rabiʿa in 206/821. The testament immediately acquired a large circulation,[12] and although Pseudo-Māwardī does not cite it, he was almost certainly familiar with it. Later Persian works perpetuate the form of the sage advice of a father to his son or of an elderly king to his heir, and they mirror the semblance of intimacy between author and addressee. The *Pandnāmeh* ('Book of Advice') attributed to Sebüktigin (r. 366–87/977–97), a general under the Samanids and the father of Sultan Maḥmūd of Ghazna, takes the form of an advisory testament to the author's son (*īn ast naṣīḥat va-vaṣiyyat-i man*, 'this is my counsel and testament'),[13] and the much longer *Qābūsnāmeh* ('Book of Qābūs', 475/1082–3) of the Ziyarid ruler Kaykāʾūs (r. *c.* 441–80/1049–87 in the Caspian regions of Tabaristan and Gurgan) constitutes the solicitous father's counsel to his son Gīlānshāh, whom the author seeks to prepare for the various eventualities that might befall him.

Though in some respects informed by the moralising genres of the *waṣiyya* and *andarz*, *Naṣīḥat al-mulūk* departs from the pattern of direct address and approaches its unnamed recipient in an oblique manner. With continual invocations of 'the king', 'the resolute king', 'the religiously observant king' or 'the virtuous kings', the author employs the third person (sometimes in the plural form) to offer advice through the use of statements. These statements sometimes commence with implicitly imperative formulations, such as *wa-yajibu ᶜalā l-malik* ('it is incumbent upon the king') or *wa-yanbaghī anna l-malik* ('it is fitting that the king'), but the indirect nature of the author's address removes the appearance of intimate acquaintance between author and recipient and conveys an effort to persuade rather than to exhort.

A second contributor, and companion, to the book-length mirror was the *adab* anthology or encyclopaedia. Exemplified by the collections of Ibn Qutayba and the Andalusian writer and anthologist Ibn ᶜAbd Rabbih (246–328/860–940), both of whom privileged the topic of power (*sulṭān*) by placing it first, the encyclopaedic anthology offered a collection of narrative materials, aphorisms and verses organised according to subject matter.[14] Such anthologies were arranged for the instruction and enjoyment of a readership with broad interests, and especially for individuals whose professional and personal positions required them to demonstrate familiarity with and add to the store of such material.[15] The incorporation of such *akhbār* (narrative reports) and *ashᶜār* (verses of poetry) into works dedicated to various topics constituted one of the principal hallmarks of tenth-century Arabic prose.[16] Pseudo-Māwardī was among the first authors of a book-length mirror to adopt the approach of the anthologists in his assembling, and shaping to his purpose, of a large assortment of *akhbār* and *ashᶜār*.[17] Whereas in his testament Ṭāhir b. al-Ḥusayn had employed only a very small number of exclusively Qurʾānic citations, Pseudo-Māwardī, as Chapter 2 will demonstrate, adduced explicit quotations ascribed to authorities of diverse provenance and association. These materials illuminate the cosmopolitan cultural world in which Pseudo-Māwardī and his audience participated, and they indicate the incidental function of his mirror as a mechanism for cultural transmission. The primary and ostensible function of offering counsel on the subject of governance linked the authors and audiences of mirrors in a shared remembrance of the past. Invocation of the experiences and pronouncements of bygone kings and sages, adduced by way of indirect commentary on the circumstances of the present, constitutes a prevalent feature of the advisory genre.[18] Pseudo-Māwardī displays a creative engagement with the past in his discursive exposition and in his careful choice of illustrative materials, which he renews and reinvigorates.

Although the lack of extant sources obviates definitive demonstration, I shall propose that the philosophical treatise constituted a third component in the genesis of *Naṣīḥat al-mulūk*. Pseudo-Māwardī employs the intellectual procedures of logical deduction, linguistic analysis and point-by-point enumeration. It is quite likely that the several Kindian compositions devoted to *siyāsa*, governance, informed the organisation, contents and method of the Pseudo-Māwardian work.[19] Of the nearly three hundred titles of al-Kindī's works listed by Ibn al-Nadīm, about ten are described as his books on matters related to governance (*kutubuhu al-siyāsiyyāt*), a category that subsumed ethics as well as politics.[20] Al-Kindī's students, al-Sarakhsī (d. 286/899) and Abū Zayd al-Balkhī (d. 322/934) also composed works devoted to *siyāsa*. Al-Sarakhsī produced a *Kitāb al-Siyāsa al-kabīr* ('Greater Book of Governance'), a *Kitāb al-Siyāsa al-ṣaghīr* ('Lesser Book of Governance'), as well as works titled *Ādāb al-mulūk* ('Customs of Kings') and *Zād al-musāfir wa-khidmat al-mulūk* ('Provisions for the Traveller and the Service of Kings').[21] Abū Zayd al-Balkhī, according to most writers from Ibn al-Nadīm onwards, composed a *Kitāb al-Siyāsa al-kabīr* and a *Kitāb al-Siyāsa al-ṣaghīr*; additionally, Yāqūt and al-Ṣafadī list a *Kitāb Adab al-sulṭān wa-l-raᶜiyya* ('Instruction for the Ruler and the Subjects'), and al-Ṣafadī also records a work titled *Faḍl al-mulk* (*al-malik*) ('Excellence of Kingship' [or 'of the King']).[22] Al-Ṣafadī refers to a *Kitāb al-Siyāsa* ('Book of Governance') composed by al-Balkhī for a certain Yānis al-Khādim, who was 'at that time governor of Balkh' (*wa-huwa idh dhāka wālī Balkh*).[23] Although the lack of surviving texts prevents demonstration of the hypothesis, it seems likely that the cluster of writings produced by al-Kindī and his intellectual descendants represented a distinctive approach to the subject of governance. A later exponent of the Kindian tradition in the eastern regions, Abū Zayd al-Balkhī's student Ibn Farīghūn, composed an instructive work, *Jawāmiᶜ al-ᶜulūm* ('Compendium of the Sciences') in a 'ramified' form (*tashjīr*); Pseudo-Māwardī's technique of numbering his points might lend itself to a similar presentation.[24]

Of particular significance to the literary context that produced *Naṣīḥat al-mulūk* is the oeuvre of Ibn al-Muqaffaᶜ (d. *c.* 139/757), a major contributor, through his translations from Middle Persian and his compositions in Arabic, to the formation of Arabic literary culture. Pseudo-Māwardī displays a thorough familiarity with the Arabic versions of Middle Persian *andarz*, for which Ibn al-Muqaffaᶜ was a principal mediator. As the examples of his quotations from, and allusions to, the 'Testament' of Ardashīr, discussed in Volume I, already suggest, Pseudo-Māwardī incorporates large numbers of explicit quotations from this repertoire, which also informed much of the conceptual and lexical framework of his presentation. Only a portion of Middle Persian *andarz* was concerned exclusively with kingship; much of the literature offered moral guidance appropriate for all humanity. In keeping with this outlook, Pseudo-Māwardī frequently remarks that a virtuous practice concerns all persons, but is especially important for kings, since their conduct affects everyone else.[25] He almost certainly possessed a thorough acquaintance with the writings of Ibn al-Muqaffaᶜ, whom he cites once by name and to whom he perhaps alludes when he refers to *ṣāḥib Kalīla wa-Dimna*, 'the author of *Kalīla wa-Dimna*'.[26] By means of his translations from Middle Persian and his compositions in Arabic prose,[27] Ibn al-Muqaffaᶜ sought to convey the wisdom of the past for the benefit of the people of his time; in *(Kitāb) al-Ādāb al-kabīr* ('Greater Book of Rules of Comportment'), he praised the writings of previous generations in fulsome terms and portrayed his work as a replication of their insights for the purposes of his contemporaries (*al-nās*).[28] While his text is replete with inter-textual references, Ibn al-Muqaffaᶜ does not include explicit quotations in *al-Ādāb al-kabīr*; his unacknowledged 'quotations' are fully integrated into his composition.[29] The book reflects Ibn al-Muqaffaᶜ's sensitivity to the perilous role of the royal counsellor when he encourages the prince to heed disagreeable advice from qualified persons: 'Accustom yourself to patience in the face of those who disagree with you and offer advice, and to swallowing the bitterness of their words and justice (*ᶜawwid nafsaka al-ṣabra ᶜalā man khālafaka min dhawī l-naṣīḥa wa-l-tajarruᶜ li-marārat qawlihim wa-ᶜadlihim*); (but) do not facilitate such access except to people of intellect, seniority and manly virtue (*illā li-ahl al-ᶜaql wa-l-sinn wa-l-muruwwa*).'[30] *Naṣīḥat al-mulūk* reflects the continuing importance of the Middle Persian repertoire, adapted into Arabic through the literary activities of Ibn al-Muqaffaᶜ and other writers of the late Umayyad and early Abbasid periods, in shaping ideas and providing a prestigious and authoritative vocabulary for literary expression pertaining to kingship and governance in the tenth-century eastern regions. *Kitāb al-Saᶜāda wa-l-isᶜād* ('Book of Felicity and the Production of Felicity'), the work of an otherwise unknown individual named Ibn Abī Dharr,[31] reflects a cultural context similar to that of Pseudo-Māwardī. It is telling that Ibn Abī Dharr cites the *Khudaynāmeh* ('Register of the Kings'), the Sasanian royal chronicle, in adducing a variant of the first part of Ibn al-Muqaffaᶜ's advice: 'It is fitting that you accustom yourself to patience in the face of opposition from a person endowed with judgement and counsel' (*yanbaghī an tuᶜawwida nafsaka al-ṣabra ᶜalā khilāf dhī l-raʾy wa-l-naṣīḥa*).[32]

In a more overt demonstration of the significance that he attached to the role of the royal adviser, Ibn al-Muqaffaᶜ ventured into the uncertain terrain of the uninvited subordinate when he undertook the composition of an unsolicited work of counsel in response to the exigencies of a specific historical moment. He wrote his epistle *Kitāb* (or *Risāla fī*) *al-Ṣaḥāba* ('Book on the [Ruler's] Companions', *c.* 136/754) for the benefit of a caliph whom, prudentially, he did not identify by name.[33] Nor did he address his intended audience in the direct manner characteristic of the *waṣiyya*. He understood the sensitive nature of addressing advice to a ruler who was unlikely to welcome implicit criticism, and took pains to situate his writings in the context of the royal duty to receive and heed counsel. In *Risāla fī l-ṣaḥāba*, Ibn al-Muqaffaᶜ emphasises the moral responsibilities of a group among the caliph's companions (*ṣaḥāba*), 'specialists in (juristic) understanding, normative practice, customs and counsel, [persons] who instruct, strengthen and remind the people in their midst, cause them to perceive error, fortify them against ignorance, restrain them from innovations, caution them against strife, and investigate their affairs' (*ahl al-fiqh wa-l-sunna wa-l-siyar wa-l-naṣīḥa muʾaddibūna muqawwimūna yudhakkirūna wa-yubṣirūna al-khaṭaʾ wa-yuᶜizzūna ᶜan al-jahl wa-yamnaᶜūna ᶜan al-bidaᶜ wa-yuḥadhdhirūna al-fitan wa-yatafaqqadūna umūr ᶜāmmat man huwa bayna aẓhurihim*).[34] As the following pages will show, Pseudo-Māwardī, fully cognisant of the danger that he, too, courted in composing an unsolicited and implicitly critical work of counsel, sought, through the adoption of the strategies employed by his predecessor, to create a moment in which it might yet find a reception.

While his perspective and vocabulary were clearly shaped by his region's inherited wisdom, Pseudo-Māwardī's *Naṣīḥat al-mulūk* exhibits few points of formal resemblance with Middle Persian *andarz*. It includes, for instance, very few gnomic sentences expressed in terms of riddles or numerical formulations. Rarely, Pseudo-Māwardī's quotations from older materials, such as the 'Wisdom of the House of David' (*ḥikmat Āl Dāʾūd*) and *Kalīla wa-Dimna*, display the technique of enumeration ubiquitous in Middle Persian *andarz*; in one example, he reports:

> They have said: I found in the 'Wisdom of the House of David': It is appropriate for the intelligent person that he should not neglect four hours: an hour in which he takes account (*yuḥāsib*) of his self, an hour in which he communes with his Lord, an hour in which he secludes himself with his trusted people who are honest with him regarding his faults and advise him regarding his self, and an hour in which he attends to his pleasures in that which is licit and appealing; for this (last) hour is an assistance against those (former) hours and a respite for hearts.[35]

Pseudo-Māwardī employs this enumerative technique only if it appears in his chosen citations. As previously stated, he frequently numbers his points, or the components of an issue that he proceeds to expound; several examples of this characteristic appear in his fifth, sixth and seventh chapters, corresponding to Chapters 3, 4 and 5 in this volume. But Pseudo-Māwardī employs this technique in order to organise and sequence the facets of his arguments, and not to provide an axiomatic number-driven encapsulation in the manner of Middle Persian *andarz*.

Notwithstanding the various literary and intellectual strands that contributed to the composition of *Naṣīḥat al-mulūk*, it remains, in its form, content and method, a mirror of striking individuality.

The Preface

Pseudo-Māwardī, like Ibn al-Muqaffaʿ, strives to win a receptive audience for his advisory project, and he uses the introduction to *Naṣīḥat al-mulūk* as a means to establish a cooperative relationship with his readers and listeners. The introduction, as Peter Freimark observes, connects the work to its context.[36]

Pseudo-Māwardī begins his book in this manner:

> We open with praise of God. In Him we place our trust, and on Him we call for assistance towards every objective; and we beseech Him for success and support.
>
> We say: Among the factors that induced us to compose this book – in addition to what we knew of God's prompting – may His mention be exalted – of the intelligent (*al-ᶜuqalāᵓ*) among His servants to seek recompense, and the ascendancy in the natures of the virtuous (*ṭabāᵓiᶜ al-fuḍalāᵓ*) of a love for the perpetuation of memory – were God's words, may He be exalted and glorified: 'And when God took a covenant (*mīthāq*) with those who had received the Book, (He said) You are to expound it to humankind, and not to hide it' (3: 187). And His words: 'Those who hide the clear proofs and guidance that We have sent down, after We had made it clear to humankind in the Book, God curses them and those who curse, curse them' (2: 159).
>
> Next, (there is) that which we have related (*rawaynā*) from our Prophet, may God bless him and grant him peace: 'He who possesses knowledge and conceals it, God will restrain him with a bridle of fire on the Day of Resurrection.'[37] We have also related from him: 'Religion is counsel' (*innamā al-dīn al-naṣīḥa*). He was asked, 'For whom, O Messenger of God?' He replied, 'For the sake of God and His Messenger, and for the benefit of the leaders of the Muslims and their community as a whole' (*lillāh wa-li-rasūlihi wa-li-aᵓimmat al-muslimīn wa-jamāᶜatihim*).[38]
>
> It is related from Jarīr b. ᶜAbdallāh that he said: 'I pledged allegiance to the Messenger of God and committed myself to hear and obey, and to sincere counsel for every Muslim' (*ᶜalā al-samᶜ wa-l-ṭāᶜa wa-l-nuṣḥ li-kull muslim*).[39]
>
> Kings are the most appropriate of people to whom counsels (*naṣāᵓiḥ*) should be directed, and the most fitting to receive words of admonition (*mawāᶜiẓ*),

since in their goodness (*ṣalāḥ*) lies the goodness of the subjects and in their corruption (*fasād*) the corruption of the world (*barriyya*). On this matter the earliest kings (*al-mulūk al-awwalūn*) used to say: 'A good ruler is better than a time of abundance.'[40] They said: 'He who misleads (*ghashsha*) the leader (*imām*) deceives the common people, even if he fancies himself a (sincere) counsellor (*munāṣiḥ*) to the common people.' And they used to say: 'He who deceives (*ghashsha*) the agent (*ᶜāmil*) never (sincerely) advised an act.'[41]

An illustrious sage (*jalīl min al-ḥukamāʾ*) once said, 'Of God's claim(s) (*min ḥaqq Allāh*) over humanity, (recognition of) the divine unity and obedience (*al-tawḥīd wa-l-ṭāᶜa*) are mandatory, and of the ruler's claim(s) (*min ḥaqq al-sulṭān*), affection and counsel (*al-wadd wa-l-naṣīḥa*) (are mandatory).'[42]

It used to be said, 'He who withholds his counsel from the ruler, his illness from the doctors, and his sorrow from his brothers betrays himself.'[43]

They said: Kisrā Abarwīz [= Khusraw II Parvīz, r. 591–628] used to say: 'He who does not do right by his king, despite his dependence on him for his own harm or benefit, does not do right by himself, and he who is not right with himself has no good in him.'[44]

For in counselling the ruler (*fī naṣīḥat al-sulṭān*) lies counsel for all, and in counselling the whole lies guidance towards the well-being (*maṣlaḥa*) of the world altogether, and the ordering of the affairs of the whole. Accordingly the person who dispenses it (advice) hopes for the reward of the temporal world and the world to come, and for recompense in the realms of life and death. For this reason it was customary among the prophets that God would send them to the kings of peoples or to their (entire) communities (*ilā mulūk al-umam aw jamāᶜatihim*), rather than to the individuals among their subjects one after another. (He acted in this way) because the person of the king alone suffices for everyone who is within his kingdom and under his governance, and because when the ruler (*al-rāᶜī*, shepherd) inclines towards a path (*madhhab*) the subjects (*al-raᶜiyya*, flock) incline towards it also, and when the king exercises restraint in (a mode of) conduct (*idhā zahuda fī sīratin*) the common people exercise restraint in it as well. The careers of most of the pseudo-prophets (*amr akthar al-mutanabbiʾīn*), who have desired the corruption of the world and of religion (*fasād al-dunyā wa-l-dīn*), have followed the same path.

So we wrote this book of ours as a counsel for kings (*naṣīḥatan lil-mulūk*) and as a demonstration of love for them (*iẓhāran li-maḥabbatihim*), in solicitude for them and for their subjects (*ishfāqan ᶜalā anfusihim wa-raᶜāyāhum*). We hope that he who comes across this book of ours with its contents of truthful advice (*ṣādiq al-naṣīḥa*) and forceful admonition (*balīgh al-mawᶜiẓa*), and gives it a share of his attention by glancing at it, reflecting on it and paying attention to it, will know that we are among his greatest friends in (terms of) counsel (*ᶜalima annā min aᶜẓam awliyāʾihi lahu naṣīḥatan*) and among his most loyal servants and supporters in (terms of proffering) assistance (*wa-ablagh khadamihi wa-aᶜwānihi lahu maᶜūnatan*).[45] For the kings (*mulūk*) and leaders (*sāsa*) who accept this counsel and act in accordance with it, God will join their temporal kingship to the eternal in the Abode of Permanence and the Place of the Righteous, in a dominion that never vanishes away and a felicity that never perishes, where pleasure is never mixed with pain, happiness never clouded by care, joy never mingled with sorrow, wealth never overtaken later by poverty, and health is such that sickness is not to be feared. (By such observance) he will attain the fullest extent of his aspirations, and the pinnacle of his desires. Moreover, it (the book and the advice it contains) will do much to relieve him of (his dependence on) soldiers, assistants, commanders and cavalrymen (*al-junūd wa-l-aᶜwān wa-l-quwwād wa-l-fursān*), and to protect him against attacks from his enemies and the ruses of his opponents. It will win him an abundance of friends, and unleash for him, and on his behalf, voices of praise and prayer (*alsinat al-thanāʾ wa-l-duᶜāʾ*), in support of, and in affection for him.[46]

It will make his kingdom prosperous, his days full and flourishing, his élites (*khawāṣṣ*) content, his subjects obedient and quiescent, his lands peaceful, his roads secure, his wealth (*amwāl*) copious, his enemies conquered and subdued, his stature rising during his lifetime and his memory enduring after his death. It will banish from him excessive preoccupations, and rid him of oppressive burdens, for if a wished-for bounty eludes him in his life, if a portion of that which he desires evades him, God will compensate him for it with something of higher value and greater importance, something more complete, more beneficial, more abundant and more splendid, according to God's true promise and true speech: God does not break His promises (*wa-llāh lā yukhlifu l-mīᶜāda*).[47]

But we have not limited ourselves in our book to our own opinions, and we have not relied in anything that we have said or mentioned on our own inclinations (*lā naᶜtamidu fī shayʾin naqūluhu ᶜalā hawānā*) without adducing proofs for it from God's speech – may He be exalted and glorified – as sent down in His Book; the sayings of His Messenger, peace be upon him, as transmitted in the traditions related from him (*fī sunanihi wa-āthārihi*); then (*thumma*) the conduct of the early kings (*siyar al-mulūk al-awwalīn*) and of the leaders of the past (*al-aʾimma al-māḍīna*), the Rightly Guided Caliphs (*al-khulafāʾ al-rāshidīn*), the ancient sages of bygone communities and ages past (*al-ḥukamāʾ al-mutaqaddimīn fī l-umam al-khāliya wa-l-ayyām al-māḍiya*). For these persons are the most deserving of being imitated (*awlā bi-l-taqlīd*) in that which they said, followed in that which they related, and emulated in that which they established as an example.[48]

We saw fit to gather the material that we intended to assemble into ten chapters:

Chapter One: On urging the acceptance of counsels;

Chapter Two: Clarification of the lofty nature of kingship and kings, and the qualities that they should adopt, the qualities that are appropriate to their stations and correspond to their ranks;

Chapter Three: Clarification of the factors that cause disorder (*ikhtilāl*) and corruption (*fasād*) to appear in kingdoms and in the conditions of kings;

Chapter Four: Aphorisms of exhortation (*fuṣūl min al-mawāᶜiẓ*) that are beneficial, provide a cure for the hardness of hearts, and facilitate recovery from the sicknesses induced by the passions and the illnesses that arise from the appetites;

Chapter Five: On the governance and discipline of the self;

Chapter Six: On the governance of the élites, including the ruler's family and children, relatives, retainers (*khadam*) and troops;

Chapter Seven: On the governance of the common people and managing the people of the kingdom;

Chapter Eight: On managing, collecting and dispensing wealth;
Chapter Nine: On managing enemies;
Chapter Ten: On establishing intentions (*niyyāt*) and seeking interpretations (*taʾwīlāt*) for several matters that many scholars and men of rational intellect (*al-ʿulamāʾ wa-l-ʿuqalāʾ*) consider reprehensible and concerning which kings should possess a clear understanding.[49]

As this section shows, Pseudo-Māwardī begins his book with a brief doxology.[50] Following this statement of praise for God, Pseudo-Māwardī explains his act of composition and, with the support of Qurʾānic texts, Prophetic ḥadīth, and wise sayings transmitted from ancient kings and sages, seeks to situate it in the context that he shared with his audience. He introduces the first pair of Prophetic utterances in his book with the phrase *rawaynā*, 'we have related', and thereby signals his position as an authority in the transmission of ḥadīth on the subject of *naṣīḥa*.

Having established, through his quotations from the sacred sources, the universal obligation of *naṣīḥa*, Pseudo-Māwardī asserts the particular appropriateness of offering counsel to kings, for which purpose he turns from the sacred sources to human wisdom. He invokes three sayings that he attributes in generic fashion to 'the ancient kings', introduced by the phrases *wa-li-dhālika mā kāna al-mulūk al-awwalūn yaqūlūna, wa-qālū, wa-kānū yaqūlūna* ('in this vein the ancient kings used to say', 'they said', 'they used to say').[51] These three aphorisms, in the course of which sincere advice is counter-posed to deception, appear, similarly marked as examples of inherited wisdom, in *ʿAhd Ardashīr*.[52] Given their appearance as unattributed remarks in *ʿAhd Ardashīr*, it is possible that Pseudo-Māwardī, like the transmitter(s) of *ʿAhd Ardashīr*, knew them as detached maxims rather than as identifiable 'quotations'. Yet, whereas in the body of his book, Pseudo-Māwardī cites frequently and explicitly from *ʿAhd Ardashīr*, the value of which he praises on more than one occasion, it is a feature of his introduction and epilogue that he refrains from identifying the specific provenance of his non-sacred sources. He follows this trio of 'quotations' from 'the ancient kings' with further maxims, attributed to an unidentified 'great sage' or 'illustrious philosopher' (*jalīl min al-ḥukamāʾ*) and ancient oral lore (*wa-kāna yuqālu, wa-qālū*, 'it used to be said'); the last of these examples concerns Kisrā Abarwīz (= the

Sasanian monarch Khusraw II Parvīz, r. 591–628), the sole speaker other than the Prophet whose name is specified in the introduction.[53] The lack of specificity in the introduction and epilogue, in contrast to much of the body of *Naṣīḥat al-mulūk*, lends a different quality to these framing sections, which employ allusion in order to foster the audience's receptivity to the presented work.

Pseudo-Māwardī next asserts the dependence of the entirety of the people on their kings, who set an example for their subjects. Kings' need to rectify themselves, in their inner and outer lives, because their subjects would follow their example, for good or ill, was a well-established theme in late antique wisdom literature, and Pseudo-Māwardī is likely to have encountered it in the oral and written literatures of his region.[54] Because his subordinates respond to his behaviour and their subordinates respond in turn to counsel, the king was, in effect, to counsel his subjects, and such counsel constituted a religious and moral obligation. Introducing the linkage of kingship and religion, Pseudo-Māwardī avers that God sent His prophets not to individuals, but to the kings of the nations or to entire communities, and that most pseudo-prophets had adopted the same strategy. Though fleeting, Pseudo-Māwardī's reference to pseudo-prophets, and his implied warning that pseudo-prophets had sought out kings, hint at the forceful exposition of the dangers of heterodoxy that will follow.[55] Pseudo-Māwardī describes his composition as an offering of sincere advice for kings (*naṣīḥatan lil-mulūk*), and it is possible that it was this phrase that inspired the librarian or owner to label the single manuscript with the 'title' 'Counsel for Kings' by which it is known today.[56] Pseudo-Māwardī also describes his work as a gesture of 'love' for kings and a mark of his 'solicitude for them and for their subjects'. His language, which recapitulates the 'affection and counsel' due to rulers according to the utterance of the illustrious philosopher, also evokes the posture of voluntary service, which depended on love, treated in Volume I.[57] In this regard it is notable that Pseudo-Māwardī describes himself, almost certainly in a metaphorical sense, as a member of the king's *khadam*, 'servants' or 'retainers', and *aʿwān*, 'assistants', groups that occupied positions of close proximity to the king and were accordingly well situated to offer counsel.

Pseudo-Māwardī's Method

Pseudo-Māwardī concludes his introduction with a statement of his method and his table of contents. He announces his intention not to limit himself to his personal opinions and inclinations, but to support his arguments with proofs drawn from God's words as revealed in His Book, the sayings (*aqāwīl*) of His Prophet as transmitted in his *sunan* and *āthār*, and next (*thumma*) the ways of conduct (*siyar*) of the early kings (*mulūk*), past leaders (*aʾimma*), Rightly Guided Caliphs (*khulafāʾ*) and ancient sages (*ḥukamāʾ*) of past nations and former times.[58] Pseudo-Māwardī's use of *thumma* introduces a defining principle, whereby he distinguishes between two levels of authority: the divine word and the divinely inspired model of the Prophet constitute the prior category of authority, while insight into human experience, whether articulated by honoured Muslim caliphs and imams or esteemed non-Muslim (or pre-Islamic) kings, sages or philosophers, constitutes the latter category. The pairing reflects the Qurʾānic categories of *kitāb* and *ḥikma*, 'the Book' and 'Wisdom', both divinely given but distinct from one another, the former restricted to prophets but the latter extended also, according to the dominant interpretation, to sages such as Luqmān.[59] It is possible that, through his familiarity with the oeuvre of Ibn al-Muqaffaʿ and other figures who preserved and perpetuated the heritage of the ancient Iranian (and Zoroastrian) past, the pairing of *dēn* (religion) and *xrad* (wisdom, New Persian *khirad*) further informed Pseudo-Māwardī's patterns of thought.[60] At the beginning of each chapter, Pseudo-Māwardī is consistent in the observance of his stated principle of precedence. In the body of his chapters, however, he intersperses materials drawn from the sacred sources and from the inheritance of expressions of human wisdom, as subsequent chapters will show.

Pseudo-Māwardī's stated abjuring of personal opinion in favour of textual authorities conveys his intention to ensure the strongest and widest possible reach of his persuasion. Perhaps in a reflection of the contested status in the early tenth century of personal judgement (*raʾy*), especially in juristic and theological contexts, Pseudo-Māwardī announces his rejection of an approach that risked the disagreement of parts of his audience. It might be noted that he almost invariably designates materials transmitted from the

Prophet as *sunan* (sing. *sunna*) and *āthār* (sing. *athar*), rather than as *ḥadīth* and *aḥādīth*.[61] This usage is consistent with common practice in the early tenth-century eastern regions (*mashriq*); al-Ḥakīm al-Tirmidhī, who lived into this period, stated that in his youth he studied *ᶜilm al-āthār*, meaning ḥadīth, and *ᶜilm al-raʾy*, by which he meant jurisprudence.[62] The Ḥanafiyya, the dominant legal–theological grouping in Pseudo-Māwardī's milieu, often employed the terms ḥadīth and *athar* synonymously; for example, the Ḥanafī al-Ṭaḥāwī (d. 321/933) in Egypt composed not only a *Bayān mushkil al-ḥadīth* ('Elucidation of the Problematic Parts of the Ḥadīth'), but also a *Kitāb Maᶜānī l-āthār* ('The Meanings of Traditions').[63]

Pseudo-Māwardī's introduction prepares his audience for an unsolicited work of advice that will be sincere and well intentioned, but not altogether pleasing to its recipient. It situates his initiative in a moral as well as a literary context; it provides the foundation for the following chapters, prefigures themes that will recur prominently in later sections, and announces a form and a method intended to enhance the work's discursive efficacy.

Urging the Acceptance of Counsels

The perennial conundrum to which Pseudo-Māwardī applied himself in *Naṣīḥat al-mulūk* received thorough and subtle treatment at the hands of his later contemporary Firdawsī, who, as Dick Davis has shown, explored every possible answer to the question of the proper response of the good, noble and wise person who finds himself subject to a foolish or misguided king.[64] Central to Pseudo-Māwardī's response, as this chapter has already suggested, was the duty of subjects to offer sincere counsel to the ruler and the reciprocal duty of the king to receive and heed salutary advice. It is to this latter responsibility that he devotes his first chapter.

In a summary paraphrase of his introduction, he observes at the outset, 'We have already mentioned that which is incumbent on men of learning, intellect, religiosity and virtue, those who enjoin upon themselves God's command, His precepts, His judgements and His injunctions, in terms of offering advice to kings and leaders (*naṣīḥat al-mulūk wa-l-aʾimma*); we have explained that this practice combines advice for all (*naṣīḥat al-kāffa*), and the élite and the common people benefit from it.'[65] After these remarks, he enumerates six reasons for kings being the most fitting of people to accept advice and listen to admonition (*inna-hum aḥaqq al-nās bi-qabūl al-naṣīḥa wa-samāᶜ al-mawᶜiẓa*):

Firstly: that thereby they may raise themselves above any similarity to the foolish and ignorant, the badly brought up and poorly behaved, the incapable of distinguishing between that which brings them benefit (*manāfiᶜ*) and that which brings them harm (*maḍārr*), or of differentiating between that which wins them praise (*maḥāmid*) and that which earns them censure (*madhāmm*); and above the level of the person whose passions (*shahawāt*) have taken possession of him and whose desire (*hawan*) overwhelms him to the point that it seizes his heart, and he finds himself among those whose hearts do not comprehend, whose eyes do not see and whose ears do not hear [cf. Q 7: 179]. It is incumbent on those possessed of high aspirations and lofty souls that by means of their aspiration they should rise above and transcend this state.

Secondly: that they should become desirous of the results of counsels (*an yarghabū fī natāʾij al-naṣāʾiḥ*), for advice constitutes guidance towards the paths of righteousness (*subul al-rashād*) and a conveyance towards the attainment of correctness (*sadād*). These results will earn him praise in this life and in the life to come, in his beginnings (in this world) and in his afterlife (in the hereafter).

Thirdly: they are the people occupied with the greatest number of affairs and encumbered with the greatest burdens. They are also the least likely of people to conduct their affairs themselves, or to witness conditions in the most distant of their provinces with their own eyes. Not every one whose assistance is sought offers help, and not every governor (*wālin*) assumes responsibility for that which is entrusted to his control.

Fourthly: they are the least likely of people to associate with scholars in their assemblies or to attend the sessions of renunciants, preachers and jurists (*innahum abᶜad al-nās min mujālasat al-ᶜulamāʾ wa-ḥuḍūr majālis al-zuhhād wa-l-wāᶜiẓīna wa-l-fuqahāʾ*), those by whom minds are sharpened and eyes made to see, and by whom persons are made mindful of deceit. The reason for this situation is that kings are concealed (secluded) from these individuals,[66] and prevented and preoccupied from conferring with them (*fa-hum ᶜanhum maḥjūbūna wa-ᶜan mufāwaḍatihim mamnūᶜūna mashghūlūna*).

Fifthly: They are the least likely of people to heed admonition, follow reminders (of the consequences of their actions) and accept advice when it runs counter to their desires, for in their case, or the generality of them, might (*ᶜizz*), wealth (*tharwa*), safety (*amn*), power (*maqdara*), boldness (*jurʾa*), enjoyment (*mutᶜa*), delight (*surūr*) and pleasure (*ladhdha*) have conquered them.[67] All of these qualities lead to the hardening of hearts and a refusal to learn the sciences, although it is in them that their success (*najāḥ*) lies; and to an aversion against receiving admonition, even though it is there that their well-being (*ṣalāḥ*) resides.

Sixthly: they among all the people have the smallest portion of sincere counsellors and sympathetic well-wishers, for most of those who surround them, namely their viziers, assistants and boon-companions, speak to them only in accordance with their desires, and they do not bring up anything that does not correspond with their opinions out of fear for their lives, in order to protect their persons, in an effort to further their ambitions and maintain their ranks. This situation arises from the fact that most of those who attach themselves to kings' courts, frequent their palaces and expend themselves in service (*khidma*) to them are seekers of this world and dealers in its vanities. They incline with the world where it inclines and they subside with it when it subsides.[68]

The idea that the counsellor should guide the ruler towards discrimination between the beneficial and the harmful is apparent, as Andras Hamori has indicated, in *Kalīla wa-Dimna* and the works of Ibn al-Muqaffaᶜ;[69] it is also evident in al-Taghlibī's *Akhlāq al-mulūk*, better known as *Kitāb al-Tāj*, a ninth-century composition that preserves earlier materials, including, like *Naṣīḥat al-mulūk*, vestiges of Sasanian texts.[70] The counterpoint of utility or benefit (*nafᶜ*, *manfaᶜa*) and injury or harm (*ḍarar, maḍarra*), introduced in Pseudo-Māwardī's preface in the previously cited saying of Khusraw Parvīz, also forms a basic conceptual and lexical underpinning for large areas of theological and philosophical discourse. As he proceeds with his six-pointed enumeration, Pseudo-Māwardī makes clear that the king is impeded from receiving and heeding sound advice by three factors. First, as his use of the passive voice (*maḥjūbūna, mamnūʿūna, mashghūlūna*, 'concealed', 'prevented', 'preoccupied') implies, kings are prevented from attaining access to counsel through their seclusion, symbolised by the screen or curtain (*ḥijāb*) that marked their status and separated them from their subordinates, and the obstructions placed between rulers and their publics by the persons who surrounded them.[71] In this category Pseudo-Māwardī specifies viziers, 'assistants' (*aʿwān*) (these two categories are paired throughout *Naṣīḥat al-mulūk*) and boon companions; the *ḥājib*, chamberlain, enforcer of the *ḥijāb*, is also presumably implicated. Secondly, kings, intent on the delights of the world, are likely to choose pleasurable pursuits in preference to the hearing of unpalatable advice. Thirdly, persons in a position to provide sincere advice were likely to keep their distance from the political authorities, and especially from a royal court that they suspected of engaging in disapproved behaviour. These points echo Pseudo-Māwardī's impressions, conveyed elsewhere, of conditions at Naṣr's court,[72] and prefigure his direct engagement with these matters subsequently in his mirror.

Pseudo-Māwardī develops further his contrast of sincere or truthful counsel and manipulative deception:

> True advice (*ḥaqq al-naṣīḥa*) does not involve the pursuit of passion, nor is it among the properties of the truth (*min khāṣṣat al-ḥaqq*) to correspond to desires. How could it be so, when God, great and glorious, has said, 'If the Truth had followed their desires, then the heavens and the earth and everything in them would have been corrupted' (23:71), and the Prophet has said, 'What I fear most of all for my community is passion and excessive expectation.' It used to be said, 'Passion is the ruin of judgement.'[73] They say, 'Passion (*hawan*) is so-called because it plunges (*yuhwī*) its owner into perilous situations (*mahālik*).'[74] An ancient scholar said, 'The intelligent person should know that judgement and passion are mutually hostile adversaries. Human beings are likely to postpone judgement and rush (in the pursuit of) passion; he (the person of rational intellect) should resist that (practice), and seek to keep his passion waiting while he complies with (the indications of) his judgement.'[75]

For these reasons, while kings do not lack for persons who will advise them, who will examine matters of income and expenditure, disbursement, taxes and outlays, who will indicate to them that which is of immediate expedience, and counsel them on outwitting their enemies and opposing their adversaries, few kings find someone who will advise them in their religion, show them what is blameworthy in their affairs as well as what is praiseworthy, remind them of their ultimate end, and convey to them the reports of their weakest subjects concerning the bad conduct of the élite and retinue (*sūʾ adab al-khāṣṣa wa-l-ḥāshiya*), the injustice of those of high standing and might towards the meek and humble.

For this reason much of the deceit of viziers (*ghishsh al-wuzarāʾ*) is directed towards the foundation of kingship. They hold that it is not fitting for the king to be a secretary, because the secretarial function is a craft (*ṣināʿa*); nor that he be an accountant, because accountancy is a profession (*mihna*). They have even said that he should not enquire into religious knowledge (*ʿilm*) or jurisprudence (*fiqh*), or investigate the differences (of theological and juristic opinion) among people so that he should be able to recognise error from correctness among the religious paths (*madhāhib*) of the community (*milla*), because to do so would alienate the common people from him and divide the hearts of the subjects away from him. They have even said it is not necessary for the king to be a valiant warrior, for that is among the tasks of the military leaders (*asāwira*). They have said that if the king commits himself to fighting, he may perish, and that as long as he still has his army, there is no need for him to risk his own life. As long as he survives, he will not lack for persons who will fight on his behalf and sacrifice their own life's blood in his place . . .

There are many such matters that derive – as the intelligent person will realise when he ponders them, and the person of discernment when he contemplates them – from the design of deceitful viziers and assistants (*annahā min waḍʿ al-ghāshshīn min al-wuzarāʾ wa-l-aʿwān*), who care not a whit if the king is devoid of every virtue (*faḍīla*) and divested of every fine quality (*manqaba*) and knowledge (*maʿrifa*). Consequently, he (the king) resembles a shackled prisoner, humiliated and defeated in their hands. They will do as they please with his property and the possessions of his subjects, they will administer in the kingdom as they wish, and they will innovate in the religious community according to their misleading notions

> (*al-ahwāʾ al-muḍilla*) and their unjust ordinances (*al-aḥkām al-jāʾira*) as they see fit.[76]

In this passage, Pseudo-Māwardī develops his previous allusions to the perils of deceit, a vice that he associates with the king's viziers and 'assistants' in particular. He draws attention to their efforts to detach the king from every area of his governance, in terms of administrative matters, religious affairs and the conduct of warfare. Pseudo-Māwardī's remarks are compatible with the impression that he admired the practices of the earlier generations of Samanid amirs, who, according to his portrayal, dispensed justice, promoted religious scholarship and conducted military campaigns.[77] With the ascendancy during Naṣr's youth of experienced viziers and members of the *khāṣṣa* to positions of great power, Pseudo-Māwardī implies that they had rendered the ruler unfit to govern and had, by design, reduced him to dependency.

Pseudo-Māwardī proceeds to adduce examples of kings, caliphs and imams who, in exemplary fashion, had opposed such efforts at manipulation and appreciated truthful counsel concerning their faults and defects:

> Among the resolute kings, and the caliphs and leaders (*aʾimma*), there were many who opposed this manner of conduct and eschewed this path. In their case, the dearest of people to them were those who were most truthful regarding their faults, the closest to them were those who counselled them most sincerely, and the most exalted of people, in these rulers' estimation, were those who warned them regarding their faults (*ʿuyūb*), made them see their sins (*dhunūb*), enjoined on them the gathering of sincere counsels and the acceptance of admonitions, and stipulated in their testaments (*ʿuhūd*) the knowledge of (sincere) counsel (*nuṣḥ*) from deception (*ghishsh*) and of the (sincere) counsellor (*al-nāṣiḥ*) from the (deceitful) imposter (*al-ghāshsh*), as well as (the ability to discern) those from whom he should accept (counsels), and how he should put them into practice.

> Among the reported utterances (*āthār*) of the Persian kings, that which has been gleaned of their judgements (*mā ujtuniya min ārāʾihim*), and that which they described in books of their customs (*āʾīn*), is (the report) that they said: 'The people most likely to face difficulty and remorse are those who are most recalcitrant towards (their) counsellors.' They said: 'Take

> from among your scholars and advisers a mirror (*mirʾāt*) for your natural characteristics (*ṭibāʿ*) and your actions, just as you take polished iron (as a mirror) for the appearance of your face; for you are in greater need of well-being (*ṣalāḥ*) with regard to your natural characteristics and deeds than for the improvement of your face, and the learned counsellor is more truthful and more indispensable than polished iron.'[78] The Prophet summarised this (point) in his saying (*qawl*), 'The believer is the mirror of his brother believer.'[79]

Strengthening the universal aspect of his argument, Pseudo-Māwardī, intermingling his two broad categories of sources, refers to the counsels, testaments and books of customs and conduct of the Persian kings (*mulūk al-ʿajam*). He proceeds to cite *ʿAhd Ardashīr*, which he introduces, in his first explicit reference, as 'of high importance and great value' (*al-jalīl al-khaṭr al-ʿaẓīm al-qadr*) and 'a model for kingship' (*dustūr al-mulk*); he follows these quotations with citations from Shāpūr's testament to his son.[80] Among other texts, including citations ascribed to Aristotle and ʿAlī, he cites the Prophetic ḥadīth, 'He who deceives is not one of us,'[81] and two maxims ascribed to 'the sages of the Arabs' (*ḥukamāʾ al-ʿarab*): 'Your brother is he who counsels you' and 'Counsel your brother'.[82] Then Pseudo-Māwardī proceeds:

> Everything that God has sent down in His Book and placed on the tongue of His Prophet, and that He has commanded should be adopted and followed; next, that which the wise philosophers (*al-ḥukamāʾ*) have commended to those who have come after them, the first of them to the last, by way of an eloquent word of wisdom (*ḥikma bāligha*) or a beneficial word (of counsel) (*kalima nāfiʿa*), or a salutary exhortation or a directive word of guidance – it is nothing but sincere counsel (*naṣīḥa*). In this way the prophets, upon them be peace, used to say and reiterate to their peoples, 'I have counselled you', 'I counsel you', 'I am a true counsellor to you', and 'My counsel would be of no avail to you, if I wished to counsel you'.[83] The people of religion, intellect, knowledge and excellence have accepted (their counsels) with gratitude in their hearts, conveyed them on their tongues, perpetuated their forms in their collections of poetry and books (*fa-kāna . . . yukhallidūna rusūmahā fī dawāwīnihim wa-kutubihim*), and praised the speaker of advice over the passing of the days.[84]

Turning by way of illustration to the conduct of exemplary rulers, Pseudo-Māwardī asserts that many caliphs, feeling themselves vulnerable to defects of character, asked the learned to advise and admonish them. In Pseudo-Māwardī's narratives, it is not courageous individuals who present their counsel, unbidden, to rulers, but caliphs who initiate the exhortation; their pious interlocutors respond, usually in a reticent manner, to the request:[85]

> Many of the caliphs, when they sensed in themselves vanity, boorishness, pride or cruelty, asked the scholars to counsel them and admonish them. Concerning [the Abbasid caliph] Abū Jaᶜfar al-Manṣūr (r. 136–58/754–75), we have heard that he said to [the specialist in exegesis, law and Prophetic tradition] Sufyān al-Thawrī [97–161/716–78],[86] 'Admonish me – but be brief!' Sufyān said, 'O Commander of the Faithful, imagine that your urine were obstructed and would not flow unless you ransomed your entire dominion for it.' The caliph said, 'I would sacrifice my entire dominion for it.' Sufyān said, 'Of what use, then, is a dominion of such worth as this?'[87]

Pseudo-Māwardī's version of this *khabar* omits the frequently reported prior exchange between the caliph and the renunciant. In most versions, the protagonists are Caliph Hārūn al-Rashīd (r. 170–93/786–809) and the ascetic Ibn al-Sammāk (d. 183/799) to whom Pseudo-Māwardī will also refer.[88] In the later version of the Iberian religious scholar, jurist and littérateur Muḥammad b. al-Walīd al-Ṭurṭūshī, also known as Ibn Abī Randaqa (*c.* 451–520/1059–1126), Hārūn is about to drink some water; Ibn al-Sammāk asks what, if the water were withheld from him, he would give to receive it, and the caliph responds that he would give up his kingdom for it. Ibn al-Sammāk then asks whether, if the water were prevented from leaving his body, the king would ransom it with his kingdom, and the caliph answers that he would. The ascetic responds, 'There is no good in a dominion that is not even equal (in value) to a drink or a urination.'[89] Pseudo-Māwardī has condensed the narrative, which evidently also circulated in association with Sufyān al-Thawrī and al-Manṣūr.[90] He proceeds to further examples:

> ᶜAmr b. ᶜUbayd [80–144/699–761, the ascetically inclined theologian linked with the beginnings of the Muᶜtazila][91] entered the presence of Abū Jaᶜfar (al-Manṣūr). The latter said to him, 'Admonish me.' He admonished

> him with a lengthy discourse, and opened it by saying, 'Had this authority (*amr*) endured for those who preceded you, then it would not have reached you. God has given you this world in its entirety, so purchase your soul from Him (for the price of) a portion of it (the world). Know that He is your observer and your questioner as to the atom's weight's-worth of good and bad, and that the community of Muḥammad will be your prosecutors on the Day of Resurrection. God will not be content with you except in that with which you would be content for yourself; you would never be content with regard to yourself unless you were treated with justice, and He will not be content with you unless you (exercise) justice towards the subjects. Beyond your gate are fires kindled by injustice.' (This passage belongs to) a long speech that he composed and (was part of) the extensive practice of censure (*ᶜitāb*) that passed between them.[92]

ᶜAmr b. ᶜUbayd, who features in this sequence, occupies a conspicuous position in *Naṣīḥat al-mulūk*. Pseudo-Māwardī includes the second Abbasid Caliph al-Manṣūr, who had become caliph in 136/754, among the praiseworthy caliphs, in significant measure on account of his receptiveness to ᶜAmr's exhortations.[93] It is likely that Pseudo-Māwardī admired ᶜAmr due both to his reputation for austerity and exhortation, and his involvement in rational theology. With Wāṣil b. ᶜAṭāᵓ (d. 131/748–9), ᶜAmr features in accounts of the origination of the Muᶜtazila.[94] Like other figures associated with the beginnings of the movement, ᶜAmr's conception of legitimate leadership required a rigorous standard of moral probity. During the rebellion of the ᶜAlid Muḥammad b. ᶜAbdallāh al-Nafs al-Zakiyya ('The Pure Soul') in 145/762–3, many members of the Muᶜtazila supported Muḥammad's claim and rallied to his brother Ibrāhīm b. ᶜAbdallāh in Basra. ᶜAmr b. ᶜUbayd, whose political inclinations differed from those of Wāṣil and who had initially refused to recognise the claim of anyone whose 'justice' he had not tested, appears to have remained loyal to al-Manṣūr, and several of his companions followed his example.[95] Pseudo-Māwardī's references to ᶜAmr emphasised the high standards to which ᶜAmr held the caliph, reminded his audience of the transience of worldly power and conveyed to them the conditional nature of the ruler's claim to legitimate sovereignty.

Pseudo-Māwardī continues with a third example:

> Hārūn al-Rashīd said to Ibn al-Sammāk [d. 183/799],[96] 'Admonish me.' He replied, 'Know that you are not the first caliph to die.' He said, 'Tell me more.' He said, 'Had those who came before you not died, then that which you now enjoy would not have passed to you.' He said, 'Tell me more.' He then recited in verse . . .
>
> For you will leave nothing behind among the people
> And will be accompanied by nothing but your deeds.[97]

Pseudo-Māwardī's exemplary narratives involve caliphs who request advice and admonition, and were moved by the reproof that they received. In their receptivity to reminders of the conditional and transient nature of their power, these caliphs offer the present amir and his audience models of meritorious royal conduct. In order to intensify the effect of these models, Pseudo-Māwardī refers next to the example of 'the early kings' (*al-mulūk al-awwalūn*). In a fashion similar to his introduction of the 'Testament of Ardashīr', Pseudo-Māwardī describes and situates the correspondence of Alexander and Aristotle at his first mention of it:

> Such were the early kings. Alexander frequently asked the philosophers (*ḥukamāʾ*) to supply him on his journeys with (wisdom) to which he could have recourse in his sovereignty, and he constantly wrote to his teacher (*ustādh*) Aristotle, who replied to him with admonitions and conveyed counsels to him. We shall mention some of Aristotle's admonitions to Alexander and his counsels for him at their proper places in our book. Among his writings to him were (counsels) designed to bring him closer (*yuqarribuhu*) to his Creator and to benefit him in his final return (in the afterlife).[98]

After citing a number of examples of Aristotle's advice, Pseudo-Māwardī concludes his first chapter:

> Were we to pursue this subject among the accounts of the kings and leaders (*akhbār al-mulūk wa-l-aʾimma*), the book would grow long. We have only selected that which we have mentioned in the light of our purpose in this book of ours, (namely) to manifest sincere advice and truth in admonition. There is no surety that it will not contain some elements that will prove

> contrary to the opinion of certain possessors of kingdoms and provinces (*dhaw[ū] al-mamālik wa-l-wilāyāt*) who incline towards the passions and amuse themselves with pleasures. Their ears will reject our advice and their hearts will recoil from it. But it is not permissible for the person who wishes for advice to measure it against his desire; rather, it is necessary that he measure both the advice and his desire against that which is right (*ḥaqq*) and that which rational intelligence (*ᶜaql*) requires. Where these two things are in conformity with the advice, he should accept it; and where they conflict with it, he should oppose it. Sometimes that which weighs heavily on one's nature (*ṭabᶜ*) and is odious to the heart is more praiseworthy in terms of the ultimate outcome, more salutary in terms of the final end, more abundant in the reward (that it brings), and better in terms of the enduring remembrance (that it creates). God, great is His mention, said, 'It may be that you hate a thing in which God has placed much good' (Q 4: 19) and He said, 'It may be that you hate a thing that is good for you, and it may be that you love a thing that is bad for you' (Q 2: 216).[99]

In this fashion, cautioning his audience that sincere advice need not coincide with desire and that they should make rightfulness (*ḥaqq*) and rational intelligence (*ᶜaql*) their yardstick in assessing both the advice and their desires, Pseudo-Māwardī prepares them for the critical commentary that ensues.

The Concept of *Naṣīḥa*

Pseudo-Māwardī devotes his introduction and his first chapter to the topic of *naṣīḥa*, 'sincere advice' or 'counsel', and its opposite, *ghishsh*, 'deception'. As several examples presented in Volume I indicated,[100] the contrast between sincerity and deception, a feature of Middle Persian *andarz*, forms a recurrent theme throughout *Naṣīḥat al-mulūk*.[101] The offering of counsel contributed to the moral duty of commanding the good and prohibiting the reprehensible (*al-amr bi-l-maᶜrūf wa-l-nahy ᶜan al-munkar*), the imperative of which Pseudo-Māwardī, in accordance with Muᶜtazilite principles, affirms. Counsel provided a means of discharging this responsibility 'by the tongue'.[102] In Baghdad, this mode of performing the duty was particularly associated during Pseudo-Māwardī's lifetime with a Ḥanbalī orientation, expressed in an affirmation of the central importance of ḥadīth and sometimes an affiliation with Ḥanbalī jurisprudence.[103] As a Ḥanafī, Pseudo-Māwardī differed from the Ḥanbalīs in his juristic and in his intellectual–epistemological disposition, but shared the commitment to austerity (*zuhd*) and a spiritually focused detachment (*warac*) that also accompanied the Ḥanbalī orientation. Tellingly, for individuals inclined towards this perspective, to withhold advice constituted a form of deception.[104] As his illustrative texts make clear, for Pseudo-Māwardī the contrast of sincerity and deception that featured prominently in writings of Middle Persian provenance combined with and supported the Qur'ānic passages and theological and legal constructions that shaped his conception of counsel.

Like the Ḥanbalīs, Pseudo-Māwardī draws upon the Prophetic example as documented in ḥadīth. He wrote in the same region as, and within memory of, the lifetimes of several of the great specialists in Prophetic tradition.[105] In particular, Abū cĪsā al-Tirmidhī (210–79/825–92) and Abū Dā'ūd al-Sijistānī (202–75/817–89), compilers of two of the 'six books' considered authoritative amongst Sunni Muslims, lived and taught in proximity to Pseudo-Māwardī's place of residence; indeed, Abū Dā'ūd spent an important period of his life in Balkh.[106] Most of the ḥadīth related by Pseudo-Māwardī in this chapter appear in al-Tirmidhī's *al-Jāmic al-ṣaḥīḥ* ('Compendium of Sound Ḥadīth') or the *Sunan* ('Collected Exemplary Practices') of Abū Dā'ūd, or in both collections. The ḥadīth that Pseudo-Māwardī adduces in his introduction and first chapter emphasise the general nature of the responsibility to offer counsel; they do not address the particular matter of offering advice to rulers. They accord with the maxim *akhūka man ṣadaqaka al-naṣīḥa*, 'Your brother is he who is truthful in his advice to you', so widespread that the Khurasani compiler and explicator of proverbs al-Maydānī al-Naysābūrī (d. 518/1124) included it in his collection with the gloss, 'This (proverb) refers to advice in matters of religion and the world.'[107] (Al-Maydānī also included in his collection the ḥadīth *inna l-dīn al-naṣīḥa*, 'Religion is counsel', which Pseudo-Māwardī cites in the opening section of his introduction.[108]) The discharging of the responsibility of counsel for the benefit of a public audience nevertheless occasioned some controversy. It is evident from Pseudo-Māwardī's reference to 'assemblies of renunciants, preachers and jurists' (*majālis al-zuhhād wa-l-wācizīna wa-l-fuqahā'*) that such gatherings, for purposes of moral edification and exhortation, though regarded in some circles as an innovation (*bid*ᶜ*a*), were a feature of his milieu. It was scholar-preachers in Samarqand and later in the cities of Iraq and Syria who traced the activities of exhortation and admonition to the Prophet and the first generations among his followers. Slightly later in the tenth century, the theologian and moralist Abū l-Layth al-Samarqandī deemed the *majlis al-*ᶜ*iẓa*, a public assembly for the purposes of exhortation, permitted. Persons who objected to such assemblies based their judgement on the ḥadīth, 'Only a person in command, a person ordered [to do so] or a dissembler exhorts the people' (*lā yaquṣṣu* ᶜ*alā l-nās illā amīr aw-ma*ᵓ*mūr aw-murā*ᵓ*in*).[109] Abū l-Layth, however, relates various ḥadīth in support of the practice. Caliph ᶜUmar reportedly permitted Tamīm al-Dārī (d. 40/660–1) – a Companion and a primary transmitter of the ḥadīth [*innamā*] *al-dīn al-naṣīḥa* – to exhort the people, for purposes of 'reminding' them (of the reward and punishment of the afterlife), every Saturday, and ᶜAbdallāh Ibn Masᶜūd (d. *c.* 32/652–3), a Companion and source of one of the earliest readings of the Qurᵓān, is reported to have 'reminded' the people every Friday evening.[110] Abū l-Layth enumerates the qualities required in the person who undertakes this task,[111] since, if their words were to carry authority, the pronouncers of exhortation, whether in the form of *qaṣaṣ* (narrative recitation), *tadhkīr* (reminding), *wa*ᶜ*ẓ* (exhortation) or *naṣīḥa* (counsel), required appropriate and recognised authorisation.[112]

If the relationship of *wā*ᶜ*iẓ* and *maw*ᶜ*ūẓ*, the exhorter and the exhorted, implied the superior moral standing of the former over the latter, the counsellor's conveyance of improving advice to the ruler likewise implied a moral inequality. The apparent reversal of power expressed in the structure of the encounter accompanied the exposure of the counsellor to the risks of the monarch's displeasure. The counsellor's predicament entailed ethical as well as pragmatic issues. In a setting in which the relationship between men of religion and rulers was a contentious subject, it is quite likely that Pseudo-Māwardī sought to persuade not only rulers of their need to solicit advice from qualified and disinterested persons, but also men of learning and wisdom of their duty to offer counsel to monarchs.

In the spectrum of opinions regarding the offering of counsel to rulers, Pseudo-Māwardī took an intermediate position that was perhaps somewhat closer to one end of the range than the other. Many scholars tended to accommodate the ruler and his functionaries, and even to cede the duty of 'commanding right', *al-amr bi-l-maʿrūf*, almost entirely to the authorities; at the other end of the spectrum, some scholars supported confrontation of the authorities, either through rebuke or through rebellion.[113] Pseudo-Māwardī did not consider contact with rulers to be damaging in principle; on the contrary, he felt it incumbent even in the case of a corrupt and misguided ruler to attempt to return him to virtue and righteousness. But whereas, as Michael Cook has observed, biographical and anecdotal materials record numerous 'sympathetically presented examples of pious Muslims harshly rebuking rulers, governors and their henchmen, often at great risk to themselves',[114] Pseudo-Māwardī's narratives, cited above, depict a milder approach. Indeed, they convey a certain reluctance on the part of the counsellor, whom the ruler finds it necessary to encourage by repeated requests for admonition. The counsellors in Pseudo-Māwardī's examples avoid outright rebuke; instead, they remind the ruler of the transience of his power and the gravity of the moral burden that his sovereignty places upon him. Moreover, although he cites a number of Prophetic materials related to counsel, Pseudo-Māwardī omits the frequently cited ḥadīth 'The finest *jihād* is to speak the truth (*kalimat ḥaqq*) in the presence of an unjust ruler (*sulṭān jāʾir*)'.[115] His advice took the form of 'engaged resistance';[116] he advocated the offering of counsel, but practised it within constraints.

At the other end of the spectrum, Pseudo-Māwardī's views differed from those of Abū Sulaymān Ḥamd b. Muḥammad al-Khaṭṭābī al-Bustī (319–88/931–98), the eminent *muḥaddith*, *faqīh* and *adīb*, and author of commentaries on the ḥadīth collections *Ṣaḥīḥ al-Bukhārī* ('The Compendium of Sound Ḥadīth' of al-Bukhārī) and *Sunan Abī Dāʾūd* ('The Transmitted Prophetic Reports' of Abū Dāʾūd). Born in Bust, in the eastern region of Sistan, al-Khaṭṭābī was perhaps a child during the later years of Pseudo-Māwardī's life.[117] Al-Khaṭṭābī commented on the meaning of the ḥadīth *inna al-dīn al-naṣīḥa* in the following terms:

> *Naṣīḥa* is a word by which is designated the sum of that which constitutes the wishing of good to the advisee (*manṣūḥ*). [It is not possible to express this meaning by a single word that encompasses it and combines its meanings other than it (the word itself)]. The root of *nuṣḥ* in linguistic

> terms is *khulūṣ* (clarity, purity, sincerity). It is said: 'I have purified the honey' (*naṣaḥtu al-ᶜasal*) when I have purified it (*khallaṣtuhu*) of wax. So the meaning of 'the counsel of God Almighty' (*naṣīḥat Allāh taᶜālā*) is soundness of belief (*ṣiḥḥat al-iᶜtiqād*) in His unicity, and sincerity of intention (*ikhlāṣ al-niyya*) in worshipping Him. Counsel with regard to the Book of God (*al-naṣīḥa li-kitāb Allāh*) is faith in it and acting in accordance with its contents. Counsel with regard to His Prophet (*al-naṣīḥa li-rasūlihi*) is belief in his prophecy and showing obedience to him in that which he commands and forbids. Counsel with regard to the leaders of the Muslims (*al-naṣīḥa li-aʾimmat al-muslimīn*) is to obey them in that which is right (*an yuṭīᶜahum fī l-ḥaqq*) and not to countenance rebellion against them (*al-khurūj ᶜalayhim*) [by the sword when they are unjust (*idhā jārū*)]. And counsel with regard to the generality of the Muslims (*al-naṣīḥa li-ᶜāmmat al-muslimīn*) is to guide them to their best interests (*irshāduhum ilā maṣāliḥihim*).[118]

In this interpretation of the Prophetic call for *naṣīḥa*, al-Khaṭṭābī removes the potential for direct interaction with the ruler. He reduces the obligation of counsel, in the case of the ruler, to the demonstration of obedience as far as such obedience is consistent with obedience to God, and to abstention from rebellion even in cases where obedience to the ruler conflicted with just conduct. In *al-ᶜUzla* ('Withdrawal'), in a chapter devoted to the corruption of leaders and the transmitted materials related to the limiting of contact with them, al-Khaṭṭābī quoted the previously cited ḥadīth in which the Prophet equates the speaking of truth in the presence of unjust power with *jihād*, but at the same time advocates abstention from association with the authorities (*al-iqlāl min ṣuḥbat al-salāṭīn*). He contrasts the past, in which a figure such as al-Ḥasan al-Baṣrī exemplified sincerity in his counsel and effectiveness in his admonition, to the present, and exclaims in rhetorical lament, 'Would that I knew who today might enter the presence of kings in order to correct their falsehood, who would speak words of justice to them while attending their *majālis*, who would counsel them; and who among them (kings) would (allow himself to) be counselled.' In the absence of such persons, al-Khaṭṭābī submitted that in the present time it was preferable to minimise contact with rulers (*an tuqilla min mukhālaṭatihim*).[119] Significantly, al-Khaṭṭābī also recorded Sufyān's utterance, 'Eschew the passions, and beware of the authorities' (*iyyāka wa-l-ahwāʾ [wa] iyyāka wa-l-sulṭān*).[120]

In an environment in which many persons concerned for their virtue considered contact with rulers repugnant and opted for dissociation from them, Pseudo-Māwardī not only dissented, but also, unusually, composed a mirror. In his willingness to associate with rulers, coupled with his belief that to do so necessitated the speaking of true advice, he follows the apparent position of his fellow citizen the theologian and administrator Abū l-Qāsim al-Kaʿbī. The remnants of al-Kaʿbī's writings contain some indications of his perspective in this matter. In his *Tafsīr*, al-Kaʿbī interpreted the Qurʾānic 'those in authority among you' (*ūlī l-amr minkum*, Q 4:59) as the temporal rulers (*al-umarāʾ*), and he included several materials that reflected the spectrum of opinion with regard to association with and service under rulers in *Qabūl al-akhbār* ('Acceptance of Reports').[121] *Naṣīḥat al-mulūk* constitutes a literary enactment of *al-amr bi-l-maʿrūf*, by which Pseudo-Māwardī sought to improve the king's moral standing and his conduct towards his subjects in the interests of universal *maṣlaḥa*. The term *maṣlaḥa* embraces several meanings related to being, becoming or rendering good, sound or beneficial; it coincides to some extent with the concepts of *khayr*, 'good', and *nafʿ* or *manfaʿa*, 'utility', both of which also feature quite frequently in *Naṣīḥat al-mulūk*. In certain contexts, it possesses a technical sense; in other cases, it carries a broader set of meanings related to welfare, well-being and the social good. In juristic parlance, *maṣlaḥa* connotes the general or public good, as opposed to *maḍarra* or *mafsada*, harm or injury. This usage is related to the legal principle of *istiṣlāḥ*, a procedure that, in cases for which specific scriptural injunctions were lacking, involved the use of reason and discretionary opinion (*raʾy*) in order to devise legal rulings that promoted the public interest. The practice of *istiṣlāḥ* is associated with the Medinese jurists and with the Ḥanafīs of eighth-century Iraq; and Ibn al-Muqaffaʿ advocated its use in *Risāla fī l-ṣaḥāba*.[122] As Ibn al-Muqaffaʿ's usage might suggest, the principle carried political as well as legal significance. Asma Afsaruddin has demonstrated that despite its relatively rare appearance as an explicitly political concept in the early literature, a political understanding of *maṣlaḥa* was a pervasive feature of political and social discourse even in the centuries before the concept attained its expansive definition in the works of al-Ghazālī.[123]

For intellectual, moral and pragmatic reasons, it was essential to Pseudo-Māwardī's presentation that he devote his preface and his first chapter to the duty of counsel (*naṣīḥa*). In these opening sections of his mirror, Pseudo-Māwardī presents a thorough and multifaceted portrayal of counsel and its obverse, dishonesty or deception. He establishes its indispensability by means of his characteristic combination of rational point-by-point argument with abundant attestations from the sacred sources, human wisdom and historical experience. The extensive and thorough attention that he devotes to *naṣīḥa* at the outset of his work conveys not only his conviction, but also his determined endeavour to gain a hearing for his work, which, as he forewarns his audience, may not conform to their desires, but will guide them towards well-being in this world and the world to come, and, through the power of the royal example, will improve the lives of the entirety of the population.

2

Sources and Authorities: The Living Meaning of Ancient Wisdom

Pseudo-Māwardī's Sources

Privileged among Pseudo-Māwardī's diverse materials, as he announces in his preface, are the sacred sources of the Qur'ān and the Prophet's *sunna.* His audience's familiarity with the Qur'ānic text allowed him to cite passages and employ allusions for a combination of structural, conceptual, literary and aesthetic purposes. Pseudo-Māwardī's engagement with the Qur'ānic text is most conspicuous in the hundreds of explicit quotations that appear, often in clusters, at prominent points in his book.

After the Qur'ān and Prophetic *sunna* (Pseudo-Māwardī cites well over a hundred Prophetic ḥadīth), the largest number of attributed quotations, by a considerable margin, in *Naṣīḥat al-mulūk* is fifty-odd citations ascribed to Aristotle, to whom he refers as Arisṭāṭālīs. In the next level of frequency are quotations ascribed to or narratives concerning the Sasanian King Ardashīr (r. *c.* 224 or 226–242), and the Rightly Guided Caliphs ᶜUmar b. al-Khaṭṭāb and ᶜAlī b. Abī Ṭālib. Following this set of speaker-protagonists in frequency are the Sasanian monarch Sābūr (Shāpūr, r. 239 or 240–270 or 273), the Umayyad Caliph Muᶜāwiya, the Abbasid Caliph Abū Jaᶜfar al-Manṣūr and the ascetically inclined theologian ᶜAmr b. ᶜUbayd (often together), and the caliphs Hārūn al-Rashīd and al-Maᵓmūn. In *Naṣīḥat al-mulūk*, this diverse set of figures convey their instruction in their verbal articulations, reported as *ḥikam*, and in their exemplary experience, narrated in the form of *akhbār.*

Indeed, at his first mention of certain sources, namely, the 'Testament of Ardashīr' (*ᶜAhd Ardashīr*), the 'Testament of Shāpūr' (*ᶜAhd Sābūr*) and the Aristotelian–Alexandrine epistolary materials, Pseudo-Māwardī affirms their remarkable value. Among other texts, he cites the 'Testament' (*ᶜahd*) of an Indian king, on two occasions identified as Sāb.t.r.m; the *Āʾīnnāmeh*, a work translated, as its title makes clear, from Middle Persian; the collection of fables *Kalīla wa-Dimna*; and an unidentified *Kitāb ʾs.hāmat al-mulūk*.[1] As his source for additional utterances of Ardashīr and axioms ascribed to the sage Buzurgmihr, and for an account pertaining to the period of the Umayyad Caliph ʿAbd al-Malik, Pseudo-Māwardī identifies al-Wāqidī (d. 207/822), the historian and specialist in *fiqh*, who enjoyed the patronage of the vizier Yaḥyā b. Khālid al-Barmakī (d. 190/805).[2] In a similar fashion, in his epilogue he identifies the historian al-Madāʾinī (b. 135–*c*. 215–228/752–*c*. 830–43) as an authority on the books of the ancients.[3]

In introducing certain quotations, Pseudo-Māwardī indicates clearly that he has encountered the materials in written texts (*qaraʾnā* ('I have read')). In other instances, he reports his citations with the observation that 'it is related from' (*ḥukiya ʿan*) or 'among the sayings of . . .' (*min aqāwīl* . . .). Such formulations suggest that he participated in the complex interplay between written and oral forms of circulation that underlay the compilation of several of the period's texts, such as the anthologies of *adab* and the production of various collections of wise sayings, in Arabic and Persian. Gregor Schoeler has inferred that at the base of many of the materials included in several written collections were 'jottings', read or recited in the presence of students who heard or noted them down. They were neither purely oral transmissions nor quotations from formally composed books; the oral and the written interacted in a dynamic symbiosis.[4] The transmission of written and oral materials in a parallel and to some extent interactive process is likely to have contributed to the extensive 'unacknowledged borrowing' of Persian *andarz*, advice and moral counsel, that Shaul Shaked has demonstrated in Ibn al-Muqaffaʿ's works.[5] Probably a reflection of his audience's deep familiarity with the material, the same phenomenon is evident in *Naṣīḥat al-mulūk*, alongside Pseudo-Māwardī's careful attribution of many of his quotations to their sources. Just as by means of *iqtibās*, allusion to Qurʾānic texts, he was able to employ numerous Qurʾānic formulations without signalling their scriptural reference, he was able to employ language redolent of Middle Persian antecedents confident in its compelling connotations for his audience.

This chapter is dedicated to the non-sacred sources identified and cited in *Naṣīḥat al-mulūk*. Associated with *al-ʿajam*, *al-hind* and *al-ʿarab*, the materials that he cites represent the perennial wisdom accumulated in the course of history and transmitted within and across multiple communities. Subsequent chapters seek to show how Pseudo-Māwardī instilled in these materials, the meanings of which were fluid and multiple, connotations that permitted his audience to apprehend his allusions to contemporary circumstances.[6]

Pseudo-Māwardī's receptivity to materials that carried Iranian and Indic associations should be distinguished from the particular enthusiasm for the Iranian heritage that contemporaries described as *shuᶜūbī*, that is, supportive of the equality of Arabs and non-Arabs (especially Persians), or indeed of the superior cultural standing of the latter.[7] His respect for the Iranian past and its culture was not of an exclusionary kind, nor did he privilege Iranian materials among the diverse sources that he brought together in his mirror. Instead, his appreciation of a diverse repertoire of wisdom suggests an affinity with the outlook of the philosopher al-Kindī, who expressed his gratitude to the purveyors of knowledge regardless of their allegiances or the sources of their learning.[8] Pseudo-Māwardī apparently shared the disposition of his contemporary the philosopher and littérateur Abū Zayd al-Balkhī, who refused to elevate either the Arabs or the non-Arabs over the other.[9] Pseudo-Māwardī, whose native language was Persian, participated in an inclusive intellectual–cultural discourse that was distinct from the sentiments that stimulated the development of Persian as a medium for the preservation and reinvigoration of the Iranian cultural heritage. He wrote in Arabic, promoted the study and use of the Arabic language, disparaged Persian stories, and quoted a substantial amount of Arabic, but no Persian, poetry.[10] He cited his materials, including materials that carried Iranian and Indic associations, in Arabic; for him, these sources had entered the vast repertoire of materials brought together in Arabic for the benefit of the multi-ethnic, multi-linguistic and multi-confessional societies of his time. Parts of *Naṣīḥat al-mulūk* might suggest a response to the energetic promotion of New Persian and the Iranian cultural legacy. Their 'excessive' *shuᶜūbiyya* was perhaps among the reasons for Pseudo-Māwardī's antipathy to the viziers of his era; according to al-Tawḥīdī (d. 414/1023), 'al-Jayhānī', probably Abū ᶜAbdallāh Muḥammad b. Aḥmad, exemplified such exaggerated display.[11] It is therefore with the cultural landscape that this review of Pseudo-Māwardī's sources of human wisdom begins.

The Reclamation of the Iranian Past

Pseudo-Māwardī lived during a period when the Samanids, no less than their rivals in the west, the Buyids, engaged intensely with the 'Iranian past'. By this phrase I refer to the diverse cultural legacy largely constructed during the Sasanian period and assimilated, transposed and reinterpreted in the early centuries of the Islamic era, especially in the regions associated with the territorial category of 'Iran'.[12] Members of the Buyid dynastic family, located in western Iran and Iraq, identified themselves with the Sasanians, whose earlier central domains they now occupied and whose traces were apparent in the landscape. With unmistakable symbolic design, ᶜAḍud al-Dawla (r. 338–72/949–83) famously left a pair of inscriptions (dated 344/955–6) at the ancient site of Takht-i Jamshīd or Persepolis, and linked his and his dynasty's rule to that of the Sasanians.[13] The Buyids sponsored writing only in Arabic. The Samanids, by contrast, and equally energetically some of the *mulūk* within their domains, promoted both Arabic letters and the development of a Persian literature in an increasing range of genres.[14] Having begun with poetry, literary activity in (New) Persian expanded to include the adaptation of established Arabic texts, and most conspicuously, the prestigious *History* and *Tafsīr* (Qurʾānic exegesis) of al-Ṭabarī.[15]

The production of adaptations into Persian also encompassed texts previously rendered into Arabic from increasingly inaccessible or lost Middle Persian versions. Among the works in this category, *Kalīla wa-Dimna* and the *Sindbādnāmeh* ('Book of Sindbād'), both of which carried Indic as well as Persian associations, and both of which the poet Abān al-Lāḥiqī reportedly turned into verse,[16] constitute leading examples. According to the 'Older Preface' (346/957) that preceded the *Shāhnāmeh* commissioned by Abū Manṣūr Ibn ᶜAbd al-Razzāq, Naṣr II commissioned his vizier Balᶜamī to render the Arabic *Kalīla wa-Dimna* into Persian, and then ordered the poet Rūdakī to transpose Balᶜamī's Persian prose into Persian poetry.[17] It was also said to be Rūdakī who undertook the versification in Persian of the *Sindbādnāmeh*.[18] The renewed expression in Persian of *Kalīla wa-Dimna* and the *Sindbādnāmeh*, with both of which Pseudo-Māwardī was familiar, coincided with the contemporaneous collection and recording of Iranian lore evident in the composition of *shāhnāmeh*s.[19] The most remarkable and lasting product of this initiative is, of course, the *Shāhnāmeh* of Firdawsī (329–410 or 416/940–1019 or 1025). Although Firdawsī completed his epic in approximately 400/1010, during the reign of Maḥmūd of Ghazna (r. 388–421/998–1030), he began it under the Samanids, and it represented the culmination of a process of *shāhnāmeh* writing to which several literary figures of the Samanid period had contributed.[20] In this case, the traditional narratives associate the initiation of the process not with the Samanid court, but with regional *mulūk*, especially in the city of Tus. It was in Tus that Abū Manṣūr al-Maᶜmarī, in compliance with the directive of Ibn ᶜAbd al-Razzāq, oversaw the composition of a prose *Shāhnāmeh*, which reached completion in 346/957.[21] If the more proximate associations of the transmitted materials were, as in the case of the *Khudaynāmeh* ('Register of Kings'), to a large extent Sasanian, the project of reformulation also encompassed distinctively regional cultural materials, such as the Sistani cycle of stories concerning the heroes (*pahlavāns*) of Zabul, especially Zāl and his son Rustam.[22] Vestiges of the Iranian past continued to appear in Arabic as well as in Persian media in the Samanid domains. Al-Khwārazmī found it appropriate to include definitions in Arabic for the terms *mōbadh* (glossed as *qāḍī al-majūs*, 'judge of the Zoroastrians'), *mōbadhān mōbadh* (*qāḍī l-quḍāt*, 'chief judge') and *hirbadh* (*khādim al-nār*, 'attendant of the [sacred] fire'), as well as numerous technical terms from Persian, in his compendium *Mafātīḥ al-ᶜulūm* ('Keys of the Sciences').[23]

As Olga Davidson has indicated, the narratives concerning this florescence of Persian literature display an elaborate patterning: each work of Persian verse represents the culmination of a process initiated through the stimulus of a Samanid king, executed through the labour of a celebrated vizier, and perfected through the genius of the quintessential progenitor of New Persian poetry, Rūdakī.[24] These patterns endowed literary activity in Persian with a pedigree in the wisdom of the past and a nimbus of prestige in the present. Pseudo-Māwardī attests to the popularity at the courts of Persian stories (*afsānaqāt*), such as *Hazār afsān* ('Thousand Stories') and the 'Book of Sindbād'.[25] In keeping with the poetic norms and literary techniques of the Classical Arabic repertoire, he discouraged the use of fiction, as well as love stories, in the education of princes, for whom clarity with regard to 'truth' (*ṣidq*) over 'falsehood' (*kidhb*) was imperative.[26] His attitude towards *Kalīla wa-Dimna* was more complicated, and demonstrates the discernment with which he selected his materials for quotation. In the case of *Kalīla wa-Dimna*, the composite collection that grew, it is commonly supposed, on the basis of Arabic versions of a Middle Persian rendering of the Sanskrit *Pañcatantra*, Pseudo-Māwardī differentiates between the book's narrative and aphoristic components, and restricts his quotations to the latter. Pseudo-Māwardī was similarly selective in his evocations of the kings of the past. Although he may not have lived to see the completion of the Abū Manṣūrī *Shāhnāmeh*, he certainly observed the interest that stimulated it, and was familiar with the oral culture that preserved its stories of kings and heroes. His numerous quotations of the pronouncements of Iranian kings and references to their recorded actions, however, involve exclusively Sasanian monarchs; in other words, he adduces only fully historical figures.[27] His low opinion of the pedagogical value of Persian stories perhaps extended to the mythological and legendary narratives of the Pishdadi and Kayani kings, the dynasties featured in the earlier stages of the epic, and to the tales of the heroes of the Sistani cycle, the family of Zāl and Rustam, linked with the ancestral lands in Zābul.

The *Dihqāns* and Persian Moralia

As demonstrated in Volume I, the earlier Samanid amirs, whose ancestral heritage linked them with the *dahāqīn* (pl. of *dihqān*), depended heavily on this group's local authority, based on their long-standing status as landowners, and their considerable military strength.[28] The *dihqāns*' enduring identity as a distinct category was linked to their continuing attachment to their Iranian cultural patrimony. The process of compiling *shāhnāmehs*, for which the city of Tus appears to have provided a principal centre, owed much to the involvement of the region's cultural custodians.[29] According to the 'Older Preface', Ibn ᶜAbd al-Razzāq instructed his leading administrator (*dustūr*) and assistant (*chākar*) Abū Manṣūr al-Maᶜmarī to 'gather the owners of books among the landlords (*dihqānān*), sages (*farzānigān*) and men of worldly experience (*jahāndīdigān*) from the various towns' with a view to the production of a 'book' (*nāmeh*).[30] In the lifetime of Pseudo-Māwardī, the *dihqāns* retained a reputation not only for their knowledge of the histories of the kings and heroes of Iran, as their recruitment for the composition of *shāhnāmehs* attests, but also for their fluency in the wisdom of antiquity.

In the long aftermath of the conquests in Iran, the *dihqān*s had, as scholars have recognised, assumed the functions of cultural intermediaries. It seems that the appreciation of ancient wisdom sometimes provided a meeting ground for the indigenous élites and more recently settled populations, and articulations of wisdom and counsel reportedly formed a significant component in the intercultural exchange that the *dihqān*s facilitated. Abū l-Layth al-Samarqandī related a report in which Ibn Ziyād (= al-Rabīᶜ b. Ziyād al-Ḥārithī, ᶜAbdallāh b. ᶜĀmir's commander, who led the first Arab incursion into Sistan in 31/651–2)[31] asked a *dihqān* (*rajul min al-dahāqīn*) for his definition of *muruwwa*, and received the *dihqān*'s fourfold reply.[32] In a similar example, also set in Sistan, ᶜAbd al-ᶜAzīz b. ᶜAbdallāh, the Umayyad governor of the province, requested from Rustam b. Mihr-Hurmuzd al-Majūsī a portion of the 'words of wisdom' (*sukhanān-i ḥikmat*) for which the *dihqān*s were renowned.[33] This positive association of the *dihqān*s with perennial wisdom perhaps contributed to Amir Ismāᶜīl's esteem for the sound judgement and sagacity of Aḥmad b. Sahl, who, in another telling indication, reportedly commissioned a certain Āzādsarv to collect the stories of Rustam.[34]

The attachment to and conservation of the wisdom of the past found expression in the moralising element in the region's developing Persian literary corpus.[35] Although, as de Fouchécour has indicated, it was compiled later than the early tenth-century date implied by its attribution, the Persian collection known as *Pandnāmeh-yi Māturīdī* ('Book of Advice of Māturīdī'), a compilation of homiletic aphorisms in ten chapters, preserves older materials, and exemplifies the strong appeal and broad dissemination of edifying maxims. Several examples from this collection suggest axiomatic encapsulations of theological–philosophical principles that would accord with a Māturīdī, Muᶜtazilite and Kindian orientation (*sar-māyeh-yi ᶜumr-i khod tawḥīd shinās* ('recognise your life's capital in the profession of the divine unity'), *ᶜaql-rā bunyād shumar* ('count rational intellect as a foundation'), *az taqvā zād-i ākhirat sāz* ('make godliness the provision of the afterlife')).[36] The cultivation of wisdom found particular expression in the region's Persian poetry, from the ninth-century fragments of Ḥanẓala Bādghīsī and Abū Salīk Gurgānī to the abundant poetic production of the tenth century.[37] Considerable portions of the tenth-century poetry of

Rūdakī, Shuhayd-i Balkhī and Daqīqī (d. *c.* 366/976), among others, display a marked predilection for moral instruction and wise meditation,[38] and the *Āfarīnnāmeh* (completed in 336/947) of Abū Shakūr Balkhī, a long poem dedicated to Nūḥ b. Naṣr and like Firdawsī's *Shāhnāmeh* in the metre *mutaqārib*, established a model for extended compositions of moralising verses.[39] The later tenth-century poet Maysarī, a physician and known as Ḥakīm, composed verses described by the copyist of the unique manuscript as his 'advice and counsel', *pand-o naṣīḥat*.[40] Firdawsī, a *dihqān* and a poet, incorporated numerous examples of wisdom into his *Shāhnāmeh*, including the speeches of kings on the occasion of their accession and royal testaments delivered to various audiences, especially from father to son at the time of the transfer of power from the former to the latter. The *Shāhnāmeh* is also replete with Firdawsī's poetic reflections on the fickle nature of worldly affairs, the transience of power, strength and good fortune, and the concomitant imperative of ethical conduct that alone offers the opportunity for an enduring reputation.[41] For Firdawsī, the stories of Iran's kings and heroes were replete with moral implications, inseparable from the maxims and verses that in concise fashion expounded their meanings.[42]

The rootedness of this varied regional culture of moral exhortation, in its many forms and registers, rendered it an effective element in the 'contract' between rulers, their powerful vassals and executives, and the people on whose periodically active cooperation the holders of power depended. The latter's patronage of projects that involved the promotion of these materials facilitated the creation of bridges with and among multiple constituencies. In a slightly later example than the cases mentioned in the preceding pages, the Amir Nūḥ b. Manṣūr (r. 365–87/976–97) is said to have instructed Ibn Sīnā to produce a translation of a Persian *Ẓafarnāmeh* ('Book of Victory'), the contents of which conveyed Buzurgmihr's counsels and sayings in reply to Anūshīrvān's questions.[43] The repeated depictions of the amirs, their viziers and vassals as the initiators of the transfer of such ancient wisdom to media accessible to their subjects indicate, no less than claims of ancient lineage, the legitimising prestige that accrued to the powerful through their association with the enlightened sages of the past and present.

These examples establish the prevalence and continued attachment of meaning to articulations of wisdom of diverse provenance, the precise transmission of which mattered less to the communities that had assimilated them into their repertoires than their timeless antiquity, which, by contrast, the authors who adduced them invariably emphasised. The mobility and mutability of such materials are particularly clearly illustrated in the case of collections such as *Kalīla wa-Dimna*, *Bilawhar wa-Būdhāṣaf* and *Sirr al-asrār*, which included texts that had traversed substantial cultural distances and that continued to adapt as they passed in the medieval and early modern periods from Arabic into numerous classical and vernacular languages. As the remainder of this chapter describes, *Naṣīḥat al-mulūk* participates in the continuing processes of adaptation and dissemination of a large and diverse repertoire of materials in the early tenth century.

The Epistolary Cycle of Aristotle and Alexander

Pseudo-Māwardī's references to and quotations from Aristotle are restricted to the philosopher's purported correspondence with Alexander. As a later chapter will indicate, parts of *Naṣīḥat al-mulūk* reflect an indirect suffusion of Aristotelianism, which is almost entirely separate from the apocryphal counsels that circulated in association with Aristotle's name.[44] Instead, the body of pseudo-Aristotelian maxims and anecdotes that circulated in Arabic and feature prominently in *Naṣīḥat al-mulūk* constitute speaking witnesses of late antique and medieval syncretism.[45] These pseudo-Aristotelian materials grew incrementally over the course of centuries and enjoyed an extremely wide and sustained diffusion.

Without exception, Pseudo-Māwardī's Aristotelian-attributed quotations derive from prose versions of the apocryphal correspondence of Alexander and Aristotle, and from narrative accounts of Aristotle's advice to his royal pupil.[46] Most of the passages that Pseudo-Māwardī ascribes to the Aristotelian–Alexandrine correspondence find parallels in the text known as *al-Siyāsa al-ᶜāmmiyya* ('General Governance'), Chapter Eight in the composite 'Epistolary Cycle' that survives in two fourteenth-century manuscripts. *Al-Siyāsa al-ᶜāmmiyya*, which probably circulated separately as well as in multipartite compositions, constituted a major component of the pseudo-Aristotelian *Sirr al-asrār*, known in various recensions in Arabic and passed into Latin, Hebrew and numerous vernacular languages of Eurasia.[47] Pseudo-Māwardī appears to have had direct access to *al-Siyāsa al-ᶜāmmiyya*, and in a version that is likely to antedate the text that appears as Chapter Eight in the fourteenth-century compilations.

The Aristotelian–Alexandrine corpus occupies a strikingly large portion of Pseudo-Māwardī's body of human wisdom. By contrast, Ibn Qutayba and, in Iberia, Ibn ᶜAbd Rabbihi, in their extensive collections *ᶜUyūn al-akhbār* and *al-ᶜIqd al-farīd* ('The Unique Necklace'), respectively, cite a mere two quotations each ascribed to Aristotle.[48] Pseudo-Māwardī possessed a thorough knowledge of *al-Siyāsa al-ᶜāmmiyya*, and occasionally introduced his Alexandrine–Aristotelian texts with brief contextualising notices. For example, his first extended quotations are prefaced with the statement, 'Alexander was constantly writing to Aristotle, his teacher, who wrote to him with *mawāᶜiẓ* (exhortations) and *naṣāʾiḥ* (counsels), which we shall mention at the appropriate place(s) in our book. Aristotle's writings were designed to bring Alexander closer to his Creator and benefit him in the afterlife.'[49] Pseudo-Māwardī also knew various narrative accounts associated with Alexander's campaigns and governance. These materials probably derived from written and oral texts related to an Arabic, or possibly a (hypothetical) Middle Persian, version of Pseudo-Callisthenes.[50] On a small number of occasions, Pseudo-Māwardī cites or refers to Alexander independently of Aristotle.[51]

Pseudo-Māwardī adduces his Aristotelian–Alexandrine materials as a distinct body of wisdom. He does not situate them within, or liken them to, the generic categories of wisdom literature associated with, for example, *al-ᶜarab, al-furs* and *al-hind* (loosely, Arabs, Persians and Indians). There is no evidence that he identified them with a 'Greek' provenance or perceived them as 'Greek'; indeed, the term *yūnān* never appears in his text, and the Greek philosophers who appear regularly in Arabic gnomologia are largely absent from *Naṣīḥat al-mulūk*. Plato appears on only three occasions, two of which derive from Chapters Twelve and Thirteen, ascribed to Plato, of the pseudo-Aristotelian *Siyāsa al-ᶜāmmiyya*.[52] At the same time, *Naṣīḥat al-mulūk* reflects indirect affinities with ideas current in Greek medical and philosophical writings.

Middle Persian *Andarz* in Early Arabic Literature and in *Naṣīḥat al-mulūk*

The most extensive surviving examples of the Middle Persian *andarz* relating to kings and kingship take the form of 'testaments', known to Pseudo-

Māwardī as *ᶜuhūd.* These compositions include *ᶜAhd Ardashīr*, preserved in Arabic, and the 'Letter of Tansar', preserved in a late Persian version.[53] The former, whether as a complete work or as extracts, was familiar to many writers in Arabic in the early centuries. The latter, according to the thirteenth-century historian of Tabaristan Ibn Isfandiyār, who stumbled upon it in Khwarazm, belonged among the Arabic translations of Ibn al-Muqaffaᶜ.[54] It passed unmentioned among the early writers and evidently circulated little, although Parvaneh Pourshariati has concluded that Balᶜamī knew and made use of the 'Letter of Tansar' in his 'History'.[55] *Naṣīḥat al-mulūk* confirms the disparity in the distribution of the two works: Pseudo-Māwardī knew *ᶜAhd Ardashīr* thoroughly and cited it on numerous occasions, whereas his book reveals no indication of familiarity with the 'Letter of Tansar'. Several additional works of *andarz* were translated, and numerous examples, such as the accession speeches and testaments (*ᶜuhūd*) of Sasanian monarchs other than Ardashīr, appear in dedicated sections and adduced citations in works of Arabic and Persian prose.[56]

Pseudo-Māwardī's use of his materials emerges in greater relief when juxtaposed with the contrasting patterns evident in the *ᶜUyūn al-akhbār* of the ninth-century littérateur (*adīb*) Ibn Qutayba. The differences reflect in part the varying cultural repertoires available in the locations in which the two authors lived and worked. Ibn Qutayba, whose family may have come from Marv, was born in Kufa, held a judgeship in Dinavar from about 236–56/851–70, and spent most of his later life in Baghdad.[57] Unlike Pseudo-Māwardī, he spent most of his productive life in Iraq, which constituted the focus of his cultural activities. The authors' usages of their Greek-, Iranian- and Indic-associated materials also reflect, in part, the different audiences for, and purposes of, their compositions. For both authors, the inclusion of a significant volume of materials of non-Arabic provenance co-existed with an unequivocal attachment to Arabic.[58]

Naṣīḥat al-mulūk also shares many of its illustrative materials with the mid-ninth-century collection known under the title of *Kitāb al-Tāj fī akhlāq al-mulūk* ('Book of the Crown on the Characteristics of Kings'). This *Kitāb al-Tāj*, a text produced for Caliph al-Mutawakkil's courtier and diplomat al-Fatḥ b. Khāqān (d. 247/861–2) and traditionally associated with the authorship of al-Jāḥiẓ (d. 255/868), is, as Gregor Schoeler established, the composition of Muḥammad b. al-Ḥārith al-Taghlibī (or al-Thaᶜlabī) (d. 250/864). Al-Taghlibī was a contemporary of al-Fatḥ b. Khāqān, to whom he dedicated the book.[59] *Kitāb al-Tāj* (also) circulated under the title *Akhlāq al-mulūk* ('The Characteristics of Kings'), as attested in the writings of al-Masᶜūdī (d. 345/956) and Ibn al-Nadīm, and as Ibn Razīn indicates in his twelfth-century abridgement.[60] *Kitāb al-Tāj* combines materials concerned with the customs and ceremonies of the Sasanian, Umayyad and early Abbasid courts. Al-Taghlibī cites few textual sources; characteristically, he presents his materials without reference to outside authorities. A later section of the present chapter explores the relationship between *Kitāb al-Tāj* and *Naṣīḥat al-mulūk*, which makes no reference to a text of this name.

The Testament of Ardashīr

Of all Sasanian writings, the text known as the 'Testament of Ardashīr' (*ᶜAhd Ardashīr*), ascribed to the founding monarch of the Sasanian dynasty, was perhaps the most widely known in the early centuries of the Islamic era.[61] Authors' frequent acknowledgement of this text, presented as Ardashīr's prescriptive statement for his son Shāpūr, attests to its prestige and authority. In his historical narrative *al-Akhbār al-ṭiwāl* ('Long Accounts'), the scholar and lexicographer Abū Ḥanīfa al-Dīnawarī (Pers. Dīnavarī) described the enduring value associated with the 'Testament' in his description of Ardashīr:

> It was Ardashīr who perfected the *āʾīn* (customs, mores) of the kings. He arranged the ranks (*rattaba al-marātib*), established patterns of behaviour (*aḥkama al-siyar*) and investigated affairs both great and small (*tafaqqada ṣaghīr al-amr wa-kabīrahu*), until he had positioned each thing in its place. He enjoined his well-known testament upon the kings (*wa-ᶜahida ᶜahdahu al-maᶜrūf ilā l-mulūk*), and they imitated it, persisted in it, found blessing in preserving it and acting in accordance with it, and made it their lesson and the focus of their attention (*kānū yamtathilūnahu wa-yalzamūnahu wa-yatabarrakūna bi-ḥifẓihi wa-l-ᶜamal bihi wa-yajᶜalūnahu darsahum wa-nuṣb aᶜyunihim*).[62]

Pseudo-Māwardī identified the text as the testament that Ardashīr had composed as 'a model for kingship' (*dustūr al-mulk*), and he further described it as being 'of high importance and great value' (*al-jalīl al-khaṭr al-ᶜaẓīm al-qadr*).[63]

Pseudo-Māwardī integrates numerous quotations from this esteemed text into his exposition, to which he invariably refers as *ᶜahd*, the term by which the *ᶜAhd Ardashīr* describes itself.[64] He often comments on the testament's specific relevance to his points (*wa-qad ḥakā Ardashīr dhālika ᶜan nafsihi fī ᶜahdihi ḥaythu qāla* ('In his testament Ardashīr recounted this on the basis of his own experience when he said'), *wa-laqad dhakara dhālika Ardashīr fī ᶜahdihi wa-jaᶜalahu min khāṣṣ faḍāʾil al-mulūk ḥaythu qāla* ('Ardashīr mentioned this in his testament and placed it among the distinctive virtues of kings when he said'), *wa-qad dalla ᶜalā jihat al-ṣalāḥ fī dhālika Ardashīr al-malik fī ᶜahdihi ḥaythu qāla* ('the king Ardashīr indicated the path towards well-being in this respect in his testament when he said')),[65] and in one place he praises its exceptional aptness for his purposes (*wa-qad qāla Ardashīr fī hādhā l-maᶜnā kāmilan jāmiᶜan li-ᶜāmmat mā dhakarnā wa-huwa* . . . ('On this matter, Ardashīr pronounced a complete and comprehensive statement that encompassed the generality of that which we have mentioned, and that is . . .')).[66]

ᶜAhd Ardashīr circulated in more than one version; Shaul Shaked has indicated the possible co-existence of two independent versions.[67] The 'Testament' known to Pseudo-Māwardī differed in some respects from the version published in Iḥsān ᶜAbbās' edition. It is likely to have been similar in structure; when Pseudo-Māwardī quotes with particular praise Ardashīr's 'first section', the cited passage appears at the opening of ᶜAbbās' edition of *ᶜAhd Ardashīr* as well.[68] Occasionally, Pseudo-Māwardī cites extracts from the, or a, testament (*ᶜahd*) of Ardashīr that do not appear in the published version of *ᶜAhd Ardashīr*, nor among the additional scattered utterances of Ardashīr that ᶜAbbās published in the same volume. Pseudo-Māwardī's attributed passages perhaps derive from the alternative version of the *ᶜAhd* posited by Shaked, or from an altogether different *ᶜahd* similarly ascribed to Ardashīr, who is reported in various works of *adab* to have delivered 'testaments' to a plurality of audiences.

Pseudo-Māwardī cites not only Ardashīr's *ᶜahd*, but also Ardashīrian reports for which the author does not refer to a document. He introduces these materials by means of phrases such as 'It is related of Ardashīr that he used to say . . .' (*fa-qad ḥukiya ᶜan Ardashīr annahu kāna yaqūlu* . . .), a formulation that conveys the author's indirect access to the information.[69] It is likely that these materials circulated in interconnected oral and written forms, and that they were assembled into written collections of varying degrees of formality and levels of circulation. In an example of a more formal collection, for which the author-compiler's name added to its authority, Pseudo-Māwardī in one instance cites an utterance of Ardashīr on the authority of al-Wāqidī.[70]

It is striking that in a number of the cases in which Pseudo-Māwardī invokes Ardashīrian materials without reference to the monarch's *ᶜahd*, these materials find parallels in *Kitāb al-Tāj*. Several of these citations, though not presented in *Naṣīḥat al-mulūk* as part of the *ᶜahd*, appear also in ᶜAbbās' edition of *ᶜAhd Ardashīr*. The inverse also occurs: in at least one instance, an utterance that Pseudo-Māwardī ascribed to Ardashīr's 'testament' appears similarly ascribed in *Kitāb al-Tāj*, but not in ᶜAbbās' published edition.[71] Al-Taghlibī and Pseudo-Māwardī, it appears, were familiar with a version of *ᶜAhd Ardashīr* that differed from the published text. Both authors also had access to additional reports concerning Ardashīr. *Kitāb al-Tāj* provides parallels for the two instances in which Pseudo-Māwardī refers to, and commends, Ardashīr's instituted practices of governance. The first of these examples concerns the Sasanian kings' sleeping habits,[72] and the second concerns the kings' hearing of grievances twice a year, in conjunction with the two major festivals, held at the spring and vernal equinoxes, Nawruz and Mihragan.[73] Pseudo-Māwardī presents his accounts of these practices in a manner that suggests their general familiarity in his milieu.

Of all the Sasanian monarchs, it is Ardashīr whom Pseudo-Māwardī cites most frequently and most carefully. By contrast, Ibn Qutayba barely refers to Ardashīr, and his few references to him are less specific and usually indirect. There is, in fact, little evidence in *ᶜUyūn al-akhbār* that Ibn Qutayba knew *ᶜAhd Ardashīr* as an independent text. Ibn Qutayba's *Kitāb al-Sulṭān* ('Book of Authority', the first of the ten books of which *ᶜUyūn al-akhbār* is composed) contains only two quotations from Ardashīr, and both are ascribed to unspecified *kutub al-ᶜajam*, 'books of the Persians'.[74] Ibn Qutayba also recounts episodes involving Ardashīr, for which he identifies his source as *Siyar al-ᶜajam* ('Accounts of the Conduct of the Persians').[75] The first of the pair of quotations represents Ardashīr's written communication to his subjects (*qaraʾtu fī baᶜḍ kutub al-ᶜajam kitāban li-Ardashīr bn Bābak ilā l-raᶜiyya*, 'I have read in one of the books of the Persians a composition by Ardashīr, son of Bābak, to his subjects').[76] The second quotation represents Ardashīr's communication 'to his son' (*wa-fī kitāb min kutub al-ᶜajam anna Ardashīr qāla li-bnihi* ('it is recorded in a Persian book that Ardashīr said to his son')), and reproduces the best known of all the pronouncements associated with Ardashīr, namely, his assertion of the pairing and mutual dependence of sovereignty and religion.[77] It seems probable that the 'book(s) of the Persians' in which Ibn Qutayba read Ardashīr's utterances consisted of a collection (or collections) of the monarch's dispersed sayings and the more widely remembered extracts from *ᶜAhd Ardashīr*. The likelihood of this conjecture is further indicated in the coincidence of Ibn ᶜAbd Rabbihi's inclusion of virtually identical materials, similarly described, in *al-ᶜIqd al-farīd*.[78] Some collections of this kind probably incorporated materials ascribed to other Sasanian kings as well.[79] Despite the apparent vagueness of a term such as *kutub al-ᶜajam*, Ibn Qutayba's techniques of quotation were by no means imprecise. In the two instances in question, Ibn Qutayba referred to Ardashīr's communications not as *ᶜuhūd*, but as *kutub*: in the first case, the text that he cites refers to itself as Ardashīr's *kitāb*;[80] in the second case, Ibn Qutayba identifies the extract, drawn from the *ᶜAhd Ardashīr*, as Ardashīr's words 'to his son'.

The 'Testament' of Shāpūr

Somewhat less widely known than *ᶜAhd Ardashīr* among authors in Arabic was a 'Testament' of Shāpūr (*ᶜAhd Sābūr*), usually described as a testament to his son Hurmuz(d), and sometimes to his son and successors.[81] The testament was familiar to al-Masᶜūdī[82] and Firdawsī.[83] Pseudo-Māwardī knew the 'Testament' of Shāpūr as an independent text and cited it, with careful acknowledgement, in four instances.[84] Again he makes plain the high esteem in which he held this expression of the wisdom of the Iranian past. On one occasion, he cites Shāpūr's 'Testament' with the favourable endorsement with which he introduced *ᶜAhd Ardashīr* and *Kalīla wa-Dimna*: 'With these meanings or the generality of them, the king Sābūr b. Ardashīr began his valuable and estimable testament to his son, when he said . . .'[85]

By contrast, neither Ibn Qutayba nor Ibn ᶜAbd Rabbihi cited the 'Testament' of Shāpūr in their anthologies, although Ibn Qutayba knew that Shāpūr had articulated such as testament when, at the time of his death, he summoned his son Hurmuz and designated him as his successor.[86] The most continuous, though incomplete, rendering of *ᶜAhd Sābūr* in Arabic appears in the *Taʾrīkh ghurar al-siyar* of al-Thaᶜālibī, who knew it as a 'long testament' (*ᶜahd ṭawīl*) from which he reproduced excerpts, one of which, concerning the collection of the *kharāj*, bears some resemblance to one of Pseudo-Māwardī's citations.[87]

The *Kitāb al-Saᶜāda wa-l-isᶜād* of Ibn Abī Dharr, whose work reflects a milieu similar to that of Pseudo-Māwardī but about whom nothing further is known, contains an especially large number of citations from *ᶜAhd Sābūr*.[88] In several instances, Ibn Abī Dharr cites the *ᶜAhd* through the *Khudaynāmeh*, the royal chronicle of the Sasanian era which, it is to be inferred, contained a version of the text.[89] There are no exact coincidences between the passages cited in *Naṣīḥat al-mulūk* and *Kitāb al-Saᶜāda wa-l-isᶜād*, although in a single case, related to the need for the king to avoid acquiring a reputation amongst his viziers for susceptibility to passion, Ibn Abī Dharr appears to record a truncated version of Pseudo-Māwardī's lengthier quotation.[90]

The 'Testament' of Anūshīrvān

The reign of Khusraw I Anūshīrvān (r. 531–79) is reported to have seen the compilation of several works of *andarz*. Two extant works in Middle Persian and others in Arabic are ascribed to the king himself. Ibn al-Nadīm records four texts allegedly composed by Anūshīrvān. Three of these compositions are designated 'testaments', two of which were addressed to his son, Hurmuz.[91] On a single occasion and in a general fashion, Pseudo-Māwardī refers to a 'Testament' of Anūshīrvān. He writes, 'We have read similarly in the "Testament(s)" of Anūshīrvān and Shāpūr regarding the exaltation of religion, its defence, and striving to preserve and protect it' (*wa-ka-dhālika qaraʾnā fī ᶜahd Anūshīrwān wa-Sābūr min taᶜẓīm al-dīn wa-l-dhabb ᶜanhu wa-l-ijtihād fī ḥimāyatihi wa-ṣiyānatihi*).[92] Pseudo-Māwardī's formulation, which perhaps reflects some textual corruption in the process of transmission, indicates that he had read the text(s) in question.

Pseudo-Māwardī cites Anūshīrvān in contexts that perhaps reflect the interplay of oral and written exchange in his environment. For example, without acknowledgement of a source, he names Anūshīrvān as the exponent of a 'circle of justice', a formulation that portrays justice as the indispensable foundation of the social and political order, in the form, 'Kingship is dependent on the soldiery, the soldiery depends on funds, funds derive from the lands, the lands are made prosperous through cultivation, and cultivation cannot be achieved without justice.'[93] In another instance, he narrates, in anonymous fashion and perhaps an indication of the prevailing oral culture (*qālū*), Anūshīrvān's celebrated sending of an envoy to one of his enemies, and his prediction of victory on the basis of the hostile king's disposition to jest over earnestness.[94] Elsewhere, apparently on the authority of Ibn al-Muqaffaᶜ, he reports Anūshīrvān's axiomatic response to the Byzantine emperor (Qayṣar), who asked how he governed his kingdom.[95]

By comparison, Kisrā Anūshīrvān, sometimes invoked simply as Kisrā, is a far more dominant presence in Ibn Qutayba's *ᶜUyūn al-akhbār* than in *Naṣīḥat al-mulūk*. The first of Ibn Qutayba's references to the monarch occurs at the very outset of his text, where he relates a ḥadīth, complete with *isnād*, in which the Prophet receives news of Kisrā's death.[96] On three occasions, Ibn Qutayba relates episodes involving Anūshīrvān for which, as in the case of his references to Ardashīr, he cites *kutub al-ᶜajam* ('books of the Persians').[97] Ibn Qutayba also cites the king's correspondence with his lords of the marches (*marāziba*, pl. of *marzubān*).[98] In many instances, Kisrā appears as a speaker of memorable utterances as well as an interlocutor, usually with his minister Buzurgmihr, who responds sagely to the monarch's questions.[99]

When Pseudo-Māwardī invokes Anūshīrvān, he identifies him by name rather than by the generic appellation Kisrā, common to the references of Ibn Qutayba and other writers in Arabic.[100] An exception to this specificity occurs in the epilogue, where, as previously noted, Pseudo-Māwardī's technique is in contrast to the discursive and carefully documented approach of his book. In this location, the author refers to a 'Kisrā', otherwise unspecified, in an exchange with the kings of Greece, China and India on the subject of speech.[101] Since, in the various versions of this well-known story, none of the kings is identified as an individual, Pseudo-Māwardī's exceptional use of the term Kisrā is explicable, and suggests the particular character and purposes of his epilogue.[102]

Khusraw Parvīz (Abarwīz)

Pseudo-Māwardī cites a single utterance ascribed to Khusraw Parvīz.[103] Already mentioned, this utterance appears in his preface, where Pseudo-Māwardī introduces it with the non-specific formula 'they said' (*qālū*), a reference to oral sources, common knowledge or a written report that reached him without a named authority. Pseudo-Māwardī also includes Khusraw Parvīz in his list of the Sasanian kings who adopted the prudential custom of sleeping in different and unpredictable locations.[104] Like several other citations and references that appear in *Naṣīḥat al-mulūk* in contexts that suggest general and dispersed knowledge, very possibly in circulation as oral lore, both these passages also appear in al-Taghlibī's *Kitāb al-Tāj*. The parallels suggest a common repertoire on which both authors drew.

In another contrast between the materials cited in *Naṣīḥat al-mulūk* and *ᶜUyūn al-akhbār*, Ibn Qutayba cites a particularly large number of sayings of Khusraw Parvīz. Furthermore, Ibn Qutayba frequently indicates that he had read some of these pronouncements in Khusraw Parvīz's written communication to his son Shīrūya (Shīrawayh) (*qaraᵓtu fī kitāb Abarwīz ilā bnihi Shīrawayh*, 'I read in Khusraw Parvīz's letter to his son Shīrawayh'),[105] and others in '*al-Tāj*' or '*Kitāb al-Tāj*'.[106] The four quotations ascribed to Khusraw Parvīz in *al-ᶜIqd al-farīd* occur in *ᶜUyūn al-akhbār* as well. Like Ibn Qutayba, Ibn ᶜAbd Rabbihi locates three of his citations from Khusraw Parvīz amongst the king's communications with his son Shīrawayh; he further identifies *al-Tāj* as the source for one of these examples. Again coinciding with Ibn Qutayba, Ibn ᶜAbd Rabbihi cites a communication addressed by Khusraw Parvīz to his treasurer, a passage that Ibn Qutayba stated that he had read in *al-Tāj*.[107] The *Kitāb al-Tāj* from which Ibn Qutayba drew his quotations from Khusraw Parvīz was evidently not the work of al-Taghlibī, since the latter author included none of the passages that appear in *ᶜUyūn al-akhbār*.[108] Ibn Qutayba's source apparently included not only Khusraw Parvīz's writings to Shīrawayh, but also his communications with his treasurer (*ṣāḥib bayt al-māl*) and his chamberlain (*ḥājib*).[109] Rarely, Ibn Qutayba relates an episode or account concerning Khusraw Parvīz without identifying its provenance.[110]

Buzurgmihr

The identification of Buzurgmihr with the epitome of wise counsel was probably well established in the late Sasanian period, and was a fixture by the time that the Arabic versions of *Kalīla wa-Dimna* were in production. The figure of Buzurgmihr combined the sagacity of the moral counsellor with the experience of the resolute minister; his personification of these manifestations of wisdom pervades the earliest compositions in Persian, and finds lengthy documentation in the *Shāhnāmeh* of Firdawsī.[111] Despite Buzurgmihr's prominence in other works in Arabic, Pseudo-Māwardī, whose avowed preference for historical rather than legendary materials has been mentioned, invokes the figure in only two instances. In the first case, adduced probably on the basis of oral reports (*ruwiya ᶜan*, 'it is related from'), he evokes Buzurgmihr b. al-Bukhtakār *ḥakīm al-ᶜajam*, 'the sage of the Persians'; in the second, on the authority of al-Wāqidī, he records Buzurgmihr's commendation or testament to his son.[112]

By contrast, Buzurgmihr, often in conjunction with Anūshīrvān, appears prominently in *ᶜUyūn al-akhbār*. Ibn Qutayba usually invokes Buzurgmihr as the exponent of sage aphorisms; he appears three times in this capacity in Ibn Qutayba's 'Book of Knowledge and Elucidation' (*Kitāb al-ᶜIlm wa-l-bayān*).[113] In several instances, these formulations consist of question and answer; Buzurgmihr provides wise responses to questions posed to him,[114] frequently by Anūshīrvān.[115] Anūshīrvān also appears in exchanges with Buzurgmihr subsequent to his imprisonment of the minister.[116]

Kitāb al-Āʾīn

Like several other authors in Arabic, Pseudo-Māwardī was familiar with and cited a text that he knew as *Āʾīnnāmeh* or *Kitāb Āʾīnnāmeh*.[117] The generic designation *āʾīnnāmeh* derives from the Middle Persian *ēwēn nāmag* or 'book of manners', a category that subsumed writings of a religious as well as a non-religious orientation.[118] The topics addressed in books of *āʾīn* appear to have been both various and specific. Surviving examples of texts described as *āʾīn* treat rules of etiquette at the royal court and among the great families, customs and conduct, skills, arts and sciences. Among the non-religious works, certain examples dealt with the game of chess, the sports of archery or polo; others dealt with weaponry and the rules of warfare.[119] Al-Masᶜūdī, writing in 345/956, provided the Arabic explanatory gloss *kitāb al-rusūm*, 'book of customs' or 'book of protocols'. He reported that the Persians possessed a book called *kahnāmāh* (*gahnāmāh*) that detailed the ranks, 600 of them, of the kingdom of Fars, and that this *gahnāmāh* formed part of the *Āʾīnnāmāh*, a colossal (*ʿaẓīm*) work in thousands of pages, complete copies of which only the *mōbadh*s and other holders of high authority (*dhawū l-riʾāsāt*) possessed.[120] Often considered a product of the genre is al-Taghlibī's *Kitāb al-Tāj fī akhlāq al-mulūk*, parts of which convey the *āʾīn* of the Sasanian court and address topics similar to those in the *Āʾīn* of Ardashīr. In 1966, Mario Grignaschi published an Arabic work of *āʾīn* presented, after an introduction of the circumstances of the composition, in the voice of Ardashīr. Among the topics treated in this text are the four divisions of the day, appropriate dress, the etiquette of eating and drinking, and the management of women, children and the extended household.[121] Grignaschi noted that the sparse evidence available suggests that works of *āʾīn* did not necessarily contain historical accounts and anecdotes, but that such materials might have been added through the combination of several books of *āʾīn*, possibly, he suggests, by the translator Ibn al-Muqaffaʿ, who, according to Ibn al-Nadīm, translated an *āʾīnnāmeh fī l-āʾīn*, 'a book called *āʾīnnāmeh*, on the subject of manners and customs'.[122] It is quite likely that the work of Ibn al-Muqaffaʿ provided Pseudo-Māwardī with his source.[123]

Pseudo-Māwardī was aware that the Sasanian kings possessed a number of books of *āʾīn*. In one instance he refers to 'the Persian kings . . . and that which they described in their books of *āʾīn*' (*mulūk al-ʿajam wa-mā ujtuniya min ārāʾihim wa-waṣafūhu fī kutub āʾīnihim*).[124] This phrase introduces the previously cited maxim: 'The people most disposed to difficulty and regret are those who are most recalcitrant towards their advisers.' It is notable that whereas most writers in Arabic refer to *kutub al-āʾīn*, Pseudo-Māwardī, apart from the previously cited instance, employed the Persian form *Āʾīnnāmeh*; it is conceivable that he knew, or knew of, the text(s) in a Persian form. He knew, or knew of, the *Āʾīnnāmeh* as a written text, on two occasions using the Arabic-cum-Persian formulation *Kitāb Āʾīnnāmeh*. He does not indicate that he has read the work himself. He introduces a pair of citations, both of which encourage association with the learned, in the passive voice (*wa-maktūb fī āʾīnnāma*, 'it is written in [the or a] book of manners and customs'). He introduces further quotations, concerned with the avoidance of elevating persons of low status or demoting persons of high status, and with the abandonment of excessive royal seclusion, through similar statements (*fī kitāb āʾīnnāmeh*, 'in the book "The Book of Manners and Customs"').[125] The topics addressed in Pseudo-Māwardī's citations convey counsel to rulers; the extracts encourage the king to display proper attentiveness to the persons with whom he interacts, to profit from their advice and learning, and to observe the norms of expected royal conduct. It is possible that the *ā'īnnāmeh* known to Pseudo-Māwardī bore some resemblance to the example briefly cited by al-Thaʿālibī, who adduced quotations concerned with the ranks of the persons (*marātib al-nās*) admitted into the ruler's *majlis*.[126]

Ibn Qutayba also knew and cited a *Kitāb al-Ā'īn*, which he, unlike Pseudo-Māwardī, often introduced with the explicit formula, 'I have read in the *Ā'īn* . . .'[127] The *Kitāb al-Ā'īn* known to Ibn Qutayba included sections that treated more specific customs and manners in the courtly setting, such as the etiquette of eating and dietary advice (the discouragement, for example, of the consumption of garlic and onions), as well as matters pertaining to service in the palace.[128] The citations in *ʿUyūn al-akhbār* and *Naṣīḥat al-mulūk* do not coincide. It is likely that Pseudo-Māwardī, who elsewhere remarks specifically on his lack of expertise and interest in matters of courtly protocol,[129] adopted the more generally edificatory and practical materials from the corpus known to him, perhaps still close to its Middle Persian antecedents.[130]

Kitāb al-Tāj

Just as several texts known under the rubric of *ā'īn* appear to have circulated in the early centuries of the Islamic period, more than one text associated with the designation *al-tāj*, which similarly suggested a generic marker rather than a title, appear to have been available in Arabic forms.[131] References and quotations imply that these writings were associated with the culture of the Sasanian royal court. The extent to which Arabic works designated *kutub al-tāj* represented translations of Middle Persian texts is uncertain; the *Kitāb al-Tāj fī akhlāq al-mulūk* ('Book of the Crown on the Characteristics of Kings') of al-Taghlibī certainly conveys, as part of its eclectic subject matter, Sasanian customs, as well as reports of the practices of Umayyad and Abbasid caliphs and their administrators. Muḥammadī has proposed four distinct *kutub al-tāj* apparently rendered into Arabic: *Kitāb al-Tāj fī sīrat Anūshīrwān* ('Book of the Crown on the Conduct of Anūshīrvān'); the *Kitāb al-Tāj* cited by Ibn Qutayba; *Kitāb al-Tāj wa-mā tafā'alat bihi mulūkuhum* ('Book of the

Crown and that which their kings took as auguries'); and the *Kitāb al-Tāj* on which the *Kitāb al-Tāj fī akhlāq al-mulūk*, the work of al-Taghlibī, was constructed.[132] Two of these items, the first and the third, appear in *al-Fihrist* of Ibn al-Nadīm. The first is listed among the translations into Arabic of Ibn al-Muqaffa^c under the title *Kitāb al-Tāj fī sīrat Anūshīrwān*, and was published in Grignaschi's article in *Journal Asiatique* in 1966;[133] the third appears in Ibn al-Nadīm's listing of Persian books 'on the true accounts and tales of their kings' (*fī l-siyar wa-l-asmār al-ṣaḥīḥa allatī li-mulūkihim*).[134] Maxim-like quotations from a *Kitāb al-Tāj* also appear in Ibn Abī Dharr's *Kitāb al-Saᶜāda wa-l-isᶜād*.[135]

As observed in the preceding pages, Ibn Qutayba's *Kitāb al-Tāj* was distinct from al-Taghlibī's *Kitāb al-Tāj fī akhlāq al-mulūk*. Especially prevalent among the materials included in Ibn Qutayba's *ᶜUyūn al-akhbār* as quotations from a *Kitāb al-Tāj* are, as indicated above, passages that convey the commendations of Khusraw Parvīz to his son Shīrawayh, or sometimes to his principal officials.[136] Lecomte proposed that by the time Ibn al-Nadīm compiled *al-Fihrist*, an association with the more commonly invoked Khusraw I Anūshīrvān had displaced an earlier association with Khusraw II Parvīz; both monarchs were commonly referred to as 'Kisrā'.[137]

Pseudo-Māwardī neither mentions nor cites a *Kitāb* (or *kutub*) *al-Tāj*, but he relates a number of materials that coincide with the contents of the ninth-century *Kitāb al-Tāj fī akhlāq al-mulūk* of al-Taghlibī. A preponderance of the texts common to both works appear in *Naṣīḥat al-mulūk* with the prefatory phrase *wa-ḥukiya* ('it is related'), which is likely to imply the author's allusion to materials that amounted to general knowledge, broadly disseminated by a combination of oral and written media. The materials that appear in both texts include accounts related to the Sasanian and the early Islamic eras. Some of the common materials are associated in both locations with Ardashīr. In one instance, as indicated above, Pseudo-Māwardī cites a passage as a quotation from 'Ardashīr's Testament' (*wa-qad qāla Ardashīr fī ᶜahdihi*) that does not appear in the published version of *ᶜAhd Ardashīr*.[138] In another instance, Pseudo-Māwardī records Ardashīr's attentiveness to the daily and nocturnal activities of his *ᶜāmma* and *khāṣṣa* with the introductory formula *wa-ka-dhālika ḥukiya ᶜan Ardashīr min mulūk al-ᶜajam* ('similarly it is related regarding Ardashīr among the Persian kings').[139] In a previously mentioned example, Pseudo-Māwardī relates the practice of the Sasanian kings (*wa-ḥukiya fī siyar mulūk Āl Sāsān*, 'it is related regarding the conduct of the Sasanian kings'), and specifies, in this order, Ardashīr, Shāpūr, Bahrām Gūr, Yazdagird, Khusraw Parvīz and Anūshīrvān; although the text is not identical, the same chronological sequence of Sasanian monarchs appears in al-Taghlibī's *Kitāb al-Tāj*.[140]

Other parallel texts concern the early caliphs, such as ᶜUmar, whose exceptional knowledge with regard to occurrences in his domains Pseudo-Māwardī introduces, after presentation of God's knowledge of the Unseen and the divinely bestowed insight of the angels and the Prophet, with the phrase *fa-ammā ᶜan khulafāʾihi al-rāshidīn fa-ḥukiya ᶜan ᶜUmar* ('as for his Rightly Guided Caliphs, it is related regarding ᶜUmar').[141] Next the author notes the similar discernment of the 'king' Muᶜāwiya (*wa-kāna Muᶜāwiya min al-mulūk ka-dhālika*, 'among the kings, Muᶜāwiya was similar'), and his administrator and governor Ziyād b. Abīhi's imitation of Muᶜāwiya's example in this regard (*wa-qtafā atharahu fī dhālika Ziyād bn Abīhi*), for which he relates a widely reported narrative concerning a petitioner's astonishment at Ziyād's foreknowledge of his affairs.[142] The accounts in the two books are similar, but presented in a different framework. The fuller account in *Kitāb al-Tāj* includes a reference to ᶜUmar's letters to his governors (*ᶜummāl*), and the observation that in his scrutiny of his subjects' secrets, ᶜUmar governed the subjects as Ardashīr had governed (*fa-sāsa siyāsat Ardashīr bn Bābak fī l-faḥṣ ᶜan asrārihā khāṣṣatan*); whereas Pseudo-Māwardī added the regionally appropriate example of ᶜAbdallāh b. Ṭāhir.[143] Much of Pseudo-Māwardī's material concerning the sending of ambassadors similarly duplicates, but does not reproduce verbatim, materials recorded in *Kitāb al-Tāj*. For example, Pseudo-Māwardī opens a section with the statement, 'The early kings among the Arabs and the Persians in this matter (exercised) remarkable investigation, precise oversight and substantial examination' (*wa-kāna lil-mulūk al-awwalīn min al-ᶜarab wa-l-ᶜajam fī hādhā l-bāb istiqṣāʾ ᶜajīb wa-naẓar daqīq wa-mtiḥān kabīr*), and proceeds to relate two quotations from Ardashīr (*wa-ḥukiya ᶜan Ardashīr annahu kāna yaqūlu . . . wa-kāna yaqūlu . . .*, 'it is related that Ardashīr used to say . . . and he used to say . . .').[144] The substance of the passage, again illustrated with reference to Ardashīr, is similar in *Kitāb al-Tāj*, where, however, only *mulūk al-aᶜājim* are credited with such care.[145]

Both authors then proceed to a lengthy and almost identical account of Alexander's sending of an envoy to 'a king of the east'.[146]

Most striking among the parallel texts in the ninth-century *Kitāb al-Tāj* and *Naṣīḥat al-mulūk* is a lengthy passage concerning the Sasanian practices of holding court for the redress of grievances, *maẓālim*, on the occasions of Nawruz and Mihrajan. The passage in question appears, without indication of a source, in almost identical form in the two books.[147] Subsequently the same account appears, also without attribution, in very similar form in the Persian works, the *Siyar al-mulūk* of Niẓām al-Mulk, where it is introduced with the phrase *chunīn gūyand keh rasm-i malikān-i ᶜālam-i ᶜajam chunān būdeh ast* ('they say that the custom of the kings of the Persian world was like this'), and the *Naṣīḥat al-mulūk* of (Pseudo-)Ghazālī.[148] Later Persian writers assimilate the Samanid Amir Ismāᶜīl b. Aḥmad to the exemplary conduct of the Persian kings, especially with regard to his selfless efforts to permit the redress of his subjects' grievances.[149] It again seems probable that the earlier authors drew from a common repertoire, and that such accounts circulated in multiple forms. Ahmad Zeki Pacha, who edited al-Taghlibī's *Kitāb al-Tāj fī akhlāq al-mulūk*, identified large numbers of parallel occurrences between *Kitāb al-Tāj* and other Arabic compositions.[150]

What is perhaps most significant about the parallels between *Kitāb al-Tāj* and *Naṣīḥat al-mulūk* is the coincidence in the ordering of items in both texts. Al-Taghlibī and Pseudo-Māwardī frequently present clusters of examples in identical sequence.[151] This similarity increases the likelihood that the two authors possessed a common written source.

The *Khudaynāmeh, Siyar al-ᶜajam* or *Siyar al-mulūk*

Pseudo-Māwardī neither refers to nor cites, under this name, the *Khudaynāmeh*, reportedly translated from Middle Persian into Arabic by Ibn al-Muqaffaᶜ.[152] He was, however, almost certainly familiar with its contents. His acquaintance with the Sasanians' royal testaments, which probably circulated independently and in various collections as well as within the historiographical corpus devoted to the Persian kings, has been established; as suggested earlier in the present chapter, the author availed himself principally of these examples of wisdom to the exclusion of the narrative content that provided context for their delivery. Materials related to the Sasanian historiographical literature appear to have circulated in Arabic under various headings. Ibn Qutayba cites, always specifying that he has read it, a *Siyar al-ᶜajam* ('Chronicles of the Persians'),[153] and several writers refer to and cite a *Siyar al-mulūk* ('Chronicles of the Kings'). Among these authors, al-Jāḥiẓ mentions *Siyar al-mulūk* and the *Kārwand*[154] as books of the Persians, and, noting the high regard for these works among 'persons eagerly attached to Persian-ness' (*man yataᶜaṣṣabu lil-ᶜajamiyya*), reports, in an ironic matter, that such persons averred, 'When a person needs intellect and *adab*, knowledge of the ranks, cautionary examples and models, and fine expressions and noble meanings, let him look into *Siyar al-mulūk*.'[155] Al-Bīrūnī mentions, in addition to Ibn al-Muqaffaᶜ, several authors each of whom produced a *kitāb siyar al-mulūk*.[156] Pseudo-Māwardī refers to *siyar al-ᶜajam* and *siyar al-mulūk*, but in contexts that do not appear to designate written texts.

It is evident that Pseudo-Māwardī possessed a broad and deep knowledge of the literary repertoire transposed from Middle Persian into Arabic. His use of this repertoire was selective. In accordance with the approach that he adopts throughout *Naṣīḥat al-mulūk*, he adduces materials that he considers 'useful' and conducive to the king's welfare and his subjects' well-being (*ṣalāḥ, maṣlaḥa*). He therefore discriminated between legendary tales and reports concerning historical figures, whose wise pronouncements had acquired authority and prestige in the cultural memory of the region's peoples.

In considering the use of Iranian-associated materials in *Naṣīḥat al-mulūk*, it is instructive to remember Pseudo-Māwardī's probable background in Tukharistan. If not to the same degree as at Tus, there is evidence to suggest that Balkh supported a group of persons who dedicated themselves to the preservation and reinvigoration of the narrative traditions of the Iranian past: the records of the composition of *shāhnāmeh*s in Persian before Firdawsī include the names of Abū ᶜAlī Muḥammad b. Aḥmad al-Balkhī and Abū l-Muᵓayyad al-Balkhī (fl. late fourth/tenth century),[157] and according to some sources, Daqīqī (d. *c.* 366/976) was also born in Balkh, an assertion, whether accurate or not, that attests to the city's associations with such activities in a period not long after the presumed lifespan of Pseudo-Māwardī.[158] Pseudo-Māwardī, a Persian-speaking author of an Arabic mirror that accentuates the virtues of Arabic for a courtly audience enthusiastic in its sponsorship of literary activities in Persian, especially the poetry of Rūdakī, represented a contrasting cultural and intellectual outlook.

A similar combination of receptivity to wisdom regardless of its provenance with a discriminating appropriation of the rich cultural resources available to Pseudo-Māwardī in Balkh emerges from a consideration of his employment of Indic-associated materials, to which the following section is dedicated.

Indic-associated Sources

Several writers of the ninth and tenth centuries associated India, sometimes with Iran, as a location that had produced useful knowledge, including in the matter of politics.[159] One of the most striking features of *Naṣīḥat al-mulūk* is the particular prominence in it of materials ascribed by Pseudo-Māwardī to Indic sources. To the extent that these materials were known to the author in written forms (and in several cases, he indicates precisely that he has read them), they are quite likely, like *Kalīla wa-Dimna,* to have been conveyed to Iran in the Sasanian era and rendered from Sanskrit, and perhaps Pali, into Middle Persian, and subsequently, probably in the eighth century, into Arabic. If *Naṣīḥat al-mulūk* was indeed a product of Balkh and Tukharistan, it is similarly likely that Pseudo-Māwardī's Indic-associated materials were integral parts of a local cultural environment that he had inherited. *Naṣīḥat al-mulūk,* a product of this context, preserves materials that have otherwise been so fully reshaped in the processes of transmission that the memory of their Indic provenance has been lost. Pseudo-Māwardī's Indic-associated repertoire consists of three major sets of materials. The first comprises materials related to *Kalīla wa-Dimna*; the second, extracts from a written document known to the author as the *ᶜahd* of an Indian king to his son; the third, utterances of the Buddha.[160] To illuminate further the distinctive qualities of *Naṣīḥat al-mulūk,* the following discussion compares the use of Indic materials in the mirror with their use in Ibn Qutayba's *ᶜUyūn al-akhbār.*

Kalīla wa-Dimna

The best known of Pseudo-Māwardī's Indic-associated sources is *Kalīla wa-Dimna,* which he, like other authors in Arabic, cited on several occasions. At the core of the Arabic versions of *Kalīla wa-Dimna,* it is supposed, lies a set of stories linked indirectly to the Indian *Pañcatantra*, which belongs to the *arthaśāstra* tradition, the Indian genre related to political advice. Rendered in the Sasanian era into Middle Persian and Syriac versions, *Kalīla wa-Dimna*, in its several subsequent Arabic incarnations, contributed significantly to the formation of Arabic literary culture.[161] The figure most frequently associated with the rendering of the collection into Arabic is Ibn al-Muqaffaᶜ.[162] The large number of extant manuscripts provides evidence of the Arabic collection's popularity, but the earliest extant manuscript is dated 681/1221; the next oldest is dated 739/1339.[163] As described earlier in this chapter, the vizier Abū l-Fażl Balᶜamī is reported to have produced, in prose, the first Persian translation, which Rūdakī turned into verse. The twelfth century saw the production of new Persian translations; these twelfth-century translations, undertaken by Muḥammad al-Bukhārī for the Zangid atabeg of Mosul Sayf al-Dīn Ghāzī (r. 541–4/1146–9) and by Naṣr Allāh Munshī for his Ghaznavid patron, Bahrāmshāh (r. *c.* 511–52/1117–57), survive in twelfth-century manuscripts, copied earlier, in fact, than the surviving Arabic versions.[164] Ibn Qutayba includes several quotations or close paraphrases from the work, sometimes introduced with specific reference to the collection,[165] but more commonly by means of the generic phrase 'in one of the books of the Indians'.[166] It was by the corresponding phrase *fī kutub al-ᶜajam*, as demonstrated earlier in the present chapter, that Ibn Qutayba adduced his quotations from Ardashīr and other Sasanian kings.

The early tenth-century interest in the retrieval into Persian of the culture of the Iranian past stimulated an intensified engagement with *Kalīla wa-Dimna*. Pseudo-Māwardī, who lived in an environment conducive to this project, evinced a somewhat ambivalent attitude towards the collection of fables. Like the *Shāhnāmeh*, and probably the *Khudaynāmeh* before it, *Kalīla wa-Dimna* combined narrative with aphoristic materials. In his introduction, Ibn al-Muqaffaᶜ (or the individual(s) assimilated into Ibn al-Muqaffaᶜ's persona) stated that the Indian sage Bīdpāy had incorporated into his work the knowledge necessary to human beings in matters of religion and the world, and had fashioned it to resemble other books of wisdom, in such a way that the stories of the animals offered entertainment while their utterances conveyed wisdom and *adab*.[167] At the conclusion of the collection, Ibn al-Muqaffaᶜ reiterated its function as a work of *naṣīḥa* and *maw*ᶜ*iẓa*.[168] The stories, accordingly, are positioned within a frame that asserts their edificatory value, and the maxims provide the semblance of a periodic, if often perplexing, commentary. It was the wisdom-related components of the collection that Pseudo-Māwardī considered most 'beneficial' for his purposes.

Pseudo-Māwardī cites *Kalīla wa-Dimna* with explicit approval on several occasions. In two instances, he distinguishes the 'author' of the opening part of the text for particular praise. On neither occasion does he identify the author, and given the accretion of layers of introductory materials to the collection of stories in their Arabic forms, it is not always obvious which of the persons involved in the creation and transmission of the text he had in mind. One of the two examples reads:

> How well the author of *Kalīla wa-Dimna* spoke when he commenced his book (*mā aḥsana mā ṣadara bihi ṣāḥib Kalīla wa-Dimna kitābahu*) with the words, 'The best of provisions for the young is a good education (*al-adab al-ṣāliḥ*). Its cultivation in youth, when the memory is attentive and the heart free of care, is an advantage (*ghunm*), for that which is usefully acquired (*mustafād*) in early life endures like an engraving on stone.'[169]

The second passage reads:

> In accordance with this (previously mentioned point) is that by which the author of *Kalīla wa-Dimna* began his book when he wrote, 'People may be divided into four groups, characterised by their craving for wealth (*al-raghba fī l-māl*), their desire for pleasures (*al-shahwa lil-ladhdhāt*), their quest for reputation (*ṭalab al-dhikr*) and their working for their final return (the afterlife) (*al-*ᶜ*amal lil-ma*ᶜ*ād*).'[170]

Both passages illustrate Pseudo-Māwardī's attraction to the collection's instructive material, especially as expressed in the form of maxims. Not surprisingly, they reveal that the version of the collection available to Pseudo-Māwardī differed from the text(s) available in modern printed editions. The second passage, in which the four *puruṣārtha*s, praiseworthy goals of humankind in Indic tradition (*kāma*, *artha*, *dharma* and *mokśa*, sensual pleasure, wealth or worldly status, duty and release), a theory encountered in the *dharmaśāstra*s and epics,[171] remain perceptible, bears a resemblance to texts that appear in published editions of *Kalīla wa-Dimna*, including that of Louis Cheikho, which is based on one of the earlier manuscripts.[172] In these versions, the passage indeed appears as part of a first-person narrative in the preliminary section recorded under the name of Barzawayh, presumably Pseudo-Māwardī's 'author' in this case. Pseudo-Māwardī appears to comment on the passage in a manner that suggests some familiarity with Indian teachings related to the four goals, in which the first three are grouped in ranked order, while the fourth is not only supreme but also different in kind:[173]

> The first three goals are of imminent transience yet lasting consequence (*tabiʿa*), while the fourth subsumes the first three without consequence.

By 'consequence', Pseudo-Māwardī perhaps conveys the concept of *karma*, the consequences of actions that accumulate over the course of a lifetime (or lifetimes) and determine rebirth. Adopting a more familiar lexicon, he then takes the first three categories of wealth (*artha*), pleasure (*kāma*) and good reputation (corresponding to *dharma*) and offers a figurative reinterpretation appropriate to his milieu and audience:

> There are no riches (*ghinan*) like contentment; there is no pleasure (*ladhdha*) like religious mindfulness (*taqwā*), which hastens the joy of good tidings; and there is no repute (*dhikr*) nobler than obedience to God, which makes everything appear fearful to its possessor, and in the absence of which everything is to be feared.[174]

On several occasions, Pseudo-Māwardī cites, without acknowledging a specific source, an aphorism that also occurs in *Kalīla wa-Dimna*. In many instances, these maxims appear as quotations in both places; for example, the maxim, 'He who conceals his advice from the ruler, his illness from the doctors, and his sorrow from his friends, has betrayed himself', appears in *Kalīla wa-Dimna* with the introductory phrase 'It is said' (*fa-innahu yuqālu*), and in *Naṣīḥat al-mulūk* with the similar formula 'It used to be said' (*wa-kāna yuqālu*).[175] Both occurrences suggest an authorial sense of incorporating, on a level apart from the central argument or narrative, an apposite *bon mot*, the provenance of which required no further elaboration. Rather than suppressing the 'source' of his 'quotation', it is likely that Pseudo-Māwardī, who indicated that he had not coined the formulation himself, did not regard it as a 'quotation' from an identifiable text so much as part of a common cultural currency available for his use, as it had been available to the 'author' of *Kalīla wa-Dimna*. It is indicative of Ibn Qutayba's greater remove from Indic-associated materials that when he cited the same maxim in *ʿUyūn al-akhbār*, he identified its provenance from *kitāb lil-hind* ('an Indian book').[176]

The appearance of *Naṣīḥat al-mulūk* at a time when *Kalīla wa-Dimna* was the focus of positive attention in the eastern regions provides a context for not only specific textual parallels, but also the many more general similarities between the two texts. Beyond the presence of coinciding maxims and explicit quotations, *Naṣīḥat al-mulūk* displays many characteristics that suggest an environment receptive to, and imprinted by, the Arabic *Kalīla wa-Dimna* and similar texts. Certain phrasings occur commonly in both texts, such as 'the resolute king' (*al-malik al-ḥāzim*, pl. *al-mulūk al-ḥazama*) and 'wicked viziers' (*wuzarāʾ al-sūʾ*); it is again notable that whereas Pseudo-Māwardī employs the former phrase as a matter of course, Ibn Qutayba, when he adopted it in *ʿUyūn al-akhbār*, explicitly ascribed it to *kitāb lil-hind*.[177] *Kalīla wa-Dimna* includes references to Balkh,[178] and displays an interest in renunciation of the world; an ascetic (*nāsik*) appears in several stories in *Kalīla wa-Dimna*, which is replete with warnings against the pitfalls of succumbing to pleasure. One evocative passage describes the inevitability by which pleasure turns to pain and generates sadness, just as salted water leaves the drinker thirstier than before; another conjures up a dog with a bone, attracted by the scent of meat yet finding not a morsel of it left.[179] An austere disposition pervades much of *Naṣīḥat al-mulūk*, which in one place, noting that desires, once attained, are continually replaced by new cravings, recalls, as noted in Volume I, Buddhist teachings.[180]

If, like many authors in Arabic of the early centuries, Pseudo-Māwardī held the moralising and aphoristic passages of *Kalīla wa-Dimna* in high regard, he makes little direct use of the collection's stories. He does not mention *Kalīla wa-Dimna* among the *afsānaqāt* that he considers pointless. On the other hand, it is in the context of the futility of stories that he cites a certain exegetical interpretation of the Qurʾānic verse 'And among the people are those who purchase the diversion of talk (*lahw al-ḥadīth*), so that they mislead from the path of God without knowledge' (Q 31: 6). Pseudo-Māwardī alludes to the interpretation that the verse refers to (al-Naḍr b.)

al-Ḥārith b. Kalada (d. *c.* 13/634), who gathered people together and read *Kalīla wa-Dimna* to them, and claimed that its tales were more pleasing and beautiful than the ancient stories (*asāṭīr al-awwalīn*, Q 6:25, 8: 31, 16: 24, 23: 83, 25: 5, 27: 68, 46: 17, 68: 15, 83: 13) brought by Muḥammad. According to the exegetes, God had sent down this verse in refutation of al-Naḍr's assertion.[181] Pseudo-Māwardī alludes to this episode in the context of his discouragement of the inclusion of fictitious tales among the reading matter assigned for the prince's education, for stories of this kind will benefit the prince very little (*wa-laysa yanālu fī tilka l-kutub . . . illā qalīlan*), and may even mislead him if he mistakenly believes them to be true.[182]

Pseudo-Māwardī, like Ibn Qutayba, was almost certainly familiar with other works by or ascribed to Ibn al-Muqaffaᶜ. In one instance, he includes, introduced with Ibn al-Muqaffaᶜ's name, a quotation from *al-Adab al-ṣaghīr* ('The Little Book of Etiquette').[183] Ibn Qutayba reports citations that he has read 'in a book by Ibn al-Muqaffaᶜ',[184] in 'the *Ādāb* of Ibn al-Muqaffaᶜ'[185] and 'in the *Yatīma*'.[186]

The Testament of an Indian King

Pseudo-Māwardī cites several passages from a 'testament' (*ᶜahd*) that he knew as the words of an Indian king to his son. In two instances, he supplies the name of the Indian king as Sāb.t.r.m.[187] He frequently specifies that he has examined this text himself.[188]

For a substantial number of the quotations introduced by such phrases, parallels exist in a text that circulated under Aristotle's name.[189] Usually designated *Waṣiyyat Arisṭāṭālīs ilā l-Iskandar* ('Testament of Aristotle to Alexander'), this text circulated independently and was also incorporated into larger collections of 'Aristotelian' epistolary materials. The *Waṣiyyat Arisṭāṭālīs* appears as a discrete text in the *Jāvīdān khirad* ('Eternal Wisdom') of the historian and polymath Miskawayh (d. 421/1030).[190] Miskawayh classified the contents of *Jāvīdān khirad* under the headings of the wise pronouncements (*ḥikam*) of 'the Persians', 'the Indians', 'the Arabs', 'the Greeks' (*rūm*) and 'the modern Muslims' (*al-islāmiyyīn al-muḥdathīn*). The historian and philosopher in Fatimid Egypt al-Mubashshir b. Fātik, compiler in 440/1048–9 of a collection of the wise sayings of ancient Greek philosophers, knew the pseudo-Aristotelian *waṣiyya* and cited excerpts from it in a chapter devoted to Aristotle's wise sayings and apposite utterances (*ḥikamuhu wa-ādābuhu*), but did not reproduce the continuous text.[191] The unknown author of *Muntakhab Ṣiwān al-ḥikma* ('Abbreviated Bookcase of Wisdom', compiled between 565/1169 and 639/1241), one of the two major (extant) abridgements of the lost *Ṣiwān al-ḥikma*, mentions the *waṣiyya* in his discussion of Aristotle and, like al-Mubashshir, cites its familiar opening section.[192] The later authors Ibn Abī Uṣaybiᶜa (d. 668/1270) and al-Shahrazūrī (d. 680/1281) included quotations from *Waṣiyyat Arisṭāṭālīs* in their works, *ᶜUyūn al-anbāᵓ fī ṭabaqāt al-aṭibbāᵓ* ('Sources of Tidings on the Generations of the Physicians') and *Rawḍat al-afrāḥ wa-nuzhat al-arwāḥ* ('The Garden of Rejoicings and the Amusement of Spirits'), respectively.[193] The coincidences between Pseudo-Māwardī's 'Testament of the Indian king Sāb.t.r.m to his Son' and the *Waṣiyyat Arisṭāṭālīs* known to several subsequent authors leave little doubt that all writers were concerned with the same text.

It is conceivable that Pseudo-Māwardī's Indian testament indeed derived from an Indian text, which in the course of its transmission lost its Indic associations and acquired, like many other texts, an association with Aristotle instead.[194] Yaḥyā b. Khālid b. Barmak, the caliphal vizier whose family were intimately associated with Balkh and who maintained a marked interest in the region and its cultures, commissioned translations of Sanskrit works in the late eighth century; it was he who dispatched the envoy whose report on the medicinal plants and religious cultures of India al-Kindī transcribed in a manuscript that Ibn al-Nadīm would draw on in *al-Fihrist*.[195] Kevin van Bladel has proposed that these translations included a collection of the teachings of Cāṇakya.[196] Ibn al-Nadīm records a *Kitāb Shānāq fī l-tadbīr* ('Book of Shānāq on Administration'), as well as a *Kitāb Shānāq al-Hindī fī l-adab* ('Book of Shānāq the Indian on Instructive Custom').[197] François de Blois, taking *tadbīr* to be a rendering of *nīti-* (the Sanskrit *nītiśāstra* designates a text devoted to politics and ethics), regards Ibn al-Nadīm's reference to *Kitāb Shānāq fī l-tadbīr* as indicating an Arabic translation, probably from Middle Persian, of the 'Book of Cāṇakya on statecraft'.[198] A suggestive indication of the rendering of Indian texts directly into Arabic appears in the thirteenth-century report of the historian Ibn Isfandiyār, who found a collection of *risālas* in Khwarazm, including, together with Ibn al-Muqaffaᶜ's translation of the *Letter of Tansar* from Middle Persian, an Arabic translation from an Indian language (*az hindavī bi-tāzī*) made in 197/813.[199] Ibn Isfandiyār does not specify the genre to which the translated work belonged, but its linkage with Ibn al-Muqaffaᶜ's translation of Sasanian *andarz* raises the possibility that the Indian text might have belonged to a similar genre.

Pseudo-Māwardī identified the king who composed his *ᶜahd* as 'Sāb.t.r.m', a name likely to derive from an Indian source.[200] I have proposed that the testament in question is probably related to the *Kitāb Sār.t.r.m* listed, without further information, among Ibn al-Nadīm's 'Titles of Indian books containing legends, fireside tales and sayings' (*asmāᵓ kutub al-hind fī l-khurāfāt wa-l-asmār wa-l-aḥādīth*).[201] The name almost certainly corresponds to that of the Indian king who appears in the Syriac version of *Kalīla wa-Dimna* as Š.t.p.r.m, a form reflected in certain Arabic, Hebrew and Old Spanish versions of the text as well.[202] In most of the Arabic versions of *Kalīla wa-Dimna*, the name of the king appears as Bilār or Bilādh, that name, formerly attached to another protagonist in the tale, having been substituted for Sāb.t.r.m.[203]

Pseudo-Māwardī's retention of the Indian name for the king distinguishes him still further from the Iraq-based writers, who tended to assign all materials known to them to be of Indic provenance to *kutub al-hind*. Indeed, al-Jāḥiẓ, who esteemed 'Indian books' for their treatment of 'wise sayings and secrets, customs and properties' (*kutub al-hind fī ḥikamihā wa-asrārihā wa-siyarihā wa-ᶜilalihā*), described them as products of ancient and collective transmission rather than as the works of known persons or recognised scholars.[204] The inclusion of the Indic-associated testament, acknowledged and cited as an independent text, in itself suggests Pseudo-Māwardī's close engagement with Indic cultural materials.

Most Arabic references to and citations from the work knew it as Aristotle's exhortative commendation to Alexander. Ibn Abī Dharr regarded two of the author's Indic-associated quotations as Aristotelian:

> Aristotle said: The station of the ruler with regard to the subjects resembles the station of the soul with regard to the body and the station of the head among the limbs. The ruler, despite the superiority of his station, needs the goodness (well-being) of his subjects just as the subjects need the goodness

> of the ruler. For just as there can be no well-being for the body without the soul, there is no endurance for the head after the demise of the limbs.[205]

> Aristotle said to Alexander: Your judgement does not adorn you if you speak well to the point of eloquence but fail to authenticate your speech by your action and your exterior by your interior.[206]

A telling exception to the Aristotelian transposition of the author's Indic wisdom appears in the writings of the preacher and polymath Ibn al-Jawzī (510–97/1126–1200), who, although he lived in Syria, far from any contact with Indic culture, reported one extract as the words of 'an Indian king to his son'.[207] At least one book that presented a body of wisdom associated with Indian kings was in circulation in twelfth-century Mosul, where Ibn Razīn cited a *Kitāb Ādāb mulūk al-hind* ('Book of the Customs of the Indian Kings'): 'The king should not associate with a deceitful person, nor with a liar; nor with an ignorant, greedy, slanderous, calumnious, profligate, two-faced or doubtful person, even if he is his son, his father, or a close relative.'[208]

The Buddha

On three occasions Pseudo-Māwardī mentions the Buddha, whom he describes in one instance as 'the leader (*za*ᶜ*īm*) of the Indians who is called al-Budd'.[209] Volume I, Chapter 2 explored contextual factors that might support Pseudo-Māwardī's references to the Buddha;[210] the present section addresses the texts.

Some of the selections associated by Pseudo-Māwardī with *al-budd* appear elsewhere in the corpus of Arabic literature. In one case, a saying attributed in *Naṣīḥat al-mulūk* to the Buddha appears, without attribution, in *Kitāb al-I*ᶜ*lām bi-manāqib al-Islām* of al-ᶜĀmirī (d. 381/992), a continuator of the Kindian tradition in Khurasan.[211] The two further quotations attributed to the Buddha appear in a cluster of materials adduced, under the rubric of *ba*ᶜ*ḍ siyāsat al-hind* (an Indian governmental practice or principle). The first item in this pair appears, similarly attributed to *al-budd*, in *Bilawhar wa-Būdhāṣaf*.[212] A portion of the long quotation that follows it, also attributed in *Naṣīḥat al-mulūk* to *al-budd*, appears, like so many of the quotations from the ᶜ*ahd*, attributed to Aristotle in *Waṣiyyat Arisṭāṭālīs*; another portion, or a variant of it, appears in *Bilawhar wa-Būdhāṣaf* and *Kalīla wa-Dimna*.[213]

When Pseudo-Māwardī introduces his second quotation from the Buddha in this sequence with the phrase 'and in another passage by him in this book' (*wa-fī faṣl lahu min hādha l-kitāb ākhar*), he conveys that *siyāsat al-hind* was a written text. This written text, it would seem, included a number of passages presented as the words of *al-budd* and conjoined materials that occur elsewhere in *Bilawhar wa-Būdhāṣaf* and *Kalīla wa-Dimna*.[214] In contrast to his references to the Indian king's *ᶜahd*, Pseudo-Māwardī does not, in this case, state explicitly that he had seen a copy of the text. This sequence of three passages, all apparently drawn from the source described as *baᶜḍ siyāsat al-hind*, occurs in the epilogue of *Naṣīḥat al-mulūk*, in which, as noted above, Pseudo-Māwardī adopts a less discursive and more narrative style than that evident in the body of his book.

Reference to the bibliophile Ibn al-Nadīm's list of Indian collections of stories supplies the suggestive title *Kitāb al-Budd*, although Ibn al-Nadīm again recorded no additional description of the text to which he referred. It appears in his list after *Kitāb Bilawhar wa-Būdhāṣaf* and *Kitāb Būdhāṣaf al-mufrad* ('The Single Book of Būdhāṣaf'), and scholars have long assumed that it was related to these works.[215] As noted above, one and possibly two of Pseudo-Māwardī's quotations from *al-budd* appear in the Arabic *Bilawhar wa-Būdhāṣaf*, in which *al-budd* appears only in the second part of the text. Like *Kalīla wa-Dimna* and *Sirr al-asrār*, *Bilawhar wa-Būdhāṣaf*, under various titles and with flexible contents, traversed a vast and linguistically, culturally and confessionally diverse space, its various surviving forms reflecting the different contexts and audiences that generated and transmitted them.[216] Daniel Gimaret held that the work, especially the second part, in which the references to al-Budd appear, took form in Sasanian Iran.[217] Mohsen Zakeri has further illuminated the diverse provenance of the materials that make up *Bilawhar wa-Būdhāṣaf*, and has proposed that the Arabic work was once known under the title 'The Prince and the Ascetic' (*Ibn al-malik wa-l-nāsik*), a title widely credited to the authorship of the littérateur, secretary and translator ᶜAlī b. ᶜUbayda al-Rayḥānī (d. 219/834). It is therefore highly likely that the composite work, parts of which surely had a long history before their incorporation into the text, acquired the title of *Bilawhar wa-Būdhāṣaf* only at a later stage.[218]

Pseudo-Māwardī's knowledge of the Buddha's significance among

Indian communities, and his citation of his wise pronouncements without regard for their 'idolatrous' provenance, are compatible with his presence in the proximity of Balkh and Bamiyan where Buddhist images and inscriptions were a continuing and visible part of the landscape, and with his affinity with the intellectual legacy of al-Kindī. The number, variety and specificity of his Indic-associated illustrative materials display the degree to which Pseudo-Māwardī was steeped in the ancient culture of the region. His engagement with this repertoire accompanied his equally firm commitment to the Arabic language, learning and culture. It was principally the Arabic language that had provided the vehicle for the continuing transmission and interpretation of the Iranian and Indic heritages for audiences further west. *Naṣīḥat al-mulūk* implies a context in which Indic-associated cultural materials were both prominent and prestigious.

It seems likely that the locality's oral culture preserved in memory numerous maxims, many of them quite possibly of great, and untraceable, antiquity. The Buddhist, Graeco-Bactrian, Parthian, Sasanian and Arabic-Islamic phases of the region's history over a millennium had produced through accretion a body of wisdom that, always fluid, constituted a repertoire that had passed from group to group and language to language. Pseudo-Māwardī, who did not regard wisdom as the exclusive accomplishment of any particular people or tradition, appears to have made a significant contribution to this process of assimilation, adaptation and transmission.

PART II

THE THREE GOVERNANCES: TRANSLATIONS AND COMMENTARY

3

The King's Self-governance

Chapters 3, 4 and 5 of this volume address *Naṣīḥat al-mulūk*'s three central chapters, devoted to the king's 'governance' (*siyāsa*) of his self (*nafs*), his élites (*khāṣṣa*) and the general population (*ᶜāmma*). Coinciding with the Aristotelian divisions of practical philosophy into ethics, economics and politics, subjects that concerned the Arabic- and Persian-speaking élites no less than their Graeco-Roman predecessors, the three 'governances' recur in the writings of the Kindian tradition,[1] and would find expression in al-Khwārazmī's classification under 'practical philosophy' (*al-falsafa al-ᶜamaliyya*) of three types of management (*tadbīr*): *tadbīr al-rajul nafsahu*, 'a man's management of himself', that is, the science of moral dispositions (*ᶜilm al-akhlāq*); *tadbīr al-khāṣṣa*, management of the élites, that is, management of the household (*tadbīr al-manzil*); and *tadbīr al-ᶜāmma*, management of the common people, that is, governance of the city, the community and dominion (*siyāsat al-madīna wa-l-umma wa-l-mulk*).[2]

The present chapter addresses Pseudo-Māwardī's centrally placed (fifth) and longest chapter, devoted to the king's 'governance and discipline of the self' (*siyāsat al-nafs wa-riyāḍatuhā*). The paired terms *siyāsa* and *riyāḍa* evoke training and discipline, in this case, of the lower self, the self that constituted the seat of the appetites; al-Ḥakīm al-Tirmidhī, Pseudo-Māwardī's contemporary and fellow resident of the region adjoining the Oxus, wrote a pair of treatises entitled *Kitāb al-Riyāḍa* ('Book of [Spiritual] Discipline') and *Kitāb Adab al-nafs* ('Book of the Training of the Self').[3] Pseudo-Māwardī's fifth chapter displays another important intertextual relationship with *Risālat al-maᶜāsh wa-l-maᶜād* ('Epistle on This Life and the Afterlife'), also known as *al-Akhlāq al-maḥmūda wa-l-madhmūma* ('Praiseworthy and Blameworthy Characteristics'), the work of his admired Muᶜtazilite predecessor al-Jāḥiẓ, who had, in that text, also enjoined 'discipline of the self'.[4]

The three chapters presented in Part II display Pseudo-Māwardī's technique of enumerating his points, and sometimes subsections of a point. By using numbers, Pseudo-Māwardī gave his chapters a clear structure and provided signposts for his audience. He employed copious references and quotations in order to extend and illustrate his points. Defining elements in his exposition are the sacred sources of the Qur᾿ān and Prophetic example, and the wisdom transmitted from the accumulated experience of earlier peoples and polities. The foundational principle in Pseudo-Māwardī's argument, which builds on his repeated parallels of divine and earthly sovereignty, is that the ruler should emulate the divine qualities. The idea of human emulation of the divine virtues elicited various responses in Pseudo-Māwardī's milieu; notably, the Karrāmiyya encouraged imitation of the divine attributes,[5] whereas some individuals rejected the notion, in which they suspected an implicit equation of the human with the divine.[6] In the Kindian tradition, however, such imitation constituted one of the (Platonic) definitions of philosophy, a point adduced, as this chapter will show, in *Naṣīḥat al-mulūk* as well.[7] In his fifth chapter, the subject of the present chapter in this book, Pseudo-Māwardī's approach is to urge the ruler first to attain knowledge of God, and then to employ this knowledge in his striving to imitate the divine. In a mirror image of the principle that 'he who knows himself knows his Lord', that is, that self-knowledge facilitated knowledge of the divine, Pseudo-Māwardī's conception advanced the point of view that knowledge of the divine provided guidance for humanity in the created world.

The King's Person and Conduct

Pseudo-Māwardī opens his fifth chapter by distinguishing his mirror from the genre devoted to matters of royal protocol:

> We should precede this chapter with the acknowledgement that it has not been our purpose, in this book of ours, to address topics that many persons consider to be part of good manners (*adab*), such as attendance at the royal assembly (*jalsa*), practices related to dress, mounts and partaking of food, the furnishings with which kings decorate their surroundings, and the

embellishments by which they adorn themselves – because other writers are more knowledgeable than we are about these matters, and have expatiated upon them in a fashion that exceeds our ability to describe or explain them. In addition, kings' followers (*atbāᶜ*) and the worldly-minded people (*abnāᵓ al-dunyā*) among them have already compiled many books, ancient and modern, that treat these subjects in a comprehensive manner, and exceed that which anybody among the people of this age might undertake. Yet much of what they have produced in that regard is of no use on the subject of governance and of little benefit to the ruler or his subjects.

Instead, we have wished to make this book of ours a religious book (*aradnā an najᶜala kitābanā hādhā kitāban dīniyyan*), in which we seek to show kings their best interests with regard to their lives in this world and in the world to come (*maṣāliḥ maᶜādihim wa-maᶜāshihim*), the order of their kingdoms and conditions with reference to the Book of God, Lord of the Worlds, and the exemplary practices (*sunan*) of the Prophet, the Rightly Guided Caliphs and the ancient kings; and to warn them against (the dangers of) an evil perdition, an ignoble death, unfavourable talk and the incurring of punishment both immediate and enduring.[8]

In referring to the voluminous literature, ancient and modern, devoted to the trappings of kingship, Pseudo-Māwardī probably had in mind the Sasanian books of *ēwēn* (books that treated manners, customs, skills) and the Arabic works of *rusūm* ('customs' or 'etiquette'), such as al-Taghlibī's *Kitāb al-Tāj*. His contribution, by contrast, is rather a *kitāb dīnī*, a book that situates the king's earthly life and responsibilities in relation to his eternal life. In the light of this characterisation of his purpose, it is not surprising that Pseudo-Māwardī's chapter reflects his Muᶜtazilite theological–philosophical orientation. At various points Pseudo-Māwardī alludes to all the Muᶜtazilite 'five principles' (*al-uṣūl al-khamsa*), namely, the doctrines of the divine unicity (*tawḥīd*), divine justice (*ᶜadl*), the 'promise and threat' (of reward and punishment in the afterlife) (*al-waᶜd wa-l-waᶜīd*), the 'intermediate position' (between belief and unbelief of the grave sinner) (*al-manzila bayn al-manzilatayn*), and commanding right and forbidding wrong (*al-amr bi-l-maᶜrūf wa-l-nahy ᶜan al-munkar*). As this chapter will show, Pseudo-Māwardī's exposition suggests in particular his affinity with al-Kaᶜbī and the Baghdadi Muᶜtazila.

Al-Kaᶜbī, a Ḥanafī jurist as well as the leading Muᶜtazilite theologian in Khurasan during the first half of the tenth century, belonged to a family with administrative and secretarial experience. His father had known Caliph al-Maᵓmūn's governor ᶜAbdallāh b. Ṭāhir, whose conduct, writings and verses Pseudo-Māwardī cites, and al-Kaᶜbī himself served as a secretary to Muḥammad b. Zayd Dāᶜī of Tabaristan (d. 287/900), as well as, many years later, as vizier to Aḥmad b. Sahl, the Samanid general appointed governor of Khurasan during the reign of Naṣr II. Like Abū Zayd al-Balkhī, al-Kaᶜbī had studied in Baghdad and eventually returned to Khurasan.[9] While al-Kaᶜbī served as Aḥmad b. Sahl's vizier, Abū Zayd, having declined the office of vizier, worked as one of his secretaries; both enjoyed high status with the governor, and al-Kaᶜbī, whose salary was higher, instructed the treasurer to augment Abū Zayd's salary with a substantial portion of his own earnings.[10] Few of al-Kaᶜbī's writings survive, but the portion of his *Maqālāt* ('Doctrines') that treats the Muᶜtazila is available in published form, and significant sections survive in the heresiographical work of the tenth-century Ismaᶜili writer Abū Tammām.[11] Al-Kaᶜbī's contemporary al-Māturīdī, and the later Muᶜtazilite theologians Abū Rashīd al-Nīsābūrī[12] and ᶜAbd al-Jabbār (d. 415/1025), record, and customarily refute, several of his doctrines. The surviving materials and reports provide suggestive evidence for the intellectual–religious mentality reflected in *Naṣīḥat al-mulūk*.

The Virtue of *Taqwā* and its Components

Before any other attribute, Pseudo-Māwardī urges the king to cultivate the virtue of *taqwā Allāh* (godliness, consciousness of God, fear of God):

> The first thing that is incumbent on the king who is concerned with the affairs of his subjects and solicitous of the protection of his realm (*ḥimāyat ḥawzatihi*) and the prosperity of his domain (*ᶜimārat bayḍatihi*) is *taqwā Allāh*, for it is the most excellent quality that has been commended by the virtuous and learned, an *ᶜiṣma* (source of protection) for him who (seeks) protection by it,[13] a sanctuary (*ḥirz*) for him who holds fast to it, a refuge for him who takes refuge in it, a (source of) safety for him who realises it, a beauty for him who clothes himself in it, a glory for him who seeks honour in it (*ᶜizz li-man iᶜtazza bihā*), a source of dignity (*mahāba*) for him who

> assumes it, a weapon for him who arms himself with it, a treasure for him who acquires it, a virtue for him who pursues it. In addition to all these things, it is His injunction (*waṣiyya*), the Glorious and Exalted, to His creation and His command that He has imposed upon them, as well as the commendation (*waṣiyya*) of the prophets and messengers, the righteous servants of God, the virtuous kings of the past and the ancient sages among the people of every nation (*jīl*) and community (*milla*), and every religion (*dīn*) and sect (*niḥla*).[14]

The Qurʾānic concept of *taqwā* is as multifaceted as it is pervasive, and difficult to capture in a single English word.[15] Often rendered as 'piety', its sense is perhaps better conveyed in Fred Donner's phrase 'mindfulness of God and the Last Day',[16] 'consciousness' or 'fear' of God,[17] or, if a single word is to be selected, E. K. Rowson's 'godliness'.[18] In Pseudo-Māwardī's presentation, *taqwā* is a timeless and universal value, common to every people and religion. To emphasise its universality, Pseudo-Māwardī supports his point by citing first, in accordance with his established hierarchy, a number of Qurʾānic passages, and next the verses of certain poets whom he explicitly identifies as *jāhilī*, that is, poets active in the period before the Qurʾānic revelation and prophetic mission of Muḥammad (introduced with the phrase, 'One of the [pre-Islamic] poets of the *jāhiliyya* said, in his ignorance [*jāhiliyya*] and unbelief [*kufr*] . . .'), followed by quotations attributed to Plato, Aristotle, Ardashīr and 'a wise Indian king'.[19] Indeed, Pseudo-Māwardī's presentation of *taqwā* perhaps reflects an engagement with the theological question of whether individuals who lived before the Prophet's mission were subject to punishment for their unbelief.[20] He defines *taqwā* in the following terms:

> The meaning of *taqwā* that God has mentioned and commended in those who act in accordance with it is the choosing (*īthār*) of obedience to God and refraining from disobedience against Him. The pious person (*al-taqī*) is the obedient person (*al-muṭīʿ*), the obedient person is the believer (*al-muʾmin*), and the believer is the person who submits (*al-muslim*), because all these names are God's words of praise (*hādhihi l-asmāʾ kulluhā madāʾiḥ Allāh*) for those who merit them through good works (*al-afʿāl al-ṣāliḥa*) and virtuous efforts (*al-masāʿī al-fāḍila*).[21]

In referring to the individual's 'choosing' (*īthār*) to obey God, Pseudo-Māwardī assumes that human beings possess the capacity to choose and perform their actions. Among the doctrines on which the Muᶜtazila were in agreement, according to al-Kaᶜbī, was that God did not create the actions of human beings, rather individuals acted according to divine commands or prohibitions by the capacity (*qudra*) that God had created for them.[22] This doctrine is central to the Muᶜtazilite understanding of divine justice, which required that human beings be accountable for the actions that occasioned God's reward or punishment.

In this passage, Pseudo-Māwardī also alludes to the relationship of actions (in obedience or disobedience to the divine commandments) to the individual's status as a believer and as a Muslim.[23] The Muᶜtazila regarded obedience (in performance of the stipulated actions and in some cases the supererogatory ones) as an integral component of faith.[24] Al-Kaᶜbī groups the Muᶜtazila among the 'people who maintain that the acts of obedience all are a component of faith' (*inna l-ṭāᶜāt kulluhā īmān*).[25] Without addressing in explicit terms the effects of disobedience on the status of the believer, Pseudo-Māwardī, like al-Kaᶜbī, asserts the identification of obedience with belief when he equates the obedient person with the Muslim. Probably implicit in Pseudo-Māwardī's formulation is the Muᶜtazilite doctrine of 'the intermediate position' (*al-manzila bayn al-manzilatayn*), according to which the individual who commits a major sin occupies neither the category of *kufr*, unbelief, nor that of *īmān*, faith, but rather that of *fisq*, sinfulness or unrighteousness.[26] Pseudo-Māwardī mentions the major sin, the *kabīra*, slightly later in his exposition, and, implicit in this instance, it informs his presentation of *taqwā*. Al-Kaᶜbī explained that the person who commits major sins (*murtakib al-kabāʾir*) no longer merits the 'noble name of faith and Islam' (*lā yastaḥiqqu an yusammā bi-l-ism al-sharīf alladhī huwa al-īmān wa-l-Islām*), but nor does he merit the name of unbelief (*kufr*); rather he deserves the name of unrighteousness (*fisq*).[27] The issue has to do with the qualifications for inclusion within the community of 'believers', within the community of 'Muslims', and expectations of reward or punishment in the afterlife. Pseudo-Māwardī employs the same verb, *istaḥaqqa*, and the plural forms *asmāʾ* ('names') and *madāʾiḥ* ('terms of praise'), a phrasing that corresponds closely with al-Kaᶜbī's formulation. ᶜAbd al-Jabbār explained his position in terms that resemble and clarify Pseudo-Māwardī's allusive language. The later Basran Muᶜtazilite proposed that, apart from the figure of the Prophet, the human being who merited divine reward was designated by the titles of *muᵓmin* (believer), *barr* (good), *taqiyy* (godly, god-fearing) and *ṣāliḥ* (righteous), as opposed to the individual who merited divine punishment, who carried the appellation of *kāfir* (unbeliever) or *fāsiq* (wrongdoer).[28] According to ᶜAbd al-Jabbār, if it was inappropriate to describe the sinful Muslim as *kāfir*, it was likewise inappropriate to describe him as *muᵓmin*, since the latter designation, through the revelation of the Qurᵓān, had become a laudatory 'name' (*ism al-madḥ*). Consequently, the perpetrator of a major sin (*ṣāḥib al-kabīra*) was called neither *muᵓmin*, contrary to the position of the Murjiᵓa, nor *kāfir*, contrary to the doctrine of the Kharijites, but rather *fāsiq*. In language reminiscent of Pseudo-Māwardī's formulation, ᶜAbd al-Jabbār held that the title (*ism*) of *muᵓmin* applied to persons who deserved praise (*madḥ*), honour (*taᶜẓīm*) and assistance (*muwālāt*), so that it was not possible to apply the appellation to *ṣāḥib al-kabīra*.[29]

Pseudo-Māwardī next presents a five-part formulation of the components of *taqwā*. He demonstrates his firm conviction of the necessary integration of three realms of experience: knowledge, faith and action. In a precisely articulated and Muᶜtazilite-inflected presentation, he asserts that precise performance of religious obligations is essential, but that action without proper belief, itself premised in right understanding, will not be accepted:

> *Taqwā* embraces many acts that can be divided into five divisions.
>
> Firstly: True knowledge of God, Glorious and Exalted (*maᶜrifat Allāh jalla wa-ᶜazza ḥaqqa maᶜrifatin*): as one and eternal, unique and singular, wise and generous, merciful and beneficent, truthful and powerful, and omniscient; so that the one who knows Him has no doubt (*ḥattā lā yashukka ᶜārifuhu*).[30] Next, that he should name Him by His beautiful names (*bi-asmāᵓihi l-ḥusnā*) and describe Him by His lofty attributes (*bi-ṣifātihi l-ᶜulyā*); so that he does not add to them anything that He has rejected from Himself and does not deny from Him any aspect of His nature (*khulq*); that he not assign any partner to Him in (the world of) His creation, nor any equal (*nadīd*) among them, nor any likeness in any aspect or quality (*maᶜnā*).[31] And he should know that He is beneficent (*barr*) to His servants

> and merciful (*raḥīm*) to His creation. He does not impose on them more than they can bear, wishes for them only that which comes easily, punishes them only in cases of sin, and judges them only in accordance with truth. He speaks to them and is content for them only with truthfulness. (He should know) that His judgement is true and His power decisive; and that out of His mercy for His creation and His solicitude towards them (*ḥusn naẓarihi lahum*) He has sent prophets bearing good tidings and warning, and He has sent down according to that which He has revealed among them the clearly understandable Book that will guide them to the Abode of Delight (*dār al-naᶜīm*) and warn them against painful chastisement.[32]

Pseudo-Māwardī assigns the primary position in his anatomy of *taqwā* to knowledge of God (*maᶜrifat Allāh*), which constituted the first of the Muᶜtazilite 'five principles' (*al-uṣūl al-khamsa*).[33] Knowledge, especially knowledge of God, was a foundational concern of all theologians and philosophers. The Muᶜtazila and the Ashᶜariyya, a theological school named after Abū l-Ḥasan al-Ashᶜarī (r. 260–324/874–936) and combining elements of the rationally based (*ᶜaqlī*) dialogical technique with transmitted (*naqlī*) knowledge, were particularly concerned with knowledge, both *maᶜrifa* (Erkenntnis) and *ᶜilm* (Wissen); the emerging Māturīdiyya, like the Murjiʾa more interested in faith than knowledge, also contributed to the field of epistemology, in part in refutation of the views of the Muᶜtazila.[34] The theologians distinguished between, on the one hand, primary (*ibtidāʾī*) or necessary (*ḍarūrī*) types of knowledge and, on the other, acquired (*iktisābī*), voluntary (*ikhtiyārī*) or theoretical (*naẓarī*) knowledge.[35] Definitions and distinctions involved the question of the means by which knowledge of a subject might be attained. In some cases knowledge might be attainable by means of *mushāhada*, 'sensory perception', or *idrāk*, 'perception' or 'apprehension'; in other cases it might be attainable by means of *tafakkur*, 'deliberation', and *naẓar*, 'rational speculation'.[36] *ᶜIlm* and *maᶜrifa*, variously understood and distinguished from one another, constituted the principal terms used to analyse knowledge;[37] a related concept, *iᶜtiqād* or 'conviction', very possibly entered into theological discourse with the teachings of al-Kaᶜbī.[38]

The earlier Muᶜtazilite Abū l-Hudhayl al-ᶜAllāf (*c.* 135–227/752–841) considered human knowledge of God to be *a priori*, and implied that it might embrace unbelievers, even those who did not possess a scripture; in their good actions, unbelievers might also obey God.[39] Al-Kaᶜbī held distinctive views regarding *maᶜrifa*, and formulated a definition of *ᶜilm* to which Muᶜtazilite writers continued to refer.[40] He developed the view that knowledge of God was *dalālatan*, arrived at by proof and inference, rather than *ḍarūratan*, manifestly or 'necessarily' evident by means of (sensory) witness (*mushāhada*) or perception (*idrāk*), and that this distinction applied to knowledge of God in this life and in the next.[41] He defined human knowledge as *iᶜtiqād al-shayʾ ᶜalā mā huwa bihi*, 'the conviction that the thing is as it truly is'.[42] Pseudo-Māwardī's contemporary in Samarqand, al-Māturīdī, proposed and treated at length three bases of *maᶜrifa*: *ᶜiyān*, *akhbār* and *naẓar*, the evidence of the senses, transmitted reports and rational enquiry.[43] Māturīdī theologians and later Muᶜtazilites refuted, modified or added qualifications to al-Kaᶜbī's definition of knowledge.[44] ᶜAbd al-Jabbār, partly in reaction against al-Kaᶜbī's acceptance of emulation (*taqlīd*), articulated the doctrine that knowledge of God (*maᶜrifat Allāh*) was neither *a priori* (*ḍarūratan*) nor amenable to sensory perception (*mushāhadatan*), but must be attained by means of deliberation (*tafakkur*) and rational speculation (*naẓar*).[45] He conceived of *ᶜilm* as a subcategory of *iᶜtiqād*, and regarded *maᶜrifa* and *iᶜtiqād* as virtually synonymous.[46]

These questions and categories, employed to explicate the necessity of human knowledge of God, underlie Pseudo-Māwardī's treatment of his first constituent of *taqwā*, which conveys his view that *maᶜrifat Allāh* formed the basis from which faith and actions proceeded. It is not fully evident from this passage whether, like Abū l-Hudhayl, he regarded *maᶜrifat Allāh* to be *a priori*, or whether, like ᶜAbd al-Jabbār, he held it to be attainable only by means of *naẓar*. Elsewhere, however, Pseudo-Māwardī makes clear that, as al-Kaᶜbī held, God could not be known by way of sensory perception (*mushāhada*) or apprehension (*idrāk*).[47]

Pseudo-Māwardī urges the ruler to imitate God to the extent that his divinely given capacity allows. His imitation must begin with knowledge. In Pseudo-Māwardī's exposition, knowledge of God forms the basis or ground of all knowledge, including self-knowledge. One of his illustrious Balkhī predecessors, the renunciant Shaqīq al-Balkhī, had said, 'Were a man to live two hundred years, if he does not know (*yaᶜrifu*) four things, then he is fit for nothing other than the Fire (of Hell). The first of these things is knowledge of God Almighty (*maᶜrifat Allāh taᶜālā*), and the second, knowledge of himself (*maᶜrifat nafsihi*); the third thing is knowledge of God's work (*maᶜrifat ᶜamal Allāh taᶜālā*) and the fourth knowledge of the enemy of God and knowledge of your enemy (*maᶜrifat ᶜaduww illāh wa-maᶜrifat ᶜaduwwika*).'[48] Of related interest is al-Māturīdī's opening of his discussion of *maᶜrifat al-rabb*, knowledge of the Lord, with the principle of *man ᶜarafa nafsahu ᶜarafa rabbahu*, 'he who knows himself knows his Lord', from which he proceeds to discuss different conceptions, among Muslims and non-Muslims, of how human self-knowledge is related to knowledge of God.[49]

For Pseudo-Māwardī as for al-Kaᶜbī, knowledge of God was synonymous with knowledge of His unicity (*tawḥīd*), the first of the Muᶜtazilite five principles.[50] Also compatible with al-Kindī's views, his description of God resembles the doctrine of the Baghdadi Muᶜtazila, who employed adjectival attributes to convey the indivisible and eternal divine nature without ascribing to Him entities or faculties (*inna l-bāriᵓ lam yazal ᶜāliman . . . bi-nafsihi lā bi-ᶜilmin*, 'the Creator remains eternally knowing . . . in Himself, not through a faculty of knowledge').[51] Pseudo-Māwardī's omission from his list of divine attributes of the adjectives *samīᶜ* and *baṣīr*, hearing and seeing, is consistent with the conception of al-Naẓẓām (d. between 220/835 and 230/845) and of al-Kaᶜbī, for whom God's seeing and hearing were identical to His knowing; by contrast, the Muᶜtazilites Abū l-Hudhayl, Abū ᶜAlī al-Jubbāᵓī (d. 303/915–16) and his son Abū Hāshim (d. 321/933) described God by these attributes.[52] Muᶜtazilites of the Basran and Baghdadi branches disagreed over the matter of 'attributes of essence' (*ṣifāt al-dhāt*) and 'attributes of action' (*ṣifāt al-fiᶜl*), a problem that concerned the scholars of Samarqand as well: the author of a text ascribed to al-Māturīdī, probably the work of Abū l-Layth al-Samarqandī, wrote of the *mashāyikh Samarqand* that (some) averred of God that He was 'knowing and possesses knowledge, by which He is described in eternity; powerful and possesses power, by which He is described in eternity; speaking and possesses speech, by which He is described in eternity' (*ᶜālim wa-lahu ᶜilm wa-huwa mawṣūf bihi fī l-azal wa-qādir wa-lahu qudra wa-huwa mawṣūf bihā fī l-azal wa-mutakallim wa-lahu kalām wa-huwa mawṣūf bihi fī l-azal*).[53]

In a reflection of the Muᶜtazila's second principle, that of divine justice, Pseudo-Māwardī emphasises the beneficent and merciful character of God's interaction with humankind. Like al-Kaᶜbī and in accordance with the Qurᵓānic text, he refers to God's imposing on His servants only that which they can bear. Al-Kaᶜbī stated in explicit terms that God did not punish His servants for failing to fulfil an obligation that lay beyond their capacity.[54] The point anticipates Pseudo-Māwardī's second component of *taqwā*, namely, faith (*īmān*):

> Secondly: Faith (*al-īmān*) in His angels, books and messengers, in the responsibility for carrying out His precepts and (the practices) that the Prophet brought, in (God's) revivification and resurrection (of humankind), reward and punishment, the (divine) promise and threat, and everything of which the believers must be convinced (*mā yajibu ᶜalā l-muᵓminīn iᶜtiqāduhu*).[55] For this (faith) is the basis of the religion (*asās al-dīn*) and the root of the acts of the believers. God will not accept a deed done in ignorance of Him or doubt of Him, in error regarding His attributes and acts, in ascribing evil to Him or assigning partners to Him in it, regardless of its (the act's) duration or repetition (*wa-in ṭāla wa-kathura*).[56]

In treating faith after knowledge, Pseudo-Māwardī conforms to the tendencies of Muᶜtazilite and Ashᶜarī theologians as opposed to Murjiᵓī and Māturīdī writers, whose primary interest lay in faith.[57] His use of the term *iᶜtiqād*, conviction, recalls al-Kaᶜbī's definition of knowledge. Under the rubric of faith, Pseudo-Māwardī enumerates distinctive Muᶜtazilite doctrines, such as the 'promise and threat' of divine reward and punishment. Like al-Kaᶜbī, who listed the 'promise and threat' among the doctrines on which the Muᶜtazila were agreed, Pseudo-Māwardī held that God does not fail to fulfil His pronounced promise and threat, does not judge unjustly, and does not charge His servants with that which exceeds their capacity or that of which they lack knowledge.[58] In accordance with the Muᶜtazilite conception of divine justice (*ᶜadl*), Pseudo-Māwardī asserts that God does not enact evil. ᶜAbd al-Jabbār, for example, described all divine actions as characterised by *ḥusn*, goodness, and asserted that God never performed an evil act (*qabīḥ*).[59]

In his presentation of the third component of *taqwā*, Pseudo-Māwardī addresses the obedience to which he linked the status of the believer and the Muslim in his introductory remarks:

> Thirdly: Upholding the performance of the precepts (*farāʾiḍ*), which are prayer, alms, fasting, pilgrimage, exertion in the path of God (*jihād fī sabīl Allāh*), and commanding right and forbidding wrong, according to their conditions and at the set times, in the proper places and in their complete forms, in accordance with the capacity to perform them (*istiᶜādat al-qudra ᶜalayhā*) and the removal of the exemptions that exclude them (*irtifāᶜ al-maᶜādhīr dūnahā*). Further, avoidance of the gross sins (*kabāʾir*) against which God has warned humankind with eternal (hell)-fire, mandated exemplary punishment and stipulated penalties, such as fornication, false accusation, exacting usurious interest and bribes, unjust appropriation of the wealth of orphans, killing, oppression, the consumption of wines, playing (the game of chance) *maysir*, and acts of obscenity (*al-fawāḥish*) both blatant and hidden.[60]

Pseudo-Māwardī's third component of *taqwā* concerns actions, which issue from the previous foundations of knowledge and faith. In keeping with Muᶜtazilite doctrine, Pseudo-Māwardī assumes that human beings act in accordance with the capacity for action with which God has endowed them, and are consequently responsible for the actions that they choose to perform. Human beings, and especially individuals who aspired to *taqwā*, were required to perform the obligatory acts of obedience and to abstain from forbidden acts, and Pseudo-Māwardī's lists of actions in these categories recall Qurʾānic passages. His category of obligations includes 'commanding right and forbidding wrong', one of the Muᶜtazilites' 'five principles',[61] and a topic on which al-Kaᶜbī held distinctive views, perhaps related to his administrative experience under Aḥmad b. Sahl.[62] His treatment of the major sins recalls the understanding of Abū l-Hudhayl (d. 227/841), who equated major sins with the acts that incurred the statutory penalties.[63] In accordance with the Muᶜtazilite principle of the divine threat, Pseudo-Māwardī avers that the individual who commits major sins incurs eternal punishment in the afterlife. Among the doctrines on which the Muᶜtazila were agreed, according to al-Kaᶜbī's account, was that God's forgiveness of the person who committed acts of disobedience (*murtakib al-maᶜāṣī*) depended on his repentance, and that the individuals consigned to hellfire remained in it forever.[64] Indeed, al-Kaᶜbī composed a treatise devoted to 'the threat [of divine punishment] of sinners', against which al-Māturīdī composed a *Kitāb Radd al-Kaᶜbī fī waᶜīd al-fussāq* ('Book in Refutation of al-Kaᶜbī on the Threat of Divine Punishment of Sinners').[65] Al-Māturīdī held that a person who committed a major sin remained a believer; while the grave sinner was not necessarily secure against divine punishment, only unbelievers faced eternal punishment.[66] Pseudo-Māwardī appears to have shared the views of al-Kaᶜbī on the matter, and, as will be shown in the following pages, addressed the consequences of the sinner's repentance and abandonment of sin at a later point in his chapter.

In his treatment of the fourth component of *taqwā*, Pseudo-Māwardī addresses the duties of the ruler in particular:

> Fourthly: Executing God's statutes, carrying out His ordinances among His servants, upholding equity (*qisṭ*) in His lands, observing His servants' rights (*al-ḥukm bi-l-ḥaqq*) with regard to their lives, wealth, persons (*fī . . . ashᶜārihim wa-abshārihim*), womenfolk and honourable reputations; avoiding injustice and transgression against them and partiality among them; following the Prophet in his manifest practices (*fī sunanihi al-ẓāhira*) and in his widely attested and beneficial conduct (*[fī] sīratihi al-mustafīḍa al-nāfiᶜa*), that God has made as a mark (*shiᶜār*) for the *umma* and as signs (*imārāt*) for the community (*milla*) where no textual injunction is found in the Book; for many of them (these practices) are precepts (*farāʾiḍ*) and many of them are requirements (*mawājib*), (although) some of them are more firmly established than others (*baᶜḍuhā ākadu min baᶜḍin*). God has commanded their adoption from the Prophet and their receptive acceptance from him by His words, 'Whatever the Prophet brings you, accept it, and whatever he forbids, refrain from it' (59: 7), and 'Obey God and obey the Prophet' (3: 132).[67]

Pseudo-Māwardī addresses the ruler's duties towards his subjects in terms that begin with divine injunctions, not limited to the statutory commandments, but extended to include equity and justice in all aspects of his governance, and the prevention of injustice. He adds to these injunctions the imitation of the example of the Prophet, and the embrace of practices that God has communicated by way of signs rather than scriptural commands. In keeping with Muᶜtazilite inclinations, Pseudo-Māwardī conveys the paramountcy of the divine revelation, invokes God's provision of marks and signs, and acknowledges the uneven foundation on which the transmitted Prophetic corpus rested.[68]

Pseudo-Māwardī's fifth component of *taqwā* likewise involves behaviour, and includes divine and Prophetic prescriptions:

> Fifthly: Taking heed of the instructive models that God has provided and following the example of His Prophet in them (*al-taᵓaddub bi-ādāb Allāh wa-l-iqtidāᵓ bi-nabiyyihi fīhā*), for God does not lay down anything conducive to the well-being of His creation (*ṣalāḥ khalqihi*) in their living and their dying, the beauty of their lives in this world and the next, by means of which they may attain a virtue or avoid a vice, without guiding them to it, urging them to it and disclosing it to them in His Book and the practices of the prophets among His creation (*fī kitābihi wa-sunan al-anbiyāᵓ min khalqihi*). For there is nothing that brings humanity towards greater nearness and proximity to Him (*yuqarribu wa-yuzlifu ladayhi*) in the afterlife that is not also a virtue to its agent (*faḍīla li-fāᶜilihi*), a mark of nobility (*sharaf*), an adornment (*zīna*) and a source of praise (*midḥa*) in this world; and nothing among that which He has forbidden and of which He has urged renunciation in this world (*lā shayᵓa mimmā nahā ᶜanhu wa-zahhada fīhi fī l-dunyā*) that is not also a vice (*radhīla*) and a (mark of) baseness (*danāᵓa*) in both (worlds), for the underpinnings of this world are connected to the underpinnings of the next (*asbāb al-dunyā mawṣūla bi-asbāb al-ākhira*); in the good (*ṣalāḥ*) of one lies the good of the other, in the corruption (*fasād*) of one the corruption of the other.[69]

In his fifth component of *taqwā*, Pseudo-Māwardī urges the ruler to cultivate the virtues that God has commended, directly or by implication, but that fall short of commandments. They find demonstration in the lives of the prophets and will earn the king not only a reward in the next life, but also praise in the present world. The two worlds, he asserts, are integrally connected, and the benefit of cultivating the virtues is the goodness or well-being, *ṣalāḥ*, of humankind. This point establishes the foundation for Pseudo-Māwardī's ensuing section devoted to the imitation of divine qualities and the cultivation of attributes that God has commended. It links his presentation of the scriptural basis for the cultivation of *taqwā* with the exemplary conduct of virtuous human beings.

His anatomy of *taqwā* illustrates clearly Pseudo-Māwardī's participation in the Muᶜtazilite discourse of his region, in which al-Kaᶜbī's teachings predominated. Although, as al-Māturīdī's numerous rebuttals of al-Kaᶜbī's teachings indicate, the scholarly cultures of Balkh and Samarqand were interconnected, and although despite differences in matters of doctrine, the two cultures shared several general characteristics, Pseudo-Māwardī's alignment with the Baghdadi branch of the Muᶜtazila emerges quite clearly.

In a transitional passage, Pseudo-Māwardī continues:

> Upholding religion is not incumbent on kings alone, but kings are prior in this regard and best positioned to implement and adopt the religion's prescriptions (*ādāb*), for several reasons, among them:
>
> As we have mentioned, God's favours towards kings are more apparent and their benefits to them more abundant, so that it is fitting for them to be more grateful, and more obedient, and quicker to (respond to) His commands and prohibitions.
>
> In addition, the position (*maqām*) in which God has placed kings is that of defender of the realm of religion and upholder of the affairs of the Muslims (*al-dhābb ᶜan ḥawzat al-dīn wa-l-qāʾim bi-umūr al-muslimīn*). If the king damages something that is entrusted to him and to which he is bound, and if no one else among his subjects is prepared to take responsibility for it, it is lost; whereas if large numbers of the subjects cause damage to something, but the king takes responsibility for it, it is not lost.
>
> Furthermore, as we have stated previously, the king's act becomes many acts, and his word becomes many words (*fiᶜl al-malik afᶜāl wa-qawluhu aqwāl*), since when the king performs an act, he is imitated in his action, his orders are followed, his words become normative traditions (*sunan*) and his actions normative practices (*siyar*) that endure over the course of time and the succession of days. If he acts well, the reward is his; if he acts wickedly, the burden accrues to him . . .[70]
>
> In addition, if he becomes known for *taqwā* and religion, the hearts of the subjects will love him, the *khāṣṣa* and *ᶜāmma* will be united in their assent

> towards him (*ittafaqat ͨalayhi kalimat al-khāṣṣa wa-l-ͨāmma*), the people involved in religion (*ahl al-dīn*) and those concerned with it will wish to approach and associate with him, and they will trust in his justice. If they see him act in an approved manner (*maḥbūb*), they will thank him for it, and if they see him act in a disapproved fashion (*makrūh*) they will excuse him of it, as long as he has acted in accordance with that which religion has made incumbent upon him and that the Lord of the Worlds has commanded of him.
>
> In addition, it will increase the awe (*mahāba*) in which he is held in the hearts of his enemies, for religion, righteousness, guidance and temperance instil loftiness in souls and awe in hearts and eyes. This is something that has become known through witnessing (*mushāhadatan*) and evident through observation (*muͨāyanatan*).[71]

In this section, Pseudo-Māwardī recapitulates several of his central themes. He extends his understanding of the reciprocal relationship between favour and gratitude to assert the king's exceptional debt of gratitude to God.[72] Kings are, as part of their particular status, responsible for the well-being of their subjects; the king's example is a powerful tool, since his practice becomes a pattern for emulation; the king needs his subjects' love in order to govern effectively; and his subjects' love, grounded in his positive reputation, renders him powerful against his enemies.[73] Pseudo-Māwardī's urging of the king to attain true knowledge and express it in his virtuous conduct recalls al-Kindī's efforts to renew the role of the philosopher, who by virtuous living would indicate the path towards universal knowledge and the highest felicity.[74]

The Divine Qualities

Pseudo-Māwardī turns next to the virtues and praiseworthy qualities (*al-faḍā'il wa-l-ma'āthir wa-l-manāqib wa-l-mafākhir*) that are indispensable to the king in matters of religion and governance (*fī l-diyāna wa-l-siyāsa*). Assuming, in Kindian fashion, the harmony of religiously and rationally based knowledge, Pseudo-Māwardī describes the king's governance as *al-siyāsa al-ḥikmiyya al-milliyya*, 'governance based on rational and religiously derived principles', or 'governance related to the generality of humankind and to the (Muslim) religious community in particular'. The epithets *ḥikmī* and *millī* evoke the categories of knowledge that would find full elaboration in the writings of al-ᶜĀmirī, who later in the tenth century divided the sciences into the contrasting but complementary categories of *al-ᶜulūm al-milliyya* ('the sciences peculiar to a specific religious community') and *al-ᶜulūm al-ḥikmiyya* ('the philosophical sciences').[75] The categories would also recur in the writings of the later Māturīdī theologian Abū l-Muᶜīn al-Nasafī (d. 508/1114), who referred to *anwāᶜ al-ᶜulūm al-milliyya wa-l-ḥikmiyya* ('types of religious and philosophical sciences').[76]

In an evocation of the correspondences between the divine model and human potential, Pseudo-Māwardī begins his recitation of the virtues that are indispensable to kings with the attribute of knowledge (*ᶜilm*):

> Knowledge is among the most resplendent of virtues in importance, highest in rank and loftiest in station. How could it be otherwise, when God has been pleased to describe Himself by it and has made it among the first epithets of praise by which He has praised (Himself) to His creation? . . .[77]
>
> In matters pertaining to crafts (*ṣināᶜāt*), governances (*siyāsāt*) and ranks (*marātib*), people differ in excellence according to their action (*ᶜamal*) and their intellect (*ᶜaql*), which is the mother and source of knowledge (*umm al-ᶜilm wa-aṣluhu*). Intellect is to no avail unless it is trained (*murabban*) and strengthened (*muqawwan*) with useful knowledge (*al-ᶜilm al-mustafād*). The learned possess a lofty stature in (people's) hearts and their names enjoy eminence in people's breasts. Furthermore, knowledge is indispensable in every religion (*diyāna*), governance (*siyāsa*) and craft (*ṣināᶜa*). It is fitting that the king should not spurn this noble virtue, nor disregard it, nor position himself in ignorance of its path or bereft of its adornment, in addition to that which we have mentioned concerning his indispensable need for it (*min ḥājatihi l-ḍarūriyya ilayhi*).[78]

Anticipating a theme that he develops further elsewhere, Pseudo-Māwardī links governance with craftsmanship, which requires the craftsman's mastery of an appropriate body of knowledge. Pseudo-Māwardī alludes to the hierarchical enumerations of the sciences in which branches of knowledge were classified according to their 'usefulness' (*nafᶜ*).[79] Most writers who attended to this topic distinguished between the Arabic-Islamic and 'foreign' or 'ancient' sciences, in the parlance of al-Khwārazmī, the categories of 'the sciences of the religious law and the related Arabic sciences' (*ᶜulūm al-sharīᶜa wa-mā yaqtarinu bihā min al-ᶜulūm al-ᶜarabiyya*) and 'the sciences of non-Arab peoples, including the Greeks and other peoples' (*ᶜulūm al-ᶜajam min al-yūnāniyyīn wa-ghayrihim*).[80] Pseudo-Māwardī, by contrast, at no point invokes this distinction. He asserts merely, in a Muᶜtazilite-inflected passage, that the science that is highest in value and utility in the realms of *dīn* and *dunyā* is *ᶜilm al-dīn*, 'the science of religion':[81]

> Absolute knowledge (*al-ᶜilm al-muṭlaq*)[82] is a general category (*jins*), beneath which are several kinds (*anwāᶜ*), and various forms (*ṣuwar*) that differ in excellence according to their usefulness (*nafᶜ*) and exaltedness (*jalāla*). Accordingly, those who specialise in them contend for precedence (*yatafāḍalu bihā ᶜālimūhā*), for there is no craft (*ṣināᶜa*), however small or ample its value (*miqdār*) and however great or little its utility (*nafᶜ*), that does not comprise a science (*ᶜilm*) that its practitioners know. It is not within human capacity to apprehend every branch of knowledge, nor to attain every science. Since there is no expectation that he master all of the branches of knowledge, the best approach for the intelligent person is that he choose among them the most exalted in value, the greatest in purport, and the most comprehensive in its usefulness in the spheres of religion and the world. No type of knowledge is more deserving of this description than the science of religion (*ᶜilm al-dīn*) by which nearness to God, great is His mention, is attained, the hereafter earned and a store towards it prepared; and no science is of greater suitability for kings, nor a greater provision for them in their governance of the kingdom and their preservation of religion, than the religious sciences, that in their sum fall into five parts.[83]
>
> The first division is the science of the divine unity (*ᶜilm al-tawḥīd*), that is, knowledge of God (*maᶜrifat Allāh*), great is His mention, and the sciences of divinity (*ᶜulūm al-ilāhiyya*) that we have previously mentioned.
>
> The second division is the relating of the traditions (*āthār*) of the Messenger of God and the transmission of his narrative reports (*akhbār*), which constitute the principles of the ordinances (*uṣūl al-aḥkām*) and foundations of (the categories of) the licit and illicit (*mabānī l-ḥalāl wa-l-ḥarām*). These trans-

> mitted materials include the practices (*sunan*) and biographical accounts (*maghāzī*) of the Prophet; knowledge of the principles, origins, consolidation and genesis of the religion (*ma*ᶜ*rifat uṣūl al-diyāna wa-makhārijihā wa-ithbātihā wa-bad*ᵓ *kawnihā*); the practices (*sunan*) of its caliphs, the governance (*siyāsa*) of its amirs, and the sayings (*aqāwīl*) of its scholars.
>
> The third division is the science of jurisprudence, which constitutes knowledge of the religious community (*ma*ᶜ*rifat al-milla*) and the practices (*sunan*) of the sharīᶜa.
>
> The fourth division is the science of admonitions (ᶜ*ilm al-mawā*ᶜ*iẓ*) that instil mindfulness of the next world and promote the attainment of divine reward and the pursuit of the good (*ṭalab al-khayr*).
>
> The fifth division is the science of language, without which no one of these sects nor the people of any group (*lā . . . firqa min hādhihi l-firaq wa-lā ahl niḥla min al-niḥal*) can aspire to become consummate in its craft (*kāmilan fī ṣinā*ᶜ*atihi*), or excellent in its religious observance, teachings or doctrine (*fāḍilan fī diyānatihi wa-madhhabihi wa-maqālatihi*), since by it (language) (a person) comes to know the order of God's speech (*naẓm kalām Allāh*) and the traditions (*āthār*) of His Prophet, and he becomes acquainted with the implications of His oration (to humankind) and the meanings of His Book (*mawāqi*ᶜ *khiṭābihi wa-ma*ᶜ*ānī kitābihi*).
>
> These are all the divisions of the religious sciences.[84]

Pseudo-Māwardī's five divisions of ᶜ*ilm al-dīn* recall his five constituents of *taqwā*. Both enumerations begin with knowledge of God (*ma*ᶜ*rifat Allāh*), equated with the doctrine of the divine unicity (*tawḥīd*); as will be seen shortly, Pseudo-Māwardī identifies the pursuit of this knowledge with the discipline of rational theology, ᶜ*ilm al-kalām*. His reference to the 'sciences of divinity', I suggest, evokes al-Kindī's category of 'divine knowledge' (*al-*ᶜ*ilm al-ilāhī*).[85] Contrary to the customary presentation of language as a 'tool' or 'instrument' (*āla*), necessary for pursuit of the sciences but subsidiary to them, Pseudo-Māwardī, perhaps in a reflection of the Kindian tradition, does not employ this term; he presents language as lower in rank, but not different in kind from the preceding four sciences.[86] Turning to the practical matter of the acquisition of the sciences, he begins with the fifth, language, since without it, none of the others would be possible:

> The order in which (the prince) should pursue (the branches of) knowledge requires that he should begin with instruction in language, which should be committed to memory in his early years, in the bloom of youth and eagerness, when his memory is most powerful and his heart clear of the (encumbrances) that sovereignty will place upon it once he accedes to his rule and becomes preoccupied with the governance of his kingdom and caring for his subjects.

Elsewhere, Pseudo-Māwardī elaborates at some length on the Arabic language and the optimal methods for non-specialists, such as kings, in acquiring proficiency in it. He displays a pronounced interest in linguistic matters, in consistency with a mentality permeated by Kindian philosophy and Muᶜtazilite theology.[87] In this instance, Pseudo-Māwardī observes that only if he possesses a good knowledge of Arabic can the king attain a correct and discerning understanding of religion, which consists first in the mastery of dialectical theology (*ᶜilm al-kalām*):

> Once he has reached physical and intellectual maturity and attained full religious responsibility (*idhā balagha wa-ᶜaqala wa-lazimathu ḥujjat Allāh*), the prince should begin with *ᶜilm al-dīn* (the science of religion), the path to which is *ᶜilm al-kalām* (the science of rational theology), until he has acquired what he needs to know, ignorance of which he cannot afford, and neglect of which is not permitted for an intelligent person (*ᶜāqil*), for it is the first of the sciences in order of precedence.[88]

In an exposition that reflects his Muᶜtazilite point of view, Pseudo-Māwardī enumerates six reasons for the assertion that the science of theology possesses priority among the religious sciences:[89]

> It is prior firstly because rectitude in it constitutes faith and felicity (*al-iṣāba fihi īmān wa-saᶜāda*), and error in it constitutes unbelief and misery (*al-khaṭaʾ fihi kufr wa-shaqāwa*). It is incumbent on the human being that he should hasten to pursue the thing that involves the greatest (potential) harm (*ḍarar*) and the greatest (potential) benefit (*nafᶜ*).[90]

> For a second reason: It is the noblest of the sciences in its essence (*fī dhātihi*) and the most excellent of the arts in its particularities, because it entails enquiry concerning God and His signs (*al-baḥth ᶜan Allāh wa-ᶜan āyātihi*). Its subject matter (*maᶜlūm*, that which is known) is He, glorious and exalted. Whatever the science, the nobler, loftier, more excellent and elevated its subject matter, the nobler and more excellent the knowledge of it, and no subject matter is nobler than that which this science investigates and by which it derives proofs concerning it (Him).[91]

Adduced in Pseudo-Māwardī's first point, the categories of utility and harm, which allude to the earthly life and the life after death, pervade *Naṣīḥat al-mulūk*, in keeping with the philosophical–theological discourse concerned with epistemology.[92] Pseudo-Māwardī's second point, in illustration of a common point of view, recapitulates the ranking of the sciences on the basis of the status of the objects of their study.[93]

> For a third reason, it constitutes enquiry (*baḥth*) concerning religion (*diyāna*) and defence (*dhabb*) of the religious community (*milla*) that, as we have clarified, constitute the root of the kingdom and the foundation of prosperity, the axis of governance (*quṭb al-siyāsa*) and the well-being (*ṣalāḥ*) of this world and the next.[94]
>
> For a fourth reason, the king stands in need of (such knowledge) and will avail himself of it in crowded assemblies (*al-majālis al-ḥāfila*) and dense gatherings of his troops (*al-ᶜasākir al-kathīfa al-jāmiᶜa*) at times of warfare, sometimes against people of opposing religious communities (*ahl al-milal al-mukhālifa*) and sometimes against people in revolt and rebellion (*ahl al-baghy wa-l-ᶜiṣyān*). The ruler needs to know whether combat against them is licit for him and violence against them permitted to him, because if he triumphs over them through injustice and oppression (*bi-ẓulm wa-jawr*) then he has lost; if he vanquishes them by means of (injustice and oppression) he is himself vanquished; and if he defeats them by (means of injustice and oppression) he is defeated.
>
> The king also needs to engage them (his opponents) in religious argument and disputation, and to call them to faith and obedience (*yaḥtāju ilā . . . daᶜwatihim ilā l-īmān wa-l-ṭāᶜa*). The established custom (*sunna*) is to

> advance the call (*taqdīm al-da*ᶜ*wa*) and set forth the proof (*iqāmat al-ḥujja*) at the time of conflict. If the king lacks knowledge of his religion and his *madhhab*, he will be defeated (in argument) and eclipsed (*maḥjūb*); and sometimes his adversary's arguments may sow dissension among his assembly, scatter his army and corrupt the hearts of his friends (*awliyā*ᵓ) against him.[95] This is one of the stratagems that kings do not cease to employ and to which they have recourse at the moment when the army encounters (its adversary) and the two sides confront one another.[96]

Pseudo-Māwardī's third and fourth points move from the abstract to the practical realm of the king's governance. The religious sciences equip the king to perform his royal functions, including the defence of the *milla*, by means of disputation,[97] and if necessary and permissible, by force. His insistence that the king may legitimately resort to force only under strictly delineated conditions is consistent with Pseudo-Māwardī's Muᶜtazilite affiliation.[98] In cases of internal dissent, a knowledge of theology will enable the king to detach his adversary's supporters to his own camp; by the same token, if the ruler is ill-equipped to answer the claims of religious opponents, he risks the defection of his troops to the other side. To illustrate his points, Pseudo-Māwardī cites crucial moments in the early history of the Muslim community. First, he mentions ᶜAlī's use of argumentation (*ḥijāj*) to divide the Companions Ṭalḥa and al-Zubayr, who opposed him at the Battle of the Camel, and later the Kharijites, who seceded from his party (*shī*ᶜ*a*).[99] Next, he mentions Abū Bakr's use of argumentation in seeking permission to fight *ahl al-ridda*, the groups who, upon the death of the Prophet, sought to leave the community.[100] Lastly, he refers to Muᶜāwiya's deployment of doubt (*shubha*) 'in the form of proof' (*fī ṣūrat al-ḥujja*) to triumph over ᶜAlī and divide his supporters at Siffin. The Battle of Siffin, in which the forces of ᶜAlī and Muᶜāwiya confronted each other, took place in 36/657. In the course of the battle, Muᶜāwiya's Syrian troops, on the verge of defeat, employed the ruse of hoisting Qurᵓānic verses (or possibly entire Qurᵓāns) on their spears, a signal that spread confusion and led to a termination of hostilities, followed by recourse to arbitration.[101] To emphasise the universal nature of his argument, Pseudo-Māwardī also cites Aristotle's correspondence with Alexander.[102]

Pseudo-Māwardī continues with the fifth and sixth points in his enumeration of reasons for the precedence to be accorded to the science of theology:

> The fifth reason is that by it he guards against the stratagems of those who misrepresent and fabricate (*min ḥiyal al-mumawwihīn wa-l-mumakhriqīn*), and the enemies of sovereignty and religion, among the *zanādiqa* and *mulḥid[ū]n*, whose intent, as we have mentioned, is sometimes to aim initially at kings, in order to corrupt them, seize them (*ightiyāl*) and hunt them, then to utilise them for the corruption of the subjects; and sometimes to aim at the subjects and corrupt them against the king, to divide their allegiances, sow dissension among them (*shaqqa ᶜaṣāhum*), and to raise conflict between them (the subjects and the king). Both cases involve the destruction of the pillars of the community (*hadam arkān al-milla*) and the uprooting of the religion and the kingdom (*istiʾṣāl al-diyāna wa-l-mamlaka*). The ordinances of the science of religion include guarding against such corruption and fortification against this (kind of) (destructive) manifestation. Among the most hideous of things for the king is that an enemy of his religion and sovereignty should aim at him; while he flees from the proof of the distinguished and learned (*al-ᶜālim al-khāṣṣī*) and the assault of the common and ignorant (*al-jāhil al-ᶜāmmī*), his enemy chases him as if he were hunting wild animals and birds until he extricates him from his religion, ruins his afterlife for him, destroys his kingdom, and he (the king), being ignorant of the root of his religion and impotent to aid his *madhhab*, surrenders these things to him.[103]

In his fifth argument for the king's need for a knowledge of theology, Pseudo-Māwardī resumes his warnings, articulated forcefully in his third chapter, regarding the deceptive strategies that he imputes to the *zanādiqa* (it is in this context that the term appears) and *mulḥids* who seek to subvert the king's sovereignty for their own purposes and to undermine the established religion.[104] Pseudo-Māwardī portrays *kalām* as the king's best means of defence against such groups.[105] He observes that heretics sometimes seek to infiltrate and seduce the élites, and sometimes foment discontent and seek adherents among the common people, observations that might suggest that he alluded not only to the spread of heterodoxy at the court, but also to local revolts. The passage anticipates the later tenth-century description of al-ᶜĀmirī, who enumerated three types of stratagem employed in efforts to undermine individuals' religious convictions and induce them to seek an alternative affiliation.[106]

Pseudo-Māwardī continues with his sixth reason:

> The sixth reason is that the foundation (*aṣl*) and method (*ṭarīq*) of the science of religion (*ᶜilm al-dīn*) consist in inference by means of analogy (*istidlāl bi-l-shāhid ᶜalā l-ghāʾib*), by that which is agreed upon against that which is subject to disagreement (*bi-l-muttafaq ᶜalayhi ᶜalā l-mukhtalaf fīhi*), and the method of logical deduction (*istikhrāj al-raʾy*). This (technique) constitutes the true science of governance (*ᶜilm al-siyāsa ᶜalā l-ḥaqīqa*), the method appropriate for the rational investigation of consequences (*al-naẓar fī l-ᶜawāqib*) and for disputation with officials, secretaries and viziers (*munāẓarat al-ᶜummāl wa-l-kuttāb wa-l-wuzarāʾ*).[107]

In this final argument for the ruler's preferential study of *ᶜilm al-dīn*, Pseudo-Māwardī advises that the method involved in theological reasoning was precisely the method that the king needed to master in order to govern, and in particular to assess, discern and refute arguments advanced to him by his officials, secretaries and viziers. Pseudo-Māwardī's implication that members of these groups sought to mislead the king served partly to displace the burden of his criticism from the person of the king to his counsellors. Pseudo-Māwardī describes his method in the language familiar from rationalist and especially Muᶜtazilite expositions of analogical and deductive reasoning, often expressed in formulations that included the manifest or 'present' (*shāhid*) and the unknown or 'absent' (*ghāʾib*).[108] Al-Kaᶜbī, who defined *istidlāl*, the derivation of proof, as 'joining one known item to another (known item) in order that the evidence for a (new) known item should result' (*ḍamm maᶜlūm ilā maᶜlūm li-yantuja l-badīha minhā maᶜlūman*), composed a treatise entitled *Kitāb* [*Kayfiyyat*] *al-istidlāl bi-l-shāhid ᶜalā l-ghāʾib* ('Book of [the Procedure for] Deriving Proof by Analogy from the Present to the Absent'), which occupied a prominent place in his intellectual outlook.[109] For many of the Muᶜtazila, *istidlāl* was synonymous with *naẓar*,[110] and it was through this technique of analogical reasoning that human beings possessed the capacity to know God. The technique involved the drawing of inferences with regard to the qualities of the 'hidden', that is, the divine by means of analogies with the visible world.[111] Pseudo-Māwardī extends the scope of *istidlāl* in an assertion of its invaluable application to the king's governance. By mastering the technique of drawing inferences, based on the knowledge attained by experience and observation and its extrapolation by means of logical deduction, the king acquires the ability to foresee outcomes and consequences, and to resist and countermand the misguided intentions of the élites in his administration. Incidentally, the passage provides a description of Pseudo-Māwardī's distinctive and consciously deployed method of argument throughout *Naṣīḥat al-mulūk*.

Having enumerated six reasons for the priority of *ᶜilm al-kalām*, Pseudo-Māwardī addresses the remaining divisions of *ᶜilm al-dīn*. He resumes:

> If the king wishes to increase his knowledge and profit further from its pursuit and accumulation, he should proceed in the order that we have mentioned and the sequence that we have laid down. We have already proposed that the first thing that brings further advancement is the relating of traditions (*āthār*), and knowledge of the reports (*akhbār*) of the Prophet, the exemplary persons among his Companions (*ahl al-qudwa min aṣḥābihi*), and the Rightly Guided Caliphs after him; and the accounts of their lives and conduct (*akhbār al-siyar wa-l-maghāzī*), for in this body of knowledge lies confirmation of the first branch and the most noble science [namely, the science of theology], because by it he (the king) will attain knowledge of the roots of the religious community (*milla*), its beginning, the virtues of its Prophet, his signs (*āyāt*) and miracles (*muᶜjizāt*), the excellent qualities of his sharīᶜa, his religion and religious community, the interpretation of the Book revealed to him and that which is difficult in it (*tafsīr kitābihi wa-mushkilihi*) and the meanings of his traditions (*āthār*).
>
> He should cultivate this knowledge so that it will not be possible for a forger to invent a (Prophetic) saying against him (*fa-lā yumkinu li-muzawwir tazwīr ḥadīth ᶜalayhi*), nor for the people of a religious community to claim a virtue for their *madhhab* or a fine quality for their *milla* without him having at his disposal something yet better in his religion and his sharīᶜa. Nor can they claim a fine conduct for the kings of the nations for which he is at a loss to find the likes of it in the conduct of his caliphs, for he who is acquainted with the conduct of the caliphs, the reports of the viziers and the transmitted reports of the rulers of Islam (*man ᶜarafa siyar al-khulafāʾ*

> *wa-akhbār al-wuzarā° wa-āthār al-umarā° al-islāmiyyīn*) will not be misled by the accounts (*akhbār*) of the earlier communities and the transmitted reports of the past kings, except in the case of human beings who wilfully give preference to falsehood over truth and deliberately (choose) the forged over the verified, and incline away from right direction towards deviation out of resistance (*ᶜinād*) and slander (*buht*). And that is a disease for which the doctor (*ṭabīb*) is incapable of a remedy and a madness for which the physicians (*ḥukamā°*) despair of a cure.[112]

After theology, according to Pseudo-Māwardī, the king should study the traditions of the Prophet and the transmitted reports of the Companions and early caliphs. This sequence amounts to the conjoining of rationally derived (*ᶜaqlī*) knowledge and transmitted (*naqlī*) knowledge in a system in which rationality informs the use of transmitted textual materials, including Prophetic ḥadīth. Pseudo-Māwardī's arrangement of these primary sources of knowledge, the respective merits of which were subject to substantial dispute during his lifetime, align him with the position of al-Kaᶜbī, who similarly asserted the priority of rational speculation and questioned the uncritical use of ḥadīth.[113] The king should attend to the distinguishing history and culture of his religious community, especially, but not exclusively, as transmitted in the Prophet's legacy, so that he will not fall prey to persons who wish to distort it to him by claiming Prophetic utterances (ḥadīth) that have no foundation or, if their allegiances or sentiments lie outside the community, to portray another community's exemplars as superior to his own. Pseudo-Māwardī's treatment of the problem of forgery, in this instance an allusion to the science of ḥadīth, anticipates the later Kindian al-ᶜĀmirī's treatment of forged reports (*akhbār muzawwara*) foisted on authoritative persons for purposes of undermining and provoking divisions within religious communities. In al-ᶜĀmirī's presentation, forgery is one of the techniques employed by persons whose desire is to falsify religion and weaken its foundation (*tazyīf al-dīn wa-tawhīn asāsihi*).[114]

Pseudo-Māwardī's reference to claims advanced in favour of earlier communities and the kings of the past recalls his holding up of Caliph al-Ma°mūn with the words, 'If this community were to compete with other nations (*sā°ir al-umam*) over their kings', they would find him superior in every respect to any rivals that other nations might invoke.[115] Although the passage contains one of Pseudo-Māwardī's few positive references to viziers, possibly in part for reasons of rhyme (*khulafā*ᵓ . . . *wuzarā*ᵓ . . . *umarā*ᵓ), his point perhaps alludes to the excessively *shu*ᶜ*ūbī* sensibilities imputed to al-Jayhānī,[116] and the enthusiastic engagement with the Iranian past expressed in the collection and composition of *shāhnāmehs*, in progress during Pseudo-Māwardī's lifetime. If this inference is correct, it perhaps illuminates al-ᶜĀmirī's references, in the same context, to *ta*ᶜ*aṣṣub malakī* (attachment based on claims to power) and *ta*ᶜ*aṣṣub nasabī* (attachment based on claims to kinship).[117]

In a manner similar to his concluding arguments in favour of theology, Pseudo-Māwardī completes his recommendations for the study of the transmitted corpus of the Islamic past with a comment on its value in the cultivation of virtue and the execution of effective governance:

> In the knowledge and hearing of *akhbār* lie a companionship (*uns*) that exceeds all other companionship, an education (*adab*) that surpasses every other education, and a subject matter (*sabab*) that clarifies praiseworthy and reprehensible moral dispositions (*al-akhlāq al-maḥmūda wa-l-madhmūma*). The activity also facilitates the knowledge of just and unjust governances (ᶜ*ilm al-siyāsāt al-*ᶜ*ādila wa-l-jā*ᵓ*ira*); the inference of knowledge concerning the designs of men, the manners of kings (*ādāb al-mulūk*), and the various *madhhabs* (*funūn al-madhāhib*); a knowledge of the transmitters (*al-ma*ᶜ*rifa bi-l-rijāl*), the drawing of lessons through [the vicissitudes of] time (*al-i*ᶜ*tibār bi-l-zamān*), an understanding of the ordinances (*al-fiqh fī l-aḥkām*), and knowledge of the licit and the forbidden (*al-*ᶜ*ilm bi-l-ḥalāl wa-l-ḥarām*).[118]

Having presented in turn the ᶜ*aqlī* sciences of rational theology and the *naqlī* study of transmitted materials, Pseudo-Māwardī treats the third of his sciences of religion, the science of jurisprudence:

> If the king wishes to increase his knowledge, then (he should turn to) the science of jurisprudence (ᶜ*ilm al-fiqh*), which is the science of the religious laws and ordinances (ᶜ*ilm al-sharā*ᵓ*i*ᶜ *wa-l-aḥkām*), for it is an obligation (*farḍ*) on every Muslim and a (source of) beauty for everyone, and it is indispensable to kings and leaders especially (*wa-lā ghaniyya bi-l-mulūk*

wa-l-aʾimma khuṣūṣan ʿanhu), for they are obliged to investigate the grievances of the subjects and the population (*al-naẓar fī maẓālim al-raʿiyya wa-l-bariyya*), to listen to their claims, proofs, oaths and testimony (*samāʿ daʿāwīhim wa-bayyinātihim wa-aymānihim wa-shahādatihim*), and to pronounce on them. Sometimes the amir is responsible for the ritual prayer, or receives written notices pertaining to the collection of the obligatory donations of alms (*zakawāt*) and charitable donations (*ṣadaqāt*), or is resorted to in matters of marriage and matrimony, sales and inheritances, and other types of ordinances (*sāʾir funūn al-aḥkām*). Sometimes something concerning the division of booty and spoils (*shayʾ min qismat al-maghnam wa-l-fayʾ*), or the allocation of the wealth of the kingdom to its proper places, is brought before him. Consequently it is most fitting for the king to pursue this virtue, so that he is not in the position of the ignorant person who needs a jurist (*faqīh*) or a judge (*qāḍī*) in the science in which he is a specialist, and (yet) which is general to all his subjects, and in which is (lodged) the foundation of his governance (*qiwām siyāsatihi*); nor is he dependent on a judge (*qāḍī*) or a jurisconsult (*muftī*) for every new occurrence (*nāzila*) and eventuality (*ḥāditha*). It is not fitting that he deprive himself of a virtue to the attainment of which he finds a path, and that he rely instead on a competent person (*kāfī*) to fulfil the obligation for him and a deputy (*nāʾib*) to whom he delegates responsibility in his place; for if he acts in this way, then someone else will have surpassed him in this virtue and will have preceded him in reaching this praiseworthy quality. Furthermore, if he acquires a satisfactory degree of juristic understanding it will make it possible for him to pursue independent reasoning (*ijtihād*) and rational enquiry (*naẓar*) in his own right, to seek proofs for them, and to interpret according to his judgements (*in balagha min al-fiqh mablaghan murḍiyyan amkanahu al-ijtihād wa-l-naẓar li-nafsihi wa-ṭalab al-ḥujaj lahā wa-l-taʾwīl li-ārāʾihi*), because in his interpretation (*taʾwīl*) he will limit himself to that which is permitted to him. It will also prepare him by means of juridical strategies (*bi-l-ḥiyal al-fiqhiyya*) to flee from much of what is forbidden to that which is licit (*min al-ḥarām ilā l-ḥalāl*), and from the false to the true (*min al-bāṭil ilā l-ḥaqq*). In (this knowledge) he will possess a proof in his religion, an adornment in his kingdom, a remover of suspicions (*tuham*) and doubt (*rayb*) from himself, and success (*najāt*) in his afterlife.[119]

The precedence that Pseudo-Māwardī assigns to *kalām* over *fiqh* mirrors the priority that he invests in knowledge and faith as necessary prerequisites for the divine acceptance of right actions.[120] It situates him in a theological–philosophical grouping distinct from that of al-Fārābī, who, in *Iḥṣāʾ al-ᶜulūm* ('Enumeration of the Sciences'), reversed Pseudo-Māwardī's order of the two sciences.[121] Nevertheless, jurisprudence is especially useful to the king, since it prepares him to assume leadership in religious matters when necessary. Pseudo-Māwardī's inventory of the activities in which the ruler may be required to lead or adjudicate seems in keeping with the patterns attested for the early Samanid amirs, who acquired some training in ḥadīth, led the prayers at the funerals of eminent scholars and presided over sessions of *maẓālim* in person.[122] They also undertook responsibilities that, as Pseudo-Māwardī describes, required a degree of juristic understanding. Naṣr I, for example, received a document related to a charitable endowment (*waqf*), which he was able to authenticate and implement in a beneficial manner.[123]

Furthermore, an adequate familiarity with *fiqh* permitted the ruler to engage in *ijtihād*, *naẓar* and *taʾwīl* for himself, since his knowledge would prevent him from deviating from the permissible.[124] Pseudo-Māwardī's encouragement of individual participation in these exercises coincides with Muᶜtazilite tendencies to reject or restrict *taqlīd*, the following of precedent without rational enquiry into it or its alternatives.[125] To arrive at the truth by means of *ijtihād* required exertion and effort; *naẓar* involved not merely quiet meditation, but active speculation, associated with dialogue and argument.[126] Pseudo-Māwardī's exposition is somewhat reminiscent of Ibn al-Muqaffaᶜ's advice to the caliph, whom the earlier writer exhorted to assert religious authority and adjudicate in matters of religious law.[127] Like other aspects of Pseudo-Māwardī's counsel, his depiction of the ruler's involvement in the religious life of the community assimilates the application of distinctive theological–philosophical perspectives, the inheritance of his region's perennial wisdom and the remembered practices of the early Saminid amirs.

The final branch of religious learning to which Pseudo-Māwardī turns is that of the knowledge of ethical exhortations:

> Next is the knowledge of admonitions and moral reminding (*ᶜilm al-mawāᶜiẓ wa-l-tadhkīr*).[128]

Pseudo-Māwardī refrains from further treatment of this 'science', since, as he reminds his readers, he has already demonstrated by means of exposition and the adducing of authoritative statements that the king is the neediest of persons for it. Furthermore, he had devoted the entirety of his previous (fourth) chapter to *mawāʿiẓ*.[129]

In concluding this section of his exposition, Pseudo-Māwardī attends briefly to other branches of knowledge, and observes:

> There is no other branch of knowledge that does not involve evident enjoyment and benefit, such as medicine, arithmetic, geometry and astronomy. But the science of religion is prior, more excellent, more elevated and noble than any other, and especially in the virtuous king and the perfect ruler, on account of the extent of his need for it and the community's dependence on it (him). Moreover it is prior because the king can find other people to calculate, measure, practise medicine and write for him, but he will not find anyone who, in his stead and on his behalf, can achieve conviction in that which is correct (*man yaʿtaqidu ʿanhu al-ṣawāb*), repel doubt, aspire to a fortunate afterlife and defend the religion – as well as for the other qualities that we have mentioned and the reasons that we have traced.[130]

In this passage, Pseudo-Māwardī differentiates the sciences of medicine, arithmetic, geometry and astronomy from the branches of 'the science of religion', to which he assigns priority. His conception of the sciences recalls al-Kindī's classification of the first set of subjects under the category of 'human knowledge' (*al-ʿilm al-insānī*) as opposed to, and subordinate to, 'divine knowledge' (*al-ʿilm al-ilāhī*).[131] In a reflection of the Muʿtazilite principle of individual exertion towards the goal of religious truth, he presents the science of religion as the one science that no one else could acquire for him. Pseudo-Māwardī's near contemporary the theologian Abū l-Layth al-Samarqandī, who acknowledged all knowledge as good in God's sight, regarded *ʿilm al-fiqh*, in the Ḥanafī–Māturīdī sense of *al-fiqh fī l-dīn*, religious understanding, as most important, on the somewhat similar grounds that it facilitated the learning of the other sciences and constituted the support of the religion.[132]

Acquiring Knowledge

Pseudo-Māwardī follows his presentation of the religious sciences appropriate to kings with a discussion of the means of their acquisition. He instructs the king that he cannot acquire knowledge of these sciences without, on the one hand, associating with scholars and, on the other, study of their books:

> It is not possible to profit from these sciences other than by the provision of two matters: firstly, holding sessions with the scholars and philosophers among the people of every category (*mujālasat al-ᶜulamāᵓ wa-l-ḥukamāᵓ min ahl kull ṭabaqa*); secondly, investigation of books devoted to religion (*al-naẓar fī kutub al-diyāna*), and attention to learning and studying them. The excellent king must hold frequent sessions with the ᶜulamāᵓ and jurists of every category (*min kull ṭabaqa min hādhihi l-ṭabaqāt*). In his times of leisure, his assembly (*majlis*) should not be without books that he examines and in which he seeks companionship. He should know that the company of the ᶜulamāᵓ when they attend his *majlis* is no less (valuable) than the company of musicians, singers, jesters and entertainers; rather, it is more dignified, more virtuous, finer, nobler, and a source of greater adornment and beauty, on account of the opportunity it provides for the acquisition of (divine) reward, the provision of fine stores (towards the afterlife) and a fine reputation that will endure over the course of time; as well as the attachment of the élites, the affection of the common people and the inclination of the ᶜulamāᵓ, who are the noblest category of the subjects in rank and the most elevated in degree.[133]

Pseudo-Māwardī emphasises that the ᶜulamāᵓ and philosophers (*ḥukamāᵓ*) in the king's assembly should represent every category (*ṭabaqa*), possibly a reference to the various *ᶜaqlī* and *naqlī* branches of the sciences, or possibly a reference to differing legal, theological and philosophical perspectives. His emphasis on the inclusivity of areas of expertise or points of view should perhaps be understood as subject to his principle of the 'sum', the basic tenets on which all members of the community should agree.[134]

Encouragement of the king to associate with the ᶜulamāᵓ finds a place in most mirrors for princes. Pseudo-Māwardī acknowledges, however, that the ᶜulamāᵓ might not wish to associate with the king. His mirror emphasises the reciprocal responsibilities of monarchs and subjects, and offers arguments for the subjects to engage with rulers, as well as for rulers to heed the well-intentioned counsel of their advisers. Pseudo-Māwardī also advises the king to study in private, and to master, presumably through silent study (*muṭālaᶜa*), books devoted to religious subjects.[135] He follows this advice with quotations from the 'Testament' of Sāb.t.r.m, King of India, to his son; the 'proclamations' (*manshūrāt*) of Plato; the wise sayings (*ḥikam*) of the Ancients; ᶜUmar b. al-Khaṭṭāb; the counsels of *al-ḥakīm* (Aristotle) to Alexander; two short utterances of Ibn al-Muᶜtazz (247–96/861–908), the Abbasid prince and poet; and a pair of passages from the *Āᵓīnnāmeh*.[136] The pair of aphorisms of Ibn al-Muᶜtazz are: 'A human being's knowledge is his lasting offspring' (*ᶜilm al-insān waladuhu al-mukhallad*) and 'The ignorant person is a child even if he is advanced in years, and the learned person is an elder even if he is a youth' (*al-jāhil ṣaghīr wa-in kāna shaykhan wa-l-ᶜālim kabīr wa-in kāna ḥadathan*).[137]

After adducing this eclectic set of attestations to the universal esteem for knowledge, Pseudo-Māwardī resumes his arguments for the benefits that the attendance of scholars at royal gatherings will bring about:

> In the prominent placement (*tamakkun*) of the ᶜulamāᵓ and the people of religion among the persons present in the ruler's assembly (*majlis al-sulṭān*) lies a means of curtailing the ambitions of enticers (*ghuwāt*) given to corrupt (heterodox) beliefs and destructive innovations, which, as we have mentioned, are among the causes of corruption in the religion and the kingdom, and the collapse of the pillars of the religious community (*tadāᶜī arkān al-milla*). It is incumbent on the virtuous king and intelligent ruler that he should not neglect this relationship and replace this category (the ᶜulamāᵓ and men of religion) with the corrupt category of effeminate persons, singers and similar types. The virtuous king and intelligent ruler (should) not neglect (scholars in favour of) people who stain his honour (*ᶜirḍ*), sovereignty and intellect by pimping, the mention of people's womenfolk (*ᶜawrāt al-nās*), infatuation with youths and women (*al-tawājud ᶜalā l-ghilmān wa-l-niswān*), or passionate love and the beloved (*al-ᶜishq wa-l-maᶜshūq*), for all of this is foolishness and weakness. Through

> his aspiration, the high-minded person should elevate himself above and distance himself from these matters – especially topics that the poets of this age have originated (*lā siyyamā mā aḥdatha shuʿarāʾ hādhā l-zamān*), for they lodge debauchery and unbelief in their verses, and infuse them with their corrupt *madhāhib*. Through their poetry they entice their listeners to seek pleasures and follow desires, by way of ease and relaxation, boldness and insolence, and making light of religion and its laws, and of the religious community and its duties (*al-istikhfāf bi-l-dīn wa-sharāʾiʿihi wa-l-milla wa-waẓāʾifihā*). All of that is damaging to the root of religious conviction and to religion (*dhālika kulluhu muḍirr bi-aṣl al-iʿtiqād wa-amr al-diyāna*). Holding assemblies with the likes of such people, and frequent association with such depraved persons (*andhāl*) give rise to limited aspirations, bad habits and a tendency to resemble them. The scholars, philosophers and people of religion (*al-ʿulamāʾ wa-l-ḥukamāʾ wa-ahl al-dīn*) have never ceased to be wary of assemblies (in which such persons are present), to announce their opposition to them, and to commend (instead) sessions with noble and honourable people (*mujālasat ashrāf al-nās wa-jillatihim*), to liken the companion to his companion, and to deem the associate indicative of his associate.[138]

Pseudo-Māwardī urges the king to associate with people whose company will encourage his virtue, and to avoid the company of persons trained to cater to his pleasures. Pseudo-Māwardī follows these remarks with Qurʾānic verses, including verses that liken the world to 'play and diversion' (*laʿb wa-lahw*), in order, as he states, to repel rational persons (*al-ʿuqalāʾ*) from it and cause the virtuous (*al-fuḍalāʾ*) to renounce it.[139] Next he cites the 'Testament' of Ardashīr, in a passage that dissociates play and diversion from the moral dispositions of kings. In quotations that emphasise the affinities among companions and the consequent importance of seeking edifying companionship and avoiding association with persons whose company is detrimental, Pseudo-Māwardī adduces two Prophetic ḥadīth, a saying of ʿAlī, an utterance ascribed to 'a littérateur', a saying of Ardashīr, the verse of an unidentified poet who hit the mark (*baʿḍ al-shuʿarāʾ al-muṣībīn*) and a verse that he attributes to the sixth-century poet Ṭarafa b. al-ʿAbd.[140]

In terms that are likely to have alluded to the court of Naṣr II and the regional courts of the Samanid domains, Pseudo-Māwardī criticises certain aspects of the culture that they fostered. He associates the king's courtiers with moral corruption and religious dissidence, and disparages the musicians, singers, poets, jesters and entertainers, whose presence, he holds, alienates the learned and virtuous and leaves the king exposed to the schemes of ambitious heretics. Pseudo-Māwardī singles out the poets of his day, whose verse, he avers, was characterised by indecency (*fuḥsh*) and unbelief (*kufr*), the corruption of religious perspectives (*madhāhib*), the glorification of sensual pleasures and a general contempt for religion. Poetry that treated the themes of love and wine found appreciative audiences in the ninth- and tenth-century courtly *majlis*, and the Persian poet Rūdakī, at Naṣr's court, devoted many poems to these themes.[141] Numbers of Pseudo-Māwardī's contemporaries believed that the poets at the court alluded to heterodox and *bāṭinī* themes in their verses; and certain high-ranking Ismaᶜilis, such as the vizier al-Muṣᶜabī and the general and *dāᶜī* Ḥusayn b. ᶜAlī, composed poetry, in Persian and Arabic.[142] Later in his chapter, with reference to al-Jāḥiẓ, Pseudo-Māwardī returns to the subject of poets and denigrates the venality of panaegyrists in particular.[143]

Against *Taqlīd*

In a particularly pointed passage, Pseudo-Māwardī moves from his advice to his royal addressee to pursue religious understanding in person to an exhortation that he eschew the passive following of a religious perspective selected by other people:

> It is incumbent on the king and indeed on anyone who loves learning the sciences, especially the knowledge that pertains to religious observance and conviction (*ᶜilm al-diyāna wa-l-iᶜtiqād*), that he should not follow anyone else's religion without question (*allā yuqallida aḥadan dīnahu*). Nor should he accept anyone else's *madhhab* except after deliberation, reflection, consideration of its evidentiary proof, debate, explication and discussion (*wa-lā yaqbala minhu madhhabahu illā baᶜda tadabbur wa-tafakkur wa-ḥujja wa-munāẓara wa-tabayyun wa-mubāḥatha*). He should adopt neither a hostile nor a partial attitude towards any of the *madhāhib* until he has witnessed its evidentiary proofs, and established the indications of its

soundness or corruption (*illā baᶜda shuhūd al-shawāhid wa-qiyām al-dalāʾil ᶜalā ṣiḥḥatihi aw fasādihi*).

If he belongs to a *madhhab* in which he grew up, that he has accepted and chosen, and of which he is convinced, he should not transfer (his allegiance) from it to another one unless he has examined both the one from which he wishes to depart and the soundness of the one to which he seeks to transfer. If in his view the corruption of a *madhhab* has become clear, he should not persist in it out of stubbornness or zealous attachment (*fa-lā yajibu an yuᶜānida fīhi wa-yataᶜaṣṣaba lahu*).[144] Nor should he consider the abundance and numbers of its people, or the eminence of its adherents and polities (*lā yanẓuru fīhi ilā kathrat ahl wa-ᶜadad wa-ᶜizzat aṣḥāb wa-duwal*), for these items are material factors that often deceive the gullible and ignorant, and dupe the common people and the heedless (*hādhihi asbāb kathīran-mā taghurru l-aghmār wa-l-juhhāl wa-takhdaᶜu al-ᶜawāmm wa-l-aghfāl*). All these factors find a ready market in the context of what is false just as they sell well in the context of what is true (*hiya kulluhā qad tanfuqu fī l-bāṭil kamā tanfuqu fī l-ḥaqq*).

Instead, what is necessary is that he investigate the soundness of the *madhāhib* through their arguments (*dalāʾil*) and judge them on the basis of their evidentiary proofs (*shawāhid*), which are, in sum, the Book, affirmation of the truth (*taṣdīq*) of which is mandatory; the *sunna*, following which is recommended (*mandūb*); reason (*ᶜaql*), the verification of which is agreed upon (*al-ᶜaql al-mujmaᶜ ᶜalā taṣdīqihi*); and the consensus of the community (*ijmāᶜ al-umma*), to which probity (*ᶜadāla*) bears witness. Persistence in falsehood is universally regarded as reprehensible, and insistence (in error) in the face of the appearance of the truth constitutes stupidity in everyone's opinion. There is no sense (*maᶜnā*) discernible to reason in either of them, nor is there any benefit (*fāʾida*) to be expected from either of them. The desired outcome of knowledge (*ᶜilm*), rational investigation (*naẓar*), clarification (*tabayyun*) and thought (*fikr*) is the attainment of truth (*iṣābat al-ḥaqq*), and its aim is the grasping of what is correct (*al-ẓafar bi-l-ṣawāb*). Once he has attained this goal, there is no sense (*maᶜnā*) in resistance (*ᶜinād*) to, denial (*juḥūd*) of, or squandering the objective that he has desired and sought.[145]

In this section, Pseudo-Māwardī insists that the king should not follow the religious path of anyone else unless he has subjected it to thorough study and comparison against alternatives. To engage in this kind of examination required training in the methods that he had described earlier in his chapter. Pseudo-Māwardī rejects the practice of *taqlīd* in the case of the king, and insists on his rational engagement, his examination of evidentiary proofs and his testing of arguments. His extension of the requirement to 'anyone who loves learning the sciences' need not imply that he considered *ijtihād* and *naẓar* mandatory for everyone. In this regard, as indicated in Volume I, he probably agreed with al-Kaᶜbī, who considered *taqlīd* permissible for the common people (*al-ᶜāmma*), upon whom the pursuit of theological detail was not an obligation.[146] Some other Muᶜtazilites held more stringent views; Abū Rashīd al-Nīsābūrī, who abandoned al-Kaᶜbī's circle for that of the Basran Muᶜtazilite ᶜAbd al-Jabbār, rejected *taqlīd* altogether and held that only conviction arrived at through intellectual exertion could produce tranquillity, or *sukūn al-nafs*.[147] Muᶜtazilites were not the only intellectual figures in Pseudo-Māwardī's environment to disapprove of *taqlīd*. Al-Māturīdī also discouraged it, and the later Māturīdī theologian Abū l-Muᶜīn al-Nasafī (d. 508/1114) rejected *taqlīd*, that is, the following or acceptance of a doctrine that was not founded on evidence (*dalīl*), as a basis for faith, to arrive at which required laborious effort (*mashaqqa*), the consideration of evidentiary proofs and the repelling of doubt by means of thought, reflection and discrimination.[148]

Pseudo-Māwardī's assertion that the aim of religious reflection is to arrive at the truth (*iṣābat al-ḥaqq*) also recapitulates the language of al-Kindī, who emphasised the integration of the theoretical and practical disciplines of philosophy. Al-Kindī stated: 'The aim (*gharaḍ*) of the philosopher (*faylasūf*) is, with respect to his knowledge (*fī ᶜilmihi*), to attain the truth (*iṣābat al-ḥaqq*), and with respect to his action (*fī ᶜamalihi*), to act rightly (*al-ᶜamal bi-l-ḥaqq*).'[149] The king, Pseudo-Māwardī held, should strive for identical goals.

In hierarchical order, Pseudo-Māwardī details four sources of evidentiary proofs: the Qurᵓān, the *sunna*, reason (*ᶜaql*) and consensus (*ijmāᶜ*). Frequently linked with *naẓar* or *istidlāl*, as in Pseudo-Māwardī's exposition, *ᶜaql*, in Muᶜtazilite writings, constitutes the basis for knowledge that is 'necessary' or self-evident.[150] Without defining its range, Pseudo-Māwardī adduces as his fourth principle *ijmāᶜ*, a principle that some Muᶜtazilites limited to the sphere of jurisprudence and considered potentially at odds with *ᶜaql*.[151]

Like Caliph al-Maʾmūn, whom Pseudo-Māwardī praised for this quality, kings should 'choose' the *madhhab* to which they commit themselves.[152] This choice should arise from conviction achieved through mental exertion, disciplined examination and deliberation. The king, Pseudo-Māwardī avers, should not allow himself to be swayed by large numbers, prominent political or social status, or the presence of states (*duwal*) affiliated with a particular *madhhab*. Although persons lacking in discernment might respond positively to these factors, they indicated neither truth nor falsehood. These points must have conjured in the minds of Pseudo-Māwardī's audience the success of the Ismaᶜili *daᶜwa* not only in the Samanid domains, but also in the Fatimid caliphate of North Africa and Egypt, the Qarmaṭī polity in al-Bahrayn and the Ismaᶜili polities of the Caspian regions and Sind.

Perhaps most pointedly, Pseudo-Māwardī instructs the ruler that if the error and corruption of a *madhhab* have become plain to him, he should not persist in his falsehood but should abandon it for the truth:

> It is not permissible for the king that his heart should feel such pride, disdain, haughtiness and arrogance that they inhibit him from submitting to his opponent (*khaṣm*) (in debate) or from conceding to his superior argument, if the error of his *madhhab* has become clear to him and its corruption manifest. He who investigates, debates, ponders or deliberates, with the result that the error of his *madhhab* and the falsehood of his doctrine (*maqāla*) become clear to him, enjoys the finest victory, the greatest good fortune, and the most abundant lot; indeed, he possesses good fortune and benefit wholly and entirely.
>
> Aristotle said: Any king who persists in his opinion after its error has become apparent to him undermines himself and assists his enemies. Any king who acts out of insistence (in his error) is alone in his delusion, and he is close to perdition.[153]
>
> In accordance with that which has been proposed earlier in our book, a group of the enemies of religion and the opponents of the religious communities have employed artful means. They have said in the books that they have compiled and the trickeries (*makhārīq*) that they have concocted

> that it is not appropriate for the governing king to preoccupy himself with the investigation of the *madhāhib*, nor to align himself with one to the exclusion of another; nor should he assist the one that is strongest in its proof and firmest in its evidentiary testimony (*lā yanṣur aqwāhā dalālatan wa-athbatahā shahādatan*). They have purported that such activity contributes to the division of the community against him, turns the hearts of many of the subjects away from him, and scatters the opinions of the common people against him. We have explained that this argument is a weak stratagem and a feeble and foolish ruse, and we have revealed in several ways the virtues comprised in the science of religion that result in the well-being of the kingdom and kingship (*al-faḍāʾil allatī taʿūdu bi-ṣalāḥ al-mamlaka wa-l-mulk*). That which these people have described amounts to a declaration that the king should be an ignorant unbeliever (*an yakūna kāfiran jāhilan*), careless and heedless of his interests in this earthly life and in the next, and of the fine qualities in his religion and in the mundane world.
>
> But experience has proven the opposite (*ʿalā khilāf hādha jarat al-ʿāda*), as have the enduring accomplishments witnessed (*al-āthār al-mushāhada*) on the part of the prophets, caliphs and virtuous kings over the course of the days and the succession of the ages and eras. In fact, the kings whom we have mentioned have defended their religions (*kān[ū] dhābbīna ʿan adyānihim*), assisted their religious communities (*nāṣirīn li-milalihim*), fought for their communities' moral characteristics (*akhlāq*), struggled in their paths, called (people) to (join) them, and held in contempt and punished those from whom they observed the innovation of a corrupt *madhhab* or an erroneous doctrine (*maqāla*). In the preceding part of our book, we have mentioned that the generality of the caliphs followed *madhāhib*, held (religious) views (*kānū yadhhabūna madhāhib wa-yaqūlūna aqāwīl*) that they pursued and to which they were devoted, and engaged in disputation; only a very few of them acted in a manner contrary to this (*madhhab*).[154]

In this return to the thrust of the arguments he advanced in his third chapter, Pseudo-Māwardī appeals to the ruler to resist the manipulative arguments of 'a group of the enemies of religion and the opponents of the religious communities' and to engage, against their urging, in rational enquiry into the proofs of the *madhāhib*. If he were to find his *madhhab* erroneous and corrupt, he should not persist in it but should renounce it. Pseudo-Māwardī's effort to persuade the king to take charge of his religious life in a rational manner represented, in part, an exercise in the performance of his duty to offer counsel. It is also possible that contemporaries believed Naṣr to be undecided or open to persuasion. Ibn al-Nadīm, who was closer in time to the events than al-Thaᶜālibī or Niẓām al-Mulk, reported that Naṣr II later repented of his conversion. Pseudo-Māwardī, turning from argument to illustration, completes this section with a reminder to his audience of the prophets, caliphs and virtuous kings whose cases he had detailed in his third chapter. Their examples demonstrated that exemplary conduct in matters religious and mundane was possible for prophets, caliphs and kings alike.

Continuing his references to the experiences of earlier peoples and the pronouncements of earlier wise philosophers, Pseudo-Māwardī cites two passages from Aristotle's correspondence with Alexander,[155] and then turns to Ardashīr, who, he avers, addressed the issue 'completely and comprehensively' (*kāmilan jāmiᶜan*) when he said:

> It is not fitting for the king to concede to the ascetics and pseudo-prophets (*lil-nussāk wa-l-mutanabbiʾīn*) that they are prior in religion, nor more solicitous of it, nor fiercer in their defence of it than he is. And it is not appropriate for the king that he place the ascetics beyond his command and prohibition in their asceticism and their religion, for the departure of the ascetics or of anyone else other than the ascetics from his command and prohibition is a disgrace (*ᶜayb*) for the king and a disgrace for the kingdom, a wound (*thulma*) that the people will count as clear evidence of harm to the king and those after him.[156]

> And he [Ardashīr] said: Know that the intelligent man who is deprived (*al-ᶜāqil al-maḥrūm*) will enlist his tongue against you, and it is the sharper of his two swords. The most severe harm that he can inflict on you by his tongue is by directing it in artifice towards religion (*mā ṣarafa al-ḥīla fīhi ilā al-dīn*). As he adduces arguments concerning religion and displays outward indignation for religion, directs his outrage on behalf of religion and his appeal to it, he will prove more attractive (in recruiting) followers, believers, advisers and supporters than you, because people's distaste is directed

> towards kings and their love and compassion are directed towards the weak and the overwhelmed.[157]

Pseudo-Māwardī discusses the king's internal enemies, who include 'the intelligent man who is deprived', in a later treatment of the varieties of disaffection among the common people with which the ruler must contend. With these long quotations from Ardashīr, Pseudo-Māwardī concludes this second major section of his longest chapter.

From Knowledge to Action: Imitation of the Divine

The preceding exposition of *ᶜilm al-dīn* arose from Pseudo-Māwardī's observation that God had described Himself by the attribute of 'knowing', and his assertion that the ruler should imitate the divine in the cultivation of this primary divine quality. These assumptions provided the context for his consideration of the types of knowledge appropriate for kings. In the remainder of his chapter, Pseudo-Māwardī addresses the actions that should flow from the ruler's knowledge:

> It is incumbent upon the king – once he has learnt the branches of knowledge that we have mentioned, and his conviction in the principles of religion has been rendered sound, his knowledge (*maᶜrifa*) of God strengthened, his justice and wisdom verified, and he has achieved a cleaving to *taqwā* as we have described and attained the path of guidance – that his efforts (*masāᶜin*), actions (*afᶜāl*), ways of conduct (*siyar*) and utterances (*aqwāl*), the manners (*ādāb*) by which he behaves, the modes of governance (*siyāsāt*) that he employs, and the customs (*ᶜādāt*) that he chooses to adopt and follow should be drawn from two areas.
>
> One of the two areas is the emulation of God, great and glorious, in His actions, and in that which He has displayed through the proofs of His wisdom in the traces of His creation (*mā aẓhara min dalāʾil ḥikmatihi fī āthār ṣanᶜatihi*) by way of correct speech and sound action, insofar as it is possible for him to perceive it (*fīmā yajūzu lahu idrākuhu*), and (as far as) his searching and striving for it prosper, his ability (*maqdara*) reaches and his capacity (*ṭāqa*) extends. For that is the loftiest point to which his aspirations can rise and the furthest extent to which his hope can reach; and in addition, it is one of the definitions of *falsafa* and one of the meanings of *ḥikma*.

> Secondly, he should carry out that which he is commanded to accomplish, in gratitude to Him, great and glorious, for His bounties, and recognition of His excellent favours, since, as we have mentioned previously, that gratitude takes precedence for the king, and is most fitting to the elevation of his station and the nobility of his rank.[158]

In this transitional passage, Pseudo-Māwardī connects the king's intellectual preparation to his responsible conduct. Much of his language remains theological and philosophical in character. His allusions to ability and capacity, *maqdara* and *ṭāqa*, which he understands as divinely given faculties that empower human beings to choose and to act, conform to the Mu^c^tazilite perspective according to which it was inconceivable that God should impose an obligation on His creatures that lay beyond their capacity (*al-taklīf bimā lā yuṭāq*).[159] As Pseudo-Māwardī acknowledges, his appeal to the king to model his conduct upon the divine attributes recapitulates the ancient, initially Platonic understanding of philosophy as imitation of the divine. This passage reflects further Pseudo-Māwardī's affinity with the Kindian tradition: al-Kindī had recorded this interpretation among his definitions of philosophy in his 'On Definitions', and had distinguished the divine qualities of wisdom, power, justice, goodness, beauty and truth.[160]

Wisdom

Pseudo-Māwardī proceeds to wisdom, the second divine quality, after knowledge, that he urges the king to imitate:

> Since he knows, recognises, affirms with conviction and comprehends that God has described Himself with the quality of wisdom (*waṣafa nafsahu bi-l-ḥikma*), and the indications of His evidentiary proofs in His creation indicate that He is wise (*ḥakīm*), he should exert himself in order to earn this name and profit from this epithet as far as he is capable of it and in accordance with the degree of assistance that he receives from his Creator and Maker and Initiator and Nurturer.
>
> The meaning of *ḥakīm* occurs in the Arabic language in two ways: one of them is in the sense of 'knowing' (*^c^ālim*); and the most knowing (*^c^alīm*) is He from whom nothing is hidden. The other is that he performs to perfection (*muḥkim*) in his actions and speech, with no disparity in his

> action, no contradiction in his moral character, and no fault, corruption, frivolity or error in his judgement (*ḥukm*).[161]

The Muᶜtazilite conception of God's commands and prohibitions, which Pseudo-Māwardī shared, links them to His wisdom. In the exposition of ᶜAbd al-Jabbār, God displayed His wisdom in creating His creatures (*wajh al-ḥikma fī btidāʾihi l-khalq*) and in imposing obligations upon them (*wajh al-ḥikma fī l-taklīf*) for the purpose of the common good, or well-being, *maṣlaḥa*.[162] In accordance with His wisdom, God's actions were directed towards a specific purpose, and He was exempt from all acts of evil (*lā yajūzu an yakhtāra fiᶜl al-qabīḥ . . . innahu munazzah ᶜan kull qabīḥ*), since He is *ghaniyy*, devoid of need.[163] Pseudo-Māwardī's description of God in his account of *maᶜrifat Allāh* likewise dissociated Him from evil, and he identifies God's wisdom in His imposing of His commands and prohibitions in the opening passages of his sixth chapter.[164]

The scholars of Samarqand also addressed the matter of divine wisdom, which they, like Pseudo-Māwardī, found reflected in the created world. Al-Māturīdī associated divine *ḥikma* with the proper positioning, apportioning and balance of all things, that is, with the creation of a properly ordered cosmos.[165] He also invokes divine wisdom, however, in his refutation of the Muᶜtazilite doctrine of the 'optimal', *al-aṣlaḥ*, to which Pseudo-Māwardī inclined.[166] Abū l-Muᶜīn al-Nasafī (d. 508/1114) would discuss the meanings of *ḥikma* and *ḥakīm*, first in lexicographical terms (*fī l-lugha*) and, secondly, according to the judgement of the theologians (*ᶜalā raʾy al-mutakallimīn*), in terms reminiscent of Pseudo-Māwardī's exposition. Abū l-Muᶜīn adds that according to some people, the *ḥakīm* is the person who restrains himself from acts of passion or evil, and that this view derives from the wisdom of the Persians (*ḥikmat al-furs*). It is also said, he reports, that *ḥikma* is *maᶜrifat al-ashyāʾ bi-ḥaqāʾiqihā wa-waḍᶜuhā bi-mawāḍiᶜihā*, 'knowledge of the true natures of things and placing them in their rightful positions', and that it encompasses knowledge (*ᶜilm*) and action (*ᶜamal*) together. The presentation, like numerous portions of Pseudo-Māwardī's exposition, coincides with the views of al-Kindī and his intellectual descendants.[167]

Pseudo-Māwardī explicates the two meanings of the divine epithet *ḥakīm* that he has reported:

> As for the meaning of (*ḥakīm* in the sense of) *al-ᶜālim*, we have mentioned and clarified that it is incumbent on the king that he acquire knowledge, prefer it, benefit from it, choose it, specialise in the noblest in stature among its branches, the greatest of them in usefulness, the clearest of them in establishing proofs (*abyanuhā ḥujjatan*), and the most general in promoting well-being (*aᶜammuhā ṣalāḥan*).
>
> As for the other meaning (of *ḥakīm*, i.e., in the sense of *muḥkim*), we say, it is incumbent on the king in the exaltedness of his stature and the loftiness of his position that he exert himself so that all his actions should be serious with no jesting in them, and should consist of wisdom (*ḥikma*) without frivolity (*ᶜabath*) in them . . .[168]

Pseudo-Māwardī explores the implications of royal jocularity with reference to a variety of texts. Among them are a citation from the testament of 'an Indian philosopher-king', and several aphoristic reports: When Alexander was asked the sign of enduring sovereignty, he replied, 'Seriousness in all matters'; when asked the sign of its passing, he said, 'Jesting'; in ancient days, people said, 'Seriousness is the seed of nobility'. Pseudo-Māwardī deploys these texts to show that kings' jesting is predictive of their defeat and fall.[169]

Generosity

Pseudo-Māwardī continues with the divine attribute of generosity:

> Since the king knows by the (revealed) word or by demonstrative evidence (*khabaran aw dalālatan*) that God, glorious and great, is generous, by His preference of him (the king) over His creation in His bestowal of enormous bounties and momentous favours, he should strive in his effort to merit this epithet and to realise its meaning (*ijtahada fī saᶜy istiḥqāq hādhā l-ism wa-idrāk hādhā l-maᶜnā*) as far as he is capable and to the extent of his ability. For no one among God's creatures lacks that thing (*mawjūd*) that enables him to practise generosity. This observation is in accordance with people's well-known praise of the generous person and their rebuke of the miserly person over the course of time and the succession of days, among every people and category, the people of every religion and sect, in every tongue and language (*fī kull jīl wa-ṭabaqa wa-ahl dīn wa-niḥla wa-bi-kull lisān wa-lugha*).[170]

Having stressed the universal and timeless esteem in which human beings have held knowledge, wisdom and generosity, Pseudo-Māwardī turns to the divine attribute that he especially associated with kingship:

Power

> Since he knows that God, glorious is His mention, has described Himself with the attribute of power (*qudra*), and praised Himself to His creation by the attribute of strength (*quwwa*), and that He has indicated these qualities by His evidentiary proofs and unassailable indications (*dalla ʿalā dhālika bi-shawāhidihi al-ẓāhira wa-dalāʾilihi al-qāhira*); and he also knows that God has charged him with vengeance against his enemies and the disobedient among His creation, with judging among them and dispensing equity to the oppressed against the oppressor among them, he should strive to realise this virtuous attribute according to the degree of his ability and the utmost of his power.
>
> His path to this end is that he should be pleased to employ the tools of courage (*ālāt al-shajāʿa*) and should learn the arts of warfare and combat, until he reaches a point where he can attain this virtue (of power) and merit this fine quality (of strength), and deserve this epithet (powerful, strong) in contest, jumping, horsemanship, running, racing, archery, training the physical self in severe endurance (*tamrīn al-nafs ʿalā l-ṣabr al-shadīd*) and the bearing of heavy weapons, as he is appointed for that set of tasks.[171] For by such means the human being gains in strength (*quwwa*) and in power (*qudra*), just as by learning a science and benefiting from the knowledge of persons who combine intellect with deeds (*taʿallum al-ʿilm wa-l-istifāda min ahl al-ʿuqūl wa-l-afʿāl*) he gains in reason (*ʿaql*) and knowledge (*ʿilm*).[172]

More than any other quality, the possession of power distinguished kings from their subjects. In consistency with his primary purpose in *Naṣīḥat al-mulūk*, Pseudo-Māwardī simultaneously urges the king to exercise self-control in his deployment of power, the appropriate uses of which were limited to defence and the upholding of justice. To convey the voluntary restraint that the king should display, notwithstanding the boundless power at his disposal, he invokes a further set of divine qualities:

The king knows that God, blessed and exalted, notwithstanding His power over the hastening (of punishment) of the disobedient among His creation and His strength over the chastisement of the tempters (*ghuwāt*) among His creatures, has described Himself by forbearance (*ḥilm*), and has indicated it by word and by reason (*khabaran wa-ᶜaqlan*); and, while He has never ceased to know (*kāna wa-lam yazal ᶜāliman*) of His creatures' disobediences and unbelief, their rejection of His favours and their fabrications against Him, He is forbearing towards them, and is not quick with His punishment. Furthermore He has described Himself by this attribute when He said, 'Indeed, God is most forgiving and forbearing' (2: 235; 3: 155), and He said, 'And God is most knowing and most forbearing' (33: 51). He praised His prophet Abraham for the same quality when He said, 'Indeed, Abraham was kind-hearted and forbearing' (9: 114). Accordingly He has made it incumbent upon him that he follow Him and His Prophet in this regard, in not rushing to punish the sinner (*mundhib*), nor to take revenge against the criminal (*mujrim*) until the truth of the matter has been reached, (the possibility of) pardon foreclosed, and the hope for repentance and forgiveness cut off. His extraordinary power and limitless dominion should not move him to iniquitous vengeance and hasty reprisal, nor should he abandon the custom of waiting before inflicting punishment. Let him remember God's power over him, the abundance of His gifts to Him, and His goodness to him. Let him remember also his manifold disobedience to God and God's forbearance of him, so that he should not treat those subject to his power (*man taḥta yadihi*) in a manner different from that which he loves in God's action (towards him). He should act in the light of his knowledge of people's praise for and exaltation of the forbearing person, and their blame for the opposite (of forbearance) and their disdain for the person who possesses that opposing characteristic.[173]

Likewise, since he finds that God, glorious is His mention, has described Himself by the attribute of forgiveness (*ᶜafw*) of the sinner, pardon (*ṣafḥ*) of the criminal and the forgiveness (*ghufrān*) of sins – for He has said, 'God is forgiving and merciful' (2: 218, 225; 4: 25), and 'God is ever forgiving and merciful' (4: 96, 100; 33: 5, 50, 59, 73) – notwithstanding that which we have mentioned of the manifold disobediences of His servants, the several types of their resistance (*anwāᶜ ᶜunūdihim*), the various sorts of their ingratitude, their defiance of His commands and their commission of the acts that He has restricted, He has made it incumbent that He be imitated in this act (of forgiveness). He (the king) should accustom himself to forgiveness for many wrongdoers and to investigation of the (explanatory) excuses of criminals. He should search for excuses for them, accept their repentance and overlook their misdemeanours (*ᶜatharāt*), as long as they have not transgressed a statutory limit (*ḥadd*) that must be upheld, or committed a major offence (*ᶜaẓīma*) that entails breach of the sharīᶜa or infringement of the practices of the community, or that impairs the arrangement of the affairs of the general public and the prosperity of the resources of the kingdom (*taᶜūdu naqḍan bi-l-sharīᶜa wa-naqḍa sunan al-milla wa-taqdaḥu fī intiẓām umūr al-ᶜāmma wa-ᶜimārat asbāb al-mamlaka*). Such clemency is most effective in the (person of) noble stature (*fa-inna dhālika ablagh fī l-makruma*), especially desirable for the person possessed of elevated rank and power (*bi-dhī l-rifᶜa wa-l-maqdura*), closest to fulfilling the obligation of loyalty towards persons whom he has fostered (*aqrab min istīfāᵓ al-ṣanīᶜa*) and seeking to conciliate persons worthy of respect (*istiᶜṭāf dhawī l-ḥurma*). Kings, philosophers, the great and the virtuous have not ceased to praise and be praised for this quality . . .[174]

Moreover he finds God, blessed is His name, observant of the innermost secrets (*sarāᵓir*) of His servants, that which they make manifest and that which they conceal, that which they display publicly and that which they keep secret in their disobediences, iniquities, sins, aberrations, depravities and unbelief, yet in many cases He does not declare them, expose or make external show of their hidden secrets. He has described Himself accordingly when He said, '(He is) Knower of the Unseen, and He does not reveal His secret to anyone, Except to any prophet whom He has chosen' (72: 26–7). He told a story concerning His prophet Jacob, who said to Joseph (Yūsuf), 'Do not relate your dream to your brothers, lest they plot against you; Satan is a clear enemy of humankind' (12: 5). It is related from the Prophet, 'Avail yourselves in your affairs of secrecy; for everyone who possesses a benefit is the subject of envy'; and when he wished to undertake a journey he concealed it from other people.[175] (Given these examples) it is incumbent on the king, for all the nobility of his stature and the elevation of his station, that he should accustom himself to keeping secrets, so that no one should observe him . . .[176]

In some circumstances there is no alternative but to disclose a secret, and the intelligent person will find no strategy to avoid it, so let him select for his disclosure persons of experience, intellect, religion, excellence, trustworthiness and sincere advice (*ahl al-khibra wa-l-ᶜaql wa-l-dīn wa-l-faḍl wa-l-amāna wa-l-naṣīḥa*), persons whom he does not suspect of divulging his secret, and whom he instructs to conceal the matter that concerns him.[177]

Similarly, since he finds that God, glorious is His mention, has described Himself by truthfulness (*ṣidq*), and has commanded it . . . and He has forbidden lying (*kidhb*) and censured it . . . He has made it incumbent on him that he imitate God and His prophets in this regard, purge his speech and talk from untruth, refrain from it and avoid pollution by it. Since he finds that God, glorious is His mention, has purified His speech of indecency and obscenity of the kind from which, deeming them impure, souls recoil in disgust and bodies shudder, and that He eschews certain expressions . . . it is incumbent on the king that he draw in his behaviour on the instructive example of God, exalted and glorious (*wajaba ᶜalā l-malik an yataᵓaddaba bi-adab Allāh jalla wa-ᶜazza*) in the refinement of his expressions (*tahdhīb alfāẓihi*) and abstention from the mention of obscenity, impurity, ribaldry, abuse, foulness and indecency of the kind that require penalty, abrogate probity, indicate a bad habit and a base origin and upbringing, necessitate the punishment of the Fire in the afterlife and perpetuate an ugly reputation and hostile talk.[178]

Similarly the king observes that God has described Himself by the attribute of accomplishing His promise and fulfilling His covenant (*injāz al-waᶜd wa-l-wafāᵓ bi-l-ᶜahd*) . . . and ordered His servants to praise Him for it and petition Him for it . . . and He has ordered His servants: 'Fulfil God's covenant when you have made a covenant with Him' (16: 91) . . . People have never ceased to praise and be praised for the fulfilment of pacts and the executing of promises, and they have censured and been censured for the opposite of that.[179]

Pseudo-Māwardī employs the theme of imitation to persuade the king to exercise restraint in his personal and political conduct. While all the divine attributes are absolute, the uses of divine power, he argues, display the tempering interaction of God's limitless forbearance and forgiveness. In the world, it is kingship that involves the greatest resources, and accordingly the king's actions, modelled after divine acts, should display a measured quality.

Divinely Enjoined Virtues

Still founding his argument on Qur'ānic texts, Pseudo-Māwardī turns from the divine attributes to attributes that God has urged His servants to cultivate. He begins, in linked sequence with the previously mentioned divine virtue of the fulfilment of promises, with gratitude for bounties:

> Among (the attributes that the king should cultivate) is gratitude for bounties (*shukr al-niᶜma*), acknowledging the rightful claim of persons entitled to protection (*maᶜrifat ḥaqq al-ṣanīᶜa*), and compensating good deeds (*mukāfāt ᶜan al-ḥasana*). God, exalted and glorious, has described Himself by this attribute and ordered His servants to adopt it when He says, 'God is responsive and most knowing' (4: 147), 'God is responsive and forbearing' (64: 17); and He has said to His slaves, 'Give thanks to Me and do not be ungrateful' (2: 152), and 'If you give thanks, I shall give you more' (14: 7). It is incumbent on the king that he should emulate this example by which God has described Himself and to which He has urged His creatures.
>
> They have said: the meaning of gratitude is that to God, and to those above you, it takes the form of obedience; to equals, it takes the form of reciprocity; and to those beneath you, it consists of conferring benefits (*ifḍāl*) to them, kindness (*iḥsān*) to them, and knowledge of that by which they become closer (*yataqarrab*) to you.[180]

This passage, in which the virtue of the fulfilment of promises (*al-wafāʾ bi-l-ᶜahd*) is immediately followed by that of gratitude for favours (*shukr al-niᶜma*), recapitulates Pseudo-Māwardī's urging of the ruler to honour the rightful claims of persons who have acquired the status of his *ṣanīᶜa*, persons subject to his 'protection'.[181] As Volume I indicated, this cluster of concepts governed the king's relations with his *khāṣṣa*, who constituted the first level of the intermediaries on whom his governance depended. As Chapter 4 will show, themes of loyalty and gratitude recur in Pseudo-Māwardī's next chapter, devoted to the king's *khāṣṣa*.

Pseudo-Māwardī continues with further virtuous qualities for which he adduces scriptural authority. His next quality also draws on God's instructive example as well as His command:

> And since he finds God pure of obscenities, elevated above forbidden things, and sanctified against injustices, he should exert himself in attaining this attribute to the extent that he is capable and in accordance with the depth of his power. He should purify himself of base desires and forbidden appetites that damage honour and manly virtue and are prohibited in the religious community (*milla*) and the religious law (sharīᶜa); for they are sources of shame and disgrace, and a path to the punishment of the Fire. God, glorious is His mention, has rejected them from Himself and prohibited them from His servants . . . We have clarified that it is incumbent, in the lofty standing of kings, their elevated station and the height of their ranks, that they elevate themselves above (these defects), and protect their honour from becoming sullied by them . . .[182]

> Among the things that God has commanded is resistance of the passions and pursuit of that which is right (*mukhālafat al-hawā wa-mutābaᶜat al-ḥaqq*). For God great and glorious says, 'As for him who feared to stand before His Lord and restrained his soul from passion (*nahā l-nafs ᶜan al-hawā*), for him the Garden [of Paradise] shall be his refuge' (79: 40–1), and 'If the truth had followed their desires, the heavens and the earth and those who dwell in them would have fallen into corruption' (23: 71). The Prophet said, 'The worst that I fear for my community is passion and excessive ambition; passion distracts from the truth and excessive ambition causes people to forget the next life.'[183]

> Among the attributes that God has commanded is humility (*tawāḍuᶜ*) and abandonment of arrogance (*tark al-takabbur*). God, glorious is His mention, has forbidden arrogance and announced that He does not love it in His servants: 'God does not love him who is proud and boastful' (4: 36). He told a story from Luqmān the sage (*al-ḥakīm*): 'Do not walk with

arrogance in the land' (31: 18); and He said: 'Do not walk in the land with pride; you shall never rend the earth nor reach the height of the mountains' (17: 37). It is related from the Prophet that God said, 'Grandeur (*kibr*) and majesty (*ᶜaẓama*) are my cloak (*ridāʾī*). Whoever challenges Me in My clothing, I am displeased with him.'[184] The Prophet said, 'He who is humble unto God, God will raise him up.'[185] In accordance with this quality's potential for endearing the *khāṣṣa* and the *ᶜāmma*, inclining the hearts of the entire population, sowing love amongst the subjects, and following the exemplary practices (*sunan*) of the Prophet in his conduct, the intelligent have never ceased to say, 'Humility is among the acts of the noble.' Aristotle said, 'Arrogance marks the epitome of failure' (*al-badhakh raʾs al-fashal*).[186] We have devoted sufficient attention to this topic in the 'Chapter of Admonitions' to obviate the need for further discussion and additional materials.[187]

Among the qualities that the king should cultivate is the maintenance of a straight path (*istiqāmat al-ṭarīqa*), so that he should not become reckless with the bounty (*niᶜma*) afforded to him in times of plenty, nor should he despair in times of straitened circumstances. This disposition is among the qualities to which God has urged humankind and that He has praised, in His words: 'That you should not grieve over that which escapes you, nor rejoice over that which has been given to you' (57: 23). Accordingly, it is among the moral dispositions (*akhlāq*) for which the sages have extolled men at the greatest length, and the praiseworthiness of which they have depicted with the greatest frequency . . .[188]

Patient endurance (*ṣabr*) is a sublime quality (*bāb jalīl*) that only the most perspicacious and astute of men is able to attain. One of the two parts of this virtue is patience in the face of adversities and calamities. God, glorious and exalted, has praised the patient and enjoined the quality of patience when He said, 'Endure patiently that which afflicts you' (31: 17), and 'The patient in affliction, adversity and in times of trouble' (2: 177). He has praised such persons when He said, 'It is they who are sincere, and they who are godly (*al-muttaqūn*)' (2: 177) . . . The multiple groupings of people (*aṣnāf al-nās*), notwithstanding the difference of their paths (*madhāhib*), their different social categories (*ṭabaqāt*) and natures (*ṭabāʾiᶜ*), and the dis-

> parity of their circumstances, agree in their preference for this quality, and in counting it among the loftiest of virtues and noblest of traits.[189]

In this commendation of patient endurance, again supported with the assertion of its universal acclaim, Pseudo-Māwardī refers to people's 'natures' (*ṭabāʾiʿ*, sing. *ṭabīʿa*). The Baghdadi Muʿtazila developed the concept of natures, and certain students of al-Naẓẓām, including al-Jāḥiẓ, were known as *aṣḥāb al-ṭabāʾiʿ* ('proponents of the concept of natures'). Al-Kaʿbī attributed to al-Jāḥiẓ a doctrine concerning *ṭibāʿ* (innate nature or character), namely, that knowledge was part of human nature (*inna l-maʿrifa ṭibāʿ*).[190] Al-Kaʿbī, himself in the intellectual lineage of al-Naẓẓām, also developed an elaborate understanding of the concept of 'natures'. He asserted that God had given to human beings the capacity (*qudra*) to gain ascendancy over and restrain their nature(s) (*ṭibāʿ*), just as He had created sexual desire (*shahwat al-nikāḥ*) in them, but He had also, in many instances, ordered them to resist it.[191] It is not entirely clear whether Pseudo-Māwardī employs the term 'nature' in a specific or technical sense, or in a general sense, but it is possible that in this respect, as in other aspects of his writing, his conception of nature(s) reflected the teachings of the Baghdadi Muʿtazila and echoed the perceptions of his esteemed predecessor al-Jāḥiẓ.

The hypothesis gains some support from the similarity of Pseudo-Māwardī's chapter devoted to the governance of the self and al-Jāḥiẓ's 'Epistle on this Life and the Afterlife'. Following the previously cited passage, Pseudo-Māwardī resumes his exposition of the virtues with a passage highly reminiscent of the words of al-Jāḥiẓ:

> Among the praiseworthy qualities is the adoption of resolve (*ḥazm*) and the strengthening of determination (*ʿazm*), wariness (*ḥidhr*) against blundering into affairs without clear understanding of the opportunity (*min ghayr tabayyun al-furṣa*), and avoidance of beguilement by persons who call for trust in God (*tawakkul*), when he ought to prepare himself for any eventuality (*wa-huwa wājid ilā l-iḥtiyāṭ sabīlan*) and search for evidence to support his judgement (*wa-ʿalā wajh al-raʾy dalīlan*). That pattern of behaviour leads to ruin. God, exalted and glorious, said: 'Do not hurl (yourselves) by your own hands to perdition' (2: 195). Furthermore God, glorious and exalted, ordered the alteration of the form of prayer, which is a pillar of the

> religion, in the context of conflict with the enemy and the fear of assault and bloodshed when He said, 'When you are among them and you have established the prayer for them, let (only) a group of them stand with you (in prayer), and let them take their weapons. When they have prostrated themselves, let them fall behind you', (and so on) until the end of the verse (4: 102). It is related from the Prophet that he said, 'Hobble her and trust in God' . . .[192]

Pseudo-Māwardī suggests in this passage that *tawakkul* (*ᶜalā Allāh*), dependence on God, while enjoined in the Qurʾān, can, if taken to excessive lengths, lead to deleterious inaction. The king should not be deceived by appeals to *tawakkul* that amount to calls for non-interference in matters that require his resolute action. To illustrate the point he reminds his audience of the divine injunction to modify the arrangements for the obligatory prayer as a precautionary measure when the early Muslims were confronted with the danger of imminent attack. He cites the Prophet's advice when an interlocutor asked him if he should allow his camel to roam and trust in God (that she would not stray or come to harm), or if instead he should tether her and trust in God; the Prophet answered by affirming the latter choice. The examples establish Pseudo-Māwardī's point that the virtue of reliance on God requires consideration of the context and the potential consequences of action and inaction. Al-Jāḥiẓ, whom Pseudo-Māwardī cites slightly later in this chapter, wrote in a very similar fashion on this theme. Al-Jāḥiẓ had written as follows:

> Be on your guard lest Satan deceive you away from resolve (*ḥazm*) by presenting deliberation in the semblance of *tawakkul*, thereby preventing you from the exercise of due caution (*ḥidhr*) and leaving you slow to act according to your capacities. For God only commanded *tawakkul* in situations where the possibility of strategic solutions had been eliminated, and where, after all pretexts had been submitted, judgement would run its course. In this manner He revealed His Book and established His *sunna*. For He said: 'Take precautions' (4: 71), and 'Do not hurl (yourselves) by your own hands to perdition' (2: 195). The Prophet said, 'Hobble her and trust in God.' When asked, 'What is resolve?' (*ḥazm*), he replied 'precaution' (*ḥidhr*).[193]

In a similar fashion, and with the use of several of the same authoritative examples, Pseudo-Māwardī presents *tawakkul* as an impediment to deliberate and determined action. Al-Jāḥiẓ alludes to the Qur'ānic presentation of *tawakkul* as the best defence against Satan, who insinuates himself into the secret conversations of human beings (58: 10), yet he warns that Satan sometimes employs *tawakkul* against human interests. The ḥadīth, 'Hobble her and trust in God', refers to the Prophet's pragmatic advice to combine prudence – hobble a camel lest she stray – with trust in God's arrangement of affairs. At the time when Pseudo-Māwardī wrote, the concept of *tawakkul* had assumed considerable prominence and occasioned controversy, since some Muslims – especially some of the early Sufis – went to very great lengths to live according to its purport. The Karrāmiyya, as previously mentioned, rejected the practice of earning a living, on the principle that God would provide; the shaykhs of Samarqand had already rejected this development in *al-Sawād al-aᶜẓam*.[194] Pseudo-Māwardī too adopts a critical stance towards *tawakkul*, and this passage makes clear his endorsement of active resolve, *ḥazm*, over passive expectation. The king should not allow himself to be diverted from active intervention in the interests of the common good.

Pseudo-Māwardī continues with an analysis of *ḥazm*:

> One of the two parts of *ḥazm* is the adoption of a suspicious outlook (*sū' al-ẓann*), and employing the resources of the soul and the intellect to foresee and prepare for the worst. For this reason it became established among the customary practices (*akhlāq*) of kings that the places in which they slept and took their siestas were not known. It is related in the accounts of the Sasanian kings, including Ardashīr, Shāpūr, Bahrām Gūr, Yazdagird, Khusraw Parvīz and Anūshīrvān, that for each king forty beds were prepared. Among these forty, not a single one would cause anyone who might consider it or look at it from afar to suspect that it was the bed specially intended for the king. It also happened sometimes that he would not sleep in any of them, but would rather lay his head on his arm and sleep in a place where no one expected him and no one suspected his presence.[195] Furthermore God commanded His Prophet in this matter when He communicated to him (*nuzūl al-waḥy*) the polytheists' designs, plotting and

> intentions against him, and he absented himself from his bed [and ᶜAlī slept in his place].[196]
>
> The second aspect of *ḥazm* consists of consultation with people of sound judgement, excellence, knowledge, intellect, religion, trustworthiness, temperance and experience, and with specialists in the matter about which he seeks to consult, whether it is a matter concerning religion or this world . . . Intelligent people (*ahl al-ᶜuqūl*) have never ceased to take refuge in consultation in every matter that befalls them and to praise the person who behaves in this fashion; and (similarly) to blame the person who is high-handed (overly confident) in his judgement and pursues his whims . . . It is not permitted to the king that he neglect this quality and turn away from it in disregard, despite the loftiness of his position and the elevation of his rank and the greatness of (his) stature in many matters, (since) it forms part of following the command of God and imitating His Prophet.[197]

These examples illustrate the timeless quality of the virtue of prudential precaution. Through foresight and deliberate action ᶜAlī, at risk of his life, had ensured the Prophet's safety by taking his place in his bed; the Sasanian kings avoided danger by concealing the location of their sleeping places at all times. An essential component of resolve, furthermore, is consultation with persons fit to advise on the matter at hand. Consultation ensures that action, when taken, will be appropriate to the situation and will be effective. The familiarity of these two definitions of resolve is evident from the appearance of both of them in the collection of proverbs of al-Maydānī.[198]

After this discussion of the virtues enjoined by God upon humanity and their significance for kings, Pseudo-Māwardī turns to the virtue, prefigured in his 'straight path' (*istiqāmat al-tarīqa*), of balance, tantamount to justice, which, in Aristotelian fashion, he relates to the adoption of the 'middle path':

> Another aspect of this matter is balanced conduct (*al-ᶜadl fī l-sīra*), and the middle path (*sulūk al-wāsiṭa*), avoiding the extremities of the virtues and the transgression of boundaries, and inclining to the abandonment of excess and deficiency (*tajannub aṭrāf al-faḍāʾil wa-mujāwazat al-ḥudūd wa-l-mayl ilā tark al-ifrāṭ wa-l-tafrīṭ*), for the praiseworthy path lies between them (*fa-inna l-ṭarīqa al-maḥmūda baynahumā*). Courage (*shajāᶜa*) lies between reckless-

> ness and timidity, religious devotion (*ᶜibāda*) between shamelessness and reclusivity, resolve (*ḥazm*) between pedantry and negligence, generosity (*jūd*) between parsimony and dissipation, forbearance (*ḥilm*) between impulsivity and self-abasement, humility (*tawāḍuᶜ*) between sycophancy and arrogance, independence of need (*ghinā*) between opulence and poverty.[199]

Pseudo-Māwardī's treatment of balance evokes the Aristotelian understanding of justice as a virtue that lies at the point of equipoise between extremes.[200] By his inclusion of several virtues that he has already treated (forbearance, generosity, humility), he conveys the comprehensive nature of justice. Unlike the later moral philosopher Miskawayh, he does not cite the Platonic conception of the cardinal virtues, related to the three faculties of the soul, and the sum of which produces justice.[201] Pseudo-Māwardī continues with a varied set of examples of moderation, the middle point between extremes:

> God has clarified this point in His Book, for He said to His Prophet: 'Neither keep your hand fettered to your neck, nor extend it fully, lest you sit down weary and aggrieved' (17: 29). He said: 'And those who, when they spend, are neither profligate nor miserly; there is a firm support between the two' (25: 67). And He said, in that which He transmitted from Luqmān in his admonitions to his son: 'Do not turn your cheek in contempt towards people, nor walk with arrogance in the land' (31: 18). God prompted His servants to pray for the combination of the good things of the present life and the afterlife, for He said: 'And among them are those who say: Our Lord, give us that which is good in this world, and that which is good in the hereafter' (2: 201); and God said, 'So remain mindful of God to the extent that you are able' (64: 16).[202]
>
> The Messenger of God said to ᶜAbdallāh b. ᶜAmr b. al-ᶜĀṣ [son of ᶜAmr b. al-ᶜĀṣ, the Companion, military leader and governor of Egypt under ᶜUmar], when the news reached him that he was fasting during the day and staying awake during the night, 'If you act in this manner, you will ruin your eyes and exhaust yourself; rather rise and sleep, fast and break your fast.'[203] He said, 'The best of people are the middling type, those who neither overreach nor lag behind,'[204] and 'This religion is firm, so apply yourselves to it in kindness.'[205] The *Āʾīnnāmeh* records the pronouncement,

> 'Do not exalt a small person, nor belittle a great person; do not forget the proper design and degree (*al-qaṣd wa-l-qadr*) in all your affairs, for he who oversteps his degree is blamed, even if his beginnings were praised.'[206] The Arabs used to say, 'Love your beloved gently, for it may be that he will become loathsome to you one day; and loathe the person whom you dislike lightly, for it may be that he will become beloved to you one day' . . .[207]

These examples, representative of Pseudo-Māwardī's catholic repertoire, emphasise the virtue of moderation. In continuity with his treatment of *tawakkul*, they suggest the error that exaggeration in a virtue brings about.

In the next section, Pseudo-Māwardī provides an example of a vice that, by inference, he relates to deviance from the middle path:

> Of this kind (*jins*) is envy, for God, glorious and exalted, has censured envy in more places than one in His Book, and ordered humanity to take refuge from the evil of the envious. He said: 'Or do they envy the people for that which God has given them of His bounty? We have given the People of Abraham the Book and Wisdom, and We have given them great dominion' (4: 54), by way of making it known, the Glorious and Exalted, that envy neither benefits the envier nor harms the envied.

> It is related from the Prophet that he said, 'Beware of envy, for, like a barber (*ḥāliqa*), it 'shaves'; I do not mean that it shaves hair, but rather that it shaves religion.'[208] Ardashīr said, 'It is inappropriate for the king to envy, unless it is the kings of nations for their excellent administration (*ḥusn al-tadbīr*).'[209]

> On the forbidding of this vice there are many transmitted reports. The envier has never ceased to be censured among the ᶜulamāᵓ and considered ignorant among persons of rational intelligence, on account of the harm that the jealous person brings upon himself without causing harm to others, his making his life a misery and his self-inflicted deprivation of the pleasures of his existence.[210]

Pseudo-Māwardī returns to the qualities that the ruler should cultivate and their practical values:

> Among these qualities is circumspection in complicated matters (*al-tathabbut fī l-umūr al-mushkila*), seeking clarification in obscure situations, and the adoption of deliberation and slowness (to action) (*isti^cmāl al-taʾannī wa-l-tuʾada*). God has commanded such conduct in His Book, since He said, 'If a dissolute person (*fāsiq*) brings you news, verify it, lest you attack a people in ignorance and later regret what you have done' (49: 6). He also said to His Prophet, 'Do not hasten with the Qurʾān before its revelation to you has been concluded' (20: 114). It is related from the Prophet that he said, 'Haste is from Satan, and deliberation is from God.'[211]

> The king's unrushed deliberation in matters should not be the result of stupidity or laziness, but rather of reflection and caution in order to avoid the slips to which the hasty person is prone and the failure that befalls the negligent, and out of desire for the rectitude of the person of reason (*raghbatan fī iṣābat al-ʿāqil*). It is related from the Prophet that he said, 'If you wish to accomplish an affair, reflect on its consequences; if it proceeds according to rectitude (*rushd*), then pursue it; if it deviates into transgression (*ghayy*), then abandon it.'[212]

> It is related from Qutham b. Jaʿfar b. Sulaymān [member of the Abbasid family, appointed to Medina and Basra] that Ḥusayn al-Khādim said to him, 'I testify by God, I was so close to (Hārūn) al-Rashīd while he was hanging on to the coverings (*astār*) of the Kaʿba, that my clothes touched his clothes and my hand his hand. (I heard him) say in his supplication to His Lord: "O Lord God, I beg for guidance regarding the execution of Jaʿfar b. Yaḥyā [the Barmakid]". Five or six years after that, he killed him.'[213]

These quotations emphasise the importance of deliberation and prefigure the regret that follows ill-considered and impetuous action. The *khabar* refers to Caliph Hārūn's seemingly abrupt and inexplicable decision to dismiss and execute his leading administrator and foster-relative, Jaʿfar b. Yaḥyā the Barmakid in 187/803; Hārūn also dismissed and executed most other members of the powerful family. The fall of the Barmakids (whom Pseudo-Māwardī mentions favourably) generated numerous exemplary narratives, many of which portray it as a paradigmatic instance of the capriciousness of royal power and sign of the danger involved in proximity to it. Pseudo-Māwardī's spare telling assumes his audience's familiarity with these narratives, and highlights the moral burden that the act placed upon the caliph, who reportedly suffered deep subsequent remorse.[214] Inviting his audience to reflect upon this *khabar*, Pseudo-Māwardī guides their response in his next remarks:

> It is incumbent on the virtuous king that no act should issue from him without his deliberation and reflection over its rightness (*rushd*) and error (*ghayy*), its goodness and wickedness, so that he chooses the good in it and leaves aside the wicked. If he decides on a bad action then certainly he should postpone it, whereas if he decides to act well he should hasten to do so, for if a bad action eludes him it will not harm him and its omission might benefit him, whereas if a good action eludes him it will harm him and will not benefit him. In fact, sometimes regret over a good action not performed accumulates against him and the sorrow of it compounds against him. If he accomplishes something good and executes a good act, he should praise God for His kind promoting of his success in it (*ᶜalā ḥusni tawfīqihi lahu*), His assistance (*maᶜūna*) to him towards it, and His guidance (*hidāya*) to him in it; and if he accomplishes a bad action and acts wickedly he should regret it, beg God's forgiveness and repent of it to Him, for God does not reckon pardon to any of His servants unless they seek forgiveness and abandon repetition (of the offence). There is no repentance by divine mercy towards him except after his repentance of his disobedience to Him (*lā tawbata bi-l-raḥma ᶜalayhi illā baᶜda tawbatihi min al-maᶜṣiya lahu*).[215]
>
> It is related from the Prophet that he said, 'There is no minor sin (*ṣaghīra*) if it occurs repeatedly, and no major sin (*kabīra*) if it is accompanied by seeking forgiveness.'[216]
>
> If different opinions occur to him and shifting factors compete with one another in his judgement, then it is necessary that he begin with consideration of religion, which advances him towards his heavenly reward and preserves for him his store for the afterlife. Then (in his decision-making) he should consider the noble qualities (*makārim*), the memory of which will endure for him and the reporting of which will be positive for him. It is not appropriate for him to disdain that which perpetuates fine remembrance

> and pleasing praise, for God, glorious and mighty, despite His elevation far above the possibility that benefits and harms or pains and pleasures might affect Him, desires gratitude from His creatures, requires it from them, and mandates it for them, for He said, 'Give thanks to Me and do not be ungrateful' (2: 152), and He said to His Prophet, 'As for the bounty of your Lord, speak of it' (93: 11). God magnified His favour upon His Prophet when He elevated his reputation, for He said: 'We have raised for you your reputation' (94: 4).

In this section Pseudo-Māwardī amplifies his earlier references to 'the promise and the threat' with the clarification that God's mercy co-exists with and does not override His justice. In accordance with Muᶜtazilite doctrine, he states explicitly that divine mercy obviates the threat of eternal punishment only in cases of repentance and transformation in the individual's behaviour.[217] The passage also clarifies Pseudo-Māwardī's conception of the divine bestowal of capacity, and His provision of assistance (*maᶜūna*) and success (*tawfīq*), whereby human beings are enabled to perform their meritorious actions.[218]

Pseudo-Māwardī continues with the theme of lasting reputation:

> The intelligent among the kings of the worlds and the virtuous among the believers have never ceased to strive for this quality (a high reputation), and to expend efforts in order to attain it. They have purchased it with their bodies, wealth, souls and possessions (*yashtarūnahā bi-l-abdān wa-l-amwāl wa-l-arwāḥ wa-l-amlāk*). They have seen that an enduring memory constitutes a perpetuation for the person remembered, so that many kings and sages have contrived strategies to this end. Some among them have sought it by the construction of strong and remarkable buildings, and fine images cut into the mountains and rocks, and painted in buildings and houses, that endure over the course of the ages; others among them have sought it through the compiling of books and composing works pertaining to the sciences, the usefulness of which will accrue to the king's lasting reputation and perpetuate his remembrance over the course of time and the passing of the years and ages; others among them have sought it by manifesting just governances and cultivating virtuous praiseworthy qualities; others among them have sought it by worshipful devotion (*ᶜibāda*) and reflection (*tadabbur*) and summoning (other people) to these activities (*al-daᶜwa ilayhi*), so

as to attain this world and the next. This quality is among the noblest of the qualities that indicate high aspiration in the quest for a lasting reputation, because its possessor rises by his aspiration to eternal life and bliss everlasting (*ilā baqāʾ al-abad wa-l-naᶜīm al-sarmad*). Even if he does not find a fine reputation in this transient abode and this passing and ephemeral life, the person who is strong in determination (*al-qawī al-ᶜazm*) devises a means to attain it in the Abode of Permanence. All of the people remember Abraham, upon him be peace, for he said, 'Let me be well spoken of (*lisān ṣidq*) in later generations. And place me amongst the inheritors of the Garden of Delight' (26: 84–5).[219]

Ardashīr mentioned this matter in his 'Testament', and reckoned it among the distinctive virtues of kings when he said, 'Know that the king's clothing and foodstuffs are comparable to the clothes and foods of the ordinary people (*al-sūqa*), or rather that the pleasure that both parties take in their attainments in these matters is the same. The superior excellence of the king over the common people lies only in his power over the acquisition of praiseworthy qualities and his strength in exercising fine characteristics. If the king wishes, he acts well, whereas the ordinary people lack this capacity.'[220]

Aristotle said to Alexander, 'Act with a view to the generations who will follow you, for their praise will outlive you.'[221]

Having affirmed several praiseworthy paths towards the garnering of a fine and lasting reputation, Pseudo-Māwardī recapitulates his criticism of poets' flattery of their royal patrons. The image reflected in flattering verse, he avers, is a poor substitute for the enduring reputation that he encourages the king, through merit, to seek. Because the poet depends for his remuneration (in the form of 'favour', *niᶜma*) on his patron's pleasure, he will inevitably exceed the boundaries of truthfulness in his praise, in the pursuit of 'increase':[222]

It is not fitting for the virtuous king to despise this noble and lofty quality of lasting reputation; rather it is necessary that he should desire it in its most excellent, lofty, noble and lasting aspects. He should strive so that his fine reputation should find expression on the tongues of the truthful (*ᶜalā alsinat al-ṣādiqīn*), whose dishonesty is not supposed, and the virtuous, whose rise to eminence results from their personal efforts (*yasmūna bi-anfusihim*).

> Such persons are not known for frivolity (*laᶜb*), and do not seek profit or the satisfaction of their needs through the marketing of praise and commendation – as is the case with effeminate persons, jesters and entertainers. Praise from the likes of these last people is in reality a form of censure, and their laudations are rebukes, because they freely praise the reprehensible person as long as he pays them, and they castigate the praiseworthy if he denies them. Moreover, they do not accept an excuse, overlook a misdemeanour or forgive a slip. In addition, according to the Book of God, they are not entitled to a share (*qisṭ*) nor to a portion (*sahm*) of God's wealth, so if the king gives to them in a manner that satisfies them, he displeases God, great is His mention, and disappoints the virtuous and the people of religion. The Prophet said, 'If you see panaegyrists, scatter dust in their faces.'[223]
>
> ᶜAmr b. Baḥr [al-Jāḥiẓ], may God have mercy upon him, spoke in excellent fashion in a section of his book where he said, 'Know that the public proclamation of fine qualities is unworthy of you unless it takes the form of speech carried on the tongues of people of manly virtue, honesty and dependability (*ᶜalā alsinat ahl al-murūʾāt wa-dhawī l-ṣidq wa-l-wafāʾ*), persons whose speech is wholesome in people's hearts, whose words are trusted and whose reports are believed; persons who, when they speak, speak honestly and when they praise, praise modestly, and who extol in proportion to experience.' The lavishing of praise in proportion to favour (*ᶜalā qadr al-niᶜma*) generates dishonesty in people's hearts, and encourages the pursuit of increase (*ṭalab al-mazāʾid*). The panaegyrists' praises in your presence (*thanāʾ al-mādiḥīna laka fī wajhika*) are simply markets that they set up [for profit]. They flatter you in their commerce and in their praise they incur no cost, while their utterances find no market among the people. They are people who turn (their listeners) away from the paths of noble qualities, and impede the pursuit of elevated goals. So repair to a seedbed in which the branches grow and the fruit is pure (*fa-rtadda li-nafsika maghrisan tanmū fīhi furūᶜuhā wa-tazkū thamaratuhā*).[224]

With respectful acknowledgement, Pseudo-Māwardī reproduces a substantial passage from al-Jāḥiẓ's *Risālat al-maᶜāsh wa-l-maᶜād* ('Epistle on Life in this World and the Hereafter'), also known as *al-Akhlāq al-maḥmūda wa-l-*

madhmūma ('Praiseworthy and Reprehensible Characteristics'), dedicated to the judge Muḥammad b. Aḥmad Ibn Abī Dūʾād (d. 239/854).[225] The affinity between al-Jāḥiẓ and Pseudo-Māwardī, whose Muᶜtazilite sensibilities informed their constructions of virtues and vices, is explicitly evident in this section of *Naṣīḥat al-mulūk*. Elsewhere, both authors employed commercial metaphors, and in different contexts both cited the maxim, 'Power (*sulṭān*) is a market. Markets only attract the goods that will sell well'.[226]

Pseudo-Māwardī continues to reproduce sections of al-Jāḥiẓ's text as he goes on to describe the links between panaegyric and profit. In his next section, Pseudo-Māwardī departs from the oblique third-person form of address to the direct address of the second-person singular:

> Your disbursement (*nafaqa*) should not go to waste; you should spend only for the sake of that which advances a good reputation or to hasten the kind of praise that proves beneficial. When you encounter affairs and they appear pressing and equally weighted in this regard, it is incumbent that you should attend to the greatest of them in import, the noblest of them in value, and the greatest of them in potential harm (*ḍarar*) should it slip away; for occupation with small matters over large ones is harmful to the great and small alike, and entails loss and negligence. If they are equal in this regard, then attend to the most proximate in its potential for positive results and the most likely of attainment, for the practice of distancing that which is close (*tabᶜīd al-qarīb*) and bringing close that which is far (*taqrīb al-baᶜīd*) is extremely difficult, involves serious breach, and results in waste and negligence.[227]

> These topics comprise a sufficient summation (*jumla kāfiya*) in the matter of efforts and deeds, the weighing of actions and attending to affairs. In them lies the completion of the personal virtues (*al-faḍāʾil al-nafsāniyya*), both their roots and the general matters that cannot be avoided among their branches. We have mentioned them, supported them with evidence, and drawn attention to that which concerns kings and other people in this time, since there is no end to them and they cannot be encompassed.[228]

In this passage, Pseudo-Māwardī reiterates his method of adherence to matters of general agreement and to guiding principles, rather than to the matters of application and inference that occasion disagreement and conflict. In the concluding passage of this longest of his chapters, Pseudo-Māwardī repeats his observation that his exposition, primarily intended for the benefit of a royal audience, applies to rulers and subjects alike:

> There is nothing that kings and subjects, rulers and ruled (*al-ruʾasāʾ wa-l-marʾūsūn*) need in religion or this world but that I have found a firm principle (*aṣl muḥkam*) and clear tradition (*athar bayyin*) for it in the Book of God and the *sunna*, *siyar* and *akhbār* of the Prophet, either in the form of an incontestable text wherein lies no doubt (*immā naṣṣan lā mukhālafata lahu wa-lā shubhata fīhi*), or in an indication that can be easily derived or a general concept the explication and interpretation of which is possible (*immā dalālatan yashulu istikhrājuhu aw-mujmalan yumkinu sharḥuhu wa-tafsīruhu*). How could it not be thus, when God, blessed and exalted, has said: 'We have neglected nothing from the Book' (6: 38), and 'We sent down to you the Book as a clarification of every thing' (16: 89). Whoever lays claim to a philosophy (*ḥikma*) or a science (*ʿilm*) that opposes, conflicts with, contradicts or rejects that which is in God's Book represents the epitome of ignorance (*jahl maḥḍ*) and utter disgrace (*ʿayb baḥt*), and is devoid of wisdom (*ḥikma*).[229]

Pseudo-Māwardī asserts the guiding value of the sacred sources for kings and subjects alike. He also expresses, in defence of rationalism, the view that philosophy (*ḥikma*) conforms to revelation. It is possible that a desire to distinguish his *ḥikma* from that of some contemporaries, such as, perhaps, al-Rāzī, underpins his insistence that *ḥikma* that did not conform to the sacred word was not true wisdom at all. The passage might also suggest that, in consistency with the Kindian tradition, he regarded philosophy as a tool available for the accomplishment of the same aims as revelation.[230] He proceeds to detail the four previously mentioned foundations for knowledge, the Qurʾān, the Prophetic sunna, rational speculation and consensus:

> God has commanded His creation to every goodness and virtue and has forbidden every evil, sin and vice . . . Exalted is His mention, He has urged humanity to all goodness and pointed in a comprehensive way to every excellence (*fa-ḥaththa jalla dhikruhu ʿalā kulli khayrin wa-dalla mujmilan*

ᶜalā kulli faḍlin); moreover He has disseminated much of this on the tongue of His Prophet. Everything of the Prophet's *akhbār* that is sound, and everything of his traditions (*āthār*) that is firm (*thabata*) on the tongues of the transmitters (*ruwāt*), is part of God's stipulations in a text (*naṣṣa Allāh ᶜalayhi*) according to this order (*ᶜalā hādhā l-tartīb*). For He has said: 'That which the Prophet has brought you, adopt it; and that which he has forbidden from you, renounce it' (59: 7), and He said: 'Obey God and obey the Prophet and those in authority among you' (4: 59). When, at God's command, we follow the traditions (*āthār*) and biographical accounts of His Prophet, we find in them every effective piece of wisdom (*ḥikma bāligha*),[231] every illustrious deed (*manqaba jalīla*), every nobility (*sharaf*) and virtue (*faḍīla*), every form of fine behaviour (*adab ḥasan*) and every pious saying (*qawl muttaqin*), every strong principle among the principles of religion, and clear knowledge (*ᶜilm bayyin*).[232]

Then the Prophet indicated the search for truth in the consensus of his community (*ijmāᶜ ummatihi*), and among the learned of his Companions, for he said, 'My community shall not agree upon an error,'[233] 'Follow those who come after me, Abū Bakr and ᶜUmar,'[234] and 'My Companions are like the stars; whomever among them you follow, you shall be led aright.'[235] He gave preference to each of his Companions in accordance with that by which God had distinguished him in terms of virtue, and had given him in terms of glorious deeds; so the Prophet indicated to us that we should take knowledge from them after him, and follow them in that which they did right (*al-iqtidāᵓ fīmā aṣābū bihim*). When we pursue their reports (*akhbār*) and follow their traditions (*āthār*), we find in them every piece of wisdom (*ḥikma*), every expression of austerity (*zuhd*) and worship (*ᶜibāda*), every form of virtuous conduct (*sīra fāḍila*) and every noble deed (*manqaba sharīfa*).[236]

Then there have not ceased to be in the religious community of Islam (*millat al-Islām*), praise be to God, scholars who teach its Book, explicate its difficult parts, deduce its principles, derive its cases, and support them with manifest proofs and powerful pieces of evidence (*ᶜulamāᵓ yuᶜallimūna kitābahā wa-yufassirūna mushkilahā wa-yufarriᶜūna uṣūlahā wa-yastakhrijūna ḥawādithahā wa-yuḥāmūna ᶜanhā bi-l-ḥujaj al-ẓāhira wa-l-dalāᵓil al-qāhira*).

> Kings, even if some of them incline to this world and are dazzled by its adornments and vanities, have not ceased to call for the preservation of the community's origin and the defence of its core (*al-difāᶜ ᶜan bayḍatihā*), and to promote the external aspects of its religious law (*ẓawāhir sharīᶜatihā*). They have established remarkable modes of conduct (*siyar ᶜajība*) and left wonderful traces (*āthār gharība*). If the king who is concerned with the well-being (*ṣalāḥ*) of his kingdom follows them, and the summoner who is mindful of the affairs of his subjects (*al-dāᶜī al-muhtamm bi-umūr raᶜiyyatihi*) knows of them, he will find in each of these topics everything he needs in terms of the ordinances of his governance, the disciplining of his self and the improvement (*iṣlāḥ*) of his kingdom, and at the same time he will garner for himself consciousness of his Lord (*taqwā rabbihi*), success in his final end, and a favourable reputation during his lifetime and after his death, by the assistance of God and His will, power and strength.[237]

In this passage, Pseudo-Māwardī asserts the four principles of Qurʾān, the Prophetic example, the consensus of the early scholars and rational speculation or analogy. He summarises the sources on which he has drawn to present the topic of the king's governance and discipline of his self.

In these final sections, Pseudo-Māwardī, who insists on the timeless and universal character of his advice, affirms the positive quality of kingship and the meritorious accomplishments of kings through the ages. His chapter intersperses materials that engage the specifically Muslim historical memory and materials that engage the diverse and multi-confessional regional memory of which the *milla* forms a part. This juxtaposition expresses Pseudo-Māwardī's conception of the affinities among communities and underlines his portrayal of the Muslim community as privileged by virtue of *tafḍīl* rather than exceptional in kind. The periodic specificity of his language is framed by the multiple discourses – scriptural, exegetical, philosophical, rational-theological, literary and poetic – that he unites in his presentation.

The force of Pseudo-Māwardī's exposition in his fifth chapter is to urge the king to exercise self-restraint. Since, as he points out more than once in the course of his mirror, the king is not subject to any 'restraining hand', his submission to constraints of his power can only be voluntary. By means of moral suasion, Pseudo-Māwardī seeks to impress upon the king the compound benefits of such self-limitation. To this end he constructs a Qurʾānic framework for his chapter, and intersperses scriptural, prophetic, narrative, aphoristic and poetic materials in order to convey the universal affirmation, supported by revelation and reason, of the self-control that he urges on the king.

Pseudo-Māwardī opens his chapter with an account of *taqwā*, from which he proceeds to a five-part model of the religious sciences. In his ranking of the branches of *ʿilm al-dīn*, Pseudo-Māwardī's emphasis on theology reflects his insistence on the role of rationality in religious knowledge. His preference for theology over jurisprudence is perhaps also related to his view, shared with some other Ḥanafīs, that the principal distinction among religious communities lies in the particularities of their laws (*sharāʾiʿ*). In the context of the *milla*, he urges the king to support the exoteric (*ẓāhirī*) meanings of the law rather than the esoteric (*bāṭinī*) interpretations advanced by several of his contemporaries. In the next section of his chapter, Pseudo-Māwardī addresses, in turn, selected divine qualities that the king, in accordance with a definition of philosophy, should emulate, followed by qualities divinely enjoined upon humankind. He also urges, explicates and demonstrates his method of logical inference and sequential presentation of his arguments. The premise of his exposition, stated explicitly at various points in his mirror, is that the king's moral well-being is an essential prerequisite for the well-being of his kingdom and subjects.

Throughout his fifth chapter, Pseudo-Māwardī follows his stated method of articulating his argument and adducing a hierarchy of supporting texts that not only illustrate his points, but also develop them. In conjunction with his numerous Qurʾānic quotations, Pseudo-Māwardī employs a diverse array of sacred and non-sacred materials, and alludes to contemporary intellectual and social developments. A secondary framework for his presentation derives from the philosophical conception of virtue as the perfect mean between polar vices. In short, Pseudo-Māwardī deploys the entire array of available intellectual and cultural resources in communicating his points in this most substantial chapter of his 'religious book'.

4

The Governance of the Élites

Pseudo-Māwardī's sixth chapter develops several themes shared with late antique writers, contemporaries such as Qudāma b. Ja^cfar, and later specialists in ethics, such as Miskawayh and Naṣīr al-Dīn Ṭūsī (597–672/1201–74). Grammatically singular, the feminine noun *khāṣṣa*, like its counterpart *^cāmma*, represents a collectivity. An individual member of the collectivity might be described as *khāṣṣ*, and a plurality of such individuals as *khawāṣṣ*. Derived from the root *kh-ṣ-ṣ*, the term *khāṣṣa* evokes, in relation to the ruler, 'special' or 'distinctive' status, as opposed to the 'common' or 'general' status of the *^cāmma*.[1]

The singular and collective form of the term *khāṣṣa* partially obscures the internally differentiated and hierarchical nature of the composite grouping to which it referred. Underlying Pseudo-Māwardī's treatment of the *khāṣṣa* are the principles of *tafḍīl*, 'preference', patterned after the divine creation, and *taqrīb*, 'bringing close', a reflection of favour, expressed in degrees of proximity to the king's person. These principles created a system of differentiation articulated in terms of a vertical hierarchy, on the one hand, and a circular radius, on the other. Degrees of proximity to the centre of the polity found expression in spatial and physical terms, in the positions assigned to individuals and groups within the royal precinct and in the context of royal audiences,[2] and in symbolic terms, by means of representation of the king beyond the sphere of the royal household. Pseudo-Māwardī's repeated references to 'the noble and the base, the distant and the close' (*al-sharīf wa-l-waḍī^c wa-l-aqṣā wa-l-adnā*) reflect his conception of relative status within the social hierarchy and relative degrees of proximity.

Like many medieval writers, Pseudo-Māwardī assigns the king to a central and intermediary position in a cosmic hierarchy ordered by degrees. Above him are the angels and prophets, whose positions in the cosmic hierarchy provide a mirror for the social order. In the cosmic order, as seen in Volume I, the angels occupy the closest position to God; in the social order, the king's courtiers occupy the positions closest to the monarch. God selects and makes some of His creatures close (*jaʿalahum aqrab al-khalq*), kings draw some of their *khāṣṣa* close (*yuqarrib*).³ Pseudo-Māwardī portrays a hierarchy of proximity created through relationship – blood relatives, foster-relatives, 'assistants' and appointed officials – and expressed in varying degrees of spatial proximity to the palace and the royal presence.

In connection with the themes of preference and proximity, which shape Pseudo-Māwardī's chapter, a third theme, the centrality of relationships of *khidma* and *iṣṭināʿ*, recurs in his exposition of governance of the *khāṣṣa*. Relationships of *khidma* and *iṣṭināʿ* encompassed several groupings. Among them, the ruler's *khadam* occupied a high position within the hierarchy of the *khāṣṣa*; they acted on behalf of the king, who depended on them.⁴ They are likened to extensions of the king's body; as a king advises his son in a pseudo-Platonic testament, 'Know that your *khadam* occupy the place of your limbs, by which you give and retract, and of your senses, by which you judge that which you perceive.'⁵ A further sub-group within the *khāṣṣa* consisted of the king's *ḥāshiya* or *ḥasham*, his 'retainers' or military 'retinue'.⁶ The members of these groups were assimilated to the royal household through the social mechanism of *iṣṭināʿ*, which involved the patron's fostering of his 'creature' or 'protégé' (*ṣanīʿa*), who in return owed his *ṣāniʿ* obedience and gratitude.⁷ The terms *khadam* and *ḥasham* frequently occur together, partly in a reflection of their overlapping meanings and partly for reasons of rhyme.⁸ The *khadam* and *ḥāshiya* or *ḥasham* differ, however, in the extent of their dependence on the ruler and their physical proximity to his person. The former category included leading military commanders and the heads of wealthy regional families; these individuals, who possessed the capacity to raise large numbers of troops, frequently contracted relationships of *khidma* with the ruler, but their presence at the court, like their representation of the king and his interests, was intermittent, and subject to the ruler's summons. Members of the ruler's *ḥāshiya* or *ḥasham*, by contrast, were assimilated in the likeness of foster-children into the royal household, and were in permanent attendance at the court.

Pseudo-Māwardī begins his chapter with an extended portrayal of the divinely instated hierarchical order, organised according to the principle of *tafḍīl*.[9] As observed in Volume I, Pseudo-Māwardī depicts God's creation of the angels as His *junūd* and *aᶜwān*, His armies and assistants, and this image prefigures his portrayal of the *khāṣṣa* as the *junūd* and *aᶜwān* of the king. He proceeds to explain that the king should select and train his *khāṣṣa* in the same manner that God selected and trained the angels and His prophets:

> It is incumbent on the king that he train and govern his *khāṣṣa* (*an yurawwiḍa ᶜalayhi wa-yasūsa bihi khāṣṣatahu*) in the same fashion, according to his capacity (*ṭāqa*) and the extent of his strength (*quwwa*).[10]

Continuing his theme of following the divine example and the divine commandments, Pseudo-Māwardī urges the king to replicate the patterns of divine governance in his earthly governance. Just as God has established a graded order, in which the angels are closest to Him in physical and symbolic terms ('the nearest in station and closest in rank', *aqrab al-khalq ilayhi manzilatan wa-adnāhum . . . martabatan*), and prophets follow the angels, the king should arrange the categories of his subjects in accordance with their qualities and characteristics. God chose prophets to act as His stewards or trustees (*umanāʾ*), and entrusted to them the well-being of His created world. As the present chapter will show, the concept of *amāna*, trustworthiness, recurs throughout Pseudo-Māwardī's discussion of the king's *khāṣṣa*.

After these introductory remarks, Pseudo-Māwardī continues:

> According to the extent of his capacity (*ṭāqa*) and the limit of his strength (*quwwa*), the king should position his *khāṣṣa* in relation to himself in the place of the tool (*āla*) to the craftsman (*ṣāniᶜ*). Without this tool, it is not possible for the craftsman to execute any of his crafts (*ṣināᶜāt*) or to accomplish any of his desires (*irādāt*), because if the tool is impaired (*al-āla idhā fasadat*), then the craftsman's work[11] becomes impaired, and his execution, skill, precision and proficiency become far more difficult.

In a metaphor that appears elsewhere in his mirror, Pseudo-Māwardī employs the language of craftsmanship to describe the ruler's governance, and implies an analogy with the divine craftsman, whose creative construction (*ṣanᶜa*) he had evoked in the previous set of passages.[12] Pseudo-Māwardī impresses on the king the imperative of maintaining the well-being and reliability of his human instruments. He continues:

> The king should also devote his highest attention to his *khāṣṣa* because the larger part of his affairs is entrusted to them and tied to them, while they in turn are related to him and compared to him. Their modes of conduct (*ādāb*) point to his conduct (*adab*); their moral dispositions (*akhlāq*) allow for inferences of his disposition (*khulq*); their religion provides an indication of his religion, and he will be judged, favourably or unfavourably, according to that which is witnessed from them. The situation is not like this in the case of the common people (*ᶜāmma*), because for each one of them there is a lord, a father, a teacher, an instructor, or a trainer who attends to his situation and who prepares him according to that which his condition can bear and his capacity can attain, and according to his choice, his aspiration, his preference and his effectiveness in his training and discipline (*ᶜalā . . . tadbīrihi fī l-riyāḍa wa-l-siyāsa*).[13]

In likening the *khāṣṣa* to the king-craftsman's 'tool', Pseudo-Māwardī accentuates the contrast between the *khāṣṣa* and the *ᶜāmma*: the king conducts his governance by means of the *khāṣṣa*, with whom he stands in a direct relationship; his relationship with the *ᶜāmma*, on the other hand, is indirect, mediated by the *khāṣṣa*, who, just as he models himself on God, model themselves on him. The *ᶜāmma* are involved in networks of relationships with lords, teachers and master craftsmen that exclude the king.

After this preliminary exposition, Pseudo-Māwardī embarks on the first major section of his chapter. This section details the proper upbringing and education, or training, of the *khāṣṣa*:

> God, glorious is His mention, ordered the instruction of the *khāṣṣa* by textual means (*amara Allāhu bi-taʾdīb al-khāṣṣa naṣṣan*) in His Book . . . and the Prophet established practices (*sanna al-nabī*) for the boy's education (*taʾdīb al-ṣabī*), his formation through circumcision and his instruction in the Qurʾān. The ᶜulamāʾ permitted (*rakhkhaṣa al-ᶜulamāʾ*) striking the boy to inculcate toughness and as a punishment before the age at which the ordinances became incumbent upon him, and the duties of the religion applied to him . . . The Prophet ordered the exaction of *zakāt al-fiṭr* [the alms due at the celebration of the breaking of the fast at the end of the month of Ramadan] from the boy, and the ᶜulamāʾ authorised its exaction from the wealth of the orphan, in order to educate him and form him in goodness and religion.[14]

In this passage, Pseudo-Māwardī distinguishes, as he had in his previous chapter, between scriptural authority (*amara Allāhu . . . naṣṣan*) and exemplary and normative Prophetic conduct (*sanna al-nabī*), to which he adds a third rank of authority, the scholarly extension of permission (*rakhkhaṣa al-ᶜulamāᵓ*) to matters not addressed in either the scriptural or Prophetic corpora. It was this last category of authority that, as Pseudo-Māwardī acknowledges, allowed for corporal punishment of children who had not yet reached the age of maturity or *taklīf*, that is, the age at which the full religious obligations of adulthood became binding upon them. The provision, also in Bryson's *Oikonomikos*, extant in a tenth-century Arabic version and perhaps known to Pseudo-Māwardī, was, of course, in keeping with the educational philosophies and practice of numerous pre-modern societies. It recurs in ethical treatises, sometimes in contexts that suggest a familiarity with Bryson. By drawing attention to the lack of Qurᵓānic or Prophetic sanction for the corporal punishment of children in the course of instruction, Pseudo-Māwardī perhaps sought to limit the practice. As later sections of the present chapter will show, Pseudo-Māwardī devoted extensive attention to matters of pedagogy; it is possible that, like Abū Zayd al-Balkhī, who likewise treated the teaching of children in his writings, he had been a teacher himself.[16] The purposes and techniques of education also concerned al-Jāḥiẓ, who had encouraged the gentle treatment of students, and it is possible that Pseudo-Māwardī's affinities with his Muᶜtazilite predecessor extended to educational matters.[17] Pseudo-Māwardī's implied reservations with regard to the physical punishment of children who had not reached the age of legal responsibility were shared by the slightly later theologian Abū l-Layth al-Samarqandī (d. 373/983), who, in presenting the qualities of teachers who aspired to attain a divine reward for their labours, would stipulate the observance of five practices, including the limited use of beating, which the teacher should not exceed.[18]

Pseudo-Māwardī proceeds:

> God chose for the companionship (*ṣuḥba*) of His Prophet various groups (*aqwām*). He made them his helpers and assistants (*jaᶜalahum lahu anṣāran wa-aᶜwānan*), and ordered him to instruct them, correct them, train them and teach them, to make them desirous (of reward) and fearful (of

punishment) through admonition, to condition them by reminding (them) until they became the most worthy of his *umma* in virtue, the most consummate of them in excellence, and the most elevated of them in degree. They became trustworthy (*umanāʾ*), godly (*atqiyāʾ*), learned (*ʿulamāʾ*) and wise (*ḥukamāʾ*), loyal (*abrār*), worshipful (*ʿubbād*) and observant (*aḥbār*), calling for the good and rebuking the reprehensible (*munādīn bi-l-maʿrūf wa-zajjārīn ʿan al-munkar*), exerting themselves for God's sake (*mujāhidīn fī llāh*) and following the prophets of God, may God have mercy upon them . . .[19]

The King Ardashīr indicated the way of well-being (*ṣalāḥ*) in this matter in his 'Testament' when he said, 'Every king has a group of close companions (*biṭāna*), and every man among his companions has his own group of companions. In this way the entire population of the kingdom are brought together. If he (the king) orders his group of companions in accordance with rectitude (*ʿalā ḥāl al-ṣawāb*), each man among them will order his group of companions in like manner, so that the generality of the subjects (*ʿāmmat al-raʿiyya*) will be brought together.'[20]

Aristotle said to Alexander, 'For your own sake, cleave to those of your *khadam* with whom you are pleased.' And he said, 'Adorn your affair among the common people. Inspect your army, and act as if they were your limbs, and the gate through which you may accomplish the humiliation of your enemy. Guard against any harm befalling them, and treat them well, for in their well-being lies well-being for the subjects and the attainment of victory. Strengthen the weak among them and you will strengthen your affair; empower the poor among them and you become powerful.'[21]

In an echo of his portrayal of God's selecting and fashioning of his angels and prophets, Pseudo-Māwardī's citing of the Prophet's example in instructing his Companions accentuates the central and essential virtue of trustworthiness or dependability (*amāna*). Just as God had selected His prophets as *umanāʾ*, trusted stewards over His creatures, the Prophet produced among his Companions a group of *umanāʾ*, trusted and trustworthy persons. Similarly the wise kings and sages of the past had urged care in the selection and elevation of the persons to whom they entrusted their affairs. In his citing of passages from the 'Testament of Ardashīr' and the Aristotelian–Alexandrine correspondence, Pseudo-Māwardī illustrates the role of the *khāṣṣa* in binding the king to his subjects. His *khāṣṣa* are close and connected to him; they in turn are connected to their subordinates, who are connected to persons subordinate to them, in a pattern that links the entirety of the kingdom in networks of interdependent relationships. Proper management of these networks results in well-being (*ṣalāḥ*), the outcome to which Pseudo-Māwardī directs his advice throughout his mirror.

The Categories of the King's *Khāṣṣa*

In the next section of his chapter, Pseudo-Māwardī subdivides the ruler's *khāṣṣa* into five ranked parts:

> The virtuous king should follow the command of God in the governance of his *khāṣṣa*, his family (*ahl*), his retinue (*ḥāshiya*), his armies (*junūd*) and his notables (*aᶜyān*),[22] and follow the example of His Prophet.
>
> The king's *khāṣṣa* to whom we refer in this instance consist of categories that are constructed in such a way that some of them are more special than others (*ᶜalā ṭabaqātin buniyyat baᶜḍahum akhaṣṣa min baᶜḍin*). The most special among them to him (*akhaṣṣuhum bihi*) are his children (*wulduhu*), and his *khadam* among his relatives and his family members. Next are his domestic and military slaves (*ᶜabīduhu wa-mamālīkuhu*), and the élite members of his military staff and his guards (*khāṣṣ fityānihi wa-ghilmānihi*).[23] Next are his viziers and his secretaries, and the stewards who oversee the tasks of his palace (*wuzarāʾuhu wa-kuttābuhu wa-kufāt ashghāl ḥaḍratihi*). Then there are his army and his senior commanders, his cavalry and soldiers (*junduhu wa-quwwāduhu wa-asāwiratuhu wa-muqātilūhu*). Next are his officials (*ᶜummāl*), to whose assistance he has recourse in ensuring the welfare of his kingdom beyond his gate and his palace, and outside his central and established place of residence (*ᶜummāluhu alladhīna yastaᶜīnu bihim fī iṣlāḥ mamlakatihi al-nāʾiya ᶜan bābihi wa-dārihi wa-l-khārija ᶜan markazihi wa-qarārihi*).[24]

Pseudo-Māwardī depicts the king at the centre of a ranked yet interrelated group that consists of several constituents. They are, first, the members of his family, bound to him through consanguinity and marriage; this group might include relatives bound to him in *khidma*; secondly, the ranks of persons whose connections to the ruler derived not from familial or marital relationships, but, initially, from acquisition, and who constituted, by ties of patronage and loyalty, extensions of his family;[25] thirdly, the administrative or civilian élites who surrounded him and discharged his affairs *in situ*; fourthly, the military élites, distinguished in this instance from the civilian administration and settled, in the case of many of his senior commanders, in their own domains, whether familial properties or gifts from the ruler in the form of 'favour' (*niᶜma*); and, fifthly, his official representatives, who were dispersed across his dominions.[26]

As Volume I sought to demonstrate, the appearance of concentrated power in the person of the king co-existed with a system of indirect governance dependent on cooperation across levels of status and authority. It is difficult to assign precise meanings to some of the terms by which Pseudo-Māwardī refers to groupings amongst the *khāṣṣa*, and to determine the degree to which the terms might have overlapped. The terms *ᶜabīd* and *mamālīk* convey a background in slavery, whether personal or inherited; individuals assimilated to the groups designated by these rubrics nevertheless varied considerably in rank. The terms *fityān* and *ghilmān* are ambiguous in this regard, and similarly embraced wide disparities in rank and privilege; a later passage in this chapter, however, indicates that the *ghilmān* were recent additions to the ruler's household, and suggests their servile status.

As I have suggested in relation to previous examples, the repertoire of materials incorporated into Arabic from Middle Persian, such as the 'Testament' of Ardashīr, contributed to Pseudo-Māwardī's articulation of the political culture that he observed. This literature contains numerous references to the monarch's wives, children, close relatives, viziers, confidants, companions, helpers, 'assistants', counsellors, persons who seek proximity, jesters and personal attendants (*azwāj, awlād, quranāʾ, wuzarāʾ, akhdān, aṣḥāb, anṣār, aᶜwān, mutanaṣṣiḥūn, mutaqarribūn, muḍḥikūn, mutazayyinūn*),[27] to *al-ahl wa-khawāṣṣ al-ḥidāth wa-l-aᶜwān wa-l-khadam* ('family members, the élites among his retainers, assistants and persons pledged in service'), and to the 'training of the king's companions and assistants' (*taʾdīb al-ikhwān wa-l-aᶜwān*),[28] and provided a vocabulary, even as, with changing conditions, the meanings of the terms evolved. In one example, Pseudo-Māwardī employs the designation *asāwira*; this term, derived from Persian and employed in the sense of 'cavalrymen', finds further attestation in the Samanid context in the slightly later *Mafātīḥ al-ᶜulūm* ('Keys of the Sciences') of al-Khwārazmī, who defines it as 'the plural of *al-uswār*, that is, *al-fāris* (the cavalryman)'.[29] In Pseudo-Māwardī's period and milieu, the term required no explanation.

In his list of categories among the *khāṣṣa*, Pseudo-Māwardī distinguishes between the officials in the king's immediate vicinity and those dispatched to or resident in more distant locations. His distinction corresponds to the account of the contemporary historian Narshakhī, according to whom Naṣr II ordered the construction in Bukhara, in the ancient vicinity of the Rīgistān where kings had built palaces since antiquity, of a new palace, at great expense and of great loveliness, for himself, and 'at its door' a palace for his officials (*sarā-yi ᶜummāl*), each of whom had his own dīvān 'next to the sulṭān's palace' (*bar dar-i sarā-yi sulṭān*).[30] The royal court was not fixed, but moved periodically from one site to another.[31] According to a celebrated account, Naṣr b. Aḥmad, who frequently spent the summer months with his army in Samarqand and elsewhere, developed a fondness for the city of Herat and involved his troops in an extended period of settlement there. Their desire to return to their families in Bukhara prompted Rūdakī to seek to persuade the king by means of one of his most famous poems.[32]

Narshakhī's description of the construction of the royal precincts in the Rīgistān reflects the conception of the king's presence as a central focus of power, to which increasingly distant social categories were linked in succession. This understanding, recalling an ancient pattern, found physical expression in the architecture of the palace and the buildings that surrounded it.[33] Pseudo-Māwardī assumes such spatial and symbolic expressions of the arrangements of power in his exposition of the king's governance of his *khāṣṣa*.

This listing of the graded categories that composed the king's *khāṣṣa* introduces Pseudo-Māwardī's detailed advice regarding the king's treatment of each group. He begins with the king's children, and provides an exceptionally full description of the proper formation of princes.

The Education of Princes

Infancy and Early Childhood

Pseudo-Māwardī begins his treatment of the king's governance of his *khāṣṣa* with the care and instruction of princes. He expresses the king's responsibilities in this regard in terms of his children's 'rights' or 'claims' (*ḥuqūq*) against him, in other words, parents' responsibilities towards their children.[34] Parts of his advice recall the Arabic *Oikonomikos* of Bryson and anticipate later treatments in Persian. Since the process of preparing a future king begins at the moment of conception, Pseudo-Māwardī begins his discussion with the choice of a mother:

> Among the first rights of the child is that the king should select his mother and choose among his womenfolk, before conception, a woman who is beautiful, noble, religious, modest, intelligent in her affairs, pleasing in her moral dispositions, experienced in the exercise of reason and fully compatible with her husband in his conditions . . .[35]
>
> It is the custom among the members of every religion and religious community (*ahl kull dīn wa-milla*), among every people (*jīl*), and among the adherents of every sect (*niḥla*), to seek equals in the matter of marriage and betrothal (*ṭalab al-kufāt fī bāb al-nikāḥ wa-l-inkāḥ*). Religion has made this custom a religious law (*sharīʿa min al-sharāʾiʿ*). The purpose of all of this is to strive for nobility of lineage (*najābat al-nasal*), to select carefully for female (*ṭurūqa*) and male (*faḥl*) in consideration of their nobility in descent, since this nobility passes from one generation to another; and in order to avoid the pollution of lineage (*tadnīs al-nasab*).
>
> The king, with the loftiness of his status and the elevation of his position, is the foremost of people to desire this virtue and to search for this fine quality for his children. Perhaps the king's son will succeed him, and it is the king's hope that his son will assume his position and take his place, and rule over a group (*jamāʿa*) of the people of his kind (*jins*), his womenfolk and his servants (*khadam*), whom only God can count. He should prepare him (to undertake) the cultivation of God's lands, the governance of His servants and the protection of His religion.

If he acts in this fashion (and desires such an outcome), it is incumbent on him that he seek to engender the child according to the prescriptions of the *sunna* and the descriptions of the philosophers (*ahl al-ḥikma*). He should avoid intercourse when in a state of drunkenness, carelessness, drowsiness and lassitude, and throughout the sexual act he should devote his intention to the conception of the child. He should take refuge from the accursed Satan, and focus his intention on the hope that perhaps God will provide him with a child who will worship God and affirm His unicity (*laᶜallahu yarzuqahu man yaᶜbud Allāh wa-yuwaḥḥiduhu*),[36] who will promote the welfare of the created world (*ṣalāḥ al-khalq*) in upholding the right (*iqāmatan lil-ḥaqq*), support for the truth, seeking benefit for God's servants and prosperity for the lands.

It is related that ᶜAmr b. ᶜUbayd said to his wife, when she was breast-feeding one of her sons, 'In suckling your child, do not be like the female animal, who by her suckling becomes attached to her offspring out of the compassion of kinship. Rather let your purpose in suckling him be your aspiration for God's reward, and the hope that by your suckling, a creature who will perhaps affirm God's unity and worship Him will live.'[37]

Among the factors involved in the selection of a wife, Pseudo-Māwardī invokes the principle of *kafāʾa*, the equality of the partners in marriage. Criteria for assessing such equality varied considerably from one legal grouping to another. In his references to *najābat al-nasal* and *tadnīs al-nasab*, Pseudo-Māwardī, in consistency with his Ḥanafī orientation in matters of law, emphasises the social dimensions of *kafāʾa*.[38] His discussion indicates that in his society, it was not only from the female partner's point of view that the marriage was required to satisfy the criteria for equality; in this case, it was the male partner whose status, and the status of whose children, required the safeguard of *kafāʾa*. In a possible reflection of ancient and continuing royal customs in his region, the author situates this requirement for social equality in the context of 'the people of every religion and religious community' (*ahl kull dīn wa-milla*). The local significance of what Julia Bray has termed 'the aristocratic principle' is borne out by al-Thaᶜālibī's emphasis on the importance of a well-born wife in *Ādāb al-mulūk*.[39]

Next in his treatment of infancy, Pseudo-Māwardī turns to the choice of a fitting and pleasing name for the child:

> When the child is born, the first of his father's favours and acts of kindness to him should be to adorn him with a good name (*ism*) and a fine and noble patronymic (*kunya*). A fine name makes an impression on people's souls at its first hearing. In this way God commanded His servants and mandated upon them that they call upon Him by the Beautiful Names (*al-asmāʾ al-ḥusnā*), and describe Him by the Exalted Attributes (*al-ṣifāt al-ʿulyā*), for He said, 'Say: Call upon Allah, or call upon the Merciful (*al-Raḥmān*); whichever one you call upon, His are the most beautiful names' (17: 110), and 'God's are the most beautiful names. Call upon Him by them, and cast aside those who abandon His names' (7: 180). The Prophet chose and selected the names of his children with the greatest care. Later, Muḥammad b. al-Ḥanafiyya [son of ʿAlī b. Abī Ṭālib and Khawla, a woman of the Banū Ḥanīfa] bore his name and his *kunya* in order to honour and ennoble him, and out of respect and reverence for him. The Prophet, upon him be peace, forbade that anyone else among the Muslims should combine his name and his *kunya*,[40] and said, 'The names dearest to me are ʿAbdallāh (Servant of God) and ʿAbd al-Raḥmān (Servant of the Merciful)'.[41]
>
> The criteria for choosing in this matter consist of three things. The first of these things is that the name should be selected from among the names of the people of the child's religion, the prophets and messengers and the righteous servants of God. This practice is intended to foster closeness to God, resplendent is His name, by instilling love for these figures in the children who bear their names; to perpetuate their names; and to follow the example of God, glorious is His name, in choosing those names for His friends (*awliyāʾ*), and that which the religion has brought. We have related from the Prophet on the topic of the most beloved of names to God, that they are 'ʿAbdallāh and names similar to it'.[42]
>
> The second criterion is that the name should consist of few letters and should be light on the tongue, easy to pronounce, and quick to grasp upon hearing . . .
>
> The third factor is that the name should be beautiful in meaning and appropriate to the condition of the named. It should be current among the names

> of the people of his category and religious community and the people of his station (*an yakūna . . . jāriyan fī asmāʾ ahl ṭabaqatihi wa-millatihi wa-ahl martabatihi*).[43]

In stipulating these three criteria for the selection of a name, Pseudo-Māwardī addresses its edificatory and instructional potential for the person who bears it, as well as the importance of its appropriateness for the individual's social category and status, and the confessional group to which he belongs. He quotes a poem of Abū Nuwās, in which the poet, affirming the appeal of simplicity in a name, alludes to the additional letter *wāw* that appears in the written form of the name ᶜAmr.[44]

Recalling a first- and second-century debate regarding the merits of breastfeeding, Pseudo-Māwardī expresses the preference that the child's mother care for him in his early years, noting that this practice accords with the divine pronouncement and with the order of the natural world. He allows, however, for the services of a wet-nurse if the mother should be unable to feed her own child:

> The proper way to nurse the child is that his mother should breastfeed him, for that is the most effective form of nursing and the most respected, the least likely to occasion a mixing of the humours (*abᶜad min mumāzajat al-akhlāṭ*), and the most dignified, in accordance with the words of God, blessed and exalted: 'Mothers shall suckle their children for two complete years' (2: 233). This arrangement is, firstly, that which God has mentioned, and at the same time it is the natural order for human beings and for all the animals (*al-amr al-ṭabīᶜī lil-insān wa-sāʾir al-ḥayawān*). If an impediment prevents this arrangement, then it is imperative that he expend the same degree of care in choosing a wet-nurse as he did in the choice of the mother. He must ensure that she be in good health and free from chronic illness (*ṣaḥīḥa min zamāna muʾidda*), aggressive sickness intermittent or persistent (*ᶜilla ᶜādiya ᶜāriḍa aw-lāzima*), clean of skin and sound of body, free of hidden disease, base descent or bad character; because it is the milk that nourishes the child, lends form to his flesh and causes his bones to grow, and endows him with the temperament (*mizāj*) that the difference of natures (*gharāʾiz*) and dispositions entails.[45] The correct way is that the period assigned for breastfeeding should reach its full term, and not exceed

> it, for God, glorious and exalted, has imposed a limit and a termination to it: 'Mothers shall suckle their children for two full years, for those who wish to complete the nursing' (2: 233). Anything after the completion of the period is a corruption and enters the realm of the unnecessary.[46]

In his preference for maternal breastfeeding over the employment of a wet-nurse, Pseudo-Māwardī reflects contemporary medical knowledge of its benefits for child and mother. His emphasis on the serious nature of the choice of a wet-nurse, in the event that it should be necessary, reflects the view that the wet-nurse participated equally in the formation, including the formation of character, of the infant.[47] Indeed, the foster relationship created through suckling (*riḍā*ᶜ) is, in legal terms, the equivalent of a blood relationship, and imposes the same limitations on permissible marriage partners (Q 4: 23).[48] In addition, the passage supplies further attestation of Pseudo-Māwardī's respect for the workings of nature and the significance that, like al-Kaᶜbī, he ascribed to the natural qualities (*ṭabā*ʾ*i*ᶜ) that conditioned the human body and ensured the perpetuation of the species.[49]

His criteria by which a wet-nurse should be selected reflect Pseudo-Māwardī's familiarity with the medical philosophy, primarily associated with Galen and diffused across the ancient Mediterranean world, western Asia and Iran, of the humours (*akhlāṭ*) and temperaments (*amzija*). According to this philosophy, the human body consists of an intermixture of four elemental humours, blood, phlegm, yellow bile and black bile, each of which possesses two natures or qualities, hot or cold and dry or moist. Each humour, moreover, was associated with one of the four seasons, and a 'temperament'. In a healthy body, the four humours co-exist in equilibrium, and sustain the distinctive temperament (*mizāj* or *ṭab*ᶜ) of each individual; illness occurs as a result of an imbalance among the humours and, by extension, temperament.[50] By the end of the ninth century, the system had become the most widely employed explanatory medical principle and the basis for almost all learned Arabic medical discourses.[51] Al-Kaᶜbī, with several of whose teachings Pseudo-Māwardī appears to have agreed, adopted the principle of the four natures out of which God had created all bodies subject to coming into and passing out of existence. These natures shifted, in such a way that one of them might become transformed into another.[52] Al-Kaᶜbī also addressed the qualities of heat and cold, moisture and dryness.[53] As a fellow-participant in the theological–philosophical culture of the early tenth century, Pseudo-Māwardī might have engaged in some medical study, but the theory of the humours had, by his lifetime, entered the general field of Arabic literary culture, and several writers whose expertise did not lie in medicine adopted the principle in their writings.[54] Abū l-Layth al-Samarqandī, in a work that addressed many topics in an edificatory spirit and, like *Naṣīḥat al-mulūk*, displays an affinity with the repertoire of *adab*, devoted a chapter of his *Bustān al-ᶜārifīn* to the quality of the 'natures' of the human being, and describes the four natures of dryness, moisture, heat and cold, and the four bodily fluids of black and yellow bile, blood and phlegm.[55] Also in the later part of the tenth century, al-Khwārazmī would report the theory in an informed manner in his *Mafātīḥ al-ᶜulūm*,[56] and al-ᶜĀmirī would refer to the theory of the humours in *Kitāb al-Amad* ('Book of the Afterlife').[57]

Upbringing and Education

After his discussion of the care of the newborn, Pseudo-Māwardī addresses the prince's early years:

> Attention should be given to the child's upbringing and education. He should wear clothes that resemble the clothing of the kings before him and in his region (*nāḥiya*). The best and finest garments should be chosen for him, suitable for standing for as long as he is receiving instruction, and for jumping and riding, since he has no alternative but to practise these activities.
>
> When he reaches the appropriate age for education and instruction, then the way to proceed is that he should begin – in this *milla* especially – with instruction in the Qurʾān with (as part of his education in) the Arabic language (*taᶜlīm al-Qurʾān maᶜa al-lugha al-ᶜarabiyya*), for it is the language in which God sent down His Book, and in which He proclaimed the laws of His religion (*sharāʾiᶜ dīnihi*) and the precepts of His community (*farāʾiḍ millatihi*). It is also the language in which His Prophet articulated and taught his *sunna*, in which religious and philosophical, earnest and humorous books have been composed (*bihā ullifat al-kutub al-dīniyya wa-l-ḥikmiyya wa-l-jiddiyya wa-l-hazliyya*), and in which their (the community's) correspondence (*rasāʾil*), as well as the documents (*ṣukūk*) that

> God has established as records of trust (*wathā᾽iq*) among them, have been written – so there is no choice for the growing child in this *milla* other than to learn it; otherwise he will be ignorant of religion and deficient among the religious communities (*kāna . . . manqūṣan fī l-milal*).
>
> In addition, this language possesses virtue of a kind that no other language has, in terms of eloquence (*faṣāḥa*), clarity (*bayān*), elegance (*ṭalāwa*) on the tongue and sweetness (*ḥalāwa*) of sound and to the ear; its many inflections (*taṣārīf*) and the ability of its grammar to convey complexities (*iḥtimāl al-maqāyīs al-naḥwiyya*); the amplitude of its expressions and the intermediate number of its letters between paucity and many; and the likes of these qualities. Were the language to be learnt solely for the sake of its beauty and acquired out of admiration, it would be entirely fitting. For these reasons, the Persian kings (*mulūk al-ᶜajam*) used to learn it, and many of them used it in times of ceremonial gatherings and in assemblies for the adornment of their courts.[58]

Pseudo-Māwardī's discussion of Arabic, its necessity to kings 'especially in this religious community', and his emphasis on the language's versatility and many virtues suggest an environment in which several languages were in use. It is possible that the arguments advanced for the prince's need to acquire Arabic reflect controversies surrounding the expanding uses of New Persian at the Samanid court and within the Samanid domains in the tenth century. Later in the century, Abū l-Layth al-Samarqandī would also address the superiority of Arabic to other languages, particularly Persian.[59] A full century later, the scientist and polymath al-Bīrūnī (362–442/973–1050 or later), a native speaker not of Dari but of Khwarazmian, famously considered Persian a vehicle fit only for fables and epics, and inadequate as a medium for serious intellectual discourse,[60] and Pseudo-Māwardī's use of the Persian-derived word *afsānaqāt*, 'stories', in the following pages confirms its associations with collections of fictional narratives. Arabic retained its primacy in the religious sciences, and in most areas of intellectual and scholarly discourse. In a reflection of his fluency in the varied repertoire of Arabic literary culture, Pseudo-Māwardī values the versatility of Arabic, which lent itself to the composition of books on religious and philosophical subjects (*al-kutub al-dīniyya wa-l-ḥikmiyya*), a formulation that, as elsewhere in *Naṣīḥat al-mulūk*, implies a distinction but complementarity between *dīn* and *ḥikma*, and books intended for serious or entertaining, contemplative and pleasurable purposes.

In a continuing demonstration of his proficiency in the Arabic language and its varied literature, Pseudo-Māwardī addresses the optimal method for teaching and acquiring the language:

> The way to teach the language is that the instructor should aim for the lightest approach, namely the lightest of its books, and for the easiest, namely the easiest of its compilations and compositions. He should not preoccupy the sons of kings with the strange and unusual or with the foreign (linguistic) irregularity (*lā yushghil awlād al-mulūk bi-l-gharīb al-waḥshī wa-l-nādir al-ajnabī*), nor with the fine points of grammar or the rules of prosody (*daqāʾiq al-naḥw wa-dawāwīn al-ʿarūḍ*), for these elements will distract the prince from the language's meanings. He should learn expressions (*alfāẓ*) solely for the purpose of understanding them, for if the human being expends his life in learning (numerous) expressions, the meanings will elude him; except in the case of persons who adopt the language as a craft (*ṣināʿa*), such as littérateurs (*udabāʾ*), teachers, instructors and grammarians.[61]

> In order to facilitate his learning of the language, he needs to avail himself of the transmitted poetry of the Arabs, the accounts of their battles (*ayyām*) and their narrative reports (*akhbār*). The correct method in this approach is that aphoristic verses – verses that contain wisdom, the divine unicity and religion (*al-ashʿār al-ḥikmiyya allatī ḍammat al-ḥikma wa-l-tawḥīd wa-l-dīn*), and urge the cultivation of knowledge, austerity (*zuhd*), courage, generosity and fine moral dispositions – should be recited and taught to him, and he should commit them to memory; to the exclusion of verses that contain mention of fornication, intercourse, passionate love (*ʿishq*)[62] and indecency (*fuḥsh*), and of satirical poems (*ahājī*) that include false accusation of marriageable women (*qadhf al-muḥṣanāt*) and the mention of people's womenfolk (*ʿawrāt*). The purpose of this practice is that he should grow up in knowledge of the virtues, with a love for the acquisition of praiseworthy qualities, and that he should become accustomed to them. At the same time the technique combines for him the benefit(s) of eloquence (*faṣāḥa*) and clarity (*bayān*), knowledge of the commonplace in speech and much of the unusual (*gharīb*) as well, and an understanding of the virtuous meanings.[63]

Pseudo-Māwardī emphasises poetry's double instructional importance. Committing poetry to memory rooted it in the young person's mind, where it would accumulate into a repertoire of reflections and reminders on which he could draw throughout his life. It also provided him with models of clarity of expression and literary skill. The poetry that the prince committed to memory should be of an edificatory nature, so that it would furnish him with admirably formed expressions of virtue that would guide his conduct in the future. By implication, Pseudo-Māwardī discourages the teaching of the *khamriyya* ('wine ode'), love poetry and *hijā*ʾ (satire), and encourages the genres known as *ḥikma* and *zuhdiyyāt* (verses devoted to wisdom and austerity).[64] Miskawayh would similarly encourage children's memorising of reports and poems of an edificatory rather than a frivolous character, and would denigrate poetry related to passionate love (*ᶜishq*) 'and those who pursue it'; and his successor Naṣīr al-Dīn Ṭūsī would explicitly discourage children's exposure to the poetry of Imruʾ l-Qays and Abū Nuwās, whose verses in other genres Pseudo-Māwardī cites readily on several occasions.[65]

Pseudo-Māwardī continues with a detailed curriculum for the young prince:

> Among the narrative reports (*akhbār*) that he should commit to memory are the biographical reports concerning the Prophet and the transmitted accounts concerning the caliphs (*akhbār al-maghāzī wa-l-siyar wa-āthār al-khulafā*ʾ), rather than the accounts (*āthār*) of lovers and books of stories (*kutub al-afsānaqāt*), such as the 'Book of Sindbād' (*Kitāb Sindbād*), the 'Thousand Stories' (*Hazār afsān*) and similar collections. For he will find amusement in these books, and he will become distracted by them more than he will derive benefit from them. By means of the former recommended materials he will reach the level of the ᶜulamāʾ, rise to the position of the jurists in his religion, take precedence among the people of his kingdom and his religious community, and excel in his governance; whereas through the latter kind of books he will acquire very little of this kind of knowledge. Furthermore, he might imagine that the stories in those books are true and suppose them to be real (*laᶜallahu an yataṣawwara mā fī tilka l-kutub min al-afsānaqāt ṣidqan wa-yaẓunnahu ḥaqqan*). That would constitute foolishness and ignorance on his part, and he would proceed in ignorance of the principles of his religion,

> and heedless of the virtues and fine qualities of his religious community. Those books and fireside tales (*asmār*) will not benefit him in his governance and his exercise of authority (*fī siyāsatihi wa-ḥukūmatihi*), and he will find they provide him with no help for conducting debates in his religion (*ᶜalā munāẓarātihi fī dīnihi*), or for his disquisitions in his assemblies ([*ᶜalā*] . . . *mubāhātihi fī maḥāfilihi*) or for his enquiry into the grievances of his subjects ([*ᶜalā*] . . . *naẓarihi fī maẓālim raᶜiyyatihi*).
>
> Concerning the meaning of God's words: 'And among the people is a person who buys the diversion of talk in order to mislead from the path of God without knowledge' (31: 6), an exegete (*baᶜḍ ahl al-tafsīr*) said that the purport of this verse was that [the merchant, a contemporary of the Prophet] (al-Naḍr b.) al-Ḥārith b. Kalada [d. *c.* 2/624] purchased the book *Kalīla wa-Dimna*. He used to gather the people and read it to them, and to claim that it was more delightful and finer (*aladhdh wa-aḥsan*) than the ancient stories (*asāṭīr al-awwalīn*) that Muḥammad had brought. So God, glorious and exalted, sent down this verse in refutation of him.[66] The Prophet said, concerning the transmission of poetry, 'There is wisdom (*ḥikma*) to be derived from poetry',[67] and 'There is magic in clarity of expression (*bayān*)'.[68] He also said, 'Poetry is the *dīwān* (register) of the Arabs', and he said, 'In poetry there are wise sayings.'[69]
>
> They have reported that [the Umayyad caliph] ᶜAbd al-Malik b. Marwān said to his sons' tutor, 'Show them poetry so that they will become generous and glorious.'[70] It is also related that he said, 'I am astonished at the person who relates forty verses of ᶜAntara [the valiant sixth-century poet-hero]; how is it that he is not among the bravest of people? I am similarly astonished at the person who recites forty verses of Ḥātim al-Ṭāʾī [sixth-century poet and paragon of generosity] and yet is not among the most generous of people, or forty verses from Labīd [sixth-century poet who died a Muslim in 40/660–1, renowned for the wisdom of his verses] and yet is not among the wisest of people.'[71]

In this example of Pseudo-Māwardī's constructive references to Umayyad figures, he cites ᶜAbd al-Malik, father of four future caliphs, in order to promote a curriculum designed to serve the dual functions of linguistic instruction and character formation. Literature that was primarily entertaining, that, by its fictional nature, 'distracted' its audience from actuality failed to assist, and potentially impeded, the prince's preparation for addressing the responsibilities of governance, including the convening of theological debates, courtly gatherings and sessions for the redress of grievances. It is instructive to compare the similar but more detailed curriculum recommended in Abū Zayd al-Balkhī's student Ibn Farīghūn's *Jawāmiᶜ al-ᶜulūm* ('Compendium of the Sciences'), an encyclopaedic work designed principally for the use of secretaries. Ibn Farīghūn added to the subjects enumerated in *Naṣīḥat al-mulūk* the 'books and biographical accounts of the Persians, such as the "Testament" of Ardashīr Bābakān, the orations (*khuṭab*) of Anūshīrvān, and the record of the *Kārnāmeh* (probably *Kārnāmak i Artaxšēr i Pāpakān*, "Book of Deeds of Ardashīr Son of Bābak"), which can be used in matters of governance and political affairs and in holding *maẓālim* (courts of redress) for the subjects.'[72] These texts, as has been observed, feature prominently in *Naṣīḥat al-mulūk*.

Pseudo-Māwardī continues his treatment of the prince's instruction with a brief summary, to be expounded later, of his physical education:

> The sons of kings have no choice but to practise swordsmanship (*thaqāfa*), archery, the throwing of the javelin, horsemanship, running and racing, until, when the prince reaches the requisite maturity, he should begin his instruction in knowledge and understanding in religion according to the order that we have mentioned.[73]

At this point, Pseudo-Māwardī addresses the choice of an excellent teacher for the prince:

> It is necessary that the king exert himself in choosing the prince's teacher and instructor with the same degree of effort that he applied to the selection of the mother and the wet-nurse; or rather an even greater degree, since the child adopts more of his moral dispositions (*akhlāq*), (positive) traits of character (*shamāʾil*), manners (*ādāb*) and habits (*ᶜādāt*) from his teacher than from his father, because he spends more time in his sessions with him and studies for longer periods of time with him. Moreover, when he is delivered to his teacher, the child is ordered to follow his example completely and to observe his commands utterly. In these circumstances the king should not

be content simply for the instructor and teacher to be capable of reciting the Qurʾān, memorising the language or transmitting poetry (*an yakūna qāriʾan lil-Qurʾān wa-ḥāfiẓan lil-lugha wa-rāwiyan lil-shiʿr*). In addition he should be godly (*taqīy*), scrupulous (*wariʿ*), modest, religiously observant, virtuous in his dispositions, self-controlled (*adīb al-nafs*) and pure of heart (*naqī l-jayb*); he should be knowledgeable of the dispositions (*akhlāq*) and customs (*ādāb*) of kings, cognisant of all the principles of religion and jurisprudence (*fiqh*), fully versed in that which, as we have mentioned, he needs to teach, according to the proper order. If anything of that which we have mentioned eludes him, godliness (*tuqan*), religion and religious understanding (*fiqh*) should not elude him, for these qualities, as we have explained in the preceding chapter, govern every aspect of behaviour (*adab*). Were the boy (*ghulām*) to grow up devoid of the *ādāb* of kings but instructed in these qualities, it would be easier for him to acquire knowledge of kings' *ādāb*, learn their dispositions, and accustom himself to their habits (*ʿādāt*) than to eliminate his bad habits, acquired in opposition to these qualities.

It is necessary that the prince be forbidden in the strictest terms and prevented by the strongest measures from falling into doubt (*rayb*), and from associating with persons given to doubt, such as jesters, mockers and youths lacking in good breeding (*adab*). In addition, no person should utter abuse in front of him, in his assembly or in his presence (*fī majlisihi wa-bi-ḥaḍratihi*), nor speak in obscenity, falsehood, indecency or slander. Anyone who does anything of that sort should be disciplined and punished for it, so that he will draw a lesson from it and be restrained from it.[74]

Pseudo-Māwardī emphasises the acquisition of habits, and the shaping role that the teacher, and other persons in the young person's environment, play in his formation. Accordingly, he impresses upon the king the necessity to ensure that his children are surrounded by persons who observe high standards of virtue in their speech and in their behaviour. In a resumption of his previous chapter, Pseudo-Māwardī stipulates that whatever competencies the teacher might lack, it is imperative that he should possess the virtue of *taqwā* (here, *tuqan*), which, with religion and religious understanding, provide the ground for all the other components of virtuous conduct. His insistence that the prince avoid associating with persons given to scepticism (*rayb*) perhaps echoes his concern that the king should strive for certainty in religious matters and act in accordance with his firm conviction.[75]

Pseudo-Māwardī then resumes the topic of the prince's physical training:

> Next, he should not succumb to every temptation nor indulge in every comfort, lest his joints slacken and his stamina weakens. Instead, he should strengthen and toughen his limbs, and he should be instructed to expose his hands and face. When told to compete in running and racing, he should be left alone (to practise) time after time. He should strike with the polo stick on foot and on horseback if he lacks strength, for such activities will lighten his body, make it sounder, and stimulate his body's innate heat, which will consume the moisture (*fa-inna dhālika mimmā yukhaffifu badanahu wa-yuṣaḥḥiḥuhu wa-yuhīju fī jismihi al-ḥarāra al-gharīziyya allatī tudhību l-ruṭūba*), extinguish many of the causes of chronic illness (*al-ᶜilal al-zamāniyya*), and protect him from the habit of weakness and lassitude (*wa-yadfaᶜu ᶜanhu ᶜādat al-ᶜujz wa-l-daᶜa*).[76]

Consistent with late antique treatments of education, Pseudo-Māwardī prescribes an intensive physical programme. His treatment of the topic coincides with the philosophical–medical teachings associated with al-Kaᶜbī, who discussed the human body's generation of heat, and ascribed the body's physical weight, reduced through its natural heat, to moisture.[77] Also notable is Pseudo-Māwardī's inclusion of polo (*ṣawlajān*)[78] among the activities that the young members of the *khāṣṣa* should be encouraged to pursue. The game, likely to have originated in the eastern regions under the Parthians, became under the Sasanians a part of the appropriate training for young princes, a purpose to which the Middle Persian romance *Kārnāmag ī Ardashīr*, recommended in Ibn Farīghūn's *Jawāmiᶜ al-ᶜulūm*, testifies.[79] Al-Taghlibī's *Kitāb al-Tāj* addresses the etiquette of playing polo with the king,[80] and the game is attested for the Saffarids, Samanids and Ghaznavids.[81] Abū Manṣūr al-Thaᶜālibī records the Bukharan poet Abū l-Ḥusayn Muḥammad b. Muḥammad al-Murādī's verses on the occasion of a sudden downpour that interrupted Naṣr b. Aḥmad's game of polo,[82] as well as a detailed narrative involving games of polo at the court of Manṣūr b. Nūḥ (r. 350–65/961–76).[83] Although some later Iranian writers would regard polo as a futile and possibly reprehensible game and form of entertainment, an example of the *la*ʿ*b wa-lahw* against which Pseudo-Māwardī elsewhere cautions the king, he evidently did not, in keeping with his regional culture, regard it in this light.[84] In Pseudo-Māwardī's milieu, polo featured among the expected pursuits of kings, but was not limited to princes: Abū Zayd al-Balkhī composed a *Kitāb Ṣawlajān al-kataba* ('Polo for Secretaries').[85] Towards the end of the following century, Kaykāʾūs, the Ziyarid ruler in the Caspian provinces and author of the Persian *Qābūsnāmeh*, would caution his son against excessive indulgence in polo, largely on account of its physical dangers; he advises his son to limit his participation in the game to twice a year.[86]

Pseudo-Māwardī continues with the prince's learning of appropriate manners:

> He should also be educated in his manner of sitting, riding, dressing, and composure, and trained with the disciplines that we have mentioned in the chapter on the governance of the self. This path should be recommended to him and he should be ordered to pursue it . . . It used to be said, 'He who instructs his son in a fine custom confounds his enemy.'[87]

> One of the sages said to his children, 'O my sons, pursue instruction so that if you become kings you shall excel, if you become middling in status you shall lead the people, and if you become poor you shall live by the excellence of your conduct' . . .[88]

> How well the author of *Kalīla wa-Dimna* (*ṣāḥib Kalīla wa-Dimna*) spoke when he began his book with the words, 'The best of provisions for the young is a good education (*al-adab al-ṣāliḥ*), gained in youth while the memory is attentive and the heart is free of care; that which is acquired in childhood endures like an engraving on stone' . . .[89]

> In a Persian book,[90] we have found this saying: 'From a fine education an effective intellect is acquired, and from an effective intellect good habits, from good habits a praiseworthy nature, from a praiseworthy nature good conduct, from good conduct the satisfaction of the Lord, and from the Lord's satisfaction lasting sovereignty.' The Persians also said, 'From a bad education a corrupt intellect is attained, and from corruption of intellect bad habits, from bad habits a vile nature, from a vile nature bad conduct, from bad conduct a bad reputation and the wrath of God, and from the

> wrath of God and His displeasure, everlasting humiliation.' They have said, 'Education is the adornment of the noble and a sign of their nobility; for those without nobility it is an instrument and a tool for the discharge of tasks; and it is a support for kings, who cannot dispense with it.' ᶜAbdallāh b. al-Muᶜtazz said, 'Education is the adornment of your intellect, so adorn your intellect as much as possible.'[91]

Pseudo-Māwardī's presentation of the upbringing and education of princes anticipates the treatment of these subjects in several later works of Persian literature. Several elements in *Naṣīḥat al-mulūk* recur in the eleventh-century *Qābūsnāmeh*. Kaykāᵓūs opens his chapter devoted to the upbringing of children (*dar ḥaqq-i farzand va-ḥaqq-shinākhtan*, 'on the rights of children and the fulfilment of these rights') with an emphasis on the importance of the choice of a pleasing name (*nām-i khush*), which he describes as 'one of the duties of fathers to their children' (*az jumleh-yi ḥaqq-hā-yi pedarān bar farzandān*).[92] The father should entrust his children to intelligent and affectionate nurses, observe the rites of circumcision, and instruct his son to memorise the Qurᵓān. As the child grows older, if the father belongs to the bearers of weapons (*ahl-i silāḥ*), he should instruct him in the arts of horsemanship and weaponry; if he is a member of the subject population (*raᶜiyyat*), he should instruct him in a trade (*pīsheh*). This last point represents a departure from Pseudo-Māwardī's *Naṣīḥat al-mulūk*, for, although the latter author does not assume that the sons of kings will, or necessarily should, succeed their fathers, he does not detail their instruction in a craft. Sebüktigin, military commander and father of the Ghaznavid Sultan Maḥmūd, acknowledges the possibility that his son might, or might not, become an amir when he qualifies his advice with the clause, 'Perhaps one day God Almighty will make you an amir, as He did me' (*agar tu-rā khudāy taᶜālā hamchūn man amīrī rūzī gardānad*).[93] Pseudo-Māwardī's treatment in Arabic of the nurturing, upbringing and education of princes draws on centuries of regional cultural traditions, and is also likely to have transmitted them.

Composition of the *Khāṣṣa*

After this full discussion of the upbringing and education of princes, Pseudo-Māwardī turns to the other categories that he has distinguished within the *khāṣṣa*. His treatment follows his initial listing of five groups, addressed in order of their proximity to the ruler. He begins with the first and closest group, members of the extended dynastic family:

> As for the group of his relatives and close family members, God glorious and exalted, in more than one place in His Book, has commanded giving them gifts, drawing them close (*taqrīb*) and extending kindness and favour to them . . . Even if the people (*qawm*) are dissolute (*fujjār*), it is incumbent on every Muslim to nurture his relationships with his family members and relatives with joy, drawing them close, showing them goodness, making them welcome, offering care and aid (*bi-l-bishr wa-l-taqrīb wa-l-birr wa-l-tarḥīb wa-l-muʾāsāt wa-l-muʿāwana*). As for kings, they especially should follow this virtue and adopt this noble characteristic. The virtuous and intelligent among them have never ceased to command it, practise it, commend it and praise it, and to count it a generous trait, a source of glory, an occasion for pride and remembrance, a cause for boasting in the face of ill-intentioned persons and a source of support in the face of opponents . . .[94]

Pseudo-Māwardī instructs the king that familial bonds outweigh other differentiating factors among individuals, even in cases of *fujūr*, dissolute behaviour; the point perhaps reflects the Muʿtazilite view of the 'intermediate stance' of the sinner.[95] It is highly probable that for Pseudo-Māwardī, like many of his contemporaries, ties of familial relationship also overrode confessional identities. In his edificatory work of some decades later, Abū l-Layth al-Samarqandī would include reports in which the Muslim and the *kāfir* are equal in certain situations, among them if they are relatives;[96] and that there is no objection to giving gifts and honouring relatives among the protected non-Muslim population of *ahl al-dhimma*.[97] The statement suggests not only the continuing presence of non-Muslim populations later in the tenth century, but also a significant degree of contact among members of different confessional groups.

Next, Pseudo-Māwardī turns to the second group among the *khāṣṣa*, the ruler's *khadam* and *ḥasham*:

> As for the needs of the *khadam* and the retinue (*ḥasham*): there must be in the palace instructors and teachers who will teach the *ghilmān*, *khadam*,

> *fityān* and *ḥasham* as much of the Qur'ān and the religion as each person's condition can bear; remind them time after time of God; inform them of the principles of the religion, the religious laws (*sharā'iᶜ*), and the performance of the prayers with complete ritual purity (*ṭuhūr*), bowing (*rukūᶜ*) and prostration (*sujūd*); explicate to them the religion's supererogatory acts (*nawāfil*) and its branches; teach them fine moral dispositions and praiseworthy acts; admonish them, remind them and instil in them fear of the Fire (of Hell); call them to Paradise and the Abode of Permanence; and urge them to *jihād*. The instructor should restrain them from corruption and bad habits, and from committing the major sins (*kabā'ir*) that God has forbidden, such as fornication and false accusation. If one of them commits a sin (*dhanb*) out of inadvertence and negligence, then the way to proceed is to turn aside and feign inattention. If one of them commits a minor sin (*ṣaghīra*) that does not incur one of the statutory penalties, or bring about corruption against the kingdom and the religion, then the appropriate response is exhortation, reproach, arousing distaste for it and deterrence. If the individual repents of the misdemeanour, abandons it and turns remorsefully to God, then he should receive pardon and forgiveness for it. If on the other hand he returns to it, then he merits punishment (*ᶜuqūba*) and chastisement (*tankīl*), according to his obstinacy and persistence, and in proportion to the degree of the crime and sin.
>
> If the king is a person who is especially mindful of religion, then it is necessary in his governance that there should be with him, at his court and in his palace (*bi-ḥaḍratihi wa-fī dārihi*) someone who asserts the doctrine of the divine unicity (*min ahl al-tawḥīd*) and possesses religious understanding (*al-fiqh fī l-dīn*) who will teach the *ghilmān* the roots of theology and acquaint them with its general principles, and increase the level of his teaching for anyone in whose nature (*ṭabᶜ*) he perceives a capacity to accept such increase, and from whom he expects aptitude for learning.[98]

The implied context for this passage is the Samanids' practice of acquiring and training large numbers of *ghilmān*, most of whom were Turkic in background, although Pseudo-Māwardī makes no mention of their ethnicities or native languages. Pseudo-Māwardī enumerates four categories, *ghilmān*, *khadam*, *fityān* and *ḥasham*; it is difficult to assess the degree of precision with which he distinguished among these groups, which he appears to have listed in this fashion partly for considerations of rhyme. The context nevertheless indicates that these persons were new Muslims, and Pseudo-Māwardī advises the ruler regarding their optimal integration into an Islamic cultural sphere. *Ghilmān* might fulfil a variety of functions in the palace or in the royal armies; the author's diversified vocabulary is likely to correspond to a diversity of posts and activities, as well as a range of levels of status and prestige. As Pseudo-Māwardī's reference to their preparation for *jihād*, the only specific indication of the goal of their training, suggests, military activities often constituted a significant portion of the *ghilmān*'s responsibilities. As Roy P. Mottahedeh has described, the *ghilmān* acquired by the ruler assumed the position of his foster children, a powerful relationship, as Pseudo-Māwardī's earlier treatment of the wet-nurse and foster-mother already indicated. The relationship of foster-parent and foster-child, frequently termed *iṣṭinā*ᶜ, involved, like *khidma*, a bond of reciprocity. Military *ghilmān* owed their training, equipment and social positions to the ruler, their patron or *ṣāni*ᶜ, to whom they were taught to display obedience and gratitude.[99] In this case, in the light of the fate of Aḥmad II at the hands of his *ghilmān*, apparently guards with access to the ruler's person at all times, it is quite likely that the term carried its earlier Sogdian meaning, and that, following Central Asian custom, some of the *ghilmān* served in the amir's personal bodyguard.[100]

This passage also provides further indications of Pseudo-Māwardī's theological position in the matter of sin. As in previous sections, he distinguishes in this context between major and minor sins.[101] In accordance with Muᶜtazilite doctrine, he held that either kind of sin necessitated repentance and cessation.[102] His reference to *ahl al-tawḥīd* may, indeed, simply refer to the Muᶜtazila, and Pseudo-Māwardī is perhaps advocating the retention of a Muᶜtazilite theologian at the court. In terms of the appropriate royal response, however, he strongly encourages the disregard of accidental errors and misdemeanours, and the gentle correction of minor infractions. He conveys an awareness of the dislocation suffered by the new members of the royal household, and encourages patience and forbearance, as well as persistence, in facilitating their acculturation and integration. The description of the training of the slaves at the court anticipates the celebrated and detailed account of Niẓām al-Mulk, who also counselled a generous attitude of tolerance and readiness to pardon minor and inadvertent indiscretions.[103]

In another indication of his Muᶜtazilite perspective, Pseudo-Māwardī includes the *nawāfil*, supererogatory acts, in the instruction of the *ghilmān*, and it is possible that in his view they, in addition to the prescribed acts of obedience (*al-ṭāᶜāt al-farāʾiḍ*), comprised faith (*īmān*). The Muᶜtazilite theologians Abū l-Hudhayl and ᶜAbd al-Jabbār subscribed to this doctrine.[104] The passage also provides another suggestion of Pseudo-Māwardī's interest in the idea of 'natures'; in this instance, he asserts that each individual possessed a distinct 'nature' that was amenable in varying degrees to the shaping role of education.

Principles of Governance

In the remainder of his chapter, Pseudo-Māwardī enumerates ten qualities or principles that the king should apply in his dealings with the categories that comprise the *khāṣṣa*:

> It is necessary, in his formation (*taqwīm*) of the entirety of the *khāṣṣa*, that he avail himself of ten principles:
>
> Firstly, he should proclaim to them all – the *khāṣṣ* and the *ᶜāmm*, the far and the near among them (*aqṣāhum wa-adnāhum*) – that he expects each one of them to adopt these enumerated qualities that we have mentioned, to the extent of the capacity of each one among them, and that he holds himself to the same expectation.[105]
>
> Secondly, he should bestow on them their allowances (*arzāq*), stipends (*jirāyāt*), salaries (*waẓāʾif*) and gifts (*ᶜaṭiyyāt*) so that they are not late and past their proper times. He should give generously to them so that they will be relieved of the temptation to injustice towards the subjects and the coveting of their wealth. The king must ensure that the *khāṣṣa* are sufficiently supplied in terms of their most important needs, such as their riding animals, their horses, their servants, their weapons and their mounts.[106] It is essential that the assessment (*taqdīr*) of their needs in these matters should be of a good standard, evenly placed (*mutawassiṭ*) between excess (*isrāf*) and deficiency (*taqtīr*), for in such moderation lie several aspects of

> well-being (*ṣalāḥ*) and good (*khayr*) that will repay the king's attention by bringing order to the conditions of the kingdom and ease for the ruler and the ruled (*al-rāᶜī wa-l-raᶜiyya*).[107]

Pseudo-Māwardī's first principle establishes the same standards of behaviour for the king and for all members of his *khāṣṣa*, in accordance with their capacity. (In accordance with Pseudo-Māwardī's frequently evoked Muᶜtazilite doctrine, human beings cannot be held responsible for actions that lie beyond their capacity.) In asserting the king's adoption of the same standards that he requires from his *khāṣṣa*, Pseudo-Māwardī alludes to the power of the king's example to compel the good behaviour of his subjects and thereby to effect the betterment of his kingdom.

Pseudo-Māwardī's second principle asserts the king's commitment to abide by his obligations towards his *khāṣṣa* by prompt and ample payment and recompense. Contemporary observers and later writers reported that the Samanids acquitted themselves unusually well in this regard. Ibn Ḥawqal, writing a few decades later than Pseudo-Māwardī but incorporating much of al-Iṣṭakhrī's earlier account, commented on the generosity of the Samanids' stipends, despite the paucity of their tax revenues. At the time of his visit (during the reign of Manṣūr b. Nūḥ), he observed that the amir dispensed an allowance (*ṭamaᶜ*, pl. *aṭmāᶜ*) first to his *ghilmān*, his *khāṣṣa* and his senior commanders (*quwwād*), and then to the remainder of his administrators (*sāʾir al-mutaṣarrifīn*). He also observes, with admiration, that several of the Samanids' appointed officials received equal allowances (*rizq al-qāḍī ka-rizq ṣāḥib al-barīd wa-l-ᶜāmil ᶜalā jibāyat al-amwāl min al-banādira wa-wālī al-maᶜūna*, 'the judge's allowance is the same as that of the officer of the intelligence department, the official responsible for the collection of taxes and the chief of security').[108] According to al-Khwārazmī, *arzāq*, the first term used in Pseudo-Māwardī's list of types of compensation, denoted the type of pay-allowances issued by the Dīwān (Persian Dīvān) of Khurasan, namely, the Samanids, whereas the Dīwān of Iraq, namely, the Buyids, issued pay-allowances termed *razaqāt*.

Conspicuously absent from Pseudo-Māwardī's account is the term *iqṭāʾ*, which denoted an administrative grant of land or fiscal entitlement over the revenues of parcels of land; the term, in this sense, was already widely used in western Iran and Iraq during the Buyid period. *Iqṭāᶜ* is treated in some detail, however, in the *Mafātīḥ al-ᶜulūm* of al-Khwārazmī, who wrote shortly after 367/977; by that date, it would seem that this system of land-holding had appeared in eastern Iran as well.[109] The *Pandnāmeh* attributed to Sebüktigin suggests that the institution was established at the time of the composition of that text,[110] and Niẓām al-Mulk, who lamented its detrimental effects, remembered the time of the 'former kings', by whom he referred to the Samanids and Ghaznavids, who had compensated their officials by means of direct payments in cash (*bīstgānī*), rather than by means of *iqṭāᶜāt.*[111] Pseudo-Māwardī's reference to various kinds of direct payments is consistent with the evidence of these near-contemporary accounts, which suggest that *iqṭāᶜ* became established only later in the tenth century. His emphasis on the timely payment of officials' allowances and wages, in the interests of ensuring their continued loyalty and preventing them from exploiting the subject population, suggests that the kind of abuses that would so concern Niẓām al-Mulk were already widespread and not unique to the institution of *iqṭāᶜ*.

Pseudo-Māwardī's third principle for the governance of the *khāṣṣa* concerns their status and advancement:

> Thirdly, he should not advance any member of his *khāṣṣa* by a leap, nor elevate a base person (*waḍīᶜ*) among them. He should not delay advancement for anyone, nor demote anyone who possesses worth except according to his merit in terms of his seniority, his personal experience, his competence or his wealth. He should not promote or demote out of inclination or caprice, nor in injustice towards anybody. For if the members of the *khāṣṣa* know that he will reward them according to their merit, they will compete with one another to gain greater proximity to the king, vie with one another in quickness to obedience (*idhā ᶜarafū dhālika tanāfasū fī abwāb al-qurba wa-tashāḥḥū ᶜalā ḥusn al-ṭāᶜa*), and hasten to display their experience and competence. If they are intelligent, the experienced person will not demand a greater increase (*ziyāda*) than that which is proportionate to his experience, and the person who falls short will not covet that which is not due to him. Everyone will be satisfied with his treatment by the king, and content with his position.[112]

The importance of advancing persons only according to observable merit, and not on the basis of personal inclination or affection, anticipates Niẓām al-Mulk's lament that in his age men devoid of merit or of noble birth had assumed positions for which they were neither qualified or deserving.[113] The *Pandnāmeh* of Sebüktigin also urges the ruler to clarify each person's work, since God has particularised each person in his attributes (*ṣifātī*) and distinctive qualities (*khāṣṣiyatī*). The ruler should recognise the status (*martabeh*) of each person, since the vizierate would not be fitting for a groom (*sutūrdān*), even if the latter possessed the necessary tools and equipment (*ālat va-ᶜuddat*). The king should never fall short in this matter and should never assign one man's work to another; if the appropriate individual is unavailable, he should seek the services of another person of his family (*az ahl va-bayt-i ū*).[114] Pseudo-Māwardī recommends that the king should advance and demote individuals in a predictable manner, in accordance with their stations and with their demonstrated talent; he should resist the urge to act impetuously or out of partiality. This advice suggests Pseudo-Māwardī's awareness of the fragile equilibrium between the king and his *khadam*, and seems intended to avert the sense of grievance that might, as the examples of Ḥusayn b. ᶜAlī and Aḥmad b. Sahl demonstrated, incline the *khadam*, and perhaps individuals at lower levels among the *khāṣṣa*, to rebel. Consistent with this interpretation, Pseudo-Māwardī's evocation of the concept of 'increase' (*ziyāda*) alludes to the escalating expectations characteristic of relationships of *khidma*, and his recommendation suggests a strategy for containing and managing this phenomenon.[115]

Pseudo-Māwardī's fourth and fifth principles aim to prevent the *khāṣṣa* from committing acts of injustice and address the proper manner of dealing with their transgressions:

> Fourthly, he should not permit any of them to commit any kind of injustice (*ẓulm*), great or small, towards the subjects. The king should instruct them of his judgement in this regard in writing, orally and in practice (*kitāban wa-shifāhan wa-istiᶜmālan*). He should inform them that there is no difference between them and the rest of the subjects in terms of God's ordinances and judgements (*aḥkām Allāh wa-qaḍāyāhu*), and that this matter is a divinely ordained precept (*farḍ min Allāh*) and accordingly cannot be modified or changed. Religion requires the dispensing of equity (*naṣafa*) and justice (*maᶜdala*), and equal treatment (*taswiya*) among the

> noble and the base and the far and the near, in order to restrain them from injustice and maltreatment towards the subjects. Injustice to the subjects incurs punishment in this world and the next, as well as a bad reputation, the sowing of enmity and hatred in their hearts, the ruination of the kingdom, the flight of its people, the stimulation of the enemy's covetousness for it, and much arbitrariness (*istibdād kathīr*) on the part of the *khāṣṣa* in the kingdom and in the province(s) (*al-mamlaka wa-l-wilāya*). These conditions entail the demise of (royal) awe (*mahāba*) and the scattering of (the subjects') allegiances (*tafarruq al-kalima*). In addition, if that custom (of injustice) becomes current among the king's *khadam*, it is extremely difficult to eliminate it among them, other than by creating degrees and ranks (*illā bi-tadrīj wa-tartīb*), extreme care (*ᶜināya shadīda*), much kindness (*rifq kathīr*) and the replacement (*istibdāl*) of a number of them with other people, and these measures involve grave danger.[116]
>
> Fifthly, he should practise forgiveness among them for minor transgressions (*ṣaghāʾir dhunūbihim*) and for crimes that occur out of inadvertency, negligence and error. He should not blame them for every slip, punish every mistake or vent his anger on every occasion. For such clemency is more likely to advance noble behaviour; it is more appropriate for persons of high status and power, more effective in perpetuating kindness and beneficence (*abqā lil-iḥsān wa-l-ṣanīᶜa*), more likely to promote love (*maḥabba*), banish disaffection and hatred, and further the conciliation of persons of esteem (*istiᶜṭāf dhī l-ḥurma*). The most deserving of persons among whom the king should apply this principle are his *khadam*, by whom he attacks his enemies, by whom he is connected to the well-being (*ṣalāḥ*) of the subjects and the prosperity of his kingdom, and to whom he entrusts his lifeblood.[117]

Pseudo-Māwardī's fourth principle continues his advocacy of equal and predictable treatment for the king's *khāṣṣa*, who are less likely to act in an opportunistic manner or to rebel against the king's authority if he appears to act in a fair and consistent manner. In a contemporaneous example, he had praised Amir Aḥmad II for his impartial administration of justice among the near and the far, the noble and the base, that is, among the entirety of the subjects.[118] His fifth principle indicates the distinct position and prestige of the *khadam* among the various constituent groupings of the king's *khāṣṣa*. Pseudo-Māwardī impresses on his royal audience the need to treat the *khadam* in particular with lenience and clemency in order to encourage their affection and loyalty. The urging of clemency, and especially the overlooking of minor infractions, also features prominently in al-Taghlibī's *Kitāb al-Tāj*.[119] Pseudo-Māwardī, however, addresses the theme at greater length and in specific terms. Indeed, he introduces a further inventory of six features pertinent to his larger principle of overlooking minor faults:

> Firstly: he should investigate the path (*madhhab*) of the *khāṣṣa*, as well as the sins and acts of disobedience that they are committing, and observe them closely until he knows the situation;
>
> Secondly, he should overlook that which it is permissible to overlook, and act as if he does not know;
>
> Thirdly, he should restrict punishment to the least that will suffice for the infraction, and perform it by way of deterrence and correction;
>
> Fourthly, he should incline towards pardon rather than punishment, as long as the infraction does not reach the level of a major sin (*kabīra*) in religion or a cause of corruption in the dominion (*fasād fī l-mulk*);[120]
>
> Fifthly, he should proceed slowly in meting out punishment and postpone it, as long as to do so does not amount to neglect or cause loss, or result in rewarding or excusing the offender. He should follow this course of action in order to allow a sinner or a criminal to repent, a suspect to adduce a proof or an innocent person to come forward with a pretext;
>
> Sixthly, he should not succumb to partiality if the case concerns one of God's statutory limits (*ḥudūd Allāh*): if a perpetrator commits an act that incurs a statutory penalty, and if a person acts in such a way that necessitates that he be punished for his action, the king must execute the penalty against him.[121]

In these six subsections of his treatment of royal clemency, Pseudo-Māwardī advocates a minimalist, moderate and systematic approach in dealing with the transgressions of the *khāṣṣa*. First, the king should attain accurate knowledge of the infraction; the advice that the king should investigate the 'path' or *madhhab* of the *khāṣṣa* is likely to refer in a general manner to their patterns of behaviour. After he has ascertained the details of the situation, the king should react in as limited a manner as possible by moving through a sequence of possible responses, of which the first option is simply to ignore the misdemeanour. He should make ample allowance for the transgressor's remorse and for extenuating circumstances. Only in cases of transgression of divine statutes, and only if the proof is indubitable, is the king obliged to uphold the rights due to God and, if all the conditions are met, to punish accordingly. Pseudo-Māwardī follows his outline of six procedures with a sequence of Qurʾānic verses that move through the same stages of ascertaining the truth before moving to judgement, forgiveness, the overlooking of minor and unintentional infractions, the postponement of punishment, and only lastly, if the commission of a crime has been manifestly proven, punishment:

> All of these principles derive from God's instructive example (*adab*), by which He has educated (*addaba*) His creation, and from His descriptive qualities (*awṣāf*), by which He has described Himself (*waṣafa bihā nafsahu*). God, great and glorious, says, with regard to the first of these virtues [in reference to the full and accurate record of each person's deeds as they face divine judgement], '[When the two (angels) who keep the account,] one sitting on the right, one on the left, take it down, There is not a word he utters but an observer is ready (to make note of it)' (50: 17–18). [On the Day of Judgement] '[The ledger (of their deeds) would be placed before them. Then you will see the sinners terrified at its contents, and say:] "Alas, what a written revelation this, which has not left unaccounted the smallest or the greatest thing!"' (18: 49).[122] He has said to His Prophet, 'Adopt forgiveness, enjoin kindness and turn away from the ignorant' (7: 199). He said, 'Let them forgive and pardon. Do you not long for God to forgive you? God is forgiving and merciful' (24: 22). On the forgiveness of minor sins and (infractions) that occur unintentionally, He has said, 'If you avoid the major things that are forbidden to you, We shall pardon your bad deeds' (4: 31). He said, 'God will not censure you for unintentional mistakes in your oaths. But He will censure you for that which your hearts have earned' (2: 225). On the postponement of punishment, He has said, 'Were God to censure people for that which they have earned, He would not leave

> a living beast on the face of the earth; but He grants them a reprieve until an appointed term' (35: 45).
>
> The Prophet said, 'Avoid the penalties (*ḥudūd*) in cases of doubt.'[123] God said, 'Known to Him is the treachery of the eye, and what the breasts conceal' (40: 19), and 'Whether you say a thing aloud or inaudibly, He has knowledge of the secret and the hidden' (20: 7). He said, 'No three persons confer secretly but He is the fourth among them, and no five but He is the sixth' (58: 7). On punishment in cases for which the claim has been verified and the wrongful deed manifestly proven, He said, 'But when they roused Our anger We inflicted retributive punishment' (43: 55), and '[And when We destroy a human habitation We send Our command to (warn) its people living a life of ease;] and when they disobey, the sentence against them is justified, and We destroy them utterly' (17: 16).[124]

In his treatment of punishment, Pseudo-Māwardī again urges the king to model his conduct on the divine example. His Qur'ānic passages, some of which allude to the narratives of punishment visited upon individuals and communities who persisted in arrogance and disobedience, emphasise God's forbearance as well as His justice. God judges only in full knowledge of His servants' actions; He fulfils His promise and threat, and rewards forgiveness. In emphasising the need to postpone judgement until all aspects of a case had become clearly established and to punish in a manner proportionate to the offence, Pseudo-Māwardī perhaps had in mind Naṣr's reputation for impetuous and severe punishments;[125] he was probably aware of specific cases of the Amir's ill-treatment. Divine punishment, unlike that of many kings, was neither precipitate nor arbitrary. In addition, Pseudo-Māwardī cites the ḥadīth that called for the suspension of the *ḥudūd* in cases of doubt. The 'doubt canon' had been widely applied in judicial practice for some centuries before its tenth-century establishment as a foundational text in this ḥadīth, which Pseudo-Māwardī cites without qualification.[126] He continues:

> It is incumbent on the virtuous king that he model Himself on God in all of these qualities, and abide by His commands in these characteristics . . . For this procedure tests excuses, severs the ambitions of the *khāṣṣa*, the *ʿāmma* and the *ḥāshiya*, and prevents calamities. The desire to spare (*ibqāʾ*) his

> *khadam* or relatives and partiality for his *khāṣṣa* and kin should not prevent the king from implementing appropriate punishment . . . Rendering judgement in such matters should be in accordance with truth and certainty, not whim (*hawan*) and suppositions (*ẓunūn*).[127]

Although he seeks to avoid the infliction of punishment as far as possible, Pseudo-Māwardī argues that if necessary, it should be administered fairly and without discrimination. Mindful of the dangers of divine punishment and of a poor reputation among his fellow human beings if he acts wrongly with regard to conflict and punishment, Pseudo-Māwardī's moral concerns reflect his alignment with parties that on the one hand sought to limit the severity of punishments and on the other promoted a moral egalitarianism in the enforcement of criminal law.[128] He returns to the enumeration of his sixth point:

> Sixthly, he should not leave them idle and without employment (*farāghan lā shughla lahum*) for long days and successive periods of time, with no activities other than rest, eating, drinking and leisure. He should employ them in an occupation that results in a praiseworthy outcome and returns a useful profit to the kingdom and the religion in some way or another, such as *ghazw*, *jihād*, swordsmanship, racing, archery, tossing and throwing, or performing a service or learning something about appropriate behaviour (*adab*) and goodness (*khayr*). Long repose, ease, leisure and devotion to comfort soften their joints, pamper their bodies, cause them to gain weight, and accustom them to impotence, cowardliness, weakness and laziness. In addition, people have mentioned several kinds of corruption in connection with long inactivity, such as excessive drinking, quarrelsomeness, killing, injury and calumny. It used to be said: It is not fitting for the intelligent person to spend his life engaged in any pursuit apart from these three: enhancing his life in this world, advancing towards the next life, or seeking pleasure of a kind that it is not forbidden. Nevertheless, the resolute philosophers of every sect (*firqa*) have belittled the third kind of activity, and have blamed the person who has made pleasure his greatest concern and most frequent occupation.[129]

Pseudo-Māwardī's sixth principle recalls the 'Testament' of Ardashīr, which relates the incipient demise of polities to leaving the subjects without any recognised occupation or work (*bi-ghayr ashghāl maʿrūfa wa-lā aʿmāl maʿlūma*).[130] Pseudo-Māwardī cautions that idleness causes the troops to lapse in their readiness for battle. The forms of activity that he proposes anticipate some of the materials included in the later *Tanbīh al-ghāfilīn* of Abū l-Layth al-Samarqandī, who includes, after chapters devoted to the excellence of military activities (*faḍl al-ghazw wa-l-jihād*) and of the *murābiṭ* (a person who serves in the military outpost, *ribāṭ*), a chapter devoted to the excellence of throwing and riding (*al-ramy wa-l-rukūb*), followed by the proper conduct of the raid (*adab al-ghazw*).[131] In addition, Pseudo-Māwardī prescribed continued instruction in good behaviour and moral conduct.

According to Pseudo-Māwardī's seventh principle, the king should select and favour certain especially trusted individuals:

> Seventhly, he should distinguish among them individual members (*khawāṣṣ*) specifically for purposes of consultation, and associate with them. They should constitute a link (*wāsiṭa*) between him and them [the *khāṣṣa* as a group]. They should act as 'assistants' (*aʿwān*) to him in relation to the rest of them, and as spies (*ʿuyūn*) against them, in case anyone should seek to initiate an action (*aḥdatha muḥdith*) or plot (*kāda kāʾid*) against him. He should select persons for this purpose only after examination, experience and testing, and after ascertaining the individual's demonstration of sincere counsel (*naṣīḥa*), compassion, temperance, trustworthiness (*amāna*), participation, cooperation, ability to keep secrets, and loyalty to the ruler (*wafāʾ lahu*) and to those associated with him.
>
> Such has been the practice (*sunna*) and custom (*ʿāda*) in every prophetic mission, every religion, kingdom and settlement (*fī kull nubuwwa wa-diyāna wa-mamlaka wa-ʿimāra*), the maintenance of which has needed soldiers and armies (*junūd wa-juyūsh*). None of these collectivities remains firm without the institution of degrees and ranks (*tadrīj wa-tartīb*), and the transferring of individuals from one degree (*daraja*) to the one closest to it. This pattern most resembles God's good practice (*adab*), and is most indicative of following His example in His successive bestowal(s) of protection from sin (*ʿiṣam*) and divinely granted success, His granting of reward and support, and His knowledge of that which benefits and that which does not benefit the individual whom He has elevated and the person who aspires to such elevation.

> God said, at the beginning of this topic, 'God chooses among the angels messengers, and from among humankind' (22: 75), and He said, 'God has taken the covenant of the Children of Israel and We have raised from them twelve chieftains' (5: 12). He said, 'Moses chose of his people seventy men for Our appointed time' (7: 155), and 'O Moses, I have preferred you over humankind by My messages and My speech (to you)' (7: 144).
>
> The Prophet chose a group among his Companions for his vizierate (*wizāra*) and for consultation (*mushāwara*). He chose a small band among his Companions for the Pledge of Good Pleasure [*bayᶜat al-riḍwān*, a pledge of support to the Prophet, taken at al-Ḥudaybiya in 6/628],[132] and a group for his service, a group for leading the army, a number for his messages and correspondence and a group to serve as his deputies over the provinces. He chose for the community's leadership (*imāma*) after him a small group whom he named, saying, 'If you designate Abū Bakr as successor, you will find him strong in his religion, but weak in his body; if you appoint ᶜUmar as successor, you will find him strong in his religion and strong in his body; if you appoint ᶜAlī as successor, you will find him a right guide and rightly guided' (*wajadtumūhu hādiyan mahdiyyan*).[133] At the same time, God gave preference to some of the angels over others. In God, His angels and His messengers are a model and an example.[134]

In this passage, Pseudo-Māwardī returns to the theme of *tafḍīl*, the granting of preference. God not only elevated the angels as a category above the other categories of His creation, but also chose amongst the angels, whom He arranged in a hierarchy.[135] Consistent in his appeal that the monarch model his behaviour on that of God and His Prophet, Pseudo-Māwardī urges the ruler to exercise sound judgement in selecting certain members from among his *khāṣṣa* for his particular trust. He states explicitly that these individuals should function as intermediaries – a link – between him and 'the rest', namely, the remainder of the *khāṣṣa*, and he explains the ruler's need for persons with whom to consult with reference to their role as informants.

Pseudo-Māwardī's inclusion of the ḥadīth regarding the leadership of the community, with its acknowledgement of Abū Bakr and ᶜUmar and its allusion to the special status of ᶜAlī, is consistent with the political outlook reported of al-Kaᶜbī, who, like most of the Baghdadi Muᶜtazila, regarded ᶜAlī as superior to Abū Bakr, but did not reject the legitimacy of the first three caliphs.[136] Although, as seen in Volume I, other aspects of *Naṣīḥat al-mulūk* probably indicate his alignment with *ahl al-sunna wa-l-jamāʾa* rather than with any of the branches of Shiʿism, it is likely that Pseudo-Māwardī shared al-Kaʿbī's pro-ʿAlid sentiment. Al-Kaʿbī was sympathetic to the stance of Zaydī Shiʿism, which did not condemn ʿAlī's predecessors in the caliphal office, and according to which any qualified descendant of ʿAlī through Ḥasan and Ḥusayn might claim the imamate, rather than a single line of designated successors. Al-Kaʿbī regarded Quraysh as holding first claim to legitimate leadership (*imāma*), but also brooked the possibility of investiture of a non-Qurashī if there were fear of imminent civil war (*fitna*).[137]

Having addressed the selection of trustworthy confidants among his *khāṣṣa*, Pseudo-Māwardī, in his eighth point, turns to the king's need for accurate information with regard to the conduct of his troops:

> Eighthly, he should require the disclosure of dissolute behaviour (*fusūq*), the drinking of wines, and the playing of *maysir* (a game of chance) among his troops, so that he can alter (*yughayyir*) any conduct considered reprehensible (*makrūh*) in religion.
>
> God has commanded this practice in more than one place in His Book, and we have cited a number of these verses in the preceding parts of our book. We have related from the Prophet that he said, 'There has been no people (*qawm*) among whom acts of disobedience were performed, and who were capable of changing (*qadarū an yughayyirū*) it but did not change, but that God punished them all.'[138] He also said, 'You are commanded to the good and forbidden from wrong, or God will bestow power over you on the wicked among you, and furthermore when the good among you call upon Him in prayer, there will be no answer for them.'[139] This was after God's words, 'Those amongst the Children of Israel who disbelieved were cursed by the tongue of David, and Jesus, the son of Mary, on account of the fact that they disobeyed and used to transgress. They did not restrain one another from wrong that they did. How wicked is that which they used to do' (5: 78–9).[140]

This passage provides an example of Pseudo-Māwardī's call for the ruler's support for the maintenance of the religious law, a practice for which, as observed in Volume I, he distinguished Ismāʿīl b. Aḥmad.[141] The ḥadīth that Pseudo-Māwardī relates on his own authority in the preceding section implies that failure to intervene in cases of disobedience is detrimental for the entire community. The required intervention is implied in the verb *ghayyara*, to 'change'. In this context, Pseudo-Māwardī probably understood the verb in a more specific sense, to 'put right' or 'rectify', since, as his ensuing examples demonstrate, he associated his advice with one of the five Muʿtazilite principles, the duty of commanding right and forbidding wrong, *al-amr bi-l-maʿrūf wa-l-nahy ʿan al-munkar*.[142] His next ḥadīth expresses an explicit exhortation to perform the duty, presented as a commentary on the Qurʾānic verses 5: 78–9.[143] Pseudo-Māwardī adduces examples of ancient wisdom that support this piece of advice:

> Aristotle wrote to Alexander: 'Rebuke (*ankir*) dissolute behaviour, for its spread causes the community to perish, and it is a characteristic particular to the lowly beasts (*huwa min khawāṣṣ al-dawābb al-daniyya*).' He also said, 'Investigate the appearance of dissolute behaviour and drunkenness among your troops, for these two things are the key to weakness, and in them lies the degradation of strength.'
>
> I say: More than one of the armies of kings has experienced this phenomenon (*hādhā l-maʿnā*) and found the matter to be just as Aristotle said: I mean that the appearance of dissolute behaviour was indeed a sign of the imminence of perdition and the proximity of ruin.[144]

In this last comment, Pseudo-Māwardī gives explicit voice to the role of his region's inherited wisdom, in this case the pseudo-Aristotelian repertoire, in shaping his perception of the conditions of his time. As previous examples have shown, he moves from the timeless and abstract to the immediate and concrete, without, in most cases, identifying in an explicit manner the contemporary application of his point.

Pseudo-Māwardī's ninth and tenth principles urge the king to maintain his contact with the *khāṣṣa*, to allow them to approach him, and to care for them and their families:

> Ninthly, he should treat them gently and at certain times he should lower his wing for them,[145] spread his wing for the far and near among them

and the *khāṣṣ* and the *ᶜāmm*. He should facilitate permission for them to enter his presence, and to express their petitions to him time after time. He should not seclude himself (*iḥtijāb*) from them to the point that it causes their estrangement (*waḥsha*), nor should he keep them waiting for lengths of time that will inevitably occasion their resentment and indicate the king's arrogance (*khuyalāʾ*) and pride (*nakhwa*).[146]

Tenthly, he should pledge himself to the support of their sick, their aged, the orphans of their dead and their heirs in cases of loss. He should replace their riding animals that have perished in his battles, and compensate them for their weapons and horses, and their possessions. If they know that he will attend to their needs and trust him to do so, they will be generous with themselves and that which is theirs. If they are confident of the opposite, they will withhold anything that they acquire and delay in exposing themselves to danger out of compassion for their families and children. This good practice (*adab*) is part of the *adab* of God, great and glorious, and in it is a model that derives from Him. For God has said with regard to this matter . . . 'Surely God does not let the recompense of those who do good go to waste. There is not a sum, large or small, that they spend, not a piece of land that they traverse (in the service of God) which is not put down in their favour, so that God could reward them for what they had done' (9: 120-1).[147]

For everyone who expends funds or strives in the way of God (*yasᶜā fī sabīl Allāh*), whether his effort be small or large, God hastens to bring a reward for him in posterity (*khalaf*), and in praise (*madḥ*), success (*tawfīq*) and grace (*luṭf*); and He grants him an abundant reward in His pardon and mercy. He will be compensated in Paradise, as far as he does nothing to compromise his reward through the commission of unbelief (*kufr*) or a major sin (*kabīra*). The speaker for a delegation to [the Umayyad caliph] Sulaymān b. ᶜAbd al-Malik [r. *c.* 96–9/715–17] said: 'You have caused us to love life and to belittle death, and so we beseech you on behalf of our posterity, those who will succeed us' . . . And on this matter, Aristotle said, 'Distribute wealth according to the needs of those who are in need of assistance (*maᶜūna*)'.[148]

The last pair of Pseudo-Māwardī's ten general principles enjoins kindness and accessibility. The two items reiterate his earlier specification that the ruler's responsibilities extend to the families of his *khāṣṣa*, and assert the king's responsibility for replacing their losses, of human and animal lives and property, in military activities undertaken at the king's behest. Pseudo-Māwardī points out that such treatment benefits the ruler, since it reinforces the loyalty and willingness to cooperate of his *khāṣṣa*, on whom he depends. The passage also recapitulates Pseudo-Māwardī's Muᶜtazilite-inflected sense of divine justice, according to which, in the afterlife, God compensates each individual according to his or her actions in the present life, and this divine compensation, whether in the form of reward or punishment, lasts for eternity. In the course of his mirror, Pseudo-Māwardī refers to heavenly reward (*thawāb*);[149] praise (*madḥ*);[150] divine conferral of success (*tawfīq*), by which God enables and assists the performance of acts of obedience; and divine favour (*luṭf*). This last concept is associated in particular with ᶜAbd al-Jabbār, who, noting that the terms *tawfīq* and *ᶜiṣma* were sometimes employed in the same sense,[151] held that divine favour made it possible for human beings to act well and avoid evil.[152]

Pseudo-Māwardī's recommendation that the king should provide proper compensation not only to the members of his *khāṣṣa*, but also to their family members and dependants, and that he should provide for their needs and make good their losses, concludes his enumeration of ten general principles involved in the governance of the *khāṣṣa*.[153] Throughout his presentation of these principles, Pseudo-Māwardī makes clear in his eclectic illustrations that human wisdom, scriptural and Prophetic texts were in accord: he states a point, then traces its logic with reference to Qurᵓānic texts, Prophetic ḥadīth and examples from the wisdom of the past and historical experience.

Specialised Groupings and Functions

After this summary of ten general principles, Pseudo-Māwardī turns to the practical tasks of governance and the role of the king's *khāṣṣa* in carrying them out:

> The king cannot dispense with a particular group of persons (*al-akhaṣṣ*), and particularly those persons who are most distinguished among his *khadam*

> (*al-akhaṣṣ min khadamihi*) in order to discharge the most important of his affairs, such as collecting the wealth of the kingdom, and disbursement of it among the armies (*juyūsh*) and in accordance with persons' rightful claims (*fī sabīl al-ḥuqūq*).[154]

In a continuation of Pseudo-Māwardī's theme of *tafḍīl*, this passage addresses the ruler's distinction of certain members of his *khāṣṣa* for specific purposes. He introduces the topic of the categories and individuals whom the king appoints directly, and who participate in the maintenance of the kingdom:

> In the maintenance of the kingdom and the great provinces (*fī iqāmat al-mamlaka wa-l-wilāyāt al-ᶜaẓīma*), it is impossible to dispense with viziers, deputies, secretaries, commanders of armies, overseers of military affairs, directors of police, leaders (of communities), officers of the guard, conveyers of information, (fiscal) agents and judges (*lā budda . . . min wuzarāᵓ wa-khulafāᵓ wa-kuttāb wa-aṣḥāb juyūsh wa-ᶜāriḍīn wa-aṣḥāb shuraṭ wa-nuqabāᵓ wa-aṣḥāb ḥaras wa-aṣḥāb akhbār wa-wukalāᵓ wa-quḍāt*).[155]

Pseudo-Māwardī's reference to 'the kingdom' (*al-mamlaka*) and 'the great provinces' (*al-wilāyāt al-ᶜaẓīma*) implies a distinction between the 'kingdom' of the Samanid amirs, with its capital in Bukhara, and the dispersed regions governed by members of the extended Samanid family, as well as members of other dynastic families and established landed families, such as the Āl Muḥtāj or Chaghanids. This inference finds support in a later passage in which Pseudo-Māwardī refers to the 'provinces (*wilāyāt*) over which the ruler appoints individuals',[156] and in his notable use of the plural and indefinite forms for the offices that he proceeds to enumerate. His presentation is consistent with the image of a system replicated across vast expanses of land at differing levels.

For the eleven positions that Pseudo-Māwardī lists as indispensable to the workings of governance, reference to the accounts of Narshakhī and al-Khwārazmī proves instructive.

The historian Narshakhī, a contemporary of Pseudo-Māwardī, enumerated a similar number of administrative offices (*dīvān*s) located in the officials' premises (*sarā-yi ᶜummāl*) that Amīr-i Saᶜīd ('The Fortunate Amir') Naṣr b. Aḥmad had had constructed next to ('at the door of') his own palace on the ancient royal site known as the Rīgistān. The amir had ordered the complex to be built so that 'every official would have a *dīvān*'. Narshakhī's list, at least in the much later extant version of his 'History', consisted of an ordered sequence of the *dīvān-i vazīr* (the vizier's office), the *dīvān-i mustawfī* (the treasurer's office), the *dīvān-i ᶜamīd al-mulk* (the office of correspondence), the *dīvān-i ṣāḥib-shuraṭ* (office of the chief of police), the *dīvān-i ṣāḥib-i muᵓayyid* (unidentified); the *dīvān-i sharaf* (= *ishrāf*)[157] (office of inspection), the *dīvān-i mamlakeh-yi khāṣṣ* (office of the ruler's private lands), the *dīvān-i muḥtasib* (office of the public inspector), the *dīvān-i awqāf* (office of religious endowments) and the *dīvān-i qażāᵓ* (the Persian form of the Arabic *qaḍāᵓ*) (office for the administration of justice).[158]

Al-Khwārazmī, who possessed specialised knowledge of Samanid administrative affairs and procedures, lists the following divisions among the secretarial staff: the *kuttāb dīwān al-kharāj* (secretaries of the department of the land-tax); the *kuttāb dīwān al-khazn* (secretaries of the department of the treasury); the *dīwān al-barīd* (office for the gathering and relaying of information); the *kuttāb dīwān al-jaysh* (secretaries of the department of the army); the *dīwān al-ḍiyāᶜ wa-l-nafaqāt* (department of estates and expenditures); the *dīwān al-māᵓ* (department of irrigation); and the *kuttāb al-rasāᵓil* (secretaries of correspondence).[159]

The collective information supplied by Narshakhī, al-Khwārazmī and Pseudo-Māwardī permits certain brief remarks regarding the categories enumerated in *Naṣīḥat al-mulūk*:

wuzarāᵓ: viziers. Pseudo-Māwardī adopts this term rather than the term *kātib*, scribe or secretary, in use earlier in his lifetime. The premises of the amir's viziers were located in the precincts of the palace.

khulafāᵓ: deputies. The amirs appointed deputies when they were absent from the capital. In the early period, they appear to have chosen members of the dynastic family. Narshakhī reports that Ismāᶜīl, at the beginning of his conflict with Naṣr, left Bukhara for Samarqand, and left as his deputy (*khalīfeh*) in Bukhara his nephew Abū Zakariyyā Yaḥyā b. Aḥmad b. Asad.[160] He reports further that when Naṣr II in [3]13/925 left Bukhara for Nishapur, he appointed Abū l-ᶜAbbās Aḥmad b. Yaḥyā b. Asad Sāmānī in the capital as his deputy.[161] The term *khalīfa* also means 'successor'. When Nūḥ b. Asad died, he appointed his brother Aḥmad b. Asad as his *khalīfeh*, and when Aḥmad died, he made his son Naṣr *khalīfeh*, all of them governing in Samarqand.[161]

kuttāb: secretaries. When the term stands alone, it connotes primarily the secretaries involved in the king's correspondence, al-Khwārazmī's *kuttāb al-rasāʾil*. Later in his chapter, in a manner similar to al-Khwārazmī's acknowledgement of various groupings within the secretarial staff, Pseudo-Māwardī refers to 'the agents and collectors of taxes among the secretaries' (*al-wukalāʾ wa-jubāt al-amwāl min al-kuttāb*).

aṣḥāb juyūsh: the ruler's standing military personnel, including, but probably not restricted to, commanding officers and senior staff.[163]

ʿāriḍūn: officials in charge of military affairs, chiefly the mustering and inspection of troops and the administration of the troops' allowances and salaries. This group corresponds to al-Khwārazmī's *kuttāb dīwān al-jaysh*, secretaries of the department of the army.

aṣḥāb shuraṭ: police commandants. By deed of appointment from the ruler, this group consisted of persons who, in cooperation with specific other men, especially local notables, undertook the responsibility for policing.[164]

nuqabāʾ: probably the *nuqabāʾ al-ashrāf*, the 'marshals of the nobility', namely, the descendants of the Prophet and his family, the *ahl al-bayt*. The *nuqabāʾ al-ashrāf* oversaw genealogical, material and moral matters pertaining to the *ahl al-bayt*; their duties included the proper administration of the *awqāf* established for the *ashrāf*. By the end of the ninth century, all the larger towns had *naqīb*s, who fell under the supervision of a chief *naqīb*, the *naqīb al-nuqabāʾ*.[165]

aṣḥāb ḥaras: officers of the guard, including the ruler's bodyguards. According to C. E. Bosworth, under the Ghaznavids, who probably continued Samanid and Abbasid practice in this regard, the *amīr-i ḥaras* (the corresponding Persian term) or commander of the guard maintained discipline at court and around the precincts of the palace.[166]

aṣḥāb akhbār: 'conveyers of information'. The term refers to the office of the *mukhbir*, 'intelligencer', an agent of the *barīd*, the postal and intelligence service, whose functions and activities perhaps overlapped with Pseudo-Māwardī's *ʿuyūn wa-mushrifūn*, mentioned subsequently.[167]

wukalāʾ: apparently agents involved in the collection of revenue, possibly a specialised grouping within the ranks of the *kuttāb*. Pseudo-Māwardī's list omits the *ᶜummāl*, who are perhaps subsumed within or overlap with this category. The term also perhaps denotes the individuals responsible for the running of the palace.[168] Under the Ghaznavids, the *vakīl-i khāṣṣ*, as he is designated in Persian sources, held the responsibility for the smooth functioning of the palace service and the supplying of its needs in matters pertaining to finance, expenditure and provisioning.[169]

quḍāt: judges, appointed by the king.

Having listed the categories of office holders whom the ruler required for the execution of his governance, Pseudo-Māwardī proceeds to guide the ruler in his appointments to these posts and to detail the qualities required in each group.[170]

The Qualities Required in the Holders of Offices

Pseudo-Māwardī follows his listing of the eleven categories of personnel indispensable to the functioning of the kingdom and great provinces with a presentation of the qualities required in these assistants to and participants in his governance:

> The king should exert himself in choosing the members of these categories among persons of competence (*min ahl al-kufāt*), resourcefulness (*istiqlāl*), perspicacity (*shahāma*), trustworthiness (*amāna*), temperance (*ᶜiffa*), religious observance (*diyāna*), intellect (*ᶜaql*) and nobility of descent (or firmness in judgement, *aṣāla*).[171]
>
> Among these qualities are some that only certain individuals, to the exclusion of others, need to possess. Among the qualities that it is necessary for the entire group to possess are religion, intellect, trustworthiness, competence (*kifāya*) and resourcefulness in that which is bound to him and entrusted to him. They all require these qualities because they include persons to whom the king entrusts his life and his soul (*rūḥ*), persons whom he entrusts over his *khadam* and his womenfolk (*ḥaram*), persons to whom he entrusts his secret affairs, and with whom he enters into consultation in matters momentous in import and high in value; persons whom he entrusts

with his religion and his afterlife, and persons whom he entrusts with his possessions and treasuries.

If a person is not restrained by religion (*dīn*) from committing treachery (*khiyāna*), his trustworthiness (*amāna*) is dependent on (his) current desire or imminent fear. It is not unlikely that his trustworthiness will recede when his desire and fear recede, and incline as they incline. Sometimes a bad habit will move him to resist the conditions of desire and fear, transgress their limits, and make light of them. If he is not trustworthy he will betray the king (*idhā lam yakun lahu amāna khāna*), and if he betrays him in the likes of these matters, he frequently occasions comprehensive harm or fundamental corruption.

If a person is not intelligent, he may wish to be of benefit but inadvertently cause injury. He may wish to protect but in fact cause harm, to adorn but in fact disfigure, or to do good but in fact behave disagreeably. And if he does not possess competence in that which is entrusted to him and to which he is bound (*kifāya bi-mā fuwwiḍa ilayhi wa-ᶜuṣṣiba bihi*), the matter will fall into ruin and disorder.

These qualities should predominate among his virtues: noble descent (or firmness of judgement, *aṣāla*), effectiveness in management and evaluation (*ḥusn al-tadbīr wa-l-taqdīr*), excellence of talent and intuition (*jūdat al-qarīḥa wa-l-badīha*), and a good ability to draw inferences by means of analogy between the manifest and the hidden and from the past regarding the future (*ḥusn al-istidlāl bi-l-shāhid ᶜalā l-ghāʾib wa-l-māḍī ᶜalā l-ātī*).[172]

In this passage, in which he prescribes the qualities essential in every appointed official, regardless of his specialisation, Pseudo-Māwardī emphasises religion, intellect and competence, and also *amāna*, trustworthiness. Recapitulating the model of the angels and prophets, he insists that the king's *akhaṣṣ* must be persons of loyalty and must abide by their commitments. This quality depends on the prior requirement of 'a religion' (he does not stipulate a particular religion). In his final requirement, Pseudo-Māwardī invokes the Muᶜtazilite principle of analogical inference, expanded from its application from the mundane to the divine to encompass the past and the present; that is, the king should appoint persons skilled in the perception and application of the lessons of the past to the unfolding events of the present.

Having addressed these qualities, necessary in every administrator and official, Pseudo-Māwardī treats the specific requirements for particular roles:

> Then there are specific qualities for every division among the governmental practices (*al-rusūm al-sulṭāniyya*):
>
> Among the persons on whom the exercise of governance depends are persons in whom an excellent knowledge of literary culture (*adab*) and language, a fine hand and clarity of expression, facility of presentation and excellence of talent are necessary: that person is the secretary (*kātib*).
>
> Another group consists of persons in whom an excellent knowledge of accounting and matters of income and expenditure are needed: they are the agents and the collectors of taxes among the secretaries (*al-wukalāʾ wa-jubāt al-amwāl min al-kuttāb*).
>
> Another group consists of persons in whom bravery, endurance, astuteness, courage, and skill and experience in battle are needed: they are the cavalry (*asāwira*) and the military leaders (*aṣḥāb al-juyūsh*).
>
> Another group consists of persons in whom the predominant characteristics of knowledge (*ʿilm*), understanding (*fiqh*), religion (*diyāna*), temperance (*ʿiffa*), trustworthiness (*amāna*), awareness (*dirāya*), probity (*ʿadāla*), decency (*ṣiyāna*), and familiarity with the ordinances, statutory limits, precepts and stipulations (*shurūṭ*), are required: that person is the judge (*qāḍī*).
>
> It is necessary that the king select the governors of his districts (*wulāt aʿmālihi*) and the collectors of his taxes (*jubāt amwālihi*) in accordance with these principles. He should know that he will not find anyone who is complete with every virtue and outstanding in every excellent quality, but he should select for each type of work the person who is best suited for it and most fit for the position, even if there is a lack or shortcoming in that person in other respects. For the king will not find anyone so refined that there is no fault in him, or so perfect that there is no deficiency in him, and

> if he does not employ persons with some failings, affairs will fall into neglect and obstruction.[173]

Having addressed the requirements, in terms of skills and personal qualities, for these posts, the author enumerates five principles that the ruler should apply in his dealings with his appointed administrators:

> The king, having demonstrated excellence in his selection (*ḥusn al-ikhtiyār*) and firm judgement (*aṣāla*) in employing these persons, should have recourse to their proper installation, according to five characteristics:
>
> Firstly, he must direct them all towards justice and equity (*bi-l-ᶜadl wa-l-inṣāf*), adherence to the precepts of the sharīᶜa and the statutory limits of the religious community (*ḥudūd al-milla*). He must remind them of the threat of the Fire [of Hell] against anyone who transgresses in these matters, or oppresses, wrongs or treats persons unjustly, just as he directs them to fulfil their responsibilities towards the subjects (*bi-istīfāʾ mā yajibu lahu ᶜalā l-raᶜiyya*) and to examine their affairs in a thorough manner. The king should not allow anyone to ruin the subjects, nor permit anyone among them to take a single dirham unless it is his due, for if he allows an official to behave in this way, then that person will allow those beneath him – since for every appointed official (*ᶜāmil*) there is an *ᶜāmil*, and for every overlord (*ṣāḥib*) there is a *ṣāḥib* – to covet from him, just as he covets from those above him. If the situation develops in this way, then the few persons who follow this path will grow to be many, and that situation will cause harm to the subjects and bring no benefit to the ruler. In fact, the problem is likely to increase and multiply, to the point that the official deals so unjustly with the subjects that they perish, and in their perishing lies also the perdition of their king and their ruler. For the subjects' houses and bodies are like (mineral) deposits and cultivable plots of land for the rulers' treasuries, and roots (sources) for them. If the root is destroyed, the branch will be destroyed too, and if the material substance (*mādda*) is cut off from the deposit and the root, the contents of the treasuries will dissipate and disappear. This situation has been compared to the likeness of streams that flow into a pool; if their source of water is cut off, it will not be long before the water in the pool begins to decrease and disappear, especially if the flow of water out of the pool remains constant and if those persons who seek its water are many.

> Nothing is more likely to sever the paths of wealth from the treasuries and storehouses than oppression, injustice and transgression of due claim(s) and established custom (*ta*ᶜ*addī l-ḥaqq wa-l-rasm*).
>
> [The Tahirid ruler] ᶜAbdallāh b. Ṭāhir [r. 213–30/828–445] observed this phenomenon when he said, 'The land-tax is the pillar (ᶜ*imād*) of sovereignty. Nothing renders it abundant like justice, and nothing renders it paltry like injustice.'[174]

Pseudo-Māwardī's insistence that the king's agents act justly in the collection of revenue from the subjects recapitulates the theme of the interconnected nature of the components of the polity expressed in 'circles of justice', formulaic expressions that asserted the interdependence of rulers and their subjects, and the necessity of justice to balance the interests of the constituent social groups.[175] Indeed, he proceeds to cite a circle of justice shortly.

On the subject of financial exactions, Pseudo-Māwardī proceeds to address in detail the various religiously mandated contributions:

> Among that which God – glorious and great – has made incumbent upon His servants are charitable contributions (*zakawāt*) and donations (*ṣadaqāt*) that He has established by the most powerful evidentiary testimony (*a*ᶜ*ẓam shāhid*), the clearest indication and the finest example. For God, glorious and exalted, only requires a portion of His servants' possessions (*juz*ᵓ *min ajzā*ᵓ*ihā*): a tenth (ᶜ*ushr*) of the fruit of the lands (*thamarat al-araḍīn*) for which they are not burdened with the costs of irrigation, and half of a tenth (*niṣf al-*ᶜ*ushr*, i.e., 5%) of the produce of lands that encumber them with such costs; or the light land-tax (*al-kharāj al-khafīf*) on the necks of livestock that graze on the lands (*riqāb al-araḍīn*); and a quarter of a tenth (*rub*ᶜ *al-*ᶜ*ushr*, i.e., 2.5%) of their gold and silver (*min ṣawāmatihim*). Of their camels that are few in number, a male animal (of another species) is due (*qarm min sawā*ᵓ*imihim al-qalīla al-*ᶜ*adad*); but if there are many camels, then a tenth of a tenth (ᶜ*ushr al-*ᶜ*ushr*, i.e., 1%) is due, or whatever is closest to that proportion in the form of sheep and other animals.
>
> He has imposed mandatory contributions only in the case of wealth that bears fruit, or wealth that is potentially fruitful. In a similar manner (*li-dhālika*) God has imposed the poll-tax (*jizya*) on the unbelievers of the

> covenanted people (*kuffār ahl al-dhimma*): He has imposed it (the *jizya*) only upon persons who are strong and working, or prosperous and rich. Moreover, He has delayed the payment of *zakāt* for a period of time in order to make it possible for His servants to increase, promote fruitfulness, foster growth and augment the possessions on which *zakāt* is due (*al-ziyāda wa-l-tathmīr wa-l-namāʾ wa-l-takthīr*). All these principles exist in order to ensure the durability of the substance of their possessions, for the benefit of their roots in the lands that they own, out of consideration and gentleness towards them, and in order to alleviate their burdens.[176]

Pseudo-Māwardī displays a detailed knowledge of the legal rulings concerning the religiously sanctioned forms of taxation, principally *zakāt* and *ṣadaqa*, both of which have a Qurʾānic basis. He describes the application of the *ᶜushr*, a tenth or tithe, and parts thereof to various kinds of possessions. He emphasises the restricted levels of each of these levies, including the *jizya* or poll-tax applied to non-Muslim communities; the law required that individuals should not be taxed beyond their means, and rates of taxation should not be so high that the tax-payers are unable to increase the productivity of their lands or their means of livelihood. Having already cited ᶜAbdallāh b. Ṭāhir, Pseudo-Māwardī cites two examples of Sasanian wisdom to this effect:

> Shāpūr b. Ardashīr explained this principle in his 'Testament' when he said, 'The soundness and expectation of the land-tax depend on the cultivation of the lands and the promotion of increase in the crops. The way to create a surplus and to attain the greatest productivity in this matter entails promoting the well-being (*istiṣlāḥ*) of the people, showing justice, equity and kindness towards them, and assisting them towards that which lies in their path, encouraging them by augmenting their livelihoods and lightening their burdens. For some matters are causative reasons for other matters; the common people are the resources of their élites (*ᶜawāmm al-nās bi-khawāṣṣihim ᶜudda*), and every group among them stands in clear need of the one next to it.'[177]

> Anūshīrvān said, 'Sovereignty depends on troops, the troops on wealth, wealth derives from the lands, the lands flourish by virtue of prosperity (*ᶜamāra*), and prosperity cannot be sustained without justice.'[178]

> For reasons of this sort, the virtuous kings ensure the circulation of wealth among the kings, troops and subjects in the course of one year according to three parts: one part should be in the treasury (*bayt al-māl*), one part in the hands of the army and military commanders (*al-jund wa-l-quwwād*), and one part in the hands of the subjects.
>
> The king concerned for the prosperity of his kingdom and solicitous of the affairs of his province should know that he has no more implacable enemy, none stronger against him or more powerful among his opponents than his official (*ᶜāmil*) if he is unjust and oppressive, and his deputy (*khalīfa*) if he is excessive and tyrannical, because his official and *khādim* are capable of harm that none of his enemies has the power to inflict. Moreover, the official exposes the king to ignominious words (*luʾm al-uḥdūtha*) that stain his honour and sully his name over the course of time, and corrupt his subjects against him. This damage is of a kind that an enemy, whatever stratagem he might employ against him, is unlikely to have the power to accomplish. Then the channels of his income are cut off, the sources of his abundance and the springs of his wealth ruined. This situation stimulates the ambitions of the king's distant enemies and his foreign adversaries (*yuṭmiᶜu fīhi aᶜdāʾahu al-abᶜadīn wa-munābidhīhi al-ajnabiyyīn*). In all of this the official pays no attention to his local leader (*raʾīs*) or to his *sulṭān* as he hastens to acquire a paltry sum of money and a trifling amount of forbidden wealth. The resolute king should not retain a single one of his officials in such conditions, nor perpetuate him in office against them.[179]

In a continuation of the theme of the mutual dependence of ruler and subjects, Pseudo-Māwardī argues that injustice on the part of the king's officials eventually results in the decay of the kingdom and its vulnerability to subversion from within or attack from external enemies. Pseudo-Māwardī's second principle urges the king to take appropriate action, after ascertaining the accuracy of the allegation, against any of his officials guilty of corruption and extortion, and to rectify the wrong to the oppressed:

> Secondly, if he discovers anything of this sort in anyone among his officials, he should dismiss him and replace him, after clarifying the truth concerning his affair without haste and harshness. He should punish him with a

> punishment that corresponds to the form of his condition and the extent of his crime. He should demand restitution from him of that which he took by injustice and return it to its owner. For the application of justice against the oppressor is more effective and powerful than the infliction of injustice against the wronged. Under these conditions the wronged person expects recompense and mercy, and is not fearful of incurring on that account a burden and harmful consequences; and the oppressor fears punishment, suffers disgrace and deserves punishment and chastisement. This arrangement is in accordance with that which God, glorious and exalted, has announced concerning Himself in His Book: 'My covenant does not encompass the oppressors' (*lā yanālu ᶜahdī al-ẓālimīna*, 2: 124); He does not adopt those who lead astray as a support (cf. 18: 51).[180] It is incumbent on the king who receives from God great favour (*jalīl al-niᶜma*) in regard to himself and his kingdom that he not oppose the command of God in his sovereignty nor resist Him in his authority by including in his covenant (*ᶜahd*) a person not encompassed in God's covenant (*ᶜahd*), or by taking as a support amongst His servants a person whose support God has announced is not to be taken.[181]

Continuing to draw on Qurʾānic texts to organise his presentation, Pseudo-Māwardī urges the ruler to ensure that his behaviour conforms to the divine model and the divine commandments by excluding oppressors from his 'covenants'; that is, the ruler should dismiss from office any official who has committed injustice against the subjects. He prescribes a method for ascertaining whether an injustice has occurred:

> Thirdly, he should place spies, observers and supervisors (*ᶜuyūn wa-mushrif [ū]na wa-azimma*) over each one of his officials, secretly and openly. He should choose trustworthy agents and the elders of the districts (*umanāʾ al-nās wa-mashāyikh al-kuwar*),[182] learned and righteous persons (*ᶜulamāʾ[u] hā wa-ṣulaḥāʾ[u]hā*), and people of temperance and modesty. They should follow the official's tracks (*āthār*) and relay reports concerning him (*akhbār*) to the king. The path of the trusted confidants and spies (*al-umanāʾ wa-l-ᶜuyūn*) should be their path (the path of those under surveillance), and the way of the former should be their way. If they encounter any official in an unjust, criminal, iniquitous or suspicious act, they should avoid haste in the

matter and allow him the opportunity to establish his innocence, so that the substance of the reports concerning him may be relayed and verified.

> The generality of the people are disposed by nature (*maṭbūᶜūn*) to envy and enmity, prone to wickedness in thought and deed (*muwakkalūn bi-sūᵓ al-ẓann wa-l-fiᶜl*), except for him whom God has protected from corruption (*man ᶜaṣṣama[hu] Allāhu min al-fasād*) and granted success through guidance (*waffaqahu lil-rashād*).[183] God does not order judgement (*qaḍāᵓ*) until the reality has emerged clearly and the truth has become manifest, so a man should fear God in rendering judgement and consider carefully that which he does and says.[184]

The passage recapitulates the ancient theme of surveillance of the king's officials, articulated, as this last passage shows, with some reference to a theological–philosophical conceptual framework of 'natures'. Much more briefly, and without reference to Qurᵓānic texts, theological doctrines, historical experience, wisdom or poetry, the *Pandnāmeh* of Sebüktigin urges the future ruler to monitor his tax officials; if he finds that an *ᶜāmil* has taken revenues dishonestly, he should recover the funds and restore them, punish the offender and then reinstate him; if he is a man of rational intelligence (*agar mard-i ᶜāqil ast*), this single experience will alert him and he will cease to deceive; if, on the other hand, he commits the offence again, he should be dismissed.[185]

Pseudo-Māwardī continues:

> Fourthly, in the case of the provinces (*wilāyāt*) over which he appoints individuals, he should appoint persons to them in accordance with the rightful claims due to their service (*bi-ḥaqq al-khidma*). He should not engender covetousness in any of his officials by his appointment of him to a province. Instead, he should be generous with his stipulated remuneration (*yudirru ᶜalayhi rizqahu al-marsūm*) in kindness (*bi-l-maᶜrūf*) when he directs him to his appointment over the district. He should determine the appropriate amount that suffices to benefit the appointee so that he may continue to apply himself to his assigned tasks, rather than obliging him to apply himself to deriving benefits for himself (through tax-farming).

> In both of these cases lies much corruption, because if the official (*ᶜāmil*) knows that his appointment is in accordance with the claims attendant on

> his relationship of *khidma* and a compensation (*mukāfaʾa*) to him for it (in lieu of a generous stipend), he will become covetous over the subjects and it will be the ruler who has instigated his covetousness; he will suppose that everyone under his authority represents the fruit of his service (*thamrat khidmatihi*) and the due profit of his work. And if the king covets the funds collected by his official, then the latter will become more covetous towards those who are subordinate to his authority, and he will not be satisfied unless he has taken from his subjects – in whom, we have mentioned, lie the prosperity of his dominion and the deposit of his treasuries – twice the amount that the king bestows on him.[186]

In this passage, Pseudo-Māwardī again raises his concern regarding the appointment of governors who, installed in their provinces, availed themselves of the opportunity to line their own pockets in place of or in a supplement to their salaries.[187] Rather than referring to *iqṭāᶜ*, Pseudo-Māwardī employs the phrase *wallā qaḍāʾ*, to appoint to authority, and it seems likely that the chief reference is to governorships of major provinces, *wilāyāt*. In a late account by the distant writer Ibn al-Zubayr, the term *iqṭāᶜ* appears in reference to the period of Naṣr II, where the holders of *iqṭāᶜāt* are described as 'holders of land-grants, who have been assigned estates for supporting themselves, for financing the upkeep of their mounts and weapons, and supporting their families and dependants' (*aṣḥāb al-iqṭāᶜāt alladhīna uqṭiᶜū ḍiyāᶜan takūnu maʾūnatahum wa-maʾūnata dawābbihim wa-silāḥihim wa-ᶜiyālihim wa-man nazala ᶜalayhim minhā*).[188] It is likely that Ibn al-Zubayr substituted a term appropriate to his own period in his account of a practice that existed, but had not yet become widespread or acquired this designation.

The passage in *Naṣīḥat al-mulūk* anticipates the problems that later writers, such as Niẓām al-Mulk, would identify in grants of *iqṭāᶜ* instead of monetary compensation. Niẓām al-Mulk follows Pseudo-Māwardī in insisting that the *mushrif* and the *ṣāḥib-khabar*, and indeed all officials, should be paid adequate and regular salaries, in order to place them above susceptibility to corruption; the advantage of having trustworthy *mushrifs* amply compensates for the expenditure on their salaries, and their pay should come from the central treasury, not from provincial funds or levies on the people; this arrangement maintains their direct dependence on the ruler.[189] The problem of a governor who took his appointment as an incentive to supplement his salary, and still sent a portion to the ruler, was the abuse that Pseudo-Māwardī wished to forestall.

Pseudo-Māwardī concludes this section with a fifth and final piece of advice for the king in his dealings with his appointed officials:

> Fifthly, he should not seek to increase the number of his officials (*ᶜummāl*), and he should not appoint more of them over the subjects than absolutely necessary; because increasing their numbers above that which is needed gives rise to several forms of corruption:
>
> The first is that as their numbers increase, the cost to the treasury for their allowances and provisions also multiplies (*kathurat arzāquhum wa-muᵓanuhum ᶜalā bayt al-māl*), so that the kingdom's wealth becomes employed for purposes other than its foremost necessities and most fitting priorities, and the treasury suffers damage.
>
> Secondly, if they grow numerous, the volume of their correspondence (*mukātaba*) and written communications (*kutub*) also increases, as well as the number of letters against them from the king's trusted agents (*kutub al-umanāᵓ ᶜalayhim*), their complaints and the claims against them. That correspondence will preoccupy the king and divert him from matters that are more important, more deserving, more proper and more appropriate for his attention.
>
> Thirdly, when they become more numerous, it becomes increasingly unlikely that they will all conform in rectitude, decency, trustworthiness, righteousness, temperance and modesty, since trustworthy agents (*umanāᵓ*) and competent persons (*kufāt*) are few and rare in every age, time, moment and era, so it is inevitable that as the number of officials grows, their conditions with regard to these characteristics (*fī hādhihi l-maᶜānī*), and the qualities that are needed in them and from them, will vary.
>
> So it is necessary that he manage with as small a number of them as he can and as comes easily, and that he spread the work among them as far as he is capable. This approach constitutes a mode of following God through emulating Him, in that God sent His messengers only one after another,

> over long consecutive periods and diminishing passages of time, according to the urgent need of His creatures altogether, for the dissemination of the religious law and in order to bridge the interval. And in every covenant (*fī kull ᶜahd*) that the Prophet concluded, he appointed only one leader (*imām*), and he said to them: 'If two amirs receive pledges of allegiance, then kill the other one of them.'[190]

In his last point, Pseudo-Māwardī argues against the proliferation of appointments for reasons of efficiency, cost and the quality of the individuals' service. This topic concludes his treatment of the governance of the *khāṣṣa*:

> Whoever disciplines his *khāṣṣa* by these principles, trains his *ḥāshiya* by them, and employs them among his officials (*ᶜummāl*), I hope that these means will fulfil the *khāṣṣa*'s due claim in their education and formation, and God's claim with regard to them; and that he will improve them and be improved by them (*wa-aṣlaḥahum wa-uṣliḥa bihim*), if God wills – and in Him lie strength, might, vigour and power.[191]

This remark concludes Pseudo-Māwardī's sixth chapter, the second of the three dedicated to the three *siyāsāt*.

In this chapter, and throughout *Naṣīḥat al-mulūk*, Pseudo-Māwardī's overriding purpose is to persuade the ruler to exercise self-control in the personal and political realms. Self-control required the habitual adoption of a cautious, reflective and gradual approach. With regard to the king's *khāṣṣa*, for example, Pseudo-Māwardī insists on the patient and painstaking gathering of information, and strongly discourages punishment in cases where doubt remains or extenuating circumstances might mitigate the gravity of an individual's crime. He impresses upon his royal audience the acute moral responsibilities entailed in the exercise of power, especially for purposes that involved the physical or material harm of individuals; he therefore urged the king to observe scrupulous standards in determining if, and when, his use of power might be appropriate, justified or necessary.

Pseudo-Māwardī drew the conceptual framework for his quite detailed discussion of specific points from the principles of *tafḍīl*, the concept of preference that underpins the hierarchical order, and *qurb* and *taqrīb*, closeness and bringing close, the concepts that give spatial expression to the ruler's governance and his delegation of responsibilities. In the cosmic hierarchy, the king occupies the central position between the heavenly realms and the earth; it is he who bears the burden of responsibility, in trust, for the well-being of God's servants, his subjects. In the context of the kingdom, the king occupies the central point in a circle, surrounded by individuals and groups at increasing degrees of removal. His descriptions of the personnel who make up the king's *khāṣṣa* confirm and supplement the limited information available with regard to the education of princes and the administrative structures of the Samanid domains. Pseudo-Māwardī's descriptive and prescriptive treatments of these arrangements are linked to an assortment of authorities, sacred and human, that reflect his customary eclecticism: Qur'ānic passages, Prophetic traditions and the transmitted accounts of the early Muslim community, Aristotle's advice to Alexander, the Sasanian kings and sages, Indian wisdom, reports and pronouncements of narratives concerning figures of modern history and verses of poetry. These materials not only provide illustrative proof-texts; they also furnish conceptual tools, as Pseudo-Māwardī's lexical choices frequently reflect. The result of Pseudo-Māwardī's densely supported exposition is an integrated presentation replete with rich cultural resources that reflect the cosmopolitanism of his milieu and his audience.

5

The Governance of the Common People

The seventh chapter of *Naṣīḥat al-mulūk* and the third in Pseudo-Māwardī's sequence of *siyāsāt* is devoted to the common people or *ᶜāmma*. It provides numerous examples of Pseudo-Māwardī's use of texts, vehicles of meanings that were neither singular nor static; he moulds the meaning of his texts by integrating them into his argument and by juxtaposing them with other texts, in order to create a cumulative and collective effect. Pseudo-Māwardī opens his chapter with a reminder of the ruler's moral injunction to imitate the divine attributes and follow the divine commandments. Invoking God's instructive conduct (*ādāb Allāh*), he emphasises the divine qualities of mercy and justice. He reiterates the king's central responsibility to maintain his obligation to abide by his promises, to meet his subjects' rightful expectations, and to strive continually to exhibit greater generosity towards them. Only in rare cases does Pseudo-Māwardī endorse punishment; much more commonly he counsels the restoration of reciprocal ties of loyalty. Like the previous chapter, chapter seven of *Naṣīḥat al-mulūk* demonstrates the model of cooperation and necessary mutual dependence between the ruler and his subjects, more particularly the subjects who mediate between the royal person and the population at large.

The chapter opens in Pseudo-Māwardī's usual manner, with a sequence of Qurʾānic quotations. Again, Pseudo-Māwardī employs these quotations in order to organise his argument, and groups them into three divisions. The first cluster of Qurʾānic fragments emphasises God's self-description as merciful and just. The second group demonstrates God's distinguishing of His Prophet by the same characteristics, compassion and fairness (*qisṭ*). The third consists of Qurʾānic texts that affirm human accountability and reject the notion of divine injustice:

We have already mentioned previously in our book that it is incumbent on the excellent king and consummate ruler (*al-malik al-fāḍil wa-l-sāʾis al-kāmil*) that he imitate God, insofar as His servants possess the capacity to perceive the divine model and to the extent that effort and exertion allow, and that he observe His command, and encourage that which He has encouraged and praised.

God has described Himself as using mercy (*raḥma*) and justice (*ʿadl*) towards His creatures, for He has said: 'And He is merciful towards the believers' (33: 43); 'Know that God is most forgiving and most merciful' (5: 34); 'The Most Merciful and Most Compassionate' (1: 3).

Then He extolled the Prophet with this epithet of praise and favoured him with this virtue, for He said of him: '[An Apostle from amongst you has come to you. Any sorrow that befalls you weighs upon him; He is eager for your happiness,] full of concern for the faithful, compassionate and kind' (9: 128); 'Muḥammad is the Prophet of God; and those with him are stern against the disbelievers but compassionate among themselves' (48: 29); 'It was through God's mercy that you dealt with them gently' (3: 159); 'Verily God has enjoined justice (*ʿadl*), the doing of good (*iḥsān*), and the giving of gifts to your relatives; and forbidden indecency, impropriety and oppression' (16: 90); 'Do not allow hatred of a people to induce you to deviate from justice; deal justly, for that is closer to godliness' (*huwa aqrabu lil-taqwā*) (5: 8).

And He, the Great and Glorious, in describing Himself as using justice (*ʿadl*) and rejecting from Himself injustice (*ẓulm*) and oppression (*jawr*), said: 'O you who believe! Be upright in fairness (*qisṭ*), testifying to God, even if it is against yourselves or your parents and relatives' (4: 135); 'We shall set the scales of justice (*al-mawāzīn al-qisṭ*) on the Day of Resurrection, so that none (*nafs*) will be wronged in the least; and even if it were equal to a mustard seed in weight We shall take it (into account). We are sufficient for computation' (21: 47); 'Your Lord is never unjust to (His) servants' (41: 46); 'God did not wrong them [the unbelievers, on the Day of Judgement]; they wronged themselves' (16: 33); 'God does not wish injustice (*ẓulm*) to the creatures of the world (*al-ʿālamīn*)' (3: 108).[1]

These passages emphasise the principles of divine mercy and the Prophet's compassion. Paired with the qualities of mercy and compassion are justice and equity. Pseudo-Māwardī chooses Qurʾānic texts that affirm the principle, foundational to Muʿtazilite theology, of divine justice, and its corollary, the responsibility of human beings for the actions that God will judge. Divine justice and the impossibility of divine injustice, to which, in Pseudo-Māwardī's interpretation, Qurʾānic texts also point, are central elements of Muʿtazilite doctrine. Having established the divine and Prophetic qualities of mercy and justice as models for the ruler's emulation, Pseudo-Māwardī reminds his audience of kings' responsibilities towards their subjects, and the contingency of the subjects' obligation to obey their authority:

> It is related from the Prophet: 'There is no ruler (*wālin*) who rules over a community (*yalī jamāʿatan*) but that when the Day of Resurrection comes, his hands shall be bound; his justice will release him, and his tyranny will cause him to perish.'[2]

> It is related regarding the Commander of the Faithful ʿUmar b. al-Khaṭṭāb that when he dispatched his officials (*ʿummāl*), he set out with them. He was on foot while they were mounted. When he wished to part from them, he said: 'Fear God: We are not placing you in command over the blood of the Muslims, nor over their properties, their persons or their honourable reputations. Rather we charge you to perform the prayer with them at its appointed times, to fight with them against their enemies, to judge among them according to the truth, and to distribute their stipends among them by justice. We charge you not to beat the Arabs and thereby humiliate them, nor to withhold from them their rights and thereby deprive them (*lā tamnaʿūhum ḥaqqahum fa-taḥrimūhum*), nor to detain them in the lands of the enemy and thereby torment them.'[3]

> He said: The Prophet of God David used to say: 'Remember the hungry when you are satiated, remember the naked when you are clothed.'

> [The Companion of the Prophet and prolific transmitter of Prophetic traditions] Abū Hurayra [d. *c.* 58/678] related from the Prophet that he said, 'If you are a ruler (*amīr*), a ruler's vizier, a person who enters the presence of a ruler, or a person with whom a ruler consults (*mushāwir amīr*), then do

not oppose my *sunna*; for any ruler, ruler's vizier or person admitted to the presence of a ruler who opposes my *sunna* and conduct (*sīra*), on the Day of Resurrection the Fire will take him from his place and he will proceed towards the Fire.'[4]

Al-Qāsim b. ᶜAbd al-Raḥmān [b. ᶜAbdallāh b. Masᶜūd, d. 116/734][5] said: 'When ᶜUmar dispatched his officials (*ᶜummāl*), he said, "I am not sending you as tyrants (*jabābira*), I am only sending you as (prayer-)leaders (*aᵓimma*). Do not beat the Muslims and thereby humiliate them, do not injure and oppress them, do not detain them [far from their families] and torment them, and promote the rightful claims of the Muslims (*idarraᵓū li-ḥaqq al-muslimīn*)", by which he meant stipends (*al-ᶜaṭāᵓ*).'[6]

We have found in a testament of the Indians: Justice is God's balance on earth (*inna al-ᶜadla mīzān Allāh fī l-arḍ*), by means of which the weak receive their due from the powerful (*yuᵓkhadhu bihi lil-ḍaᶜīf min al-shadīd*) and the deserving (the duly entitled claimant) (*muḥiqq*) from the false claimant (*mubṭil*). He who upsets God's balance from its purpose, namely in order to uphold equity (*qisṭ*) among His servants, will find himself reduced to the utmost degree of poverty; he is deluded with regard to God to the utmost degree of deception. So, avail yourself in your exercise of justice of two characteristics: seeking guidance (*ṭalab al-hudā*) and firmness in affairs (*al-tathabbut fī l-umūr*).[7]

Then there is that which God has made incumbent for the believers in their relations with one another (*mā awjaba Allāhu lil-muslimīn baᶜḍahum ᶜalā baᶜḍin*), as God said: 'The believers are brothers; so make peace among your brethren' (Q 49: 10). The Prophet said: 'The believer is the brother of the believer; he neither forsakes him nor oppresses him.'[8] He said: 'I am commanded to fight against the people until they say, "There is no god but God". When they profess it, they secure protection for their lives and possessions from me, except for rightful claims to their wealth and their account according to God.'[9] And he said: 'The believers are like an edifice, one part of which strengthens the other part.'[10]

The king who shares the faith of his subjects (*al-malik al-mushārik fī l-īmān li-raᶜiyyatihi*) should display this attribute of kindness in his conduct with them and his treatment of them (*muᶜāmalatuhu iyyāhum*) should be of this character.[11]

Pseudo-Māwardī adduces an eclectic set of further materials to support and illustrate his twinned principles of compassion and justice. Predominant among these texts, after the sacred sources of the Qurʾān and Prophetic traditions, are utterances of and narratives concerning the second Rightly Guided Caliph ᶜUmar. ᶜUmar's dispatching of his *ᶜummāl* (sing. *ᶜāmil*), a category that in this early period encompassed several governmental and military responsibilities,[12] became a model in later works of *adab* as well as in political and juridical writings, including the *Kitāb al-Kharāj* ('Book of the Land-Tax') of the Ḥanafī jurist Abū Yūsuf (d. 182/798).[13] Pseudo-Māwardī, a Ḥanafī whose knowledge of tax-related law was observed in the previous chapter, is likely to have been familiar with Abū Yūsuf's text. Pseudo-Māwardī also cites his 'Indian testament', in which justice is likened to God's balance on the earth, that is, in the present life, and the king responsible for its maintenance; he should therefore ascertain the truth regarding the cases brought before him, by 'seeking guidance', and having determined the situation, he should act decisively, by 'firmness in affairs'.[14] The purpose of Pseudo-Māwardī's quotations and allusions in these opening pages is to emphasise to his audience that clemency and kindness are necessary accompaniments to justice, and that it is on the basis of these principles that the king should govern the common people. His quotations also remind the king that he shares with every individual among his subjects a common humanity and should approach them in mutual cooperation: on this basis he should support them all, as fellow believers in the case of his Muslim subjects, and as fellow human beings and protected members of his population in the case of his non-Muslim subjects. In this vein the citations emphasise the limits of the ruler's authority against his subjects, his duties towards them, and their due expectations of justice and equity from him.

Pseudo-Māwardī continues with an example, related on his own authority, from the Prophet:

> At a previous point in our book, we have already related from the Prophet that he said, 'Each one of you is a shepherd (*rāᶜin*) and each of you is responsible for his flock (*raᶜiyya*) [subjects]' (*kullukum rāᶜin wa-kullukum*

> *mas*ʾ*ūl* ᶜ*an ra*ᶜ*iyyatihi*).[15] We have instructed [the reader] that the shepherd and the flock, and the ruler and the ruled (*al-sā*ʾ*is wa-l-masūs*), are both nouns of apposition (*asmā*ʾ *al-iḍāfa*):[16] neither can endure without the other; and the shepherd's need of the flock [subjects] is not less than the flock's [subjects'] need for the shepherd; likewise in the case of the king (*al-malik*) and the dominion (*al-mulk*). It is for this reason that the subjects have been likened to the body and the ruler to the head, and it has been said, 'If the subjects perish, the ruler (*al-rā*ᶜ*ī*) perishes; if they are corrupt, the condition of the ruler falls into corruption. Whenever a deficiency enters among them, with regard to their possessions and their lives, that deficiency rebounds against him.'[17]
>
> One of the kings of old said: If the ruler seeks the corruption of the subjects, he is as unlikely to possess the power (*qudra*) to seek his own improvement as the head is likely to endure after the demise of its bodily supports (*arkān*); except that the ruler is better positioned to improve the corrupt subjects and corrupt the good subjects than the subjects are to improve or corrupt the ruler, by virtue of his power over them, and the weakness of their power over him.[18]

Pseudo-Māwardī's introduction of the ancient metaphor of the body politic alludes in yet another way to the hierarchical yet interdependent relationships among the constituents of the polity. These passages prepare his audience for his exposition of the common people's indispensable contributions to the whole, and the king's dependence upon them. It is at this point that Pseudo-Māwardī describes the king's dependence on his ᶜ*āmma* as no less important than his dependence on his *khāṣṣa*. This passage was reproduced and discussed in Volume I, Chapter 4,[19] where I suggested that Pseudo-Māwardī's social description portrays the need for mutual cooperation between the ruler and the groups that functioned as intermediaries between the dynastic level of governance and the population. Pseudo-Māwardī classifies the wealthy, the *dahāqīn*, the religious scholars and jurists, judges and ascetics, elders and notables among the ᶜ*āmma*, and associates them all with the kingdom (*mamlaka*) rather than with the king. By contrast, the king's 'assistants' (*a*ᶜ*wān*), his *khadam* and his troops (*junūd*) belong to the *khāṣṣa*, and, like the king's material possessions, they are 'his'. The description portrays the *khāṣṣa* as extensions of the ruler's person, assimilated into his household or located in close proximity; whereas the categories that comprise the common people are dispersed across the *mamlaka*, whether in familial estates or in urban neighbourhoods. As constituent groupings among the *ʿāmma*, these categories are entitled by rightful claims to the ruler's justice.

A recurrent feature of Pseudo-Māwardī's treatment of the *ʿāmma*, as some of his introductory quotations presaged, is his drawing of an analogy in kind between the ruler and his subjects. Where he depicted the king's relationship to his *khāṣṣa* in terms of proximity, by blood or foster relationship and by advancement, and in familial, spatial and symbolic terms, Pseudo-Māwardī develops his theme of social interdependence by emphasising the common humanity of ruler and ruled:

> The subjects and the ruler (*al-raʿiyya wa-l-rāʿī*) are united in closeness of kind and affinity (*qurb al-mujānasa wa-l-munāsaba*), similarity of nature, form and kinship (*mushākalat al-ṭabīʿa wa-l-ṣūra wa-l-ḥāma*); and affinity (*munāsaba*) necessitates compassion and inclination. In addition, he owes them the rights (*ḥaqq*) due to the religious community (*milla*) and the covenant of protection (*dhimma*), for God has made the believers brothers, and the *dhimma* a trust (*amāna*). Obedience is incumbent on them only on condition of justice, the fulfilment of that which he has promised, compassion and mercy (*innamā yajibu ʿalayhim al-ṭāʿa bi-sharīṭat al-maʿdala wa-l-wafāʾ bi-l-ʿahd wa-l-raʾfa wa-l-raḥma*). For it is related from the Prophet that he said: 'Quraysh have a claim against you: if they seek mercy they should be treated mercifully, if they submit to arbitration (or judgement) they should receive justice, and if they conclude pacts they should be fulfilled (*in ʿāhadū wufū*). Whoever does not act in this way, then the curse of God, the angels and all the people will be against him; his action will not be accepted from him in any fashion.' And he said: 'There is no obligation to obedience upon the creature in disobedience to the Creator' (*lā ṭāʿata li-makhlūqin fī maʿṣiyat al-khāliq*). And he said: 'Obedience is due only in return for goodness' (*innamā al-ṭāʿa fī l-maʿrūf*).[20]

This passage reiterates several of Pseudo-Māwardī's central themes. The king is like his subjects in kind (*jins*) and in 'nature' (*ṭabīʿa*), and his affinity (*munāsaba*) with them requires his sympathetic treatment of them. His debt of responsibility involves the entirety of his subjects, Muslim and non-Muslim alike, as his references to *milla* and *dhimma* specify. Pseudo-Māwardī reiterates, with reference to a previously cited ḥadīth, that the subjects' duty of obedience depended on the ruler's compliance with obedience to God. He introduces additional ḥadīth that identify the subjects' rightful claims, which include clemency, justice and the fulfilment of covenants. The king's claim (*ḥaqq*) to his subjects' obedience and cooperation ('love') was contingent on his honouring of the pledges and promises (*ᶜuhūd*) that he had contracted with them. The qualities of *wafāᵓ* and *amāna* were essential to the maintenance of the social relationships through which the king's governance was conducted and the subjects' lives rendered secure; breach of these principles risked the severance of the king's bonds with the intermediaries on whose active support his governance depended.[21]

Pseudo-Māwardī resumes his exposition with reference to the metaphor of the craftsman:

> At the same time, every master craftsman (*ṣāniᶜ*) and aspiring apprentice (*sāᶜin*, lit. runner) in the world must of necessity possess knowledge (*maᶜrifa*) of a craft (*ṣināᶜa*) in which he is skilled, a tool (*āla*) that he employs, a material (*mādda*) that he imprints according to his intended design, and a purpose (*gharaḍ*) that he seeks to accomplish in the fruit of his action. The craft of the king is governance (*siyāsa*), and his science (*ᶜilm*) is his proficiency in it. His material(s) and tool(s) are his army (*jund*), his 'assistants' (*aᶜwān*), his officials (*ᶜummāl*), and his *khadam*, and his material(s) (*mādda*) are his subjects. The fruit of his action is the reward that he earns from Almighty God in the Abode of Felicity in eternity, and a fine reputation after his death and during his lifetime in both the future and the here and now (*fī l-ghāᵓib wa-l-shāhid wa-l-ātī wa-l-ḥāḍir*). The adornment of his action, and the excellence in it that indicates his proficiency and pre-eminence in his craft are the prosperity of his kingdom (*ᶜimārat mamlakatihi*) and the well-being of his subjects (*ṣalāḥ ḥāl al-raᶜiyya*). It is necessary that the king act, persevere and strive in accordance with this set of principles, for if he opposes, eschews, abandons or turns away from this path, he will destroy his capital (*raᵓs māl*), which is the material (*mādda*) [of his craft], and will nullify the fruit of his action. [In fact,] he will dem-

> onstrate his ignorance of his craft, and that is a most patent loss (*dhālika abyan al-khusrān*).[22]

Pseudo-Māwardī's extended application of the metaphor of craftsmanship, I suggest, displays his affinity with the Kindian tradition.[23] This passage of *Naṣīḥat al-mulūk* is the third and most lengthy instance in which Pseudo-Māwardī adduces the conceptual world of crafts. In his initial portrayal of kingship, he had already likened some of the king's subjects to 'material' (*mādda*) and others to a 'tool' (*āla*); the ruler, he stated, employed the 'tool' to shape the 'material' and thereby produce an image or 'form' (*ṣūra*) according to the degree of his skill in his craft, his proficiency in (fulfilling) his 'purpose' (*gharaḍ*) and his intention (*niyya*).[24] He also compared the *khāṣṣa* with the tool of the craftsman (*ṣāniᶜ*) in his previous chapter.[25] The passage reproduced above bears comparison with Abū Zayd al-Balkhī's description of kingship as a craft (*ṣināᶜa*), for which the craftsman, like any other artisan (*ṣāniᶜ*), requires five things that constitute its causes (or properties) (*khamsat ashyāʾ takūnu ᶜilalan lahā*): its material (*mādda*), form (*ṣūra*), motion (*ḥaraka*) or agent (*fāᶜil*), purpose (*gharaḍ*) and tool (or instrument) (*āla*).[26] Abū Zayd al-Balkhī opens his presentation with the observation that governance is a craft that accomplishes 'the prosperity of the land and the protection of the human beings in it' (*ᶜimārat al-bilād wa-ḥimāyat man fīhā min al-ᶜibād*), and he identifies its purpose as 'the permanence and duration of the common good' (*baqāʾ al-maṣlaḥa wa-dawāmuhā*). These formulations recall Pseudo-Māwardī's 'prosperity of his kingdom and the well-being of his subjects'. Whereas Abū Zayd al-Balkhī's portrayal remains abstract, Pseudo-Māwardī explicitly identifies the 'material', 'tool' and 'product' of the king's craftsmanship with elements of the body politic and the objectives of his governance.

Pseudo-Māwardī continues with a characteristically diverse set of exemplary texts:

> It is related from [the Companion of the Prophet] Abū Hurayra that he said: An hour's justice is better than sixty years of worship, spent keeping vigil during the nights and fasting during the day; and the injustice of an hour in government (*ḥukm*) is greater before God than the sins of sixty years.[27]

> Similarly, it is related concerning many of the kings of the Persians that they used to say: It is fitting that the righteous king (*ḥaqīq ᶜalā al-malik al-ṣāliḥ*) should pray for the righteous subjects (*an yadᶜuwa lil-raᶜiyya al-ṣāliḥa*). It is not fitting for the subjects to pray for the righteous king, because the prayer closest to God (*aqrab al-duᶜāʾ ilā llāh*) is the prayer of the righteous king.[28]

> We have read in one of the chronicles of the Indians: None is more beneficial for God's servants (*aṣlaḥ li-ᶜibād Allāh*), and none more fortunate in earning God's satisfaction (*riḍwān Allāh*) than the ruler who acts righteously. Nor is anyone more corrupting to God's servants and to himself than the ruler who acts corruptly. For the ruler occupies the same place in relation to the subjects as the soul (*rūḥ*) to the body that possesses no life without it, and he occupies the place of the head in relation to the limbs (*arkān*) that have no capacity to endure except by it. Notwithstanding the superiority of his position, it is needful that the ruler attend to the improvement of the subjects, just as it is needful for the subjects to seek the improvement of the ruler, for the strength of each one of them increases the strength of the other, and the weakness of each one of them hastens the weakening of the other.[29]

Pseudo-Māwardī presents texts that emphasise the king's primary responsibilities towards his subjects, and that depict the mutuality of the relationship. In specific terms they evoke the relationship expressed in the practice of public prayer. The offering of public prayer (*duᶜāʾ*) for the ruler's well-being and longevity featured among the duties of the subjects. A public demonstration of the population's acceptance of the king's authority and of their willingness to display their loyalty to him accompanied, but was distinct from, the subjects' duty to acknowledge the ruler's suzerainty in the weekly *khuṭba* that followed the congregational prayer on Fridays. As shown in Chapter 1, in his preface, Pseudo-Māwardī encouraged his royal addressee to heed his advice, noting that it would garner for him an abundance of friends, and 'unleash for him, and on his behalf, voices of praise and prayer in support of him and in affection for him' (*wa-aṭlaqa fīhi wa-lahu alsinat al-thanāʾ wa-l-duᶜā al-maḥrūḍ ᶜalayhi wa-l-marghūb fīhi*).[30] The duty to offer *duᶜāʾ* on behalf of the ruler and sometimes his dynasty provides an illustration of Pseudo-Māwardī's theme of the subjects' 'love' of their monarch. It also falls among the practical means by which the population fulfilled the duty of manifesting 'gratitude' for the benefit of royal sovereignty.[31]

Seeking to convince his royal audience to exercise restraint in his governance, Pseudo-Māwardī asserts that the responsibilities and claims of rulers and their subjects are reciprocal. The ruler's claim to his subjects' prayers on his behalf remained current only as long as he earned their loyalty through his justice and trustworthiness. Indeed, urban communities sometimes reversed their prayer and, in public demonstrations of discontent, directed their petitions for the removal of unjust or corrupt rulers. If a figure of high moral and religious standing instigated such negative public prayer, his act carried considerable authority. The previously mentioned case of the *muḥaddith* Abū Yaᶜlā ᶜAbd al-Muᵓmin b. Khalaf (259–346/873–957) of Nasaf provides an example of a well-known and widely admired individual, a descendant of a Companion of the Prophet and member of a family of transmitters of ḥadīth, who had travelled widely in Transoxiana, Khurasan, Iraq and Syria in order to hear and write down ḥadīth, and had a reputation for the performance of miracles (*karāmāt*).[32] The possibility that such persons might offer public prayer for the removal of a ruler or pray for his perdition constituted a further motivation for rulers to cultivate scholars and renunciants, whom Pseudo-Māwardī listed among the groupings on whose cooperation the ruler depended.[33] The case provides an illustration of the ruler's forfeiture of his subjects' obedience and cooperation if he failed to govern according to the agreed upon expectations.

After this evocation of the mutual needs of rulers and their subjects, Pseudo-Māwardī addresses the specific claims of the subjects in their relationship to the ruler:

> Among the rights of the subjects from the imam (*min ḥaqq al-raᶜiyya ᶜalā l-imām*) – since He has commanded them to obedience, counsel and support (*bi-l-ṭāᶜa wa-l-naṣīḥa wa-l-muᵓāzara*), to paying taxes and providing supplies (*al-akhrija wa-l-muᵓna*), the *jizya* (poll-tax) of the *ahl al-dhimma* (protected peoples) and the *zakāt* (alms) of the *ahl al-milla* (the Muslim community) – is that he exalt their religion, conduct them according to its paths and signposts, and uphold among them the prayers for the feasts, Fridays and [religious, seasonal or regional] festivals (*an . . . yuqīma fihim al-ṣalawāt min al-aᶜyād wa-l-jumaᶜāt wa-l-mawāsim*); that he defend their

> territory (*ḥawza*), fulfil their petitions, and fight their enem(ies) on their behalf; that he make their lands prosperous and their roads safe, maintain (with the protected communities) their covenant of protection (*an . . . yaḥfaẓa dhimmatahum*), deliver justice to the wronged among them from their oppressor(s), and to the weak among them from the strong, and preserve for them their possessions and their persons; that he uphold among them God's statutes, that He has stipulated for them and against them, without leniency, inclination or partiality; that he provide liberally in fulfilment of their due claims (*ḥuqūq*) from the treasury, according to the (Prophet's) practice (*ᶜalā mā jāᶜat bihi al-sunna*) and that which the sharīᶜa has mandated for them. If the ruler does not fulfil the subjects' due claim(s) against him, yet still demands his claim from them, he is the leading oppressor and the most unjust tyrant. God great and glorious has made (the holder of) power an arbiter among them (*wa-qad jaᶜala Allāhu ᶜazza wa-jalla al-sulṭāna ḥakaman baynahum*), an arbiter who restrains some of them from others; how is this to be accomplished by one who oppresses and inflicts harm? [The exemplary figure] al-Ḥasan al-Baṣrī said: He only made (the holder of) power (*al-sulṭān*) as a means of supporting His religion (*nāṣiran li-dīnihi*); what, then, of the one by whom injustice is permitted as if it were licit?[34]

Urging the king to rule justly, Pseudo-Māwardī specifies the reciprocal responsibilities of the subjects and their rulers. The subjects' duties include obedience and the rendering of counsel, and take the concrete form of the submission of their taxes and provisions. The ruler's responsibilities include the upholding of the ritual and legal requirements of the Muslim community (*ahl al-milla*), the protection of the non-Muslim communities (*ahl al-dhimma*), the defence of the realm, the promotion of prosperity and security within his territories, and the fulfilment of his subjects' needs, according to their due claims, from his treasury. Niẓām al-Mulk would recapitulate Pseudo-Māwardī's point that the ruler, after the exaction of the taxes due to him, had no further rights over the persons or possessions of his subjects.[35]

Pseudo-Māwardī gives prominence to the theme of trust throughout *Naṣīḥat al-mulūk*. The ruler is the steward or trustee over his subjects. He is responsible, for a fleeting period of time, for their well-being; eventually, the subjects' divine master will hold him accountable for his conduct towards them. The concept follows the Qurʾānic association of sovereignty, *mulk*, with God: God is 'the owner of sovereignty', *mālik al-mulk* (Q. 3: 26), and earthly kings derive their turns in power according to God's will.[36] It also continues the region's ancient wisdom. Ibn Abī Dharr, author of *Kitāb al-Saʿāda wa-l-isʿād*, cited Anūshīrvān's articulation of the point:

> Kings are the trustees of God (*umanāʾ Allāh*) in His earth and over His creatures. The first thing to which an executor (*al-muʾtaman*) should attend is the preservation of that which has been entrusted to him.[37]

In his treatment of the interdependence and mutual obligations of ruler and subjects, Pseudo-Māwardī seeks to persuade the ruler to exercise his power in accordance with the divine principles of justice and fairness. He turns next to the practical implementation of the ruler's duties.

The Ten Requirements in the Ruler's Conduct

Following the method that he had adopted in his treatment of the *khāṣṣa*, Pseudo-Māwardī enumerates ten items that concern the ruler's governance of his *ʿāmma*:

> We shall now gather, under ten headings, the items to which the king must attend in this regard. We shall expound these topics, support them with proofs, and explicate them from the point of view of the well-being that they induce.
>
> Among these ten items, some concern both the *khāṣṣa* and the *ʿāmma*, because the king's *khāṣṣa*, according to the degree of their familiarity with the king (*ʿalā miqdār al-taʿāruf*), are, in relation to those apart from them, commoners (*ʿāmma*) . . . Others are unique to the *ʿāmma* to the exclusion of the *khāṣṣa*.[38]
>
> Of the items that encompass the *khāṣṣa* and the *ʿāmma* is, as we have mentioned, inducing, urging and encouraging observance of the external aspect of the law (*al-ḥaml ʿalā ẓāhir al-sharīʿa wa-l-ḥathth ʿalayhā wa-l-targhīb fīhā*), showing honour towards those who are observant in this matter and holding them in reverence (*iẓhār karāmat al-mutadayyinīn ʿalayhi*

> *wa-jalālatihim ᶜindahu*); preventing displays of corruption and debauchery, such as games of chance (*maysir*), the drinking of wines, drunkenness and dissoluteness, false accusation, excessive lamentation over the dead (*al-niyāḥāt al-fāḥisha ᶜalā l-mawtā*),[39] and every act that is forbidden and reprehensible in the religion, as well as that which is subsumed in the areas of *ḥisba* [the maintenance of public morals] and (the duty of) commanding the good and forbidding the reprehensible (*al-amr bi-l-maᶜrūf wa-l-nahy an al-munkar*).[40]

Upholding the requirements of the religious law in the public sphere, a royal responsibility that, in keeping with his Muᶜtazilite orientation, he has emphasised repeatedly, constitutes the first of Pseudo-Māwardī's list of necessary qualities. As he has done throughout his mirror, he employs numerous terms involving the root *ẓ-h-r*, to manifest or display openly, and conveys the ruler's duty to observe the categories of mandatory and forbidden activities, and to maintain in the public arena standards of decency and moral behaviour associated with the injunctions of *ḥisba* and 'commanding right and forbidding wrong'. His list of infractions is largely Qurʾānic, or grounded in Prophetic tradition.

Pseudo-Māwardī proceeds to his second item:

> The second matter, also mentioned previously, concerns the protection of the subjects' heartland (*bayḍa*) and the preservation of their territory (*ḥawza*), and confronting their enemies and those who rebel against them (*mujāhadat aᶜdāʾihim wa-l-bāghīn ᶜalayhim*). The king's performance of these duties should be adequate to ensure that the subjects' means of livelihood become abundant, that they are secure from assault (*maᶜarra*) by their enemies, and able to attend to their means of earning a living. Also, he should promote the prosperity of the kingdom, facilitate their ability to pay their land-taxes (*akhrija*), additional duties (*waẓāʾif*), charitable donations (*ṣadaqāt*) and levies (*ḍarāʾib*) to the treasury,[41] encourage the increase of their families and the growth of the population, the permanently settled and the newcomers (*wa-yukaththir ahlahā wa-yuᶜaẓẓim sawādahā min al-muqīmīn wa-l-ṭāriʾīn*), by procreation and reproduction. This kind of governance belongs to the good practice (*adab*) of God, great and glorious, and is a distinctive characteristic (*khāṣṣa*) of the prophets, imams and kings.[42]

The second aspect for which rulers are responsible to their subjects includes the preservation of their lands against external enemies and rebels, and the promotion of their prosperity and material well-being. Pseudo-Māwardī explains that the subjects' ability to submit their taxes in accordance with their duties depends on the king's active attention to their security; he also perhaps implies that their ability to cultivate their lands and generate revenue depends on their release from military service. The taxes listed in this passage differ from the exclusively religious dues of *zakawāt* and *ṣadaqāt* enumerated in Pseudo-Māwardī's sixth chapter.[43] Ibn Ḥawqal remarked on the Samanids' recourse to ancient patterns for the assessment of local sums and allocations: 'They possess ancient (records of) established local donations, fiscal lists and daily registers' (*lahā ᶜibar qadīma wa-dustūrāt wa-rūznāmajāt*), which, he implies, facilitated the distribution of allowances with equity and consistency, with neither shortfall nor excess.[44] To illustrate the solicitude with which the ruler should observe his responsibility towards his subjects, Pseudo-Māwardī reports an account concerning Caliph Hārūn al-Rashīd:

> It has reached us concerning Caliph Hārūn al-Rashīd that he set out by night during one of his journeys and military expeditions (*fī baᶜḍ asfārihi wa-ghazawātihi*). Snow overtook him, and afflicted him. One of his companions said to him, 'Will you not consider, O Commander of the Faithful, the hardship (*jahd*) that we are in, while the subjects are at rest?' He said, 'Be quiet. It is for them to sleep and for us to keep vigil: the shepherd must keep his flock and suffer for them.'[45]

Thirdly, Pseudo-Māwardī addresses the preservation of order and security in the kingdom. Urging the king to adopt a moral stance in matters of criminal justice, he concentrates on the need for equal treatment, without regard to status or relationship, and for punishment suitable to the offence:

> The third matter is the elimination of those who frighten, abuse and corrupt the subjects, and preventing their access to them . . . The ruler should not be swayed by mildness, nor by inclination towards a criminal into partiality in this matter, for partiality towards them is tantamount to the

abandonment of partiality for himself, and allowing criminals to persist leads to the perdition of the subjects . . .

At the same time, Islam has imposed restrictions on killing, and prevented and forbidden severe punishment; for it is among the rights of the people against the king that he should not punish anyone out of prejudice (*taʿaṣṣub*) or anger (*taghaḍḍub*), but only as a means of instruction (*taʾdīb*) and in obedience to religion (*tadayyun*). The correct method is that the king should not oppose the decree of his religion in the matter of punishment. He should look into the upholding of these statutory penalties, and the correction of criminals among the subjects. He should examine and investigate (suspected offenders), and should not impose any kind of punishment on anyone without clear proof (*bayān*) and evidence (*burhān*).[46]

As for those among them for whom imprisonment is required, it is necessary that he should examine their conditions and investigate their affairs in three respects. Firstly, he should not imprison anybody unless he has ascertained that his imprisonment is required. Secondly, he should maintain prisoners during their confinement by the provision of food and clothing, for they are a group who are prevented from caring for themselves and from striving to meet these basic needs. Not all of them have money to spend or a friend to attend to them, so the sufficing of their needs and their maintenance are the responsibility of the imam, who is the friend of the Muslims, and the *sulṭān*, [who] is a friend to him who has no friend (*al-imām alladhī huwa walī l-muslimīn wa-l-sulṭān walī man lā walīya lahu*).[47] Thirdly, he should examine them continually, because a sinner may experience remorse or a criminal repent; a truthful person's claim may receive the acknowledgement of his adversaries, or a liar may regret his falsehood. There may be some among them whose families are in dire straits, since they have depended on his labour for their provisions, on his toil for their support, and on his earning(s) for their livelihood. There is also the sick person who has no nurse to care for him and no physician to attend him.

Imprisonment is among the most serious of punishments, and punishments should be applied only in proportion to their crimes. It is not permitted

> for the ruler to treat criminals guilty of minor transgressions as if they were equal to those who have committed major crimes, and to subject both groups to permanent banishment, exile, fettering and expulsion. The only exception arises in the case of a person who persists, for whom imprisonment is necessary to prevent him from corruption in the earth (*fasād fī l-arḍ*), and who then neither desists nor repents.[48]

Having urged, in keeping with the citations that he adduced at the beginning of his chapter, the principles of clemency and justice, Pseudo-Māwardī urges the ruler to implement fair punishments, to be swayed neither by attachment to nor distaste for the criminal, and to avoid excessive measures of retribution. His discussion of imprisonment and his attention to the rights and fair treatment of prisoners are particularly noteworthy. The plight of prioners was a matter of public concern; as ᶜAbdallāh b. Ṭāhir demonstrated in the acts that accompanied his repentance, the release of prisoners was meritorious.[49] I suggest that Pseudo-Māwardī wrote in the light of his personal observation and solicitude on behalf of a prisoner, or prisoners, whom he considered to have been unfairly treated. The textual evidence of *Naṣīḥat al-mulūk* and the conditions of Pseudo-Māwardī's milieu provide a number of possibilities. Naṣr II's great-uncle Isḥāq, of whom Pseudo-Māwardī held a high opinion, had been imprisoned after the defeat of his challenge to the young amir's accession; the military governor Aḥmad b. Sahl had been imprisoned and mistreated under his Saffarid overlord ᶜAmr b. al-Layth and, when in the suppression of his later rebellion against Samanid suzerainty, Aḥmad was imprisoned again, he died in detention; Pseudo-Māwardī's fellow citizen al-Kaᶜbī, who had served as Aḥmad's vizier, was imprisoned in the course of the same events; the scholar and municipal leader Saᶜīd b. Ibrāhīm al-Raʾīs al-Nasafī, whose detention elicited the ḥadīth-scholar Abū Yaᶜlā's public prayer for his release, was subjected to examination (*miḥna*) in connection with the apparently violent disturbances described as 'the factionalism of the Qarmaṭīs' (*taᶜaṣṣub al-qarāmiṭa*).[50] It seems quite possible that Pseudo-Māwardī was acquainted with some of these individuals, and likely that he was familiar with the reports of their ordeals.

Next, Pseudo-Māwardī turns to the ruler's responsibility for establishing justice towards all his subjects:

The fourth requirement is that he should render judgement among them in their grievances and their petitions (*an yaḥkuma baynahum fī maẓālimihim wa-daᶜāwīhim*). He should hear their proofs and testimonies according to the Book of God, great and glorious, and the *sunna* of His Prophet, and that which the truth (the rightful claim) and legal judgement mandate (*mā yūjibuhu al-ḥaqq wa-l-ḥukm*).[51]

He should exert himself in the selection of judges (*ḥukkām*), and appoint only persons who are religiously observant and upright (*al-dayyin al-ᶜafīf*), knowledgeable and learned in jurisprudence (*al-ᶜālim al-faqīh*), resourceful and trustworthy (*al-arīb al-amīn*), dignified and composed (*al-waqūr al-razīn*), as stated in the previous chapter. He should direct the judge to immerse himself in investigation, rational enquiry and finding for the weak against the strong, not to rush to judgement before the completion of the investigation and enquiry, nor to delay after the firm establishment of proof and consolidation of the evidence. For in both those cases lie neglect and omission. The judge should not render judgement out of inclination, nor stray from the path of justice out of partiality towards the person awaiting judgement, lest he judge against himself, and make him his adversary on the Day of Resurrection, in the presence of One whom inclination does not cause to waver, and in whose sentences injustice (*ḍaym*) never occurs. That approach has never ceased to be God's charge (*waṣiyya*) to His prophets and the substance of His commands delivered to His friends (*awliyāᵓ*). For He said: 'O David, We have made you a deputy (*khalīfa*) in the earth, so judge among the people according to the truth, and do not follow passion, lest it divert you from the path of God' (38:26).[52]

The essential prerequisite in the matter of the *qāḍī* and the *ḥākim* is that the ruler should appoint him on terms that provide him with ample and comfortable allowances (*al-arzāq al-wāsiᶜa al-hanīᵓa*), so that he has no need for and will not covet the possessions of the subjects (*raᶜiyya*); for avidity for the goods of the lower world, especially in these times of ours, has become a habit among the ᶜulamāᵓ (*qad ṣāra ᶜādatan lil-ᶜulamāᵓ*), quite contrary to what ought to be the case with them. It is related from the Prophet that he said, 'Anyone who increases in knowledge and also increases in cupidity for the world, increases only in distance from God, while God increases in dislike of him.'[53]

Aristotle summed the whole matter up when he said: 'The judge (*ḥākim*) is a lord (*sayyid*) to those over whom he holds authority (*sayyid* ᶜ*alā man waliyahu*), so in the judge, four qualities should come together, namely, that he be modest (*ḥayyiy*), scrupulous (*wari*ᶜ), knowledgeable (ᶜ*ālim*) and not hasty (*ghayr* ᶜ*ajūl*). Know that the judge brings adornment to judgement (*ḥukm*) by his justice, and sullies it by the pollution of cleaving to a path other than the correct path.' He also said, 'Be wary of the judge who has an appetite for talk, for such a person is not well suited for the exercise of judgement (*ḥukūma*). The perfection of this matter requires that the king make the judge free of need for the possessions of the subjects (*ra*ᶜ*iyya*), and that he make his allowances (*arzāq*) ample for him. The king should make himself available to the judge whenever counsel (*naṣīḥa*) is forthcoming from him, and he should not hasten to promote him. If you (the king) disapprove of anything in his treatment of the affairs of the subjects, then investigate him, just as the judge investigates, in accordance with the established *sunna*; and induce him to follow the established pattern of judgement. If he is well liked among the people and your reproach of him concerns your affairs specifically, then conceal it and promote someone else for his fine standing and knowledge; when the latter becomes well-known and familiar among the people, then dismiss the first with the evident and strong proof (*al-ḥujja al-ẓāhira al-qawiyya*) that you hold against him.'[54]

The juxtaposition of Pseudo-Māwardī's remarks concerning judges with his quotation of Pseudo-Aristotle's summary (*faṣl jāmi*ᶜ) indicates the degree to which the latter repertoire informed his advice on this topic. He employs some of the same vocabulary, which he explicitly applies to the conditions of his time by asserting the bad habit prevalent among the ᶜulamāᵓ of his day of taking money from the subjects. His inclusion of Pseudo-Aristotle's remarks concerning the removal of judges who are well liked among the population are of particular interest, and perhaps prompted, by way of association, Pseudo-Māwardī's next quotation, which is the lengthy letter dispatched by the second Rightly Guided Caliph, ᶜUmar, to Abū Mūsā al-Ashᶜarī, a Companion of the Prophet and military leader. ᶜUmar appointed Abū

Mūsā al-Ashᶜarī governor of Basra and Kufa on different occasions, but a series of complaints against him were brought to ᶜUmar and to his successor ᶜUthmān. Nevertheless, Abū Mūsā enjoyed the support of the Kufan population, who requested his appointment as governor in 22/642–3 and again in 34/654–5; on the latter occasion, the inhabitants of Kufa drove out the existing governor, Saᶜīd b. al-ᶜĀṣ. Pseudo-Māwardī reproduces the text of ᶜUmar's letter in full:

> It is incumbent that the qāḍī not neglect to use the contents of the letter of the Commander of the Faithful ᶜUmar b. al-Khaṭṭāb to Abū Mūsā al-Ashᶜarī, for it constitutes the beginnings of the science of the judge's office (*fa-innahu awāʾil ᶜilm al-qaḍāʾ*). He wrote to him:
>
> To proceed (*ammā baᶜd*):[55] the office of judge (*al-qaḍāʾ*) is an established duty (*farīḍa muḥkama*) and a practice (*sunna*) that should be followed. So if you are presented with this office, you must understand that there is no profit in speaking truthfully without acting accordingly. Deal equally with the people in your presence (*fī wajhika*), your legal assembly (*[fī] majlisika*) and in your justice (*[fī] ᶜadlika*), so that no noble person covets your partiality, nor any weak person fears your injustice. The supply of proof (*bayyina*) is the responsibility of the plaintiff (*man iddaᶜā*), and the swearing of the oath (*yamīn*) the responsibility of the defendant (*man ankara*). Reconciliation (*ṣulḥ*) among Muslims is permissible, except in the case of a reconciliation that would prohibit the lawful or render lawful the prohibited. Your judgement in a case yesterday should by no means prevent you from returning to reconsider it (*rājaᶜta fīhi*), if you see fit, in order to render judgement according to the truth, guided by your sense of right (*li-rushdika*). For truth is eternal, and reversing a decision in accordance with the truth is better than persisting in falsehood. The exercise of comprehension (*fahm*) is appropriate in the case of issues that produce trouble in your breast, and are not addressed in the Qurʾān and the *sunna*. Master the issues that are similar and comparable (*al-amthāl wa-l-ashbāh*), then draw analogies (*qis*) in affairs on that basis; attend to that which is most pleasing to God and most closely resembles the truth in your view. Establish for the plaintiff a set period of time; if in that time he presents a proof, he has acted in accordance with his right (*ḥaqq*); if not, then judge against him, for that

is the clearest response in obscurity and the most effective in cases of difficulty. Muslims are deemed to be persons of probity (*ᶜudūl*) one to another, except in the case of a person who has been chastised in accordance with a statutory penalty, is proven to have given false testimony, or is suspected of ties of clientage (*walāʾ*) or family relationship (*qarāba*), for God turns away their secrets and rejects their doubts.

Be wary of irritation, agitation, taking offence at people and hostility towards the adversaries in situations that call for the truth, for which God has stipulated a reward and which improves your stores (for the future life). For whoever is sincere in his intention towards God (and acts in the light of) his relationship with Him, even if it entails acting against himself, God will recompense him for (the consequences that such action might produce) in terms of his relationship with the people (*al-nās*); whereas whoever fabricates for the sake of the people (*al-nās*) when God knows that the opposite is true, God will not spare him (*yashunnuhu Allāh*). Do not entertain thoughts of recompense from any source other than God, whose heavenly reward brings ready sustenance and the treasuries of His mercy. Farewell.[56]

Perhaps by way of association, Pseudo-Māwardī adduces further evidence of ᶜUmar's authority in matters of the judgeship when he cites a second letter:

They said: He [ᶜUmar] wrote to [his governor in Damascus, later the first Umayyad caliph] Muᶜāwiya b. Abī Sufyān:

'To proceed, I am writing you a letter to avoid neglecting you or myself in performing a good action, and in it I stipulate five things. If you understand them, you will make your religion sound and you will position yourself well for the most excellent possibilities of your appointed lot. When two adversaries come before you, it is your responsibility to establish what is a just piece of evidence (*al-bayyina al-ᶜādila*) and a decisive oath (*al-yamīn al-qāṭiᶜa*). Bring close (*adni*) the weak party so that his heart becomes strong and his tongue will loosen. Make a pact with the stranger; for if you do not make a pact with him, he will abandon his claim (*ḥaqq*) and return to his people, and he who does not bring forward his case forfeits his claim. You are enjoined to bring about reconciliation between people where the proper judgement is not clear to you.'[57]

This extensive treatment of the office of the judgeship is separate from Pseudo-Māwardī's treatment of the ruler's redress of grievances, to which he turns later in the chapter.[58]

After this treatment of the qualities required in judges and the practice of rendering judgement, Pseudo-Māwardī proceeds to his fifth point:

> The fifth requirement is that you should know the categories and ranks of the people (*ṭabaqāt al-nās wa-marātib[u]hum*): the sons of kings (*abnāʾ al-mulūk*), the nobles (*al-ashrāf*), those with lineages and acquired merits and their children (*dhaw[ū] l-ansāb wa-l-aḥsāb wa-awlāduhum*); the scholars and ascetics and their relatives (*al-ʿulamāʾ wa-l-nussāk wa-dhaw[ū] hum*); the wealthy and the owners of estates and lands (*al-aghniyāʾ wa-arbāb al-ḍiyāʿ wa-l-araḍīn*); the merchants, craftsmen and artisans (*al-tujjār wa-l-ṣunnāʿ wa-l-mahana*); and the men of degrees (*aṣḥāb al-aqdār*) among them. The king should arrange them in their ranks and situate them in their places, and give abundantly to each category its rightful claim in proportion to their stations (*ʿalā maqādīr asbābihim*) and their ranks, in joy, to foster closeness, show kindness and effect a proper arrangement (*bi-l-bishr wa-l-taqrīb wa-l-irfāq wa-l-tartīb*). For such treatment will stimulate them to compete with one another in precedence (*tasābuq*) in seeking the good, and to vie with one another in the acquisition of excellence in their particular situations, and that is a causal factor in the ordering of their affairs, the harmonious arrangement of their conditions, and the cultivation of sweetness of disposition in their souls. If they are treated in the opposite manner, it will lead them to harbour resentment against the ruler (*sulṭān*) and to bear him a grudge, because when a person who perceives in himself an excellence in terms of nobility, knowledge, courage, distinction, bravery or competence finds that his rightful claim is ignored, and that which he deserves and merits is withheld from him, this manner of treatment will offend him and cause vexation, and embitter him and cause rancour. It will seem to him that he has been deprived of a compelling claim (*ḥaqq wājib*) and a binding obligation (*dayn lāzim*), and that he has been oppressed with a great injustice (*ẓulm ʿaẓīm*). He who possesses the power will choose to defend himself against this injustice (*ikhtāra dafʿahu ʿanhā*) if he finds a way to do so. And even if he does not find a way, his obedience will be that

> of someone who feels loathing but is compelled, oppressed and overpowered, and not the obedience of someone who acts voluntarily and out of love (*muḥibb mukhtār*).[59]

This passage, discussed in Volume I, lists the categories among the *ᶜāmma* whose consent to his authority and willing obedience the king requires. It includes groups whose status lies in their inherited merit, in their wealth, in acquired merit and in their economic productivity. The *ᶜāmma*, as the passage makes clear, do not include labourers, other than the stated groups, agricultural workers, or the poor or indigent, presumably since these groups were not in a position to play a mediating role. To earn the loyalty and cooperation of these essential groups, the king must fulfil his subjects' due expectations by way of recompense and advancement. Pseudo-Māwardī's terms *taqrīb*, to 'bring close', *irfāq*, 'kindness' and *tartīb*, 'proper arrangement' reflect the theme of proximity, and perhaps refer, for the higher ranks among the categories of the people (*ṭabaqāt al-nās*), to a summons to the ruler's presence to initiate or renew ties of *khidma* and *wafāʾ*.[60] His depiction of the change of heart that persons of substance experience when their merits are overlooked recalls the rebellions of Naṣr's high-ranking and long-standing commanders.[61] Pseudo-Māwardī reiterates the point that the ruler should not assume his subjects' unconditional loyalty; if slighted or injured, it is possible, if the means and the opportunity are available to them, that they will resist. He continues with texts that evoke differing degrees of merit:

> God made this matter incumbent in His Book, clarified it to His Prophet and made it part of His religion when He said: 'Lower your wing to those among the believers who follow you' (26: 215),[62] and 'Those among you who spent and fought before the victory are not equal (with those who did not); those persons are greater in degree than those who spent and fought afterwards' (57: 10). He said: 'The believers who stay behind, other than those who have suffered harm, are not equal with those who struggle in the way of God with their wealth and their lives; God has favoured by a degree those who strive with their possessions and their lives over those who remain behind' (4: 95). And He said: 'Are those who know equal with those who do not know? Only persons of understanding remember' (39: 9). He said, 'The inhabitants of the Fire are not equal with the inhabitants of

> Paradise' (59: 20), and He said, 'Or do those who commit evil deeds reckon that We shall make them like those who believe and perform good deeds, equal to them in life and in death? How wrongly they judge!' (45: 21).[63]

In this context, Pseudo-Māwardī's texts imply that the king should exercise discernment among his subjects and richly reward loyal service. Some of the Qurʾānic quotations allude to the Muslims who fought with the Prophet against the early community's enemies. It is possible that Pseudo-Māwardī alludes in particular to the military commanders who had won victories on behalf of the Samanids and received inadequate recompense from the amir. These individuals sometimes responded by rejecting Samanid overlordship and asserting their independent power. The hypothesis that Pseudo-Māwardī had such persons in mind is strengthened by his next sequence of texts, which urge the overlooking of offences committed by prominent individuals:

> The Prophet said: 'Overlook the transgressions of persons of stature.'[64] He spread his cloak for Qays b. ʿĀṣim al-Minqarī [d. 47/667, leader of the delegation of Tamīm to the Prophet, reputed for his generosity and forbearance] and said, 'When the noble person of a group comes to you, treat him nobly.'[65] He said on the Day of the Conquest [of Mecca, 8/629]: 'Whoever enters the house of Abū Sufyān [d. 32–4/653–5, leading merchant of Quraysh and opponent of the Prophet in the years before the taking of Mecca] is safe.'[66] And he said to him: 'There are all kinds of game in the belly of the wild ass.'[67]

> On the (Battle) Day of Ḥunayn [8/630], he gave many of those whose hearts were to be conciliated (*al-muʾallafa qulūbuhum*)[68] more than he gave to many of the excellent persons among the believers, then he praised every group according to its situation, invited each one according to that which he deserved, favoured each person among his Companions with that which he merited, and chose him for that for which he was worthy. In God lies a model and in the Prophet an example. This is a subject related to governance (*hādhā bāb min al-siyāsa*) in which lies great (potential) benefit (*kathīra manfaʿatuhu*) and great (potential) damage (*ʿaẓīma maḍarratuhu*).[69]

In his last example, Pseudo-Māwardī seems to imply an equation between the higher ranking intermediaries, including, perhaps, those who had rebelled and had been imprisoned or executed, and the Qurʾānic *al-muʾallafa qulūbuhum*, persons whose hearts the Prophet sought to win through generosity and the bestowal of privilege. Abū Sufyān played a leading role in the Meccan and Qurashī resistance to the Prophet and his community in the years preceding the Muslims' taking of Mecca in 8/629. When the Muslims entered the city in a bloodless victory, the Prophet not only refrained from retribution, but also extended great honour to Abū Sufyān, by declaring his house a safe haven, as Pseudo-Māwardī mentions. Abū Sufyān, who had possibly become a Muslim shortly before the conquest of Mecca, and his sons Muᶜāwiya and Yazīd were among *al-muʾallafa qulūbuhum*. By implying a parallel between this group and the higher categories among the *ᶜāmma*, Pseudo-Māwardī suggests to his audience that the king's disaffected servants might, by good and generous treatment, redouble their loyalties in his service, just as Abū Sufyān, having joined the Prophet, assisted him in various ways, including as an emissary.[70] The proverb, 'There are all kinds of game in the belly of the wild ass', associated with hunting and employed by the Prophet in his conciliatory conversation with Abū Sufyān, suggests the latter's special status among his peers.[71] In a further example of the particular importance of winning the support of the disaffected, Pseudo-Māwardī reproduces another of Caliph ᶜUmar's communications to Abū Mūsā al-Ashᶜarī:

> It is related of ᶜUmar b. al-Khaṭṭāb that he wrote to Abū Mūsā al-Ashᶜarī: 'To proceed: The people (*al-nās*) still have chiefs (*wujūh*) who remember their needs, so honour the chiefs of the people under your jurisdiction. It suffices the weak Muslim man that he be treated fairly in justice (*ᶜadl*) and division (*qism*).'[72]

This example emphasises the need for the king to secure the loyalty of persons whose support and cooperation are indispensable to him, and to extend exceptional favour to them:

> Kings have not ceased to commend the preservation of this quality and to commend persistence in its maintenance. If you follow their books (*kutub*) and testaments (*ᶜuhūd*), you will not find a single comprehensive testament or complete book that omits it.

> For example, Ardashīr said in his testament (*ᶜahd*), 'Direct your conversation to the people of high ranks (*ahl al-marātib*), your generosity to the people engaged in *jihād (ahl al-jihād)*, and (model) your modes of conduct on the people of religion (*ahl al-dīn*).'[73]
>
> Aristotle wrote to Alexander: 'Defend the people of manly virtues (*ahl al-murūʾāt*) and those who possess ancient precedence in goodness (*qadīm fī l-khayr*). If their present conditions decline, their ancestors remain a source of pride to them, and in terms of nobility, it should suffice you that the sons of kings incline towards you.' And he said, 'Do not reveal the hidden concerns of the people of degrees and pride (*ahl al-aqdār wa-l-anafa*), for the shame of it will rebound against your sovereignty.'[74]
>
> They said: Ardashīr said: Treat the free (noble) people (*aḥrār al-nās*) with pure affection (*mawadda*), for they cannot tolerate degradation; treat the common people (*al-ᶜāmma*) with a mixture of encouragement and fear; and treat the base people (*al-sifla*) with unmixed fear.[75]
>
> . . . Aristotle wrote to Alexander: 'Advance those who are renowned for their scrupulousness (*waraᶜ*), and use them to discharge the needs of the common people (*al-ᶜāmma*).'[76]

After this sequence of quotations, which indicate the universality of Pseudo-Māwardī's advice, he addresses the sixth requisite, the curbing of injustice:

> The sixth point is that the king should protect the common people (*al-ᶜāmma*) from his own injustice, and the injustice of his companions and retinue (*ẓulm aṣḥābihi wa-ḥāshiyatihi*), and that he should eradicate his own covetousness and their covetousness of the Muslims' possessions, their womenfolk and their persons (*ᶜan amwāl al-muslimīn wa-furūjihim wa-ashᶜārihim wa-abshārihim*). He himself should deal justly with them, since we have made clear the corruption that lies in oppression and the well-being (*ṣālaḥ*) that lies in its opposite. This is a matter of the first priority for the king, since it involves honour, seeking the well-being (*istiṣlāḥ*) (of himself and his subjects), sound opinion and astute judgement; for he holds power over them, and the oppression of a human being who is subject to his power and sovereignty is a source of shame and baseness.

If the subjects (*raᶜiyya*) oppress one another, the *sulṭān* is their place of retreat, their succour, their refuge and their source of assistance. If he is unjust, the subjects have no recourse because there is no restraining hand over him. It will become a habit that is difficult to eliminate, and a practice that is almost impossible to abandon. He should behave according to this quality, by which I mean justice (*ᶜadl*), in following the command of God and imitating Him, and accustoming himself to the habits of the righteous among His prophets and His friends (*bi-sunan al-ṣāliḥīn min anbiyāᵓihi wa-awliyāᵓihi*), following the path of the surpassing sages (*sulūkan li-sabīl al-ḥukamāᵓ al-mubarrizīn*), in accordance with God's promise (*mā waᶜada*) to the just of an ample reward and noble recompense in the afterlife, and His threat (*wa-awᶜada*) to the unjust of painful chastisement and severe punishment . . .[77]

The Commander of the Faithful ᶜUmar brought a case before Zayd b. Thābit [d. 45/665, a Companion of the Prophet, one of the Prophet's scribes and qāḍī under ᶜUmar and ᶜUthmān] for judgement, swore an oath against his adversary, and they both reached agreement. The Commander of the Faithful ᶜAlī brought a case before Shurayḥ [b. al-Ḥārith b. Qays al-Kindī, d. *c.* 72–99/691–718, an early qāḍī of Kufa], his qāḍī, for judgement; Shurayḥ pronounced two decrees, and ᶜAlī abided by the legal obligation placed upon him after the verdict.[78]

The Prophet said: 'Fear God in the matter of grievances (*maẓālim*), for injustice constitutes darkness on the Day of Resurrection' . . .[79]

We have read in the testament (*ᶜahd*) of an Indian king to his son: Know that, in the case of the person from whom you have suffered an injustice (*maẓlima*) or against whom you have acted excessively in punishment, that which you have brought upon yourself is more severe than that which you have brought upon him. For the traces left by the injuries of this world are effaced and will disappear, whereas the injuries incurred from sins stick to men's souls until retribution (*qiṣāṣ*) removes them.[80]

In the same way, the resolute kings (*al-mulūk al-ḥazama*) have never ceased to commend this matter, to enjoin it in their testaments (*ᶜuhūd*), to fill their books (*kutub*) with it, and to transmit it in the records (*āthār*) of their conduct (*siyar*). The Sasanian kings, whose traces (*āthār*) have endured over the course of time, had two days in the year, [the festivals of the spring and autumn equinoxes] Nawruz and Mihrajan,[81] on which they appeared for the *khāṣṣa* and the *ᶜāmma*. On those two days no one, great or small, noble or base, was denied access to them. The king ordered that the call should go out throughout the kingdom some days before he sat for the redress of grievances, so that he would be ready for the people by the day of gathering, and the wronged parties could prepare their proofs, write their statements and summon their adversaries. Sometimes, out of fear of humiliation, maltreatment and severe punishment, many persons who had committed acts of injustice reached agreement before that day, and they returned their unjustly taken seizures and compensated the aggrieved parties for the consequences. When the day came, the *mōbadhān*, who was their chief qāḍī, commanded that a man be designated from his trusted companions to stand at the *Bāb al-ᶜāmma*, the gate for the reception of the general population. He was not to prevent anyone from entering the king's presence. The king's herald (*munādin*) called to announce that if anyone should prevent a man from raising his grievance, he had disobeyed God and opposed the custom (*sunna*) of the king; and anyone who disobeyed God invited hostility from Him and from the king. The king commanded that the people be granted permission to enter and their petitions (*riqāᶜ*) taken. He examined them attentively. If any petitioner held a grievance against the king, his case was taken up first and put before every other grievance. The king would summon the leading *mōbadh* (*al-mōbadh al-kabīr*), the chief administrator (*dabīrbādh*) and the head priest of the fire temples (*raʾs sadanat buyūt al-nīrān*),[82] then a herald (*munādin*) would rise and proclaim: 'Let those whose complaint lies against the king stand aside', and they withdrew. The king stood with his adversaries, and even knelt (*yajthū*) in front of the *mōbadh*. He said: 'O *mōbadh*, there is no sin greater before God than the sin of kings. They are entrusted with subjects (*raᶜāyā*) only in order that they should repel injustice (*ẓulm*) from them, and defend the heartland of the kingdom (*bayḍat al-mulk*) against the tyranny of oppressors and the iniquity of the unjust. If they are oppressive tyrants, then those beneath them are entitled to raze the fire temples, and plunder whatever shrouds are in the sarcophagi. This assembly (*majlis*) that you have called, in which I am a lowly servant (*ᶜabd dhalīl*), resembles the assembly in which you will appear before God tomorrow. If you have shown preference to God over the world, He will prefer you; and if you have shown preference to the king, He will punish you.' The *mōbadh* would praise him and speak to him handsomely. Sometimes he would say, 'When God desires the felicity of His servants, He chooses for them the best among the people of the earth; and when He desires to teach them of his stature, He makes him utter the words that have passed over your lips.' Then the *mōbadh* looked into the king's affair and enjoined upon his adversaries truth and justice. If he found a true grievance against the king, he held him to account for it; if not, he detained the individual who had complained falsely against him, and punished him, and announced against him: 'This is the reward of one who wished to disgrace the kingdom and slander it falsely.' When he had finished with the grievances of the king, the latter rose and prostrated himself before God (*sajada li-llāh*) for a long time, and praised God greatly for the grievances that had received redress and the burdens that had been lifted. Then he put the crown on his head and sat on the throne of sovereignty, and turned his attention to his closest companions, his *khāṣṣa* and his relatives (*ilā qurābatihi wa-khāṣṣatihi wa-ḥāmmatihi*). He said: 'I began with myself and have dispensed justice accordingly only so that no covetous person should seek partiality from me. Whoever has a claim, let him return to his adversary in the matter, either in reconciliation or otherwise.' So in terms of his rightful claim, the closest of the people (*aqrab al-nās*) to the king was like the most distant of them, and the strongest of them like the weak among them.[83]

They said: The people did not cease to follow these procedures from the time (*ᶜahd*) of Ardashīr until Yazdagird the Sinner [Yazdagird I, r. 399–420][84] came to rule over them. Yazdagird altered this conduct in the matter of justice. He killed his father, and his affairs proceeded as they did. Then Bahrām Gūr [= Bahrām V, r. 421–38] restored some of the earlier mode of conduct in matters of justice and equity, even though a predilection for diversion and play (*al-lahw wa-l-laᶜb*) predominated in him in most respects.[85]

This section, more heavily narrative than most of Pseudo-Māwardī's discursive text, reproduces, without indication of a source, in almost verbatim fashion materials that also appear in *Kitāb al-Tāj*. As indicated in Chapter 2, it seems likely that Pseudo-Māwardī had independent access to the materials that appear in both texts. He continues with further materials that exhort rulers to redress their subjects' wrongs or depict the lengths to which exemplary kings have gone to display their justice:

> The wise philosopher (*al-ḥakīm*) [Aristotle] wrote to Alexander: The best course for you, O Alexander, is that you should sit for the redress of grievances for the common people (*ᶜāmma*) altogether at the turn of the year. Adhere to the custom of the Indians, for it is praiseworthy; examine that which reaches you, investigate it thoroughly, dispense admonitions to them (the common people) from time to time, and stipulate the times for their gatherings. Aristotle also said: This practice makes for fine conduct as long as you do not allow the period between sessions to lapse, for if something of that sort were to occur over the years and months, people would quietly and unconcernedly commit injustice and oppression until the time of the session. How many a wronged person dies before being able to seek restitution for his claim, and how many an oppressor flees! How many a weak person becomes powerless, how many a truthful person falls ill, and how many a stranger returns to his country and thus forfeits his claim!
>
> It is essential that the king perform this duty over the course of weeks and months. In that time he must ensure that the people who have sought satisfaction have the opportunity to attain it, once he has strengthened his hand and his resolve, and warned the adversaries regarding the decisive threat (*waᶜīd*); or he should inform the parties that such is his judgement, that he has examined the case for indications of neglect, weakness, favouritism or inclination, as we have clarified elsewhere in this book.[86]

Pseudo-Māwardī adduces a variety of illustrative texts to depict the excellent reputation that adheres to royal fairness towards the lowliest of the king's subjects:

> Among the transmitted records of the Persians (*min maᵓthūr āthār al-ᶜajam*) on this subject is that when Kisrā [Khusraw Anūshīrvān] was building the columned hall at Ctesiphon (*al-īwān bi-l-Madāᵓin*), a poor old woman happened to have a house in a corner where they planned to construct

the square of the building. So they asked if they could buy it from her for several times its value, to the extent that she would have had enough dinars to cover the entire surface of that house. She refused, and she said, 'I would rather be near the king than have all this money.' They built it (the hall) with a break in the square. When the edifice had been erected, she came to the king and she said, 'I did not do what I did out of acquisitiveness for property, nor because I wished to vex the king; rather I did it out of my love (*maḥabba*) (for the king), so that the king, by virtue of his sufferance of me, and his equity and his kindness towards me, would continue to possess a praiseworthy quality that will leave an imprint and a virtue (reports of which) will spread over the passing of the days and across the face of time; so that it will prove better for him, and more lasting to his memory, than this building, despite the loftiness of its elevation, the vastness of its design, the solidity of its foundation and the strengths of its pillars.' He thanked her for that act, and he regarded it as a favour (*ṣanīʿa*) on her part, indeed a remarkable favour; and he ordered that she should be honoured and treated with the utmost hospitality.[87]

Qaḥṭaba b. Ḥumayd reported: I was standing by the side of the Commander of the Faithful al-Maʾmūn when he was sitting for a session of *maẓālim*. He sat until nearly sunset, when a woman dressed in tattered rags approached. She stumbled over her clothes and said, 'Peace be upon you, O Commander of the Faithful, and the mercy and blessings of God', and he, having glanced at Yaḥyā b. Aktham [d. 242/857, qāḍī l-quḍāt, Chief Judge of Baghdad, and adviser and boon companion to al-Maʾmūn],[88] said, 'May peace be upon you also; speak, may God have mercy upon you.' And she said [in verse]:

O good and just one, one to whom right guidance (*rushd*) has been vouchsafed
O leader by whom the land is made resplendent
To you, who are bound in sovereignty, a widow brings her complaint:
A lion has assailed her, and she can never prevail against it.
He has altogether robbed me of my estate, which was formerly protected
And he has separated from me my family and children.

Al-Maʾmūn replied to her [in verse]:

> That which you have said is beyond patience and endurance;
> It has distressed me to the bottom of my heart.
> But now it is time for the mid-day prayer; so depart,
> And appear before me again on the appointed day:
> At the Saturday *majlis*, if the session is so determined for us
> I shall recompense you in this matter, and if not, then at the Sunday *majlis*.

> Qaḥṭaba continued: So she turned away, and when Sunday came, al-Maʾmūn sat for the redress of grievances. He returned to the session only on account of her, and the first person who called for him was the woman. She approached in that same clothing and greeted him. Al-Maʾmūn returned her greeting. Then he said, 'Where is your adversary?' She gestured towards the caliph's son al-ʿAbbās. He said, 'O Aḥmad', meaning Ibn Abī Khālid [= Aḥmad b. Abī Khālid (d. 211/826–7), vizier under al-Maʾmūn], 'Take him by the hand and seat him with her, so that they can confront one another.' The woman began to raise her voice over the voice of the son of the Commander of the Faithful. Yaḥyā b. Aktham said, 'Gently; do not raise your voice over that of the son of the Commander of the Faithful.' The caliph said, 'Let her be, for the truth has rendered her articulate and falsehood has silenced him.' Then al-Maʾmūn judged (in favour of) the restoration of her estate. He censured al-ʿAbbās for his injustice to her, and said, 'O Aḥmad, write (instructions for) the return of her estate to her, and write to the official there that she should be treated kindly and provided for generously, and conveyed to her family.'[89]

Pseudo-Māwardī's texts convey the point that the paradigmatic figures Anūshīrvān and al-Maʾmūn, renowned for their justice and virtue, earned their fine repute by their willing self-subjugation to scrupulous fairness. The narratives employ the *topos* of the powerful yet magnanimous ruler confronted by the lone, poor and elderly woman whose faith in the ruler's justice prompts her to seek redress against the depredations of his agents.[90] The royal figures display the virtues of forbearance and humility towards the most defenceless and marginal members of the subject population.

Pseudo-Māwardī continues with his seventh requisite:

> The seventh point is that the king should appoint observers (*an yajʿala ʿalā al-raʿiyya ʿuyūnan*) over the subjects to infiltrate all of their ranks (*ṭabaqāt*), and spies (*jawāsīs*) to gather reports and pursue information about them, especially in places of doubt and suspicion (*mawāḍiʿ al-ẓinna wa-l-tuhma*), just as he does when rulers, who are his peers and neighbours, oppose him (*al-munābidh[ū]n lahu*) and become his adversaries and enemies – as kings have done in every time and age.[91]
>
> He should strive to ensure that the person charged with the security of their area should perform the task in secret and realise the trust placed in him, for that is part of perfected administration, effective determination and correct governance. In such practice lies instruction in the *adab* of God and following the models of God's actions. We have included a preliminary mention of this matter in earlier parts of our book, and we repeat it in affirmation and support . . .[92]

Suggesting, as an example of the divine *adab* to which he refers, that God, notwithstanding His omniscience, instructs His angels to record the deeds of His servants, Pseudo-Māwardī relates the accomplishments of ʿUmar, Muʿāwiya and Ziyād, among other rulers, in attaining thorough and accurate information regarding their subjects. To these materials he adds the mention of ʿAbdallāh b. Ṭāhir, who went out incognito at night in order to learn his subjects' opinions of him and his officials.[93] He continues:

> Similarly among the kings of the Persians, it is related of Ardashīr that when he woke in the morning, he knew everything that had happened during the night to anyone in the capital of his kingdom, as well as within his palace (*fī qaṣabat mamlakatihi wa-ḍimn dārihi*), whether it concerned his *ʿāmma* or his *khāṣṣa*; and when it was evening, he knew everything that they had done during the morning. He often used to say to the lowliest and highest of his servants: Yesterday at your house such and such an incident occurred, and you were doing such and such. Many people used to say that an angel from heaven came to him and informed him about these actions.[94]
>
> A bedouin man was asked about one of their rulers (*suʾila aʿrābī ʿan wālin lahum*). He replied, 'Who is the like of him? By God, he does not close his

> eyelids; he sends out spies over his spies, so that when he is absent it is as if he were present, and the person of good conduct is safe while the person of bad conduct is fearful.'[95]

This section, concerned with the king's need for thorough and accurate information, especially with regard to the behaviour of his officials, who represent him, supports Pseudo-Māwardī's earlier insistence that the king should judge and act upon his judgement only when he possesses a full understanding of the circumstances. He turns next to his eighth point:

> The eighth point is that he should relax his seclusion (*ḥijāb*), be lenient in permitting access, and instruct his chamberlains (*ḥujjāb*) and door-keepers (*bawwābūn*) that they should not impede from access to him anyone bearing news, any petitioner bearing a grievance, or any person wishing to give counsel (*mutanaṣṣiḥ*) who appears at the time of his sitting in audience (*julūs*). These people should be permitted to see him or their arrival announced to him without delay, for there are certain affairs the delay of which causes great corruption and severe damage. Among these matters are some the delay of which and the omission of which cannot be repaired, nor their correction accomplished. Of this kind are religious matters that require attention, action and opportune performance at the appropriate times, for all religious acts, or the generality of them, are timed, and if an action escapes him, he misses much good, a large reward, fine praise and pleasing remembrance.
>
> At the same time, this matter entails something that is among the greatest benefits in justice, in attention to the subjects, and in the improvement of the *khāṣṣa* and the *ᶜāmma*: it is that when the *khāṣṣa* know and feel that the king is accessible and responsive to his subjects, their avidities towards the subjects and their maltreatment, oppression and subjugation of them decrease. Then the king becomes secure from the machinations of his viziers and their arbitrary exercise of power in disregard of him (*istibdāduhum bi-l-sulṭān dūnahu*), and he acquires a safeguard against unexpected events, surprise attacks by his enemies, and various kinds of harm . . .[96]
>
> The king should know that strict seclusion (*shiddat al-ḥijāb*) alienates people of noble virtues and high aspirations, causes offence to the protégé

> (*ṣanīᶜa*), leads to corruption for the subjects (*raᶜiyya*) and arouses suspicion. Everything that we have mentioned on this subject has already been described by virtuous kings and viziers in their books and recorded by poets in their verses . . .[97]

Using the well-known verses of Maḥmūd al-Warrāq (d. *c.* 225/840), Pseudo-Māwardī warns the king that excessive distance from his subjects alienates them, prevents him from administering justice and creates an environment in which his *khāṣṣa* exploit their subordinates and bring ruin to the kingdom:

> It is said in the Book *Āʾīnnāmeh*: It is not fitting for the king that he be strict in his seclusion (*ḥijāb*), for it indicates pride and a bad disposition, and generates aversion. It causes that which may be good to appear loathsome and fine deeds to be forgotten, and it brings to mind bad deeds. Moreover, it deprives the *sulṭān* of the benefits that the person who appears to see him might bring; for he stands in greatest need of these benefits in matters of knowledge and action . . .[98]

> A certain Indian king said in his testament: Know that the action of a ruler is not complete unless his knowledge of the subjects (*raᶜiyya*) is complete. His knowledge of the subjects will not be complete unless the subjects come to him of their own accord, and those who are closer (*adnā*) to him inform him regarding those who are more distant from him. This situation will not come about unless the king ensures that his gates (*abwāb*) are open, unless he displays gentleness, and unless he investigates grievances (*maẓālim*). If the king behaves in this way, the officials (*ᶜummāl*) will fear him and be restrained from injustice (*ẓulm*), and the people (*al-nās*) will deal equitably with one another without the need for intervention from their greatest ruler (*dūna wālīhim al-aᶜẓam*). The ruler will be proven effective with regard to both that which he undertakes in person and that which the people (*al-nās*) undertake without resorting to his involvement.[99]

Pseudo-Māwardī's treatment of the detrimental effects of royal seclusion provides a framework for his extended discussion, in his ninth item, of the varieties of disaffection rife among the *ᶜāmma*:

The ninth point is that the king should not make his investigation of affairs and his attention to them, in the areas that we have mentioned and the matters that we have enumerated, concerning his *khāṣṣa* and his *ᶜāmma*, his troops and his subjects, into a game or a diversion (*laᶜban wa-lahwan*), or treat them in a predatory or frivolous manner (*salban wa-hazlan*). Instead, he should undertake them in order to attain accurate knowledge of the relevant points (*maᶜrifat al-ḥaqāʾiq*) and award to all parties the recompense due to them by right (*qaḍāʾ al-ḥuqūq*), in order to reward the doer of good and punish the wrongdoer, to bring close (*taqrīb*) the sincere adviser (*nāṣiḥ*) who is distant and make distant the deceiver who is near, to provide for needs and remedy deficiencies, to profit from opportunities, to hasten to accomplish that the neglect of which is to be feared, and to attend to that the postponement of which would cause harm. Further, he should attend to these matters in order to raise up the friend, subdue the foe, and manage the case of the hidden enemy in the midst of the subjects (*raᶜiyya*), among whom there are several types of people: the intelligent person who is deprived (of suitable opportunity) (*ᶜāqil maḥrūm*),[100] the adversary engaged in dispute, the truthful person who has been wronged, the innovator (*mubtadiᶜ*) whose opinions are contrary to those of the common people (*ᶜāmma*) and the king and who seeks tirelessly to draw the king and the kingdom into confusion, the generous person (*karīm*) who is restricted and the person of merit who is rejected, the noble person (*sharīf*) who is alienated and the wise person (*ḥakīm*) whose value is ignored, the virtuous person (*fāḍil*) whose share of advancement and elevation is prevented, the ascetic (*nāsik*) who regards it as a religious duty to urge the ruler and his subjects (*al-rāᶜī wa-l-raᶜiyya*) to renounce whatever reprehensible practices (*manākīr*) have come to his attention, the villain (*fātik*) who in the ugliness of his conduct and the wickedness of his nature plots treachery against the king and who awaits a turn in fortune (*dāʾira*) that will accomplish for him that which he wishes and hopes, to which his nature and the evil of his conduct incline him. Then there is the case of the person who once enjoyed favour and status, or authority and force (*dhī niᶜma wa-rafᶜa aw sulṭān wa-manᶜa*), but who lost that fortunate position (*niᶜma*) to the king and whose turn in power (*dawla*) was brought to an end by means of the king's *dawla*.

> All of these types of people are enemies of the king and the kingdom, and of the ruler and the subjects. Moreover, since they are in the midst of the kingdom and at the heart of the realm (*bayḍa*), they are far better positioned to lead the king into dangers and much more powerful in combat against him than his external enemies and opponents who are distant from his palace and his residence.[101]

Pseudo-Māwardī, whose audience could doubtless relate these categories of disaffection to specific cases, addresses each variety of opposition:

> The method of rectifying this situation is for the king to look into the causes that elicited the disaffected person's opposition and prompted him to fabricate his plot, to instigate harm, to plan his deception and to harbour enmity. If the cause lies in an injustice that affected him or an enmity that was visited upon him, then the way to address the matter is for the harm to be removed from him and for him to be compensated, so that he will return to his former condition and the cause of his disappointment will cease. If his disaffection derived from deprivation and alienation (*wa-in kāna dhālika min ḥirmān wa-jafwa*), then the method to adopt is that the disaffected should be given their due rights and treated kindly (*an yuʿṭū ḥuqūqahum wa-yuḥsana ilayhim*). If it arose from the effort to fulfil an aspiration or the desire for an elevation in rank the achievement of which, and the attainment of their hopes for which, are permitted for them according to the established practices of the kingdom and the ordinances of the sharīʿa (*yajūzu fī rusūm al-mamlaka wa-aḥkām al-sharīʿa*), then the method to adopt is to grant them relief in the matter and to cease withholding it from them.
>
> If none of this is possible, and the disaffected person appears to be deceived in his desire and his expectations, then the way to treat the matter is to show him and persuade him, by way of pleasant encounters and discreet exchanges, of the impossibility of his achieving the rank to which he aspires; and he should be acquainted with his appropriate degree and guided towards the abandonment of such hopes.
>
> If the cause of disaffection lies in an ancient hostility and the passing of a turn in power (*li-ʿadāwa qadīma wa-dawla zāʾila*), then the king should

act to correct it by showing favour (*birr*), congeniality (*īnās*), encouraging closeness (*taqrīb*) and kindness (*iḥsān*), and, where appropriate, investment with an office (*taqlīd*); for hearts are moulded by love for those who treat them well and antipathy towards those who mistreat them.

If a person's disaffection stems from opposition in religion, then the method that the ruler should adopt is to enquire into his religion and his *madhhab*, his opinion (*raʾy*) and his doctrine (*maqāla*). If it is true (*in kāna ḥaqqan*), then the correct thing for the king to do is to agree with him, and to desist from opposition (*muʿānada*) to it. This action is among the most abundant of good fortunes that an individual can attain, and the greatest of lots that he can win. It is the most appropriate course for the virtuous king and the just ruler, and for every intelligent administrator (*hiya awlā al-ashyāʾ bi-l-malik al-fāḍil wa-l-sāʾis al-ʿādil wa-kull mudabbir ʿāqil*), for returning to the truth is better than persistence in falsehood.

If, however, the disaffected person's calling is false and his *madhhab* corrupt (*in kāna daʿwāhu bāṭilan wa-madhhabuhu fāsidan*), then the method to adopt is to summon him to the truth secretly. The ruler should dispatch surreptitiously to him a group who will enable him to understand the religion and inform him of the truth, in the hope that such instruction will cause him to recant, prevent him (from obstinacy in his falsehood) and bring about his reform (*yuṣliḥ bihi*). If that approach does not rectify him, then the path to pursue is to summon him to attend the ruler's *majlis* and require his presence at his gathering (*maḥfil*), and order him to debate (*munāẓara*) in the matter; to adduce proofs against his theological position, and to expose the futility of his *madhhab* and the weakness of his doctrine (*maqāla*) for the enlightenment of the *khāṣṣ* and the *ʿāmm*. The king should disseminate that information amongst the population (*jumhūr*), so that they will understand it and be on their guard against it.

Then the king should investigate the extent of the offender's innovation (*bidʿa*), and the degree of corruption in his doctrine (*maqāla*). If his *madhhab* is such that he deserves to be killed, then he should be killed, if after being asked to repent of it he clings to it and insists in it; then the king will be relieved of him. If he merits correction (*taʾdīb*), the king should correct

> him; if he deserves imprisonment, he should imprison him. This matter concerns exclusively the principles of the religion and the mother of the sharīᶜa. It does not concern the branches, ordinances and legal questions (*fī uṣūl al-diyāna wa-umm al-sharīᶜa dūna l-furūᶜ wa-l-aḥkām wa-l-masāʾil al-fiqhiyya*); in these matters, he may worship God in accordance with or in opposition to the laws of a particular school. If the king acts in this way, I hope that he will repel harm, protect the kingdom and its people from shame, and remove a temptation to sedition (*fitna*).[102]

In this section, Pseudo-Māwardī provides a detailed programme for reconciliation between the king and his disaffected subjects. Seeking to restore concord in every possible case, he proposes deliberate, staged interventions. His distinction between the major principles of the religion and its theological and legal branches reflects his alignment with the minimalist point of view.[103] Pseudo-Māwardī refrains from identifying his typologies of disaffection with particular figures. Yet it seems likely that he had specific persons and cases in mind. Consideration of the context in which he wrote renders it possible to speculate in this regard; it is not possible to move beyond suggestion, however.

> If it is the reversal of circumstances or upsetting of conditions from one quarter or another (*taqārub al-aḥwāl min jiha wa-tabāyunuhā min ukhrā*) that have occasioned a person's envy, rebellion and hostility, the king should know that this situation stimulates a contemptible disposition and acts deemed reprehensible in terms of religion and manly virtue (*muruwwa*), harmful and shameful to the perpetrator and devoid of benefit. If there is nothing to be done, the way to proceed is that the king should make efforts to ensure that no group (*jamāᶜa*) should assemble on his opponent's account, and that neither power (*shawka*) nor substance (*ᶜudda*) should reach his gang (*shirdhima*) (of supporters). He should divide them in their intentions, their thoughts and their persons. He should occupy a group among them with an activity, invest a party among them with appointed positions, and give gifts to others. He should punish his opponent's obstinacy (*ᶜinād*). He should adopt these measures according to the individuals' situations and earlier stations, through management and determination in kindness and affability, observation of conditions and events, and thorough

investigation in every time and period and day and hour. If they do not reform, then the way to proceed in the matter is to admonish them and warn them. If that is of no use, if things come to a head, wickedness appears and the matter has ceased to be concealed and secret and instead becomes generally known, then the path to adopt is the same as the path to be taken in the case of external enemies against the religious community (*milla*) or rebels (*bāghūn*) within it. We will clarify this matter sufficiently in the chapter devoted to the management of enemies, by God's will.[104]

These passages, where Pseudo-Māwardī presents an extended description of the kinds of disaffection that rulers may confront among their subjects and the recommended procedures for rectifying various situations, are highly likely to allude to contemporary circumstances. The reference to 'reversals of circumstances' is likely to connote the alienation experienced when one dynastic family, or one branch of a dynastic family, replaces another and members of the first are faced with loss of power and stature. Pseudo-Māwardī's detailing of the varieties of discontent finds an immediate context in the large numbers of rebellions that Naṣr faced from diverse individuals and constituencies. It was not only the large numbers of individuals who rebelled during Naṣr's reign, but also the forceful suppression of the revolts that attracted the comment of contemporary and later writers. Al-Iṣṭakhrī wrote of Naṣr b. Aḥmad, 'His force and subjugation of anyone who opposed him in his rule and the strength of his state were known, so that if anyone raised a challenge to his rule he invariably subdued him and prevailed.'[105] Gardīzī observed the large numbers of rebels (*khavārijīyān*) who revolted during Naṣr's reign, and added that his armies triumphed over them all.[106] Ibn al-Athīr offers the same observation, and furthermore supplies a list of the individuals and groups who rejected Naṣr's claims to their obedience:

Among those who rebelled against obedience to Naṣr were the people of Sijistan; his great-uncle, Isḥāq b. Aḥmad b. Asad, at Samarqand, and his two sons Manṣūr and Ilyās, the sons of Isḥāq; Muḥammad b. al-Ḥusayn b. Mutt; Abū l-Ḥasan b. Yūsuf; al-Ḥusayn b. ᶜAlī al-Marwarrūdhī; Muḥammad b. Ḥayd; Aḥmad b. Sahl; Līlī b. Nuᶜmān of the ᶜAlids in Tabaristan, encountered by Sīmjūr with Abū l-Ḥasan b. al-Nāṣir, and Qaratigin and Mākān b. Kākī; his brothers Yaḥyā, Manṣūr and Ibrāhīm

> revolted against him, the children of Aḥmad b Ismāʿīl; Jaʿfar b. Abī Jaʿfar; Ibn Dāʾūd; Muḥammad b. Ilyās; Naṣr b. Muḥammad b. Mutt; Mardāwīj and Wushmgīr, the sons of Ziyār. [Al-Amīr] al-Saʿīd [= Naṣr II] was victorious and triumphant over them all.[107]

Ibn al-Athīr's list includes individuals who correspond to many of Pseudo-Māwardī's categories. They include family members of varying degrees of closeness, military commanders, vassals and rivals, and their resistance sometimes continued through more than one generation. In one example, Mākān b. Kākī, member of a local dynastic family in Gilan, at times aligned with the Samanids, but eventually shifted his allegiances and rejected Samanid suzerainty; the Samanid vassal Abū ʿAlī Chaghānī defeated Mākān, who was killed in 329/940. The case of Muḥammad b. Ilyās bears a resemblance to the examples of Ḥusayn b. ʿAlī and Aḥmad b. Sahl. Like them, Muḥammad b. Ilyās was one of Naṣr's commanders. His family appears to have owned land in Sughd, although they had established their power in Kirman in the period before Naṣr's reign. Muḥammad b. Ilyās had incurred Naṣr's displeasure and had been imprisoned, but Abū l-Fażl Balʿamī interceded on his behalf and secured his release. Muḥammad was then sent on a campaign to Gurgan. When in 317/929 Naṣr's brother Yaḥyā rebelled, Muḥammad b. Ilyās joined his side. After the rebellion faltered and the amir's brothers dispersed, Yaḥyā sought to enter Nishapur, but Mākān, at that time a Samanid vassal and governor of the city, denied entry to Yaḥyā. Muḥammad b. Ilyās then made common cause with Mākān and took over the city when Mākān left for Gurgan. During Mākān's absence Muḥammad b. Ilyās admitted Yaḥyā to Nishapur. In 317/929 Yaḥyā, who had held the governorship of Samarqand in 306/918–19, was proclaimed amir, and named in the *khuṭba.* Naṣr marched on Nishapur in 320/932, and Muḥammad b. Ilyās withdrew to Kirman and established his authority there.[108] These cases provide examples of the repeated opposition that Naṣr faced from several of his high-ranking commanders and from members of well-established landed families.

It seems highly likely that Pseudo-Māwardī alluded to these various types of disaffection when he provided his list of types of people who might feel alienated from the established authorities, and might, if opportunity presented itself, rebel against them. His audience would have interpreted the mirror in the light of prevailing conditions, and perceived his urging of the king, as far as possible, to seek reconciliation. In the case of persons whose disaffection was religious in nature, he suggests that if the ruler found their doctrines to be correct, it was he who should change his disposition. He continues to encourage the king to ascertain the full information regarding each case, and to exercise restraint and clemency:

> Everything that we have mentioned finds a model in the management (*tadbīr*) by which God has managed (*dabbara*) the affairs of His creatures and the instructive examples (*ādāb*) by which He has instructed (*addaba*) them. It derives from the indicative proofs (*dalāʾil*) that He has established, since the Eternal – glorious is His mention – is ever-knowing of those among His creation who oppose Him, those among His creatures who resist His command and deviate from obedience to Him, and those among His servants who seek to keep Him away. That knowledge did not prevent Him from creating them, shaping them, originating them, fashioning them and bestowing on them the bounties of life, sound minds and strong limbs, and favouring each one of them with that which He knew was best (*aṣlaḥ*) for him. He called them to obedience to Him. Then, after they began to show hostility, to display opposition, to adopt gods other than Him, to worship idols with Him (*ʿibādat al-aṣnām maʿahu*), and, many of them, to commit all sorts of obstinacy (*ʿunūd*) and ingratitude (*kunūd*), He showed them His signs (*dalāʾil*), adduced His proofs (*shawāhid*), dispatched messengers (*rusul*) to them, revealed books (*kutub*) to them, delivered good news to them and warned them (*bashsharahum wa-andharahum*), promised and threatened them (*waʿadahum wa-awʿadahum*), called them to that in which lies their salvation and gave them as a respite a time in which clarity (*tabayyun*), deliberation (*tadabbur*), reconsideration (*murājaʿa*) and reflection (*tafakkur*) were possible. He did not hasten to censure them until He had verified their word and despaired of their return to obedience. Firm resolve (*ḥazm*) does not permit and proper administration (*tadbīr*) does not allow that the king should make light of this matter, notwithstanding the exalted nature of his status and the grand stature of his authority, or that he should neglect it out of delusion regarding his power over those persons among his subjects and in the midst of his kingdom. For the beginning of

> wickedness is but a small misdemeanour, and many a pouring rain has as its beginning a mere shower.[109]

In this passage, shaped by his Muᶜtazilite understanding of divine justice, Pseudo-Māwardī again encourages the king to model his sovereignty on the divine pattern. God, like earthly kings, contends with His creatures' disobedience and ingratitude. His eternal knowledge of those of His creatures who would resist His command did not deter Him from creating them and bestowing favours upon them, each according to the principle of the 'optimal' (*al-aṣlaḥ*). He continued to provide them with both revelation and the rationality that would enable them to discern the truth, and He allowed them countless opportunities to heed His promise and threat. Kings likewise should provide their disobedient servants with ample opportunity to return to their service. They should censure them only if the impossibility of their return to obedience has been established beyond doubt.

In this allusive section, Pseudo-Māwardī evokes an extensive disaffection among the population, and suggests the inadequacy of Naṣr's coercive responses to signs of his subjects' unease. Implicitly, he appeals for the rehabilitation of servants who had rejected their overlords' suzerainty but who, in the past, had provided them with invaluable support. In several cases, the amirs reinstated family members who had challenged their rule and the military governors who had withdrawn their allegiance,[110] but in other cases, rebellious vassals were subjected to prolonged imprisonment. During his absence from Bukhara, Naṣr had detained his brothers in the citadel. In a reflection of the social discrimination that often pertained in matters of criminal justice, an inequality against which Pseudo-Māwardī argued in his urging of fair treatment without regard to rank or relationship, members of the lower social groups, such as the cook who released Naṣr's brothers and facilitated their revolt, were subjected to brutal forms of execution.[111]

Pseudo-Māwardī encourages the king to remain alert to the conditions of his subjects; if he is well informed regarding their conditions, he is in a position to prevent or forestall dissatisfactions. His previously adduced example of *al-muʾallafa qulūbuhum* indicated for his audience the likelihood that in many cases magnanimity and generosity might establish or re-establish unity and equilibrium in the polity. Yet the king should remain vigilant, and should know that in cases of unrelenting disobedience, efforts at reconciliation would prove ineffective. He develops this point with reference to the category of *munāfiqūn*, the 'hypocrites' reputed to have assented outwardly to the Prophet's teachings but to have resisted inwardly:

> God . . . cautioned His Prophet against this kind of enemy in terms stronger than He had employed in His warnings to him regarding external and distant enemies, and He described them with a wrath that He omitted in His treatment of the polytheists who fought against him (*ahl al-ḥarb min al-mushrikīn*). For He said: 'When you see them, their figures please you, and when they speak, you listen to their speech. Yet they are like the wooden paneling of a wall . . .' (63: 4) . . .[112] In many verses of this kind, God described the condition of the 'hypocrites' (*munāfiqūn*), who belonged among the number of those who made peace with the Prophet, and made an appearance of faith in him and of obedience to him.
>
> The poet who spoke the following verses understood this situation:
>
> Do not despise the smallest of things;
> Things that appear small will tomorrow become large
> Know also that the large things that you (now) behold
> Were once small.

By invoking the *munāfiqūn*, Pseudo-Māwardī reminds his audience of the dangers to be expected from contemporary instances of internal dissent, embodied in figures whose appearance of allegiance, he implies, masked subversive ambitions. Guiding his audience's interpretation of his meaning, he alludes to the earlier experience of the Abbasid *daʿwa*, active in Khurasan in the very regions that now formed the Samanid polity. He cites the poetic warnings of Naṣr b. Sayyār, the Umayyad governor, who, lamenting the Umayyads' neglect of the mounting threat to their authority, foresaw the dynasty's overthrow:

> Concerning the first appearance of the *daʿwa* of the Banū l-ʿAbbās, the poet said:
>
> I see amidst the ashes the flash of live coals
> On the point of rising into a blaze

For fire may be kindled with (a mere) two sticks of wood.
Words precede war;
If not extinguished, they conceal a war that is
In busy preparation, enough to turn a youth's hair white
A preparation that reveals its brilliance
Its kindling palace and crown.
I say in astonishment, Would that I knew
Whether Umayya [the dynasty that the Abbasids were to overthrow] were awake or sleeping?
You [Umayyads] are distant from a land in which the lowliest of the people have become mighty
And the most noble among them suppressed.[113]

They (the Umayyads) slept and did not awaken, and the matter turned out as the poet said . . .

There has been no prophetic mission (*nubuwwa*) or religion (*diyāna*), nor any kingdom (*mamlaka*) or civilisation (*ᶜimāra*) in the world that did not begin weak, and subsequently grew strong.[114]

Having alerted his audience to pay attention to signs of rivalry and dissent, even if they currently appear insignificant in scale, Pseudo-Māwardī warns the king against over-reliance on his capacity to suppress internal challenges by means of force. Indeed, the use of force is likely to result in an escalation of conflict:

The powerful king (*al-malik al-muqtadir*), complacent in his might, his assistants (*aᶜwān*), his military contingents (?) (*jamāᶜāt*), his treasuries (*khazāʾin*), his resources (*ᶜudda*) and his equipment (*ᶜatād*), should not suppose that he will be able to address these kinds of crises or rectify these kinds of faults by sheer strength, severity, force, brutality and killing. On the contrary, that approach sometimes fans and intensifies the flames of war, renders the evil more forceful, and aggravates the conflict. Proper governance lies between gentleness and force, and kindness is more effective than violence. The correct path in administration (*tadbīr*), wisdom (*ḥikma*), welfare (*maṣlaḥa*) and governance (*siyāsa*) is for the king to favour gentleness over force and inducement over punishment, and not to rush into conflict when he finds a way to prevent it. For God, Blessed and Almighty, has said in His Book: 'We have tested them with good things and evil things, for perhaps they will return (*laᶜallahum yarjiᶜūna*)' (7: 168), and He said, 'We test you with the evil and with the good, as a temptation (*fitna*)' (21: 35).

It has been said: [Display] force without violence, and gentleness without weakness . . .[115]

Ibrāhīm b. al-ᶜAbbās wrote to the people of Homs:

To proceed (*ammā baᶜd*): The Commander of the Faithful sees it as part of God's claim (*ḥaqq*) against him in his responsibility for managing events that he adopt three principles, each one of which takes precedence over the next: the first consists of exhortation (*waᶜẓ*) and vigilance (*tanbīh*); the next consists of cautioning (*īᶜād*) and warning (*taḥdhīr*); the last resort is to intervene in events if the harm will not depart by any other means.[116]

[The poet said]:

First, patience. If patience does not suffice, try warning.

If that too is inadequate, only then resort to decisive resolution.

God, great is His mention, said, with regard to the first point (encouraging patience and clemency): 'It was by God's mercy that you (O Muḥammad) were lenient with them; had you been severe and rough-hearted they would have scattered from round about you. So pardon them, seek forgiveness on their behalf, and consult them in affairs; and when you have reached a decision, place your trust in God' (3: 159).[117] He said, 'Banish evil with that which is better' (23: 96). Then He said: 'Then, (in the case of) the person for whom hostility exists between him and you, it will be as if he were a close and compassionate friend' (41: 34). And He commanded the Prophet to give (a portion of the spoils) to those whose hearts were to be reconciled . . .

So, in this wise, the king should seek to conciliate his enemies and to attract the hearts of the people who bear him ill-will.[118]

This ninth principle of the ruler's governance of the *ᶜāmma* addresses the management of opposition and conflict within the realm, and recapitulates several of the themes introduced in the context of the ills that beset kings and their kingdoms, and their remedies. In an early tenth-century context, Pseudo-Māwardī's list of the types of person who constitute, actually or potentially, the king's enemies within his kingdom is suggestive of the breadth of the resistance facing Naṣr: men of intellect and learning disbarred from the ruler's presence; persons who have been aggrieved without redress; persons of merit whose expectations have been disappointed; scions of dynastic families displaced by or subordinated to the king; ascetics performing the duty of *al-amr bi-l-maʿrūf wa-l-nahy ʿan al-munkar*; rebels and criminals. Pseudo-Māwardī's ninth principle urges the king to seek the return to loyalty of persons who have rebelled, and to overlook all but the most egregious offences in the interests of the reintegration of the social network that, once broken, severs a succession of relationships in addition to the personal bond of ruler and *khādim*. The king is obligated to fulfil fair expectations on the part of the persons on whose loyalty and skill, and on whose willingness to commit their human and financial resources on his behalf, his position depends. If he is inattentive, or assumes his might will be sufficient to overwhelm internal opposition, he should remember the fate of the Umayyads.

As for rebels whose resistance to the ruler stems from differences in religion, they too should be encouraged to return to the polity. The king should first enquire into the nature of the religious difference; if he finds his opponent's position to be correct, he should align himself to it and renounce his false path.[119] Pseudo-Māwardī's depiction suggests his sympathy with most of the categories that he enumerates among the disaffected, and he impresses upon the king that effective governance requires magnanimity, clemency, patience and 'kindness', in order to win the subjects' 'love'. Governance of a discontented population by means of force, he implies, will not succeed; it will engender greater resistance that will erupt at an opportune time. I have suggested that Pseudo-Māwardī had in mind particular individuals and particular situations. His repeated urging of the amir to employ the positive strategies of generous gifts, appointments to appropriate posts and the reinforcement of ties – the probable implication of 'drawing someone near' (*taqrīb*) – represented a contrast to the haste and severity with which Naṣr reputedly meted out punishment and crushed opposition. Indeed, Pseudo-Māwardī implies that in some cases the rebels and opponents of the king may be in the right, and it is the king who should acknowledge his fault and rectify it.

Pseudo-Māwardī concludes his chapter devoted to governance of the common people with a discussion of his tenth and final point:

> The tenth requirement is that the king should not empower some of the subjects (*raᶜiyya*) and common people (*ᶜāmma*) over others, and he should not set up in the kingdom any commander (*[al]lā yajᶜala fī l-mamlaka āmiran*) other than himself and his deputies (*khulafāʾ*). For no one is more cruel in his victory, more wicked in his guardianship (*riᶜāya*) or more severe in the exercise of power than a commoner (*ᶜāmmī*) if he attains leadership (*riyāsa*) or assumes authority (*waliya wilāya*). It sometimes happens that if a commoner attains that position, then others like him will envy him, someone who is of his kind will covet his station, and each of them will acquire a following, and that leads to a vast trouble against the *sulṭān*, and an enormous offence against the kingdom.

Pseudo-Māwardī advises the king to maintain the established ranks among the common people and to avoid situations in which a commoner could attain the opportunity to treat his fellow commoners as subordinates.

> Rather, in the loftiness of his aspiration, the perfection of his power, the strength of his force, the purity of his moral dispositions, the fineness of his habits, the rectitude of his management and the nobility of his judgements, the king should be a king. In his humility before God, his mildness, his upholding of his religion, his fear of his Lord, his mindfulness of the demise of his turn in power (*dawla*) and his reflection on his eventual end, he should be an ascetic (*nāsik*). In his closeness (*qurb*) to his subjects, his gentleness to the people of his kingdom (*ahl mamlakatihi*) and his kindness to the people of his province (*ahl wilāyatihi*), he should be a commoner (*ᶜāmmī*). In the acuity of his thought and the precision of his examination into the components (*asbāb*) of his sovereignty, he should be a lowly person (*sūqī*). In his knowledge of that which has been entrusted to him and bound to him in terms of justice among his subjects, he should be a learned jurist (*ᶜālim faqīh*).[120]

Pseudo-Māwardī implies that the king should embrace the roles of his subjects: he should be, in the true senses of the terms, a king, an ascetic, a common person, a lowly person, a jurist. The reference to the *sūqa*, apart from the *ᶜāmma* reveals that the latter category excluded persons who lacked independence, such as agricultural labourers, the poor and indigent. Yet the king should recognise the claims of every constituency among his subjects. Having begun his treatment of the *ᶜāmma* with the observation that the king is like his subjects in kind, Pseudo-Māwardī concludes by encouraging the king to cultivate the best qualities associated with each category.

Pseudo-Māwardī concludes his seventh chapter with an expression of his hope that the king who models his behaviour (*sīra*) on these ten points and governs his subjects accordingly will achieve virtue in his governance (*faḍīlat al-siyāsa*), discharge the rightful claims of the kingdom (*ḥaqq al-mamlaka*), earn God's divine reward and the lasting praise of the intelligent. The king should take instruction (*taᵓaddub*) from the divine model, as far as he is capable of apprehending it through rational consideration of God's signs, indications and proofs, His speech and His acts; and from the wisdom of human experience, accumulated over time, articulated in the words and exemplary conduct of kings and sages of the past.[121]

This seventh chapter in *Naṣīḥat al-mulūk* represents the third and final section in Pseudo-Māwardī's cluster of chapters devoted to the three 'governances', of self, élites and common people. Throughout these chapters Pseudo-Māwardī presents a consistent argument that proceeds from one point to the next, often enumerated so that each point takes its place in a developing intellectual system. He demonstrates his logic through the use of Qurᵓānic verses, examples of the Prophet's actions and words, situations encountered by the caliphs and their responses, the practices and declarations of kings in earlier communities, and the advice of wise counsellors. The juxtaposition of these assorted texts is significant. Their meanings, individually, are fluid; it is through his placement of them at particular points in the course of his exposition, and his movement from one text to the next that Pseudo-Māwardī imbues his resources with meaning, creates impressions and emphases, and guides his audience's associations with the conditions of the contemporary historical context. Occasionally, he states explicitly that the points he has made are relevant to the current conditions of the kingdom. He refrains, however, from identifying individuals or groups, and leaves it to his audience to draw appropriate inferences.

Conclusion

This book has concentrated on an early Arabic mirror for princes and its contexts. It has explored the mentality of the unidentified author, the intellectual, cultural and religious currents that shaped his perspective, and the circumstances in which he wrote, on the basis of the evidence furnished by the mirror itself and the parallels that it displays with the works of other, especially contemporary authors. The study has suggested a number of outcomes.

The dating and locating of *Naṣīḥat al-mulūk*'s composition to tenth-century Balkh, already established by Aḥmad and Anṣārī, have been confirmed, and the evidence for them augmented. *Naṣīḥat al-mulūk* offers a regional as well as a theological–intellectual perspective, and supplements the fairly limited repertoire of materials currently available for the study of the Samanid domains during the earlier part of the tenth century. Aḥmad's suggestion of Abū Zayd al-Balkhī's authorship and Anṣārī's positing of the authorship of a student of Abū l-Qāsim al-Kaᶜbī al-Balkhī are insightful in their linking of Pseudo-Māwardī with the circles of these two dominating figures in the intellectual life of early tenth-century Balkh. If the name of the author cannot, given the information currently available, be proven definitively (Anṣārī's proposal seems entirely plausible but is, for the time being, unverifiable), it is reasonable to conclude that Pseudo-Māwardī was a Balkhī, and that he shared the mentality of, and almost certainly knew, both of his illustrious fellow-citizens.

Pseudo-Māwardī was an engaged and thoughtful observer of kingship, and incidentally of countless other topics, but rather than being attached to the court or resident in the capital, he wrote from the remove of a major regional city. He wrote, furthermore, in response to a moment of seemingly widespread discontent on the part of various constituencies among the population. This sense manifested itself in pronounced disaffection and frequent rebellions, whether political or religious in appearance (in Pseudo-Māwardī's terms, whether directed towards *riyāsa* or *diyāna*). Both the frequency and in several cases the gravity of these eruptions may indicate not only the aspirations and ambitions of their leaders, but also the active or passive support of considerable numbers of ordinary people. Pseudo-Māwardī appears to have linked this time of crisis to the mounting discontent of the Samanids' provincial governors and military leaders, and to reports that the polity had fallen into, or was on the brink of falling into, the hands of an élite motivated to transform it in ways that stimulated fear and resistance among prominent urban constituencies. The evidence of the text supports the hypothesis that Pseudo-Māwardī wrote in the decades when the Isma^cili *da^cwa* in the Samanid realm was at its most active and visible, and that *Naṣīḥat al-mulūk* expressed the conviction of local intellectual leaders that the king, surrounded by Isma^cilis at the court, had either joined their cause or failed to recognise the threat to political stability that the *da^cwa* posed.

Yet Pseudo-Māwardī's mirror is a work less of protest than of persuasion. *Naṣīḥat al-mulūk* warns the king of the consequences that await him and his subjects if he continues to suppress dissent and disaffection by means of force and retaliation. He implies also that the religious-intellectual outlook of the courtly élite fell outside the 'minimal' set of convictions that he considered a necessary basis for the maintenance of political equilibrium and social cohesion. His mirror offers the king the opportunity and the incentive to change.

Pseudo-Māwardī's act in writing finds a context in the various expressions of resistance that occurred in the region during his lifetime. Members of powerful and wealthy families, established regional lords and military leaders with command over the loyalties of large numbers of soldiers enjoyed a high level of independence from the state. Compelled by bonds of *khidma* to serve the ruler when called upon, they were in a position to retract their support when they perceived the ruler to have breached his pledge of *wafā*ʾ. In such situations, these individuals possessed various choices (or opportunities), including rebellion and defection. Naṣr's reign witnessed many episodes of rebellion from individuals in these categories. Their motives were various and there appears to be no evidence to suggest that heterodox allegiances played any role in them. One of the disaffected, Ḥusayn b. ᶜAlī, a former benefactor of Abū Zayd al-Balkhī, was an Ismaᶜili, and assumed the leadership of the Ismaᶜili *daᶜwa*; but it is not clear if or how his role in the *daᶜwa* and his rebellion might have been related. In at least one case, that of Aḥmad b. Sahl, who suppressed Ḥusayn's revolt and not long afterwards rebelled himself, there is a high likelihood that Pseudo-Māwardī was acquainted with the rebellious governor and was at the very least knowledgeable regarding his situation: numismatic evidence demonstrates that Aḥmad had governed in Balkh for a period of years before his appointment to the governorship of Khurasan, in which capacity he employed Abū l-Qāsim al-Kaᶜbī and Abū Zayd al-Balkhī. Pseudo-Māwardī places great emphasis on the ruler's responsibilities for the fulfilment of the recognised claims (*ḥuqūq*) of his *khadam*, and it is likely that his insistent reminders of this obligation were not merely rehearsals of an abstract principle, but arose from immediate observation.

Urban constituencies, and their leading figures among the intermediaries on whom the king depended, also responded to the prevailing perception of crisis. Several reports, including the suggestive testimony of Pseudo-Māwardī, make clear that several intellectuals, scholars and renunciants absented themselves from the court, turned inwards and grew alienated from it. Abū Zayd al-Balkhī excused himself from compliance with the amir's summons to Bukhara on the grounds that his fear of crossing the Oxus prevented him from doing so.[1] Religious leaders went so far on occasion as to pray publicly for the demise of the current executives. Pseudo-Māwardī responded, in recapitulation of a gesture enacted by his admired predecessor Ibn al-Muqaffaᶜ, by composing a work of advice.

Pseudo-Māwardī's choice of response demonstrates the potential and perils of the advisory genre. In their ostensible purpose, mirrors necessarily imply that, despite his power, the ruler stands in need of advice and cannot dispense with his counsellors. Their *raison d'être* consists in the persuasion of the ruler to accept and impose, of his own volition, limits to his power. The writer of the mirror brings to the task his experience, his learning, his moral authority and his rhetorical skill. Chances of failure were high, as the case of Ibn al-Muqaffaᶜ, among many others, demonstrated.[2] But the mirror remained a meaningful medium of communication between subject and ruler because both parties inhabited a mentality in which kings, to be effective as well as virtuous, needed to govern in accordance with self-imposed disciplines. The prevalence of this understanding required rulers to recognise its cultural and moral force, even when their behaviour reflected competing impulses and principles. As a consequence, mirrors, however presented and received, retained their currency across vast expanses of time and distance, and the genre proved to be adaptable to a variety of purposes.

Pseudo-Māwardī knew that his chances of winning the king's ear were low, and that he exposed himself to danger in the attempt. He acknowledges the fear of reprisal that prevented many persons in the king's company from expressing any sentiment other than that which they believed he wished to hear. He refers repeatedly to kings' subordinates following the royal example, and states explicitly that their imitation resulted not necessarily from agreement – their outward presentation might well be strategic – but from their concern for self-preservation and their perceived self-interest. In Pseudo-Māwardī's assessment, it was precisely the fact that the king's conduct and disposition brought in its wake the waves of imitative behaviour amongst his *khāṣṣa*, from the categories in closest proximity to his person to the groups at the furthest remove, that rendered the king powerful.

Clear-sighted in his undertaking, Pseudo-Māwardī presented his mirror as a work of counsel and an expression of 'love'. His motivation arose in considerable measure from his Muᶜtazilite convictions, which required the commanding of right and the forbidding of wrong. The offering of counsel constituted a recognised method of discharging this duty, and Pseudo-Māwardī devotes not only his preface, but also his first chapter to the reciprocal duties of king and subjects in receiving and offering advice. In its discursive strategy *Naṣīḥat al-mulūk* mixes flattery with resistance.[3] Pseudo-Māwardī's second chapter adopts a deferential posture in its affirmation of the elevated status of kings. It is not until his third chapter, devoted to the kingdom's problems and their solutions, that Pseudo-Māwardī embarks in an explicit fashion on his commanding of right. His mirror, in accordance with the paradoxical nature of the genre, argues that to rule well, the king must be ruled. To this end, Pseudo-Māwardī places the king within a system of cosmic correspondences; he prescribes a programme that, flatteringly, likens the king's position in the polity to that of God in the cosmos, but also conveys the interdependent nature of his relationship with his subjects, over whom his power, in appearance limitless, was both contingent and restricted. Like Firdawsī, who, within the framework of a poetic exploration of sovereignty secreted a nuanced, implicitly critical and frequently dispiriting portrayal of kings,[4] Pseudo-Māwardī demonstrated the mirror's potential as a vehicle for the expression of resistance against the arbitrary exercise of royal power. In *Naṣīḥat al-mulūk*, Pseudo-Māwardī displays the full potential of the genre in his careful choice and arrangement of exemplary texts, by means of which he alluded to contemporary developments that could not be addressed in an explicit manner.

In the course of his counsel, Pseudo-Māwardī addresses a great variety of topics, including the education of children, breastfeeding, the 'natures' specific to individuals, the health and strength of the body, the fair treatment of prisoners, the poetry of the day, techniques of language instruction, music and taxation. His mirror, like many later examples, possesses an encyclopaedic quality and conveys a complex mentality in which Muᶜtazilite and Kindian intellectual techniques, principles and terminology converged with deeply rooted late antique concepts and metaphors, some disseminated across vast expanses of Eurasia, some regional in character. To a degree, in uniting rationalist theological–philosophical concepts and vocabulary with the rich cultural heritage of eastern Iran, Pseudo-Māwardī adopted a posture demonstrated in the writings of other Muᶜtazilites, including individuals especially likely to have shaped his understanding: Abū Isḥāq al-Naẓẓām took an interest in Iranian religion, and perhaps knew Persian; al-Jāḥiẓ, who was acquainted with *kutub al-ᶜajam*, cited Ibn al-Muqaffaᶜ and 'wisdom'; and Abū l-Hudhayl al-ᶜAllāf, who argued that an unbeliever might obey God in his good actions, held *Jāvīdān khirad*, 'perennial wisdom', in high esteem and cited it at a gathering at which al-Jāḥiẓ was also present.[5] The extent and depth of the integration evinced in *Naṣīḥat al-mulūk*, with its often scriptural points of departure, its logical methods of argument and its underpinnings in Middle Persian *andarz*, are exceptionally striking. A principal point of convergence among these various strands of discourse is the concept of *ṣalāḥ* or *maṣlaḥa*: thoroughly supported by scripture and wisdom, by revelation and reason, welfare, well-being and the public good dominate the intertwined political, social and religious-philosophical outlook evident in Pseudo-Māwardī's mirror.

If there is little doubt that Pseudo-Māwardī wrote during Naṣr's reign and with the amir in mind, it is unlikely that he intended the book exclusively for the amir's personal perusal. His use of the third person spared the king the indignity of direct address, but it also allowed the author to present his arguments to a public audience rather than to a circumscribed and intimate one. When in his preface Pseudo-Māwardī suggests that whoever might come across his book, that person would find him a well-intentioned counsellor, he follows a convention, but he also invites an unlimited readership. It is possible that he wrote with multiple potential audiences in mind. Local rulers, princes and members of the élites might profit from the book's lessons. Scholars who had kept their distance from the court might find in it an exhortation to abandon their reticence and to participate in the political culture by means of moral persuasion.

There appears to be no record regarding the reception of *Naṣīḥat al-mulūk*, and whether it, in any form or by any channel, reached either a primary or a secondary audience during its author's lifetime remains unknown. This situation is by no means unusual; indeed, it seems that after their initial presentation, many mirrors were deposited, unread, in royal libraries. In some cases the books had perhaps already fulfilled their immediate purposes: they had created the occasion for the ruler to display his legitimacy by observing the model of magnanimous kingship, and for the writer to secure remuneration and perhaps employment. I have suggested that *Naṣīḥat al-mulūk* anticipates later advisory works produced by authors who lived in, or were shaped by, the religious–intellectual culture of the region, such as the Arabic *Ādāb al-mulūk* of al-Thaʿālibī (d. 429/1038) and the Persian *Siyar al-mulūk* Niẓām al-Mulk (d. 485/1092). It appears that the mirror made its way from eastern Iran to Iraq and further west, and at an unknown point acquired its attribution to al-Māwardī. When Ibn al-Jawzī, who preached for the benefit of rulers and large urban audiences, composed a work of counsel for Caliph al-Mustaḍīʾ (r. 566–75/1170–80), he resumed several of the themes addressed in *Naṣīḥat al-mulūk* and adopted a vocabulary that echoes formulations employed in the earlier text.[6] It is possible that the book found an audience among the *wuʿʿāẓ*, preachers, who selected and transmitted aspects that served their purposes (Pseudo-Māwardī had, after all, included an entire chapter dedicated to *mawāʿiẓ*, admonitions). Whatever its trajectory, the mirror is quite likely to have undergone certain modifications, such as the addition of the verse of Ibn Khālawayh,[7] in the course of its passage. *Naṣīḥat al-mulūk* nevertheless retained its mixed body of late antique wisdom, and accordingly provided a channel for the preservation and dissemination of an exceptionally full and varied repertoire of cultural materials. It had travelled far beyond the location of its initial composition by the time it came to the attention of the Ottoman bureaucrat who commissioned the surviving copy.

Puzzling and paradoxical in many respects, mirrors for princes have often struck modern readers as repositories of hackneyed truisms, examples of perennial wisdom, reproduced in a pattern of thoughtless repetition or in conformity with an audience's expectations.[8] The *Naṣīḥat al-mulūk* of Pseudo-Māwardī, I have attempted to show, reflects and comments critically on the polity inhabited by the author and his audience, alludes to specific persons and events, and demonstrates the potent meaning that ancient and familiar materials, narrative and aphoristic, could acquire when deployed in distinct historical and literary situations. While the constant themes of advice literature have endured since antiquity in diverse cultural milieux, many examples of the genre are strikingly individual, and the meaning of a motif, however often it has been invoked before, is shaped with each utterance by the particularities of time, place, author and audience. Mirrors for princes, as *Naṣīḥat al-mulūk* demonstrates, evoke and participate in a long-standing literary, cultural and political continuum, on the one hand, and carry immediate and specific connotations, on the other.

Notes

Chapter 1

1. Neguin Yavari has drawn attention to the resemblances in subject matter among mirrors produced in almost entirely unconnected environments ('Mirrors for Princes or Hall of Mirrors', p. 49; *Advice for the Sultan*, p. 23).
2. A significant point of comparison might be the anonymous mid-tenth-century work known as *Siyāsat al-mulūk* ('The Governance of Kings'), composed during the Buyid period apparently by a secretary (Sadan, 'New Source'; Sadan and Silverstein, 'Ornate Manuals or Practical *Adab*?'). In fifty folios, this work, which the present author has not seen in its entirety, would appear to be roughly half the length of *Naṣīḥat al-mulūk*. The published portion of the text (Sadan, *Nouvelle source*) and the studies of Sadan and Silverstein suggest a text quite different in character.
3. On the characteristics of a 'book', see Günther, 'Assessing the Sources', pp. 78–9. On the authorial prresence in works of *adab*, see Hoyland, 'History', p. 23. Pseudo-Māwardī makes no allusions to other books that he might have written.
4. On the ten-chapter version of *Kalīla wa-Dimna*, see *Taʾrīkh al-Yaʿqūbī*, I: 88–9; for the 'Long Form' of *Sirr al-asrār*, see Manzalaoui, 'Facts and Problems', p. 148. Although the extant manuscripts date from later periods, Manzalaoui found that the 'Long Form' probably appeared in the later tenth century (p. 193).
5. Ibn Qutayba, *ʿUyūn al-akhbār*, 'Muqaddimat al-muʾallif', I, *ʿayn*.
6. Most of the compositions listed under the title *ʿahd* (pl. *ʿuhūd*) in Ibn al-Nadīm's *al-Fihrist* are connected to Sasanian figures. Among the listings are *ʿAhd Ardashīr*, listed in two places (once placed first in a list of books included because of their excellence (*jūda*), I: ii: 391, and once among the names of books devoted to the *mawāʿiẓ* (exhortations), *ādāb* (edifying sayings) and

ḥikam (wise maxims) of the Persians, Greeks, Indians and Arabs, II: i: 349); and three *ᶜuhūd* of Kisrā (= Khusraw I) (*ᶜAhd Kisrā ilā bnihi Hurmuz yūṣīhi ḥīna aṣfāhu al-mulk wa-jawāb Hurmuz iyyāhu* ('Khusraw's "Testament" to his son Hurmuz, left to him when he selected him for sovereignty, and Hurmuz's reply'), II: i: 349; *ᶜAhd Kisrā ilā man adraka al-taᶜlīm min banīhi* ('Khusraw's "Testament" to those of his sons who comprehended instruction'), II: i: 349; *ᶜAhd Kisrā Anūshīrwān ilā bnihi alladhī yusammā ᶜishsh al-balāgha* ('Khusraw Anūshīrvān's "Testament" to his son, called the "Nest of Eloquence"'), II: i: 350). Cf. Shaked, 'Andarz'.

7. Harmsen, *Die Wasiya als literarisches Genre*, pp. 50–8; cf. Dietrich, 'Das politische Testament'. Cf. Gilliot, '*In consilium deduces me*', pp. 487–98.
8. Ibn Qutayba, *ᶜUyūn al-akhbār*, II: 226.
9. See further Cook, *Early Muslim Dogma*, pp. 6–7; Beeston, 'Parallelism'; Meisami, 'Oratory'; Qutbuddin, '*Khuṭba*', esp. pp. 207–8; and below, Chapter 5.
10. Abū Ḥanīfa (attrib.), *al-ᶜĀlim wa-l-mutaᶜallim*, p. 8; see also p. 34. For further examples, see the renunciants' speeches reported in Abū Nuᶜaym, *Ḥilyat al-awliyāᵓ*, VIII: 14, 18 (Ibrāhīm b. Adham), 90 (Fuḍayl b. ᶜIyāḍ), 206 (Ibn al-Sammāk), 241 (Yūsuf b. Asbāṭ).
11. Al-Ṭabarī, *Taᵓrīkh*, VIII: 582.
12. Al-Ṭabarī, *Taᵓrīkh*, VIII: 582, 591.
13. Nāẓim, '*Pand-Nāmah*', pp. 614, 621.
14. See Kilpatrick, 'Adab Encyclopedia'; Leder and Kilpatrick, 'Researcher's Sketch Map'.
15. Cf. Kilpatrick,'Encyclopedias, Medieval'; Ali, *Arabic Literary Salons*.
16. Mubarak, *La prose arabe*, pp. 35, 73–8. On the use of *akhbār*, cf. Kilpatrick, 'Ashᶜab'.
17. Often combined; cf. Leder, 'Prosa-Dichtung', pp. 30–41; Gruendler, 'Verse and Taxes', pp. 89–96; for Persian stories, see Toorawa, 'Defining *Adab*', pp. 290–304.
18. Cf. Arkoun, 'Éthique et histoire'; Meisami, 'Past in Service of the Present'; Ferster, *Fictions of Advice*, pp. 4, 8 and passim.
19. See Marlow, 'Abū Zayd al-Balkhī'.
20. Ibn al-Nadīm, *al-Fihrist*, II: i: 191–2.
21. Ibn al-Nadīm, *al-Fihrist*, I: ii: 459; II: i: 197; al-Tawḥīdī cites al-Sarakhsī's *Āᵓīn khidmat al-mulūk* in *al-Baṣāᵓir wa-l-dhakhāᵓir*, IV: 117. Cf. Biesterfeldt, 'Aḥmad ibn aṭ-Ṭaiyib as-Saraḫsī', pp. 150, 151–3, 153–6.
22. Ibn al-Nadīm, *al-Fihrist*, I: ii: 428-31; Yāqūt, *Muᶜjam al-udabāᵓ*, I: 275 (No.

92); al-Ṣafadī, *al-Wāfī bi-l-wafayāt*, VI: 409–10. Ibn Ḥajar lists a single *Kitāb al-Siyāsa* for Abū Zayd al-Balkhī, as well as a work titled *Adab al-sulṭān* (*Lisān al-mīzān*, I: 283).

23. Al-Ṣafadī, *al-Wāfī bi-l-wafayāt*, XVII: 26; the information occurs in the biography devoted to al-Kaᶜbī, who criticised the work in question. Yānis al-Khādim remains unidentified (Rosenthal, 'Abū Zayd al-Balkhī on Politics', p. 288).
24. Ibn Farīghūn, *Jawāmiᶜ al-ᶜulūm*; cf. Biesterfeldt, 'Arabisch-islamische Enzyklopädien'.
25. See, for example, his remarks in his introduction, below, Chapter 2, p. 12.
26. NM-A, p. 391 (ᶜAbdallāh b. al-Muqaffaᶜ); pp. 220, 234 (*ṣāḥib Kalīla wa-Dimna*).
27. Ibn al-Nadīm, *al-Fihrist*, I: ii: 367–9.
28. Ibn al-Muqaffaᶜ, *al-Ādāb al-kabīr*, in *Āthār Ibn al-Muqaffaᶜ*, pp. 279–80. On this work, see Kristó-Nagy, *La pensée d'Ibn al-Muqaffaᶜ*, pp. 187–210.
29. Cf. Shaked, 'Notes', esp. pp. 31–40.
30. Ibn al-Muqaffaᶜ, *al-Ādāb al-kabīr*, p. 283. Cf. Hamori, 'Prudence'.
31. In the light of the findings of Rowson (*Muslim Philosopher*, pp. 15–17) and more recently Wakelnig (*Feder, Tafel, Mensch*, pp. 35–9; 'Die Weiterführung', p. 181), I refer to the author of *Kitāb al-Saᶜāda wa-l-isᶜād* as Ibn Abī Dharr rather than following Minovi's earlier and widely accepted attribution of the text to al-ᶜĀmirī ('Muqaddima', *al-Saᶜāda wa-l-isᶜād*).
32. Ibn Abī Dharr, *Kitāb al-Saᶜāda wa-l-isᶜād*, p. 432.
33. On the practice of prudential silence with regard to the dedication of writings that implied criticism, see Touati, 'La dédicace des livres', esp. pp. 325, 350. It is assumed that Ibn al-Muqaffaᶜ composed the epistle for the benefit of the second Abbasid Caliph al-Manṣūr, presumably at a date between the caliph's accession in 136/754 and the author's execution in *c.* 139/757 (van Ess, *Theologie und Gesellschaft*, II: 24; Kristó-Nagy, *La pensée d'Ibn al-Muqaffaᶜ*, pp. 214–17). In a seeming reference to al-Manṣūr, Ibn al-Muqaffaᶜ describes his addressee as austere, open to advice and living in expectation of a future life, and suggests that these qualities encourage potential advisers to approach him with suggestions (*Āthār Ibn al-Muqaffaᶜ*, pp. 345–6; Pellat, *'Conseilleur' du calife*, pp. 18–19; cf. Goitein, 'Turning Point', p. 153).
34. Ibn al-Muqaffaᶜ, *Risāla fī l-ṣaḥāba*, in *Āthār Ibn al-Muqaffaᶜ*, p. 360 = Pellat, *'Conseilleur' du calife*, pp. 60–3. See further Zaman, 'The Caliphs, the ᶜUlamāᵓ, and the Law', p. 5.
35. NM-A, pp. 315–16; cf. NM-Ḥ, p. 444 and n. 1097. On the *Ḥikmat* (*Āl*)

Dāᵓūd, see Khoury, *Wahb b. Munabbih*, esp. pp. 258–63, 266–8. Ibn Qutayba cites the passage reproduced here, on the authority of Wahb b. Munabbih, who relates having found it in *Ḥikmat Dāᵓūd* (*ᶜUyūn al-akhbār*, I: 279-80; cf. Khoury, *Wahb b. Munabbih*, p. 259). The quotation appears without attribution in *al-Adab al-ṣaghīr* (*Āthār Ibn al-Muqaffaᶜ*, p. 323), and in Miskawayh's *Jāvīdān khirad*, pp. 71–2, as part of *faṣl min kalām ḥakīm ākhar fārsī* ('Passage from the words of another Persian sage'; on this text, see Zakeri, 'ᶜAlī Ibn ᶜUbaida ar-Raiḥānī', p. 93). A similar passage appears in the *Waṣiyyat Aflāṭūn* ('Plato's Testament'); cf. Badawī, *Platon en pays d'Islam*, p. 244. For a further example of a numerical saying, see Pseudo-Māwardī's quotation from *Kalīla wa-Dimna*, which lists six things from which the ruler should be secure (NM-A, p. 387).

36. Freimark, *Vorwort*, p. 12. The preface to *Naṣīḥat al-mulūk* does not, however, conform to the tripartite schema described in Freimark's study (*Vorwort*, p. 23).
37. NM-A, p. 43. Abū Dāᵓūd, *Sunan* in *ᶜAwn al-maᶜbūd*, X: 91–2 = *Kitāb al-ᶜIlm*, *Bāb* 9, No. 3641; al-Tirmidhī, *al-Jāmiᶜ al-Ṣaḥīḥ*, III: 459 (= *Kitāb al-ᶜIlm*, 3: *Bāb mā jāᵓa fī kitmān al-ᶜilm*, No. 2649); Ibn Māja, *Sunan*, I: 157–9 = *Muqaddima*, *Bāb* 24, Nos 261, 264, 265, 266; Aḥmad b. Ḥanbal, *Musnad*, XVI: 293, 351, Nos 10487, 10597 (on the authority of Abū Hurayra). In each case, Pseudo-Māwardī's versions of the ḥadīths that he cites in his preface vary slightly from those in the standard collections.
38. NM-A, p. 43. The ḥadīth is widely attested with multiple lines of transmission. Al-Bukhārī, *Ṣaḥīḥ*, I: 17 (= *Kitāb al-Īmān*, *Bāb* 43); Muslim, *Ṣaḥīḥ*, p. 43 (= *Kitāb al-Īmān*, *Bāb* 23, Nos 95, 96 (= No. 55)); Abū Dāᵓūd, *Sunan*, in *ᶜAwn al-maᶜbūd*, XIII: 288 = *Kitāb al-Adab*, *Bāb* 67, No. 4923; al-Tirmidhī, *al-Jāmiᶜ al-Ṣaḥīḥ*, III: 75–6 = *Kitāb al-Birr wa-l-ṣila*, 17: *Bāb mā jāᵓa fī l-naṣīḥa*, No. 1926; al-Nasāᵓī, *Sunan*, VII: 156–7; al-Dārimī, *Sunan*, II: 195 (= *Kitāb al-Riqāq*, *Bāb* 40); Aḥmad b. Ḥanbal, *Musnad*, V: 318, No. 3281 (Ibn ᶜAbbās, in a version that lacks the final *ᶜāmmat al-muslimīn*); XIII: 335–6, No. 7954 (Abū Hurayra); XXVIII: 138–41, 146–8 (Nos 16940, 16941, 16942, 16945, 16947 (Tamīm al-Dārī)); al-Bayhaqī, *Ṣaḥīḥ al-jāmiᶜ*, III: 75–6. In Pseudo-Māwardī's transmission, the word *jamāᶜa* replaces the customary *ᶜāmma*.
39. NM-A, p. 44. *Ṣaḥīḥ al-Bukhārī*, I: 17 = *Kitāb al-Īmān*, *Bāb* 43; *Ṣaḥīḥ Muslim*, 43–4 = *Kitāb al-Īmān*, *Bāb* 23, Nos 97, 98, 99 (= No. 56); al-Tirmidhī, *al-Jāmiᶜ al-ṣaḥīḥ*, III: 75 (= *Kitāb al-Birr wa-l-ṣila*, 17: *Bāb mā jāᵓa fī l-naṣīḥa*, No. 1925); Abū Dāᶜūd, *Sunan* in *ᶜAwn al-maᶜbūd*, XIII: 288–9 = *Kitāb al-*

Adab, *Bāb* 67, No. 4923; *Sunan al-Nasāʾī*, VII: 140 = *Kitāb al-Bayʿa*, *Bāb* 6; al-Dārimī, *Sunan*, II: 117 (= *Kitāb al-Buyūʿ*, 9: *Bāb fī l-naṣīḥa*, No. 2540); *Musnad al-Imām Aḥmad*, XXXI: 533, 535, 557, 572, Nos 19195, 19229, 19199, 19258; 500–1, 529, 556, 566–7, Nos 19162, 19163, 19191, 19228, 19245, 19248 (Jarīr b. ʿAbdallāh); al-Ābī, *Nathr al-durr*, IV: 236.

40. *ʿAhd Ardashīr*, p. 53 (*wa-qad qāla al-awwalūna minnā: rashādu l-wālī khayr lil-raʿiyya min khiṣb al-zamān*, 'those who came before us said, the rectitude of the ruler is better for the subjects than a time of abundance'); Ibn Qutayba, *ʿUyūn al-akhbār*, I: 5 (*kānat al-ḥukamāʾ taqūlu: ʿadl al-sulṭān anfaʿ lil-raʿiyya min khiṣb al-zamān*, 'the sage philosophers used to say, the ruler's justice is of greater use to the subjects than a time of abundance'); al-Masʿūdī, *Murūj al-dhahab*, I: 298 (*kāna [Anūshīrwān] yaqūlu: ṣalāḥ amr al-raʿiyya anṣar min kathrat al-junūd wa-ʿadl al-malik anfaʿ min khiṣb al-zamān*, 'Anūshīrvān said, the well-being of the subjects is of greater assistance than a large number of troops, and the king's justice is of greater use than a time of abundance').
41. *ʿAhd Ardashīr*, p. 75 (*wa-man ghashsha al-imāma fa-qad ghashsha al-ʿāmma wa-in ẓanna annahu lil-ʿāmma nāṣiḥ wa-kāna yuqālu lam yanṣaḥ ʿamalan man ghashsha ʿāmilahu*). Pseudo-Māwardī's two quotations follow the order of *ʿAhd Ardashīr*.
42. Cf. Miskawayh, *Jāvīdān khirad*, p. 14 (*fī ḥaqq Allāh ʿazza wa-jalla al-taʿẓīm wa-l-shukr wa-fī ḥaqq al-sulṭān al-ṭāʿa al-naṣīḥa*, 'the rights of God include exaltation and gratitude, and the rights of the ruler include obedience and counsel').
43. Ibn al-Muqaffaʿ, *Kalīla wa-Dimna*, in *Āthār Ibn al-Muqaffaʿ*, p. 120; Ibn Qutayba, *ʿUyūn al-akhbār*, I: 92; al-Mubashshir, *Mukhtār al-ḥikam*, p. 257 (in a slightly extended form and ascribed to Baṭlamiyūs).
44. Al-Taghlibī, *Kitāb al-Tāj*, p. 95.
45. The functions of the *awliyāʾ* and *aʿwān* are uncertain: cf. Volume I, pp. 104, 131. For the Abbasid context, see Montgomery, *Al-Jāḥiẓ*, p. 40.
46. A reference to the mutual responsibilities of rulers and subjects; it was a duty of the subjects to pray for the ruler and a manifestation of their 'love' for him (see below, pp. 206–7).
47. NM-A, p. 46. Cf. Q. 3: 9 (*inna llāha lā yukhlifu l-mīʿāda*), 194 (*innaka lā tukhlifu l-mīʿāda*); 13: 31 (*inna llāha lā yukhlifu l-mīʿāda*); 39: 20 (*lā yukhlifu llāhu l-mīʿāda*).
48. NM-A, p. 46.
49. NM-A, p. 47.

50. Pseudo-Māwardī writes, 'We open with praise of God . . . and on Him we call for assistance', perhaps an echo of Q 1, 'The Opening'. The doxology consists of praise of God alone, and omits the invocation of blessings on the Prophet; this feature is not unusual in ninth-century epistles (see Montgomery, *Al-Jāḥiẓ*, pp. 199, 201–2).
51. NM-A, p. 44.
52. Two of the citations adduced without specific attribution in *Naṣīḥat al-mulūk* appear in a similar fashion in *ᶜAhd Ardashīr* (*wa-qad qāla al-awwalūna minnā, wa-kāna yuqālu*) (*ᶜAhd Ardashīr*, pp. 53, 75).
53. The saying is introduced in al-Taghlibī's *Kitāb al-Tāj* by the phrase *wa-yaqūlu* (*Kitāb al-Tāj*, p. 95).
54. See, for example, Miskawayh, *Jāvīdān khirad*, where the sentiment appears among the wise sayings of the Iranian King Bahman (p. 62); on this text, see Zakeri, *Persian Wisdom in Arabic Garb*, I: 80–1.
55. See Volume I, Chapter 7.
56. See Volume I, Introduction, pp. 3–4.
57. See Volume I, pp. 130, 132, 134–5.
58. NM-A, p. 46.
59. Yaman, *Prophetic Niche*, pp. 4–6, 27–36, 47–60 and passim. The terms appear together in Q 2: 231, 3: 48, 4: 54, 4: 113.
60. Shaked detected this pattern in the underlying structure of Ibn al-Muqaffaᶜ's *dīn* (religion) and *ᶜaql* (reason, intelligence) ('Notes', p. 36).
61. Exceptions appear at NM-A, pp. 150, 158. Notwithstanding Pseudo-Māwardī's preference for the designations *sunan* and *āthār* (the latter term usually rendered, when applied to materials transmitted from the Prophet, as 'traditions'), the present text will sometimes employ the term ḥadīth in reference to these Prophetic materials.
62. Radkte and O'Kane, *Concept of Sainthood*, p. 15; cf. Melchert, 'Traditionist-Jurisprudents', p. 387.
63. Melchert, 'Traditionist-Jurisprudents', p. 398.
64. As Davis notes, the responses that Firdawsī explores include ' blind support of the oppressor . . . mute acceptance . . . gentle or exasperated attempts to reform the king . . . withdrawal from the court and a washing of one's hands of the whole affair, [and] outright rebellion' (Davis, *Epic and Sedition*, pp. 20–1).
65. NM-A, p. 49.
66. *Maḥjūb*, literally 'veiled', or 'concealed', 'secluded', probably a reference to the *ḥijāb*, the screen behind which caliphs from the Umayyad period onwards con-

cealed themselves from their audiences; see below, p. 21. The reference also alludes to the office of the *ḥājib* or chamberlain, the figure responsible for admitting individuals to the ruler's presence or denying them access to the monarch.

67. Compare the list of royal weaknesses rehearsed in *ᶜAhd Ardashīr* and alluded to elsewhere in *Naṣīḥat al-mulūk* (Volume I, pp. 195–7).
68. NM-A, pp. 49–51.
69. Hamori, 'Shameful and Injurious', pp. 198–200.
70. Al-Taghlibī, *Kitāb al-Tāj*, p. 71.
71. Royal seclusion, especially in the form of the ruler's concealment behind a screen, appears to have been a Sasanian practice. All the Persian kings from Ardashīr to Yazdagird secluded themselves from their boon companions by means of a curtain (*sitāra*), and Muᶜāwiya, many of the later Umayyad caliphs and the Abbasids adopted the same custom, according to al-Taghlibī (*Kitāb al-Tāj*, pp. 28, 32–44 passim). On royal seclusion and the *ḥijāb*, see al-Azmeh, *Muslim Kingship*, pp. 14, 69, 139.
72. See Volume I, p. 207.
73. Also recorded in Miskawayh, *Jāvīdān khirad*, p. 75, as part of *waṣiyyat ukhrā lil-furs* ('another Persian testament', which corresponds to the collection *al-Adab al-ṣaghīr*, ascribed to Ibn al-Muqaffaᶜ; see Zakeri, *Persian Wisdom in Arabic Garb*, I: 81).
74. Compare Ibn Qutayba, *ᶜUyūn al-akhbār*, I: 37.
75. Miskawayh, *Jāvīdān khirad*, pp. 75 (in *waṣiyyat ukhrā lil-furs*); 62 (ascribed to King Bahman). Cf. Zakeri, 'ᶜAlī ibn ᶜUbaida ar-Raiḥānī', pp. 94, 95; Zakeri has established the Middle Persian provenance of these and other axiomatic sayings that were translated by al-Rayḥānī. Compare similar phrases in Ibn Qutayba, *ᶜUyūn al-akhbār*, I: 37.
76. NM-A, pp. 51–2.
77. See Volume One, Chapter 6, esp. pp. 174–81.
78. Cf. al-Mubashshir, *Mukhtār al-ḥikam*, p. 335.
79. NM-A, p. 53 (see n. 14), following the reading in NM-Ḥ, p. 57, n. 70 (cf. MS 2447, f. 6b). Abū Dāʾūd relates the ḥadīth in the extended form: 'The believer is a mirror to the believer, and a brother to the believer; he restrains him from aberration and watches his back' (*yakuffu ᶜalayhi ḍayᶜatahu wa-yaḥūṭuhu min warāʾihi*) (*ᶜAwn al-maᶜbūd*, XIII: 260 = *Kitāb al-Adab* ('Book of Comportment'), *Bāb* 57, No. 4897). Cf. al-Tirmidhī, *al-Jāmiᶜ al-Ṣaḥīḥ*, III: 77 (= *Kitāb al-Birr wa-l-ṣila*, 18: *Bāb mā jāʾa fī shafaqat al-muslim ᶜalā l-muslim*, No. 1929). Al-Masᶜūdī includes the maxim among the Prophet's short sayings

(*Murūj al-dhahab*, II: 294); Abū l-Layth al-Samarqandī cites it among the Prophet's *amthāl* (proverbs) (*Bustān al-ᶜārifīn*, p. 86); al-Ābī includes it among the sayings of the Prophet (*Nathr al-durr*, I: 161); and Abū ᶜUbayd includes it as a ḥadīth in his collection of proverbs (*al-Amthāl* in al-Bakrī, *Faṣl al-maqāl*, p. 275).

80. NM-A, p. 54.
81. NM-A, p. 55. *Ṣaḥīḥ Muslim*, 56 = *Kitāb al-Imān* ('Book of Faith'), *Bāb* 43, No. 164 [102]; al-Tirmidhī, *al-Jāmiᶜ al-Ṣaḥīḥ*, II: 322 (= *Kitāb al-Buyūᶜ*, 74: *Bāb mā jāʾa fī karāhiyat al-ghishsh fī l-buyūᶜ*, No. 1315); Abū Dāʾūd, *ᶜAwn al-maᶜbud, Kitāb al-Ijāza*, *Bāb* 17, No. 3435 = IX: 321; al-Dārimī, *Sunan*, II: 117 (= *Kitāb al-Buyūᶜ* ('Book of Sales'), *Bāb* 10 (= *Bāb fī l-nahy ᶜan al-ghishsh*, No. 2541)); Aḥmad b. Ḥanbal, *Musnad*, I: 122, No. 5113 (Ibn ᶜUmar); XV: 232, No. 9396 (Abū Hurayra); Ibn Māja, *Sunan*, III: 52–3 (= *Kitāb al-Tijārāt*, *Bāb* 36: *al-Nahy ᶜan al-ghishsh*, Nos 2224, 2225).
82. The latter citation continues, '"If he accepts your counsel, (so much the better); if he does not accept it, deceive him". When asked, "How should I deceive him?" the sage replied, "Remain silent, and withhold your counsel from him". They considered the withholding of counsel to be a punishment for the person counselled (*al-manṣūḥ*) for his refusal to accept it' (NM-A, p. 56).
83. Q. 7: 79, 93; 7: 62; 7: 68; 11: 34.
84. NM-A, p. 56.
85. See further Cook, *Commanding Right*, p. 56.
86. Cf. van Ess, *Theologie und Gesellschaft*, I: 221–8.
87. NM-A, pp. 56–7.
88. Al-Ṭabarī, *Taʾrīkh*, VIII: 357–8 = XXX: 323; Ibn al-Athīr, *al-Kāmil*, VI: 219–20. See below, p. 27.
89. Al-Ṭurṭūshī, *Sirāj al-mulūk*, I: 27–8; cf. Ibn al-ᶜImād, *Shadharāt al-dhahab*, II: 434 (also involving Ibn al-Sammāk). See further El-Hibri, *Reinterpreting Islamic Historiography*, pp. 26–7, 92. The anecdote is somewhat similar to one recounted in *Siyar al-mulūk* (Niẓām al-Mulk, *Siyar al-mulūk*, p. 64 = 48).
90. Sufyān, like al-Ḥasan al-Baṣrī (d. 110/728), appears in several accounts as an exemplar of disinterested truth-telling in his interactions with rulers, but he is also reputed to have discouraged the practice (Cook, *Commanding Right*, pp. 50–67, esp. pp. 53–4, 65–7).
91. van Ess, 'ᶜAmr b. ᶜObayd'; van Ess, *Theologie und Gesellschaft*, II: 280–310. See also Volume I, pp. 37, 39–40, 211, 233.
92. NM-A, pp. 56–7. Cf. al-Jāḥiẓ, *al-Bayān wa-l-tabyīn*, IV: 64–5; al-Masᶜūdī,

Murūj al-dhahab, III: 303; al-Ḥuṣrī, *Zahr al-ādāb*, I: 102-3; El-Hibri, *Reinterpreting Islamic Historiography*, p. 41, n. 59.

93. NM-A, p. 103; Volume I, pp. 39–40. Many authors record how al-Manṣūr solicited admonition from ᶜAmr b. ᶜUbayd, who was well known for his closeness to al-Ḥasan al-Baṣrī (van Ess, *Theologie und Gesellschaft*, II: 297–8). See Ibn Qutayba, *ᶜUyūn al-akhbār*, II: 237; al-Masᶜūdī, *Murūj al-dhahab*, III: 302–3.
94. The two men reportedly 'withdrew' (*iᶜtazala*) from the circle of al-Ḥasan al-Baṣrī in consequence of theological differences over the status of the sinning Muslim; see van Ess, *Theologie und Gesellschaft*, II: 234, 255–60, 260–7, 305–6 (with attention to the misleading and tendentious nature of many of the reports concerning the beginnings of the Muᶜtazila).
95. Madelung, *Der Imam al-Qāsim*, pp. 72–4. Wāṣil b. ᶜAtāᵓ reportedly supported the claim to the legitimate leadership of al-Nafs al-Zakiyya fourteen years before the rebellion broke out. Al-Kaᶜbī enumerates the many Muᶜtazilites who supported Muḥammad's brother Ibrāhīm in Basra during the revolt, which ensued a year after the death of ᶜAmr b. ᶜUbayd (al-Kaᶜbī, *Faḍl al-iᶜtizāl*, pp. 117–19; Madelung, *Der Imam al-Qāsim*, p. 73 and n. 195; van Ess, *Theologie und Gesellschaft*, II: 248–53, 259, 285–95). On ᶜAmr's conception and advocacy of *al-amr bi-l-maᶜrūf* with regard to rulers, see van Ess, *Theologie und Gesellschaft*, II: 286, 293, and Cook, *Commanding Right*, pp. 53, 197.
96. The Kufan traditionist and frequent preacher (*wāᶜiẓ*) at Hārūn's court, Ibn al-Sammāk appears in many such anecdotes with the caliph; see al-Ṭabarī, *Taᵓrīkh*, VIII: 357 = XXX: 322; al-Khaṭīb al-Baghdādī, *Taᵓrīkh Baghdād*, V: 368–73; al-Ṭurṭūshī, *Sirāj al-mulūk*, I: 120; Ibn al-Jawzī, *al-Quṣṣāṣ wa-l-mudhakkirīn*, pp. 68–9, § 135; Ibn al-ᶜImād, *Shadharāt al-dhahab*, II: 376–7 (*sub anno* 183), 434.
97. NM-A, pp. 57–8. The poem (by Abū l-ᶜAtāhiya), variously recorded, appears in *Abū l-ᶜAtāhiya: ashᶜāruhu wa-akhbāruhu*, p. 273, No. 290; al-Rāghib al-Iṣfahānī, *Muḥāḍarāt al-udabāᵓ*, III: 242. Cf. Marlow, 'Performances of Advice'.
98. NM-A, p. 58.
99. NM-A, pp. 59–60.
100. See Volume I, pp. 168, 198, 199, 201. Cf. Gilliot, '*In consilium deduces me*', pp. 472–8.
101. In another example associated with Ardashīr, the contrast of *munāṣiḥūn* and *ghāshshūn* occurs in the *Āᵓīn li-Ardashīr* (Grignaschi, 'Quelques spécimens', p. 98 = 118). Pseudo-Māwardī's presentation is also reminiscent of the section

devoted to the subjects' obligation to offer counsel to the ruler (*Bāb mā yajibu ᶜalā l-raᶜiyya min naṣīḥat al-malik*) in the anonymous *al-Asad wa-l-ghawwāṣ* ('The Lion and the Diver'), pp. 44–52, esp. pp. 44–5. The allegorical narrative itself is closely related to *Kalīla wa-Dimna* (al-Sayyid, 'Fī l-taqdīm', pp. 24–31).

102. Cook, *Commanding Right*, pp. 32–5, 96.
103. With particular reference to al-Barbahārī (d. 329/941), see Cook, *Commanding Right*, pp. 114–44, esp. 114–18; and Melchert, 'Ḥanābila and the Early Sufis', p. 366.
104. Melchert, 'Asceticism to Mysticism', p. 68; see further above, n. 82.
105. Mottahedeh has noted the significance of Transoxiana and Khurasan in the development of the science of ḥadīth, and the connections with these regions of the compilers of the 'six books' (Mottahedeh, 'Transmission of Learning', pp. 66–7).
106. Pakatchi, 'Abū Dāwūd al-Sijistānī', pp. 657–66.
107. Al-Maydānī, *Majmaᶜ al-amthāl*, I: 54, No. 68. Al-Maydānī adds, from the corpus of ḥadīth (*fī baᶜḍ al-ḥadīth*), 'The man is the mirror of his brother', which he interprets to mean that when he sees something reprehensible in him, he brings it to his attention and forbids it to him (*Majmaᶜ al-amthāl*, I: 54). Cf. Ibn Qutayba, *ᶜUyūn al-akhbār*, I: 38.
108. Al-Maydānī, *Majmaᶜ al-amthāl*, I: 345, No. 1433.
109. Ibn al-Jawzī (510–97/1126–1200) would address the issue of authoritative exhortation with reference to this Prophetic saying (al-Dārimī, *Sunan*, II: 204 (= *Kitāb al-Riqāq*, 61: *Bāb fī l-nahy ᶜan al-qaṣaṣ*, No. 2779)), in the form 'Only an amir or a *maʾmūr* shall preach; (anyone else who does so) is presumptuous' (*lā yaquṣṣu illā amīr aw-maʾmūr aw-mukhtāl*). He identifies the *maʾmūr* as the individual appointed by the imam to assume the role of preacher (*man yuqīmuhu l-imām khaṭīban*), and the *mukhtāl* as the person who, without having been ordered to do so, assumes the role out of a desire for leadership (*ṭalaban lil-riyāsa*) (Ibn al-Jawzī, *al-Quṣṣāṣ wa-l-mudhakkirīn*, pp. 28–9, §§ 46–7 = pp. 114–15, §§ 46–7). Cf. Cheikh-Moussa, 'Comment s'adresser au tyran?', pp. 139–40. Ch. Pellat translates 'None but an *amīr*, a subordinate [of an *amīr*] or a proud man (*mukhtāl*) shall preach', noting that the idiom *yaquṣṣu ᶜalā l-nās* probably refers to the delivery of a *khuṭba* (Pellat, 'Ḳāṣṣ', p. 733).
110. Abū l-Layth al-Samarqandī, *Bustān al-ᶜārifīn*, pp. 23–5. Cf. Ibn al-Jawzī, *al-Quṣṣāṣ wa-l-mudhakkirīn*, pp. 22, 51, §§ 32, 96 (Tamīm al-Dārī); p. 44, §§ 81–2 (Ibn Masᶜūd).
111. Abū l-Layth al-Samarqandī, *Bustān al-ārifīn*, pp. 25–6.

112. See Cheikh-Moussa, 'Comment s'adresser au tyran?' Ibn al-Jawzī differentiated among the activities of *qaṣaṣ*, edificatory 'story-telling', preaching, *tadhkīr*, 'reminding' people of their religious and moral duties and the judgement that awaited them, and *wa*ᶜ*ẓ*, 'exhortation' (*al-Quṣṣāṣ wa-l-mudhakkirīn*, pp. 9–11, §§ 3–5), and devoted considerable attention to the manner in which such exhortation should be undertaken (*al-Quṣṣāṣ wa-l-mudhakkirīn*, p. 143, § 330 = pp. 228–9, § 330; cf. p. 228, n. 3 and p. 229, n. 3).
113. The stance of the jurist, theologian, political adviser and polymath al-Ghazālī (450–505/1058–1111) in this regard is particularly notable; see Cook, *Commanding Right*, pp. 427–68, esp. p. 431. Al-Ghazālī's 'celebration of heroic incivility to rulers' displeased Ibn al-Jawzī, among others (*Commanding Right*, p. 458); al-Ghazālī laments the lapsing of the practice, and Ibn al-Jawzī, as the passage cited later in the present chapter suggests, discourages it in the present (*Commanding Right*, pp. 140–1).
114. Cook, *Commanding Right*, p. 476.
115. Cook, *Commanding Right*, p. 6 and n. 18. On the larger corpus of traditions related to the duty, see Cook, *Commanding Right*, pp. 32–45.
116. I borrow the term from Samer Ali (*Arabic Literary Salons*, p. 156).
117. On al-Khaṭṭābī, see al-Samᶜānī, *al-Ansāb*, V: 158–9; Ibn Khallikān, *Wafayāt al-a*ᶜ*yān*, II: 214–16, No. 207. According to Ibn Khallikān and Yāqūt, al-Khaṭṭābī's given name was Ḥamd, but people commonly called him Aḥmad. Contemporaries compared him with Abū ᶜUbayd al-Qāsim b. Sallām in terms of his ᶜ*ilm* (knowledge), *adab* (literary culture), *zuhd* (austerity), *wara*ᶜ (uprightness, scrupulousness), *tadrīs* (instruction) and *ta*ʾ*līf* (composition); Yāqūt cites al-Thaᶜālibī as the source for this information. Al-Khaṭṭābī died in a *ribāṭ* on the banks of the river in Bust (Ibn al-Jawzī, *al-Muntaẓam*, VI: 397; Yāqūt, *Mu*ᶜ*jam al-udabā*ʾ, II: 486–90, No. 175 [s. v. Aḥmad], III: 1205–7, No. 428 [s. v. Ḥamd]; Sezgin, *GAS* I: 210–11).
118. Al-Khaṭṭābī, *Ma*ᶜ*ālim al-sunan* ('Landmarks of the Traditions'), IV: 125–6. The passages in square brackets represent parts of al-Khaṭṭābī's text omitted in Ibn al-Jawzī's later citation (*al-Miṣbāḥ*, pp. 181–2).
119. Al-Khaṭṭābī, *al-*ᶜ*Uzla*, pp. 133–9, esp. pp. 133–4, No. 354. See also Cook, *Commanding Right*, pp. 473–9, esp. pp. 477; cf. 50–67.
120. Al-Khaṭṭābī, *al-*ᶜ*Uzla*, pp. 134–5, No. 357; cf. 358. See further Cook, *Commanding Right*, pp. 65–7.
121. Al-Kaᶜbī, *Tafsīr*, p. 167; al-Kaᶜbī, *Qabūl al-akhbār*, pp. 229–44 and passim. For other interpretations of *ūlī l-amr*, see Crone, *God's Rule*, pp. 138, 155.

122. Ibn al-Muqaffa[c], *Āthār Ibn al-Muqaffa*[c], p. 360; Pellat, *'Conseilleur' du calife*, pp. 60–3.
123. Afsaruddin, '*Maslahah* as a Political Concept'. Al-Ghazālī located *maṣlaḥa* in his treatment of the 'objectives of the law' (*maqāṣid al-sharī*[c]*a*). In al-Ghazālī's formulation, God's purpose in revealing the divine law was, in a broad sense, *maṣlaḥa*: the sharī[c]a had as its purpose the preservation of the five elements essential to humankind's well-being, namely, religion, life, intellect, offspring and property; anything that furthered these aims constituted *maṣlaḥa* (Hallaq, *History of Islamic Legal Theories*, pp. 112–13, 130–4, 168–74 and passim; Opwis, '*Maṣlaḥa* in Contemporary Islamic Legal Theory', pp. 187–97).

Chapter 2

1. MS Arabe 2447, f. 12b. Aḥmad suggests the reading *Kitāb Siyāsat al-mulūk* ('Book of the Governance of Kings') (NM-A, p. 77, n. 74); al-Ḥadīthī substitutes *Kitāb Ā*[ɔ]*īnnāma(t) al-mulūk* (NM-Ḥ, p. 99; see nn. 171, 70).
2. NM-A, pp. 153, 390. On the Barmakids, who hailed from Balkh, and enjoyed prominence under the early Abbasid caliphs until Hārūn al-Rashīd abruptly curtailed their power in 187/803, see also Volume I, pp. 46, 81–2, 163.
3. NM-A, p. 390.
4. Schoeler, 'Die Frage der schriftlichen oder mündlichen Überlieferung'. On the status of 'notes' (*aṭrāf*) in the transmission of tradition, see further Cook, 'Opponents', esp. pp. 488–9, §§ 100–1.
5. Shaked, 'Notes', pp. 31–40.
6. Cf. Gutas, 'Classical Arabic Wisdom Literature'; Dakhlia, 'Les miroirs des princes'.
7. On the *shu*[c]*ūbiyya*, see Mottahedeh, 'Shu[c]ûbîyah Controversy'.
8. Al-Kindī, *Fī l-falsafa al-ūlā*, pp. 32–3 = Akasoy, *Die erste Philosophie*, pp. 64–5; Ivry, *Al-Kindi's Metaphysics*, p. 57; cf. Zimmermann, 'al-Kindī', p. 368; Adamson, *Al-Kindī*, p. 22.
9. It is of interest to note that among the books listed under al-Balkhī's authorship is one entitled *Akhlāq al-umam* ('Characteristics of the Nations'); al-Tawḥīdī refers to this work as a useful one (*Kitāb al-Imtā*[c], I: 212; cf. Yāqūt, *Mu*[c]*jam al-udabā*[ɔ], I: 259; Ibn Ḥajar, *Lisān al-mīzān*, I: 283). The (possibly even 'authoritative') bio-bibliographers Yāqūt and al-Ṣafadī refer to both this work and a *Ṣifāt al-umam* (Yāqūt, *Mu*[c]*jam al-udabā*[ɔ], I: 275; al-Ṣafadī, *al-Wāfī*, VI: 410). Cf. Kraemer, *Philosophy in the Renaissance of Islam*, p. 147.
10. See Volume I, p. 67, and below, pp. 156–7

11. Al-Tawḥīdī, *al-Imtā*ᶜ, I: 78–90; cf. Treadwell, 'Political History', p. 319. Cf. Margoliouth, 'Some Extracts', pp. 389–90.
12. See Volume I, pp. 18–19; Lazard, 'Rise of the New Persian Language'.
13. Blair, *Monumental Inscriptions*, pp. 34–5, No. 7; 32–3, No. 6; cf. Blair, *Islamic Inscriptions*, p. 47. See also *Monumental Inscriptions*, pp. 60–2, 118–20, Nos 18, 43; Melikian-Chirvani, 'Le royaume de Salomon'.
14. Bosworth, 'Interaction'.
15. Daniel, 'Sāmānid "Translations"'; Peacock, *Tārīkhnāma*, esp. pp. 76–105; Meisami, *Persian Historiography*, pp. 23–37.
16. Ibn al-Nadīm, *al-Fihrist*, I: ii: 370, II: i: 326; Zakeri, *Persian Wisdom in Arabic Garb*, I: 100–16.
17. Qazvīnī, 'Muqaddimeh-yi qadīm', p. 33 = Minorsky, 'Older Preface', p. 168 = pp. 265–6. See further Treadwell, 'Political History', pp. 183, 185; Meisami, *Persian Historiography*, p. 17. The 'Older Preface', the only surviving part of the 'Abū Manṣūrī *Shāhnāmeh*', commissioned by Ibn ᶜAbd al-Razzāq, appears at the front of certain manuscripts of Firdawsī's *Shāhnāmeh*. Ibn ᶜAbd al-Razzāq was Abū ᶜAlī Chaghānī's governor in Nishapur in *c.* 334/945; he joined the latter's rebellion and, like Abū ᶜAlī, cultivated relations with the Buyids (Khaleghi-Motlagh, 'Abū Manṣūr ᶜAbd al-Razzāq'; Meisami, *Persian Historiography*, p. 20).
18. Reportedly Rūdakī versified certain stories from the *Sindbādnāmeh* some years before Naṣr's successor Nūḥ b. Naṣr instructed another vizier, the ᶜAmīd Abū l-Favāris Qinārazī, to commission the translation of the *Sindbādnāmeh* from Pahlavi into Persian prose; the process reached its culmination with Azraqī Heravī's rendering of the prose version into verse in the sixth/twelfth century. See further Dānishpazhūh, 'Dībācheh'; Manṣūr, *Dīvān-i Rūdakī*, pp. 56–8; Ross, 'Rudaki and Pseudo-Rudaki'; de Fouchécour, *Moralia*, p.48 and n. 81.
19. For a list of the examples that preceded Firdawsī, see Minorsky, 'Older Preface', p. 160 = pp. 260–1 (from 'Muḥaṣṣil').
20. On the writing of *shāhnāmeh*s before Firdawsī, see Volume I, pp. 45, 69.
21. Qazvīnī, 'Muqaddimeh-yi qadīm', pp. 30, 36; Minorsky, 'Older Preface', pp. 161, 164–6, 169 = pp. 262, 264–6. Cf. Khaleghi-Motlagh, 'Abū Manṣūr Maᶜmarī'; Meisami, *Persian Historiography*, pp. 20–3.
22. See Pourshariati, *Decline and Fall*, pp. 116–18, 476 and passim, and pp. 368–78.
23. Al-Khwārazmī, *Mafātīḥ al-ᶜulūm*, p. 116.
24. Davidson, 'Testing of the *Shāhnāma*'. To the elements identified by Davidson might be added the repeated appearance in these narratives of individuals who bore the *kunya* Abū Manṣūr.

25. On *Hazār afsān*, see Ibn al-Nadīm, *al-Fihrist*, II: i: 322–4; on Sindbād al-ḥakīm, see Ibn al-Nadīm, *al-Fihrist*, II: i: 324. On *Hazār afsān* and the *Sindbādnāmeh*, see Tafażżolī, *Tārīkh-i adabīyāt-i Īrān*, pp. 297–301; de Blois, 'Sindbād'; Toorawa, 'Defining *Adab*', pp. 290–304.
26. NM-A, p. 216. See Drory, 'Three Attempts', pp. 146, 154–5; Hoyland, 'History', p. 17.
27. Cf. Drory, 'Three Attempts', p. 146.
28. See Volume I, pp. 138–40.
29. Qazvīnī, 'Muqaddimeh-yi qadīm', pp. 34–5 = Minorsky, p. 168 = p. 266; Pourshariati, *Decline and Fall*, p. 463 and n. 2613.
30. Qazvīnī, 'Muqaddimeh-yi qadīm', p. 34 = Minorsky, 'Older Preface', p. 168 = p. 266. On the application to al-Maʿmarī of the term *chākar*, see Volume I, p. 105.
31. ʿAbdallāh b. ʿĀmir (d. between 57/678 and 59/680), governor of Basra from 29/649–50 to 35/656 and from 41/661 to 44/664, advanced into Khurasan in 30–1/651, defeated the Hephthalites and occupied the province as far as Marv, Balkh and, in the following year, Herat. Between 41 and 43/661 and 663 his lieutenants pacified Sistan and Khurasan, where revolts had broken out in the first civil war.
32. According to the *dihqān*, *muruwwa*, for the *dahāqīn*, consisted of four elements: first, a man should avoid sin, for if he were sinful he became base and devoid of *muruwwa*; secondly, he should put his wealth to good use (*an yuṣliḥa mālahu*) and not squander it, for if he squandered his resources and became dependent on other people he would forfeit his *muruwwa*; thirdly, that he should assume responsibility for the needs of his family, for a man whose family members needed assistance from other people lacked *muruwwa*; and fourthly, in terms of food and drink, he should consider what was suitable and eat and drink accordingly, without exceeding that amount; observance of these four rules of conduct constituted the perfection of *muruwwa*. Abū l-Layth al-Samarqandī, *Bustān al-ʿārifīn*, p. 119.
33. *Tārīkh-i Sīstān*, p. 106 (*guft dahāqīn-rā sukhanān-i ḥikmat bāshad mā-rā az ān chīzī bi-gū-ī*). Tafażżolī noted the similarity of the cited specimens to Pahlavi *andarz* (Tafażżolī, 'Dehqān', p. 224).
34. Pourshariati, 'Parthians and the Production of the Canonical Shāhnāmas', pp. 371–2. In the *Shāhnāmeh*, the name Āzādsarv appears at the beginning of the story of Rustam and Shaghād; see the discussion in Davidson, *Poet and Hero*, pp. 48, 71. It also appears in Firdawsī's account of Nūshīrvān's dream;

Āzādsarv perceived the inability of the *mōbadh*s to interpret the king's dream, and left the court for Marv, where he discovered Buzurgmihr, who alone possessed the power to interpret it (*Le livre des rois*, VI: 192).

35. De Fouchécour, *Moralia*, pp. 19–112, esp. pp. 106–7; Ṣafā, *Tārīkh-i adabīyāt dar Īrān*, I: 133.
36. *Pandnāmeh-yi Māturīdī*, p. 49. De Fouchécour proposes an eleventh-century or perhaps early twelfth-century dating for this collection, but notes numerous parallels with the counsels of Anūshīrvān (de Fouchécour, *Moralia*, pp. 100–1).
37. Lazard, *Les premiers poètes*, I: 53 = II: 12, I: 17–18 (Ḥanẓala Bādghīsī); I: 61 = II: 21–2; I: 19 (Abū Salīk Gurgānī); Ṣafā, *Tārīkh-i adabīyāt dar Īrān*, I: 179–80 (Ḥanẓala), 181–2 (Abū Salīk).
38. Tabatabai, *Father of Persian Verse*, pp. 74–85; Lazard, *Les premiers poètes*, I: 62–9, 136–62 = II: 23–39, 141–77. Cf. Ṣafā, 'Andarz Literature', p. 17; Ṣafā, *Tārīkh-i adabīyāt dar Īrān*, I: 389–93, 408–19.
39. Lazard, *Les premiers poètes*, I: 91–127 = II: 102–26 and I: 27–30, 182. Cf. Ali, 'Abū Shakūr Balkhī'; de Fouchécour, *Moralia*, pp. 102–3; Ṣafā, *Tārīkh-i adabīyāt dar Īrān*, I: 369, 403–8.
40. Lazard, *Les premiers poètes*, I: 102–14 = II: 91–127; I: 27–30.
41. de Fouchécour, *Moralia*, pp. 22, 51–8 and passim; Meisami, '*Šâh-nâme* as Mirror for Princes'.
42. For an example of Firdawsī's mention of the *dihqān*(s) as custodians of ancient wisdom in his narrative, see *Le livre des rois*, VI: 232–7.
43. Ṣafā, 'Andarz Literature', p. 18; Muḥammadī, *al-Tarjama wa-l-naql*, p. 38; de Fouchécour, *Moralia*, pp. 28, 67–9. The amir's initiative is recorded in the preface to the *Ẓafarnāmeh*, the collection of the semi-legendary sage Buzurgmihr's wise sayings, which appears in its earliest surviving version in the *Tārīkh-i guzīdeh* ('Selected History') (730/1329) of Ḥamd Allāh Qazvīnī (*Tārīkh-i guzīdeh*, pp. 66–70). Several features of this work, which was copied frequently and versified, suggest that it preserves much older materials. The *Ẓafarnāmeh* records forty-two maxims said to have been uttered by Buzurgmihr in response to a request from Anūshīrvān for 'a work of counsels, concise in words but ample in meaning, of utility in this world and the next' (*Pīrūzīnāmeh* ('Book of Victory', a title in which the Persian word *pīrūzī* replaces the Arabic *ẓafar*), p. 54).
44. See below, pp. 126–7; Marlow, 'Abū Zayd al-Balkhī'.
45. Cf. Dubler, 'Über arabische Pseudo-Aristotelica', pp. 66, 72–5; van Bladel, 'Iranian Characteristics'.

46. On this literature, see Grignaschi, 'Les "Rasāʾil ʾAristāṭālīsa ʾilā-l-Iskandar"' (Grignaschi dated the appearance in Arabic of *al-Siyāsa al-ʿāmmiyya* to the reign of the Umayyad Caliph Hishām (r. 105–25/724–43)); Grignaschi, 'Le roman épistolaire classique'; Grignaschi, 'La figure d'Alexandre'; Manzalaoui, 'Facts and Problems'; Latham, 'Beginnings', pp. 154–64; Forster, *Das Geheimnis der Geheimnisse*; Stern, *Aristotle on the World State*. For the Aristotelian epistolary cycle in Persian, see de Fouchécour, *Moralia*, pp. 69–81.
47. On the transmutations of *Sirr al-asrār*, see Manzalaoui, 'Facts and Problems'; Grignaschi, 'La diffusion du "Secretum secretorum"'; Williams, *Secret of Secrets*; Forster, *Das Geheimnis der Geheimnisse*.
48. Compare *ʿUyūn al-akhbār*, I: 8 (*wa-qaraʾtu kitāban min Arisṭāṭālīs ilā l-Iskandar* ('I read in a book by Aristotle to Alexander'); this quotation appears in *Kitāb al-Sulṭān*); II: 108 (*qāla Arisṭāṭālīs*; this quotation, not addressed to Alexander, concerns the properties of a stone and appears in *Kitāb al-Ṭabāʾiʿ*, 'Book of Natures'). Ibn ʿAbd Rabbihi, *al-ʿIqd al-farīd*, I: 38 (*wa-kataba Arisṭāṭālīs ilā l-Iskandar* ('Aristotle wrote to Alexander'); this quotation occurs in *al-Sulṭān wa-ʿadl sāʿa* ('Sovereignty and the Justice of an Hour') = *The Unique Necklace*, I: 17); and I: 155.
49. NM-A, p. 58.
50. Ciancaglini, in a reappraisal of Th. Nöldeke's hypothesis of a Middle Persian precursor (cf. Fahd, 'La version arabe', pp. 26, 27), has found that the Syriac version of Pseudo-Callisthenes derived directly from the Greek ('Syriac Version'). Fahd speculates that materials related to the Alexander Romance might have formed part of the *Khudaynāmeh* (p. 29).
51. NM-A, p. 172 (*wa-qīla lil-Iskandar*, 'It was said to Alexander'); NM-A, pp. 356–7 (a well-known narrative sequence involving the dispatch of an envoy).
52. NM-A, p. 146 (*wa-qāla Aflāṭūn* ('Plato said')), from Chapter Thirteen of *al-Siyāsa al-ʿāmmiyya* (Maróth, *Correspondence*, p. 40); p. 161 (*fī manshūrāt Aflāṭūn*, 'among Plato's proclamations'), not found in *al-Siyāsa al-ʿāmmiyya*, but also cited as amongst Plato's *manshūrāt* in al-Mubashshir's *Muhktār al-ḥikam* (pp. 140–1) and in al-Shahrazūrī's *Nuzhat al-arwāḥ* (p. 180); p. 182 (*wa-ḥukiya ʿan Aflāṭūn*), from Chapter Twelve of *al-Siyāsa al-ʿāmmiyya* (Maróth, *Correspondence*, p. 38). Pseudo-Māwardī's introduction of these materials conveys his indirect access to them; he is unlikely to have encountered them in an independent Platonic-associated text.
53. Cf. Tafażżolī, *Tārīkh-i adabīyāt-i Īrān*, pp. 214–37.
54. See below, pp. 66–7.

55. Pourshariati, *Decline and Fall*, pp. 85–94, esp. p. 89.
56. See Shaked, 'Andarz'; Muḥammadī, *al-Tarjama wa-l-naql*; de Fouchécour, *Moralia*, pp. 19–100, passim; Browne, 'Some Account'; Grignaschi, 'La Nihāyatu-l-ʾarab', I, II.
57. Cf. Lecomte, *Ibn Qutayba*, II: 353–8.
58. Lecomte, *Ibn Qutayba*, II: 347–9, 371–6; I: 192–4.
59. On al-Fatḥ b. Khāqān, see Gordon, 'Khāqānid Families', pp. 239–41.
60. Schoeler, 'Verfasser und Titel'; Ibn Razīn, *Ādāb al-mulūk*, pp. 30, 32, 59, 102, 103, 136. I refer to the author of this book as al-Taghlibī, and to the book as *Kitāb al-Tāj*, since it is under that title that it has been published and is generally known.
61. On the large corpus of counsels that circulated under Ardashīr's name, rendered at an early date into Arabic, see al-Masʿūdī, *Murūj al-dhahab*, I: 272; Firdawsī, *Le livre des rois*, V: 294–6, 297–9, 302–9; de Fouchécour, *Moralia*, pp. 84–100. When authors, including Ibn al-Nadīm, mention or cite 'the testament of Ardashīr to his son' or 'the testament of Anūshīrvān to his son Hurmuz', it is likely that their references involve generic designations rather than fixed titles (see Volume I, p. 4).
62. Al-Dīnawarī, *al-Akhbār al-ṭiwāl*, p. 88.
63. NM-A, p. 54; see Chapter 1, p. 24.
64. NM-A, p. 80 (*qāla Ardashīr al-malik fī ʿahdihi* ('Ardashīr the king said in his testament')) = *ʿAhd Ardashīr*, pp. 60, 69; 164 (*qāla Ardashīr fī ʿahdihi*) = *ʿAhd Ardashīr*, pp. 65–6 (the initial part of the author's quotation does not appear in the published text); p. 267 (*wa-qad qāla Ardashīr fī ʿahdihi*) = *ʿAhd Ardashīr*, p. 72; p. 290 (*wa-qāla Ardashīr fī ʿahdihi*) = *ʿAhd Ardashīr*, pp. 81–2; cf. 70 (*qāla Ardashīr*) = *ʿAhd Ardashīr*, p. 58; p. 194 (*wa-qāla Ardashīr* = *ʿAhd Ardashīr*, p. 69). An additional citation appears not in ʿAbbās' edition, but in *Kitāb al-Tāj*; NM-A, p. 146 (*qāla Ardashīr fī ʿahdihi*) = *Kitāb al-Tāj*, p. 2; see further below. For the text's self-description, see *ʿAhd Ardashīr*, p. 82 (*fa-innī qad ʿahadtu ilaykum ʿahdī* ('I have enjoined my testament [charge] upon you')).
65. NM-A, pp. 177, 197, 208 = *ʿAhd Ardashīr*, pp. 72, 70, 71.
66. NM-A, pp. 168–9 = *ʿAhd Ardashīr*, p. 57.
67. Shaked, 'Notes', pp. 37–8.
68. NM-A, p. 120 (*wa-qad dhakara kathīran min hādhihi l-maʿānī Ardashīr fī awwal faṣl min ʿahdihi ḥaythu qāla* ('Ardashīr mentioned many of these topics in the beginning of his testament when he said') = *ʿAhd Ardashīr*, p. 49).
69. NM-A, p. 356 (= *ʿAhd Ardashīr*, p. 91; *Kitāb al-Tāj*, p. 122 (*wa-kāna Ardashīr*

ibn Bābak yaqūlu, 'Ardashīr the son of Bābak used to say'); NM-A, p. 165 *(qālū wa-kāna Ardashīr al-malik yaqūlu*, 'It is said that the king Ardashīr used to say') = *ᶜAhd Ardashīr*, pp. 90–1, *Kitāb al-Tāj*, p. 24 (*wa-kāna Ardashīr yaqūlu*, 'Ardashīr used to say'); p. 268 (*qālū wa-qad qāla Ardashīr*, 'It is said that Ardashīr said') (this example is attributed in later sources to Anūshīrvan, NM-A, p. 268, n. 70); p. 278 (*wa-ka-dhālika ḥukiya ᶜan Ardashīr min mulūk al-ᶜajam*) = *Kitāb al-Tāj*, pp. 167–8 (this example is a narrative report (*khabar*) rather than a reported saying).

70. NM-A, p. 153 (*wa-rawā al-Wāqidī qāla qīla li-Ardashīr*, 'al-Wāqidī related that someone said to Ardashīr').
71. NM-A, p. 146 (*qāla Ardashīr fī ᶜahdihi*) = *Kitāb al-Tāj*, p. 2. In *Naṣīḥat al-mulūk*, the quotation reads *saᶜādat al-raᶜiyya fī ṭāᶜat al-mulūk wa-saᶜādat al-mulūk fī ṭāᶜat Allāh al-mālik* ('the felicity of the subjects lies in obedience to kings and the felicity of kings lies in obedience to God the Sovereign Being'). In the version recorded in *Kitāb al-Tāj*, the word *Allāh* does not appear. The discrepancy suggests that Pseudo-Māwardī had at his disposal a somewhat more Islamicised form of the text, or that he amended it himself.
72. NM-A, p. 189 (*wa-ḥukiya fī siyar mulūk Āl Sāsān . . .*) = *Kitāb al-Tāj*, p. 124. See below, p. 125.
73. NM-A, pp. 271–2 (*qālū*) = *Kitāb al-Tāj*, pp. 159–63. Pseudo-Māwardī intervenes in the material to a greater extent than al-Taghlibī; whereas the latter mentions without explanation *al-mōbadh* (*Kitāb al-Tāj*, p. 160), Pseudo-Māwardī glosses *al-mōbadhān* with *wa-huwa qāḍī quḍātihim* ('he is their Chief Judge', NM-A, p. 271). See above, p. 39, and below, pp. 223–5.
74. On the term *ᶜajam*, in this case applied specifically to speakers of Persian, see Volume I, Introduction, p. 18.
75. Ibn Qutayba, *ᶜUyūn al-akhbār*, I: 96–7, IV: 119–20. Ardashīr also appears at I: 273, and III: 186.
76. Ibn Qutayba, *ᶜUyūn al-akhbār*, I: 7. The text that follows, addressed to the *fuqahāʾ*, *asāwira*, *kuttāb* and *dhaw[ū] l-ḥarth* (jurists, soldiers, secretaries and agriculturalists), appears among the scattered utterances of Ardashīr (*ᶜAhd Ardashīr*, pp. 87–8, No. 1). Al-Masᶜūdī reports the passage (in a variant form) as a specimen of Ardashīr's correspondence to the most distinguished categories of his subjects and officials (*khawāṣṣ min anwāᶜ raᶜiyyatihi wa-ᶜummālihi*) (*Murūj al-dhahab*, I: 272).
77. Ibn Qutayba, *ᶜUyūn al-akhbār*, I: 13 (*ya bunayya inna al-mulk wa-l-dīn akhawān . . .* ('O my son, sovereignty and religion are two brothers')); *ᶜAhd*

Ardashīr, p. 53. The report of al-Mas^cūdī confirms that this formulation was the most widely known section of Ardashīr's *waṣiyya* to his son (*Murūj al-dhahab*, I: 272). See further Shaked, 'Notes', pp. 31–40; Volume I, p. 192.

78. Ibn ᶜAbd Rabbihi, *al-ᶜIqd al-farīd*, I: 36 (*wa-qāla Ardashīr li-bnihi: yā bunayya inna l-mulk wa-l-ᶜadl akhawān* . . .) = *The Unique Necklace*, I: 16 (on this variant, see Shaked, 'Notes', p. 37); cf. *ᶜUyūn al-akhbār*, I: 13 (see above); *al-ᶜIqd al-farīd*, I: 38 (*wa-qāla Ardashīr li-aṣḥābihi*) = I: 17; I: 65–6 (*wa-kataba Ardashīr ilā raᶜiyyatihi* ('Ardashīr wrote to his subjects')) = I: 30–1; cf. *ᶜUyūn al-akhbār*, I: 7 (see above).
79. Cf. Sarah Savant's discussion, in connection with al-Masᶜūdī, of 'sourcebooks' ('Genealogy and Ethnogenesis', pp. 178–9).
80. *ᶜAhd Ardashīr*, pp. 87–8, No. 1.
81. Tafaẓẓolī, *Tārīkh-i adabīyyāt-i Īrān*, pp. 220–1.
82. Al-Masᶜūdī reports that Shāpūr left a testament (*ᶜahd*) for his son Hurmuz and those who succeeded him, and he cites the text (*Murūj al-dhahab*, I: 274). He also records a written document of Hurmuz to one of his officials, in which he stipulated that five qualities were necessary for the defence of the borders, leading armies and administering the regions: resoluteness, knowledge, courage, trustworthiness and generosity (*Murūj al-dhahab*, I: 274).
83. Firdawsī, *Le livre des rois*, V: 315–16.
84. NM-A, pp. 54–5, 78, 242. Pseudo-Māwardī also refers in a general way to his familiarity with the 'Testament of Shāpūr' when he mentions having read about the elevation, defence, protection and guardianship of religion 'in the Testament(s) of Anūshīrvan and Shāpūr', p. 108 (see further below). Pseudo-Māwardī also mentions Sābūr in a list of Sasanian kings, NM-A, p. 189.
85. NM-A, p. 78 (*wa-laqad iftataḥa bi-hādhihi l-maᶜānī aw-ᶜāmmatihā Sābūr b. Ardashīr al-malik ᶜahdahu al-jalīl al-khaṭar al-ᶜaẓīm al-qadr fī bābihi ilā bnihi ḥaythu qāla ammā baᶜdu* ('Shāpūr b. Ardashīr opened his estimable and invaluable testament with these concepts, or the generality of them, in his chapter to his son when he said, to proceed')).
86. Ibn Qutayba, *al-Maᶜārif*, p. 654 (*ᶜahida ilayhi* [= *ilā bnihi*], 'he composed a testament for him [his son]').
87. Al-Thaᶜālibī, *Histoire des rois des perses*, pp. 495-8; cf. 495-6; NM-A, pp. 242-3.
88. Ibn Abī Dharr, *Kitāb al-Saᶜāda wa-l-isᶜād*, pp. 251, 286, 294, 295, 296, 297, 298, 299, 300, 303, 315, 317, 331, 421, 427, 429, 430, 432, 435, 443, 444 (cf. Arkoun, 'La conquête du bonheur', p. 69).
89. Ibn Abī Dharr, *Kitāb al-Saᶜāda wa-l-isᶜād*, pp. 296, 298, 427, 429, 432, 435.

90. NM-A, pp. 54–5; Ibn Abī Dharr, *al-Saᶜāda wa-l-isᶜād*, p. 430.
91. Muḥammadī, *al-Tarjama wa-l-naql*, p. 34, cf. pp. 34–42; Firdawsī, *Le livre des rois*, VI: 390–94; de Fouchécour, *Moralia*, pp. 38–58, esp. pp. 56–8; Shaked, 'Andarz', p. 14.
92. NM-A, p. 108. The author adds, 'We have related [on this subject] from their reported utterances and the transmitted accounts of their actions' (*rawaynā fī āthārihim wa-akhbārihim*).
93. NM-A, p. 243; Volume I, p. 102. On circles of justice, see further Sadan, 'A "Closed-Circuit" Saying', with numerous references; for examples, see Ibn Qutayba, *ᶜUyūn al-akhbār*, I: 9 (without specific attribution); al-Masᶜūdī, *Murūj al-dhahab*, I: 277; ᶜAbbās, *ᶜAhd Ardashīr*, p. 98 (among the scattered sayings of Ardashīr, No. 16); al-Jahshiyārī, *Kitāb al-Wuzarāʾ wa-l-kuttāb*, p. 6 (ascribed to Shāpūr); Muḥammadī, *al-Tarjama wa-l-naql*, p. 117 (attributed to Anūshīrvān).
94. NM-A, p. 172.
95. NM-A, p. 392. A similar passage, not attributed to any particular ruler and not directed to the emperor, appears in Ibn Qutayba, *ᶜUyūn al-akhbār*, I: 10.
96. Ibn Qutayba, *ᶜUyūn al-akhbār*, I: 1.
97. Ibn Qutayba, *ᶜUyūn al-akhbār*, I: 149, 178–9, 339. Other references to Anūshīrvan, without mention of a source, occur at I: 6, 156, 272; III: 115 (in a poem of ᶜAdī b. Zayd al-ᶜIbādī (d. *c.* 600), Christian Arab poet at the courts of the Sasanians in Ctesiphon and the Lakhmids at al-Ḥīra), 174; IV: 50.
98. Ibn Qutayba, *ᶜUyūn al-akhbār*, I: 173.
99. Ibn Qutayba, *ᶜUyūn al-akhbār*, I: 98, 238, 281; II: 126, 129, 175; III: 191. The device of question and answer recurs with Anūshīrvān and Buzurgmihr (*Le livre des rois*, VI: 291–306; de Fouchécour, *Moralia*, pp. 28–9), and with Alexander and Aristotle (p. 30).
100. NM-A, pp. 172, 189. Cf. Morony, 'Kisrā'.
101. NM-A, p. 393.
102. *Kalīla wa-Dimna*, p. 45; Ibn Qutayba, *ᶜUyūn al-akhbār*, II: 179 (*wa-fī kutub al-ᶜajam* ('in the Persian books')). See further Shaked, 'Notes', pp. 40–9. For the traditions surrounding the 'four kings', compare Pelliot, 'La théorie des quatre Fils du Ciel', esp. pp. 106–8 (Xuanzang), pp. 116–24.
103. NM-A, p. 45 = al-Taghlibī, *Kitāb al-Tāj*, p. 95.
104. NM-A, p. 189 = al-Taghlibī, *Kitāb al-Tāj*, p. 124. See below, p. 125.
105. Ibn Qutayba, *ᶜUyūn al-akhbār*, I: 17 (*wa-qaraʾtu fī kitāb Abarwīz ilā bnihi Shīrawayh* ('I read in the book of Khusraw Parvīz to his son Shīrawayh')),

30 (*wa-qaraʾtu fī kitāb Abarwīz ilā bnihi Shīrawayh wa-huwa fī ḥabsihi* ('I read in a book of Khusraw Parvīz to his son Shīrawayh while he was in his custody')), 59 (*qaraʾtu fī kitāb Abarwīz ilā bnihi Shīrawayh* ('I read in a book of Khusraw Parvīz to his son Shīrawayh')), I: 288 (*wa-kataba Kisrā Abarwīz ilā bnihi Shīrawayh min al-ḥabs* ('Khusraw Abarwīz wrote to his son Shīrawayh during his imprisonment')); cf. I: 328 (*qāla Abarwīz li-bnihi* ('Khusraw Parvīz said to his son')).

106. Ibn Qutayba, *ᶜUyūn al-akhbār*, I: 11, 15, 45–6, 59, 84.
107. Ibn Qutayba, *ᶜUyūn al-akhbār*, I: 11 (*wa-qaraʾtu fī kitāb al-Tāj: qāla Abarwīz li-bnihi Shīrawayh wa-huwa fī ḥabsihi*, 'I read in the Book of the Crown: Khusraw Parvīz said to his son Shīrawayh while he was in his custody') = *al-ᶜIqd al-farīd*, I: 40 (*wa-qāla Abarwīz li-bnihi Shīrawayh*, 'Khusraw Parvīz said to his son Shīrawayh') = *Unique Necklace*, I: 18; *ᶜUyūn al-akhbār*, I: 15 (*wa-fī l-Tāj anna Abarwīza kataba ilā bnihi Shīrawayh min al-ḥabs* ('In *al-Tāj* it is reported that Khusraw Parvīz wrote to his son Shīrawayh from prison')) = *al-ᶜIqd al-farīd*, I: 42 (*wa-fī l-Tāj kataba Abarwīz li-bnihi Shīrawayh yuwaṣṣīhi*, 'In *al-Tāj* it is stated that Khusraw Parvīz wrote to his son Shīrawayh and exhorted him') = *Unique Necklace*, I: 19–20; *ᶜUyūn al-akhbār*, I: 59 (*wa-qaraʾtu fī l-Tāj anna Abarwīza qāla li-ṣāḥib bayt al-māl* ('I read in *al-Tāj* that Khusraw Parvīz said to the director of the treasury')) = *al-ᶜIqd al-farīd*, 22 (*wa-qāla Abarwīz li-ṣāḥib bayt al-māl*, 'Khusraw Parvīz said to the director of the treasury') = *Unique Necklace*, I: 9; *ᶜUyūn al-akhbār*, I: 288 (*wa-kataba Kisrā Abarwīz ilā bnihi Shīrawayh min al-ḥabs* ('Kisrā Abarwīz wrote to his son Shīrawayh during his imprisonment')) = *al-ᶜIqd al-farīd*, I: 41 (*wa-kataba Kisrā Abarwīz ilā bnihi Shīrawayh min al-ḥabs* ('Khusraw Parvīz wrote to his son Shīrawayh from prison')) = *Unique Necklace*, I: 19.
108. Also noted in Lecomte, *Ibn Qutayba*, p. 188. Michael Cooperson takes Ibn Qutayba's *al-Tāj* to be the work of Ibn al-Muqaffaᶜ ('Ibn al-Muqaffaᶜ', pp. 154–5).
109. Ibn Qutayba, *ᶜUyūn al-akhbār*, I: 59, 84.
110. Ibn Qutayba, *ᶜUyūn al-akhbār*, I: 299, III: 216.
111. Khaleghi-Motlagh, 'Bozorgmehr-e Boḵtagān'; de Fouchécour, *Moralia*, pp. 58–69; Firdawsī, *Le livre des rois*, VI: 190–232.
112. NM-A, pp. 152, 153. Cf. Khaleghi-Motlagh, 'Bozorgmehr-e Boḵtagān'.
113. Ibn Qutayba, *ᶜUyūn al-akhbār*, II: 120, 127, 179.
114. Ibn Qutayba, *ᶜUyūn al-akhbār*, II: 17, 122, 123, III: 6, 90, 103, 176.
115. Ibn Qutayba, *ᶜUyūn al-akhbār*, II: 175.

116. Ibn Qutayba, *ᶜUyūn al-akhbār*, II: 126, 113, 191, 295. Cf. Firdawsī, *Le livre des rois*, VI: 366–71; de Fouchécour, *Moralia*, p. 59, n. 128.
117. The copyist of the manuscript was not familiar with this title (NM-A, pp. 162, 193, 281), which the editor al-Ḥadīthī recognised correctly (NM-Ḥ, p. 57, n. 70).
118. Muḥammadī, *al-Tarjama wa-l-naql*, pp. 23–4; Tafażżolī, 'Āᵓīn-nāma'; Tafażżolī, *Tārīkh-i adabīyāt-i Īrān*, pp. 245-8 (Tafażżolī notes that the contents of the *āᵓīnnāmeh* sometimes included, alongside religious materials, narrative materials and wise aphorisms (*sukhanān-i ḥikmat*), p. 245).
119. Ibn al-Nadīm knew of various *kutub āᵓīn*: classified as writings on the subjects of horsemanship, the bearing of weapons and the equipment of war, their deployment and use among all peoples (*al-furūsiyya wa-ḥaml al-silāḥ wa-ālāt al-ḥurūb wa-l-tadbīr wa-l-ᶜamal bi-dhālika li-jamīᶜ al-umam*, II: i: 346–8), his list includes an *Āᵓīn al-ramy* ('Rules for Throwing the Javelin'), ascribed to Bahrām Gūr or Bahrām Chūbīn and an *Āᵓīn al-ḍarb bi-l-ṣawālija lil-furs* ('Rules for Playing Polo among the Persians') (*al-Fihrist*, II: i: 346).
120. Al-Masᶜūdī, *al-Tanbīh wa-l-ishrāf*, p. 104.
121. Grignaschi, 'Quelques spécimens', pp. 91–102 (Text) = pp. 111–28 (Translation). See also Tafażżolī, *Tārīkh-i adabīyāt-i Īrān*, p. 237.
122. Ibn al-Nadīm, *al-Fihrist*, I: ii: 368; Grignaschi, 'Quelques spécimens', p. 4.
123. In addition to the *Āᵓīnnāmeh* by ᶜAbdallāh Ibn al-Muqaffaᶜ (I: ii: 368), Ibn al-Nadīm records a work bearing the title *Āᵓīn* by al-Jayhānī (I: ii: 428). Ayman Fuᵓād Sayyid reads *Āᵓīn mithālāt kutub al-ᶜuhūd lil-khulafāᵓ wa-l-umarāᵓ* ('Rules Regarding Models for Written Covenants by the Caliphs and Rulers', *al-Fihrist*, I: ii: 428); the substitution of *maqālāt* ('pronouncements', 'doctrines') is proposed in the edition of Shaᶜbān Khalīfa and Walīd Muḥammad al-ᶜAwza (*al-Fihrist li-bn al-Nadīm*, I: 251). The editors also differ in their readings of the following item. Sayyid reads *Kitāb al-Ziyādāt fī Kitāb al-Nāshiᵓ fī-l-maqālāt* ('Book of Additions to al-Nāshiᵓ's Book of Doctrines'), whereas Khalīfa and al-ᶜAwza read *Kitāb al-Ziyādāt fī Kitāb Āᵓīn fī l-maqālāt* ('Book of Additions to the Book of Regulations on Doctrines'). The remaining two books of al-Jayhānī are *Kitāb al-Masālik wa-l-mamālik*, discussed in Volume I, pp. 31–2, and a *Kitāb al-Rasāᵓil* ('Book of Epistles').
124. NM-A, p. 53, NM-Ḥ, p. 57. See above, p. 23.
125. NM-A, pp. 162–3, 193, 281. At the first occurrence, Pseudo-Māwardī uses the Persian name only; at the second and third, this name appears with the Arabic word *Kitāb*.

126. *Histoire des rois des Perses*, p. 14 (*fī kitāb al-ā'īn*), p. 15 (during the reign of Jamshīd); cf. Tafażżolī, *Tārīkh-i adabīyāt-i Īrān*, p. 247.
127. Ibn Qutayba, *ᶜUyūn al-akhbār*, I: 8 ('I read in the Book of *Ā'īn* that one of the kings of the *ᶜajam* said in a *khuṭba*'; the passage is followed by a similar one introduced with *wa-naḥwahu qawl al-ᶜajam, wa-qālū*; I: 62 (in *Kitāb al-Sulṭān*); III: 221 (*qara'tu fī l-Ā'īn*), III: 278 (*qara'tu fī l-Ā'īn*) (in *Kitāb al-Ṭaᶜām* ('Book of Food')); IV: 59 (*qara'tu fī l-Ā'īn*) (in *Kitāb al-Nisā'* ('Book of Women')). See Lecomte, *Ibn Qutayba*, I: 183.
128. See Muḥammadī, *al-Tarjama wa-l-naql*, pp. 235–41, 242–8, 249–50, 257–8, 259–60; pp. 229–35, 235–41. Cf. Swain, *Economy, Family and Society*, p. 415.
129. NM-A, p. 143.
130. There are no correspondences between the passages cited in *Naṣīḥat al-mulūk* and those reproduced in Muḥammadī, *al-Tarjama wa-l-naql*, pp. 230–60. One of Pseudo-Māwardī's passages resembles a quotation in Miskawayh, *Jāvīdān khirad*, p. 72 (NM-A, p. 193, cf. NM-Ḥ, pp. 273–4, n. 624).
131. Muḥammadī, *al-Tarjama wa-l-naql*, pp. 18–27; Tafażżolī, *Tārīkh-i adabīyāt-i Īrān*, pp. 248–50.
132. Muḥammadī, *al-Tarjama wa-l-naql*, pp. 18–27, 27.
133. Grignaschi, 'Quelques spécimens', p. 4; Text, pp. 103–8 = Translation, pp. 129–35. Cf. Kristó-Nagy, *La pensée d'Ibn al-Muqaffaᶜ*, pp. 171–2, where it is suggested that the published text might represent a fragment of a longer work, possibly one that included the passages cited by Ibn Qutayba.
134. Ibn al-Nadīm, *al-Fihrist*, I: ii: 368–9, II: i: 325 (*samar*, pl. *asmār* connotes a story told in the evening). See below, p. 157.
135. Ibn Abī Dharr, *Kitāb al-Saᶜāda wa-l-isᶜād*, pp. 442, 435. Cf. Muḥammadī, *al-Tarjama wa-l-naql*, pp. 18–19.
136. Ibn Qutayba, *ᶜUyūn al-akhbār*, I: 11, 15, 45–6, 59, 84; see also I: 5, 17, 27, 30, 96. Cf. Lecomte, *Ibn Qutayba*, pp. 188–9.
137. Lecomte, *Ibn Qutayba*, pp. 188–9.
138. NM-A, p. 146: 'The felicity of the common people lies in obedience to kings, and the felicity of kings lies in obedience to [God] the Possessor [of Sovereignty]' (*fī ṭāᶜat [Allāh] al-mālik*), attributed to Ardashīr's *ᶜahd* without further identification of its addressee (see also above, n. 71).
139. NM-A, p. 278.
140. NM-A, p. 189 = al-Taghlibī, *Kitāb al-Tāj*, p. 124.
141. NM-A, p. 277 (n. 94); al-Taghlibī, *Kitāb al-Tāj*, pp. 168–9; Volume I, p. 55.
142. NM-A, p. 277 = al-Taghlibī. *Kitāb al-Tāj*, p. 169; Volume I, pp. 55–6.

143. Al-Taghlibī. *Kitāb al-Tāj*, p. 169; NM-A, p. 277. See Volume I, p. 56/
144. NM-A, p. 356 = al-Taghlibī, *Kitāb al-Tāj*, p. 122. The second quotation appears among the scattered utterances of Ardashīr (*ᶜAhd Ardashīr*, p. 92).
145. Al-Taghlibī, *Kitāb al-Tāj*, p. 122.
146. NM-A, pp. 356–7 (*wa-laqad balaghanā ᶜan al-Iskandar* ('it has reached us concerning Alexander')), *Kitāb al-Tāj*, p. 123 (*wa-yuqālu inna l-Iskandar* ('it is said that Alexander')).
147. NM-A, pp. 270–2 (see below, pp. 223–5); *Kitāb al-Tāj*, pp. 159–63 = *Le livre de la couronne*, pp. 179–81. Other references to Nawruz and Mihrajan occur on pp. 101, 149 of *Kitāb al-Tāj*.
148. Niẓām al-Mulk, *Siyar al-mulūk*, pp. 57–9 = *Book of Government*, pp. 42–4. Ghazālī, *Naṣiḥat al-mulūk*, pp. 167–70 = *Ghazālī's Book of Counsel for Kings*, pp. 102–3.
149. See, for example, Ghazālī, *Naṣīḥat al-mulūk*, pp. 122–4 = pp. 70–1; Niẓām al-Mulk, *Siyar al-mulūk*, pp. 28–9 = pp. 21–2; and Volume I, p. 49.
150. 'Taṣdīr', *Kitāb al-Tāj*, p. 69.
151. See, for example, Volume I, pp. 55–6.
152. Ibn al-Nadīm, *al-Fihrist*, I: ii: 368 (*Khudaynāmeh fī l-siyar*); also listed among the Persians' books on the true accounts and tales of their kings (*asmār ṣaḥīḥa allatī li-mulūkihim*) (II: i: 325). Cf. Shahbazi, 'On the Xwadāy-Nāmag'; Tafażżolī, *Tārīkh-i adabīyāt-i Īrān*, pp. 269–74.
153. Ibn Qutayba, *ᶜUyūn al-akhbār*, I: 96–7 (*qaraᵓtu fī siyar al-ᶜajam* ('I read in the Chronicles of the Persians')); I: 117–21 (*qaraᵓtu fī kitāb siyar al-ᶜajam*), 178–9 (*qaraᵓtu fī kitāb siyar al-ᶜajam*). The first of these citations appears in *Kitāb al-Sulṭān*; the second and third extracts appear in *Kitāb al-Ḥarb* ('Book of War'). On Ibn Qutayba's use of the works of Ibn al-Muqaffaᶜ, see Lecomte, *Ibn Qutayba*, I: 181–9.
154. Perhaps al-Jāḥiẓ refers to *Kārnāmak i Artaxšēr i Pāpakān* ('Book of Deeds of Ardashīr Son of Bābak'); cf. Volume II, pp. 158, 160.
155. Al-Jāḥiẓ, *al-Bayān wa-l-tabyīn*, III: 14. The reported sentiment resonates with the words of the Syrian poet Kulthūm b. ᶜAmr al-ᶜAttābī (d. *c*. 220/835), who visited Khurasan on three occasions for the purpose of copying Persian books (in his words, *katabtu kutub al-ᶜajam* ('I wrote out various Persian books')). When asked for an explanation, he responded, 'Are fine meanings (*al-maᶜānī*) to be found anywhere other than in Persian books and in eloquent expression? We possess the language (*al-lugha*), and they possess the fine meanings' (*wa-hal al-maᶜānī illā fī kutub al-ᶜajam wa-l-balāgha al-lugha lanā wa-l-maᶜānī*

lahum) (Ibn Ṭayfūr, *Baghdād fī taʾrīkh al-khilāfa al-ʿAbbāsiyya*, pp. 85–6; cf. Bosworth, 'Ṭāhirids and Persian Literature', pp. 105–6; my translation is based on Bosworth's). Al-Tawḥīdī cites al-ʿAttābī's expression of a related but slightly different formula to al-Maʾmūn (*al-Baṣāʾir wa-l-dhakhāʾir*, VII: 78).

156. Al-Bīrūnī, *al-Āthār al-bāqiya*, p. 99.
157. The two names perhaps refer to a single individual. Ażkāʾī, who prepared an edition of the text, suggested that since only al-Bīrūnī mentions the *Shāhnāmeh* of Abū ʿAlī al-Balkhī, that poet was perhaps identical to Abū l-Muʿayyad Balkhī (*al-Āthār al-bāqiya*, ed. Ażkāʾī, p. 114; cf. notes, pp. 497, 554–5); Khaleghi-Motlagh endorsed this proposal ('Abū ʿAlī Bal<u>k</u>ī'). Abū l-Muʾayyad al-Balkhī dedicated his *ʿAjāʾib al-buldān* ('Wonders of the Countries') to Nūḥ b. Manṣūr (r. 365–87/976–97) (Lazard, 'Abu'l-Moʾayyad Bal<u>k</u>ī'). On the composition of *shāhnāmeh*s before Firdawsī, see Qazvīnī, 'Muqaddimeh-yi qadīm', pp. 7–22; Minorsky, 'Older Preface', p. 160; Meisami, *Persian Historiography*, p. 17; and above, p. 265, n. 19.
158. Of the various places suggested for Daqīqī's birth, Khaleghi-Motlagh regards Tus as the most likely (Khaleghi-Motlagh, 'Daqīqī'). On Daqīqī, see Lazard, *Les premiers poètes*, I: 136–62 = II: 141–77, and I: 32–6.
159. Cf. Arjomand, 'Perso-Indian Statecraft'.
160. See further Marlow, 'Kings and Sages'.
161. de Blois, *Burzōy's Voyage*, p. 15; Richter, *Studien*, pp. 22–32, 34–6; Cooperson, 'Ibn al-Muqaffaʿ', p. 153.
162. Ibn al-Nadīm, *al-Fihrist*, I: ii: 368, II: i: 325–6.
163. These manuscripts have been published by ʿAbd al-Wahhāb ʿAzzām (*Kitāb Kalīla wa-Dimna*, Cairo: al-Maʿārif, 1941) and Louis Cheikho (*La version arabe de Kalîlah et Dimnah d'après le plus ancien manuscrit arabe daté* (Beirut: Imprimerie catholique, 1905), respectively. I have used a standard edition, that of ʿUmar Abū l-Naṣr, published with Ibn al-Muqaffaʿ's other writings in *Āthār Ibn al-Muqaffaʿ* (Beirut: Dār Maktabat al-Ḥayāt, 1966), sometimes supplemented with the editions of Cheikho and ʿAzzām.
164. Cf. de Blois, *Burzōy's Voyage*, pp. 1–17, 61–72; Riedel, 'Kalila wa Demna' (with further bibliography).
165. Ibn Qutayba, *ʿUyūn al-akhbār*, I: 168, 281; II: 179; III: 180, 192.
166. Ibn Qutayba almost always avers that he has read the accounts that he cites: *wa-qaraʾtu fī kitāb min kutub al-hind* ('I read in an Indian book'), I: 3; *qaraʾtu fī kitāb lil-hind*, I: 18, 19, 22, 25, 27–8, 92, 111, 112, 224, 239, 280, 291, 328; II: 7, 22, 40; III: 5, 6, 80, 107, 111, 112, 113, 161, 176; *wa-qaraʾtu fīhi* ('I

read in it'), I: 3, 19; *wa-fī kitāb lil-hind*, I: 30, 36, 45, 231, 248, 263; II: 121, 143, 173; III: 169, 191. Cf. Lecomte, *Ibn Qutayba*, I: 184. Ibn ᶜAbd Rabbih similarly introduces his citations with the formulae *wa-fī kitāb lil-hind*, *wa-min kitāb lil-hind* or *wa-qaraᵓtu fī kitāb lil-hind* ('I read in an Indian book'); see Werkmeister, *Quellenuntersuchungen*, pp. 142–5.

167. *Āthār Ibn al-Muqaffaᶜ*, pp. 53–4.
168. *Āthār Ibn al-Muqaffaᶜ*, p. 276.
169. NM-A, p. 220. See further NM-A, p. 231, n. 88.
170. NM-A, p. 234. The first two goals appear in reverse order to the standard classifications (see following note).
171. Such as the *Mānava Dharmaśāstra* = *Laws of Manu*, p. 18 (ch. 2, § 13). This text dates from between roughly 200 BCE and 100 CE.
172. *Kalîlah et Dimnah*, ed. Cheikho, p. 31; cf. *Āthār Ibn al-Muqaffaᶜ*, pp. 81–2.
173. Cf. Smith, *Classifying the Universe*, pp. 3–25.
174. NM-A, p. 234.
175. *Kalīla wa-Dimna*, in *Āthār Ibn al-Muqaffaᶜ*, p. 120; NM-A, p. 44; al-Ābī, *Nathr al-durr*, IV: 225.
176. Ibn Qutayba, *ᶜUyūn al-akhbār*, I: 92; Ibn ᶜAbd Rabbih, *al-ᶜIqd al-farīd*, I: 18.
177. For *al-malik al-ḥāzim*, Ibn Qutayba, *ᶜUyūn al-akhbār*, I: 18, 27; for *wuzarāᵓ al-sūᵓ*, see *Āthār Ibn al-Muqaffaᶜ*, pp. 139, 204, 205.
178. *Kalīla wa-Dimna*, *Āthār Ibn al-Muqaffaᶜ*, pp. 164, 252.
179. *Āthār Ibn al-Muqaffaᶜ*, p. 90. Without the metaphors, Pseudo-Māwardī's treatment of the inevitable mutation of pleasure into pain expresses a similar sentiment (NM-A, p. 130).
180. NM-A, p. 133. See Volume I, p. 235.
181. Al-Ziriklī, *al-Aᶜlām*, VIII: 33; cf. Toorawa, *Arabic Writerly Culture*, pp. 80–1.
182. NM-A, pp. 216–17. Cf. Leder, 'Conventions', pp. 38–43; Drory, 'Three Attempts'.
183. NM-A, p. 391 = *al-Adab al-ṣaghīr* (*Āthār Ibn al-Muqaffaᶜ*, p. 325); Miskawayh, *Jāvīdān khirad*, p. 73. On *al-Adab al-ṣaghīr*, see Zakeri, 'Forgotten Belletrist', pp. 93–101, where it is associated with ᶜAlī al-Rayḥānī rather than Ibn al-Muqaffaᶜ, and Kristó-Nagy, *La pensée d'Ibn al-Muqaffaᶜ*, pp. 181–5.
184. Ibn Qutayba, *ᶜUyūn al-akhbār*, I: 2.
185. Ibn Qutayba, *ᶜUyūn al-akhbār*, I: 20–1, 22, 31.
186. Ibn Qutayba, *ᶜUyūn al-akhbār*, I: 3. Ibn al-Nadīm records a *Yatīma fī l-rasāᵓil* ('Matchless Pearl on Epistles') among the works of Ibn al-Muqaffaᶜ (*al-Fihrist*, I: ii: 368–9). Cf. Lecomte, *Ibn Qutayba*, I: 181–3.

187. NM-A, pp. 161, 183.

188. NM-A, pp. 65, 78, 79, 146, 169, 171, 191, 251, 256, 270, 282, 392, 395.

189. Aḥmad and al-Ḥadīthī have indicated a number of these Aristotelian attributions, as well as other parallels, in the valuable notes that accompany their editions. See also Marlow, 'Kings and Sages'.

190. Miskawayh, *Jāvīdān khirad*, pp. 219–25.

191. Al-Mubashshir, *Mukhtār al-ḥikam*, pp. 185–222.

192. Dunlop, *Muntakhab*, p. 42.

193. Ibn Abī Uṣaybiᶜa, *Min ᶜUyūn al-anbāʾ*, I: 197; al-Shahrazūrī, *Nuzhat al-arwāḥ*, pp. 165–72, esp. pp. 166, 167.

194. van Bladel, 'Iranian Characteristics'; van Bladel, 'Bactrian Background'.

195. See Volume I, p. 84.

196. van Bladel, *Arabic Hermes*, p. 207; Sternbach, 'Indian Wisdom'; Zachariae, 'Die Weisheitssprüche'.

197. Ibn al-Nadīm, *al-Fihrist*, II: i: 326, 351.

198. de Blois, 'Two Sources', p. 96. The oldest example of the genre, known as the *Arthaśāstra*, a manual on statecraft, is believed to be the work of Kauṭilya, also called Cāṇakya, who lived in the late fourth century BCE.

199. Ibn Isfandiyār, *Tārīkh-i Ṭabaristān*, I: 7. Cf. Melville, 'Ebn Esfandīār', p. 21.

200. Cf. Marlow, 'Advice Literature in Tenth- and Early Eleventh-Century Iran', pp. 89–90.

201. Ibn al-Nadīm, *al-Fihrist*, ed. Khalīfa and al-ᶜAwza, I: 612; cf. *al-Fihrist*, ed. Sayyid, II: i: 326 (Sādīrm). Flügel listed the variants Kitāb Sādiram, Sārdum and Sārirm ('Zur Frage über die Romane', p. 732, No. 25).

202. Cf. Keith-Falconer, *Kalīlah and Dimnah*, p. xlix; *Kalîlah et Dimnah*, ed. Cheikho, pp. 178–201 (Shād.r.m); Benfey, 'Einleitung'.

203. Nöldeke, 'Zu Kalīla waDimna, pp. 799–800, and n. 2.

204. Al-Jāḥiẓ, *al-Bayān wa-l-tabyīn*, III: 14, 27.

205. Ibn Abī Dharr, *al-Saᶜāda wa-l-isᶜād*, pp. 193–4; = NM-A, p. 256. See also Maróth, *Correspondence*, p. 13; Miskawayh, *Jāvīdān khirad*, p. 220 (in *Waṣiyyat Arisṭāṭālīs lil-Iskandar*); al-Mubashshir, *Mukhtār al-ḥikam*, p. 187; Marlow, 'Kings and Sages', p. 52; al-Ābī, *Nathr al-durr*, IV: 232 (*qāla ḥakīm*).

206. Ibn Abī Dharr, *al-Saᶜāda wa-l-isᶜād*, p. 282 = NM-A, p. 78. See also Maróth, *Correspondence*, p. 13; Miskawayh, *Jāvīdān khirad*, p. 220; al-Mubashshir, *Mukhtār al-ḥikam*, p. 187; Marlow, 'Kings and Sages', p. 44.

207. Ibn al-Jawzī, *al-Miṣbāḥ al-muḍīᶜ*, p. 190.

208. Ibn Razīn, *Ādāb al-mulūk*, pp. 52–3. Little is known of this author, who

adapted and abbreviated al-Taghlibī's *Akhlāq al-mulūk* in the work cited here and at the beginning of Volume I, p. 1.

209. NM-A, pp. 78, 395.
210. See Volume I, pp 75–87.
211. Marlow, 'Kings and Sages', p. 54.
212. Marlow, 'Kings and Sages', p. 55.
213. Marlow, 'Kings and Sages', p. 55.
214. Cf. Gimaret, 'Traces et parallèles', pp. 117–20, 131.
215. Ibn al-Nadīm, *al-Fihrist,* II: i: 326. See further Lang, *Wisdom of Balahvar*, pp. 32–6; Gimaret, 'Traces et parallèles', pp. 20–1, 25; Zakeri, *Persian Wisdom in Arabic Garb*, pp. 137–41; Tafażżolī, *Tārīkh-i adabīyāt-i Īrān*, p. 301.
216. Toral-Niehoff, 'Die Legende "Barlaam und Josaphat"'; Gimaret, 'Traces et parallèles', pp. 97–8, n. 2; Pitts, 'Barlaam and Josaphat', p. 5.
217. Gimaret, 'Traces et parallèles', pp. 132–3.
218. Zakeri, *Persian Wisdom in Arabic Garb*, I, pp. 137–41.

Chapter 3

1. Wakelnig, *Philosophy Reader*, p.124; Rosenthal, 'Arabic Books and Manuscripts VI', pp.27–8; Adamson, 'Kindian Tradition'; Butterworth, 'Al-Kindī'; Daiber, 'Political Philosophy'; Swain, *Economy, Family, and Society*, pp. 75–6, 246–7.
2. Al-Khwārazmī, *Mafātīḥ al-ᶜulūm*, p. 132. Cf. Butterworth, 'Medieval Islamic Philosophy'.
3. Al-Tirmidhī, *Kitāb al-Riyāḍa wa-Adab al-nafs*; see pp. 98–100, 104–5 and passim.
4. Al-Jāḥiẓ, *Risālat al-maᶜāsh wa-l-maᶜād*, in *Rasāʾil al-Jāḥiẓ*, I: 133. Significantly, Pseudo-Māwardī opens his fifth chapter with an account of his purpose in addressing *maṣāliḥ maᶜādihim wa-l-maᶜāshihim*, 'kings' well-being in their lives and their afterlives' (NM-A, p. 143).
5. Among the Karrāmiyya (see Volume I, Chapter 5), the divine *ṣifāt* (attributes) were 'archétypes à la fois humaine et divine' (Vadet, 'Le Karramisme de la Haut-Asie', p. 42).
6. See Daiber, *Muᶜāmmar ibn ᶜAbbād as-Sulamī*, pp. 360–6. Later writers were also wary of equations between the divine and human realms: the Ḥanbalī Ibn al-Jawzī would warn his audience against the postulation of analogies between the attributes of the Creator and the characteristics of His creation (*qiyās ṣifāt al-khāliq ᶜalā ṣifāt al-makhlūqīn kufr*) (*Ṣayd al-khāṭir*, pp. 281–2).
7. Cf. Druart, 'Al-Kindi's Ethics', p. 339. See below, pp. 112, 113.

8. NM-A, p. 143.
9. van Ess, 'Abu'l-Qāsem Ka^{c}bī'. See also Volume I, pp. 88–9.
10. Yāqūt, *Mu^{c}jam al-udabā'*, I: 278.
11. See Volume I, p. 166.
12. See Madelung, 'Abū Rašīd Nīsābūrī', pp. 367–8, and Volume I, pp. 232–3.
13. Cf. Al-Ash^{c}arī, *Maqālāt*, I: 209.
14. NM-A, pp. 143–4.
15. Fazlur Rahman identifies *taqwā* as 'perhaps the most important single term in the Qur'ān', and explains its sense as 'to protect oneself against the harmful or evil consequences of one's conduct' (*Major Themes*, pp. 28–9 and passim). Izutsu, *Ethico-Religious Concepts*, pp. 195–200, renders the term as '(pious) fear of God' and classifies it, together with *shukr*, 'thankfulness', as key conceptual components of *īmān*, 'faith'.
16. Donner, *Narratives of Islamic Origins*, p. 99.
17. Melchert, 'Exaggerated Fear', pp. 283–5.
18. Rowson, *Muslim Philosopher*, p. 169.
19. NM-A, pp. 144–6 (including passages from Q. 65: 2, 3; 16: 128; 2: 194; 19: 72; 65: 4, 5).
20. van Ess, *Erkenntinislehre*, pp. 16–17.
21. NM-A, p. 146.
22. Al-Ka^{c}bī, *Faḍl al-i^{c}tizāl*, p. 63; Madelung and Walker, *Ismaili Heresiography*, p. 11 = p. 29. For al-Kindī's views, see Adamson, 'Al-Kindī and the Mu^{c}tazila', pp. 66–75, and 'Note on Freedom'.
23. See also al-Māturīdī, *Kitāb al-Tawḥīd*, pp. 57–98.
24. Al-Ash^{c}arī, *Maqālāt*, I: 211–14, § 241; Mānkdīm, *Sharḥ al-uṣūl al-khamsa*, pp. 707–8.
25. Madelung and Walker, *Ismaili Heresiography*, p. 12 = p. 30. Compare the definition of faith (*īmān*) in *al-Sawād al-a^{c}ẓam*, according to which faith is obedience, but not every act of obedience is faith, just as unbelief (*kufr*) is disobedience, although not every act of disobedience constitutes unbelief (*al-Sawād al-a^{c}ẓam*, p. 127).
26. The 'intermediate position' is also referred to as the doctrine of *al-asmā' wa-l-aḥkām* ('names and ordinances'), since it involved the 'name' (believer, unbeliever or wrongdoer), and the legal ordinances; see al-Mas^{c}ūdī, *Murūj al-dhahab*, III: 221, 222; van Ess, *Theologie und Gesellschaft*, II: 260–7.
27. Madelung and Walker, *Ismaili Heresiography*, p. 13 = p. 30; al-Ka^{c}bī, *Faḍl al-i^{c}tizāl*, p. 64.

28. Mānkdīm, *Sharḥ al-uṣūl al-khamsa*, pp. 697–8; see also al-Māturīdī, *Kitāb al-Tawḥīd*, pp. 528–31.
29. Mānkdīm, *Sharḥ al-uṣūl al-khamsa*, pp. 701–2. According to this passage, Abū l-Qāsim (al-Kaᶜbī) held that persons who committed major sins were *kuffār niᶜma*, ungrateful rejectors of divine bounty (Madelung, *Der Imam al-Qāsim*, p. 13, n. 27, cf. p. 61). See also al-Ashᶜarī, *Maqālāt*, I: 216, § 249, and the views of al-ᶜĀmirī (Rowson, *Muslim Philosopher*, p. 168 = p. 169).
30. The adjectival attributes in this passage are *wāḥid qadīm aḥad fard ḥakīm jawād raḥīm birr ṣādiq qādir ᶜalīm* (NM-A, p. 146). Cf. al-Ashᶜarī, *Maqālāt*, II: 363ff.
31. The term *maᶜnā*, in theological–philosophical discourse, extends far beyond its foundational sense of 'meaning' to encompass 'concept', 'entity', 'reason for being', 'spiritual reality'; van Ess acknowledges that the term is barely translatable (*Erkenntnislehre*, p. 92), and Monnot holds that transcription is preferable to translation (*Penseurs musulmans*, p. 39). Cf. Jihāmī, *Mawsūᶜāt muṣṭalaḥāt al-falsafa*, pp. 824–5, 825–7. I have rendered the term variously in different contexts.
32. NM-A, pp. 146–7.
33. The Muᶜtazila differed over many particulars of the matter; van Ess, *Erkenntnislehre*, esp. pp. 140–1, 160–1, 325–6, 329.
34. van Ess, *Erkenntnislehre*, pp. 10–11. The terms are van Ess'.
35. van Ess, *Theologie und Gesellschaft*, IV: 666–7.
36. On *fikr* and *tafakkur*, see van Ess, *Erkenntnislehre*, pp. 241–2.
37. In some contexts, *maᶜrifa* connoted 'awareness', knowledge derived from sensibility or perception, whereas *ᶜilm* connoted knowledge derived from intellect (Adamson, 'Knowledge of Particulars', p. 267). For al-Maqdisī, *ᶜilm* constituted an encompassing comprehension of the essence of a thing, and *maᶜrifa* connoted perception of its essence and ontological status (al-Maqdisī, *al-Badʾ wa-l-taʾrīkh*, I: 21–2 (*al-ᶜilm al-iḥāṭa bi-dhāt al-shayʾ . . . wa-l-maᶜrifa idrāk dhātihi wa-thabātihi*), cf. 19; van Ess, *Erkenntnislehre*, p. 79; cf. pp. 73, 108, 110).
38. El-Omari, 'Theology of Abū l-Qāsim al-Balḫī/al-Kaᶜbī', pp. 192–3.
39. Al-Baghdādī, *al-Farq bayn al-firaq*, p. 111; al-Baghdādī, *Uṣūl al-dīn*, p. 32 (*maᶜrifat Allāh wa-maᶜrifat al-dalīl al-dāᶜī ilā maᶜrifatihi bi-l-ḍarūriyya*); van Ess, *Erkenntnislehre*, pp. 160, 329; cf. ᶜAbd al-Jabbār, *al-Mughnī*, XII: 230. van Ess, 'Abūʾl-Hoḏayl al-ᶜAllāf', pp. 319–20.
40. Mānkdīm, *Sharḥ al-uṣūl al-khamsa*, p. 57 (*mā yuᶜrafu istidlālan lā yajūzu an*

yu^crafa illā istidlālan ka-mā . . . mā yu^crafu ḍarūratan lā yajūzu an yu^crafa illā ḍarūratan); van Ess, *Erkenntnislehre*, p. 72.

41. Al-Ka^cbī, *Faḍl al-i^ctizāl*, p. 63; Madelung and Walker, *Ismaili Heresiography*, p. 11 = p. 29; Mānkdīm, *Sharḥ al-uṣūl al-khamsa*, pp. 51–2.
42. See al-Baghdādī, *Uṣūl al-dīn*, p. 5 (*za^cama al-Ka^cbī annahu [al-^cilm] i^ctiqād al-shay^ɔ ^calā mā huwa*); El-Omari, 'Theology of Abū l-Qāsim al-Balḫī/al-Ka^cbī', pp. 162–202.
43. Al-Māturīdī, *Kitāb al-Tawḥīd*, pp. 11–21.
44. On its negative reception among the Māturīdiyya, see El-Omari, 'Theology of Abū l-Qāsim al-Balḫī/al-Ka^cbī', pp. 189–92.
45. Mānkdīm, *Sharḥ al-uṣūl al-khamsa*, p. 39; cf. pp. 48–51; ^cAbd al-Jabbār, *al-Mughnī*, XII: 325, 379; Horten, *Die Philosophie des abu Raschíd*, pp. 192–3. Contrast Abū l-Khayr al-Yahūdī's conception of *ma^crifat Allāh* (al-Tawḥīdī, *al-Muqābasāt*, pp. 174–5). Cf. van Ess, *Erkenntnislehre*, pp. 237–46, esp. pp. 239–40.
46. ^cAbd al-Jabbār, *al-Mughnī*, XII: 16, 23, 25–9, 129; van Ess, *Erkenntnislehre*, pp. 74, 79, 333–4, cf. pp. 13, 71–2. Cf. *Sharḥ al-uṣūl al-khamsa*, p. 46, where Mānkdīm, having reported ^cAbd al-Jabbār's views, observed that *i^ctiqād* could arise from *ghayr al-^cilm* as well as *^cilm*.
47. See Volume I, pp. 117–18.
48. Al-Nasafī, *al-Qand fī dhikr ^culamā^ɔ Samarqand*, pp. 237–8, No. 375.
49. Al-Māturīdī, *Kitāb al-Tawḥīd*, pp. 159–63.
50. Abū Rashīd, *Masā^ɔil*, p. 322, § 111; Horten, *Die Philosophie des abu Raschíd*, p. 182.
51. Al-Ash^carī, *Maqālāt*, II: 373–4. Cf. Mānkdīm, *Sharḥ al-uṣūl al-khamsa*, pp. 65–6; van Ess, *Erkenntnislehre*, p. 73; Adamson, 'Al-Kindī and the Mu^ctazila', pp. 49–57, and 'Conception of Being', pp. 300, 305.
52. Al-Bazdawī, *Uṣūl al-dīn*, p. 31; al-Baghdādī, *al-Farq bayn al-firaq*, p. 166. But see al-Ash^carī, *Maqālāt*, I: 141–3, who reports that al-Naẓẓām and most of the Mu^ctazila, as well as the Kharijites and most of the Murji^ɔa and Zaydiyya, hold that God is and does not cease to be hearing and seeing.
53. Daiber, *Islamic Concept of Belief*, pp. 141, 150; cf. al-Ash^carī, *Maqālāt*, II: 363–9.
54. Madelung and Walker, *Ismaili Heresiography*, p. 12 = p. 30; al-Ka^cbī, *Faḍl al-i^ctizāl*, pp. 63–4. Cf. al-Mas^cūdī, *Murūj al-dhahab*, III: 222 (*lam yukallifhum* [= *al-^cibād*] *mā lā yuṭīqūnahu wa-lā arāda minhum mā lā yaqdurūna ^calayhi*, 'God does not charge human beings with responsibilities that they lack the

capacity to perform, and He does not desire of them that which they have no power to enact'). Al-Māturīdī criticises al-Kaᶜbī's doctrines concerning God's imposing of that which lies beyond his capacity (*Kitāb al-Tawḥīd*, pp. 424–7).

55. Cf. al-Samarqandī, *al-Sawād al-aᶜẓam*, p. 30.
56. NM-A, p. 147.
57. van Ess, *Erkenntnislehre*, pp. 26–7, 161.
58. Al-Kaᶜbī, *Faḍl al-iᶜtizāl*, pp. 63–4; Madelung and Walker, *Ismaili Heresiography*, pp. 11–12 = pp. 29–30; cf. Mānkdīm, *Sharḥ al-uṣūl al-khamsa*, p. 133; pp. 122–3. Cf. van Ess, *Erkenntnislehre*, p. 159.
59. ᶜAbd al-Jabbār, *al-Mughnī*, XIV: 53; cf. al-Kaᶜbī, in *Faḍl al-iᶜtizāl*, pp. 63–4; Madelung and Walker, *Ismaili Heresiography*, pp. 11–12 = pp. 29–30.
60. NM-A, p. 148.
61. Al-Ashᶜarī, *Maqālāt*, I: 219, § 254; al-Masᶜūdī, *Murūj al-dhahab*, III: 222; Cook, *Commanding Right*, pp. 195–226.
62. Al-Kaᶜbī included the principle of *al-amr bi-l-maᶜrūf* among the doctrines on which the Muᶜtazila were agreed (*Faḍl al-iᶜtizāl*, p. 64; Madelung and Walker, *Ismaili Heresiography*, p. 13 = p. 30). His position on the performance of the duty, however, was that the use of arms to forbid wrong was permitted to ordinary people (*sāʾir al-nās*) only in contexts in which there was no imam and no one designated by the imam (in cases that required the use of force); it was not suitable in cases in which the imam or an individual deputed by him to perform the task was present except in cases of dire necessity (*ḍarūra*) (al-Ṭūsī, *al-Tibyān*, II: 549; Cook, *Commanding Right*, pp. 199, 269).
63. van Ess, *Theologie und Gesellschaft*, III: 288–9.
64. Al-Kaᶜbī, *Faḍl al-iᶜtizāl*, p. 64; Madelung and Walker, *Ismaili Heresiography*, pp. 12–13 = p. 30. Cf. al-Ashᶜarī, *Maqālāt*, II: 355–7, §§ 216, 217, 222, 225; al-Masᶜūdī, *Murūj al-dhahab*, III: 222; al-Āmidī, *Abkār al-afkār*, IV: 379; ᶜAbd al-Jabbār, *al-Mughnī*, XIV: 335; Mānkdīm, *Sharḥ al-uṣūl al-khamsa*, pp. 644–5 (the Baghdadiyya), 789.
65. Rudolph, *Al-Māturīdī*, p. 199; cf. pp. 122, 127. Al-Kaᶜbī's book is not listed in Ibn al-Nadīm's entry for al-Kaᶜbī in *al-Fihrist*.
66. Al-Māturīdī, *Kitāb al-Tawḥīd*, pp. 532–46, cf. p. 520 (on the minor sinner); Rudolph, *Al-Māturīdī*, pp. 234, 344.
67. NM-A, p. 148.
68. See El-Omari, 'Theology of Abū l-Qāsim al-Balḫī/al-Kaᶜbī', pp. 226–93.
69. NM-A, pp. 148–9.
70. NM-A, p. 149. Pseudo-Māwardī cites the Prophetic ḥadīth, 'He who institutes

a good sunna, its reward goes to him, as does the reward of those who act by it until the Day of Resurrection' (Muslim, *Ṣaḥīḥ*, pp. 118–19 (= *Kitāb al-ᶜIlm, Bāb* 6, No. 1017); and Ibn Māja, *Sunan*, I: 125 (= *al-Muqaddima, Bāb* 14: *Man sanna sunna ḥasana aw sayyiᵓa*, No. 203)).

71. NM-A, pp. 149–50.
72. See Volume I, Chapter 3.
73. On favour and gratitude, see also ᶜAbd al-Jabbār, *al-Mughnī*, XII: 430 (*wajh wujūb al-maᶜrifa wujūb shukr al-niᶜma*); cf. van Ess, *Erkenntnislehre*, p. 330.
74. See Endreß, 'al-Kindī über die Wiedererinnerung der Seele', p. 184.
75. Heinrichs, 'Classification of the Sciences', p. 132; cf. Rowson, 'Philosopher as Littérateur', pp. 52, 59; Endreß, 'al-Kindī über die Wiedererinnerung der Seele', p. 204. See also Netton, *Al-Fārābī and His School*, p. 74.
76. Al-Nasafī, *Tabṣirat al-adilla*, I: 356–61, 359; At-Tancî, 'Abû Mansûr al-Mâturîdî', pp. 8, 10.
77. NM-A, p. 151. Pseudo-Māwardī cites passages from Q. 8: 75, 9: 115, 29: 64, 58: 7; 9: 94, 105, 13: 9, 32: 6; 4: 17, 92, 104, 117, 170, 48: 26; 3: 18; 3: 7, followed by Prophetic traditions, sayings from ᶜAlī, a saying of Buzurgmihr, a saying ascribed to an unidentified philosopher (*ḥakīm min ḥukamāᵓ al-falāsifa*); an account of Alexander's request that Aristotle accompany him on his campaigns and Aristotle's refusal, followed by the advice that Aristotle offered in substitution for his presence; a report on the authority of al-Wāqidī concerning a question posed to Ardashīr and his response; Buzurgmihr's admonition to his son; and a short aphorism of Ibn al-Muᶜtazz (247–96/861–908) (pp. 151–3). Ibn al-Muᶜtazz's axiom is 'He who promotes the life of a science does not die, and he who possesses an understanding does not become impoverished' (*mā māta man aḥyā ᶜilman wa-lā iftaqara man malaka fahman*, p. 153); the first part of the phrase appears in Kratchkovsky, 'Le Kitāb al-ādāb', appendix, p. 119, line 12).
78. NM-A, p. 153.
79. Cf. Heck, *Construction of Knowledge*, pp. 1–25; Heck, 'Hierarchy of Knowledge'; Beitia, 'La classification des sciences'.
80. Al-Khwārazmī, *Mafātīḥ al-ᶜulūm*, p. 5. See Biesterfeldt, 'Arabische-islamische Enzyklopädien', pp. 46–7.
81. Al-ᶜĀmirī would express the related point that 'the religious science' (*al-ᶜilm al-dīnī*) was the basis (*asās*) upon which all the other sciences were constructed (*al-Iᶜlām bi-manāqib al-Islām*, p. 106).
82. van Ess, *Erkenntnislehre*, pp. 60, 62.

83. NM-A, p. 154.
84. NM-A, pp. 154–5.
85. *Risālat al-Kindī fī kammiyyat kutub Arisṭūṭālīs*, in *Rasāʾil al-Kindī al-falsafiyya*, p. 376; Walzer, *Greek into Arabic*, pp. 177–87.
86. See Marlow, 'Abū Zayd al-Balkhī'.
87. Cf. van Ess, *Erkenntnislehre*, p. 97.
88. NM-A, p. 155.
89. Cf. van Ess, *Erkenntnislehre*, p. 44.
90. NM-A, p. 155.
91. NM-A, p. 155.
92. Cf. al-Māturīdī, *Kitāb al-Tawḥīd*, pp. 343–6.
93. Cf. van Ess, *Erkenntnislehre*, p. 44.
94. NM-A, p. 156.
95. In this context, it is possible that the term *awliyāʾ* also connotes 'regularly paid troops' (Bosworth, 'Alleged Embassy', p. 21).
96. NM-A, p. 156.
97. Pseudo-Māwardī returns to the theme of conflict in his ninth chapter, devoted to 'the management of enemies and criminals'. In that context he reiterates the duty of the 'imam and sulṭān' to engage in or arrange disputations with religious innovators in the presence of scholars, theologians and jurists (NM-A, pp. 331–2). In accordance with the predominant Muʿtazilite stance, Pseudo-Māwardī insists on the dissenter's opportunity for repentance, which ensures God's forgiveness. His emphasis on the ruler's correct conduct with religious dissenters reflects the importance attached to the issue in his milieu. In the following century, the historian Ibn al-Balkhī, writing for the Seljuk Sultan Muḥammad I Tapar b. Malikshāh (r. 498–511/1105–18), would narrate in paradigmatic fashion the Sasanian monarch Bahrām's procedure when he wished to be rid of Mānī, 'this heretical dog' (*īn sag-i zindīq*) and his followers, so that 'this sedition and corruption' (*fitneh* and *fasād*) would subside, yet he knew that execution of a person 'was not part of justice and sovereignty' (*ʿadl* and *pādshāhī*), except in cases of compelling proof (*ḥujjat*) (Ibn al-Balkhī, *Fārsnāmeh*, pp. 76–7).
98. Cf. al-Ashʿarī, *Maqālāt*, II: 347–50, §§ 194, 195, 196, 200.
99. ʿAlī faced resistance to his caliphate from the Companions Ṭalḥa and al-Zubayr, and the Prophet's widow ʿĀʾisha, at the Battle of the Camel (36/656). Slightly later he faced the defection of a group who 'seceded', and became known thereafter as Kharijites, 'those who seceded', after he had submitted to arbitration in his conflict with the Umayyad governor of Syria Muʿāwiya.

100. Abū Bakr had faced the defection of tribes who, at the death of the Prophet, had considered their ties to the polity in Medina to be at an end; the first caliph pursued them and enforced their continuing allegiance in the campaigns known as 'the wars of apostasy' (*ridda*).
101. NM-A, pp. 156–7. The encounter at Siffin is a crucial one in terms of history and theology, since it ushered in the Umayyad caliphate and the formation of the Shiᶜa. Cf. al-Ashᶜarī, *Maqālāt*, II: 340–1, § 174; Abou El Fadl, *Rebellion and Violence*, pp. 34–7, 40–1 and passim.
102. NM-A, p. 157. Cf. Grignaschi, 'La "Siyâsatu-l-ᶜâmmiyya"', p. 111; Maróth, *Correspondence*, p. 33.
103. NM-A, pp. 157–8.
104. See Volume I, pp. 160–3.
105. See Volume I, pp. 214–15.
106. Al-ᶜĀmirī, *al-Iᶜlām*, pp. 194–6.
107. NM-A, p. 158.
108. van Ess, *Erkenntnislehre*, pp. 381–94, esp. pp. 383, 388. The principle and practice are also treated in Māturīdī, *Kitāb al-Tawḥīd*, pp. 47–50.
109. Ibn al-Nadīm, *al-Fihrist*, I: ii: 615; Yāqūt, *Muᶜjam al-udabāʾ*, IV: 1493; van Ess, 'Abuʾl-Qāsem Kaᶜbī', p. 360. Cf. Abū Rashīd, *Masāʾil*, pp. 345, 348, §§ 130, 134; Horten, *Die Philosophie des abu Raschid*, pp. 203–4; van Ess, *Erkenntnislehre*, pp. 118, 244; 16, 239–40.
110. Abū Rashīd, *Masāʾil*, p. 345, § 130.
111. van Ess, *Erkenntislehre*, pp. 381, 383.
112. NM-A, pp. 158–9.
113. See El-Omari, 'Theology of Abū l-Qāsim al-Balḫī/al-Kaᶜbī', pp. 162–202, 226–93.
114. Al-ᶜĀmirī, *al-Iᶜlām*, pp. 194–6.
115. NM-A, p.105; cf. Volume I, p. 41.
116. See above, pp. 37–8.
117. Al-ᶜĀmirī, *al-Iᶜlām*, p. 195. See also p. 165, where al-ᶜĀmirī describes *fitna*, one of three types of conflict, as strife that arises among the categories of the nations (*bayna ṭabaqāt al-umam*) on account of *taᶜaṣṣub baladī* or *taᶜaṣṣub nasabī*, factionalism over territory or lineage; see further the same author's *Kitāb al-Amad*, where he attributes fighting to avidity for political leadership (*riyāsa*) or wealth (*māl*) (Rowson, *Muslim Philosopher*, pp. 112–13, 276). Cf. Volume I, p. 202 (cf. Rowson, *Muslim Philosopher*, pp. 186–7).
118. NM-A, p. 159.

119. NM-A, pp. 159–60.
120. Cf. Mānkdīm, *Sharḥ al-uṣūl al-khamsa*, p. 126.
121. Al-Fārābī, *Iḥṣāʾ al-ʿulūm*, pp. 107–8. Cf. Reisman, 'Curriculum'.
122. See Volume I, pp. 174–81.
123. Al-Nasafī, *al-Qand fī dhikr ʿulamāʾ Samarqand*, pp. 587–8, No. 1035.
124. Al-Ashʿarī, *Maqālāt*, II: 357–8, § 226. Cf. van Ess, *Erkenntnislehre*, p. 303.
125. van Ess, *Erkenntnislehre*, pp. 242, 279, 303, 325–7 and passim. On the qualifications of *ijtihād*, see al-Ashʿarī, *Maqālāt*, II: 360, § 233.
126. van Ess, *Erkenntnislehre*, pp. 16, 20 (with reference to *jadal* and *mujādala*), 303.
127. See Zaman, *Religion and Politics*, pp. 82–5; Zaman, 'The Caliphs, the ʿUlamāʾ, and the Law', pp. 4–7; Kristó-Nagy, *La pensée d'Ibn al-Muqaffaʿ*, pp. 236–7.
128. NM-A, p. 160.
129. NM-A, pp. 85–109. The study of admonition receives recognition as a 'science' in Ottoman sources. The theologian and biographer Taşköprüzade (901–68/1495–1561) would include in his encyclopaedia entries for *ʿilm al-mawāʿiẓ* and *ādāb al-tadhkīr* (*Miftāḥ al-saʿāda*, II: 426, I: 57–60).
130. NM-A, p. 160.
131. Al-Kindī, *Risālat al-Kindī fī kammiyyat kutub Arisṭūṭālīs*, in *Rasāʾil al-Kindī al-falsafiyya*, p. 376; Walzer, *Greek into Arabic*, pp. 177–87.
132. Al-Samarqandī, *Bustān al-ʿārifīn*, pp. 27–9.
133. NM-A, p. 161. Cf. Volume I, p. 198.
134. See Volume I, pp. 218, 219.
135. See further Touati, 'Pour une histoire de la lecture', pp. 14–20.
136. NM-A, pp. 161–3.
137. The two sayings of Ibn al-Muʿtazz (NM-A, p. 162) appear in Kratchkovsky, 'Le Kitāb al-ādāb', p. 90, line 8 and p. 91, line 1. Both maxims appear, attributed to Ibn al-Muʿtazz, in al-Ābī, *Nathr al-durr*, III: 152, and in al-Ṣafadī, *al-Wāfī bi-l-wafayāt* (Bray, 'Ibn al-Muʿtazz and Politics', p. 130). For the second of the pair, see also al-Mubashshir, *Mukhtār al-ḥikam*, p. 20 (ascribed to Hermes); al-Ḥuṣrī, *Zahr al-ādāb*, I: 375 (not attributed to Ibn al-Muʿtazz; see Bray, 'Ibn al-Muʿtazz and Politics', p. 129).
138. NM-A, p. 163. On *ʿishq*, see below, p. 298, n. 62.
139. On *lahw wa-laʿb*, see Volume I, pp. 72, 235.
140. NM-A, pp. 163–6. Citations include Q 6: 68, 70, 68, 32; 47: 36 = 57: 20; 23: 115; *ʿAhd Ardashīr*, pp. 65–6 and 90–1, No. 7. For the attribution of the final verse, see NM-A, p. 166, n. 85.

141. For examples of Rūdakī's poetry that extol the excellence and pleasures of love and wine, see Tabatabai, *Father of Persian Verse*, esp. pp. 86–99, 108–9; *Dīvān-i Rūdakī*, pp. 58–62 (*madāʾiḥ*, praise poems), 63–4 (*muhājāt*, satirical poems), 66–7 (*khamriyyāt*, wine poems). Cf. Yarshater, 'Theme of Wine-Drinking', pp. 43–53.
142. A number of poets composed 'Ismaᶜili *qaṣīdas*' in Persian, and some of the Ismaᶜilis at the Samanid court, such as the vizier Muṣᶜabī, were also accomplished poets (Lazard, *Les premiers poètes*, I: 74–5 = II: 48–9 and I: 23). Nāṣir-i Khusraw in his *Jāmiᶜ al-ḥikmatayn* and the commentary on the 'Ismaᶜili *qaṣīda*' of Abū l-Haytham Gurgānī conserve examples of such poetry (Lazard, *Les premiers poètes*, I: 24–5). Lazard also remarks on the possible or alleged heterodoxy of Shuhayd-i Balkhī and Maᶜrūfī (Lazard, *Les premiers poètes*, I: 8–9, I: 21, I: 31). Al-Thaᶜālibī records the Arabic poetry, some of it heterodox, of al-Ḥusayn b. ᶜAlī al-Marwazī (*Yatīmat al-dahr*, IV: 96–7); cf. Treadwell, 'Political History', pp. 111, 190 and n. 24.
143. NM-A, p. 199, and see below, p. 133.
144. On *ᶜinād*, stubborn persistence in religious matters, see Volume I, pp. 36, 38, 206.
145. NM-A, pp. 166–7.
146. See Volume I, p. 219; Abū Rashīd, *Masāʾil*, p. 302, § 97; van Ess, *Erkenntnislehre*, pp. 45–50, esp. pp. 46 and 71–6. For a detailed discussion of al-Kaᶜbī's acceptance of *taqlīd* and al-Ashᶜarī's criticism of this trend among Muᶜtazilites, see El-Omari, 'Theology of Abū l-Qāsim al-Balḫī/al-Kaᶜbī', pp. 168–71.
147. Abū Rashīd, *Masāʾil*, p. 302, § 97; van Ess, *Erkenntnislehre*, pp. 26, 45–8, 75–6, cf. pp. 49–51. Cf. Mānkdīm, *Sharḥ al-uṣūl al-khamsa*, p. 46. Pseudo-Māwardī does not invoke *sukūn al-nafs*, mental or spiritual tranquillity, a concept criticised by al-Jāḥiẓ, who observed that erroneous conviction would also generate the feeling (ᶜAbd al-Jabbār, *al-Mughnī*, XII: 36; van Ess, *Erkenntnislehre*, p. 77).
148. Al-Nasafī, *Tabṣirat al-adilla*, I: 25–43, 26. The *mashāyikh* of Samarqand were not unanimous, however, in their rejection of *taqlīd* as a basis for faith; one tenth-century author recorded the point of view that *al-īmān bi-l-taqlīd ṣaḥīḥ* (faith accepted without examination is true) (Daiber, *Islamic Concept of Belief*, p. 68).
149. Al-Kindī, *Fī l-falsafa al-ūlā*, p. 97. Cf. Yaman, *Prophetic Niche*, pp. 6, 223; Adamson, *Al-Kindī*, p. 30; Ivry, *Al-Kindi's Metaphysics*, pp. 13, 55.
150. van Ess, *Erkenntnislehre*, pp. 16, 118, cf. p. 166.
151. van Ess, *Erkenntnislehre*, pp. 45–6; ᶜAbd al-Jabbār, *al-Mughnī*, XVII: 199: 'as

for demonstrating the legal validity of *ijmāᶜ* by a process of reason, that is inconceivable' (*fa-ammā l-istidlāl ᶜalā ṣiḥḥat al-ijmāʾ min jihat al-ᶜaql fa-baᶜīd*).

152. On al-Maʾmūn's example, see Volume I, Chapter 1, pp. 41–2.
153. Grignaschi, 'La "Siyâsatu-l-ᶜâmmiyya"', p. 120; Maróth, *Correspondence*, p. 38; Ibn Hindū, *al-Kalim al-rūḥāniyya*, p. 73.
154. NM-A, pp. 167–8.
155. NM-A, p. 168; Grignaschi, 'La "Siyâsatu-l-ᶜâmmiyya"', pp. 109, 120; Maróth, *Correspondence*, pp. 31, 38; al-Mubashshir b. Fātik, *Mukhtār al-ḥikam*, p. 193; al-Shahrazūrī, *Nuzhat al-arwāḥ*, I: 200.
156. NM-A, pp. 168–9; *ᶜAhd Ardashīr*, p. 57 (ᶜAbbās's text lists *ᶜubbād* as well as *nussāk*, and *mutabattilūn* (recluses, those who retire from the world) instead of Pseudo-Māwardī's *mutanabbiʾūn*). Cf. Shaked, 'Esoteric Trends', p. 216.
157. NM-A, p. 169; *ᶜAhd Ardashīr*, p. 56. Cf. Steppat, 'From *ᶜAhd Ardashīr* to al-Maʾmūn', pp. 452–3. Pseudo-Māwardī adds to these citations a quotation from the Testament of 'one of the kings of India to his son' (pp. 169–70).
158. NM-A, p. 170.
159. Cf. van Ess, *Erkenntnislehre*, p. 269.
160. Al-Kindī, *Risāla fī ḥudūd al-ashyāʾ wa-rusūmihā* ('On the Definitions and Patterns of Things'), in *Rasāʾil al-Kindī*, p. 172 and *Cinq épîtres*, 22 (70); Druart, 'al-Kindi's Ethics', p. 339. See further Endreß, 'al-Kindī über die Wiedererinnerung der Seele', pp. 189-97; Klein-Franke, 'Al-Kindi's "On Definitions and Descriptions of Things"'; Frank, 'Al-Kindī's *Book of Definitions*'; Berman, 'Political Interpretation'.
161. NM-A, pp. 170–1. See also Yaman, *Prophetic Niche*, pp. 22–5, 32–3, 89–91.
162. ᶜAbd al-Jabbār, *al-Mughnī*, XI: 58–60, 134 (*wajh al-ḥikma fī khalq al-mukallif annahu taᶜālā khalaqahu li-yanfaᶜahu bi-l-tafaḍḍul wa-li-yuᶜarriḍahu lil-thawāb*), p. 387 (*al-gharaḍ bi-l-taklīf huwa taᶜrīḍ al-mukallaf lil-thawāb*), p. 393. Cf. al-Ashᶜarī, *Maqālāt*, I: 200, § 217.
163. Mānkdīm, *Sharḥ al-usūl al-khamsa*, p. 66. For ᶜAbd al-Jabbār, to impute evil to God constituted *kufr* (Mānkdīm, *Sharḥ al-usūl al-khamsa*, p. 125, cf. pp. 132–3).
164. NM-A, p. 203.
165. Al-Māturīdī, *Kitāb al-Tawḥīd*, pp. 61, 152, 192–3, 266, cf. pp. 343–51. Al-Māturīdī describes two ways by which divine *ḥikma* manifests itself (al-Māturīdī, *Kitāb al-Tawḥīd*, p. 125; Rudolph, *Al-Māturīdī*, pp. 332–3). Elsewhere, al-Māturīdī equates *ḥikma* with *iṣāba*: *taʾwīl al-ḥikma al-iṣāba wa-huwa waḍᶜ kull shayʾ mawḍiʾahu wa-dhālika maᶜnā al-ᶜadl* (*Kitāb al-Tawḥīd*, p. 152).

166. See Volume I, p. 233.
167. Al-Nasafī, *Tabṣirat al-adilla*, I: 384–6. Parts of al-Nasafī's account echo al-Māturīdī's interpretation, cited above (n. 165).
168. NM-A, p. 171.
169. NM-A, pp. 171–2. Also cited is the inscription on Rustam's signet ring (see Volume I, p. 69).
170. NM-A, pp. 172–3.
171. See further below, pp. 158, 160.
172. NM-A, p. 173.
173. NM-A, p. 174.
174. NM-A, pp. 174–5. Pseudo-Māwardī adduces quotations from ʿUmar and Muʿāwiya, passages from a letter of al-Muhallab b. Abī Ṣufra, general of the seventh century and appointed as governor of Khurasan, to the governor of Iraq al-Ḥajjāj; an utterance ascribed to al-Ḥajjāj and a report concerning the Umayyad Caliph ʿUmar b. ʿAbd al-ʿAzīz (pp. 175–6).
175. Al-Suyūṭī, *al-Jāmiʿ al-ṣaghīr*, I: 216–17, No. 985. Al-Māwardī cited the ḥadīth in several places: *Adab al-dunyā wa-l-dīn*, p. 295; *Tashīl al-naẓar*, p. 159; *Qawānīn al-wizāra*, p. 226. Pseudo-Māwardī cites it again at NM-A, p. 352.
176. NM-A, pp. 176–7.
177. NM-A, p. 178.
178. NM-A, pp. 178–9. Pseudo-Māwardī cites several Qurʾānic texts and ḥadīth on the subject of *ṣidq*, and provides examples of expressions that the king should avoid lest they embroil him in double entendre.
179. NM-A, pp. 179–80.
180. NM-A, p. 181. Compare Miskawayh, *Jāvīdān khirad*, p. 76 ('Treat those above you with respect, be gentle with those beneath you, and favourable with your equals; but most importantly treat your equals favourably').
181. Cf. Mottahedeh, *Loyalty and Leadership*, pp. 82–93, 82–3, 89 and passim; see Volume I, pp. 122–4.
182. NM-A, pp. 181–2.
183. NM-A, pp. 182–3 (the first part of this ḥadīth appeared earlier in his book; see above, p. 21). The section concludes with a citation from ʿAlī and a passage from the 'Testament' of the Indian King Sāb.t.r.m.
184. Ibn Māja, *Sunan*, IV: 499 (= *Kitāb al-Zuhd*, No. 4174).
185. Ibn Māja, *Sunan*, IV: 499–500 (= *Kitāb al-Zuhd*, No. 4176).
186. Al-Mubashshir, *Mukhtār al-ḥikam*, p. 193.
187. NM-A, pp. 183–4. The reference is to the fourth chapter, NM-A, pp. 111–41.

188. NM-A, pp. 184–5.
189. NM-A, p. 186.
190. Al-Kaᶜbī, *Faḍl al-iᶜtizāl*, p. 73; Madelung and Walker, *Ismaili Heresiography*, p. 19 = p. 34.
191. Al-Murtaḍā, *Amālī*, I: 468. Cf. van Ess, 'Abu'l-Qāsem Kaᶜbī', p. 361; van Ess, *Erkenntnislehre*, pp. 136–7.
192. NM-A, pp. 188–9. Al-Tirmidhī, *al-Jāmiᶜ al-Ṣaḥīḥ*, III: 390 (= *Kitāb Ṣifat al-qiyāma wa-l-raqāʾiq wa-l-waraᶜ*, p. 60, No. 2517); al-Ābī, *Nathr al-durr*, IV: 201.
193. Al-Jāḥiẓ, *Risālat al-maᶜāsh wa-l-maᶜād*, in *Rasāʾil al-Jāḥiẓ*, I: 111–12.
194. Al-Samarqandī, *al-Sawād al-aᶜẓam*, pp. 126–7, affirms the obligation to seek economic gain (*kasb*) in times of need, against the ascetic position of the Karrāmiyya on this matter.
195. Cf. al-Taghlibī, *Kitāb al-Tāj*, p. 124 = p. 144.
196. A reference to ᶜAlī's taking the Prophet's place at night; ᶜAlī risked his life by sleeping in the Prophet's bed on the night that the Prophet left Mecca for Medina; cf. al-Taghlibī, *Kitāb al-Tāj*, p. 124 = p. 145.
197. NM-A, pp. 190–1.
198. Al-Maydānī, *Majmaᶜ al-amthāl*, I: 87, No. 215 and I: 270, No. 1106, both ascribed to or transmitted from Aktham b. Ṣayfī, a judge of the *jāhiliyya* and source of numerous wise sayings.
199. NM-A, p. 191. Cf. al-Jāḥiẓ's discussion of the relationship of the human virtues and vices to 'natures' (*Risālat al-maᶜāsh wa-l-maᶜād*, in *Rasāʾil al-Jāḥiẓ*, I: 110–11). See also above, p. 123.
200. I have discussed this presentation in a forthcoming article (Marlow, 'Abū Zayd al-Balkhī'). The passage is also noted in Hamori, 'Prudence', p. 165, n. 15.
201. This conception also appears in the writings of al-Kindī; see *Risālat al-Kindī fī ḥudūd al-ashyāʾ wa-rusūmihā*, pp. 177–9.
202. NM-A, pp. 191–2.
203. Al-Nasāʾī, *Sunan*, III: 206–7 (= *Kitāb al-Ṣiyām, al-nahy ᶜan ṣiyām al-dahr*).
204. See al-Ābī, *Nathr al-durr*, I: 277 (among the sayings of ᶜAlī b. Abī Ṭālib).
205. Al-Suyūṭī, *al-Jāmiᶜ al-ṣaghīr*, II: 520–1, Nos 2508, 2509.
206. Miskawayh, *Jāvīdān khirad*, p. 72 (in *faṣl min kalām ḥakīm ākhar fārsī*).
207. NM-A, p. 192–3. The last saying appears in al-Tirmidhī, *al-Jāmiᶜ al-Ṣaḥīḥ*, III: 110 (= *Kitāb al-Birr wa-l-ṣila*, 60: *Bāb mā jāʾa fī l-iqtiṣād fī l-ḥubb wa-l-bughḍ*, No. 1997); al-Maydānī, *Majmaᶜ al-amthāl*, I: 271–2, No. 1111, and

in the collection of Abū ᶜUbayd al-Qāsim b. Sallām, *al-Amthāl*, in the commentary of al-Bakrī, *Faṣl al-maqāl*, p. 264.

208. Al-Ābī, *Nathr al-durr*, I: 153: 'Envy and hatred shave; they shave religion, not hair' (among the sayings of the Prophet). See also Abū Dāʾūd, *ᶜAwn al-maᶜbūd*, XIII: 2445 (= *Bāb fī l-ḥasad*, No. 4882) ('Beware of envy, for it consumes good deeds just as fire consumes wood' [or plants]); cf. Ibn Māja, *Sunan*, IV: 515 (= *Kitāb al-Zuhd*, No. 4210).
209. *ᶜAhd Ardashīr*, p. 69.
210. NM-A, pp. 193–4.
211. Al-Tirmidhī, *al-Jāmiᶜ al-Ṣaḥīḥ*, III: 116 (= *Kitāb al-Birr wa-l-ṣila*, 66: *Bāb mā jāʾa fī l-taʾannā wa-l-ᶜajala*, No. 2012).
212. NM-A, pp. 194–5.
213. NM-A, p. 195. Cf. al-Taghlibī, *Kitāb al-Tāj*, p. 66.
214. Unlike the narratives that interpret the caliph's act as an example of royal injustice (Meisami, 'Masᶜūdī on Love', pp. 268–9), Pseudo-Māwardī's *khabar* portrays it as anything but impulsive (cf. Montgomery, 'Serendipity', p. 223). Significantly, he narrates it in the voice of Ḥusayn al-Khādim, a prominent member of Hārūn's *khadam* and frequently mentioned with the caliph's executioner Masrūr al-Khādim, who circulated contrasting stories of the events (Sadan, 'Death of a Princess', p. 135, nn. 5, 7). On the numerous accounts and interpretations of the fall of Barmakids, see, with the copious references cited therein, Hamori, 'Going Down in Style'; Meisami, 'Masᶜūdī on Love'; Sadan, 'Death of a Princess'.
215. NM-A, pp. 195–6.
216. Cf. Wensinck-Gardet, 'Khaṭīʾa', p. 1107. Miskawayh ascribes a similar sentiment to an anonymous Persian testament (*waṣiyya ukhrā lil-furs*): 'Know that repentance (*tawba*) never leads anyone to the Fire, and insistence (in a sin) (*iṣrār*) never leads anyone to Paradise' (*Jāvīdān khirad*, p. 75).
217. Cf. al-Ashᶜarī, *Maqālāt*, I: 214–15; al-Baghdādī, *Uṣūl al-dīn*, p. 242.
218. Mānkdīm, *Sharḥ al-uṣūl al-khamsa*, pp. 779–80; cf. al-Ashᶜarī, *Maqālāt*, I: 208.
219. NM-A, pp. 196–7.
220. NM-A, p. 197. Cf. *ᶜAhd Ardashīr*, p. 70.
221. NM-A, pp. 197–8; 336. Cf. Grignaschi, 'La "Siyâsatu-l-ᶜâmmiyya"', p. 199; Maróth, *Correspondence*, p. 37; Ibn Hindū, *al-Kalim al-rūḥāniyya*, pp. 72–3.
222. On favour (*niᶜma*) and increase (*ziyāda*), see Volume I, Chapter 3.
223. NM-A, p. 198. Al-Tirmidhī, *al-Jāmiᶜ al-Ṣaḥīḥ*, III: 330 (= *Kitāb al-Zuhd*, 54:

Bāb mā jāʿa fī karāhiyat al-midḥa wa-l-maddāḥīn, Nos 2393, 2394); Ibn Māja, *Sunan*, IV: 256 (= *Kitāb al-Adab*, 36: *Bāb al-madḥ*, No. 3742). Al-Masʿūdī, *Murūj al-dhahab*, II: 293–4, cites the Prophetic maxim and explains that it applies to dishonest praise.

224. NM-A, p. 199. The citation continues from al-Jāḥiẓ, *Risālat al-maʿāsh wa-l-maʿād* (*Rasāʾil al-Jāḥiẓ*, I: 129), from which I have emended *ahl al-riwāyāt* to *ahl al-murūʾāt* and *ūlāʾika al-ṣādiqūn* to *ūlāʾika al-ṣāddūn*.
225. On al-Jāḥiẓ's writings for, and relationship with, Ibn Abī Duʾād, see Montgomery, *Al-Jāḥiẓ*, pp. 29–30, 201–13 and passim.
226. Montgomery's translation; *Al-Jāḥiẓ*, p. 202 (from another letter to Ibn Abī Duʾād, *Kitāb al-Futyā*, 'Treatise on Legal Verdicts', in *Rasāʾil al-Jāḥiẓ*, III: 313); NM-A, p. 94; Ghazālī, *Naṣīḥat al-mulūk*, p. 109 = p. 61; al-Ābī, *Nathr al-durr*, IV: 234.
227. NM-A, pp. 199–200.
228. NM-A, p. 200.
229. NM-A, p. 200.
230. Adamson, *Al-Kindī*, pp. 44–5.
231. Q. 54: 5. See Yaman, *Prophetic Niche*, p. 84.
232. NM-A, pp. 200–1.
233. Ibn Māja, *Sunan*, IV: 367 (= *Kitāb al-Fitan*, 8: *al-Sawād al-aʿẓam*, No. 3950: 'My community shall never agree upon an error, and if you find that you differ, then follow the great community' (*al-sawād al-aʿẓam*)).
234. Al-Tirmidhī, *al-Jāmiʿ al-Ṣaḥīḥ*, IV: 447 (= *Kitāb al-Manāqib*, 16: *Fī manāqib Abī Bakr wa-ʿUmar*, No. 3662), Ibn Māja, *Sunan*, I: 80 (= *Muqaddima*, 11: *Fī faḍāʾil aṣḥāb rasūl Allāh*, No. 97).
235. Al-Ābī, *Nathr al-durr*, I: 165.
236. NM-A, pp. 201–2.
237. NM-A, p. 202.

Chapter 4

1. Aspects of Pseudo-Māwardī's treatment of the *khāṣṣa* and *ʿāmma* have been discussed in Volume I. Cf. Mottahedeh, *Loyalty and Leadership*, pp. 115–16.
2. For portrayals of the physical expression of rank in the ruler's presence, see al-Taghlibī, *Kitāb al-Tāj*, pp. 7–9 = pp. 35–7; al-Masʿūdī, *Murūj al-dhahab*, I: 267. For a study of these ideas and their various articulations in Muslim contexts, see Al-Azmeh, *Muslim Kingship*, esp. pp. 121–53.
3. NM-A, p. 203; see below.

4. See Paul, '*Khidma*', and Volume I, Chapter 3, pp. 107, 111, 122.
5. Badawī, *al-Uṣūl al-yūnāniyya*, p. 13.
6. In the Seljuk period, the term *ḥasham* sometimes referred to nomadic warriors and their chiefs, who followed a particular ruler (Paul, 'Terms for Nomads', pp. 446–54).
7. Mottahedeh, *Loyalty and Leadership*, pp. 82–93 and passim.
8. Paul, 'Terms for Nomads', p. 450 and n. 20.
9. A translation and discussion of this section appears in Volume I, pp. 97–102.
10. NM-A, p. 205.
11. Reading *ᶜamal* for *ᶜaql*, as in the manuscript (f. 45b).
12. See Volume I, Chapter 3.
13. NM-A, p. 205.
14. NM-A, pp. 206–7. Ellipses mark Qurᵓānic passages (20: 132; 7: 145; 66: 6; 26: 214).
15. Gilᶜadi, *Children of Islam*, pp. 61–6.
16. Ibn al-Nadīm, *al-Fihrist*, I: ii: 430; Yāqūt, *Muᶜjam al-udabāᵓ*, I: 294–5. Yāqūt supplies the information that Abū Zayd had been a teacher (*kāna muᶜalliman lil-ṣibyān*). Both authors record among his compositions a *Kitāb Ajwibat Abī Isḥāq al-muᵓaddib* ('Book of Answers to Abū Isḥāq the Teacher'), and Yāqūt includes among Abū Zayd's writings a defence of teachers and booksellers (*fī . . . l-muᶜallimīn wa-l-warrāqīn*) in response to an earlier work that had censured them.
17. See Günther, 'Medieval Muslim Thinkers on Educational Theory', pp. 371–3.
18. Abū l-Layth al-Samarqandī, *Bustān al-ᶜārifīn*, pp. 36–7.
19. NM-A, pp. 207–8.
20. Cf. *ᶜAhd Ardashīr*, p. 71.
21. NM-A, p. 208. Grignaschi, 'La "Siyâsatu-l-ᶜâmmiyya"', pp. 117, 113–14; Maróth, *Correspondence*, pp. 37, 34.
22. Although the manuscript clearly reads *aᶜyān* (f. 46 b), the repeated linking of *junūd* and *aᶜwān*, 'assistants', in the author's vocabulary raises the possibility of an alteration in the course of the text's transmission.
23. The exact referents of these terms are elusive, and my renderings into English provisional; further discussion follows in the present chapter.
24. NM-A, pp. 208–9. Ibn Ḥawqal likewise uses the terms *dār* and *qarār* to describe Ismāᶜīl's selection of Bukhara as his capital (*Ṣūrat al-arḍ*, p. 491); cf. NM-A, p. 283.

25. Cf. Mottahedeh, *Loyalty and Leadership*, pp. 84–9.
26. Niẓām al-Mulk's later description of the ranked order (*tartīb*) that should prevail in courtly convocations (*andar tartīb-i bār-dārān-i khāṣṣ-o ᶜāmm*) reflects some of the same distinctions among the categories of the *khāṣṣa*: the king's close relatives (*khwīshāvandān*) should enter first, followed by the most celebrated members of the *ḥasham* (*maᶜrūfān-i ḥasham*), followed in turn by the remaining categories of persons (*dīgar ajnās-i mardumān*) (*Siyar al-mulūk*, p. 159).
27. *ᶜAhd Ardashīr*, p. 52.
28. Grignaschi, 'Quelques spécimens', pp. 91–2 = p. 111; see pp. 123–4, nn. 2; p. 101 = p. 121, cf. p. 127, n. 49.
29. Al-Khwārazmī, *Mafātīḥ al-ᶜulūm*, p. 115; cf. Bosworth, 'Asāwera'.
30. Narshakhī, *Tārīkh-i Bukhārā*, p. 36. The use of the term sulṭān, apparently to designate the royal person rather than 'royalty' or 'authority' in the abstract sense, almost certainly reflects later usage and one of the later redactions of Narshakhī's much altered text (see Volume I, p. 263, n. 119). On the topography and urban design of Bukhara, including the Rīgistān, see al-Iṣṭakhrī, *Masālik al-mamālik*, p. 309; Ibn Ḥawqal, *Ṣūrat al-arḍ*, pp. 482–5, 491.
31. Bosworth, *Ghaznavids*, p. 34.
32. Niẓāmī Samarqandī, *Chahār maqāleh* ('Four Discourses'), pp. 22–4; Browne, *Literary History*, II: 15–17. Possibly Pseudo-Māwardī had this practice in mind when he repeated, as part of Yazīd III's address, the latter's pledge to avoid the protracted detention of troops away from their families (see Volume I, p. 38).
33. Cf. Winter, '"Seat of Kingship"', esp. p. 27.
34. Cf. Abū l-Layth al-Samarqandī, *Tanbīh al-ghāfilīn*, pp. 95–7 (*Bāb ḥaqq al-walad ᶜalā l-wālid*, 'the responsibilities of the father towards his child'), p. 95.
35. NM-A, p. 209, with Qurʾānic quotations (66: 5; 56: 35–7; 56: 22; 55: 56; 55: 72; 24: 3; 24: 31; 33: 33) (pp. 209–10). Pseudo-Māwardī's discussion concerns the preparation of princes for kingship; I have therefore used the male pronoun, although in some instances his advice perhaps applied to male and female children of the élites (cf. Swain, *Economy, Family, and Society*, pp. 364–421).
36. The reference to taking refuge from the accursed Satan (*al-shayṭān al-rajīm*) evokes a number of Qurʾānic passages, especially the two final chapters, Q 113 and 114, which provide the language *aᶜūdhu bi-rabb al-falak* ('I seek refuge with the Lord of the rising day') and *aᶜūdhu bi-rabb al-nās* ('I seek refuge with the Lord of men'). The passage also evokes Mary's words when

the angel appears to her to announce that she will give birth to Jesus (19: 18, 'I seek refuge in the Merciful from you'), and Mary's mother's prayer for her protection from Satan (3: 36, 'Preserve her and her children from Satan the ostracised'). (These translations are Ali's; *Al-Qur*ᵓ*ān*, pp. 560–1, 261, 55). Moreover, it is God who creates, sustains, causes to die and gives life again (Q 30: 40), and Pseudo-Māwardī's reference to the concept of God's provision (*rizq*) evokes the Qurᵓānic description of God as 'the best of providers' (*khayr al-rāziqīn*, 5: 114 and elsewhere). The reference to taking refuge from Satan, and protecting the child, if conceived, from Satan, is also reminiscent of the Prophetic ḥadīth (al-Dārimī, *Sunan*, I: 630 (*Kitāb al-Nikāḥ*, 29: *Bāb al-qawl* ᶜ*inda l-jimā*ᶜ, No. 2212)).

37. NM-A, pp. 210–11.
38. On *kafā*ᵓ*a* in *fiqh*, see Ziadeh, 'Equality (*kafā*ᵓ*ah*)'; Marlow, *Hierarchy and Egalitarianism*, pp. 30–4. Cf. Swain, *Economy, Family, and Society*, p. 374.
39. Bray, 'Local Mirror', pp. 37–8.
40. Muḥammad b. al-Ḥanafiyya's *kunya* was Abū l-Qāsim, and Pseudo-Māwardī's reference is to a Prophetic ḥadīth, 'Take my name but not my *kunya*' (al-Tirmidhī, *al-Jāmi*ᶜ *al-Ṣaḥīḥ*, III: 559–60 (= *Kitāb al-Adab*, 68: *Bāb mā jā*ᵓ*a fī karāhiyat al-jam*ᶜ *bayna sm al-nabī wa-kunyatihi*, Nos 2841, 2842)); Abū Dāᵓūd, *Sunan*, in ᶜ*Awn al-ma*ᶜ*būd*, XIII: 305 (= *Kitāb al-Adab*, 74: *Bāb fī l-rajul yatakannā bi-Abī l-Qāsim*, No. 4944). Al-Tirmidhī also includes the ḥadīth that records the Prophet's granting to Muḥammad b. al-Ḥanafiyya of a dispensation (*rukhṣa*) in this regard (No. 2843), a ḥadīth to which Pseudo-Māwardī also alludes in this passage.
41. Al-Tirmidhī, *al-Jāmi*ᶜ *al-Ṣaḥīḥ*, III: 556–7 (= *Kitāb al-Adab*, 64: *Bāb mā jā*ᵓ*a mā yustaḥabbu min al-asmā*ᵓ, No 2833–4); Abū Dāᵓūd, *Sunan*, in ᶜ*Awn al-ma*ᶜ*būd*, XIII: 292–3 (= *Kitāb al-Adab*, 69: *Bāb fī taghyīr al-asmā*ᵓ, Nos 4928, 4929); Ibn Māja, *Sunan*, IV: 249 (= *Kitāb al-Adab*, 30: *Mā yustaḥabbu min al-asmā*ᵓ, No. 3728).
42. NM-A, p. 212. Pseudo-Māwardī cites the ḥadīth on his own authority (*wa-qad rawaynā* ᶜ*anhu*). Ibn Māja, *Sunan*, IV: 249, No. 3728 (= *Kitāb al-Adab* ('Book of Good Custom'), *Bāb mā yustaḥabbu min al-asmā*ᵓ); al-Tirmidhī, *al-Jāmi*ᶜ *al-ṣaḥīḥ*, III: 556–7 (= *Kitāb al-Adab*, *Bāb mā jā*ᵓ*a mā yustaḥabbu min al-asmā*ᵓ, Nos 2833, 2834); al-Dārimī, *Sunan*, II: 174 (= *Kitāb al-Isti*ᵓ*dhān*, 60, *Bāb mā yustaḥabbu min al-asmā*ᵓ, No. 2695).
43. NM-A, pp. 211–13. Swain, *Economy, Family, and Society*, p. 407.
44. NM-A, pp. 213–14.

45. NM-A, p. 213 = NM-Ḥ, p. 304; cf. MS ff. 47b–48a.
46. NM-A, pp. 213–14. Swain, *Economy, Family, and Society*, pp. 374–6.
47. See Gilᶜadi, *Infants, Parents and Wet Nurses*, pp. 14–67, esp. pp. 53–6.
48. As Maya Shatzmiller has demonstrated for al-Andalus, employment as a wet-nurse also provided women with an opportunity for paid labour (Shatzmiller, 'Women and Wage Labour', pp. 182–8).
49. Horten, *Die Philosophie des abu Raschîd*, pp. 149–50; van Ess, 'Abuᵓl-Qāsem Kaᶜbī', p. 351.
50. Vestiges of the theory of the humours are apparent in the introductory section ascribed to Burzōy (Bāzawayh) the Physician (*al-mutaṭabbib*) in *Kalīla wa-Dimna* (*Kalîlah et Dimnah*, pp. 30–44, 31, 43).
51. Pormann and Savage-Smith, *Medieval Islamic Medicine*, pp. 41–79, esp. pp. 43–5; Conrad, 'Arab-Islamic Medical Tradition', esp. pp. 99–104.
52. Abū Rashīd, *Masāᵓil*, pp. 133–50, §§ 28–9; Horten, *Die Philosophie des abu Raschîd*, pp. 100–1, 149; van Ess, 'Abuᵓl-Qāsem Kaᶜbī', p. 361.
53. Abū Rashīd, *Masāᵓil*, pp. 232–4, §§ 71–3; Horten, *Die Philosophie des abu Raschîd*, pp. 92–4, 149.
54. Conrad, 'Arab-Islamic Medical Tradition', pp. 122–3.
55. Abū l-Layth al-Samarqandī, *Bustān al-ᶜārifīn*, pp. 236–7.
56. Al-Khwārazmī, *Mafātīḥ al-ᶜulūm*, pp. 152–83, esp. p. 181.
57. Rowson, *Muslim Philosopher*, p. 148 = p. 149.
58. NM-A, pp. 214–15.
59. Abū l-Layth al-Samarqandī, *Bustān al-ārifīn*, pp. 39–41.
60. See Richter-Bernburg, 'Linguistic shuᶜūbīya', p. 59, n. 47. Daniel has suggested that Bīrūnī's remarks may have been prompted in part by the fact that his native language was Khwarazmian ('Samanid "Translations"', pp. 278–9, n. 46).
61. NM-A, p. 215.
62. Defined by al-Kindī as 'excessive love' (*ifrāṭ al-maḥabba*), and distinguished from *maḥabba*, which is defined as *maṭlūb al-nafs wa-mutammimat al-quwwa allatī hiya ijtimāᶜ al-ashyāᵓ* ('that which the soul seeks, and that which completes the strength that [arises from] the union of things') (*Rasāᵓil al-Kindī al-falsafiyya*, pp. 175, 176). Pseudo-Māwardī follows al-Kindī in the strongly positive sense in which he employs the term *maḥabba* and the negative connotations that he associates with *ᶜishq*. See above, pp. 105, 156.
63. NM-A, p. 215.
64. See Schoeler, 'Die Einteilung der Dichtung'. Pseudo-Māwardī's poetic catego-

ries accord with the genres described in the tenth-century work of the literary specialist Isḥāq b. Ibrāhīm al-Kātib (*al-Burhān fī wujūh al-bayān* ('Proof in the Types of Clear Expression'), pp. 170–1).

65. Miskawayh, *Tahdhīb al-akhlāq*, p. 57 = p. 52; Ṭūsī, *Akhlāq-i Nāṣirī*, p. 224 = p. 168. Unlike Pseudo-Māwardī, these philosophers mention Bryson, with whose *Oikonomikos*, on the management of property, slaves, women and children, the earlier author was perhaps also acquainted (cf. Swain, *Economy, Family, and Society*, pp. 246–56).
66. Al-Naḍr b. al-Ḥārith, a merchant, reportedly challenged Muḥammad on his return from Persia by saying, 'I know stories that are better than yours, I know the stories of Rustam and Isfandiyār' (Rosenthal, 'Asāṭīr al-awwalīn'; al-Ziriklī, *al-Aʿlām*, VIII: 33).
67. Al-Dārimī, *Sunan*, II: 177–8 (= *Kitāb al-Istīdhān*, 68: *Bāb fī anna min al-shiʿr ḥikma*, No. 2704); Ibn Māja, *Sunan*, IV: 262–3 = *Kitāb al-Adab*, *Bāb* 41 (*Bāb al-shiʿr*), No. 3755 (Ubayya Ibn Kaʿb, *inna min al-shiʿr la-ḥikmatan*), No. 3756 (Ibn ʿAbbās, *inna min al-shiʿr ḥikaman*); Abū Dāʾūd, *Sunan*, in *ʿAwn al-maʿbūd*, XIII: 353–4 (= *Kitāb al-Adab*, 96: *Bāb mā jāʾa fī l-shiʿr*, No. 4989); *Musnad al-Imām Aḥmad Ibn Ḥanbal* XXXV: 88, No. 21154; 89, No. 21155; 89, No. 21156; 91, No. 21158, 91, No. 21159 (Ubayya Ibn Kaʿb, *inna min al-shiʿr ḥikmatan*).
68. *Ṣaḥīḥ Muslim*, 335 (No. 47) = *Kitāb al-Jumʿa*, *Bāb takhfīf al-ṣalāt wa-l-khuṭba*, No. 869 (*inna min al-bayān siḥran*); Abū Dāʾūd, *Sunan*, in *ʿAwn al-maʿbūd*, XIII: 351–2 (= *Kitāb al-Adab*, 96: *Bāb mā jāʾa fī l-shiʿr*, No. 4988); al-Dārimī, *Sunan*, I: 401 (= *Kitāb al-Ṣalāt*, 199: *Bāb fī qaṣr al-khuṭba* (*fa-inna min al-bayān la-siḥran*, No. 1556)). In a different form, and a possible reading in this case, the two Prophetic utterances appear as a single ḥadīth transmitted on the authority of Ibn ʿAbbās, *inna min al-shiʿr ḥukman wa-min al-bayān siḥran* (*Musnad*, IV: 245, No. 2424, 278, No. 2473; V: 25–6, No. 2824, 52, No. 2859); Abū Dāʾūd, *Sunan*, in *ʿAwn al-maʿbūd*, XIII: 354–5 (= *Kitāb al-Adab*, 96: *Bāb mā jāʾa fī l-shiʿr*, Nos 4990, 4991); al-Masʿūdī, *Murūj al-dhahab*, II: 295.
69. Cf. al-Maydānī, *Majmaʿ al-amthāl*, I: 35, No. 1; Biesterfeldt, 'Weisheit als mot juste', pp. 370–1.
70. Cf. Ibn Qutayba, *ʿUyūn al-akhbār*, II: 167.
71. NM-A, pp. 215–17.
72. Ibn Farīghūn, *Jawāmiʿ al-ʿulūm*, p. 135; Rosenthal, *History of Muslim Historiography*, pp. 35–6, 539-40. Cf. Biesterfeldt, 'Ibn Farīġūn'; Meisami, 'Why Write History in Persian?' pp. 359–60.

73. NM-A, p. 218. The reference is to the previous chapter in *Naṣīḥat al-mulūk*; see above, pp. 90–1. Abū l-Layth al-Samarqandī discussed swimming, horsemanship and throwing (*Bustān al-ʿārifīn*, p. 237; *Tanbīh al-ghāfilīn*, pp. 369–71).
74. NM-A, pp. 218–19. Cf. Swain, *Economy, Family, and Society*, pp. 490–3.
75. See Volume I, pp. 217–18.
76. NM-A, pp. 218–19. Cf. Swain, *Economy, Family, and Society*, pp. 375, 396–400, 482–9.
77. Abū Rashīd, *Masāʾil*, p. 150, § 29; Horten, *Philosophie des abu Raschíd*, pp. 148–9. Cf. Swain, *Economy, Family, and Society*, pp. 432–3.
78. The term constitutes another example of *fārsī muʿarrab* (Arabicised Persian) (Ibn Manẓūr, *Lisān al-Lisān*, II: 31). On the term *čōvēgān* to designate the stick used in the game of polo, or the game itself, and its Arabicised form *ṣawlajān*, see Nyberg, *Manual of Pahlavi*, II: 56.
79. Nöldeke, 'Geschichte des Artachšîr i Pâpakân', pp. 39–40.
80. Al-Taghlibī, *Kitāb al-Tāj*, pp. 83–4.
81. Chehabi and Guttmann, 'Origin and Diffusion of Polo', esp. pp. 385–6. I am grateful to H. E. Chehabi for supplying me with a copy of this article.
82. Al-Thaʿālibī, *Yatīmat al-dahr*, IV: 85.
83. Al-Thaʿālibī, *Ādāb al-mulūk*, pp. 105–6.
84. On the views of later writers, see Vahman, 'Bāzī'.
85. Yāqūt, *Muʿjam al-udabāʾ*, I: 275. On polo, see also Rosenthal, *Gambling in Islam*, pp. 55–6. The case of chess is equally interesting; despite disapproval of the game in some circles, Abū Zayd al-Balkhī composed a treatise devoted to it (Ibn al-Nadīm, *al-Fihrist*, I: ii: 430), and Pseudo-Māwardī did not include it in his treatment of the controversial matters associated with kings.
86. Kaykāʾūs, *Qābūsnāmeh*, pp. 96–7 = *Mirror for Princes*, pp. 85–6.
87. Al-Ābī, *Nathr al-durr*, IV: 225.
88. A variant attributed to the Umayyad Caliph ʿAbd al-Malik appears in al-Māwardī, *Adab al-dunyā wa-l-dīn*, p. 41.
89. NM-A, p. 220; *Kalīla wa-Dimna*, ed. Cheikho, p. 45; *Āthār Ibn al-Muqaffaʿ*, pp. 68–9. See above, p. 62.
90. *Wajadnā fī baʿḍ kutub al-ʿajam*, a phrase that suggests that Pseudo-Māwardī encountered the work in an Arabic translation.
91. NM-A, pp. 219–21. The verse of Ibn al-Muʿtazz appears in Kratchovsky, 'Le Kitāb al-ādāb', p. 73, line 3 (variant); Zakeri, *Persian Wisdom in Arabic Garb*, II: 20, No. 12; Bray, 'Ibn al-Muʿtazz and Politics', pp. 120, 128.
92. Kaykāʾūs, *Qābūsnāmeh*, p. 132.

93. Nāẓim, 'Pand-nāmah' ('Book of Advice'), p. 614.
94. NM-A, pp. 221–3.
95. It is possible that the passage resumes the theological question of 'the intermediate stance', al-manzila bayn al-manzilatayn, or whether sinners retained their status as Muslims. The Muʿtazila agreed that acts of disobedience compromised faith, but disagreed over whether the fāsiq remained a muʾmin (al-Ashʿarī, Maqālāt, I: 216; Mānkdīm, Sharḥ al-uṣūl al-khamsa, p. 712); see above, pp. 78–9.
96. Abū l-Layth al-Samarqandī, Tanbīh al-ghāfilīn, pp. 97–102 (Bāb ṣilat al-raḥim), 99.
97. Abū l-Layth al-Samarqandī, Bustān al-ʿārifīn, p. 118 (fī l-muʿāmala maʿa ahl al-kufr).
98. NM-A, p. 225.
99. Mottahedeh, Loyalty and Leadership, pp. 84–9.
100. Treadwell, 'Account of the Murder'; Treadwell, 'Urban Militias', pp. 133–5 (on Aḥmad's murder); de la Vaissière, Samarcande et Samarra, pp. 59–88, esp. pp. 73, 75–7; cf. Beckwith, 'Early History of the Central Asian Guard Corps'; Frye, 'Notes on the History of Transoxiana', pp. 110–12. See Volume I, pp. 104–5. On the khadam's possible role as bodyguards, see below, p. 170.
101. Cf. al-Ashʿarī, Maqālāt, I: 126, 214–15; Mānkdīm, Sharḥ al-uṣūl al-khamsa, pp. 632–8; Wensinck-Gardet, 'Khaṭīʾa'.
102. Mānkdīm, Sharḥ al-uṣūl al-khamsa, p. 794.
103. Niẓām al-Mulk, Siyar al-mulūk, pp. 141–3 = pp. 103–4. On the Samanids' training of the ghilmān, see de la Vaissière, Samarcande et Samarra, pp. 262–5; Bosworth, Ghaznavids, p. 102; Nāẓim, 'Pand-nāmah', pp. 613, 623; Bosworth, 'Alleged Embassy', pp. 17–29.
104. Mānkdīm, Sharḥ al-uṣūl al-khamsa, pp. 707–8.
105. NM-A, p. 226.
106. fī amr... silāḥihim wa-kurāʿihim; cf. al-Khwārazmī, Mafātīḥ al-ʿulūm, p. 59 (al-kurāʿ hiya al-dawābb).
107. NM-A, p. 226. On poetic treatments of taxation, see Gruendler, 'Verse and Taxes'.
108. Ibn Ḥawqal, Ṣūrat al-arḍ, pp. 469–70; on the current amir, see Ṣūrat al-arḍ, p. 472. Al-Khwārazmī enumerates three categories of allowances (arzāq) in the Dīwān of Khurasan, namely: ḥisāb al-ʿishrīniyya (four aṭmāʿ per year); ḥisāb al-jund (that is, the dīwān, consisting of two ṭamāʿ per year); and ḥisāb al-murtaziqa (three aṭmāʿ per year) (p. 65). The murtaziqa correspond to the

awliyāʾ, the regularly paid troops, in the account of the Chinese embassy (Bosworth, 'Alleged Embassy', pp. 21, 27). On the payment of judges, as well as other officials, see further Rosenthal, 'Gifts and Bribes', pp. 140–3.

109. Al-Khwārazmī, *Mafātīḥ al-ʿulūm*, pp. 59–60, 62, 65. See further Bosworth, 'Secretary's Art', pp. 116–17, 133, 138–9, 144.
110. Nāẓim, '*Pand-nāmah*', pp. 617, 625.
111. Niẓām al-Mulk, *Siyar al-mulūk*, pp. 43, 177 = pp. 32, 128–9. Cf. Bosworth, 'Secretary's Art', p. 117.
112. NM-A, p. 226.
113. Niẓām al-Mulk, *Siyar al-mulūk*, pp. 190–1, 200–1. Cf. Marlow, *Hierarchy and Egalitarianism*, pp. 129–30.
114. Nāẓim, '*Pand-nāmah*', pp. 618, 626.
115. Cf. Paul, 'Khidma'; Volume I, pp. 102–13.
116. NM-A, pp. 226–7.
117. NM-A, p. 227; NM-Ḥ, p. 323.
118. NM-A, p. 108; Volume I, pp. 47–8. The mystic Dhū l-Nūn considered the equal treatment of the strong and the weak to be one of the three marks of the good exercise of power (al-Bayhaqī, *Ṣaḥīḥ al-jāmiʿ*, III: 80)
119. Al-Taghlibī, *Kitāb al-Tāj*, pp. 99–102 = pp. 125–7.
120. Possibly an echo of the Qurʾānic concept *fasād fī l-arḍ*, corruption in the earth, which appears frequently and in various forms.
121. NM-A, pp. 227–8.
122. These verses refer to the written record of each individual's deeds, good and bad, presented to each person at the Day of Judgement; those who receive the document in their right hands will enter Paradise, and those who receive it in their left hands will enter the Fire (see further Diem and Schöller, *The Living and the Dead*, I: 159–60). The translations in this section are from Ali, *Al-Qurʾān*, pp. 447, 254.
123. NM-A, p. 229; cited again at p. 332. See Rabb, *Doubt in Islamic Law*, pp. 38, 49, 323–32 and 330, where the ḥadīth appears in the form cited in *Naṣīḥat al-mulūk*, as transmitted through Abū Ḥanīfa and ʿAlī. For ʿAlī's deference to doubt, see pp. 53–4.
124. NM-A, pp. 227–9. The translations of these verses follow Ali, *Al-Qurʾān*, pp. 400, 266, 474, 421, 241.
125. Bayhaqī, *Tārīkh-i Bayhaqī*, pp. 106–8.
126. On the concept and applications of doubt, especially in relation to the statutory penalties and other forms of punishment, see Rabb, *Doubt in Islamic Law*.

On its earlier application in criminal justice, see pp. 56-9; and for the role of doubt in Ḥanafī jurisprudence, see pp. 185–203, 323–32.

127. NM-A, pp. 229–32. The ellipses mark quotations of a Qurʾānic verse, the case of ʿUmar b. al-Khaṭṭāb's son (see Rabb, *Doubt in Islamic Law*, pp. 108, n. 20, 241 and Appendix B), a quotation from Aristotle's advice to Alexander, and a passage from *Kalīla wa-Dimna.*
128. Rabb, *Doubt in Islamic Law*, pp. 99. 132. See also Volume I, p. 136.
129. NM-A, pp. 232–3.
130. *ʿAhd Ardashīr*, pp. 61–1, and see Volume I, p. 220.
131. Abū l-Layth al-Samarqandī, *Tanbīh al-ghāfilīn*, pp. 363–72, 369–71.
132. In this year, the Prophet, with a small number of Muslims from Medina, journeyed to Mecca in order to perform the pilgrimage. Quraysh sent a force to prevent their entry into the town, and the Prophet halted at al-Ḥudaybiya, on the edge of the sacred territory, in order to negotiate. The negotiations resulted in a ten-year treaty, which included the provision that the Prophet and his followers would be permitted to return for the pilgrimage in the following year. During this period at al-Ḥudaybiya, the Prophet called upon the Muslims who had accompanied him to pledge their support; this pledge is known as the Pledge of Good Pleasure.
133. Cited in al-Māwardī, *Adab al-dunyā wa-l-dīn*, p. 138.
134. NM-A, pp. 234–5.
135. Cf. Q. 25: 25, *wa-yawma tashaqqaqu l-samāʾu bi-l-ghamāmi wa-nuzzila l-malāʾikatu tanzīlan*, 'A day when the heaven with the clouds will be rent asunder and the angels will be sent down in a grand descent.'
136. Madelung, *Der Imam al-Qāsim*, pp. 41–2, 64.
137. Al-Baghdādī, *Uṣūl al-dīn*, p. 275; van Ess, 'Abuʾl-Qāsem Kaʿbī', p. 362; Madelung, *Der Imam al-Qāsim*, pp. 35, 50. On Muʿtazilite doctrines concerning *imāma* and *tafḍīl*, see Mānkdīm, *Sharḥ al-uṣūl al-khamsa*, pp. 749–67, esp. pp. 766–7; al-Baghdādī, *Uṣūl al-dīn*, pp. 293–4.
138. Ibn Māja, *Sunan*, IV: 403, No. 4009 (= *Kitāb al-Fitan*, *Bāb* 20: *al-amr bi-l-maʿrūf wa-l-nahy ʿan al-munkar*), related in *Naṣīḥat al-mulūk* on the author's authority.
139. Al-Tirmidhī, *al-Jāmiʿ al-Ṣaḥīḥ*, III: 210 (= *Kitāb al-Fitan*, 9: *Bāb mā jāʾa fī l-amr bi-l-maʿrūf wa-l-nahy ʿan al-munkar*, No. 2169).
140. NM-A, pp. 235–6.
141. See Volume I, p. 47.
142. On the verb *ghayyara*, see Cook, *Commanding Right*, pp. 33–5.

143. For versions of the ḥadīth, see Cook, *Commanding Right*, pp. 36–7 and n. 19 (for one example, see Ibn Māja, *Sunan*, IV: 400, No. 4004 = *Kitāb al-Fitan, Bāb al-amr bi-l-maᶜrūf wa-l-nahy ᶜan al-munkar*); on the Qurʾānic verse 5: 78–9, see Cook, *Commanding Right*, pp. 15–16, 26–7.
144. NM-A, pp. 236–7. The first of the two citations from Aristotle corresponds to Grignaschi, 'La "Siyâsatu-l-ᶜâmmiyya"', p. 124, Maróth, *Correspondence*, p. 40, and *Sirr al-asrār*, in Badawī, *al-Uṣūl al-yūnāniyya*, p. 76 (considerably modified); elsewhere Pseudo-Māwardī adduces it as transmitted from Plato (NM-A, p. 182), as it appears in al-Mubashshir, *Mukhtār al-ḥikam*, p. 129; Ibn Hindū, *al-Kalim al-rūḥāniyya*, p. 19; al-Shahrazūrī, *Nuzhat al-arwāḥ*, p. 76. The second citation from Aristotle corresponds to Grignaschi, 'La "Siyâsatu-l-ᶜâmmiyya"', p. 132; Maróth, *Correspondence*, p. 46, and Ibn Hindū, *al-Kalim al-rūḥāniyya*, p. 74. The verb *ankara*, which appears in the first example, is related to *munkar*, and appears as a variant of *ghayyara* in several of the relevant ḥadīths; see Cook, *Commanding Right*, pp. 34, 36 nn. 8, 16.
145. An allusion to the Qurʾānic verse enjoining kindness to elderly parents: 'Lower unto them the wing of humility out of compassion' (17: 24).
146. NM-A, p. 237.
147. NM-A, p. 237. The translation (Q. 9: 120–1) is Ali's, *Al-Qurʾān*, pp. 175–6.
148. NM-A, pp. 237–8. For the report concerning the delegation to Sulaymān, see Ibn Qutayba, *ᶜUyūn al-akhbār*, I: 106; for the citation from Aristotle, see NM-A, p. 297; Grignaschi, 'La "Siyâsatu-l-ᶜâmmiyya"', p. 98; Maróth, *Correspondence*, pp. 25–6.
149. Compare Mānkdīm, *Sharḥ al-uṣūl al-khamsa*, p. 638.
150. Compare ᶜAbd al-Jabbār, *al-Mughnī*, XII: 444–9, XIV: 306–10 (opposed to *ᶜiqāb* and *dhamm*), cf. 450–86; Mānkdīm, *Sharḥ al-uṣūl al-khamsa*, pp. 614–19.
151. Mānkdīm, *Sharḥ al-uṣūl al-khamsa*, p. 779.
152. ᶜAbd al-Jabbār, *al-Mughnī*, XII: 415–30 XIII: 3–199, esp. pp. 9–18; Mānkdīm, *Sharḥ al-uṣūl al-khamsa*, pp. 518–25; van Ess, *Erkenntnislehre*, pp. 333, 335. Cf. al-Ashᶜarī, *Maqālāt*, II: 414–16.
153. Pseudo-Māwardī's list bears some resemblance to al-ᶜĀmirī's later enumeration of six 'things' that the king, for the purpose of his security (*li-amn nafsihi*), should 'give' in order to ensure the sincerity of (the subjects') counsel and their 'love', and six 'things' that he should 'take' in return; Wakelnig, *Philosophy Reader*, pp. 348–51. On this MS, see also Cottrell, '*L'Anonyme d'Oxford*'.
154. NM-A, pp. 238–9.

155. NM-A, p. 239.
156. See NM-A, p. 245, above, p. 170 and below, pp. 192–3.
157. Following the emendation adopted in Bosworth, 'Secretary's Art', p. 142; Bosworth, *Ghaznavids*, p. 29; Frye, 'Sāmānids', p. 144 (the text reads *dīvān-i sharaf*).
158. Narshakhī, *Tārīkh-i Bukhārā*, p. 36. Cf. Frye, 'Sāmānids', p. 144.
159. Al-Khwārazmī, *Mafātīḥ al-ᶜulūm*, p. 53.
160. Narshakhī, *Tārīkh-i Bukhārā*, p. 110.
161. Narshakhī, *Tārīkh-i Bukhārā*, p. 130.
162. Narshakhī, *Tārīkh-i Bukhārā*, pp. 105–6.
163. Frye notes the use in Arabic of *ṣāḥib juyūsh* to correspond to the Persian *sipah-sālār* (Frye, 'Sāmānids', p. 143).
164. Paul, *Herrscher, Gemeinwesen, Vermittler*, p. 94. Cf. Havemann, *Riʾāsa und qaḍāʾ*, pp. 51–7.
165. Havemann, 'Naḳīb al-ashrāf'; Bulliet, *Patricians*, esp. pp. 234–40.
166. Cf. Niẓām al-Mulk, *Siyar al-mulūk*, pp. 181–6; Bosworth, *Ghaznavids*, p. 138.
167. Cf. Bosworth, 'Secretary's Art', p. 127; Silverstein, *Postal Systems*, pp. 114–15, 125–31.
168. Cf. Frye, 'Sāmānids', p. 144; Bosworth, *Ghaznavids*, p. 68.
169. Bosworth, *Ghaznavids*, pp. 138, 68–9.
170. As Wakelnig has pointed out, Pseudo-Māwardī's enumeration is similar to al-ᶜĀmirī's later list of seven categories among the ruler's *aᶜwān* essential for ensuring the best interests of his subjects and the proper arrangement of his kingdoms (*li-maṣāliḥ raᶜāyāhu wa-intiẓām mamālikihi*) (Wakelnig, *Philosophy Reader*, pp. 344–6, p. 132 n. 333).
171. The term *aṣāla* can indicate nobility of descent or firmness (of resolve or judgement); *rajul aṣīl* can connote *lahu aṣl* ('of noble lineage') or that he is *thābit al-raʾy ᶜāqil* ('firm in opinion and intelligent') (*Lisān al-Lisān*, I: 32). I am not sure which sense of the word Pseudo-Māwardī intends, although I suspect it is another case of Bray's 'aristocratic principle', since al-Thaᶜālibī and Niẓām al-Mulk, whose mirrors closely resemble Pseudo-Māwardī's in numerous respects, repeatedly use the terms *aṣl* and *aṣīl* in the sense of 'noble lineage' and 'well born', respectively (cf. Bray, 'Local Mirror', pp. 37–8).
172. NM-A, pp. 239–40.
173. NM-A, pp. 240–1. For a similar passage, see Miskawayh, *Jāvīdān khirad*, p. 74.

174. NM-A, pp. 241–2. On ʿAbdallāh b. Ṭāhir, see Volume I, pp. 21, 56, 178. This axiom appears in Ibn Qutayba, *ʿUyūn al-akhbār*, I: 13 (attributed to Jaʿfar b. Yaḥyā, the Barmakid). The phrasing echoes one of the scattered sayings of Ardashīr (ʿAbbās, *ʿAhd Ardashīr*, p. 101, No. 24).
175. See Volume I, p. 102 and n. 22.
176. For these stipulations regarding rates of *zakāt* due on various possessions, see Zysow, 'Zakāt', pp. 410–13. *ʿUshr* is not a Qurʾānic term, but is elaborated in Islamic law, and is sometimes considered a kind of *zakāt* (Sato, 'ʿUshr'; Bosworth, 'Secretary's Art', p. 130). Compare the detailed descriptions of later tenth-century Samanid taxes and imposts in al-Khwārazmī, *Mafātīḥ al-ʿulūm*, pp. 58–62; Bosworth, 'Secretary's Art', pp. 130–9.
177. Al-Jahshiyārī (d. 331/942), scholar, writer and chamberlain at the Abbasid court, also cites this passage as a quotation from Shāpūr's *ʿahd* (testament) to his son (*Kitāb al-Wuzarāʾ wa-l-kuttāb* ('Book of Viziers and Secretaries'), p. 6).
178. See Volume I, p. 102 and n. 22.
179. NM-A, pp. 242–4.
180. A reference to Q 18: 51, where God speaks in the first person (*wa-mā kuntu muttakhidha l-muḍillīna ʿaḍudan*, 'I would not take as helpers those who lead [men] astray', in Ali's translation (*Al-Qurʾān*, p. 255)).
181. NM-A, p. 244.
182. The unit of the *kūra* (pl. *kuwar*) also appears in al-Khwārazmī, *Mafātīḥ al-ʿulūm*, p. 60; Bosworth, 'Secretary's Art', p. 135.
183. Ibn al-Muqaffaʿ used the same phrase (*qad ʿaṣṣama Allāh amīr al-muʾminīn*) of his addressee in *Risāla fī l-ṣaḥāba* (Pellat, '*"Conseilleur" du calife*, p. 17).
184. NM-A, pp. 244–5.
185. Nāẓim, '*Pand-nāmah*', pp. 616, 625.
186. NM-A, pp. 245–6. The passage continues; see MS f. 56b, NM-A, pp. 245–6, NM-Ḥ, pp. 346–7.
187. Cf. Paul's study of a 'second phase' in practices related to taxation, when the central state largely abandoned involvement through, for example, periodic assessments, and the institution of the *iqṭāʿ* was 'introduced' (*Herrscher, Gemeinwesen, Vermittler*, pp. 66–92, esp. pp. 75, 86).
188. Ibn al-Zubayr, *al-Dhakhāʾir wa-l-tuḥaf*, p. 143; cf. Treadwell, 'Urban Militias', pp. 140–1, and n. 45.
189. Niẓām al-Mulk, *Siyar al-mulūk*, pp. 84, 85–96; Bosworth, *Ghaznavids*, p. 94.
190. NM-A, pp. 246–7, and n. 152; NM-Ḥ, p. 348 n. 848. The ḥadīth appears in Muslim, *Ṣaḥīḥ*, p. 806 = *Kitāb al-Imāra, Bāb idhā būyiʿa li-khalīfatayn*, No.

1853; al-Bayhaqī, *Ṣaḥīḥ al-jāmiᶜ*, III: 70. Al-Māwardī cites the same ḥadīth in *Adab al-dunyā wa-l-dīn*, where, after observing that the entire community (*al-jumhūr*) adopts the view that the establishment of two imams in the same time is not permitted according to the religious law (*lā yajūzu sharᶜan*), he supplies two variants: *ruwiya ᶜan al-nabī . . . annahu qāla: idhā būyiᶜa amīrāni fa-wallū aḥadahumā, wa-ruwiya fa-aqtilū al-akhīra minhumā* (*Adab al-dunyā wa-l-dīn*, p. 138).

191. NM-A, p. 247.

Chapter 5

1. NM–A, pp. 249–50. I have followed Ali in several of these translated verses (*Al-Qurʾān*, pp. 176, 442, 67, 236, 278, 62).
2. Similar ḥadīth appear in al-Bayhaqī, *Ṣaḥīḥ al-jāmiᶜ*, III: 72–3; al-Dārimī, *Sunan*, II: 107, No. 2515; al-Suyūṭī, *al-Jāmiᶜ al-ṣaghīr*, IV: 1607, Nos 8007, 8008.
3. NM-A, pp. 250–1. The first part of ᶜUmar's oration appears in Ibn Abī Dharr, *Kitāb al-Saᶜāda wa-l-isᶜād*, p. 244.
4. The phrase *mushāwir amīr* is a reference to the *shūrā*, the small consultative group that advised the early caliphs, in a continuation of Arabian practice.
5. A descendant of the celebrated Companion Ibn Masᶜūd, al-Qāsim was *qāḍī* of Kufa in 102–3/720–1; al-Ṭabarī, *Taʾrīkh*, VI: 618 (*sub anno* 102), 620 (*sub anno* 103) = XXIV: 165, 168; al-Dhahabī, *Siyar aᶜlām al-nubalāʾ*, V: 195–6.
6. NM-A, p. 251. Cf. Abū Yūsuf, *Kitāb al-Kharāj*, p. 261.
7. NM-A, pp. 251–2. See Maróth, *Correspondence*, p. 18; Miskawayh, *Jāvīdān khirad*, p. 224; al-Mubashshir, *Mukhtār al-ḥikam*, p. 190.
8. Abū Dāʾūd, *Sunan*, in *ᶜAwn al-maᶜbūd*, XIII: 236 (= *Bāb al-muʾākhāt* ('Chapter on Fraternity'), No. 4892); al-Tirmidhī, *al-Jāmiᶜ al-Ṣaḥīḥ*, II: 393-4 (= *Kitāb al-Ḥudūd*, 3: *Mā jāʾa fī l-satr ᶜalā l-muslim*, No. 1426 (*al-muslim akhū l-muslim . . .*)); III: 76 (= *Bāb al-Birr wa-l-ṣila*, 18: *Bāb mā jāʾa fī shafaqat al-muslim ᶜalā l-muslim* ('Chapter on the Transmitted Materials Related to Muslims' Kindness to One Another'), No. 1927). Cf. Abū Dāʾūd, *Sunan*, in *ᶜAwn al-maᶜbūd*, XIII: 260 (= *Bāb fī l-naṣīḥa wa-l-ḥiyāṭa* ('Chapter on Counsel and Protection'), No. 4897).
9. Ibn Māja, *Sunan*, IV: 355–6 (= *Kitāb al-Fitan*, 1: *al-Kaff ᶜamman qāla lā ilāha illā Allāh*, Nos 3927, 3928).
10. Al-Tirmidhī, *al-Jāmiᶜ al-Ṣaḥīḥ*, III: 76 (= *Kitāb al-Birr wa-l-ṣila*, 18: *Bāb mā jāʾa fī shafaqat al-muslim ᶜalā l-muslim*, No. 1928).

11. NM-A, p. 252.
12. In later usage the scope of the term *ᶜāmil* (pl. *ᶜummāl*) became more specialised, and referred almost exclusively to the ruler's financial agents.
13. Cf. Havemann, *Riᵓāsa und qaḍāᵓ*, pp. 38–45.
14. The passage is among the several examples of this Indic-associated testament that appear in other Arabic writings in pseudo-Aristotelian guise; see above, pp. 65–8, and Marlow, 'Kings and Sages', p. 51.
15. Al-Tirmidhī, *al-Jāmiᶜ al-Ṣaḥīḥ*, II: 566 (= *Kitāb al-Jihād*, 27: *Bāb mā jāᵓa fī l-imām*, No. 1705); al-Bayhaqī, *Ṣaḥīḥ al-jāmiᶜ*, II: 71.
16. Pseudo-Māwardī's invocation of this grammatical principle is reminiscent of al-Kindī's conception of 'annexation' (*iḍāfa*), whereby two things might be extrinsically related; see Druart, 'Al-Kindi's Ethics', p. 341. See further the discussion in al-Tawḥīdī, *al-Muqābasāt*, pp. 231–2.
17. NM-A, pp. 252–3; compare Miskawayh, *Jāvīdān khirad*, p. 220, and Pseudo-Māwardī's citation elsewhere from the testament of an Indian king, NM-A, p. 65; Marlow, 'Kings and Sages', p. 44.
18. NM-A, p. 253. The quotation from the ancient king appears in *Waṣiyyat Arisṭāṭālīs lil-Iskandar*; Maróth, *Correspondence*, pp. 13–14; Miskawayh, *Jāvīdān khirad*, p. 220; Marlow, 'Kings and Sages', p. 52.
19. NM-A, pp. 253–4; see Volume I, pp. 130–1.
20. NM-A, pp. 254–5. For the ḥadīth, see al-Nasāᵓī, *Sunan*, VII: 159-60 (= *Kitāb al-Bayᶜa*, [*Bāb*] *Jazāᵓ man umira bi-maᶜṣiya fa-aṭāᶜa*); Ibn Māja, *Sunan*, III: 396–7 (= *Kitāb al-Jihād*, *Bāb* 40: *Lā ṭāᶜata fī maᶜṣiyat Allāh*, Nos 2863–5); cf. Abou El Fadl, *Rebellion and Violence*, p. 121. Cf. Abū l-Layth al-Samarqandī, *Bustān al-ᶜārifīn*, pp. 106–7.
21. On *wafāᵓ*, see Volume I, pp. 105–6; Volume II, pp. 119, 120; on *amāna*, see Volume II, p. 141.
22. *NM-A*, p. 255. The final phrase is a Qurᵓānic echo; see Q 22: 11, 39: 15 (*dhālika huwa al-khusrānu l-mubīn*, 'This is indeed a palpable loss').
23. See Marlow, 'Abū Zayd al-Balkhī'.
24. NM-A, pp. 66–7.
25. NM-A, p. 205; see above, p. 141.
26. The extract attributed to Abū Zayd al-Balkhī's *Kitāb al-Siyāsa* appears in al-Tawḥīdī, *al-Baṣāᵓir wa-l-dhakhāᵓir*, IX: 146–7 = Rosenthal, 'Abū Zayd al-Balkhī on Politics', pp. 289–90. Al-ᶜĀmirī produced a description that appears to draw heavily on his teacher's formulation (Wakelnig, 'Philosophical Fragments', pp. 234–5).

27. A staple of Persian mirrors for princes; see, for example, Ghazālī, *Naṣīḥat al-mulūk*, p. 15 = p. 14; *al-Tibr al-masbūk*, p. 96; cf. Lambton, 'Justice in the Medieval Persian Theory', p. 105.
28. NM-A, pp. 255–6. A number of ḥadīth express the same sentiment; see al-Bayhaqī, *Ṣaḥīḥ al-jāmiᶜ*, III: 70–1.
29. NM-A, p. 256. Maróth, *Correspondence*, p. 13; Miskawayh, *Jāvīdān khirad*, p. 220; al-Mubashshir, *Mukhtār al-ḥikam*, p. 187; Marlow, 'Kings and Sages', p. 53.
30. NM-A, p. 46; cf. above, p. 13.
31. Paul, '*Khidma*'; cf. Paul, *Herrscher, Gemeinwesen, Vermittler*, pp. 223–31.
32. Al-Nasafī, *al-Qand fī dhikr ᶜulamāᵓ Samarqand*, pp. 437–9, No. 756, and see Volume I, pp. 186–7. Abū Yaᶜlā appears in the *isnād* of the ḥadīth, 'Almighty God does not accept any speech without action, nor any speech or action without (right) intention, not any speech, action or intention without following the *sunna*' (p. 439). On *duᶜā-yi bad*, the Persian term for negative public prayer, see Paul, *Herrscher, Gemeinwesen, Vermittler*, p. 228.
33. See Volume I, pp. 141–2.
34. NM-A, pp. 256–7.
35. Niẓām al-Mulk, *Siyar al-mulūk*, p. 43 = p. 32.
36. Cf. Mottahedeh, *Loyalty and Leadership*, p. 185.
37. Ibn Abī Dharr, *Kitāb al-Saᶜāda wa-l-isᶜād*, p. 207.
38. NM-A, p. 257.
39. A disapproved practice; see al-Tirmidhī, *al-Jāmiᶜ al-Ṣaḥīḥ*, II: 110–11 (= *Kitāb al-Janāᵓiz*, 12: *Bāb mā jāᵓa fī karāhiyat al-naᶜy* ('Chapter on the Disapproved Nature of Excessive Lamentation'), Nos 984–6).
40. NM-A, pp. 257–8.
41. The term *waẓīfa* denoted a further, fixed payment, in addition to the *kharāj* or land-tax; *ḍarība* also denoted a further tax, in addition to the sanctioned taxes of *zakāt* or *ᶜushr*, *jizya* and *kharāj* (al-Khwārazmī, *Mafātīḥ al-ᶜulūm*, pp. 62, 59; Bosworth, 'Secretary's Art', pp. 132, 139).
42. NM-A, p. 258. Pseudo-Māwardī displays a detailed knowledge of the fiscal practices in the Samanid domains; also noted in al-Sayyid, 'al-Māwardī', p. 94.
43. See above, p. 100.
44. Ibn Ḥawqal, *Ṣūrat al-arḍ*, p. 470. Cf. al-Khwārazmī, *Mafātīḥ al-ᶜulūm*, pp. 54, 58, 60–1; Bosworth, 'Secretary's Art', pp. 121–2, 128, 135–6.
45. NM-A, pp. 258–9. Al-Thaᶜālibī narrates the same anecdote in *Ādāb al-mulūk*, p. 34 (I have adopted Bray's translation of the last line; see Bray, 'Local Mirror', p. 42). Elsewhere, the incident and the following verses (unattributed) appear

in association with ᶜUmar rather than Hārūn (al-Hamadhānī, *Takmilat Taʾrīkh al-Ṭabarī* ('Completion of al-Ṭabarī's "History"'), XI: 189; this work is one of several continuations of al-Ṭabarī's 'History').

46. NM-A, pp. 259–60.
47. A Qurʾānic echo: God is *walī alladhīna āmanū* (2: 257), 'the friend of those who believe'.
48. NM-A, pp. 260–1.
49. See Volume I, p. 178.
50. See Volume I, pp. 32–3 (Isḥāq); 112–3 (Aḥmad b. Sahl); 309 n. 116 (Saᶜīd b. Ibrāhīm al-Nasafī).
51. NM-A, p. 261.
52. NM-A, pp. 261–2.
53. NM-A, p. 262. Al-Ābī, *Nathr al-durr*, I: 189. Miskawayh records a similar utterance with a generic attribution to 'a philosopher' (*baᶜḍ al-ḥukamāʾ*): *man izdāda fī l-ᶜilm rushdan fa-lam yazdad fī l-dunyā zuhdan izdāda min Allāhi buᶜdan* ('he who increases in knowledge and in right guidance but does not increase in his austerity in the world, increases in his distance from God', *Jāvīdān khirad*, p. 167).
54. NM-A, pp. 262–3. Grignaschi, 'La "Siyâsatu-l-ᶜâmmiyya"' pp. 115–16, Maróth, *Correspondence*, p. 36.
55. This epistolary and textual formula, sometimes referred to as *baᶜdiyya*, customarily separates doxological statements, such as expressions of praise for God and His Prophet and prayers on behalf of the Prophet and his family, from the body of the preface. Accordingly it marks the beginning of the substance of oral and written communications in public discourse in Arabic. See Gacek, *Arabic Manuscript Tradition*, p. 14; Freimark, *Das Vorwort*, pp. 24–6, 72; Montgomery, *Al-Jāḥiẓ*, p. 194.
56. NM-A, pp. 263–4. Divergent versions appear in Ibn Qutayba, *ᶜUyūn al-akhbār*, I: 66; al-Jāḥiẓ, *al-Bayān wa-l-tabyīn*, II: 48–50; al-Māwardī, *al-Aḥkām al-sulṭāniyya*, pp. 71–2 = pp. 80–1.
57. NM-A, p. 264. Abū Yūsuf, *Kitāb al-Kharāj*, pp. 264–5 (addressed to Abū ᶜUbayda b. al-Jarrāḥ); al-Jāḥiẓ, *Kitāb al-Ḥijāb*, in *Rasāʾil*, II: 31 (ᶜUmar, writing to Muᶜāwiya as his governor in Syria).
58. See below, pp. 222–6.
59. NM-A, pp. 264–5.
60. See Volume I, pp. 102–7.
61. See Volume I, pp. 107–13.

62. Also alluded to above, p. 178.
63. NM-A, pp. 265–6.
64. Al-Maydānī, *Majma*ᶜ *al-amthāl*, II: 146, No. 2938; Abu ᶜUbayd al-Qāsim b. Sallām, *al-Amthāl*, in al-Bakrī, *Faṣl al-maqāl*, p. 45; al-Masᶜūdī, *Murūj al-dhahab*, II: 296; Zakeri, *Persian Wisdom in Arabic Garb*, II: 37 (No. 48). For further references see Marlow, *Hierarchy and Egalitarianism*, p. 27 and n. 78.
65. Ibn Māja, *Sunan*, IV: 240–1, No. 3712 (= *Kitāb al-Adab, Bāb idhā atākum karīmu qawmin fa-akrimūhu*); al-Ābī, *Nathr al-durr*, I: 163. For further references see Marlow, *Hierarchy and Egalitarianism*, p. 27 and n. 72.
66. The Prophet designated Abū Sufyān's house a safe haven when the Muslim forces entered Mecca in 8/629.
67. The proverb, cited by the Prophet to Abū Sufyān, appears in the collections of al-Maydānī, *Majma*ᶜ *al-amthāl* (II: 162, No. 3010) and Abū ᶜUbayd, *al-Amthāl*, in al-Bakrī, *Faṣl al-maqāl*, p. 10; al-Ābī, *Nathr al-durr*, I: 205.
68. The Qurʾānic category of *al-muʾallafa qulūbuhum* (9: 60), a term applied to former opponents of the Prophet who became reconciled by the Prophet's distribution of spoils after the Battle of Ḥunayn (8/630), in which the Muslims, victorious against the confederation of Hawāzin, had obtained very large quantities of booty. The beneficiaries included Abū Sufyān and his sons, Muᶜāwiya and Yazīd.
69. NM-A, pp. 266–7.
70. Keshk, 'Abū Sufyān'.
71. Al-Maydānī and Abū ᶜUbayd explain the proverb's coinage with reference to three hunters and their quarries. They also report that the Prophet used it in his reconciliation with Abū Sufyān, and that it entered general usage to connote a person who has been favoured over his peers (see above, n. 67).
72. NM-A, p. 267. Al-Ṭabarī, *Taʾrīkh*, IV: 203 = XIV: 106.
73. NM-A, p. 267. Cf. *ᶜAhd Ardashīr*, p. 72.
74. NM-A, p. 268. Grignaschi, 'La "Siyâsatu-l-ᶜâmmiyya"', p. 119; Maróth, *Correspondence*, p. 38; Ibn Hindū, *al-Kalim al-rūḥāniyya*, p. 73.
75. NM-A, p. 268. Compare al-Mubashshir, *Mukhtār al-ḥikam*, p. 150, where the saying appears among Plato's *manshūrāt* (proclamations), and the three social groups appear linked with the faculties of the soul. Pseudo-Māwardī follows the saying with verses on the same subject 'by one of the modern poets'.
76. NM-A, p. 269. See Grignaschi, 'La "Siyâsatu-l-ᶜâmmiyya"', p. 117; Maróth, *Correspondence*, p. 36; al-Mubashshir, *Mukhtār al-ḥikam*, p. 193.
77. NM-A, p. 269.

78. NM-A, pp. 269–70. For both individuals, the first an eminent Companion and the second a celebrated *tābi*ᶜ, member of the generation that followed the Prophet's Companions, see al-Ṭabarī, *Ta*ᵓ*rīkh, sub anno* 21 = XIV: 15–16, and nn. 84 and 87. Ibn Khallikān reports two incidents in which ᶜAlī came before Shurayḥ (*Wafayāt al-a*ᶜ*yān*, II: 460–3 (No. 290), 462).
79. Al-Tirmidhī, *al-Jāmi*ᶜ *al-ṣaḥīḥ*, III: 126 (= *Kitāb al-Birr wa-l-ṣila*, 83: *Bāb mā jā*ᵓ*a fī l-ẓulm*, No. 2030); al-Bayhaqī, *Ṣaḥīḥ al-jāmi*ᶜ, III: 82–3; al-Dārimī, *Sunan*, II: 107, No. 2516; al-Suyūṭī, *al-Jāmi*ᶜ *al-ṣaghīr*, I: 41, Nos 135, 136. These versions of the ḥadīth read *ẓulm* instead of *maẓālim*; like Aḥmad, I have followed the reading in the MS, f. 63a.
80. NM-A, p. 270; Maróth, *Correspondence*, p. 15; Miskawayh, *Jāvīdān khirad*, p. 222; Marlow, 'Kings and Sages', p. 48; Zakeri, *Persian Wisdom in Arabic Garb*, II: 784–5, No. 1718.
81. See also above, pp. 48, 58.
82. Cf. al-Taghlibī, *Kitāb al-Tāj*, p. 160.
83. NM-A, pp. 271–2. Cf. al-Taghlibī, *Kitāb al-Tāj*, pp. 159–63 = Pellat, *Le livre de la couronne*, pp. 179–82.
84. He acquired this soubriquet in the Sasanian sources, from which the term was transferred into Arabic as *al-athīm*; Yazdagird's reputation appears to have derived chiefly from the favour that he extended to religious minorities and his execution of members of the nobility (Daryaee, *Sasanian Persia*, pp. 21–2).
85. NM-A, pp. 272–3. The entire sequence appears in similar form in Niẓām al-Mulk, *Siyar al-mulūk*, pp. 57–8 = pp. 42–4, and Ghazālī, *Naṣīḥat al-mulūk*, pp. 167–70 = pp. 102–3.
86. NM-A, p. 273. Grignaschi, 'La "Siyâsatu-l-ᶜâmmiyya"', pp. 107, 118; Maróth, *Correspondence*, pp. 30, 37; cf. *Sirr al-asrār*, in Badawī, *al-Uṣūl al-yūnāniyya*, p. 78.
87. NM-A, pp. 273–4. Cf. al-Masᶜūdī, *Murūj al-dhahab*, I: 291.
88. On Yaḥyā b. Aktham, see Ibn Khallikān, *Wafayāt al-a*ᶜ*yān*, VI: 147–62 (No. 793); Sourdel, *Le vizirat* ᶜ*abbāside*, pp. 238–9; Zakeri, *Persian Wisdom in Arabic Garb*, I: 12–13.
89. NM-A, pp. 274-6. A briefer and slightly different version of this story appears in al-Māwardī, *al-Aḥkām al-sulṭāniyya*, 94-5 = 95–6. On the functions and effects of poetic utterances in Arabic *akhbār*, see Leder, 'Prosa-Dichtung', p. 8; Gruendler, 'Verse and Taxes', p. 88.
90. The *topos* appears in numerous Persian sources; see, for example, Ghazālī, *Naṣīḥat al-mulūk*, pp. 117–18 = pp. 66–7; the celebrated story of Sanjar and

the elderly woman provides a notable, and much illustrated, example (Grabar, *Mostly Miniatures*, figs 62, 63).

91. NM-A, p. 276.
92. The ellipses mark Quʾranic texts (18: 49, 50: 18).
93. This section was discussed in Volume I, p. 56.
94. NM-A, p. 278. Cf. al-Taghlibī, *Kitāb al-Tāj*, pp. 167–8 (*fī qaṣabat dār mamlakatihi*) = p. 185.
95. NM-A, p. 278. Cf. Ibn Qutayba, *ʿUyūn al-akhbār*, I: 13, where Ibn Qutayba introduces the statement with the phrase *dhakara aʿrābī amīran*, without reference to a source.
96. NM-A, pp. 278–9.
97. See Volume I, p. 198. Pseudo-Māwardī cites the verses of Maḥmūd al-Warrāq (pp. 280–1), also adduced in al-Jāḥiẓ (*Kitāb al-Ḥijāb*, in *Rasāʾil*, II: 36), and Ibn Qutayba, *ʿUyūn al-akhbār*, I: 84.
98. NM-A, p. 281.
99. NM-A, p. 282. Cf. Marlow, 'Kings and Sages', appendix II.
100. Cf. *ʿAhd Ardashīr*, p. 56, and see above, p. 111.
101. NM-A, pp. 282–3.
102. NM-A, pp. 284–5.
103. See Volume I, pp. 218–19.
104. NM-A, pp. 285–6. Pseudo-Māwardī refers to his ninth chapter, which treats the management of enemies.
105. Al-Iṣṭakhrī, *al-Mamālik wa-l-masālik*, p. 144.
106. Gardīzī, *Zayn al-akhbār*, pp. 330–6.
107. Ibn al-Athīr, *al-Kāmil*, VIII: 78–9.
108. Bosworth, 'The Banū Ilyās', p. 110.
109. NM-A, pp. 286–7. For a somewhat similar passage ascribed to *ḥakīm ākhar fārsī* ('another wise Persian philosopher'), see Miskawayh, *Jāvīdān khirad*, p. 72; the proverb appears in the same text, p. 205.
110. See Volume I, pp. 110–11.
111. See Gardīzī, *Zayn al-akhbār*, pp. 335–6. Cf. Rabb, *Doubt in Islamic Law*, pp. 74–81.
112. Several further Qurʾānic quotations follow (3: 119; 2: 14–15; 9: 42; 59: 12; 33: 19).
113. NM-A, pp. 288–9. Cf. al-Ṭabarī, *Taʾrīkh*, VII: 369, *sub anno* 129 (lines 1, 2 and 5 only, with variants) = XXVII: 83 (I have consulted this translation for the verses that appear in al-Ṭabarī's version); *ʿUyūn al-akhbār*, 1: 128; al-Jāḥiẓ,

al-Bayān wa-l-tabyīn, I: 158–9. In most versions, the speaker is identified as Naṣr b. Sayyār, the Umayyad governor of Khurasan.

114. NM-A, p. 289.
115. NM-A, p. 290. Cf. *ᶜUyūn al-akhbār*, I: 9 (ascribed to ᶜUmar b. al-Khaṭṭāb); Miskawayh, *Jāvīdān khirad*, p. 64.
116. NM-A, pp. 290–1.
117. The context for this verse is that after the Battle of Uḥud, in which the Muslims experienced a defeat, the community was divided; the verse states that the resolution of these tensions was due to God's mercy, and God commanded the Prophet to pardon, forgive and consult (al-Baghdādī, 'Consultation', p. 409).
118. NM-A, p. 291.
119. See Volume I, Chapter 7, pp. 214–24.
120. NM-A, pp. 291–2.
121. NM-A, p. 292.

Conclusion

1. Al-Muqaddasī, *Aḥsan al-taqāsīm*, p. 4; Yāqūt, *Muᶜjam al-udabāʾ*, I: 152; al-Ṣafadī, *al-Wāfī bi-l-wafayāt*, VI: 413.
2. Cf. Yavari, 'Mirrors for Princes or Hall of Mirrors?' (with particular attention to the case of Niẓām al-Mulk, who despite his power and wealth was eventually executed on the command of the Seljuk Sultan Malikshāh).
3. The terms are Ferster's in *Fictions of Advice*, p. 1.
4. Cf. Davis, *Epic and Sedition*, pp. 25–6.
5. van Ess, 'Abū Esḥāq Naẓẓām'; Cooperson, 'Al-Jāḥeẓ' (with reference to al-Jāḥiẓ, *al-Bayān wa-l-tabyīn*, I: 115–17); van Ess, 'Abū'l-Hoḏayl ᶜAllāf'. The last account appears in al-Tawḥīdī, *al-Baṣāʾir wa-l-dhakhāʾir*, VI: 123.
6. Ibn al-Jawzī, *al-Miṣbāḥ al-muḍīʾ*, pp. 160, 180, 197 and passim; see further Almagor, 'The Pious Man and the Ruler', pp. 180–1.
7. See Volume I, pp. 59–60.
8. Cf. Ferster, *Fictions of Advice*, pp. 2–3, 40.

Bibliography

ᶜAbd al-Jabbār, al-Qāḍī al-Hamadhānī, *al-Mughnī fī abwāb al-tawḥīd wa-l-ᶜadl*, ed. Muṣṭafā al-Saqqā and Ibrāhīm Madkūr (Cairo: al-Dār al-Miṣriyya lil-Taᵓlīf wa-l-Tarjama, 1960–5).

ᶜAbd al-Jabbār, al-Qāḍī al-Hamadhānī, *Tathbīt dalāᵓil al-nubuwwa*, ed. ᶜAbd al-Karīm ᶜUthmān (Beirut: Dār al-ᶜArabiyya, 1966).

Abdul Haq, 'Historical Poems in the Diwan of Abū Tammām', *Islamic Culture* 14 (1940): 17–29.

Al-Ābī, Manṣūr b. al-Ḥusayn, *Nathr al-durr* (Cairo: al-Hayᵓa al-Miṣriyya al-ᶜĀmma lil-Kitāb, 1980).

Abou El Fadl, Khaled, *Rebellion and Violence in Islamic Law* (Cambridge: Cambridge University Press, 2001).

Abū l-ᶜAtāhiya, *Abū l-ᶜAtāhiya: ashᶜāruhu wa-akhbāruhu*, ed. Shukrī Fayṣal (= *Abul Atahiya, sa vie et ses poèmes*) (Damascus: Presses de l'Université de Damas, 1965).

Abū Dāᵓūd, *Sunan*, in *ᶜAwn al-maᶜbūd: Sharḥ Sunan Abī Dāᵓūd maᶜa sharḥ Ibn Qayyim al-Jawziyya*, ed. ᶜAbd al-Raḥmān Muḥammad ᶜUthmān (Beirut: Dār al-Fikr, 1979).

Abū Ḥanīfa, *al-ᶜĀlim wa-l-mutaᶜallim riwāyat Abī Muqātil ᶜan Abī Ḥanīfa*, ed. Muḥammad Zāhid al-Kawtharī (Cairo: Maṭbaᶜat al-Anwār, 1949).

Abū Ḥanīfa, *al-ᶜĀlim wa-l-mutaᶜallim*, eds Muḥammad Rawwās Qalᶜajī and ᶜAbd al-Wahhāb al-Hindī al-Nadawī (Aleppo: Maktabat al-Hudā, 1972).

Abū Ḥanīfa, *Waṣiyyat al-Imām Abī l-Ḥanīfa al-Nuᶜmān*, ed. Abū Muᶜādh Muḥammad b. ᶜAbd al-Ḥayy ᶜUwayna (Beirut: Dār Ibn Ḥazm, 1997).

Abū l-Maᶜālī Muḥammad b. al-Ḥusaynī [b. al-Ḥusayn] al-ᶜAlawī, *Bayān al-adyān*, ed. Hāshim Rażī (Tehran, 1964).

Abū Nuᶜaym al-Iṣfahānī, Aḥmad b. ᶜAbdallāh, *Ḥilyat al-awliyāᵓ wa-ṭabaqāt al-aṣfiyāᵓ* (Beirut: Dār al-Kutub al-ᶜIlmiyya, 1967).

Abū Nuwās, *Dīwān Abī Nuwās, al-Ḥasan b. Hāniᵓ*, ed. Aḥmad ᶜAbd al-Majīd al-Ghazzālī (Beirut: Dār al-Kitāb al-ᶜArabī, c. 1966).

Abū Rashīd al-Nīsābūrī, *al-Masāᵓil fī l-khilāf bayn al-Baṣriyyīn wa-l-Baghdādiyyin*, eds Maᶜn Ziyāda and Riḍwān al-Sayyid (Beirut: Maᶜhad al-Inmāᵓ al-ᶜArabī, 1979).

Abū ᶜUbayd al-Qāsim b. Sallām, see al-Bakrī, Abū ᶜUbayd.

Abū Yūsuf, *Kitāb al-Kharāj*, ed. Iḥsān ᶜAbbās (Beirut: Dār al-Shurūq, 1975).

Adab al-mulūk fī bayān ḥaqāᵓiq al-taṣawwuf, ed. Bernd Radtke (Beirut: Orient-Institut der Deutschen Morgenländischen Gesellschaft, 1991).

Adamson, Peter, 'Before Essence and Existence: al-Kindī's Conception of Being', *Journal of the History of Philosophy* XL (2002): 297–312.

Adamson, Peter, 'A Note on Freedom in the Circle of al-Kindī', in James Montgomery (ed.), *ᶜAbbasid Studies: Occasional Papers of the School of ᶜAbbasid Studies, Cambridge, 6–10 July 2002* (Leuven: Peeters, 2002), pp. 199–207.

Adamson, Peter, 'Al-Kindī and the Muᶜtazila: Divine Attributes, Creation and Freedom', *Arabic Sciences and Philosophy: A Historical Journal* XIII (2003): 45–77.

Adamson, Peter, 'On Knowledge of Particulars', *Proceedings of the Aristotelian Society*, NS, 105 (2005): 257–78.

Adamson, Peter, *Al-Kindī* (Oxford: Oxford University Press, 2007).

Adamson, Peter, 'The Kindian Tradition: The Structure of Philosophy in Arabic Neoplatonism', in Cristina D'Ancona (ed.), *The Libraries of the Neoplatonists* (Leiden: Brill, 2007), pp. 351–70.

ᶜAdī b. Zayd al-ᶜIbādī, *Dīwān*, ed. Muḥammad Jabbār al-Muᶜaybid (Baghdad: Dār al-Jumhuriyya lil-Nashr wa-l-Ṭabᶜ, 1965).

Afsaruddin, Asma, '*Maslahah* as a Political Concept', in Mehrzad Boroujerdi (ed.), *Mirror for the Muslim Prince: Islam and the Theory of Statecraft* (Syracuse, NY: Syracuse University Press, 2013), pp. 16–44.

ᶜAhd Ardashīr, ed. Iḥsān ᶜAbbās (Beirut: Dār Ṣādir, 1967).

Aḥmad, Fuᵓād ᶜAbd al-Munᶜim, *al-Tuḥfa al-mulūkiyya fī l-ādāb al-siyāsiyya al-mansūba lil-Imām Abī l-Ḥasan al-Māwardī* (Alexandria: Muᵓassasat Shabāb al-Jāmiᶜa, 1977).

Aḥmad, Fuᵓād ᶜAbd al-Munᶜim, 'Muqaddimat al-dirāsa wa-l-taḥqīq', in al-Māwardī (attrib.), *Kitāb Durar al-sulūk fī siyāsat al-mulūk*, ed. Fuᵓād ᶜAbd al-Munᶜim Aḥmad (Riyadh: Dār al-Waṭan lil-Nashr, 1997), pp. 7–52.

Aḥmad, Fuᵓād ᶜAbd al-Munᶜim, *Abū l-Ḥasan al-Māwardī wa-kitāb Naṣīḥat al-mulūk* (Alexandria: Muᵓassasat Shabāb al-Jāmiᶜa, n.d.).

Aḥmad, Fu'ād ᶜAbd al-Munᶜim, 'Muqaddimat al-taḥqīq wa-l-dirāsa', in NM-A, pp. 5–33.

Aḥmad, Fu'ād ᶜAbd al-Munᶜim and Muḥammad Sulaymān Dā'ūd, 'Muqaddima', in *Qawānīn al-wizāra lil-Imām Abī l-Ḥasan al-Māwardī* (Alexandria: Mu'assasat Shabāb al-Jāmiᶜa, 1991), pp. 5–38.

Aigle, Denise, 'La conception du pouvoir dans l'Islam: miroirs des princes persans et théorie sunnite (XIe–XIVe siècles)', *Perspectives médiévales* 31 (2007): 17–44.

Akasoy, Anna, *Die erste Philosophie: Arabisch–Deutsch* (Freiburg: Herder, 2011).

Al-Azmeh, Aziz, *Muslim Kingship: Power and the Sacred in Muslim, Christian, and Pagan Polities* (London: Tauris, 1997).

Ali, Ahmad, *Al-Qur'ān: A Contemporary Translation* (Princeton, NJ: Princeton University Press, 1993).

Ali, Mohammad Abd, 'Abū Shakūr Balkhī', trans. Daryoush Mohammad Poor, *Encyclopaedia Islamica*, vol. II (Leiden: Brill, 2009), pp. 562–3.

Ali, Samer M., *Arabic Literary Salons in the Islamic Middle Ages: Poetry, Public Performance, and the Presentation of the Past* (Notre Dame, IN: University of Notre Dame Press, 2010).

Almagor, Ella, 'The Pious Man and the Ruler: A Literary Form in the Service of Government', *Jerusalem Studies in Arabic & Islam* 33 (2007): 179–92.

Al-Āmidī, Sayf al-Dīn, *Abkār al-afkār fī uṣūl al-dīn*, ed. Aḥmad Muḥammad al-Mahdī (Cairo: Dār al-Kutub wa-l-Wathā'iq al-Qawmiyya, 2002).

Al-ᶜĀmirī, *Kitāb al-Iᶜlām bi-manāqib al-Islām*, ed. Aḥmad ᶜAbd al-Ḥamīd Ghurāb (Cairo: Dār al-Kitāb al-ᶜArabī lil-Ṭibāᶜa wa-l-Nashr, 1967).

Amitai, Reuven, 'Towards a Pre-History of the Islamization of the Turks: A Re-reading of Ibn Faḍlān's *Riḥla*', in Étienne de la Vaissière (ed.), *Islamisation de l'Asie Centrale: processus locaux d'acculturation du VIIe au XIe siècle* (Paris: Association pour l'avancement des études iraniennes = *Studia Iranica*, Cahier 39, 2008), pp. 277–96.

Ansari, Hassan, see Anṣārī, Ḥasan.

Anṣārī, Ḥasan, 'Yek andīsheh-nāmeh-yi siyāsī-yi arzeshmand-i muᶜtazilī az Khurāsān dawrān-i Sāmānīyān', *Bar-rasī-hā-yi tārīkhī*, available at: http://ansari.kateban.com/entryprint1951.html.

Arjomand, Said Amir, 'ᶜAbd Allah Ibn al-Muqaffaᶜ and the ᶜAbbasid Revolution', *Iranian Studies* 27 (1994): 9–36.

Arjomand, Said Amir, 'Perso-Indian Statecraft, Greek Political Science and the Muslim Idea of Government', *International Sociology* 16 (2001): 455–73.

Arjomand, Said Amir, 'Medieval Persianate Political Ethic', *Studies on Persianate Societies* 1 (2003): 3–28.

Arjomand, Said Amir, 'The Salience of Political Ethic in the Spread of Persianate Islam', *Journal of Persianate Studies* 1 (2008): 5–29.

Arjomand, Said Amir, 'Evolution of the Persianate Polity and its Transmission to India', *Journal of Persianate Studies* 2 (2009): 116–20.

Arkoun, Mohammed, 'La conquête du bonheur selon Abû-l-Ḥasan al-ʿÂmirî', *Studia Islamica* XXII (1965): 55–90.

Arkoun, Mohammed, 'Éthique et histoire d'après les Tajarib al-Umam', *Atti del terzo Congresso di studi arabi e islamici* (Naples: Instituto Universitario Orientale, 1967), pp. 83–112.

Al-Asad wa-l-ghawwāṣ, ed. Riḍwān al-Sayyid (Beirut: Dār al-Ṭalīʿa lil-Ṭibāʿa wa-l-Nashr, 1978).

Al-Ashʿarī, *Maqālāt al-Islāmiyyīn wa-khtilāf al-muṣallīn*, ed. Naʿīm Zarzūr (Beirut: al-Maktabat al-ʿAṣriyya, 2009).

Pseudo-Aṣmaʿī, *Nihāyat al-arab fī akhbār al-furs wa-l-ʿarab*, ed. M. T. Dānishpazhūh (Tehran: Anjuman-i Āthār va-Mafākhir-i Farhangī, 1996 or 1997).

Ayalon, David, 'On the Eunuchs in Islam', *Jerusalem Studies in Arabic & Islam* 1 (1979): 67–124 = *Outsiders in the Lands of Islam: Mamluks, Mongols and Eunuchs* (London: Variorium, 1988), III.

Azad, Arezou, 'Female Mystics in Mediaeval Islam: The Quiet Legacy', *Journal of the Economic and Social History of the Orient* 56 (2013): 53–88.

Azad, Arezou, 'The *Faḍāʾil-i Balkh* and its Place in Islamic Historiography', *Iran* (2013): 79–102.

Azad, Arezou, *Sacred Landscape in Medieval Afghanistan: Revisiting the* Faḍāʾil-i Balkh (Oxford: Oxford University Press, 2013).

Al-Azdī, Yazīd b. Muḥammad, *Taʾrīkh al-Mawṣil*, ed. ʿAlī Ḥabība (Cairo: Lajnat Iḥyāʾ al-Turāth al-Islāmī, 1967).

ʿAzzām, ʿAbd al-Wahhāb, see Ibn al-Muqaffaʿ.

Badawī, ʿAbd al-Raḥmān, *al-Uṣūl al-yūnāniyya lil-naẓariyyāt al-siyāsiyya fī l-Islām* (Cairo: Matbaʿat Dār al-Kutub al-Miṣriyya, 1954).

Badawī, ʿAbd al-Raḥmān, *Aflāṭūn fī l-Islām = Platon en pays d'Islam* (Tehran: Muʾassaseh-yi Muṭālaʿāt-i Islāmī-yi Dānishgāh-i McGill, 1974).

Badawi, M. M., 'The Function of Rhetoric in Medieval Arabic Poetry: Abū Tammām's Ode on Amorium', *Journal of Arabic Literature* 9 (1978): 43–56.

Al-Baghdādī, ʿAbd al-Qāhir b. Ṭāhir, *Kitāb al-Farq bayn al-firaq wa-bayān al-firqa al-nājiya minhum*, ed. Muḥammad Badr (Cairo, Maṭbaʿat al-Maʿārif, 1910).

Al-Baghdādī, ᶜAbd al-Qāhir b. Ṭāhir, *Kitāb Uṣūl al-dīn* (Beirut: Dār al-Kutub al-ᶜIlmiyya, 1908; reprinted Istanbul: Maṭbaᶜat al-Dawla, 1928).

Al-Baghdādī, Aḥmad Mubārak, 'Consultation', trans. Brannon M. Wheeler, *EQ* I: 406–10.

Al-Baghdādī, Ismāᶜīl Pasha = Ismaᶜil Paşa Bağdatlı, *Īḍāḥ al-maknūn fī l-dhayl ᶜalā Kashf al-ẓunūn* = *Keşf el-zunun zeyli* (Istanbul: Milli Eğitim Basımevi, 1945–7).

Bailey, H. W., 'Iranica', *Bulletin of the School of Oriental & African Studies* 11 (1943): 1–5.

Al-Bakrī, Abū ᶜUbayd, *Faṣl al-maqāl fī sharḥ Kitāb al-Amthāl*, eds Iḥsān ᶜAbbās and ᶜAbd al-Majīd ᶜĀbidīn (Beirut: Dār al-Amāna, 1971).

Balayé, Simone, *La Bibliothèque nationale des origines à 1800* (Geneva: Librairie Droz SA, 1988).

Baldick, Julian, 'The Iranian Origin of the *futuwwa*', *Annali* – Sezione romanza, Instituto Universitario Orientale di Napoli 50 (1990): 345–61.

Bannerth, E., 'La Khalwatiyya en Égypte: quelques aspects de la vie d'une confrerie', *Mélanges de l'Institut dominicain d'études orientales du Caire* 8 (1964–6): 1–74.

Barthold, W., 'Preface to the *Ḥudūd al-ᶜālam*', trans. from the Russian V. Minorsky, in *The Regions of the World: A Persian Geography, 372 A.H. (982 A.D.)*, trans. from the Persian V. Minorsky, 2nd edn, C. E. Bosworth (London, Luzac, 1970), pp. 3–44.

Barthold, W., *Turkestan down to the Mongol Invasion*, 4th edn (London: E. J. W. Gibb Memorial Trust, 1977).

Barthold, W. [C. E. Bosworth], 'Ṭukhāristān', *EI²* X (2000), pp. 599–602.

Al-Bayḍāwī, *Anwār al-tanzīl wa-asrār al-taᵓwīl, Beidhawii Commentarius in Coranum*, ed. H. O. Fleischer (Leipzig: F. C. G. Vogelii, 1878).

Bayhaqī, Abū l-Fażl, *Tārīkh-i Bayhaqī* = *Tārīkh-i Masᶜūdī*, eds Q. Ghanī and A. A. Fayyāż (Tehran, 1945–6) = *The History of Beyhaqi (The History of Sultan Masᶜud of Ghazna, 1030–1041)*, trans. C. E. Bosworth and revd Mohsen Ashtiany (Boston, MA and Washington, DC: Ilex Foundation and Center for Hellenic Studies, 2011).

Bayhaqī, ᶜAlī b. Zayd Ibn Funduq, *Tārīkh-i Bayhaq*, ed. Aḥmad Bahmanyār (Tehran: Kitāb-Furūshī-yi Furūghī, 1960).

Al-Bayhaqī, Aḥmad b. al-Ḥusayn, *Ṣaḥīḥ al-jāmiᶜ al-muṣannif li-shuᶜab al-īmān*, ed. Muḥammad b. Riyāḍ al-Aḥmad (Beirut: Dār al-Kutub al-ᶜIlmiyya, 2013).

Al-Bazdawī, Muḥammad b. Muḥammad, *Kitāb Uṣūl al-dīn* (Cairo: Dār Ihyāᵓ al-Kutub al-ᶜArabiyya, 1963).

Beal, Samuel, *Si-yu-ki. Buddhist Records of the Western World. Translated from the Chinese of Hiuen Tsiang (A.D. 629)* (London: Kegan Paul, Trench, Trübner, 1906).

Beckwith, Christopher I., 'The Early History of the Central Asian Guard Corps in Islam', *Archivum Eurasiae medii aevi* 4 (1984): 29–43.

Beckwith, Christopher I., 'The Plan of the City of Peace: Central Asian Iranian Factors in Early ᶜAbbâsid Design', *Acta Orientalia Academiae Scientiarum Hungaricae* 38 (1/2) (1984): 143–64.

Beckwith, Christopher I., *The Tibetan Empire in Central Asia: A History of the Struggle for Great Power among Tibetans, Turks, Arabs, and Chinese during the Early Middle Ages* (Princeton, NJ: Princeton University Press, 1987).

Beeston, A. F. L., 'Parallelism in Arabic Prose', *Journal of Arabic Literature* 5 (1974): 134–46.

Beitia, A. Cortabarria, 'La classification des sciences chez al-Kindī', *Mélanges de l'Institut dominicain d'études orientales du Caire* XI (1972): 49–76.

Benfey, Theodor, 'Einleitung', *Kalīlag und Damnag. Alte syrische Übersetzung des indischen Fürstenspiegels.* Text und deutsche Übersetzung von Gustav Bickell. Mit einer Einleitung von Theodor Benfey (Leipzig: Brockhaus, 1876), pp. v–cxlvii.

Berkey, Jonathan, *The Transmission of Knowledge in Medieval Cairo: A Social History of Islamic Education* (Princeton, NJ: Princeton University Press, 1992).

Berman, L. V., 'The Political Interpretation of the Maxim: The Purpose of Philosophy is the Imitation of God', *Studia Islamica* 15 (1961): 53–61.

Bernand, Marie, 'Le *Kitāb al-Radd ᶜalā l-bidaᶜ* d'Abū Muṭīᶜ Makḥūl al-Nasafī', *Annales islamologiques* XVI (1980): 8–126.

Bernard, Paul, 'The Greek Colony at Aï Khanum and Hellenism in Central Asia', in Fredrik Hiebert and Pierre Cambon (eds), *Afghanistan: Crossroads of the Ancient World* (London: British Museum Press, 2011).

Bernheimer, Teresa, 'The Rise of *Sayyids* and *Sādāt*: The Āl Zubāra and Other ᶜAlids in Ninth- and Tenth-Century Nishapur', *Studia Islamica* 100/1 (2005): 43–69.

Biesterfeldt, Hans Hinrich, 'Abū l-Ḥasan al-ᶜĀmirī und die Wissenschaften', *XIX. Deutscher Orientalistentag* 1975 (*ZDMG* Supplement III 1977): 335–41.

Biesterfeldt, Hans Hinrich, 'Ibn Farīġūn's Chapter on Arabic Grammar in His *Compendium of the Sciences*', in K. Versteegh and M. G. Carter (eds), *Studies in the History of Arabic Grammar II* (Amsterdam: Benjamins, 1990), pp. 49–56.

Biesterfeldt, Hans Hinrich, 'Weisheit als mot juste in der klassisch-arabischen Literatur', in A. Assmann (ed.), *Weisheit* (Munich: Fink, 1991), pp. 367–86.

Biesterfeldt, Hans Hinrich, 'Arabisch-islamische Enzyklopädien: Formen und Funktionen', in Ch. Meier (ed.), *Die Enzyklopädie im Wandel vom Hochmittelalter bis zur frühen Neuzeit* (Munich: Wilhelm Fink Verlag, 2002), pp. 77–98.

Biesterfeldt, Hans Hinrich, 'Ibn Farīghūn on Communication', in Peter Adamson (ed.), *In the Age of al-Fārābī: Arabic Philosophy in the Fourth-Tenth Century* (London: Warburg Institute, 2008), pp. 265–76.

Biesterfeldt, Hans Hinrich, 'Abū Zaid al-Balḫī', in Ulrich Rudolph (ed.), unter Mitarbeit von Renate Würsch, *Philosophie in der islamischen Welt, Band I, 8.–10. Jahrhundert* (Basel: Schwabe, 2012), pp. 156–67.

Biesterfeldt, Hans Hinrich, 'Aḥmad ibn aṭ-Ṭaiyib as-Saraḫsī', in Ulrich Rudolph (ed.), unter Mitarbeit von Renate Würsch, *Philosophie in der islamischen Welt, Band I, 8.–10. Jahrhundert* (Basel: Schwabe, 2012), pp. 148–56.

Biesterfeldt, Hans Hinrich, 'Ibn Farīġūn', in Ulrich Rudolph (ed.), unter Mitarbeit von Renate Würsch, *Philosophie in der islamischen Welt, Band I, 8.–10. Jahrhundert* (Basel: Schwabe, 2012), pp. 167–70.

Bilawhar wa-Būdhāṣaf, see Gimaret, Daniel.

Al-Bīrūnī, *Taḥqīq mā lil-hind = Alberuni's India. An Account of the Religion, Philosophy, Literature, Chronology, Astronomy, Customs, Laws and Astrology of India about A.D. 1030*, ed. E. Sachau (London: Trübner, 1887).

Al-Bīrūnī, *al-Āthār al-bāqiya ᶜan al-qurūn al-khāliya*, ed. C. E. Sachau, *Chronologie orientalischer Völker von Albêrûni* (Leipzig: Brockhaus, 1923).

Al-Bīrūnī, *al-Āthār al-bāqiya ᶜan al-qurūn al-khāliya*, ed. P. Åżkāʾī (Tehran: Mīrāth-i Maktūb, 2001).

Bladel, Kevin van, 'The Iranian Characteristics and Forged Greek Attributions in the Arabic Sirr al-asrār (Secret of Secrets)', *Mélanges de l'Université Saint-Joseph* 57 (2004): 151–72.

Bladel, Kevin van, *The Arabic Hermes from Pagan Sage to Prophet of Science* (Oxford: Oxford University Press, 2009).

Bladel, Kevin van, 'The Bactrian Background of the Barmakids', in Anna Akasoy, Ch. Burnett and R. Yoeli-Tlalim (eds), *Islam and Tibet – Interactions along the Musk Routes* (Farnham: Ashgate, 2011), pp. 43–88.

Blair, Sheila S., *The Monumental Inscriptions from Early Islamic Iran and Transoxiana*, Supplements to *Muqarnas*, vol. V (Leiden: Brill, 1992).

Blair, Sheila S., *Islamic Inscriptions* (Edinburgh: Edinburgh University Press, 1998).

Blankinship, Khalid Yahya, *The End of the Jihād State: The Reign of Hishām Ibn ᶜAbd al-Malik and the Collapse of the Umayyads* (Albany, NY: State University of New York Press, 1994).

Blois, François de, *Burzōy's Voyage to India and the Origin of the Book of Kalīlah wa Dimnah* (London: Royal Asiatic Society, 1990).

Blois, F. C. de, 'Two Sources of the Handarz of Ošnar', *Iran* 31 (1993): 95–7.

Blois, F. C. de, 'Zindīḳ', *EI*² XI (2000), pp. 510–13.

Blois, F. C. de, 'Sindbād, Book of', *EAL* II (1998), pp. 723–4.

Bonebakker, S. A., 'Early Arabic Literature and the Term *adab*', *Jerusalem Studies in Arabic & Islam* 5 (1984): 389–421.

Bonner, Michael, *Aristocratic Violence and Holy War: Studies in the Jihad and the Arab–Byzantine Frontier* (New Haven, CT: American Oriental Society, 1996).

Bonner, Michael, 'Some Observations Concerning the Early Development of Jihad on the Arab–Byzantine Border', reprinted in *Arab–Byzantine Relations in Early Islamic Times*, ed. Michael Bonner (Aldershot: Ashgate, 2004), pp. 410–27.

Bonner, Michael, 'The Waning of Empire, 861–945', in Chase F. Robinson (ed.), *The New Cambridge History of Islam, vol. I: The Formation of the Islamic World Sixth to Eleventh Centuries* (Cambridge: Cambridge University Press, 2010), pp. 305–59.

Borrut, Antoine, 'Entre tradition et histoire: la genèse et diffusion de l'image de ᶜUmar II', *Mélanges de l'Université Saint-Joseph* 58 (2005): 329–78.

Bosworth, C. E., 'The Rise of the Karāmiyah in Khurasan', *Muslim World* 50 (1960): 6–14.

Bosworth, C. E., 'The Titulature of the Early Ghaznavids', *Oriens* XV (1962): 210–33.

Bosworth, C. E., *The Ghaznavids: Their Empire in Afghanistan and Eastern Iran 994–1040* (Edinburgh: Edinburgh University Press, 1963).

Bosworth, C. E., 'Abū ᶜAbdallāh al-Khwārazmī on the Technical Terms of the Secretary's Art: A Contribution to the Administrative History of Mediaeval Islam', *Journal of the Economic & Social History of the Orient* 12 (1969): 113–64.

Bosworth, C. E., 'An Alleged Embassy from the Emperor of China to the Amir Naṣr b. Aḥmad: A Contribution to Sâmânid Military History', in M. Minovi and Iraj Afshar (eds), *Yādnāmeh-yi Īrānī-yi Mīnūrskī* (Tehran, Dānishgāh-i Tihrān, 1969), pp. 17–29.

Bosworth, C. E., 'The Tahirids and Arabic Culture', *Journal of Semitic Studies* XIV (1969): 45–79.

Bosworth, C. E., 'The Ṭāhirids and Persian Literature', *Iran* VII (1969): 103–6.

Bosworth, C. E., 'An Early Arabic Mirror for Princes: Ṭāhir Dhū l-Yamīnain's Epistle to his Son ᶜAbdallāh (206/821)', *Journal of Near Eastern Studies* 29 (1970): 25–41.

Bosworth, C. E., 'The Banū Ilyās of Kirmān (320–57/932–68)', in C. E. Bosworth (ed.), *Iran and Islam* (Edinburgh: Edinburgh University Press, 1971), pp. 107–24.

Bosworth, C. E., 'The Heritage of Rulership in Early Islamic Iran and the Search for Dynastic Connections with the Past', *Iran* XI (1973): 51–62.

Bosworth, C. E., 'The Interaction of Arabic and Persian Literature and Culture in the 10th and Early 11th Centuries', *al-Abḥāth* 27 (1978–9): 59–75

Bosworth, C. E., 'The Rulers of Chaghāniyān in Early Islamic Times', *Iran* XIX (1981): 1–20.

Bosworth, C. E., 'Afšīn', *EIr* I (1985), pp. 589–91.

Bosworth, C. E., 'Aḥmad b. Sahl b. Hāšem', *EIr* I (1985), pp. 643–4.

Bosworth, C. E., 'Āl-e Afrīḡ', *EIr* I (1985), pp. 743–5.

Bosworth, C. E., 'Āl-e Farīḡūn', *EIr* I (1985), pp. 756–8.

Bosworth, C. E., 'Āl-e Maᵓmūn', *EIr* I (1985), pp. 762–4.

Bosworth, C. E., 'Āl-e Moḥtāj', *EIr* I (1985), pp. 764–6.

Bosworth, C. E., 'Khurāsān', *EI*² V (1986), pp. 55–9.

Bosworth, C. E., 'Andarāb', *EIr* II (1987), p. 10.

Bosworth, C. E., 'Asāwera', *EIr* II (1987), pp. 706–7.

Bosworth, C. E., 'Balᶜamī, Abuᵓl-Fażl Moḥammad', *EIr* III (1989), pp. 573–4.

Bosworth, C. E., 'Balḵ', ii: 'History from the Arab Conquest to the Mongols', *EIr* III (1989), pp. 588–91.

Bosworth, C. E., 'Administrative Literature', in M. J. L. Young, J. D. Latham and R. B. Serjeant (eds), *The Cambridge History of Arabic Literature, Religion, Learning and Science in the ᶜAbbasid Period* (Cambridge: Cambridge University Press, 1990), pp. 155–67.

Bosworth, C. E., 'Bukhara', ii: 'From the Arab Invasions to the Mongols', *EIr* IV (1990): 513–15.

Bosworth, C. E., 'Chorasmia', ii, 'In Islamic Times', *EIr* V (1992), pp. 516–17.

Bosworth, C. E., 'Narshakhī', *EI*² VII (1993), p. 966.

Bosworth, C. E., 'al-Sallāmī', *EI*² VIII (1995), pp. 996–7.

Bosworth, C. E., 'Sāmānids', i. 'History, Literary Life and Economic Activity', *EI*² VIII (1995), pp. 1026–9.

Bosworth, C. E., 'Samarḳand', I, 'History', *EI*² VIII (1995), pp. 1031–4.

Bosworth, C. E., *The New Islamic Dynasties: A Chronological and Genealogical Manual* (New York, Columbia University Press, 1996).

Bosworth, C. E., Sīmdjūrids', *EI*² IX (1997), p. 612.

Bosworth, C. E., 'Mirrors for Princes', *EAL* II (1998), pp. 527–9.

Bosworth, C. E., 'Sistan and its Local Histories', *Iranian Studies* XXXIII (2000): 31–43.

Bosworth, C. E., *The History of the Saffarids of Sistan and the Maliks of Nimruz (247/861 to 949/1542–3)* (Costa Mesa, CA: Mazda Publishers, 2004).

Bosworth, C. E., 'Banīdjūrids', *EI*² XII Supplement (2004), p. 125.

Bosworth, C. E., 'The Appearance and Establishment of Islam in Afghanistan', in Étienne de la Vaissière (ed.), *Islamisation de l'Asie Centrale: processus locaux d'acculturation du VIIe au XIe siècle* (Paris: Association pour l'avancement des études iraniennes, 2008), pp. 97–114.

Böwering, Gerhard, 'Covenants', *EQ* I (2001), pp. 464–7.

Boyle, J. A., 'The Alexander Romance in the East and West', *Bulletin of the John Rylands University Library of Manchester* 60 (1977): 13–27.

Bray [Ashtiany], Julia, 'Al-Muᶜtaṣim's "Bridge of Toil" and Abū Tammām's Amorium *Qaṣīda*', in G. R. Hawting, J. A. Mojaddedi and A. Samely (eds), *Studies in Islamic and Middle Eastern Texts and Traditions in Memory of Norman Calder* (Oxford: Oxford University Press, 2000), pp. 31–73.

Bray, Julia, 'Al-Thaᶜalibi's *Adab al-muluk*, a Local Mirror for Princes', in Yasir Suleiman (ed.), *Living Islamic History: Studies in Honour of Carole Hillenbrand* (Edinburgh: Edinburgh University Press, 2010), pp. 32–46.

Bray, Julia, 'Ibn al-Muᶜtazz and Politics: The Question of the *Fuṣūl Qiṣār*', *Oriens* 28 (2010): 107–43.

Bregel, Yuri, 'Turko-Mongol Influences in Central Asia', in Robert L. Canfield (ed.), *Turko-Persia in Historical Perspective* (Cambridge: Cambridge University Press, 1991), pp. 53–77.

Brockelmann, Carl, *Geschichte der arabischen Litteratur* (*GAL*) (Leiden: Brill, 1937–42).

Browne, E. G., 'Some Account of the Arabic Work Entitled "Niháyatuˀl-irab fí akhbáriˀl-Furs waˀl-ᶜArab," Particularly of that Part which Treats of the Persian Kings', *Journal of the Royal Asiatic Society* (1900): 195–259.

Browne, E. G., *A Literary History of Persia, vol. II: From Firdawsi to Saᶜdi* (Cambridge: Cambridge University Press, 1928).

Al-Bukhārī, *Ṣaḥīḥ al-Bukhārī* (Stuttgart: Thesaurus Islamicus Foundation, 2000).

Bulliet, Richard W., *The Patricians of Nishapur: A Study in Medieval Islamic Social History* (Cambridge, MA: Harvard University Press, 1972).

Bulliet, Richard W., 'Naw Bahār and the Survival of Iranian Buddhism', *Iran* XIV (1976): 140–5.

Bulliet, Richard W., 'Medieval Nishapur: A Topographic and Demographic Reconstruction', *Studia Islamica* 5 (1976): 67–89.

Bulliet, Richard W., *Conversion to Islam in the Medieval Period: An Essay in Quantitative History* (Cambridge, MA: Harvard University Press, 1979).

Bulliet, Richard W., 'Conversion to Islam and the Emergence of a Muslim Society in Iran', in N. Levtzion (ed.), *Conversion to Islam* (New York: Holmes & Meier, 1979), pp. 30–51.

Busse, Heribert, 'Iran under the Būyids', in R. N. Frye (ed.), *Cambridge History of Iran, vol. IV: The Period From the Arab Invasion to the Saljuqs* (Cambridge: Cambridge University Press, 1975), pp. 250–304.

Butterworth, Charles E., 'Medieval Islamic Philosophy and the Virtue of Ethics', *Arabica* 34 (1987): 221–50.

Butterworth, Charles E., 'Al-Kindī and Islamic Political Philosophy', in Charles E. Butterworth (ed.), *The Political Aspects of Islamic Philosophy: Essays in Honor of Muhsin S. Mahdi* (Cambridge, MA: Harvard University Press, 1992), pp. 11–60.

Cahen, Claude, 'Mouvements populaires et autonomisme urbain dans l'Asie musulmane du moyen âge', I, *Arabica* V (1958): 225–50; II, *Arabica* VI (1959): 25–56; III, *Arabica* VI (1959): 223–65 = *Mouvements populaires et autonomisme urbain dans l'Asie musulmane du moyen âge* (Leiden: Brill, 1959).

Canard, M., 'Daᶜwa', *EI*² II (1991), pp. 168–70.

Canfield, Robert L., 'Introduction: The Turko-Persian Tradition', in Robert L. Canfield (ed.), *Turko-Persia in Historical Perspective* (Cambridge: Cambridge University Press, 1991), pp. 1–34.

Canfield, Robert L., 'Theological "Extremism" and Social Movements in Turko-Persia', in Robert L. Canfield (ed.), *Turko-Persia in Historical Perspective* (Cambridge: Cambridge University Press, 1991), pp. 132–60.

Chabbi, J., 'Fuḍayl b. ᶜIyāḍ, un précurseur du hanbalisme (187/803)', *Bulletin d'études orientales* 30 (1978): 331–45.

Chabbi, J., 'Ribāṭ', *EI*² VIII (1995), pp. 493–506.

Chehabi, H. E. and Allen Guttmann, 'From Iran to All of Asia: The Origin and Diffusion of Polo', *International Journal of the History of Sport* 19 (2002): 384–400.

Cheikh-Moussa, Abdallah, 'L'historien et la littérature arabe médiévale', *Arabica* 43 (1996): 152–88.

Cheikh-Moussa, Abdallah, 'Du discours autorisé ou comment s'adresser au tyran?', *Arabica* 46 (1999): 139–75.

Cheikh-Moussa, Abdallah, 'De la "communauté de salut" à la "populace": la représentation du "peuple" dans quatre Miroirs arabes des Princes (VIIIe–XIIIe s.)', in Christian Müller and Muriel Roiland-Rouabah (eds), *Les non-dits du nom. Onomastiques et documents en terres d'Islam. Mélanges offerts à Jacqueline Sublet* (Beirut: Presses d'Ifpo, 2014), pp. 497–524.

Cheikho, L., *La version arabe de Kalîlah et Dimnah d'après le plus ancien manuscrit arabe daté* (Beirut: Imprimerie catholique, 1905; reprinted Amsterdam: Philo Press, 1981).

Chih, Rachida, 'Cheminements et situation actuelle d'un ordre mystique réformateur: la Khalwatiyya en Égypte (fin XVe siècle à nos jours)', *Studia Islamica* 88 (1998): 181–201.

Chih, Rachida and Catherine Mayeur-Jaouen, 'Introduction: le soufisme ottoman vu d'Égypte (XVIe–XVIIIe siècle)', *Le soufisme à l'époque ottomane XVIe–XVIII siècle* (Cairo: Institut français d'archéologie orientale, 2010), pp. 1–55.

Choksy, Jamsheed K., *Conflict and Cooperation: Zoroastrian Subalterns and Muslim Elites in Medieval Iranian Society* (New York: Columbia University Press, 1997).

Ciancaglini, Claudia A., 'The Syriac Version of the Alexander *Romance*', *Le Muséon*, XIV (2001): 121–40.

Colless, Brian E., 'The Nestorian Province of Samarqand', *Abr Nahrain* 24 (1986): 21–7.

Conrad, Lawrence I., 'The Arab-Islamic Medical Tradition', in Lawrence I. Conrad, Michael Neve, Vivian Nutton, Roy Porter and Andrew Wear (eds), *The Western Medical Tradition 800 BC to AD 1800* (Cambridge: Cambridge University Press, 1995), pp. 93–138.

Cook, Michael, *Early Muslim Dogma: A Source-Critical Study* (Cambridge: Cambridge University Press, 1981).

Cook, Michael, 'The Opponents of the Writing of Tradition in Early Islam', *Arabica* 44 (1997): 437–530.

Cook, Michael, *Commanding Right and Forbidding Wrong in Islamic Thought* (Cambridge: Cambridge University Press, 2000).

Cook, Michael, 'The Namesake Taboo', *Muqarnas* 25 (2008): 11–16.

Cooperson, Michael, *Classical Arabic Biography: The Heirs of the Prophets in the Age of al-Maʾmūn* (Cambridge: Cambridge University Press, 2000).

Cooperson, Michael, *Al-Maʾmun* (Oxford: Oneworld, 2005).

Cooperson, Michael, 'Ibn al-Muqaffaᶜ', in Michael Cooperson and Shawkat M. Toorawa (eds), *Arabic Literary Culture, 500–925, Dictionary of Literary Biography*, vol. 311 (Detroit: Thomson Gale, 2005), pp. 150–63.

Cooperson, Michael, 'Al-Jāḥeẓ', *EIr* XIV (2008), pp. 386–9.

Cottrell, Emily, 'L'*Anonyme d'Oxford* (Bodleian Or. Marsh 539): Bibliothèque ou commentaire?', in Cristina D'Ancona (ed.), *Libraries of the Neoplatonists* (Leiden: Brill, 2007), pp. 415–41.

Crone, Patricia, *Slaves on Horses: The Evolution of the Islamic Polity* (Cambridge: Cambridge University Press, 1980).

Crone, Patricia, 'Did al-Ghazālī Write a Mirror for Princes? On the Authorship of *Naṣīḥat al-mulūk*', *Jerusalem Studies in Arabic & Islam* 10 (1987): 167–91.

Crone, Patricia, *Pre-industrial Societies* (Oxford: Basil Blackwell, 1989).

Crone, Patricia, 'Maᶜūna', *EI²* VI (1991), p. 848.

Crone, Patricia, 'Mawlā: II: In Historical and Legal Usage', *EI²* VI (1991), pp. 874–82.

Crone, Patricia, '"Even an Ethiopian Slave": The Transformation of a Sunnī Tradition', *Bulletin of the School of Oriental & African Studies* 57/1 (1994): 59–67.

Crone, Patricia, 'The ᶜAbbāsid Abnāᵓ and Sāsānid Cavalrymen', *Journal of the Royal Asiatic Society* 3rd series 8 (1998): 1–19.

Crone, Patricia, *God's Rule: Government and Islam: Six Centuries of Medieval Islamic Political Thought* (New York: Columbia University Press, 2004).

Crone, Patricia, 'Post-Colonialism in Tenth-Century Islam', *Der Islam* 83 (2006): 2–38.

Crone, Patricia, 'Abū Tammām on the Mubayyiḍa', in Omar Alí-de-Unzaga (ed.), *Fortresses of the Intellect: Ismaili and Other Islamic Studies in Honour of Farhad Daftary* (London, Tauris, 2011), pp. 167–87.

Crone, Patricia, 'Buddhism as Ancient Iranian Paganism', in Teresa Bernheimer and Adam Silverstein (eds), *Late Antiquity: Eastern Perspectives* (Exeter: E. J. W. Gibb Memorial Trust, 2012), pp. 25–41.

Crone, Patricia, *The Nativist Prophets of Early Islamic Iran: Rural Revolt and Local Zoroastrianism* (Cambridge: Cambridge University Press, 2012).

Crone, Patricia and Martin Hinds, *God's Caliph: Religious Authority in the First Centuries of Islam* (Cambridge: Cambridge University Press, 1986).

Crone, Patricia and L. Treadwell, 'A New Text on Ismailism at the Samanid Court', in C. Robinson (ed.), *Texts, Documents and Artefacts: Islamic Studies in Honour of D. S. Richards* (Leiden: Brill, 2003), pp. 37–67.

Crone, Patricia and Masoud Jafari Jazi, 'The Muqanna Narrative in the *Tārīkhnāma*: Part I, Introduction, Edition and Translation', *Bulletin of the School of Oriental & African Studies* 73 (2010): 157–77; 'The Muqanna Narrative in the *Tārīkhnāma*: Part II, Commentary and Analysis', *Bulletin of the School of Oriental & African Studies* 73 (2010): 381–413.

Daftary, Farhad, *The Ismāᶜīlīs: Their History and Doctrines*, 2nd edn (Cambridge: Cambridge University Press, 2007).

Daiber, Hans, *Das theologisch–philosophische System des Muᶜāmmar ibn ᶜAbbād as-Sulamī (gest. 830 n. Chr.)* (Beirut, in Kommission bei Franz Steiner Verlag, Wiesbaden, 1975).

Daiber, Hans, 'The Ruler as Philosopher: A New Interpretation of al-Fārābī's View', *Mededelingen der Koninklijke Nederlandse Akademie van Wetenschappen, Afd. Letterkunde* 49/4 (Amsterdam: North-Holland, 1986), pp. 133–48.

Daiber, Hans, *The Islamic Concept of Belief in the 4th/10th Century: Abū l-Laiṯ as-Samarqandī's Commentary on Abū Ḥanīfa (died 150/767) al-Fiqh al-absaṭ, Introduction, Text and Commentary* (Tokyo: Institute for the Study of Languages and Cultures of Asia and Africa, 1995).

Daiber, Hans, 'Political Philosophy', in Seyyed Hossein Nasr and Oliver Leaman (eds), *History of Islamic Philosophy*, vol. II (London: Routledge, 1996), pp. 841–85.

Dakhlia, Jocelyne, 'Les Miroirs des princes islamiques: une modernité sourde?', *Annales: Histoire, Sciences Sociales*, 57(5) (2002): 1191–206.

Daniel, Elton L., *The Political and Social History of Khurasan under Abbasid Rule 747–820* (Minneapolis and Chicago: Bibliotheca Islamica, 1979).

Daniel, Elton L., 'Manuscripts and Editions of Balᶜamī's *Tarjamah-i tārīkh-i Ṭabarī*', *Journal of the Royal Asiatic Society* 122 (1990): 282–321.

Daniel, Elton L., 'Arabs, Persians, and the Advent of the Abbasids Reconsidered', *Journal of the American Oriental Society* 117 (1997): 542–8.

Daniel, Elton L., 'The Sāmānid "Translations" of al-Ṭabarī', in *Al-Ṭabarī, Studies in Late Antiquity and Early Islam*, vol. XV (Princeton: Darwin Press, 2008), pp. 263–97.

Daniel, Elton L., 'The Islamic East', in Chase F. Robinson (ed.), *The New Cambridge History of Islam, vol. I: The Formation of the Islamic World Sixth to Eleventh Centuries* (Cambridge: Cambridge University Press, 2010), pp. 448–505.

Dānishpazhūh, 'Dībācheh', *Tuḥfat al-mulūk*, see *Tuḥfat al-mulūk*.

Dankoff, Robert, *Wisdom of Royal Glory (Kutadgu bilig)* (Chicago, IL: Chicago University Press, 1983).

Al-Dārimī, *Sunan al-Dārimī*, eds Sayyid Ibrāhīm and ʿAlī Muḥammad ʿAlī (Cairo: Dār al-Ḥadīth, 2000).

Darling, Linda T., *Revenue-Raising and Legitimacy: Tax Collection and Finance Administration in the Ottoman Empire 1560–1660* (Leiden: Brill, 1996).

Darling, Linda T., *A History of Social Justice and Political Power in the Middle East: The Circle of Justice from Mesopotamia to Globalization* (London: Routledge, 2013).

Daryaee, Touraj, *Sasanian Persia: The Rise and Fall of an Empire* (London: Tauris, 2009).

Dāʾūd, Muḥammad Sulaymān and Fuʾād ʿAbd al-Munʿim Aḥmad, *Min aʿlām al-Islām: al-Imām Abū l-Ḥasan al-Māwardī . . . al-mufassir al-muḥaddith al-faqīh al-uṣūlī al-siyāsī al-qāḍī al-mutakallim al-faylasūf al-akhlāqī* (Alexandria: Muʾassasat Shabāb al-Jāmiʿa, 1978).

Davidson, Olga M., 'The Testing of the *Shāhnāma* in the "Life of Ferdowsī" Narratives', in L. Marlow (ed.), *The Rhetoric of Biography: Narrating Lives in Persianate Societies* (Boston, MA and Washington: Ilex Foundation and Center for Hellenic Studies, 2011), pp. 11–20.

Davidson, Olga M., *Poet and Hero in the Persian Book of Kings*, 3rd edn (Boston, MA and Washington, DC: Ilex Foundation and Center for Hellenic Studies, 2013).

Davis, Dick, *Epic and Sedition: The Case of Ferdowsi's Shahnameh* (Washington, DC: Mage Publishers, 1992).

Davis, Dick, 'The Problem of Ferdowsî's Sources', *Journal of the American Oriental Society* 116 (1996): 48–57.

Demichelis, Marco, 'Between Muʿtazilism and Syncretism: A Reappraisal of the Behavior of the Caliphate of al-Maʾmūn', *Journal of Near Eastern Studies* 71 (2012): 257–74.

Denny, F. M., 'Umma', *EI*^{2} X (2000), pp. 859–63.

Al-Dhahabī, *Siyar aʿlām al-nubalāʾ*, eds Bashshār ʿAwwād Maʿrūf and Shuʿayb al-Arnāʾūt (Beirut: Muʾassasat al-Risāla, 2001).

Al-Dhahabī, *Taʾrīkh al-Islām wa-wafayāt al-mashāhīr wa-l-aʿlām*, ed. Bashshār ʿAwwād Maʿrūf (Beirut: Dār al-Gharb al-Islāmī, 2003).

Diem, Werner and Marco Schöller, *The Living and the Dead in Islam: Studies in Arabic Epitaphs* (Wiesbaden: Harrassowitz, 2004).

Dietrich, A., 'Das politische Testament des zweiten ʿAbbasidenkalifen al-Mansur', *Der Islam* 30 (1952): 149–56.

Al-Dīnawarī, Abū Ḥanīfa Aḥmad b. Dāʾūd, *al-Akhbār al-ṭiwāl*, ed. ʿIṣām Muḥammad al-Ḥājj ʿAlī (Beirut: Dār al-Kutub al-ʿIlmiyya, 2001).

Donner, Fred M., *Narratives of Islamic Origins: The Beginnings of Islamic Historical Writing* (Princeton, NJ: Darwin Press, 1998).

Doufikar-Aerts, Faustina, *Alexander Magnus Arabicus: A Survey of the Alexander Tradition Through Seven Centuries, from Pseudo-Callisthenes to Suri* (Walpole, MA: Peeters, 2010) (= *Alexander Magnus Arabicus, zeven eeuwen Arabische Alexandertraditie*, trans from Dutch by Ania Lentz-Michaelis).

Drory, Rina, 'Three Attempts to Legitimize Fiction in Classical Arabic Literature', *Jerusalem Studies in Arabic & Islam* 18 (1994): 146–64.

Druart, Thérèse-Anne, 'Al-Kindi's Ethics', *Review of Metaphysics* 47 (1993): 329–57.

Druart, Thérèse-Anne, 'Metaphysics', in Peter Adamson and Richard C. Taylor (eds), *The Cambridge Companion to Arabic Philosophy* (Cambridge: Cambridge University Press, 2005), pp. 327–48.

Dubler, César E., 'Über arabische Pseudo-Aristotelica: Beitrag zur Kenntnis des angeblich hellenischen Wissens unter den Muslimen', *Asiatische Studien* XIV (1961): 33–92.

Ducène, Jean-Charles, 'Al-Ǧayhānī: fragments (Extraits du *K. al-masālik wa-l-mamālik* d'al-Bakrī)', *Der Islam* 75 (1998): 259–82.

Dunlop, D. M., 'Philosophical Discussions in Sijistan in the 10th Century A.D.', *Akten des VII. Kongresses für Arabistik und Islamwissenschaft, Göttingen*, 15. bis 22. August 1974, Göttingen, 1976, pp. 108–14.

Dunlop, D. M., *The Muntakhab Ṣiwān al-Ḥikmah of Abū Sulaimān as-Sijistānī*, Arabic Text, Introduction and Indices (The Hague: Mouton, 1979).

EAL = *Encyclopedia of Arabic Literature*, eds Julie Scott Meisami and Paul Starkey (London and New York: Routledge, 1998).

EI² = *Encyclopaedia of Islam New Edition* (Leiden: Brill, 1960–).

EI Three = *Encyclopaedia of Islam Three* (Leiden: Brill, 2007–).

EIr = *Encyclopaedia Iranica*, ed. E. Yarshater (London and Boston, MA: Routledge & Kegan Paul, 1985–).

El-Hibri, Tayeb, *Reinterpreting Islamic Historiography: Hārūn al-Rashīd and the Narrative of the Abbasid Caliphate* (New York: Cambridge University Press, 1999).

El-Nahal, Gamal H., *The Judicial Administration of Ottoman Egypt in the Seventeenth Century* (Minneapolis and Chicago: Bibliotheca Islamica, 1979).

El-Omari, Racha Moujir, 'The Theology of Abū l-Qāsim al-Balḫī/al-Kaᶜbī (d. 319/931): A Study of its Sources and Reception', PhD dissertation, Yale University, 2006.

El-Omari, Racha, 'Abū l-Qāsim al-Balkhī al-Kaᶜbī's Doctrine of the *Imāma*', in Camilla Adang, Sabine Schmidtke and David Sklare (eds), *A Common Rationality: Muᶜtazilism in Islam and Judaism* (Würzburg: Ergon Verlag, 2007), pp. 39–57.

El-Omari, Racha, 'Accommodation and Resistance: Muᶜtazilites on Ḥadīth', *Journal of Near Eastern Studies* 71 (2012): 231–56.

Endreß, Gerhard, 'The Defense of Reason. The Plea for Philosophy in the Religious Community', *Zeitschrift für Geschichte der Arabisch-Islamischen Wissenschaften* 6 (1990): 1–49.

Endreß, Gerhard, 'al-Kindī über die Wiedererinnerung der Seele: Arabischer Platonismus und die Legitimation der Wissenschaften im Islam', *Oriens* 34 (1994): 174–221.

Endreß, Gerhard, 'The Circle of al-Kindī: Early Arabic Translations from the Greek and the Rise of Islamic Philosophy' in Gerhard Endreß and Remke Kruk (eds), *The Ancient Tradition in Christian and Islamic Hellenism: Studies on the Transmission of Greek Philosophy and Sciences, Dedicated to H. J. Drossaart Lulofs on His Ninetieth Birthday* (Leiden: Research School CNRW, 1997), pp. 43–76.

Endreß, Gerhard and Peter Adamson, 'Abū Yūsuf al-Kindī', in Ulrich Rudolph (ed.), unter Mitarbeit von Renate Würsch, *Philosophie in der islamischen Welt, Band I, 8.–10. Jahrhundert* (Basel: Schwabe, 2012), pp. 100–3.

EQ = *Encyclopaedia of the Qurʾān*, ed. Jane Dammen McAuliffe (Leiden: Brill, 2001–6).

Esin, E., 'Tarkhan Nīzak or Tarkhan Tirek? An Enquiry Concerning the Prince of Bādghīs Who in A.H. 91/A.D. 709–710 Opposed the ᶜOmayyad Conquest of Central Asia', *Journal of the American Oriental Society* 97 (1977): 323–32.

Ess, Josef van, *Die Erkenntnislehre des ᶜAḍudaddīn al-Īcī: Übersetzung und Kommentar des ersten Buches seiner Mawāqif* (Wiesbaden: Franz Steiner, 1966).

Ess, Josef van, 'Les Qadarites et la Ġailānīya de Yazīd III', *Studia Islamica* 31 (1970): 269–86.

Ess, Josef van, *Une lecture à rebours de l'histoire du muᶜtazilisme* (Paris: Librairie orientaliste Paul Geuthner, 1984 = *Revue des études islamiques* XLVI/2-1978, XLVII/1-1979).

Ess, Josef van, 'Abu'l-Qāsem Kaᶜbī', *EIr* I (1985), pp. 359–62.

Ess, Josef van, 'Abu'l-Layṯ Samarqandī', *EIr* I (1985), pp. 332–3.

Ess, Josef van, 'ᶜAmr b. ᶜObayd', *EIr* I (1985), pp. 991–2.

Ess, Josef van, 'Abuʾl-Hoḏayl al-ᶜAllāf', *EIr* I (1985), pp. 318–22.

Ess, Josef van, *Theologie und Gesellschaft im 2. und 3. Jahrhundert Hidschra* (Berlin: Walter de Gruyter, 1991–7).

Ess, Josef van, 'Naẓẓām', *EI²* VII (1993), pp. 1057–8.

Ess, Josef van, 'Abū Esḥāq Naẓẓām', *Encyclopaedia Islamica,* vol. I (Leiden: Brill, 2008), pp. 275–80.

Fahd, T., 'La version arabe du Roman d'Alexandre', *Graeco-Arabica* IV (1991): 25–31.

Faḍl al-iᶜtizāl wa-ṭabaqāt al-Muᶜtazila, ed. Fuᵓād Sayyid (Tunis: al-Dār al-Tūnisiyya lil-Nashr, 1974).

Al-Fārābī, Abû Naṣr al-Fârâbî, *La religion: al-Milla: Texte, traduction et commentaire,* Amor Cherni (Paris: Dar Albouraq, 2012).

Al-Fārābī, *Iḥṣāᵓ al-ᶜulūm = Abū Naṣr Muḥammad ibn Muḥammad al-Fārābī,* Iḥṣāᵓ al-ᶜulūm *and* De ortu scientiarum, Texts and Studies II, collected and reprinted by Fuat Sezgin (Frankfurt am Main: Institute for the History of Arabic-Islamic Science at the Johann Wolfgang Goethe University, 2005).

Faṣīḥ Khvāfī, *Mujmal-i Faṣīḥī,* ed. Sayyid Muḥsin Nājī Naṣrābādī (Tehran: Intishārāt-i Asāṭīr, 2007).

Fażāᵓil-i Balkh, see Vāᶜiẓ, Shaykh al-Islām.

Ferrari, Cleophea, 'Ein Brückenschlag zwischen der Kindī-Tradition und der Bagdader Schule: Ibn Hindū', in Ulrich Rudolph (ed.), unter Mitarbeit von Renate Würsch, *Philosophie in der islamischen Welt,* Band I, 8.–10. Jahrhundert (Basel: Schwabe, 2012), pp. 238–43.

Ferster, Judith, *Fictions of Advice: The Literature and Politics of Counsel in Late Medieval England* (Philadelphia, PA: University of Pennsylvania Press, 1996).

Firdawsī, *Le livre des rois par Abouᵓlkasim Firdousi,* traduit et commenté par Jules Mohl (Paris: Imprimerie nationale, 1877).

Firestone, Reuven, 'Pharaoh', *EQ* IV (2004), pp. 66–8.

Fīrūzābādī, Abū Isḥāq Ibrāhīm b. ᶜAlī al-Shīrāzī, *Ṭabaqāt al-fuqahāᵓ,* ed. ᶜAlī Muḥammad ᶜUmar (Cairo: Maktabat al-Thaqāfa al-Dīniyya, 1997).

Fleischer, Cornell H., *Bureaucrat and Intellectual in the Ottoman Empire: The Historian Mustafa Âli (1541–1600)* (Princeton, NJ: Princeton University Press, 1986).

Flügel, Gustav, 'Zur Frage über die Romane und Erzählungen der mohammedanischen Völkerschaften', *Zeitschrift der Deutschen Morgenländischen Gesellschaft* 22 (1868): 731–7.

Forster, Regula, *Das Geheimnis der Geheimnisse: die arabischen und deutschen Fassungen des pseudo-aristotelischen Sirr al-asrār/Secretum secretorum* (Wiesbaden: Reichert Verlag, 2006).

Fouchécour, Charles-Henri de, *Moralia: les notions morales dans la littérature per-*

sane du 3e/9e au 7e/13e siècle (Paris: Institut français de recherche en Iran, 1986).

Fragner, Bert, 'The Concept of Regionalism in Historical Research on Central Asia and Iran (A Macro-Historical Interpretation)', in Devin DeWeese (ed.), *Studies on Central Asian History in Honor of Yuri Bregel* (Bloomington, IN: Indiana University Research Institute for Inner Asian Studies, 2001), pp. 341–53.

Frank, Tamar Zahava, 'Al-Kindī's *Book of Definitions*: Its Place in Arabic Definition Literature', PhD dissertation, Yale University, 1975.

Freimark, Peter, *Das Vorwort als literarische Form in der arabischen Literatur*, Inaugural-Dissertation zur Erlangung des Doktorgrades der Philosophischen Fakultät der Westfälischen Wilhelms-Universität zu Münster (Westfalen), Münster, 1967.

Frye, R. N., 'Notes on the History of Transoxiana', *Harvard Journal of Asiatic Studies* 19 (1956): 106–25.

Frye, R. N., *Bukhara: The Medieval Achievement* (Norman, OK: University of Oklahoma Press, 1965).

Frye, R. N., 'The Sāmānids', in R. N. Frye (ed.), *The Cambridge History of Iran, vol. IV: The Period from the Arab Invasions to the Saljuqs* (Cambridge: Cambridge University Press, 1975), pp. 136–61.

Frye, R. N., 'Bukhara', i: 'In Pre-Islamic Times', *EIr* IV (1990), pp. 511–13.

Frye, R. N., *Al-Narshakki's The History of Bukhara*, translation from the Persian abridgement (Princeton, NJ: Markus Wiener, 2007).

Fuchs, Walter, *Huei-chᶜao's Pilgerreise durch Nordwest-Indien und Zentral-Asien um 726* (Berlin: Verlag der Akademie der Wissenschaften in Kommission bei Walter de Gruyter, 1939 = Sonderausgabe aus den Sitzungsberichten der Preußlichen Akademie der Wissenschaften Phil.-hist. Klasse, 1938).

Fück, Johann W., 'Sechs Ergänzungen zu Sachaus Ausgabe von al-Bīrūnīs "Chronologie Orientalischer Völker"', *Documenta Islamica Inedita* (Berlin: Akademie-Verlag, 1952), pp. 69–98.

Gacek, Adam, 'Ownership Statements and Seals in Arabic Manuscripts', *Manuscripts of the Middle East* 2 (1987): 88–95.

Gacek, Adam, 'Technical Practices and Recommendations Recorded by Classical and Post-Classical Arabic Scholars Concerning the Copying and Correction of Manuscripts', in François Déroche (ed.), *Les manuscrits du Moyen-Orient: essais de codicologie et de paléographie* (Istanbul and Paris: Institut français d'études anatoliennes and Bibliothèque nationale, 1989), pp. 51–60.

Gacek, Adam, *The Arabic Manuscript Tradition: A Glossary of Technical Terms and Bibliography* (Leiden: Brill, 2001).

Galli, Ahmad Mohmed Ahmad, 'Some Aspects of al-Māturīdī's Commentary on the Qur᾿ān', *Islamic Studies* 21 (1982): 3–21.

Gardīzī, *Zayn al-akhbār = Tārīkh-i Gardīzī*, ed. ᶜAbd al-Ḥayy Ḥabībī (Tehran: Dunyā-yi Kitāb, 1984 or 1985).

Garel-Grislin, Julie, *Les manuscrits arabes et persans du cardinal Mazarin conservés à la Bibliothèque nationale de France*, Université de Lyon, Mémoire d'étude, Janvier 2013, Diplôme de conservateur des bibliothèques.

GAS = Sezgin, Fuat, *Geschichte des arabischen Schrifttums* (Leiden: Brill, 1967).

Geoffroy, Éric, *Le soufisme en Égypte et en Syrie sous les derniers mamelouks et les premiers ottomans: orientations spirituelles et enjeux culturels* (Damascus: Institut français de Damas, 1995).

Geoffroy, Éric, 'Le soufisme au verdict de la fatwa, selon les *Fatâwâ hadîthiyya* d'Ibn Hajar al-Haytamî (m. 974/1567)', in Rachida Chih and Catherine Mayeur-Jaouen, *Le soufisme à l'époque ottomane XVIe–XVIII siècle* (Cairo: Institut français d'archéologie orientale, 2010), pp. 119–28.

Ghazālī, *Naṣīḥat al-mulūk*, ed. Jalāl al-Dīn Humā᾿ī (Tehran: Kitābkhāneh-yi Millī, 1972) = F. R. C. Bagley, *Ghazālī's Book of Counsel for Kings* (London: Oxford University Press, 1964).

Al-Ghazālī, Abū Ḥāmid Muḥammad, *al-Tibr al-masbūk fī Naṣīḥat al-mulūk*, ed. Muḥammad Aḥmad Damaj (Beirut: Mu᾿assasat ᶜIzz al-Dīn lil-Ṭibāᶜa wa-l-Nashr, 1996).

Gilᶜadi, Avner, *Children of Islam: Concepts of Childhood in Medieval Muslim Society* (New York: St. Martin's Press, 1992).

Gilᶜadi, Avner, *Infants, Parents and Wet Nurses: Medieval Islamic Views on Breastfeeding and Their Social Implications* (Leiden: Brill, 1999).

Gilliot, Claude, 'La théologie musulmane en Asie centrale et au Khorasan', *Arabica* 49 (2002), pp. 135–203.

Gilliot, Claude, '*In consilium tuum deduces me*: le genre du «conseil», *naṣīḥa*, *waṣiyya* dans la littérature arabo-musulmane. *In Memoriam* Père Louis Pouzet, S.J.', *Arabica* 54 (2007): 466–99.

Gimaret, Daniel, 'Traces et parallèles du Kitāb Bilawhar wa Būḏāsf dans la tradition arabe', *Bulletin d'études orientales* 24 (1971): 97–133.

Gimaret, Daniel (ed), *Kitāb Bilawhar wa-Būḏāsf* (Beirut: Dār al-mashriq, 1972) = Gimaret, Daniel, *Le livre de Bilawhar et Būdāsf selon la version arabe ismaélienne* (Geneva and Paris: Librairie Droz, 1971).

Gimaret, D, 'Muʿtazila', EI² VII (1993), pp. 783–93.

Gnoli, Gherardo, 'Farr(ah)' EIr IX (1999), pp. 312–19.

Goitein, S. D., 'A Turning Point in the History of the Muslim State', *Studies in Islamic History and Institutions* (Leiden: Brill, 1968), pp. 150–67.

Golden, Peter, 'The Karakhanids and Early Islam', in Denis Sinor (ed.), *The Cambridge History of Early Inner Asia* (Cambridge: Cambridge University Press, 1990), pp. 343–70.

Gonzalez, Valerie, 'Sheba', *EQ* IV (2004), pp. 585–7.

Gordon, Matthew S., 'The Khāqānid Families of the Early ʿAbbasid Period', *Journal of the American Oriental Society* 121 (2001): 236–55.

Görke, Andreas and Konrad Hirschler, *Manuscript Notes as Documentary Sources* (Beirut: Orient-Institut Beirut, 2011).

Götz, Manfred, 'Māturīdī und sein Kitāb Taʾwīlāt al-Qurʾān', *Der Islam* 41 (1965): 27–70.

Grabar, Oleg, *Mostly Miniatures: An Introduction to Persian Painting* (Princeton, NJ: Princeton University Press, 1999).

Grignaschi, Mario, 'Quelques spécimens de la littérature sassanide conservés dans les bibliothèques d'Istanbul', *Journal asiatique* 254 (1966): 1–142.

Grignaschi, Mario, 'Les "Rasāʾil ʾAristāṭālīsa ʾilā-l-Iskandar" de Sālim Abū-l-ʿAlāʿ et l'activité culturelle à l'époque omayyade', *Bulletin d'études orientales* 19 (1967): 7–83.

Grignaschi, Mario, 'Le roman épistolaire classique conservé dans la version arabe de Sālim Abū 'l-ʿAlāʾ', *Le Muséon* 80 (1967): 211–54.

Grignaschi, Mario, 'La *Nihāyatu-l-ʾarab fī aḫbāri-l-furs wa-l-ʿarab* et les *Siyaru mulūki-l-ʿaǧam* du Ps. Ibn-al-Muqaffaʿ', Première partie, *Bulletin d'études orientales* 22 (1969): 15–67 and Deuxième partie, *Bulletin d'études orientales* 26 (1973): 83–148.

Grignaschi, Mario, 'La "Siyâsatu-l-ʿâmmiyya" et l'influence iranienne sur la pensée politique islamique', *Acta Iranica* VI, Deuxième Série, *Hommages et Opera Minora, vol. III: Monumentum H. S. Nyberg* (Leiden: Brill, 1975), pp. 33–286.

Grignaschi, Mario, 'La diffusion du "Secretum secretorum" (Sirr-al-ʾasrār) dans l'Europe occidentale', *Archives d'histoire doctrinale et littéraire du Moyen Âge* 47 (1980): 7–70.

Grignaschi, Mario, 'La figure d'Alexandre chez les Arabes et sa genèse', *Arabic Sciences and Philosophy* 3 (1993): 205–34.

Gril, Denis, *La Risāla de Ṣafī al-Dīn Ibn Abī l-Manṣūr Ibn Ẓāfir: biographies des maîtres spirituels connus par un cheikh égyptien du VIIe/XIIIe siècle* (Cairo: Institut français d'archéologie orientale du Caire, 1986).

Gruendler, Beatrice, 'Verse and Taxes: The Function of Poetry in Selected Literary *Akhbār* of the Third/Ninth Century', in Philip F. Kennedy (ed.), *On Fiction and* Adab *in Medieval Arabic Literature* (Wiesbaden: Harrassowitz, 2005), pp. 85–124.

Günther, Sebastian, 'Assessing the Sources of Classical Arabic Compilations: The Issue of Categories and Methodologies', *British Journal of Middle Eastern Studies* 32 (2005): 75–98.

Günther, Sebastian, '"Be Masters in That You Teach and Continue to Learn": Medieval Muslim Thinkers on Educational Theory', *Comparative Education Review* 50 (2006): 367–88.

Gutas, Dimitri, *Greek Wisdom Literature in Arabic Translation. A Study of the Graeco-Arabic Gnomologia* (New Haven, CT: American Oriental Society, 1975).

Gutas, Dimitri, 'Classical Arabic Wisdom Literature: Nature and Scope', *Journal of the American Oriental Society* 101 (1981): 49–86.

Gutas, Dimitri, 'Ethische Schriften im Islam', in Wolfhart Heinrichs (ed.), *Orientalisches Mittelalter* (Wiesbaden: AULA Verlag, 1990), pp. 346–65.

Ḥājjī Khalīfa = Muṣṭafā b. ᶜAbdallāh al-shahīr bi-Ḥājjī Khalīfa wa-bi-Kātib Chalabī, *Kitāb Kashf al-ẓunūn ᶜan asāmī al-kutub wa-l-funūn*, eds Muḥammad Sharaf al-Dīn Yāltaqāyā and Rifᶜat Bīlah al-Kilīsī = *Keşf-el-zunun*, eds Şerefettin Yaltkaya and Kilisli Rifat Bilge (Istanbul: Wakālat al-Maᶜārif = Maarif matbaası, 1941–3).

Hallaq, Wael B., *A History of Islamic Legal Theories: An Introduction to Sunnī* uṣūl al-fiqh (Cambridge: Cambridge University Press, 1997).

Hallaq, Wael B.,'Contracts and Alliances', *EQ* I (2001), pp. 431–4.

Halm, Heinz, *Kosmologie und Heilslehre der frühen Ismāᶜīlīya: Eine Studie zur islamischen Gnosis* (Wiesbaden: Franz Steiner, 1978).

Halm, Heinz, *Das Reich des Mahdi: Der Aufstieg der Fatimiden (875–973)* (Munich: Beck, 1991).

Al-Hamadhānī, Muḥammad b. ᶜAbd al-Malik, *Takmilat Taʾrīkh al-Ṭabarī, Dhuyūl Taʾrīkh al-Ṭabarī*, ed. Muḥammad Abū l-Faḍl Ibrāhīm (Cairo: Dar al-Maᶜārif), Taʾrīkh XI.

Hamdani, Sumaiya, 'The Dialectic of Power: Sunni–Shiᶜi Debates in Tenth-Century North Africa', *Studia Islamica* 90 (2000): 5–21.

Hamori, Andras, 'Ascetic Poetry (*Zuhdiyyāt*)', in Julia Ashtiany, T. M. Johnstone, J. D. Latham, R. B. Serjeant and G. Rex Smith (eds), *ᶜAbbasid Belles-Lettres*,

The Cambridge History of Arabic Literature (Cambridge: Cambridge University Press, 1990), pp. 265–74.

Hamori, Andras, 'Shameful and Injurious: An Idea of Ibn al-Muqaffa^{c}'s in *Kalīla wa-Dimna* and *al-Adab al-kabīr*', *Jerusalem Studies in Arabic & Islam* 32 (2006): 189–212.

Hamori, Andras, 'Going Down in Style: The Pseudo-Ibn Qutayba's Story of the Fall of the Barmakīs', *Princeton Papers in Near Eastern Studies* 3 (1994), pp. 89–125.

Hamori, Andras, 'Prudence, Virtue, and Self-Respect in Ibn al-Muqaffa^{c}', in Angelika Neuwirth and Andreas Christian Islebe (eds), *Reflections on Reflections: Near Eastern Writers Reading Literature; Dedicated to Renate Jacobi* (Wiesbaden: Reichert, 2006), pp. 161–79.

Hamori, Andras, 'Anthology', *EI Three*, available at: http://referenceworks.brillonline.com/entries/encyclopaedia-of-islam-3.

Hanna, Nelly, *In Praise of Books: A Cultural History of Cairo's Middle Class, Sixteenth to the Eighteenth Century* (Syracuse, NY: Syracuse University Press, 2003).

Harmsen, Nils, *Die Wasiya als literarisches Genre bis ins 14. Jahrhundert. Magisterarbeit an der Universität Hamburg, Fachbereich Orientalistik, Oktober 1997 Angabe* (Hamburg: Diplomarbeiten Agentur, 1999).

Hathaway, Jane, with contributions by Karl K. Barbir, *The Arab Lands under Ottoman Rule, 1516–1800* (Harlow: Pearson, 2008).

Haussig, Hans Wilhelm, *Die Geschichte Zentralasiens und der Seidenstrasse in vorislamischer Zeit* (Darmstadt: Wissenschaftliche Buchgesellschaft, 1983).

Havemann, Axel, *Riʾāsa und qaḍāʾ: Institutionen als Ausdruck wechselnder Kräfteverhältnisse in syrischen Städten vom 10. bis 12. Jahrhundert* (Freiburg: Schwarz Verlag, 1975).

Havemann, A., 'Naḳīb al-ashrāf', *EI*^{2} VII (1993), pp. 926–7.

Hawting, G. R., *The First Dynasty of Islam: The Umayyad Caliphate* AD *661–750* (London: Croom Helm, 1986).

Heck, Paul, *The Construction of Knowledge in Islamic Civilization: Qudāma b. Ja^{c}far and His* Kitāb al-Kharāj wa-ṣinā^{c}at al-kitāba (Leiden: Brill, 2002).

Heck, Paul L., 'The Hierarchy of Knowledge in Islamic Civilization', *Arabica* 49 (2002): 27–54.

Heidemann, Stefan, 'Numismatics', in Chase F. Robinson (ed.), *The New Cambridge History of Islam, vol. I: The Formation of the Islamic World Sixth to Eleventh Centuries* (Cambridge: Cambridge University Press, 2010), pp. 648–63.

Heller, B. [A. Rippin], 'Yūsha^{c} b. Nūn', *EI*^{2} XI (2002), p. 351.

Heinrichs, Wolfhart, 'The Classification of the Sciences and the Consolidation of

Philology in Classical Islam', in J. W. Drijvers and A. A. MacDonald (eds), *Centres of Learning: Learning and Location in Pre-modern Europe and the Near East* (Leiden: Brill, 1995), pp. 119–39.

Hillenbrand, Carole, 'Islamic Orthodoxy or Realpolitik? Al-Ghazālī's Views on Government', *Iran* 26 (1988): 81–94.

Hinds, Martin, 'al-Maghāzī', *EI*^{2} V (1986), pp. 1161–4.

Hinds, Martin, 'Miḥna', *EI*^{2} VII (1993), pp. 2–6.

Horten, Max, *Die Philosophie des abu Raschid (um 1068). Aus dem Arabischen übersetzt und erläutert* (Bonn: Peter Hanstein, 1910).

Howard, Douglas A., 'Ottoman Historiography and the Literature of "Decline" of the Sixteenth and Seventeenth Centuries', *Journal of Asian History* 22 (1988): 52–77.

Howard, Douglas A., 'Genre and Myth in the Ottoman Advice for Kings Literature', in Virginia H. Aksan and Daniel Goffman (eds), *The Early Modern Ottomans: Remapping the Empire* (Cambridge: Cambridge University Press, 2007), pp. 137–66.

Howard-Johnston, James, 'The Sasanians' Strategic Dilemma', in Henning Börm and Josef Wiesehöfer (eds), *Commutatio et contentio: Studies in the Late Roman, Sasanian, and Early Islamic Near East In Memory of Zeev Rubin* (Düsseldorf: Wellem Verlag, 2010), pp 37–70.

Hoyland, Robert G., 'History, Fiction and Authorship in the First Centuries of Islam', in Julia Bray (ed.), *Writing and Representation in Medieval Islam: Muslim Horizons* (London: Routledge, 2006), pp. 16–46.

Ḥudūd al-ᶜālam, trans. V. Minorsky, *The Regions of the World: A Persian Geography, 372 A.H. (982 A.D.)*, 2nd edn (London: E. J. W. Gibb Memorial, 1970).

Hurvitz, Nimrod, *The Formation of Hanbalism: Piety into Power, Culture and Civilization in the Middle East* (New York: Routledge Curzon, 2002).

Al-Ḥusaynī, Majd al-Dīn Muḥammad, *Zīnat al-majālis* (Qum: Kitābkhāneh-yi Sanāᵓī, 1963).

Al-Ḥuṣrī, Ibrāhīm b. ᶜAlī, *Zahr al-ādāb wa-thamar al-albāb* (Cairo: Dār Iḥyāᵓ al-Kutub al-ᶜArabiyya, 1953).

Ibn ᶜAbd Rabbihi, *al-ᶜIqd al-farīd*, ed. Karam al-Bustānī (Beirut: Maktabat Ṣādir, 1951–5) = *The Unique Necklace*, trans. Professor Issa J. Boullata (Reading: Garnet, 2006).

Ibn Abī Dharr = al-ᶜĀmirī, *al-Saᶜāda wa-l-isᶜād*, facsimile of copy prepared by Mujtaba Minovi (Wiesbaden: Franz Steiner, 1957–8).

Ibn Abī l-Dunyā, *Kitāb al-ᶜAql wa-faḍlihi wa-yalīhi Kitāb Dhamm al-malāhī*, ed. al-Saᶜīd b. Basyūnī Zaghlūl (Beirut: Muʾassasat al-Kutub wa-l-Thaqāfa, 1993).

Ibn Abī Uṣaybiᶜa, *Min ᶜUyūn al-anbāʾ fī ṭabaqāt al-aṭibbāʾ* (Damascus: Manshūrāt Wizārat al-Thaqāfa, 1997).

Ibn al-Athīr, *al-Kāmil fī l-taʾrīkh*, ed. C. J. Tornberg, *Ibn-el-Athiri Chronicon quod perfectissimum inscribitur* (Leiden: Brill, 1862 = Beirut: Dār Ṣādir, 1965–7).

Ibn al-Balkhī, *Fārsnāmeh*, ed. ᶜAlī Naqī Bihrūzī (Shiraz: Ittiḥādīyeh-yi Matbūᶜātī-yi Fārs, 1964).

Ibn Faḍlān, *Risālat Ibn Faḍlān*, ed. Samī al-Dahhān (Damascus: Majmaᶜ al-Lugha al-ᶜArabiyya bi-Dimashq, 1959).

Ibn al-Faqīh, *Kitāb al-Buldān*, ed. M. J. de Goeje (Leiden: Brill, 1885 = Beirut: Dār Ṣādir, 1967).

Ibn Farīghūn, *Jawāmiᶜ al-ᶜulūm = Compendium of Sciences: Jawāmiᶜ al-ᶜulūm by Ibn Farīᶜūn (Tenth Century A.D.)*, ed. F. Sezgin (Frankfurt: Maᶜhad Taʾrīkh al-ᶜUlūm al-ᶜArabiyya wa-l-Islāmiyya, 1985).

Ibn al-Farrāʾ, al-Ḥusayn b. Muḥammad, *Kitāb Rusul al-mulūk wa-man yaṣluḥu lil-risāla wa-l-sifāra*, ed. Ṣalāḥ al-Dīn al-Munajjid (Cairo: Maṭbaᶜat Lajnat al-Taʾlīf wa-l-Tarjama wa-l-Nashr, 1947).

Ibn Funduq, see Bayhaqī, ᶜAlī b. Zayd.

Ibn Ḥajar al-ᶜAsqalānī, *Tabṣīr al-muntabih bi-taḥrīr al-mushtabih*, eds ᶜAlī Muḥammad al-Bijāwī and Muḥammad ᶜAlī al-Najjār (Cairo: al-Dār al-Miṣriyya lil-Taʾlīf wa-l-Tarjama, 1966).

Ibn Ḥajar al-ᶜAsqalānī, *Lisān al-mīzān* (Beirut: Dār al-Bashāʾir al-Islāmiyya, 2002).

Ibn Ḥanbal, Aḥmad, *Musnad al-Imām Aḥmad b. Ḥanbal*, eds Shuᶜayb al-Arnāʾūt and ᶜĀdil Murshid (Beirut: Muʾassasat al-Risāla, 1993–2008).

Ibn Ḥawqal, *Kitāb Ṣūrat al-arḍ* (Leiden: Brill, 1939).

Ibn Hindū, Abū l-Faraj, *al-Kalim al-rūḥāniyya min al-ḥikam al-yūnāniyya*, ed. Muḥammad Jalūb al-Farḥān (Beirut: al-Sharika al-ᶜĀlamiyya lil-Kitāb, 2001).

Ibn al-ᶜImād, Shihāb al-Dīn ᶜAbd al-Ḥayy, *Shadharāt al-dhahab fī akhbār man dhahab*, eds ᶜAbd al-Qādir al-Arnāʾūt and Maḥmūd al-Arnāʾūt (Damascus and Beirut: Dār Ibn Kathīr, 1988).

Ibn Isfandiyār, *Tārīkh-i Ṭabaristān*, ed. A. Iqbāl (Tehran: Majlis, 1941).

Ibn al-Jawzī, Abū l-Faraj ᶜAbd al-Raḥmān, *Kitāb al-Quṣṣāṣ wa-l-mudhakkirīn*, ed. and trans. Merlin S. Swartz (Beirut: Dār al-Mashriq, 1986).

Ibn al-Jawzī, Abū l-Faraj ᶜAbd al-Raḥmān, *Ṣayd al-khāṭir*, eds al-Sayyid Muḥammad Sayyid and Sayyid Ibrāhīm (Cairo: Dār al-Ḥadīth, 1996).

Ibn al-Jawzī, *al-Muntaẓam fī ta'rīkh al-mulūk wa-l-umam* (Hyderabad: Maṭba'at Dā'irat al-Ma'ārif al-'Uthmāniyya, 1940).
Ibn al-Jawzī, *al-Miṣbāḥ al-muḍī' fī khilāfat al-Mustaḍī'*, ed. Nājiya 'Abdallāh Ibrāhīm (Baghdad: Madrasa Musā'ida – Jāmi'at Baghdād, 1976; reprinted Beirut, 2000).
Ibn Kathīr, *Ṭabaqāt al-shāfi'iyya*, ed. 'Abd al-Ḥafīẓ Manṣūr (Beirut: Dār al-Madār al-Islāmī, 2004).
Ibn Khallikān, *Wafayāt al-a'yān wa-anbā' abnā' al-zamān*, ed. Iḥsān 'Abbās (Beirut: Dār Ṣādir, 1977).
Ibn Khurradādhbih, *Kitāb al-Masālik wa-l-mamālik*, ed. M. J. de Goeje (Leiden: Brill, 1889).
Ibn Māja, Muḥammad b. Yazīd, *Sunan*, eds Maḥmūd Muḥammad Maḥmūd Ḥasan Naṣṣār (Beirut: Dār al-Kutub al-'Ilmiyya, 1998).
Ibn Manẓūr, see *LA*.
Ibn al-Muqaffa', *Āthār Ibn al-Muqaffa'*, ed. 'Umar Abū l-Naṣr (Beirut: Dār Maktabat al-Ḥayāt, 1966).
Ibn al-Muqaffa', *Kitāb Kalīla wa-Dimna*, ed. 'Abd al-Wahhāb 'Azzām (Cairo: al-Ma'ārif, 1941).
Ibn al-Muqaffa', *Kalīla wa-Dimna* in Louis Cheikho (ed.), *La version arabe de Kalîlah et Dimnah ou Les fables de Bidpai* (Amsterdam: Academic Publishers/Philo Press, 1981; reprint of Beirut, 1905).
Ibn al-Nadīm, *al-Fihrist*, eds Sha'bān Khalīfa and Walīd Muḥammad al-'Awza (*al-Fihrist li-bn al-Nadīm*) (Cairo: al-'Arabī lil-Nashr wa-l-Tawzī', 1991).
Ibn al-Nadīm, *Kitāb al-Fihrist*, ed. Ayman Fu'ād Sayyid (London, Mu'assasat al-Furqān lil-Turāth al-Islāmī, 2009).
Ibn Qutayba, *Kitāb 'Uyūn al-akhbār* (Cairo: Maṭba'at Dār al-Kutub al-Miṣriyya, 1925).
Ibn Qutayba, *al-Ma'ārif*, ed. Tharwat 'Ukāsha (Cairo: Dār al-Ma'ārif, 1981).
Ibn Razīn, 'Alī, *Ādāb al-mulūk*, ed. J. al-'Aṭiyya (Beirut: Dār al-Ṭalī'a lil-Ṭibā'a wa-l-Nashr, 2001).
Ibn Rusta, Abū 'Alī Aḥmad b. 'Umar, *al-A'lāq al-nafīsa* (Leiden: Brill, 1891).
Ibn Sīnā, *Aqsām al-'ulūm (al-'aqliyya)*, in *Tis' rasā'il fī l-ḥikma wa-l-ṭabī'iyyāt* (Cairo: Maṭba'a Hindiyya, 1908).
Ibn Sīnā, *Pīrūzīnāmeh mansūb bi-Buzurgmihr-i Bakhtagān*, Tarjameh-yi Abū 'Alī Sīnā, ed. Kāżim Rajavī (Tehran: Kitābfurūshī-yi Ibn Sīnā, 1954).
Ibn Taghribirdī, *al-Nujūm al-zāhira fī mulūk Miṣr wa-l-Qāhira* (Cairo: al-Mu'assasa al-Miṣriyya al-'Āmma lil-Ta'līf wa-l-Ṭibā'a wa-l-Nashr, 1963–71).

Ibn Ṭayfur, Aḥmad Ibn Ṭāhir al-Kātib [al-maᶜrūf bi-Ibn Ṭayfūr], *Baghdād fī taʾrīkh al-khilāfa al-ᶜabbāsiyya* (Baghdad: Maktabat al-Muthannā, 1968).

Ibn al-Zubayr, *Kitāb al-Dhakhāʾir wa-l-tuḥaf*, ed. M. Ḥamīd Allāh (Kuwait: Maṭbaᶜat Ḥukūmat al-Kuwayt, 1984).

Irwin, R., 'al-Subkī', *EAL* II (1998), pp. 737–8.

Al-Iṣfahānī, Ḥamza b. al-Ḥasan, *Taʾrīkh sinī mulūk al-arḍ wa-l-anbiyāʾ* (Beirut: Manshūrāt Dār Maktabat al-Ḥayāt, 1961).

Al-Iṣṭakhrī, *Kitāb Masālik al-mamālik*, ed. M. J. de Goeje, *Viae regnorum. Descriptio ditionis moslemicae auctore Abu Ishák al-Fárisí al-Istakhrí* (Leiden: Brill, 1870).

Ivry, Alfred L., *Al-Kindi's Metaphysics: A Translation of Yaᶜqūb ibn Isḥāq al-Kindī's Treatise 'On First Philosophy' (fī al-Falsafah al-Ūlā)* (Albany, NY: State University of New York Press, 1974).

Ivry, Alfred L., 'Al-Kindī and the Muᶜtazila: A Philosophical and Political Reevaluation' *Oriens* 25/26 (1976): 69–85.

Izutsu, Toshihiko, *Ethico-Religious Concepts in the Qurʾān* (Montreal: McGill University Press, 1966).

Al-Jāḥiẓ, *al-Bayān wa-l-tabyīn*, ed. ᶜAbd al-Salām Muḥammad Hārūn (Cairo: Maktabat al-Khānjī, 1960).

Al-Jāḥiẓ, *Rasāʾil al-Jāḥiẓ*, ed. ᶜAbd al-Salām Muḥammad Hārūn (Cairo: Maktabat al-Khānjī, 1964–79).

Al-Jahshiyārī, *Kitāb al-Wuzarāʾ wa-l-kuttāb* (Cairo: Muṣṭafā al-Bābī al-Ḥalabī wa-Awlāduhu, 1980).

Jihāmī, Jirār, *Mawsūᶜāt muṣṭalaḥāt al-falsafa ᶜind al-ᶜarab* (Beirut: Maktabat Lubnān Nāshirūn, 1998).

Judd, Steven C., 'Ghaylan al-Dimashqi: The Isolation of a Heretic in Islamic Historiography', *International Journal of Middle East Studies* 31 (1999): 161–84.

Judd, Steven, 'Reinterpreting al-Walīd b. Yazīd', *Journal of the American Oriental Society* 128 (2008): 439–58.

Jurado Aceituno, Antonio, 'La "ḫidma" selyuqí: la red de relaciones de dependencia mutua, la dinámica del poder y las formas de obtención de los beneficios', unpublished PhD dissertation, Madrid, Universidad Autónoma, 1993.

Kaabi, Mongi, 'Les Ṭāhirides: étude historico-littéraire de la dynastie des Banū Ṭāhir b. al-Ḥusayn au Ḫurāsān et en Iraq au IIIème s. de l'hégire/IXème s. J.-C.', Thèse de doctorat d'état ès lettres et sciences humaines (Paris: Université de Paris-Sorbonne, Faculté des lettres et sciences humaines, 1971).

Al-Kaᶜbī, Abū l-Qāsim, *Maqālāt = Faḍl al-iᶜtizāl wa-ṭabaqāt al-muᶜtazila*, ed. Fuʾād Sayyid (Tunis: al-Dār al-Tūnisiyya lil-Nashr, 1974), pp. 63–119.

Al-Kaᶜbī, Abū l-Qāsim, *Qubūl al-akhbār wa-maᶜrifat al-rijāl* (Beirut: Dār al-Kutub al-ᶜIlmiyya, 2000).

Al-Kaᶜbī, Abū l-Qāsim, *Tafsīr Abī l-Qāsim al-Kaᶜbī al-Balkhī* (Beirut: Dār al-Kutub al-ᶜIlmiyya, 2007).

Karev, Yury, 'Qarakhanid Wall Paintings in the Citadel of Samarqand: First Report and Preliminary Observations', *Muqarnas* XXII (2005): 45–84.

Kartanegara, R. Mulyadhi, 'The Mukhtaṣar Ṣiwān al-ḥikma of ᶜUmar b. Sahlān al-Sāwī: Arabic Text and Introduction', PhD dissertation, University of Chicago, 1996.

Al-Kātib, Isḥāq b. Ibrāhīm, *al-Burhān fī wujūh al-bayān* (Cairo: Maktabat al-Shabāb, 1969).

Kātib Chalabī, *Kitāb Kashf al-ẓunūn ᶜan asāmī al-kutub wa-l-funūn*, see Ḥājjī Khalīfa.

Kaykāʾūs, *Qābūsnāmeh*, ed. Ghulām-Ḥusayn Yūsufī (Tehran: Shirkat-i Intishārāt-i ᶜIlmī va-Farhangī, 1989) = Reuben Levy, *A Mirror for Princes: The Qābūs nāma* (London: Cresset Press, 1951).

Keith-Falconer, I. G. N., *Kalīlah and Dimnah or the Fables of Bidpai* (Cambridge: Cambridge University Press, 1885).

Kennedy, Hugh, 'al-Muwaffaḳ', *EI*^{2} VII (1993), p. 801.

Kennedy, Hugh, *The Armies of the Caliphs: Military and Society in the Early Islamic State* (London: Routledge, 2001).

Kennedy, Hugh, *The Prophet and the Age of the Caliphates*, 2nd edn (London: Pearson, 2004).

Keşf-el-zunun, see Ḥājjī Khalīfa.

Keshk, Khaled M. G., 'Abū Sufyān', *EI Three*, available at: http://referenceworks.brillonline.com/entries/encyclopaedia-of-islam-3.

Khaleghi-Motlagh, Djalal, 'Abū ᶜAlī Bal<u>k</u>ī', *EIr* I (1985), pp. 254–5.

Khaleghi-Motlagh, Djalal, 'Abū Manṣūr (Moḥammad b.) ᶜAbd-al-Razzāq', *EIr* I (1985), p. 335.

Khaleghi-Motlagh, Djalal, 'Abū Manṣūr Maᶜmarī', *EIr* I (1985), p. 337.

Khaleghi-Motlagh, Djalal, 'Amīrak Balᶜamī, *EIr* I (1985), pp. 971–2.

Khaleghi-Motlagh, Djalal, 'Borzūya', *EIr* IV (1990), pp. 381–2.

Khaleghi-Motlagh, Djalal, 'Bozorgmehr-e Bo<u>k</u>tagān', *EIr* IV (1990), pp. 427–9.

Khaleghi-Motlagh, Djalal, 'Daqīqī', *EIr* VI (1993), pp. 661–2.

Khalidi, Tarif, *Islamic Historiography: The Histories of Masᶜūdī* (Albany, NY: State University of New York Press, 1975).

Khalidi, Tarif, *Arabic Historical Thought in the Classical Period* (Cambridge: Cambridge University Press, 1994).

Khan, Geoffrey, *Arabic Documents from Early Islamic Khurasan* (London: Nour Foundation, 2007).

Khan, Geoffrey, 'Newly Discovered Arabic Documents from Early Abbasid Khurasan', in Petra M. Sijpesteijn, Lennart Sundelin, Sofía Torallas Tovar and Amalia Zomeño (eds), *From al-Andalus to Khurasan: Documents from the Medieval Muslim World* (Leiden: Brill, 2007), pp. 201–15.

Al-Khaṭīb al-Baghdādī, *Taʾrīkh Baghdād aw-Madīnat al-salām* (Beirut: Dār al-Kitāb al-ʿArabī, 1966).

Al-Khaṭṭābī al-Bustī, Ḥamd b. Muḥammad, *Maʿālim al-sunan lil-Imām Abī Sulaymān . . . al-Khaṭṭābī al-Bustī wa-huwa Sharḥ Sunan al-Imām Abī Dāʾūd*, ed. Muḥammad Rāghib al-Ṭabbākh (Aleppo: al-Maṭbaʿa al-ʿIlmiyya, 1933).

Al-Khaṭṭābī, *al-ʿUzla*, ed. ʿAbdallāh Ḥajjāj (Cairo: Maktabat al-Turāth al-Islāmī, n.d.).

Khismatulin, A., 'To Forge a Book in the Medieval Ages: Nezām al-Molk's *Siyar al-molūk* (*Siyāsat-nāma*)', *Journal of Persianate Studies* I (2008): 30–66.

Khismatulin, A., 'The Art of Medieval Counterfeiting: The *Siyar al-mulūk* (the *Siyāsat-nāma*) by Niẓām al-Mulk and the "Full" Version of the *Naṣīḥat al-mulūk* by al-G͟hazālī', *Manuscripta Orientalia: International Journal for Oriental Manuscript Research* 14 (2008): 3–31.

Khoury, R. G., *Wahb b. Munabbih, Teil I: Der Heidelberger Papyrus PSR Heid Arab 23* (Wiesbaden: Harrassowitz, 1972).

Khoury, R. G., 'Al-ʿArim', *EQ* I (2001), pp. 60–1.

Al-Khwārazmī, *Mafātīḥ al-ʿulūm*, ed. G. van Vloten, Liber *Mafâtîh al-olûm* (Leiden: Brill, 1895–1968).

Kilpatrick, H., 'A Genre in Classical Arabic: The Arabic Encyclopedia', in Robert Hillenbrand (ed.), *Union Européenne des Arabisants et Islamisants*, Proceedings of the 10th Congress, Edinburgh, September 1980 (Edinburgh: Edinburgh University Press, 1982), pp. 34–42.

Kilpatrick, H., 'Anthologies, Medieval', *EAL* I (1998), pp. 94–6.

Kilpatrick, H., 'Encyclopedias, Medieval', *EAL* I (1998), pp. 208–9.

Kilpatrick, H., 'The "genuine" Ashʿab. The Relativity of Fact and Fiction in Early *Adab* Texts', in Stefan Leder (ed.), *Story-telling in the Framework of Non-fictional Arabic Literature* (Wiesbaden: Harrassowitz, 1998), pp. 94–117.

Kinberg, Leah, 'What is Meant by *Zuhd*', *Studia Islamica* 61 (1985): 27–44.

Kinberg, Leah, 'Qurʾān and Ḥadīth: A Struggle for Supremacy as Reflected in Dream Narratives', in Louise Marlow (ed.), *Dreaming Across Boundaries: The*

Interpretation of Dreams in Islamic Lands (Boston, MA and Washington, DC: Ilex Foundation and Center for Hellenic Studies, 2008), pp. 25–49.

Al-Kindī, *Rasāʾil al-Kindī al-falsafiyya*, ed. Muḥammad ᶜAbd al-Hādī Abū Rīda (Cairo: Dār al-Fikr al-ᶜArabī, 1953).

Al-Kindî: Cinq épîtres (Paris: Centre National de la recherche scientifique, 1976).

Kirmānī, Nāṣir al-Dīn Munshī, *Nasāʾim al-asḥār min laṭāʾim al-akhbār dar tārīkh-i vuzarāʾ*, ed. Mīr Jalāl al-Dīn Ḥusaynī Urmavī 'Muḥaddith' (Tehran: Dānishgāh-i Tihrān, 1985).

Kitāb al-Tāj = *Kitāb al-Tāj fī akhlāq al-mulūk*, ed. Ahmed Zeki Pacha, *Le livre de la couronne (Kitab el Tadj)* (Cairo: Imprimerie nationale, 1914) = Charles Pellat, *Le livre de la couronne* (Paris: Société d'Édition Les Belles Lettres, 1954).

Klein-Franke, Félix, 'Al-Kindi's "On Definitions and Descriptions of Things"', *Le Muséon* 95 (1982): 191–216.

Klimburg-Salter, Deborah, 'Bāmiyān: Recent Research', *East and West* 38 (1988): 305–12.

Klimburg-Salter, Deborah, 'Bāmiyān: An Obituary and a Glance Towards the Future', *Oriental Art* XLIV (2003): 2–12.

Kochnev, Boris, 'Les monnaies de Muqannaᶜ', *Studia Iranica* 30 (2001): 143–50.

Kolesnikov, A. I., 'The Information of the Early Muslim Geographers about the Confessional Situation in Khurasan in the 9th–12th Centuries', *Studies in Arabic and Islam,* Proceedings of the 19th Congress, Halle, 1998, pp. 81–8.

Kraemer, Joel L., *Philosophy in the Renaissance of Islam: Abū Sulaymān al-Sijistānī and His Circle* (Leiden: Brill, 1986).

Kratchkovsky, Ign., 'Le Kitāb al-ādāb d'Ibn al-Muᶜtazz', *Le monde oriental* 16 (1924): 56–121.

Kristó-Nagy, István T., *La pensée d'Ibn al-Muqaffaᶜ: un 'agent double' dans le monde persan et arabe* (Paris: Éditions de Paris, 2013).

Al-Kulaynī, *al-Kāfī*, see *al-Kutub al-arbaᶜa.*

Al-Kutub al-arbaᶜa = al-Kulaynī, *al-Kāfī*; Ibn Bābawayh, *Man lā yaḥḍuruhu l-faqīh*; al-Ṭūsī, *Tahdhīb al-aḥkām*; al-Ṭūsī, *al-Istibṣār* (Qum: Anṣārīyān lil-Ṭibāᶜa wa-l-Nashr, 2003).

LA = Ibn Manẓūr, *Lisān al-ᶜarab* (Cairo: Dār al-maᶜārif, 1981).

Lambton, A. K. S., 'Justice in the Medieval Persian Theory of Kingship', *Studia Islamica* 17 (1962): 91–119.

Lambton, A. K. S., 'Islamic Mirrors for Princes', in *La Persia nel medioevo, Quaderno dell'Accademia Nazionale dei Lincei* 160 (Rome, 1971), pp. 419–42.

Lambton, A. K. S., *State and Government in Medieval Islam* (Oxford: Oxford University Press, 1981).

Lamoreaux, John C., *The Early Muslim Tradition of Dream Interpretation* (Albany, NY: State University of New York Press, 2002).

Lang, D. M., *The Wisdom of Balahvar: A Christian Legend of the Buddha* (London: Allen & Unwin, 1957).

Lapidus, Ira M., *A History of Islamic Societies*, 2nd edn (Cambridge: Cambridge University Press, 2002).

Latham, J. D., 'The Beginnings of Arabic Prose Literature: The Epistolary Genre', in A. F. L. Beeston, T. M. Johnstone, R. B. Serjeant and G. R. Smith (eds), *Arabic Literature to the End of the Umayyad Period* (Cambridge: Cambridge University Press, 1983), pp. 154–79.

Latham, J. D., 'Ibn al-Muqaffaᶜ and Early ᶜAbbasid Prose', in Julia Ashtiany, T. M. Johnstone, J. D. Latham, R. B. Serjeant and G. Rex Smith (eds), *ᶜAbbasid Belles-Lettres* (Cambridge: Cambridge University Press, 1990), pp. 48–77.

Lawrence, Bruce B., 'Shahrastānī on Indian Idol Worship', *Studia Islamica* 38 (1973): 61–73.

Lawrence, Bruce B., *Shahrastānī on the Indian Religions* (The Hague: Mouton, 1976).

The Laws of Manu, trans. Wendy Doniger with Brian K. Smith (London: Penguin, 1991).

Lazard, G., *Les premiers poètes persans (IXe–Xe siècles): fragments rassemblés, édités et traduits* (Tehran: Centre national de la recherche scientifique, 1964).

Lazard, G., 'Pahlavi, parsi, dari: les langues de l'Iran d'après Ibn al-Muqaffaᶜ', in C. E. Bosworth (ed.), *Iran and Islam, in Memory of the Late V. Minorsky* (Edinburgh: Edinburgh University Press, 1971), pp. 361–91.

Lazard, G., 'The Rise of the New Persian Language', in R. N. Frye (ed.), *The Cambridge History of Iran, vol. IV: The Period from the Arab Invasion to the Saljuqs* (Cambridge: Cambridge University Press, 1975), pp. 595–632.

Lazard, G., 'Abu'l-Moᵓayyad Balḵī', *EIr* I (1985), p. 340.

Lecomte, Gérard, *Ibn Qutayba (mort en 276/889): l'homme, son oeuvre, ses idées* (Damascus: Institut français de Damas, 1965).

Leder, Stefan, 'Prosa-Dichtung in der *aḫbār* Überlieferung: Narrative Analyse einer Satire', *Der Islam* 64 (1987): 6–41.

Leder, Stefan, 'Conventions of Fictional Narration in Learned Literature', in Stefan Leder (ed.), *Story-telling in the Framework of Non-fictional Arabic Literature* (Wiesbaden: Harrassowitz, 1998), pp. 34–60.

Leder, Stefan, 'Aspekte arabischer und persischer Fürstenspiegel: Legitimation,

Fürstenethik, politische Vernunft', in Angela de Benedictis (ed.), *Specula principum* (Frankfurt: Vittorio Klostermann, 1999), pp. 21–50.

Leder, Stefan and Hilary Kilpatrick, 'Classical Arabic Prose Literature: A Researcher's Sketch Map', *Journal of Arabic Literature* 23(1) (1992): 2–26.

Le Strange, Guy, *The Lands of the Eastern Caliphate* (Cambridge: Cambridge University Press, 1930).

Lewisohn, L., 'Taḳwā', *EI*[2] XII Supplement (2004), pp. 781–5.

Lisān al-Lisān: Tahdhīb Lisān al-ᶜarab (Beirut: Dār al-Kutub al-ᶜIlmiyya, 1993).

Little, Donald, 'A New Look at *al-Aḥkām al-sulṭāniyya*', *Muslim World* 64 (1974): 1–15.

Lowry, Joseph E., 'The First Islamic Legal Theory: Ibn al-Muqaffaᶜ on Interpretation, Authority, and the Structure of the Law', *Journal of the American Oriental Society* 128 (2008): 25–40.

Madelung, Wilferd, *Der Imam al-Qāsim ibn Ibrāhīm und die Glaubenslehre der Zaiditen* (Berlin: Walter de Gruyter, 1965).

Madelung, Wilferd, 'The Assumption of the Title Shāhānshāh by the Buyids and "The Reign of the Daylam (*Dawlat al-Daylam*)"', Part I, *Journal of Near Eastern Studies*, 28(2) (1969): 84–108; Part II, *Journal of Near Eastern Studies* 28(3) (1969): 168–83.

Madelung, Wilferd, 'ᶜIṣma', *EI*[2] IV (1978), pp. 182–4.

Madelung, Wilferd, 'Abu'l-Qāsem Esḥāq Samarqandī', *EIr* I (1985), pp. 358–9.

Madelung, Wilferd, 'Abū Rašīd Nīsābūrī', *EIr* I (1985), pp. 367–8.

Madelung, Wilferd, 'The Early Murjiʾa in Khurāsān and Transoxania and the Spread of Ḥanafism', *Der Islam* 59 (1982): 32–39; reprinted in *Religious Schools and Sects in Medieval Islam* (London: Variorum, 1985), III.

Madelung, Wilferd, 'The Spread of Māturīdism and the Turks', in *Actas do IV Congresso de Estudos Árabes e Islâmicos Coimbra-Lisboa 1968* (Leiden, 1971), pp. 109–68; reprinted in *Religious Schools and Sects in Medieval Islam* (London: Variorum, 1985), II.

Madelung, Wilferd, *Religious Trends in Early Islamic Iran* (Albany, NY: State University of New York Press, 1988).

Madelung, Wilferd, 'al-Māturīdī, Abū Manṣūr', *EI*[2] VI (1991), pp. 846–7.

Madelung, Wilferd and Paul E. Walker, *An Ismaili Heresiography: The 'Bāb al-shayṭān' from Abū Tammām's* Kitāb al-shajara (Leiden: Brill, 1998).

Makdisi, George, *The Rise of Colleges: Institutions of Learning in Islam and the West* (Edinburgh: Edinburgh University Press, 1981).

Makḥūl al-Nasafī, see Bernand, Marie.

Malamud, Margaret, 'The Politics of Heresy in Medieval Khurasan: The Karramiyya in Nishapur', *Iranian Studies* 27 (1994): 37–51.

Al-Manīnī, Aḥmad b. ᶜAlī, *Sharḥ al-Yamīnī al-musammā bi-l-Fatḥ al-wahbī ᶜalā Taʾrīkh Abī Naṣr al-ᶜUtbī* (Cairo: al-Maṭba al-Wahabiyya, 1869).

Mānkdīm, *Taᶜlīq Sharḥ al-uṣūl al-khamsa = Sharḥ al-uṣūl al-khamsa li-Qāḍī al-Quḍāt ᶜAbd al-Jabbār ibn Aḥmad*, ed. ᶜAbd al-Karīm ᶜUthmān (Cairo: Maktabat Wahba, 1965).

Manzalaoui, Mahmoud, 'The Pseudo-Aristotelian *Kitāb Sirr al-asrār*: Facts and Problems', *Oriens* (1974): 147–257.

Al-Maqdisī, al-Muṭahhar b. Ṭāhir, *Kitāb al-Badʾ wa-l-taʾrīkh*, ed. Cl. Huart (Paris: Leroux, 1899–1919).

Margoliouth, D. S., 'Some Extracts from the *Kitāb al-Imtāᶜ wal-muʾānasah* of Abū Ḥayyān Tauḥīdī', *Islamica* 2 (1926): 380–90.

Marlow, Louise, *Hierarchy and Egalitarianism in Islamic Thought* (Cambridge: Cambridge University Press, 1997).

Marlow, Louise, 'Advice and Advice Literature', *EI Three* I (2007), pp. 34–58.

Marlow, Louise, 'A Sāmānid Work of Counsel and Commentary: The *Naṣīḥat al-mulūk* of Pseudo-Māwardī', *Iran* 44 (2007): 181–92.

Marlow, Louise, 'Advice Literature in Tenth- and Early Eleventh-Century Iran and Early Persian Prose Writing', in Edmund Herzig and Sarah Stewart (eds), *Early Islamic Iran* (London: Tauris, 2012), pp. 76–101.

Marlow, Louise, 'Among Kings and Sages: Greek and Indian Wisdom in an Arabic Mirror for Princes', *Arabica* 60(1/2) (2013): 1–57.

Marlow, Louise, 'Difference and Encyclopaedism in Tenth-Century Eastern Iran', *Jerusalem Studies in Arabic & Islam* 40 (2013): 195–244.

Marlow, Louise, 'Teaching Wisdom: A Persian Work of Advice for Atabeg Ahmad of Luristan', in Mehrzad Boroujerdi (ed.), *Mirror for the Muslim Prince: Islam and the Theory of Statecraft* (Syracuse, NY: Syracuse University Press, 2013), pp. 122–59.

Marlow, Louise, 'Abū Zayd al-Balkhī and the *Naṣīḥat al-mulūk* of Pseudo-Māwardī', *Der Islam* (forthcoming).

Marlow, L., 'Performances of Advice and Admonition in the Courts of Muslim Rulers of the Ninth-Eleventh Centuries', in Evelyn Birge Vitz and Maurice Pomerantz (eds), *Courts and Performance in the Premodern Middle East 700–1600* (New York, NY: New York University Press, forthcoming).

Maróth, Miklós, *The Correspondence between Aristotle and Alexander the Great: An*

Anonymous Greek Novel in Letters in Arabic Translation (Piliscsaba: Avicenna Institute of Middle Eastern Studies, 2006).

Marquart, Joseph, *Ērānšahr nach der Geographie des Ps. Moses Xorenac^c^i* (Berlin: Weidmannsche Buchhandlung, 1901).

Martin, B. G., 'A Short History of the Khalwati Order of Dervishes', in Nikki R. Keddie (ed.), *Scholars, Saints, and Sufis: Muslim Religious Institutions in the Middle East since 1500* (Berkeley, CA: University of California Press, 1972), pp. 275–305.

Massé, H., 'Buzurgmihr', *EI*[2] I (1986), pp. 1358–9.

Al-Mas^c^ūdī, *Kitāb al-Tanbīh wa-l-ishrāf*, ed. M. J. de Goeje (Leiden: Brill, 1893; photo-offset reproduction, Beirut: Maktabat Khayyāṭ, 1965).

Al-Mas^c^ūdī, *Murūj al-dhahab wa-ma^c^ādin al-jawhar* (Beirut: Dār al-Andalus, 1984).

Al-Māturīdī, Abū Manṣūr Muḥammad, *Kitāb al-Tawḥīd* = Ebû Mansûr el-Mâtürîdî, *Kitâbü't-Tevhîd*, eds Bekir Topaloğlu and Muhammed Aruçi (Ankara: Türkiye Diyanet Vakfı Islâm Araştırmaları Merkezi Yayınları, 2003).

(Pseudo-Māturīdī), *Pandnāmeh-yi Māturīdī*, ed. Īraj Afshār, *Farhang-i Īrān-zamīn* 9 (1961): 48–67.

Marvazī, see Minorsky.

Al-Māwardī, *Naṣīḥat al-mulūk*, Bibliothèque nationale de France, MS Arabe, 2778.

Al-Māwardī, *Adab al-dunyā wa-l-dīn*, ed. Muṣṭafā Saqqā (Cairo: Maṭba^c^at Muṣṭafā al-Bābī al-Ḥalabī wa-Awlādihi, 1973) = O. Rescher, *Das kitâb 'adab ed-dunjâ wa 'ddîn' [über die richtige Lebensart in praktischen und moralischen Dingen] des Qâḍî abû 'l-Ḥasan el-Baçrî, gennant Mâwerdî* (Stuttgart, 1932).

Al-Māwardī, *al-Wizāra: Adab al-wazīr*, eds Muḥammad Sulaymān Dā^ɔ^ūd and Fu^ɔ^ād ^c^Abd al-Mun^c^im Aḥmad (Alexandria: Dār al-Jāmi^c^āt al-Miṣriyya, 1976).

Al-Māwardī, *al-Tuḥfa al-mulūkiyya fī l-ādāb al-siyāsiyya al-mansūba lil-Imām Abī l-Ḥasan al-Māwardī*, ed. Fu^ɔ^ād ^c^Abd al-Mun^c^im Aḥmad (Alexandria: Mu^ɔ^assasat Shabāb al-Jāmi^c^a, 1977).

Al-Māwardī, *Qawānīn al-wizāra wa-siyāsat al-mulk*. ed. Riḍwān al-Sayyid (Beirut: Dār al-Ṭalī^c^a lil-Ṭibā^c^a wa-l-Nashr, 1979).

Al-Māwardī, *Naṣīḥat al-mulūk*, ed. Khiḍr Muḥammad Khiḍr (Kuwait: Maktabat al-Falāḥ, 1983).

Al-Māwardī, *Kitāb Naṣīḥat al-mulūk*, ed. Muḥammad Jāsim al-Ḥadīthī (Baghdad: Dār al-Shu^c^ūn al-Thaqāfiyya al-^c^Āmma, 1986).

Al-Māwardī, *Tashīl al-naẓar wa-ta^c^jīl al-ẓafar fī akhlāq al-malik wa-siyāsat al-mulk*, ed. Riḍwān al-Sayyid (Beirut: Dār al-^c^Ulūm al-^c^Arabiyya, 1987).

Al-Māwardī, *Naṣīḥat al-mulūk al-mansūb ilā Abī l-Ḥasan al-Māwardī*, ed. Fuʾād ʿAbd al-Munʿim Aḥmad (Alexandria: Muʾassasat Shabāb al-Jāmiʿa, 1988).

Al-Māwardī, *Aʿlām al-nubuwwa*, ed. Khālid ʿAbd al-Raḥmān al-ʿAkk (Beirut: Dār al-Nafāʾis, 1994).

Al-Māwardī, *al-Aḥkām al-sulṭāniyya wa-l-wilāyāt al-dīniyya* (Cairo: Sharikat Maktabat wa-Maṭbaʿat Muṣṭafā al-Bābī al-Ḥalabī wa-Awlādihi, 1966) = Wafaa H. Wahba, *Al-Mawardi: The Ordinances of Government* (Reading: Garnet, 1996).

Al-Māwardī (attrib.), *Durar al-sulūk fī siyāsat al-mulūk*, ed. Fuʾād ʿAbd al-Munʿim Aḥmad (Riyadh: Dār al-Waṭan lil-Nashr, 1997).

Al-Maydānī, Aḥmad b. Aḥmad al-Naysābūrī, *Majmaʿ al-amthāl*, ed. Naʿīm Ḥusayn Zarzūr (Beirut: Dār al-Kutub al-ʿIlmiyya, 1988).

McChesney, R. D., 'Reconstructing Balkh: The *Vaqfiya* of 947/1540', in Devin DeWeese (ed.), *Studies on Central Asian History in Honor of Yuri Bregel* (Bloomington, IN: Indiana University, Research Institute for Inner Asian Studies, 2001), pp. 187–243.

Meisami, Julie Scott, 'Masʿūdī on Love and the Fall of the Barmakids', *Journal of the Royal Asiatic Society* 2 (1989), pp. 252–77.

Meisami, Julie Scott, *The Sea of Precious Virtues (Baḥr al-Favāʾid): A Medieval Islamic Mirror for Princes* (Salt Lake City, UT: University of Utah Press, 1991).

Meisami, Julie Scott, 'The Past in Service of the Present: Two Views of History in Medieval Persia', *Poetics Today* XIV(2) (1993): 247–75.

Meisami, Julie Scott, 'The *Šâh-nâme* as Mirror for Princes: A Study in Reception', in Christopher Balay, Claire Kappler and Ziva Vesel (eds), *Pand-o Sokhan: mélanges offerts à Charles-Henri de Fouchécour* (Tehran: Institut français de recherche en Iran, 1995), pp. 265–73.

Meisami, Julie Scott, 'Oratory and Sermons', *EAL* II (1998), pp. 593–4.

Meisami, Julie Scott, *Persian Historiography to the End of the Twelfth Century* (Edinburgh: Edinburgh University Press, 1999).

Meisami, Julie Scott, 'Why Write History in Persian? Historical Writing in the Samanid Period', in C. Hillenbrand (ed.), *Studies in Honour of Clifford Edmund Bosworth*, vol. II (Leiden: Brill, 2000), pp. 348–74.

Melchert, Christopher, 'The Transition from Asceticism to Mysticism at the Middle of the Ninth Century C.E.', *Studia Islamica* 83 (1996): 51–70.

Melchert, Christopher, 'The Ḥanābila and the Early Sufis', *Arabica* 48 (2001): 352–67.

Melchert, Christopher, 'Sufis and Competing Movements in Nishapur', *Iran* 39 (2001): 237–47.

Melchert, Christopher, 'Traditionist-Jurisprudents and the Framing of Islamic Law', *Islamic Law and Society* 8 (2001): 383–406.

Melchert, Christopher, 'The Piety of the Hadith Folk', *International Journal of Middle East Studies* 34 (2002): 425–39.

Melchert, Christopher, 'Māwardī, Abū Yaᶜlá, and the Sunni Revival', in Krzystof Kościelniak (ed.), *Prosperity and Stagnation: Some Cultural and Social Aspects of the Abbasid Period (750–1258)* (Cracow: UNUM, 2010), pp. 37–61.

Melchert, Christopher, 'Exaggerated Fear in the Early Islamic Renunciant Tradition', *Journal of the Royal Asiatic Society* 21 (2011): 283–300.

Melikian-Chirvani, A. S., 'Le royaume de Salomon: les inscriptions persanes de sites achéménides', *Le monde iranien et l'Islam* I (1971): 1–41.

Melikian-Chirvani, A. S.,'L'évocation littéraire du Bouddhisme dans l'Iran musulman', *Le monde iranien et l'Islam: sociétés et cultures* 2 (1974): 1–72.

Melville, Charles, 'Ebn Esfandīār', *EIr* VIII (1998), p. 21.

Mikhail, Hanna, *Politics and Revelation: Mawardi and After* (Edinburgh: Edinburgh University Press, 1995).

Miles, G. C., 'Numismatics', in R. N. Frye (ed.), *The Cambridge History of Iran, vol. IV: The Period from the Arab Invasions to the Saljuqs* (Cambridge: Cambridge University Press, 1975), pp. 364–77.

Minorsky, V., *Sharaf al-Zamān Ṭāhir Marvazī on China, the Turks and India* (London: Royal Asiatic Society, 1942).

Minorsky, V., 'The Older Preface to the *Shāh-nāma*', *Studi orientalistici in onore di G. Levi della Vida*, II (1956): 159–79 = *Iranica: Twenty Articles*, ed. V. Minorsky (Hertford and Tehran: Stephen Austin and Publications de l'université de Téhéran, 1964), pp. 260–73.

Minorsky, V., *Ḥudūd al-ᶜālam 'The Regions of the World': A Persian Geography 372 A.H–982 A.D.*, 2nd edn (Cambridge: E. J. W. Memorial Trust, 1970).

Miquel, A., *La géographie humaine du monde musulman jusqu'au milieu du 11e siècle* (Paris: Mouton, 1967).

Miquel, A., 'Ibn Ḥawḳal', *EI*[2] III (1971), pp. 786–8.

Miquel, A., 'al-Iṣṭakhrī', *EI*[2] IV (1978), pp. 222–3.

Mīrkhwānd, *Tārīkh-i Rawżat al-ṣafāʾ* (Tehran: Markazī-yi Khayyām Pīrūz, 1959–60).

Miskawayh, *al-Ḥikma al-khālida = Jāvīdān khirad*, ed. ᶜAbd al-Raḥmān Badawī (Cairo: Maktabat al-Nahḍa al-Miṣriyya, 1952).

Miskawayh, *Tahdhīb al-akhlāq*, ed. Qustantīn Zurayq (Beirut: al-Jāmiᶜa al-Amīrkiyya fī Bayrūt, 1966) = Constantine K. Zurayk, *The Refinement of Character* (Beirut: American University in Beirut, 1968).

Mitchiner, Michael, *The Multiple Dirhems of Medieval Afghanistan* (London: Hawkins Publications, 1973).

Muḥammadī, Muḥammad, *al-Tarjama wa-l-naql ʿan al-fārisiyya fī l-qurūn al-islāmiyya al-ūlā* (= *La traduction des livres pehlevis en arabe dans les premiers siècles de l'Islam*) (Beirut: Manshūrāt Qism al-Lugha al-Fārisiyya wa-Ādābihā fī l-Jāmiʿa al-Lubnāniyya, 1964).

Monnot, Guy, *Penseurs musulmans et religions iraniennes: ʿAbd al-Jabbār et ses devanciers* (Paris: Librairie philosophique J. Vrin, 1974).

Monnot, Guy, *Islam et religions* (Paris: Éditions Maisonneuve et Larose, 1986).

Montgomery, James E., 'Serendipity, Resistance, and Multivalency: Ibn Khurradādhbih and his *Kitāb al-Masālik wa-l-mamālik*', in Philip F. Kennedy (ed.), *On Fiction and* Adab *in Medieval Arabic Literature* (Wiesbaden: Harrassowitz, 2005), pp. 177–232.

Montgomery, James E., 'Speech and Nature: al-Jāḥiẓ, *Kitāb al-Bayān wa-l-tabyīn*, Part 1', *Middle Eastern Literatures* 11 (2008): 175–207.

Montgomery, James E., *Al-Jāḥiẓ: In Praise of Books* (Edinburgh: Edinburgh University Press, 2013).

Morony, Michael, 'Kisrā', *EI*² V (1986), pp. 184–5.

Mottahedeh, Roy P., 'The Shuʿûbîyah Controversy and the Social History of Early Islamic Iran', *International Journal of Middle East Studies* VII (1976): 161–82.

Mottahedeh, Roy P., 'The Transmission of Learning: The Role of the Islamic Northeast', in Nicole Grandin and Marc Gaborieau (eds), *Madrasa: la transmission du savoir dans le monde musulman* (Paris: AP Éditions Arguments, 1997), pp. 63–72.

Mottahedeh, Roy P., *Loyalty and Leadership in an Early Islamic Society*, 2nd edn (London: Tauris, 2001).

Mottahedeh, Roy P., 'The Eastern Travels of Solomon: Reimagining Persepolis and the Iranian Past', in Michael Cook et al. (eds), *Law and Tradition in Classical Islamic Thought: Studies in Honor of Professor Hossein Modarressi* (New York: Palgrave Macmillan, 2013), pp. 247–67.

Mubarak, Zaki, *La prose arabe au IVe siècle de l'Hégire (Xe siècle)* (Paris: Librairie orientale et américaine, 1931).

Al-Mubashshir b. Fātik, *Mukhtār al-ḥikam wa-maḥāsin al-kalim*, ed. ʿAbd al-Raḥmān Badawī (Madrid: Instituto Egipcio de Estudios Islámicos, 1958).

Mujmal al-tavārīkh va-l-qiṣaṣ, ed. Malik al-shuᶜarā Bahār (Tehran: Chāpkhāneh-yi Khāvar, 1939).

Al-Muqaddasī, *Aḥsan al-taqāsīm fī maᶜrifat al-aqālīm* (Leiden: Brill, 1967).

Al-Murtaḍā, al-Sharīf ᶜAlī b. al-Ḥusayn, *Amālī al-Murtaḍā: Ghurar al-fawāᵓid wa-durar al-qalāᵓid*, ed. Muḥammad Abū l-Faḍl Ibrāhīm (Cairo: Dār Iḥyāᵓ al-Kutub al-ᶜArabiyya, 1954).

Muslim, *Ṣaḥīḥ Muslim* (Cairo: Muᵓassasat al-Mukhtār, 2005).

Nadwi, Mawlana Syed Sulaiman, *Indo-Arab Relations: An English Rendering of* Arab o' Hind ke Ta'alluqat, trans. M. Salahuddin (Hyderabad: Institute of Indo-Middle East Cultural Studies, 1962).

Narshakhī, Abū Bakr Muḥammad b. Jaᶜfar, *Tārīkh-i Bukhārā, Tarjameh-yi Abū Naṣr Aḥmad b. Muḥammad b. Naṣr al-Qubāwī, Talkhīṣ-i Muḥammad b. Zufar b. ᶜUmar*, ed. Mudarris Rażavī (Tehran: Kitābfurūshī-yi Sanāᵓī, 1984).

Al-Nasafī, Abū l-Muᶜīn, *Kitāb al-Tamhīd li-qawāᶜid al-tawḥīd*, ed. Muḥammad Rabīᶜ Muḥammad Jawharī (Cairo: Dār al-Ṭibāᶜa al-Muḥammadiyya, 1986).

Al-Nasafī, Abū l-Muᶜīn Maymūn b. Muḥammad, *Tabṣirat al-adilla fī uṣūl al-dīn*, ed. Claude Salamé (Damascus: Institut français de Damas, 1990–3).

Al-Nasafī, Najm al-Dīn ᶜUmar b. Muḥammad b. Aḥmad, *al-Qand fī dhikr ᶜulamāᵓ Samarqand*, ed. Yūsuf al-Hādī (Tehran: Āᵓīneh-yi Mīrāth [Mirᵓāt al-Turāth], 1999).

Al-Nasāᵓī, *Sunan al-Nasāᵓī bi-sharḥ al-Ḥāfiẓ Jalāl al-Dīn al-Suyūṭī* (Beirut: Dār al-Fikr, 1930).

Nasrallah, Nawal, *Annals of the Caliphs' Kitchens: Ibn Sayyār al-Warrāq's Tenth-Century Baghdadi Cookbook. English Translation with Introduction and Glossary* (Leiden: Brill, 2007).

Nawas, John, 'Badr', *EQ* I (2001), pp. 196–7.

Naymark, Aleksandr and Luke Treadwell, 'An Arab–Sogdian Coin of AH 160: An Ikhshid in Ishtihan?', *Numismatic Chronicle* 171 (2011): 359–66.

Nāẓim, M., *The Life and Times of Sulṭān Maḥmūd of Ghazna* (Cambridge: Cambridge University Press, 1931).

Nāẓim, M., 'The *Pand-Nāmah* of Subuktigīn', *Journal of the Royal Asiatic Society* (1933): 605–28.

Netton, Ian, *Al-Fārābī and His School* (London: Routledge, 1992).

Nihāyat al-arab fī akhbār al-furs wa-l-ᶜarab, ed. M. T. Dānishpazhūh (Tehran: Anjuman-i Āthār va-Mafākhir-i Farhangī, 1996–7).

Niẓām al-Mulk, *Siyar al-mulūk (Siyāsatnāmeh)*, ed. H. S. G. Darke (Tehran: Bungāh-i

Tarjameh va-Nashr-i Kitāb, 1962) = Hubert Darke, *The Book of Government or Rules for Kings* (London: Routledge & Kegan Paul, 1978).

NM-A = *Naṣīḥat al-mulūk al-mansūb ilā Abī l-Ḥasan al-Māwardī*, ed. Fuʾād ʿAbd al-Munʿim Aḥmad, see al-Māwardī.

NM-Ḥ = *Kitāb Naṣīḥat al-mulūk*, ed. Muḥammad Jāsim al-Ḥadīthī, see al-Māwardī.

NM-Kh = *Naṣīḥat al-mulūk*, ed. Khiḍr Muḥammad Khiḍr, see al-Māwardī.

Nöldeke, Theodor, 'Geschichte des Artachšîr i Pâpakân, aus dem Pehlewi übersetzt, mit Erläuterungen und einer Einleitung versehen', *Beiträge zur Kunde der indo-germanischen Sprachen* 4 (1878): 22–69.

Nöldeke, Theodor, 'Zu Kalīla waDimna', *Zeitschrift der Deutschen Morgenländischen Gesellschaft* 59 (1905): 794–806.

Nyberg, H. S., *A Manual of Pahlavi* (Wiesbaden: Harrassowitz, 1974).

Ohlander, Erik S., '"He was Crude of Speech": Turks and Arabs in the Hagiographical Imagination of Early Ottoman Egypt', in Jane Hathaway (ed.), *The Arab Lands in the Ottoman Era: Studies in Honor of Professor Caesar Farah* (Minneapolis, MN: Center for Early Modern History, University of Minnesota, 2009), pp. 111–35.

Opwis, Felicitas, '*Maṣlaḥa* in Contemporary Islamic Legal Theory', *Islamic Law and Society* 12 (2005): 182–223.

Orfali, Bilal, 'The Art of Anthology: Al-Thaʿālibī and His *Yatīmat al-dahr*', PhD dissertation, Yale University, 2009.

Orfali, Bilal, 'The Art of the *Muqaddima* in the Works of Abū Manṣūr al-Thaʿālibī (d. 429/1039)', in Lale Behzadi and Vahid Behmardi (eds), *The Weaving of Words: Approaches to Classical Arabic Prose* (Beirut: Orient-Institut Beirut, 2009), pp. 181–202.

Orfali, Bilal, 'The Works of Abū Manṣūr al-Thaʿālibī (350–429/961–1039)', *Journal of Arabic Literature* 40 (2009): 273–318.

Orfali, Bilal, 'The Sources of al-Thaʿālibī in *Yatīmat al-Dahr* and *Tatimmat al-Yatīma*', *Middle Eastern Literatures* 16 (2013): 1–47.

Ormsby, Eric, *Theodicy in Islamic Thought: The Dispute over al-Ghazālī's 'Best of All Possible Worlds'* (Princeton, NJ: Princeton University Press, 1984).

Pandnāmeh-yi Māturīdī, ed. Īraj Afshār, *Farhang-i Īrān-zamīn* 9 (1961): 48–67.

Pasha, Aḥmad Zaki, 'Taṣdīr', *Kitāb al-Tāj*, pp. 23–83.

Pakatchi, Ahmad, 'Abū Dāwūd al-Sijistānī', trans. Shahram Khodaverdian, *Encyclopaedia Islamica*, vol. I (Leiden: Brill, 2008), pp. 657–66.

Pakatchi, Ahmad, 'Abū al-Layth al-Samarqandī', *Encyclopaedia Islamica*, vol. II (Leiden: Brill, 2009), pp. 219–28.

Paul, Jürgen, 'The Histories of Samarqand', *Studia Iranica* 22 (1993): 69–92.

Paul, Jürgen, 'Nachrichten arabischer Geographen aus Mittelasien', *Bamberger Mittelasienstudien; Konferenzakten, Bamberg 15–16. Juni 1990* (Berlin: Schwarz, 1994), pp. 179–91.

Paul, Jürgen, *The State and the Military: The Samanid Case* (Bloomington, IN: Research Institute for Inner Asian Studies, 1994).

Paul, Jürgen, *Herrscher, Gemeinwesen, Vermittler: Ostiran und Transoxanien in vormongolischer Zeit* (Beirut: In Kommission bei Franz Steiner Verlag, Stuttgart, 1996).

Paul, Jürgen, 'The Histories of Isfahan: Mafarrukhi's *Kitāb maḥāsin Iṣfahān*', *Iranian Studies* 33 (2000): 117–32.

Paul, Jürgen, 'Buchara die Edle – Traum und Wirklichkeit einer islamischen Metropole', *Städte und Monumente: Ringvorlesung des Orientwissenschaftlichen Zentrums* 6 (2003): 61–90.

Paul, Jürgen, 'Terms for Nomads in Medieval Persian Historiography', *Asiatische Studien* 60 (2006): 437–57.

Paul, Jürgen, 'Islamizing Sufis in Pre-Mongol Central Asia', in Étienne de la Vaissière (ed.), *Islamisation de l'Asie Centrale: Processus locaux d'acculturation du VIIe au XIe siècle* (Paris: Association pour l'avancement des études iraniennes, 2008), pp. 297–317.

Paul, Jürgen, 'Aḥmad b. Sahl', *EI Three* (2009), pp. 60–1.

Paul, Jürgen, 'Sanjar and Atsız: Independence, Lordship, and Literature', in Jörg Gertel, Stefan Leder, Jürgen Paul and Bernhard Streck (eds), *Nomaden und Sesshafte* (Wiesbaden: Ludwig Reichert, 2013), pp. 81–129.

Paul, Jürgen, 'Where Did the *Dihqāns* Go?', *Eurasian Studies* XI (2013): 1–34.

Paul, Jürgen, '*Khidma* in the Social History of Pre-Mongol Iran', *Journal of the Economic and Social History of the Orient* 57 (2014): 392–422.

Peacock, A. C. S., *Mediaeval Islamic Historiography and Political Legitimacy: Balᶜamī's* Tārīkhnāma (London: Routledge, 2007).

Pellat, Ch., *Le livre de la couronne* (Paris: Société d'Édition Les Belles Lettres, 1954).

Pellat, Ch., *Ibn al-Muqaffaᶜ. Mort vers 140/757. 'Conseilleur' du calife* (Paris: G-P. Maisonneuve et Larose, 1976) (= edition and translation into French of Ibn al-Muqaffaᶜ, *al-Risāla fī l-ṣaḥāba*).

Pellat, Ch., 'al-Djayhānī', *EI²* XII (Supplement), 2004, pp. 265–6.

Pellat, Ch., 'Dīnavarī, Abū Ḥanīfa Aḥmad', *EIr* VII (1996), p. 417.

Pellat, Ch., 'Ḳāṣṣ', *EI²* IV (1997), pp. 733–5.

Pelliot, Paul, 'La théorie des quatre fils du ciel', *T'oung Pao*, 2nd series, XXII (1923): 97–125.

Pessagno, J. Meric, 'Intellect and Religious Assent: The View of Abū Manṣūr al-Māturīdī', *Muslim World* 69 (1979): 18–27.

Picard, Elizabeth, 'Za^{c}īm', *EI*[2] XI (2002), pp. 402–3.

Pickthall, Muhammed Marmaduke, *The Glorious Koran: A Bi-Lingual Edition with English Translation, Introduction and Notes* (London: George Allen & Unwin, 1976).

Pines, Sh., 'A Note on an Early Meaning of the Term *Mutakallim*', *Israel Oriental Studies* 10/11 (1971): 224–38.

Pingree, David and Wilferd Madelung, 'Political Horoscopes Relating to Ninth-Century ^{c}Alids', *Journal of Near Eastern Studies* 36 (1977): 247–75.

Pitts, Monique B., 'Barlaam and Josaphat: A Legend for All Seasons', *Journal of South Asian Literature* XVI (1981): 3–16.

Pīrūzīnāmeh mansūb bi-Buzurgmihr-i Bakhtagān, Tarjameh-yi Abū ^{c}Alī Sīnā, ed. Kāẓim Rajavī (Tehran: Kitābfurūshī-yi Ibn Sīnā, 1954).

Planhol, X. de, 'Balḵ', i: 'Geography', *EIr* III (1989), pp. 587–8.

Pormann, Peter E. and Emilie Savage-Smith, *Medieval Islamic Medicine* (Washington, DC: Georgetown University Press, 2007).

Pourshariati, Parvaneh, 'Local Historiography in Early Medieval Iran and the *Tārīkh-i Bayhaq*', *Iranian Studies* 33 (2000): 133–64.

Pourshariati, Parvaneh, *Decline and Fall of the Sasanian Empire: The Sasanian–Parthian Confederacy and the Arab Conquest of Iran* (London: Tauris, 2008).

Pourshariati, Parvaneh, 'The Parthians and the Production of the Canonical Shāhnāmas: Of Pahlavī, Pahlavānī and the Pahlav', in Henning Börm and Josef Wiesehöfer (eds), *Commutatio et contentio: Studies in the Late Roman, Sasanian, and Early Islamic Near East in Memory of Zeev Rubin* (Düsseldorf: Wellem Verlag, 2010), pp. 347–92.

Pseudo-Jāḥiẓ, *Kitāb al-Tāj fī akhlāq al-mulūk*, see *Kitāb al-Tāj*.

Al-Qalqashandī, Aḥmad, *Ṣubḥ al-a^{c}shā* (Cairo: al-Maṭba^{c}a al-Amīriyya, 1915).

Qazvīnī, Ḥamd Allāh Mustawfī, *Tārīkh-i guzīdeh*, ed. ^{c}Abd al-Ḥusayn Navā$^{\circ}$ī (Tehran: Amīr Kabīr, 1983 or 1984).

Qazvīnī, Muḥammad, *Bīst maqāleh-yi Qazvīnī: Maqālāt-i adabī va-tārīkhī-yi Mīrzā Muḥammad-Khān ibn ^{c}Abd al-Vahhāb-i Qazvīnī*, ed. ^{c}Abbās Iqbāl (Tehran: Chāpkhāneh-yi Sharq, 1953–4).

Qazvīnī, Mīrzā Muḥammad, 'Muqaddimeh-yi qadīm-i Shāhnāmeh', *Bīst maqāleh-yi Qazvīnī* (Tehran: Chāpkhāneh-yi Sharq, 1958), II: 5–90 = *Bīst maqāleh-yi Qazvīnī* (Tehran, Maṭbaᶜeh-yi Majlis, 1934), pp. 1–64; reprinted in *Hazāreh-yi Firdawsī: Majmūᶜeh-yi maqālāt-i dānishmandān-i Īrān va-Īrānshināsān-i jahān bi-munāsibat-i yak hazārumīn sāl-i rūz-i tavallud-i Firdawsī, Tihrān, Dār al-funūn, 1313*, ed. Muḥammad Amīn Riyāḥī (Tehran: Muᵓassaseh-yi Muṭālaᶜāt va-Taḥqīqāt-i Farhangī, 2009 or 2010), pp. 123–48.

Qutbuddin, Tahera, '*Khuṭba*: The Evolution of Early Arabic Oration', in Beatrice Gruendler and Michael Cooperson (eds), *Classical Arabic Humanities in Their Own Terms: Festschrift for Wolfhart Heinrichs on His 65th Birthday Presented by His Students and Colleagues* (Leiden: Brill, 2008), pp. 176–273.

Rabb, Intisar A., *Doubt in Islamic Law: A History of Legal Maxims, Interpretation, and Islamic Criminal Law* (New York: Cambridge University Press, 2014).

Radtke, Bernd, 'Theologen und Mystiker in Ḫurāsān und Transoxanien', *Zeitschrift der Deutschen Morgenländischen Gesellschaft* 136 (1986): 538–49.

Radtke, Bernd, 'Ḥakim al-Termed̲i', *EIr* XI (2003), pp. 574–5.

Radtke, Bernd and John O'Kane, *The Beginning of the Affair of . . . al-Ḥakīm al-Tirmidhī*, in *The Concept of Sainthood in Early Islamic Mysticism: Two Works by al-Ḥakīm al-Tirmidhī* (Richmond: Curzon Sufi Series, 1996).

Al-Rāghib al-Iṣfahānī, *Muḥāḍarāt al-udabāᵓ wa-muḥāwarāt al-shuᶜarāᵓ wa-l-bulaghāᵓ* (Cairo: Maktabat al-Thaqāfa al-Dīniyya, 2009).

Rahman, Fazlur, *Major Themes of the Qurᵓān*, 2nd edn (Chicago, IL: University of Chicago Press, 2009).

Rapin, Claude and Pierre Hadot, 'Les textes littéraires grecs de la Trésorerie d'Aï Khanoum', *Bulletin de correspondance héllenique* 111 (1987): 225–66.

Raven, W., 'Sīra', *EI*² IX (1997), pp. 660–3.

Reisman, David C., 'Al-Fārābī and the Philosophical Curiculum,' in Peter Adamson and Richard C. Taylor (eds), *The Cambridge Companion to Arabic Philosophy* (Cambridge: Cambridge University Press, 2005), pp. 52–71.

Richter, Gustav, *Studien zur Geschichte der älteren arabischen Fürstenspiegel* (Leipzig: Hinrichs'sche Buchhandlung, 1932).

Richter-Bernburg, Lutz, 'Linguistic Shuᶜūbīya and Early Neo-Persian Prose', *Journal of the American Oriental Society* 94 (1974): 55–64.

Richter-Bernburg, Lutz, 'Ebn Hendū', *EIr* VIII (1998), pp. 29–30.

Riedel, Dagmar, 'Kalila wa Demna', ii: 'Redactions and Circulation', *EIr* XV (2011), pp. 386–95.

Riyāḥī, Muḥammad Amīn, *Sar-chashmeh-hā-yi Firdawsī-shināsī: Majmūᶜeh-yi nivishteh-hā-yi kuhan darbāreh-yi Firdawsī va-Shāhnāmeh va-naqd-i ānhā*

(Tehran: Mu᾽assaseh-yi Muṭālaᶜāt va-Taḥqīqāt-i Farhangī [Pazhūhishgāh], 1993 or 1994).

Rosenthal, Erwin I. J., *Political Thought in Medieval Islam: An Introductory Outline* (Cambridge: Cambridge University Press, 1962).

Rosenthal, Franz, 'From Arabic Books and Manuscripts VI: Istanbul Materials for al-Kindî and as-Saraḫsî', *Journal of the American Oriental Society* 76 (1956): 27–31.

Rosenthal, Franz, 'Gifts and Bribes: The Muslim View', *Proceedings of the American Philosophical Society* 108 (1964): 135–44.

Rosenthal, Franz, *A History of Muslim Historiography*, 2nd rev. edn (Leiden: Brill, 1968).

Rosenthal, Franz, *Gambling in Islam* (Leiden: Brill, 1975).

Rosenthal, Franz, 'Abū Zayd al-Balkhī on Politics', in C. E. Bosworth, C. Issawi, R. Savory and A. L. Udovitch (eds), *Essays in Honor of Bernard Lewis: The Islamic World from Classical to Modern Times* (Princeton, NJ: Darwin Press, 1989), pp. 287–301.

Rosenthal, Franz, 'Al-Kindî als Literat', *Orientalia,* NS 11 (1962): 262–88; reprinted in *Muslim Intellectual and Social History, A Collection of Essays* (Aldershot: Variorum, 1990), VI.

Rosenthal, Franz, 'Asāṭīr al-awwalīn', *EI*[2] XII (Supplement) (2004), pp. 90–1.

Rosenthal, R., 'Ebn Qotayba Dīnavarī', *EIr* VIII (1998), pp. 45–7.

Ross, E. Denison, 'Rudaki and Pseudo-Rudaki', *Journal of the Royal Asiatic Society* IV (1924): 609–44.

Ross, E. Denison, 'A Qasida by Rudaki', *Journal of the Royal Asiatic Society* 2 (1926): 213–37.

Rowson, E. K., *A Muslim Philosopher on the Soul and its Fate: Al-ᶜĀmirī's* Kitāb al-Amad ᶜalā l-abad (New Haven, CT: American Oriental Society, 1988).

Rowson, E. K., 'The Philosopher as Littérateur: al-Tawḥīdī and His Predecessors', *Zeitschrift der Deutschen Morgenländischen Gesellschaft* 6 (1990): 50–92.

Rowson, E. K., 'al-Thaᶜālibī', *EI*[2] X (2000), pp. 426–8.

Rowson, E. K. and Seeger A. Bonebakker, *A Computerized Listing of Biographical Data from the* Yatīmat al-dahr *of al-Thaᶜālibī* (Paris: Centre national de la recherche scientifique, 1980).

Rūdakī, *Dīvān-i Rūdakī,* ed. Jahāngīr Manṣūr (Tehran: Intishārāt-i Nāhīd, 1994).

Rudolph, Ulrich, *Al-Māturīdī und die sunnitische Theologie in Samarkand* (Leiden: Brill, 1997).

Sabra, A. L., 'al-Khwārazmī', *EI*[2] IV (1978).

Sadan, J., *Une nouvelle source sur l'époque būyide*, Ḥaḍāra: Texts and Studies in the Civilization of Islam (Tel Aviv: Tel-Aviv University, n.d.).

Sadan, J., 'A New Source of the Būyid Period', *Israel Oriental Studies* IX (1979): 355–76.

Sadan, J., '"Community" and "Extra-Community" as a Legal and Literary Problem', *Israel Oriental Studies* 10 (1980): 102–15.

Sadan, J., '*Ādāb* – règles de conduite et *ādāb* – dictons, maximes, dans quelques ouvrages inédits d'al-Ṯaᶜālibī', *Mélanges Dominique Sourdel* = *REI* 54 (1986): 283–300.

Sadan, J., 'A "Closed-Circuit" Saying on Practical Justice', *Jerusalem Studies in Arabic & Islam* 10 (1987): 325–41.

Sadan, Joseph, 'Death of a Princess: Episodes of the Barmakid Legend in its Late Evolution', in Stefan Leder (ed.), *Story-telling in the Framework of Non-fictional Arabic Literature* (Wiesbaden: Harrassowitz, 1998), pp. 130–57.

Sadan, J. and A. Silverstein, 'Ornate Manuals or Practical *Adab*? Some Reflections on a Unique Work by an Anonymous Author of the 10th Century CE', *Al-Qanṭara* XXV(2) (2004): 339–55.

Ṣafā, Żabīhullāh, *Tārīkh-i adabīyāt dar Īrān* (Tehran: Kitābfurūshī-yi Ibn Sīnā, 1959).

Ṣafā, Żabīhullāh, 'Andarz Literature in New Persian', *EIr* I (1985), pp. 16–22.

Al-Ṣafadī, *al-Wāfī bi-l-wafayāt* = *Das biographische Lexikon des Ṣalāḥaddīn Ḫalīl Ibn Aibak aṣ-Ṣafadī* (Wiesbaden: Kommissionsverlag Franz Steiner, 1962–).

Al-Samᶜānī, *al-Ansāb* (Hyderabad: Maṭbaᶜat Majlis Dāʾirat al-Maᶜārif al-ᶜUthmāniyya, 1962–82).

Al-Samarqandī, Abū l-Layth, *Tanbīh al-ghāfilīn wa-yalīhi Bustān al-ᶜārifīn*, ed. Ḥusayn ᶜAbd al-Ḥamīd Nayl (Beirut: Dār al-Arqam b. Abī l-Arqam lil-Ṭibāᶜa wa-l-Nashr wa-l-Tawzīᶜ, 1994).

Al-Samarqandī, Abū l-Layth, *Tafsīr al-Qurʾān al-karīm 'Baḥr al-ᶜulūm'* (Baghdad: Maṭbaᶜat al-Irshād, 1985).

Samarqandī, Abū l-Qāsim Ḥakīm, *Tarjameh-yi al-Sawād al-aᶜẓam*, ed. ᶜAbd al-Ḥayy Ḥabībī (Tehran, Bunyād-i Farhang-i Īrān, 1969).

Samarqandī, Niẓāmī ᶜArūżī, *Chahār maqāleh*, eds M. Qazvīnī and M. Muᶜīn (Tehran: Dānishgāh-i Tihrān, 1955).

Sarıbıyık, Mustafa, *Siyaset Senati* (Istanbul: Sosyal Bilimler Enstitüsü, 1996).

Sato, T., 'ᶜUshr', *EI*[2] X (2000), pp. 917–19.

Savant, Sarah Bowen, 'Genealogy and Ethnogenesis in al-Masᶜūdī's *Muruj al-dhahab*', in Sarah Bowen Savant and Helena de Felipe (eds), *Genealogy and*

Knowledge in Muslim Societies: Understanding the Past (Edinburgh: Edinburgh University Press, 2013), pp. 164–86.

Savant, Sarah Bowen, '"Persians" in Early Islam', *Annales islamologiques* 42 (2008): 73–91.

Savant, Sarah Bowen, *The New Muslims of Post-Conquest Iran: Tradition, Memory and Conversion* (Cambridge: Cambridge University Press, 2013).

Al-Sawād al-aᶜẓam see Samarqandī, Abū l-Qāsim Ḥakīm.

Al-Sayyid, Riḍwān, 'Fī l-taqdīm', in Riḍwān al-Sayyid (ed.), *al-Asad wa-l-ghawwāṣ* (Beirut: Dār al-Ṭalīᶜa lil-Ṭibāᶜa wa-l-Nashr, 1978), pp. 8–37.

Al-Sayyid, Riḍwān, 'al-Māwardī (364–450 h./974–1058 m.): al-rajul wa-l-ᶜaṣr', in Riḍwān al-Sayyid (ed.), *Qawānīn al-wizāra wa-siyāsat al-mulk* (Beirut: Dār al-Ṭalīᶜa lil-Ṭibāᶜa wa-l-Nashr, 1979), pp. 5–114.

Al-Sayyid, Riḍwān, *al-Umma wa-l-jamāᶜāt wa-l-sulṭa* (Beirut: Dār Iqrāʾ, 1984).

Al-Sayyid, Riḍwān, *Mafāhīm al-jamāᶜāt fī l-Islām* (Beirut: Dār al-Tanwīr lil-Ṭibāᶜa wa-l-Nashr, 1984).

Al-Sayyid, Riḍwān, 'Tamhīd: al-Ijtimāᶜ al-basharī: Dirāsa fī ruʾyat al-Māwardī al-ijtimāᶜiyya', in al-Māwardī, *Tashīl al-naẓar wa-taᶜjīl al-ẓafar*, ed. Riḍwān al-Sayyid (Beirut: Dār al-ᶜUlūm al-ᶜArabiyya, 1987), pp. 7–93.

Schacht, J., 'ᶜAhd', *EI*[2] I (1960), p. 255.

Schacht, J. [C. E. Bosworth], 'al-Subkī', 9: Tādj al-Dīn Abū l-Naṣr b. Taḳī al-Dīn, *EI*[2] IX (1997), pp. 744–5.

Schaeder, H. H. [C. E. Bosworth], 'Samarḳand', i, 'History', *EI*[2] VIII (1995), pp. 1031–4.

Schmidtke, Sabine, 'Neuere Forschungen zur Muᶜtazila unter besonderer Berücksichtigung der späteren Muᶜtazila ab dem 4./10. Jahrhundert', *Arabica* 45 (1998): 379–408.

Schoeler, Gregor, 'Die Einteilung der Dichtung bei den Arabern', *Zeitschrift der Deutschen Morgenländischen Gesellschaft* 123 (1973): 9–55.

Schoeler, Gregor, 'Verfasser und Titel des dem Ǧāḥiẓ zugeschriebenen sog. *Kitāb at-Tāǧ*', *Zeitschrift der Deutschen Morgenländischen Gesellschaft* 130 (1980): 217–25.

Schoeler, Gregor, 'Die Frage der schriftlichen oder mündlichen Überlieferung der Wissenschaften im frühen Islam', *Der Islam* 62 (1985): 201–30.

Schwarz, P., 'Bemerkungen zu den arabischen Nachrichten über Balkh', *Oriental Studies in Honour of Cursetji Ersachji Pavry* (London, 1933), pp. 434–43.

Serikoff, Nicolaj, 'Beobachtungen über die Marginal- und Schnitttitel in christlich-arabischen und islamischen Büchersammlungen', *Manuscript Notes as*

Documentary Sources, eds Andreas Görke and Konrad Hirschler (Beirut: Orient-Institut Beirut–Ergon Verlag Würzburg, 2011), Beiruter Texte und Studien 129, pp. 163–71.

Shaban, M. A., *The ᶜAbbāsid Revolution* (Cambridge: Cambridge University Press, 1970).

Shaban, M. A., 'Khurāsān at the Time of Arab Conquest', in C. E. Bosworth (ed.), *Iran and Islam: In Memory of the Late Vladimir Minorsky* (Edinburgh: Edinburgh University Press, 1971), pp. 479–90.

Shaban, M. A., *Islamic History: A New Interpretation* (Cambridge: Cambridge University Press, 1971).

Shahbazi, A. Sh., 'Bahrām', vii. 'Bahrām VI Čōbīn', *EIr* III (1989), pp. 519–22.

Shahbazi, Shapur, 'On the Xwadāy-Nāmag', *Acta Iranica: Papers in Honor of Professor Ehsan Yarshater* VXI (1990): 218–33.

Al-Shahrazūrī, *Taᵓrīkh al-ḥukamāᵓ: Nuzhat al-arwāḥ wa-rawḍat al-afrāḥ* (n.p., Jamᶜiyyat al-Daᶜwa al-Islāmiyya al-ᶜĀlamiyya, 1988).

Shaked, Shaul, 'Notes on the New Aśoka Inscription from Kandahar', *Journal of the Royal Asiatic Society* 2 (1969): 118–22.

Shaked, Shaul, 'Andarz and Andarz Literature in Pre-Islamic Iran', *EIr* I (1985), pp. 11–16.

Shaked, Shaul, 'From Iran to Islam: Notes on Some Themes in Transmission', *Jerusalem Studies in Arabic & Islam* 4 (1984): 31–67; reprinted in *From Zoroastrian Iran to Islam: Studies in Religious History and Intercultural Contacts* (Aldershot: Variorum, 1995), Article VI.

Shaked, Shaul, 'Esoteric Trends in Zoroastrianism', *Proceedings of the Israel Academy of Sciences and Humanities* 3, Jerusalem, 1969, pp. 175–221; reprinted in *From Zoroastrian Iran to Islam: Studies in Religious History and Intercultural Contacts* (Aldershot: Variorum, 1995), I.

Shaked, Shaul, 'Early Persian Documents from Khorasan', *Journal of Persianate Studies* VI (2013): 153–62.

Sharḥ al-uṣūl al-khamsa li-Qāḍī al-Quḍāt ᶜAbd al-Jabbār ibn Aḥmad, see Mānkdīm.

Sharon, Moshe, *Black Banners from the East: The Establishment of the ᶜAbbāsid State – Incubation of a Revolt* (Jerusalem and Leiden: Magnes Press, Hebrew University and Brill, 1983).

Sharon, Moshe, *Revolt: The Social and Military Aspects of the ᶜAbbāsid Revolution* (Jerusalem: Hebrew University, 1990).

Shatzmiller, Maya, 'Women and Wage Labour in the Medieval Islamic West: Legal

Issues in an Economic Context', *Journal of the Economic and Social History of the Orient* 40 (1997): 174–206.

Shaw, Stanford J., *The Financial and Administrative Organization and Development of Ottoman Egypt 1517–1798* (Princeton, NJ: Princeton University Press, 1962).

Silverstein, Adam J., *Postal Systems in the Pre-modern Islamic World* (Cambridge: Cambridge University Press, 2007).

Simidchieva, Marta, '*Siyāsat-nāme* Revisited: The Question of Authenticity', in B. Fragner, C. Fragner, G. Gnoli, R. Haag-Higuchi, M. Maggi, and P. Orsatti (eds), *Proceedings of the Second European Conference of Iranian Studies* (Rome, 1995), pp. 657–74.

Sims-Williams, Nicholas, *Bactrian Documents from Northern Afghanistan, vol. II: Letters and Buddhist Texts* (London: Nour Foundation in Association with Azimuth Editions, 2007).

Slane, M. le Baron de, *Catalogue des manuscrits arabes de la Bibliothèque nationale* (Paris: Imprimerie nationale, 1883–95).

Smith, Brian K., *Classifying the Universe: The Ancient Indian Varṇa System and the Origins of Caste* (New York: Oxford University Press, 1994).

Sourdel, Dominique, *Le vizirat ᶜabbāside de 749 à 936 (132 à 324 de l'Hégire)* (Damascus: Institut français de Damas, 1959).

Spitaler, A., 'Ibn Khālawayh', *EI²* III (1971), pp. 824–5.

Spuler, B., *Iran in früh-islamischer Zeit: Politik, Kultur, Verwaltung und öffentliches Leben zwischen der arabischen und der seldschukischen Eroberung, 633 bis 1055* (Wiesbaden: Steiner, 1952).

Spuler, B., 'Čaghāniyān', *EI²* II (1965), pp. 1–2.

Spuler, B., 'Gurgandj̱', *EI²* II (1991), p. 1142.

Steppat, Fritz, 'From *ᶜAhd Ardashīr* to al-Maʾmūn: A Persian Element in the Policy of the *Miḥna*', in Wadād al-Qāḍī (ed.), *Studia Arabica et Islamica: Festschrift for Iḥsān ᶜAbbās on His Sixtieth Birthday* (Beirut: American University of Beirut, 1981), pp. 451–4.

Stern, S. M., *Aristotle on the World State* (Oxford: Cassirer, 1968).

Stern, S. M., 'The Early Ismāᶜīlī Missionaries in North-West Persia and in Khurāsān and Transoxania', *Bulletin of the School of Oriental & African Studies* 23 (1960): 56–90; reprinted in S. M. Stern, *Studies in Early Ismāᶜīlism* (Jerusalem and Leiden: Magnes Press, Hebrew University and Brill, 1983), pp. 189–233.

Stern, S. M., 'Ismāᶜīlī Propaganda and Fāṭimid Rule in Sind', *Islamic Culture* XXIII (1949): 298–307; reprinted in S. M. Stern, *Studies in Early Ismāᶜīlism* (Jerusalem and Leiden: Magnes Press, Hebrew University and Brill, 1983), pp. 177–88.

Sternbach, Ludwik, 'Indian Wisdom and Its Spread Beyond India', *Journal of the American Oriental Society* 101 (1981): 97–131.

Stetkevych, S. P., *Abū Tammām and the Poetics of the ᶜAbbāsid Age* (Leiden: Brill, 1991).

Stroumsa, Sarah and Gedaliahu G. Stroumsa, 'Aspects of Anti-Manichaean Polemics in Late Antiquity and under Early Islam', *Harvard Theological Review* 81 (1988): 37–58.

Al-Subkī, Tāj al-Dīn, *Ṭabaqāt al-Shāfiᶜiyya al-kubrā*, eds ᶜAbd al-Fattāḥ al-Ḥilw and Maḥmūd Muḥammad al-Tannāhī (Cairo: Maṭbaᶜat ᶜĪsā al-Bābī al-Ḥalabī, 1964–).

Al-Subkī, Tāj al-Dīn, *Muᶜīd al-niᵓam wa-mubīd al-niqam* (Beirut: Dār al-Ḥadātha, 1983).

Subtelny, Maria Eva, 'The Making of *Bukhārā-yi Sharīf*: Scholars and Libraries in Medieval Bukhara (The Library of Khwāja Muḥammad Pārsā)', in Devin DeWeese (ed.), *Studies on Central Asian History in Honor of Yuri Bregel* (Bloomington, IN: Indiana University, Research Institute for Inner Asian Studies, 2001), pp. 79–111.

Al-Sulamī, Muḥammad b. al-Ḥusayn, *Ṭabaqāt al-ṣūfiyya* (Beirut: Dār al-Kutub al-ᶜIlmiyya, 1998).

Al-Suyūṭī, Jalāl al-Dīn, *Taᵓrīkh al-khulafāᵓ*, ed. M. ᶜAbd al-Ḥamīd (Cairo, 1969).

Al-Suyūṭī, Jalāl al-Dīn, *al-Jāmiᶜ al-ṣaghīr min ḥadīth al-bashīr al-nadhīr*, ed. Ḥamdī al-Dimirdāsh Muḥammad (Riyadh: Maktabat Nizār Muṣṭafā al-Bāz, 1998).

Swain, Simon, *Economy, Family, and Society from Rome to Islam: A Critical Edition, English Translation, and Study of Bryson's* Management of the Estate (Cambridge: Cambridge University Press, 2013).

Al-Ṭabarī, *Taᵓrīkh al-Ṭabarī = Taᵓrīkh al-rusul wa-l-mulūk*, ed. M. Faḍl Ibrāhīm (Cairo: Dār al-Maᶜārif, 1960–77) = *The History of al-Ṭabarī* (Albany, NY: State University of New York Press, 1985).

Tabatabai, Sassan, *Father of Persian Verse: Rudaki and His Poetry* (Leiden: Leiden University Press, 2010).

Tafażżolī, Aḥmad, 'Āᵓīn-nāma', *EIr* I (1985), p. 692.

Tafażżolī, Aḥmad, 'Dehqān', i, 'In the Sasanian Period', *EIr* VII (1996), pp. 223–5.

Tafażżolī, Aḥmad, *Tārīkh-i adabīyāt-i Īrān pīsh az Islām* (Tehran: Sukhan, 1997).

Al-Taghlibī or al-Thaᶜlabī, *Akhlāq al-mulūk*, see *Kitāb al-Tāj*.

Tahmi, Mahmoud, *L'Encyclopédisme musulman à l'âge classique: le Livre de la création et l'histoire de Maqdisi* (Paris: Maisonneuve et Larose, 1998).

Tamer, Georges, 'Politisches Denken in pseudoplatonischen arabischen Schriften', *Mélanges de l'Université Saint-Joseph* 57 (2004): 303–35.

At-Tancî, Mohammed b. Tavît, 'Abû Mansûr al-Mâturîdî', *Ankara Üniversitesi Ilâhiyat Fakültesi Dergisi* 4 (1955): 1–12.

Tārīkh-i Sīstān, ed. Malik al-shuʿarāʾ Bahār (Tehran: Muʾassaseh-yi Khāvar, 1935).

Tarzi, Z., 'Bāmīān', *EIr* III (1989), ii. 'History and Monuments', pp. 658–60.

Taşköprüzade, Aḥmad b. Muṣṭafā, *Miftāḥ al-saʿāda wa-miṣbāḥ al-siyāda* (Hyderabad: Maṭbaʿat Dāʾirat al-Maʿārif al-ʿUthmāniyya, 1977–).

Al-Tawḥīdī, Abū Ḥayyān, *Kitāb al-Imtāʿ wa-l-muʾānasa*, eds Aḥmad Amīn and Aḥmad al-Zayn (Cairo: Lajnat al-Taʾlīf wa-l-Tarjama wa-l-Nashr, 1939-44, 2nd printing Beirut, 1953).

Al-Tawḥīdī, *al-Muqābasāt*, ed. Muḥammad Tawfīq Ḥusayn (Baghdad: Maṭbaʿat al-Irshād, 1970).

Al-Tawḥīdī, *al-Baṣāʾir wa-l-dhakhāʾir*, ed. Wadād al-Qāḍī (Beirut: Dār Ṣādir, 1988).

Al-Thaʿālibī, *Histoire des rois des Perses = Ghurar akhbār mulūk al-furs wa-siyarihim*, Texte arabe publié et traduit par H. Zotenberg (Paris: Imprimerie nationale, 1900).

Al-Thaʿālibī, *Laṭāʾif al-maʿārif*, eds Ibrāhīm al-Anbarī and Ḥasan Kāmil al-Ṣayrafī (Cairo, Dār Iḥyāʾ al-Kutub al-ʿArabiyya, ʿĪsā al-Bābī al-Ḥalabī) = C. E. Bosworth, *The Book of Curious and Entertaining Information: The Laṭāʾif al-maʿārif of Thaʿālibī* (Edinburgh: Edinburgh University Press, 1968).

Al-Thaʿālibī, *Tuḥfat al-wuzarāʾ al-mansūb ilā Abī Manṣūr ʿAbd al-Malik b. Muḥammad b. Ismāʿīl al-Thaʿālibī*, eds H. ʿAlī al-Rāwī and I. M. al-Saffār (Baghdad: Wizārat al-Awqāf, 1977).

Al-Thaʿālibī, *Yatīmat al-dahr fī maḥāsin ahl al-ʿaṣr*, ed. Mufīd Muḥammad Qumayḥa (Beirut: Dār al-Kutub al-ʿIlmiyya, 1983).

Al-Thaʿālibī, *Ādāb al-mulūk*, ed. Jalāl al-ʿAṭiyya (Beirut: Dār al-Gharb al-Islāmī, 1990).

Thapar, Romila, *Aśoka and the Decline of the Mauryas* (Delhi: Oxford University Press, 1973, rev edn 1997).

Al-Tirmidhī, al-Ḥakīm, *Thalātha muṣannafāt lil-Ḥakīm al-Tirmidhī*, ed. Bernd Radkte, *Drei Schriften des Theosophen von Tirmiḏ* (Beirut: In Kommission bei Franz Steiner Verlag, Stuttgart, 1992).

Al-Tirmidhī, Muḥammad b. ʿAlī al-Ḥakīm, *Kitāb al-Riyāḍa wa-Adab al-nafs*, eds A. J. Arberry and Alī Ḥasan ʿAbd al-Qādir (Cairo: Maṭbaʿat Muṣṭafā al-Bābī al-Ḥalabī, 1947).

Al-Tirmidhī, Muḥammad b. ʿĪsā, *al-Jāmiʿ al-Ṣaḥīḥ wa-huwa Sunan al-Tirmidhī*, ed. Maḥmūd Muḥammad Maḥmūd Ḥasan Naṣṣār (Beirut: Dār al-Kutub al-ᶜIlmiyya, 2000).

Toorawa, Shawkat M., 'Defining *Adab* by (re)defining the *Adīb*: Ibn Abī Ṭāhir Ṭayfūr and storytelling' in Philip F. Kennedy (ed.), *On Fiction and* Adab *in Medieval Arabic Literature* (Wiesbaden: Harrassowitz, 2005), pp. 286–308.

Toorawa, Shawkat M., *Ibn Abī Ṭāhir Ṭayfūr and Arabic Writerly Culture: A Ninth-Century Bookman in Baghdad* (London: Routledge Curzon, 2005).

Tor, D. G., 'Privatized Jihad and Public Order in the Pre-Seljuq Period: The Role of the *Mutatawwiᶜa*', *Iranian Studies* 38 (2005): 555–74.

Tor, D. G., *Violent Order: Religious Warfare, Chivalry, and the ᶜAyyār Phenomenon in the Medieval Islamic World* (Würzburg: Ergon Verlag, 2007).

Tor, D. G., 'The Mamluks in the Military of the Pre-Seljuq Persianate Dynasties', *Iran* XLVI (2008): 213–24.

Tor, D. G., 'The Islamisation of Iranian Kingly Ideals in the Persianate Fürstenspiegel', *Iran* 49 (2011): 15–22.

Tor, D. G., 'The Long Shadow of Pre-Islamic Iranian Rulership: Antagonism or Assimilation', in Teresa Bernheimer and Adam Silverstein (eds), *Late Antiquity: Eastern Perspectives* (Exeter: E. J. W. Gibb Memorial Trust, 2012), pp. 145–63.

Tor, D. G., 'ᶜAyyār', *EI Three*, available at: http://referenceworks.brillonline.com/entries/encyclopaedia-of-islam-3.

Toral-Niehoff, Isabel, 'Die Legende "Barlaam und Josaphat" in der arabisch-muslimischen Literatur: Ein arabistischer Beitrag zur "Barlaam-Frage"', *Die Welt des Orients* 31 (2000): 110–44.

Touati, Houari, 'La dédicace des livres dans l'Islam médiéval', *Annales. Histoire, Sciences Sociales*, 55(2) (2000): 325–54.

Touati, Houari, *Islam et voyage en moyen âge: Histoire et anthropologie d'une pratique lettrée* (Paris: Éditions du Seuil, 2004).

Touati, Houari, 'Pour une histoire de la lecture au Moyen-Âge musulman: à propos des livres d'histoire', *Studia Islamica* 104/105 (2007): 11–44.

Treadwell, Luke, 'Ibn Ẓāfir al-Azdī's Account of the Murder of Aḥmad b. Ismāᶜīl al-Sāmānī and the Succession of his Son Naṣr', in C. Hillenbrand (ed.), *Studies in Honour of Clifford Edmund Bosworth, vol. II: The Sultan's Turret: Studies in Persian and Turkish Culture* (Leiden: Brill, 2000), pp. 397–419.

Treadwell, Luke, '*Shāhānshāh* and *al-Malik al-Muᵓayyad*: The Legitimation of Power in Sāmānid and Būyid Iran', in Farhad Daftary and Josef W. Meri (eds), *Culture and Memory in Medieval Islam: Essays in Honour of Wilferd Madelung* (London: Tauris, 2003), pp. 318–37.

Treadwell, Luke, 'The Account of the Samanid Dynasty in Ibn Ẓāfir al-Azdī's *Akhbār al-duwal al-munqaṭiᶜa*', *Iran* 43 (2005): 135–71.

Treadwell, Luke, 'Urban Militias in the Eastern Islamic World (Third–Fourth Centuries AH/Ninth–Tenth Centuries CE)', in Teresa Bernheimer and Adam Silverstein (eds), *Late Antiquity: Eastern Perspectives* (Exeter: E. J. W. Gibb Memorial Trust, 2012), pp. 128–44.

Treadwell, Luke, 'The Samanids: The First Islamic Dynasty of Central Asia', in Edmund Herzig and Sarah Stewart (eds), *Early Islamic Iran, vol. V: The Idea of Iran* (London: Tauris, 2012), pp. 3–15.

Treadwell, W. L., 'The Political History of the Sāmānid State', unpublished PhD thesis, University of Oxford, 1991.

Tuḥfat al-mulūk dar ādāb, ed. M. T. Dānishpazhūh (Tehran: Chāpkhāneh-yi Majlis, 1938).

Al-Ṭurṭūshī, *Sirāj al-mulūk*, ed. Muḥammad Fatḥī Abū Bakr (Cairo: Dār al-Miṣriyya al-Lubnāniyya, 1994).

Ṭūsī, Naṣīr al-Dīn, *Akhlāq-i Nāṣirī*, eds Mujtabā Mīnuvī and ᶜAlīriżā Ḥaydarī (Tehran: Khavārazmī, 1982) = G. M. Wickens, *The Nasirean Ethics, by Naṣīr ad-Dīn Ṭūsī* (London: George Allen & Unwin, 1964).

Al-Ṭūsī, Shaykh al-Ṭāʾifa Muḥammad b. al-Ḥasan, *al-Tibyān fī tafsīr al-Qurʾān*, eds Aḥmad Shawqī al-Amīn and Aḥmad Ḥabīb Qaṣīr (Najaf: Maktabat al-Amīn, 1957–63).

Vadet, Jean-Claude, 'Le Karramisme de la Haut-Asie au carrefour de trois sectes rivales', *Revue des études islamiques* 48 (1989): 25–50.

Vahman, Fereydun, 'Bāzī', *EIr* IV (1990), pp. 60–5.

Vāᶜiẓ, Shaykh al-Islām, *Fażāʾil-i Balkh*, ed. ᶜAbd al-Ḥayy Ḥabībī (Tehran: Bunyād-i Farhang-i Īrān, 1971).

Vajda, Georges, *Index général des manuscrits arabes musulmans de la Bibliothèque nationale de Paris* (Paris: Centre national de la recherche scientifique, 1953).

Vajda, Georges, 'Le témoignage d'al-Māturīdī sur la doctrine des Manichéens, des Dayṣānites et des Marcionites', *Arabica* 13 (1966): 1–38.

Vaissière, Étienne de la, 'Čākar', *EIr* IV (1990), available at: www.iranicaonline.org/articles/search/keywords:čākar.

Vaissière, Étienne de la, *Histoire des marchands sogdiens* (Paris: Collège de France, Institut des hautes études chinoises, 2002).

Vaissière, Étienne de la, *Samarcande et Samarra: élites d'Asie Centrale dans l'empire Abbasside* (Paris: Association pour l'avancement des études iraniennes, 2007).

Vasmer, R., 'Beiträge zur muḥammedanischen Münzkunde, I. Die Münzen der Abū Dāʾudiden', *Numismatische Zeitschrift* NS, 18 (1925): 49–62.

Vaziri, Mostafa, *Buddhism in Iran: An Anthropological Approach to Traces and Influences* (New York: Palgrave Macmillan, 2012).

Versteegh, Kees, 'Linguistic Contacts between Arabic and Other Languages', *Arabica* 48 (2001): 470–508.

Waardenburg, Jacques, 'The Medieval Period, 650–1500', in Jacques Waardenburg (ed.), *Muslim Perceptions of Other Religions: A Historical Survey* (New York: Oxford University Press, 1999), pp. 18–69.

Wakelnig, Elvira, *Feder, Tafel, Mensch: al-ᶜĀmirīs* Kitāb al-Fuṣūl fī l-Maᶜālim al-ilāhīya *und die arabische Proklos-Rezeption im 10. Jh.* (Leiden, Brill: 2006).

Wakelnig, Elvira, 'Metaphysics in al-ᶜĀmirī: The Hierarchy of Being and the Concept of Creation', *Medioevo* 32 (2007): 39–59.

Wakelnig, Elvira, 'Philosophical Fragments of al-ᶜĀmirī Preserved Mainly in al-Tawḥīdī, Miskawayh, and in the Texts of the *Ṣiwān al-ḥikma* Tradition', in Peter Adamson (ed.), *In the Age of al-Fārābī: Arabic Philosophy in the Fourth/Tenth Century* (London: Warburg Institute, 2008), pp. 215–38.

Wakelnig, Elvira, 'Die Weiterführung der neuplatonischen Ansätze', *Grundriss der Geschichte der Philosophie: Philosophie in der islamischen Welt,* Band I: 8.–10. Jahrhundert (Basel: Schwabe, 2012), pp. 170–85.

Wakelnig, Elvira, *A Philosophy Reader from the Circle of Miskawayh* (Cambridge: Cambridge University Press, 2013).

Walker, Paul E., *Early Philosophical Shiism: The Ismaili Neoplatonism of Abū Yaᶜqūb al-Sijistānī* (Cambridge: Cambridge University Press, 1993).

Walker, Paul E., *Abū Yaᶜqūb al-Sijistānī: Intellectual Missionary* (London: Tauris, 1996).

Walzer, Richard, *Greek into Arabic: Essays on Islamic Philosophy* (Cambridge, MA: Harvard University Press, 1962).

Weinberger, J., 'The Authorship of Two Twelfth-Century Transoxanian Biographical Dictionaries', *Arabica* 33 (1986): 369–82.

Weir, T. W. [A. Zysow], 'Ṣadaḳa', *EI²* VIII (1995), pp. 708–16.

Wensinck-Gardet, A. J., 'Khaṭīᶜa', *EI²* V (1986), pp. 1106–9.

Werkmeister, Walter, *Quellenuntersuchungen zum Kitāb al-ᶜIqd al-farīd des Andalusiers Ibn ᶜAbdrabbih (246/860–328/940)* (Berlin: Schwarz, 1983).

Widengren, Geo, 'Recherches sur le féodalisme iranien', *Orientalia Secuana* V (1956): 79–182.

Williams, Steven J., *The Secret of Secrets: The Scholarly Career of a Pseudo-Aristotelian*

Text in the Latin Middle Ages (Ann Arbor, MI: University of Michigan Press, 2003).
Winter, Irene J., '"Seat of Kingship"/"A Wonder to Behold": The Palace as Construct in the Ancient Near East', *Ars Orientalis* 23, *Pre-Modern Islamic Palaces* (1993): 27–55.
Winter, Michael, 'Ottoman Egypt, 1525–1609', in M. W. Daly (ed.), *The Cambridge History of Egypt, vol. II: Modern Egypt, from 1517 to the End of the Twentieth Century* (Cambridge: Cambridge University Press, 1998), pp. 1–33.
Wormser, Paul, 'La rencontre de l'Inde et de l'Égypte dans la vie et l'oeuvre du savant religieux d'expression malaise Nûruddin ar-Rânîrî (m. 1658)', in Rachida Chih and Catherine Mayeur-Jaouen, *Le soufisme à l'époque ottomane XVIe–XVIII siècle* (Cairo: Institut français d'archéologie orientale, 2010), pp. 209–33.
Yaman, Hikmet, *Prophetic Niche in the Virtuous City: The Concept of* Ḥikmah *in Early Islamic Thought* (Leiden: Brill, 2011).
Al-Yaᶜqūbī, *Kitāb al-Buldān* (Leiden: Brill, 1891).
Al-Yaᶜqūbī, *Taʾrīkh al-Yaᶜqūbī* (Beirut: Dār Ṣādir, 1980).
Yāqūt, *Muᶜjam al-buldān* (Beirut: Dār Ṣādir, 1957).
Yāqūt, *Muᶜjam al-udabāʾ: Irshād al-arīb ilā maᶜrifat al-adīb*, ed. Iḥsān ᶜAbbās (Beirut: Dār al-Gharb al-Islāmī, 1993).
Yarshater, E., 'The Theme of Wine-Drinking and the Concept of the Beloved in Early Persian Poetry', *Studia Islamica* 13 (1960): 43–53.
Yavari, Neguin, 'Mirrors for Princes or a Hall of Mirrors? Niẓām al-Mulk's *Siyar al-mulūk* Reconsidered', *al-Masāq* XX(1) (2008): 47–69.
Yavari, Neguin, *Advice for the Sultan: Prophetic Voices and Secular Politics in Medieval Islam* (Oxford: Oxford University Press, 2014).
Yücesoy, Hayrettin, 'Translation as Self-Consciousness: Ancient Sciences, Antediluvian Wisdom, and the ᶜAbbāsid Translation Movement', *Journal of World History* 20 (2009): 523–57.
Yūsofī, G. H., 'Abū Moslem K̲orāsānī', *EIr* I (1985), pp. 341–4.
Zachariae, Theodor, 'Die Weisheitssprüche des Šānāq bei aṭ-Ṭorṭūšī (Übersetzung und Kommentar)', *Wiener Zeitschrift für die Kunde des Morgenlandes* 28 (1914): 182–210.
Zakeri, Mohsen, 'ᶜAlī ibn ᶜUbaida al-Raiḥānī: A Forgotten Belletrist (adīb) and Pahlavi Translator', *Oriens* XXXIV (1994): 75–102.
Zakeri, Mohsen, *Sāsānid Soldiers in Early Muslim Society: The Origins of ᶜAyyārān and Futuwwa* (Wiesbaden: Harrassowitz, 1995).
Zakeri, Mohsen, 'From Iran to Islam: *ᶜAyyārān* and *Futuwwa*', *Proceedings of the*

Second European Conference of Iranian Studies, Bamberg, 30 September–4 October 1991 (1995), pp. 745–57.

Zakeri, Mohsen, 'Ādāb al-falāsifa: The Persian Content of an Arabic Collection of Aphorisms', *Mélanges de l'Université Saint-Joseph* 57 (2004): 173–90.

Zakeri, Mohsen, *Persian Wisdom in Arabic Garb: ᶜAlī b. ᶜUbayda al-Rayḥānī (d. 219/834) and his* Jawāhir al-kilam wa-farāʾid al-ḥikam (Leiden: Brill, 2007).

Zaman, Muhammad Qasim, *Religion and Politics under the Early ᶜAbbāsids: The Emergence of the Proto-Sunnī Elite* (Leiden: Brill, 1997).

Zaman, Muhammad Qasim, 'The Caliphs, the ᶜUlamāʾ, and the Law: Defining the Role and Function of the Caliph in the Early ᶜAbbāsid Period', *Islamic Law and Society* IV (1997): 1–36.

Zaman, Muhammad Qasim, 'Death, Funeral Processions, and the Articulation of Religious Authority in Early Islam', *Studia Islamica* 93 (2001): 27–58.

Zambaur, Edouard de, *Manuel de généalogie et de chronologie pour l'histoire de l'Islam* (Hannover 1927, reprinted 1955).

Zambaur, Eduard von, *Die Münzprägungen des Islams zeitlich und örtlich geordnet, I. Band: Der Westen und Osten bis zum Indus* (Wiesbaden: Steiner, 1968).

Zaydān, Jurjī, *Kitāb Taʾrīkh ādāb al-lugha al-ᶜarabiyya* (al-Fajjāla, Miṣr: Maṭbaᶜat al-Hilāl, 1912).

Zayn al-akhbār = Tārīkh-i Gardīzī, see Gardīzī.

Ziadeh, Farhat J., 'Equality (*kafāʾah*) in the Muslim Law of Marriage', *American Journal of Comparative Law* VI (1957): 503–17.

Zimmermann, Fritz W., 'Al-Kindī', in M. L. Young, J. D. Latham and R. B. Serjeant (eds), *The Cambridge History of Arabic Literature, Religion, Learning and Science in the ᶜAbbasid Period* (Cambridge: Cambridge University Press, 1990), pp. 364–9.

Al-Ziriklī, Khayr al-Dīn, *al-Aᶜlām* (Beirut: Dār al-ᶜIlm lil-Malāyīn, 2007).

Zysow, A., 'Zakāt', A., *EI²* XI (2002), pp. 406–22.

Index

Abān al-Lāḥiqī, 38
ʿAbbās, I., 47, 48
Abbasid(s), 35, 46, 55, 183, 240, 241
ʿAbdallāh b. ʿĀmir, 41, 266n
ʿAbdallāh b. ʿAmr b. al-ʿĀṣ, 127
ʿAbdallāh b. Ṭāhir, 5, 57, 76, 188, 189, 213, 229
ʿAbd al-ʿAzīz b. ʿAbdallāh, 41
ʿAbd al-Jabbār, 76, 78, 79, 81, 83, 108, 114, 166, 180
ʿAbd al-Malik, 36, 157
ʿAbd al-Muʾmin b. Khalaf, Abū Yaʿlā, 207, 213
ʿabīd, 145, 146
abnāʾ al-dunyā, 75
abnāʾ al-mulūk, 218
Abraham, 117, 128, 132
Abū ʿAlī Chaghānī, 237
Abū ʿAlī al-Jubbāʾī, 82
Abū Bakr, 94, 136, 176, 177
Abū Dāʾūd al-Sijistānī, 29, 31
  Sunan, 29, 31
Abū Ḥanīfa, 5
Abū Hāshim ʿAbd al-Salām, 82
Abū l-Hudhayl al-ʿAllāf, 80, 81, 82, 84, 166, 250
Abū Hurayra, 199, 205
Abū Manṣūr al-Maʿmarī, 39, 40
Abū Mūsā al-Ashʿarī, 215, 216, 221
Abū Nuwās, 151, 156
Abū Rashīd al-Nīsābūrī, 76, 108
Abū Salīk Gurgānī, 41
Abū Shakūr Balkhī, 42
Abū Sufyān, 220, 221, 311n
Abū Tammām, Ismaʿili *dāʿī*, 76
Abū Yaʿlā ʿAbd al-Muʾmin *see* ʿAbd al-Muʾmin b. Khalaf
Abū Yūsuf, 201
  Kitāb al-Kharāj, 201
Abū Zayd al-Balkhī *see* al-Balkhī, Abū Zayd
accountant, 22
ʿāda (pl. *ʿādāt*), 110, 112, 158, 159, 160, 175, 214
adab (pl. *ādāb*), 4, 6, 7, 8, 22, 36, 47, 59, 60, 62, 65, 66, 68, 73, 74, 86, 87, 99, 112, 119, 136, 142, 149, 153, 158, 159, 161, 172, 174, 175, 179, 186, 197, 201, 210, 229, 238, 251, 253n, 263n
  ~ al-mulūk, 7, 99
  sūʾ ~, 22
ʿadāla, 107, 186
adīb, 31, 45, 159
ʿadl, 8, 75, 83, 126, 187, 198, 200, 216, 221, 223, 257n, 286n; *see also* justice
admonition, 11, 13, 19, 20, 23, 27, 30, 31, 32, 91, 101, 122, 127, 144, 226, 251, 261n, 285n, 288n; *see also mawʿiẓa*
ʿAḍud al-Dawla, 38
advice, 4, 5, 6, 8, 9, 12, 13, 15, 16, 18, 19, 20, 21, 24, 27, 28, 29, 30, 31, 33, 36, 41, 42, 43, 55, 61, 63, 101, 104, 106, 119, 124, 125, 137, 145, 147, 148, 162, 169, 171, 178, 194, 196, 206, 215, 222, 245, 248, 249, 252; *see also* counsel, *naṣīḥa*, *pand*
Āfarīnnāmeh, 42
afsān, *afsānaqāt*, 39, 64, 154, 156
Afsaruddin, A., 33
ʿahd (pl. *ʿuhūd*), 4, 5, 23, 24, 35–6, 44–5, 46, 47, 48, 50, 60, 65, 67, 68, 69, 119, 120, 191, 195, 203, 204, 221, 222, 223, 253n
ʿAhd Ardashīr, Testament of Ardashīr, 8, 15, 24, 27, 35, 45, 46–9, 56, 105, 132, 144, 145, 146, 158, 174, 222, 269n8
ʿAhd Sābūr, Testament of Shāpūr, 24, 35, 49–50, 189, 271n, 306n
aḥkām, 23, 90, 99, 100, 169, 233, 235; *see also* ordinances

ahl al-aqdār, 222; *see also aṣḥāb al-aqdār*
ahl al-ᶜaql, 9, 119; *see also ahl al-ᶜuqūl*, *ᶜāqil*, *ᶜuqalāʾ*, intelligent person(s)
ahl al-baghy wa l-ᶜiṣyān, 93; *see also* rebels
ahl al-bayt, 183
ahl al-dhimma, 163, 189, 207, 208
ahl al-dīn, 88, 105, 119, 222
ahl al-fiqh, 9
ahl al-ḥikma, 149; *see also ḥakīm*
ahl al-jihād, 222
ahl al-khibra, 119
ahl al-marātib, 222
ahl al-milla, *ahl al-milal*, 93, 207, 208
ahl al-murūʾāt, 133, 222
ahl al-ridda, 94
ahl al-sunna wa-l-jamāᶜa, 177
ahl al-tawḥīd, 164, 165
ahl al-ᶜuqūl, 116, 126; *see also ahl al-ᶜaql*, *ᶜāqil*, *ᶜuqalāʾ*, intelligent person(s)
Aḥmad, F. ᶜAbd al-Munᶜim, 246
Aḥmad b. Abī Khālid, 228
Aḥmad II b. Ismāᶜīl, 165, 170
Aḥmad b. Sahl, 41, 76, 84, 169, 213, 236, 237, 248
Aḥmad b. Yaḥyā b. Asad, 182
aḥrār, 222
āʾīn, 23, 46, 53, 54
Āʾīnnāmeh, 36, 53–5, 104, 127, 231
Āʾīn of Ardashīr, 54
ᶜajam, 36, 53, 57, 58, 59, 90, 226
  kutub al- ~, 48, 49, 51, 61, 250
  mulūk al- ~, 24, 54, 56, 57, 58, 154, 270
  siyar al- ~, 48, 58, 59
akhbār see *khabar*
akhlāq, 73, 99, 110, 122, 125, 133, 142, 158, 159
  Akhlāq al-mulūk of al-Taghlibī, 20, 45, 46, 54, 55, 56, 58
  see also Kitāb al-Tāj
āla (pl. *ālāt*), 91, 116, 141, 169, 204, 205
Alexander, 3, 27, 43, 44, 58, 65, 67, 68, 94, 104, 111, 115, 132, 144, 178, 196, 222, 226
ᶜAlī b. Abī Ṭālib, 24, 35, 94, 105, 126, 150, 176, 177, 223
Āl-i Muḥtāj, 181
al-ᶜĀlim wa-l-mutaᶜallim, 5
amāna, 119, 141, 144, 175, 184, 185, 186, 203, 204
ᶜamīd al-mulk, 182
ᶜāmil (pl. *ᶜummāl*), 12, 57, 96, 145, 147, 167, 181, 182, 184, 187, 190, 192, 194, 195, 199, 200, 201, 204, 231
amīn (pl. *umanāʾ*), 141, 144, 191, 194, 209, 214
al-Amīn, 5
al-ᶜĀmirī, 68, 89, 95, 98, 99, 153, 285n
  al-Amad, 153, 287n
  al-Iᶜlām bi-manāqib al-Islām, 68
amīr-i ḥaras, 183
ᶜāmma, *ᶜāmmī*, *ᶜawāmm*, 9, 32, 47, 56, 73, 87, 88, 95, 107, 108, 118, 122, 139, 142, 144, 166, 173, 179, 189, 197, 202, 203, 209, 219, 221, 222, 224, 226, 229, 230, 231, 232, 234, 242, 244, 245; *see also* common people
al-amr bi-l-maᶜrūf wa-l-nahy ᶜan al-munkar, 28, 31, 33, 75, 178, 210, 243
ᶜAmr b. al-Layth, 213
ᶜAmr b. ᶜUbayd, 25, 26, 35, 149
analogy, 96, 137, 141, 185, 203, 216
andarz, 4, 6, 8, 10, 28, 36, 44, 45, 50, 67, 250
angels, 57, 83, 139, 140, 141, 144, 172, 176, 185, 203, 229, 296n
Anṣārī, Ḥ., 246
ᶜAntara, 157
anthology, 4, 6, 36, 49
Anūshīrvān, 42, 50, 51, 53, 55, 56, 57, 125, 158, 189, 209, 226, 228, 267n
ᶜāqil (pl. *ᶜuqalāʾ*), 11, 15, 92, 105, 111, 129, 192, 232, 234
  al-ᶜāqil al-maḥrūm, 111, 232; *see also ahl al-ᶜaql*, *ahl al-ᶜuqūl*, *ᶜāqil*, intelligent person(s), *ᶜuqalāʾ*
ᶜaql, 9, 28, 41, 89, 107, 108, 109, 116, 117, 119, 184
ᶜaqlī, 80, 98, 99, 103
ᶜarab, 24, 36, 44, 57
Arabic *see* language, *lugha*
Ardashīr, 35, 36, 46, 47, 48, 49, 56, 57, 61, 77, 105, 111, 112, 125, 128, 132, 144, 158, 222, 225, 229
Ardashīr, Testament of *see ᶜAhd Ardashīr*
ᶜāriḍ, 181, 183
Arisṭāṭālīs *see* Aristotle
Aristotle, Aristotelian, 3, 24, 27, 35, 43, 44, 65, 66, 67, 68, 73, 77, 94, 104, 109, 111, 122, 126, 127, 132, 144, 145, 178, 179, 196, 215, 222, 226
arithmetic, 102
arrogance, 109, 121, 122, 127, 173, 179
arthaśāstra, 61
arzāq, 166, 167, 194, 214, 215, 301n; *see also rizq*, stipend(s)
aṣāla, 184, 185, 187
asāṭīr al-awwalīn, 65, 157

asāwira, 22, 145, 147, 186
ascetic(s), 25, 64, 69, 111, 202, 218, 232, 243, 244; *see also nāsik*
aṣḥāb akhbār, 181, 183
aṣḥāb al-aqdār, 218; *see also ahl al-aqdār*
aṣḥāb ḥaras, 181, 183
aṣḥāb juyūsh, 181, 183, 186
aṣḥāb shuraṭ, 181, 182, 183
al-Ashᶜarī, Abū l-Ḥasan, 80
Ashᶜariyya, 80
ashrāf, 105, 183, 218
aṣlaḥ, *al-aṣlaḥ*, 114, 238, 239
asmār, 56, 67, 157; *see also* tale(s)
assembly, 19, 29, 30, 74, 93, 94, 103, 104, 105, 154, 157, 159, 216, 224, 225; *see also maḥfil, majlis, mujālasa*
assistants, 13, 16, 20, 21, 22, 23, 40, 140, 141, 143, 146, 175, 184, 202, 204, 241; *see also aᶜwān*
astronomy, 102
ᶜaṭāᵓ, 200; *see also ᶜaṭiyyāt*, stipend(s)
athar (pl. *āthār*), 14, 17, 18, 23, 57, 90, 91, 97, 98, 110, 112, 135, 136, 137, 156, 191, 223, 224, 226
  ᶜilm al- ~, 18
ᶜaṭiyyāt, 166; *see also ᶜaṭāᵓ*, stipend(s)
attributes, divine, 74, 79, 82, 83, 112–20, 150, 197
austerity, 26, 29, 136, 155, 156, 310n; *see also zuhd*
aᶜwān, 13, 16, 21, 22, 141, 143, 146, 175, 202, 204, 241; *see also* assistants
awe *see mahāba*
awliyāᵓ, 13, 94, 150, 214, 223
aᶜyān, 145
Āzādsarv, 41, 266n

Bāb al-ᶜāmma, 224
Baghdad, 28, 45, 76, 227
bāghūn, 210, 236; *see also* rebels
Bahrām-i Gūr, 57, 125, 225
Bahrāmshāh, 61
al-Baḥrayn, 109
Balᶜamī, Abū l-Fażl, 38, 45, 61, 237
balance, 114, 126, 127, 188, 200, 201
Balkh, 7, 29, 59, 60, 64, 66, 70, 87, 246, 248
al-Balkhī, Abū ᶜAlī, 59
al-Balkhī, Abū l-Muᵓayyad, 59
al-Balkhī, Abū Zayd, 7, 37, 76, 143, 158, 161, 205, 246, 248
  Adab al-sulṭān wa-l-raᶜiyya, 7
  Faḍl al-mulk, 7
  Ṣawlajān al-kataba, 161
  al-Siyāsa al-kabīr, 7
  al-Siyāsa al-ṣaghīr, 7
Bamiyan, 70
barīd, 167, 182, 183
Barmakids, 129
Barzawayh, 63
Basra, 26. 129, 216
bāṭinī, 106
bayān, 154, 155, 157, 212
bayt al-māl, 52, 190, 194
beloved, 104, 128; *see also maᶜshūq*
benefit, 8, 11, 12, 18, 19, 20, 27, 44, 65, 75, 86, 87, 92, 102, 107, 109, 115, 116, 118, 120, 128, 130, 131, 149, 155, 156, 157, 175, 185, 187, 189, 192, 220, 230, 231, 235; *see also niᶜma*
bidᶜa, 9, 30, 234; *see also* innovation
Bīdpāy, 61
Bilādh, 67
Bilār, 67
Bilawhar wa-Budhāṣaf, 4, 43, 68, 69
al-Bīrūnī, 59, 154
bīstgānī, 168
biṭāna, 144
van Bladel, K., 66
blame, 22, 73, 117, 126, 128, 170, 174; *see also* censure, rebuke
de Blois, F., 66
bodyguard, 165, 183
book *see kitāb*
boon companion, 20, 21, 227, 259n
Bray, J., 149, 305n
breastfeeding, 149, 151, 152, 250
Bryson, 143, 148, 299n
al-budd, 68, 69
Buddha, 60, 68, 69
Buddhist, 64, 70
Bukhara, 147, 160, 181, 182, 239, 248, 295n
al-Bukhārī, 31
  Ṣaḥīḥ, 31
al-Bukhārī, Muḥammad, 61
Bust, 31
Buyids, 38, 167, 168, 267n
Buzurgmihr, 36, 42, 51, 52–3, 267n, 285n
Byzantines, 51

Camel, Battle of, 94, 286n
Cāṇakya, 66
  capacity, 78, 81, 83, 84, 90, 96, 112, 113, 123, 131, 132, 140, 141, 142, 164, 166, 167, 198, 206, 241, 248, 283n; *see also qudra*

Caspian, 5, 109, 161
censure, 19, 26, 119, 128, 133, 172, 228, 238, 239; *see also* blame, rebuke
Chaghanids, 181
chākar, 40
chamberlain, 21, 52, 230, 259n; *see also ḥājib*
charitable endowment *see waqf*
Cheikho, L., 63
child, children, 14, 31, 54, 104, 140, 143, 145, 146, 147, 148–62, 165, 179, 218, 227, 250, 297n
China, 51
choice, 78, 109, 142, 148, 150, 151, 152, 154, 158, 162; *see also ikhtiyār*
circumcision, 142, 162
clemency, 118, 170, 171, 201, 204, 213, 238, 242, 243
clothing, 122, 132, 153, 212, 228; *see also* dress
commanding good and forbidding wrong *see al-amr bi-l-maʿrūf*
common people, 12, 14, 18, 22, 73, 95, 103, 107, 108, 110, 112, 132, 142, 144, 189, 197, 201, 202, 203, 209, 222, 226, 232, 244, 245; *see also ʿāmma*
compassion, 112, 149, 175, 179, 197, 199, 201, 203; *see also* mercy
consensus, 107, 108, 135, 136, 137; *see also ijmāʿ*
consultation, 126, 175, 176, 184
conviction, 79, 80, 81, 83, 96, 102, 105, 106, 107, 109, 112, 113, 160, 247, 249; *see also iʿtiqād*
Cook, M., 31
corruption, 12, 13, 14, 32, 86, 95, 104, 106, 107, 109, 114, 121, 152, 161, 164, 171, 174, 185, 190, 192, 193, 194, 202, 210, 213, 222, 230, 231, 234, 286n; *see also fasād*
counsel, 4, 5, 6, 9, 10, 11, 12, 13, 14, 15, 16, 18, 19, 21, 22, 23, 24, 25, 27, 28, 29, 30, 31, 32, 34, 36, 41, 42, 43, 44, 52, 55, 101, 104, 111, 175, 197, 207, 208, 215, 230, 249, 250, 251; *see also naṣīḥa*
counsellor, 8, 12, 20, 23, 24, 30, 31, 53, 96, 146, 245, 248, 251; *see also nāṣiḥ*
craft, 22, 89, 90, 91, 141, 155, 162, 204, 205; *see also ṣināʿa*
craftsman, 89, 141, 142, 204, 205, 218; *see also ṣāniʿ*
criminal, 117, 118, 171, 211, 212, 213, 239, 243, 286n
Ctesiphon, 226
cultural transmission, 6, 70
dāʿī, 106, 137
dalīl (pl. *adilla, dalāʾil*), 107, 108, 112, 116, 123, 136, 238
Damascus, 217
Daqīqī, 42, 59
ḍarar, 20, 92, 134; *see also maḍarra*
Dari, 154
ḍarūra, 81
ḍarūrī, 80, 89
David, 177, 199, 214
  House of ~, 10
Davidson, O., 39
Davis, D., 18
daʿwa, 93, 94, 131
  Abbasid ~, 240
  Ismaʿili ~, 109, 247, 248
dawla (pl. *duwal*), 107, 109, 232, 233, 244
debate, 106, 109, 151, 157, 158, 234; *see also* disputation, *munāẓara*
deceit, 12, 19, 22, 23, 24, 28, 68; *see also* deception, *ghishsh*
deception, 15, 21, 23, 28, 29, 34, 200, 233; *see also* deceit, *ghishsh*
dēn, 17
deputy *see khalīfa*
desire, 13, 19, 20, 21, 28, 34, 62, 64, 98, 105, 121, 123, 129, 132, 141, 147, 148, 173, 185, 233
dharma, 63
dharmaśāstra, 62
dhimma, 203, 204, 208; *see also ahl al-dhimma*
dihqān (pl. *dahāqīn*), 40–1, 42, 202, 266n
Dinavar, 45
al-Dīnawarī, Abū Ḥanīfa, 46
  al-Akhbār al-ṭiwāl, 46
direct address, 4–5, 6, 9, 251
disobedience, 77, 78, 84, 117, 118, 130, 171, 173, 177, 178, 203, 239
disorder, 14, 185
disputation, 93, 94, 96, 110, 286n; *see also* debate, *munāẓara*
dispute, 232
dīwān (Persian *dīvān*)
  administrative office, 147, 167, 181, 182, 183, 301n
  collection of poetry, 24
  register, 155, 157
Diyār Rabīʿa, 5
doctrine, 75, 76, 78, 79, 81, 82, 83, 84, 87, 91, 108, 109, 110, 114, 123, 131, 164, 165, 166, 167, 192, 199, 234, 238; *see also maqāla*

Donner, F., 77
doubt, 79, 83, 94, 100, 102, 108, 135, 159, 173, 195, 217, 229, 239
dress, 54, 74, 161; *see also* clothing
dustūr, 24, 40, 46, 211

education (of princes), 39, 62, 65, 99, 142, 143, 148, 153–62, 166, 195, 196, 250
Egypt, 18, 65, 109, 127
elder(s), 104, 191, 202; *see also mashāyikh*
employment, 152, 174, 251
encyclopaedia, 4, 6, 158, 250
enemy, enemies, 13, 15, 22, 51, 82, 88, 95, 109, 110, 112, 116, 118, 124, 144, 161, 170, 190, 199, 208, 210, 211, 220, 229, 230, 232, 233, 236, 240, 242, 243, 286n
enmity, 170, 192, 233
envy, 118, 128, 192, 235, 244
epic, 39, 40, 62, 154
epistemology, 29, 80, 93
equity, 85, 116, 169, 187, 189, 199, 200, 201, 211, 225, 227; *see also qisṭ*
evil, 75, 83, 114, 128, 135, 180, 232, 241, 242

fable(s), 36, 61, 154
fāḍil (pl. *fuḍalāʾ*), 11, 105, 232, 234; *see also* virtuous
faḍīla (pl. *faḍāʾil*), 22, 47, 86, 88, 110, 126, 134, 135, 136, 245; *see also* virtue
faith, 32, 78, 79, 80, 81, 83, 84, 92, 93, 101, 108, 166, 200, 240; *see also īmān*
falsafa, 112
faqīh (pl. *fuqahāʾ*), 19, 29, 31, 100, 214, 244
farᶜ (pl. *furūᶜ*), 133, 235
al-Fārābī, 101
  Iḥṣāʾ al-ᶜulūm, 101
farḍ, 99, 169
farīḍa (pl. *farāʾiḍ*), 84, 85, 153, 166, 216
fāris (pl. *fursān*), 13, 147
fasād, 12, 13, 14, 86, 107, 171, 192, 213, 286n; *see also* corruption
fāsiq, 79, 129
al-Fatḥ b. Khāqān, 45, 46
fayʾ, 100
faylasūf, 108
fiction, fictional, fictitious, 39, 65, 154, 158
fiqh, 9, 22, 36, 99, 100, 101, 159, 186
  ~ *fī l-dīn*, 102, 164; *see also ᶜilm al-fiqh*
Firdawsī, 18, 39, 42, 49, 53, 59, 250, 265n, 266n
firqa (pl. *firaq*), 91, 174
fisq, 78
fitna, 177, 235, 242, 287n
fityān, 145, 146, 164
  five principles, 75, 80, 82, 84, 178, 187
  see also al-uṣūl al-khamsa
flattery, 132, 249
forbearance, 117, 120, 127, 165, 173, 220, 228; *see also ḥilm*
forge, forgery, 97, 98
forgiveness, 84, 116, 117, 118, 120, 130, 164, 170, 172, 173, 242
de Fouchécour, Ch.-H., 41
Freimark, P., 11
fujūr, 163
fuḥsh, 106, 155
funerals, 101
furnishings, 74
al-furs, 44, 114, 259n, 274n; *see also* Persian(s)

gahnāmag, 53
Galen, 152
Gardīzī, 236
generosity, 115–16, 127, 155, 157, 167, 197, 220, 221, 222, 239, 271n
geometry, 102
gharaḍ, 108, 204, 205
al-Ghazālī, 33, 58, 263n, 264n
  Naṣīḥat al-mulūk, 58
Ghaznavids, 160, 168, 183, 184
ghazw (pl. *ghazawāt*), 174, 175, 211
ghishsh, 22, 23, 28; *see also* deceit, deception
ghulām (pl. *ghilmān*), 104, 145, 146, 159, 163, 164, 165, 166, 167
Gilan, 237
Gīlānshāh, 6
Gimaret, D., 69
grammar, 154, 155
gratitude, 24, 37, 88, 113, 120, 121, 131, 140, 165, 207
Greece, 51
grievance(s), 48, 58, 100, 157, 158, 169, 214, 218, 223, 224, 225, 226, 228, 230, 231; *see also maẓālim*
Gurgan, 5, 237

ḥadd (pl. *ḥudūd*), 118, 126, 171, 173, 187
ḥājib (pl. *ḥujjāb*), 21, 52, 230, 259n; *see also* chamberlain
ḥakīm (pl. *ḥukamāʾ*), 12, 14, 15, 17, 24, 27, 53, 98, 103, 104, 105, 113, 114, 115, 121, 144, 223, 226, 232; *see also* philosopher, sage
ḥākim (pl. *ḥukkām*), 214, 215; *see also* judge
al-ḥalāl wa-l-ḥarām, 90, 99, 100

Ḥanafī, Ḥanafiyya, 18, 29, 33, 76, 102, 138, 149, 201
Ḥanbalī, 28–9
Ḥanẓala Badghīsī, 41
Hamori, A., 20
ḥaqq (pl. *ḥuqūq*), 12, 21, 28, 31, 32, 79, 85, 100, 107, 108, 120, 121, 148, 149, 156, 162, 181, 188, 192, 199, 200, 203, 204, 206, 207, 208, 214, 216, 217, 218, 232, 233, 234, 242, 245, 248
Hārūn al-Rashīd, 25, 27, 35, 129, 211
Ḥasan b. ᶜAlī b. Abī Ṭālib, 177
al-Ḥasan al-Baṣrī, 32, 208
ḥasham, 140, 163, 164, 296n
ḥāshiya, 22, 140, 145, 173, 195, 222; *see also* retinue
Ḥātim al-Ṭāʾī, 157
hawan, *hawā* (pl. *ahwāʾ*), 14, 19, 21, 23, 33, 121, 174
Hazār afsān, 39, 156
ḥazm, 123, 124, 125–6, 127, 238; *see also* resolve
heat, 153, 160
Herat, 147
heterodoxy, 16, 95
ḥijāb, 21, 230, 231, 258n, 259n
ḥijāj, 94
ḥikma (pl. *ḥikam*), 10, 17, 24, 35, 41, 65, 67, 104, 112, 113, 114, 115, 135, 136, 149, 155, 156, 157, 241, 253n, 274n; *see also* philosophy, wisdom
Ḥikmat Āl Dāʾūd, 10
ḥikmī, 88, 89, 153, 154, 155
ḥilm, 117, 127; *see also* forbearance
al-hind, 36, 44, 64, 67, 68, 69, 277n
  Kitāb Adab mulūk ~, 68
  see also India(n), Indic
ḥisba, 210
Homs, 242
al-Ḥudaybiya, 176
ḥujja (*ḥujaj*), 92, 94, 100, 115, 136, 215
ḥukm, 85, 114, 205, 214, 215
ḥukūma, 157, 215
humility, 121, 122, 127, 228, 244; *see also* *tawāḍu*ᶜ
humours, 151, 152, 153
Ḥunayn, 220
Hurmuz(d), son of Shāpūr, 49
Hurmuz(d), son of Anūshīrvān, 50
Ḥusayn al-Khādim, 129, 293n
Ḥusayn b. ᶜAlī b. Abī Ṭālib, 177
al-Ḥusayn b. ᶜAlī al-Marwazī (al-Marwarrūdhī), 106, 169, 236, 237, 248, 289n
Ibn ᶜAbd Rabbih, 6, 44, 49, 52
  al-ᶜIqd al-farīd, 44, 49, 52
Ibn ᶜAbd al-Razzāq, 38, 39, 40
Ibn Abī Dharr, 9, 50, 56, 67, 209
Ibn Abī Duʾād, 134
Ibn Abī Uṣaybiᶜa, 66
  ᶜUyūn al-anbāʾ fī ṭabaqāt al-aṭibbāʾ, 66
Ibn al-Athīr, 236, 237
Ibn Farīghūn, 7, 158, 160
  Jawāmiᶜ al-ᶜulūm, 7–8, 158, 160
Ibn Ḥawqal, 167, 211
Ibn Isfandiyār, 45, 66, 67
Ibn al-Jawzī, 68, 251
Ibn Khālawayh, 252
Ibn al-malik wa-l-nāsik, 69
Ibn Masᶜūd, 30
Ibn al-Muqaffaᶜ, 8, 9, 10, 17, 20, 33, 36, 45, 51, 54, 56, 58, 59, 60, 61, 65, 66, 67, 101, 248, 250
  al-Ādāb al-kabīr, 8, 65
  al-Adab al-ṣaghīr, 65
  Risāla fī l-ṣaḥāba, 9, 33
al-Yatīma, 65; *see also Kalīla wa-Dimna*
Ibn al-Muᶜtazz, 104, 162, 285n
Ibn al-Nadīm, 7, 46, 50, 54, 56, 66, 67, 69, 111
  al-Fihrist, 56, 66
Ibn Razīn, 46, 68
Ibn Sīnā, 42
Ibn Qutayba, 4, 5, 6, 44, 45, 48, 49, 51, 52, 53, 55, 56, 59, 60, 61, 64, 65
  ᶜUyūn al-akhbār, 4, 44, 45, 48, 51, 52, 53, 55, 56, 60, 64
Ibn al-Sammāk, 25, 27
Ibn Ziyād *see* al-Rabīᶜ b. Ziyād
Ibn al-Zubayr, 193
Ibrāhīm b. al-ᶜAbbās, 242
Ibrāhīm b. ᶜAbdallāh, 26
Ibrāhīm b. Aḥmad b. Ismāᶜīl, 236–7
idrāk, 80, 81, 112, 115
ifrāṭ, 126, 298n
iḥsān, 120, 170, 198, 234; *see also* kindness
iḥtijāb, 179
ijmāᶜ, 107, 108, 109, 136; *see also* consensus
ijtihād, 50, 100, 101, 108
ikhtilāl, 14
ikhtiyār, 187; *see also* choice
ikhtiyārī, 80
ᶜilm, 22, 80, 81, 82, 89, 90, 99, 104, 106, 107, 108, 114, 116, 135, 136, 186, 204, 263n
  al-ᶜilm al-ilāhī, *al-ᶜulūm al-ilāhiyya*, 90, 91, 102
  al-ᶜilm al-insānī, 102

al-ᶜilm al-muṭlaq, 90
see also knowledge, *al-ᶜulūm al-ḥikmiyya*, *al-ᶜulūm al-milliyya*
ᶜilm al-akhlāq, 73
ᶜilm al-āthār, 18
ᶜilm al-dīn, 90, 91, 92, 96, 97, 112, 138
ᶜilm al-fiqh, 99, 102
ᶜilm al-kalām, 91, 92, 97
ᶜilm al-mawāᶜiẓ, 91, 101
ᶜilm al-qaḍāʾ, 216
ᶜilm al-raʾy, 18
ᶜilm al-sharāʾiᶜ, 99
ᶜilm al-siyāsa, *ᶜilm al-siyāsāt*, 96, 99
ᶜilm al-tawḥīd, 90
Ilyās b. Isḥāq, 236
īmān, 78, 83, 92, 93, 166, 200; *see also* faith
improve, improvement, 24, 33, 34, 137, 195, 202, 206, 217, 230; *see also iṣlāḥ*
Imruʾ al-Qays, 156
ᶜinād, 98, 107, 235; *see also* obstinacy, *ᶜunūd*
increase, 132, 133, 168, 169; *see also ziyāda*
India(n), Indic, 36, 37, 38, 44, 45, 51, 60–70, 77, 104, 115, 196, 200, 201, 206, 223, 226, 231; *see also al-hind*
indirect address, 6
ingratitude, 118, 238, 239
injustice, 22, 26, 85, 93, 121, 166, 168, 169, 170, 188, 190, 191, 197, 198, 199, 205, 208, 214, 216, 218, 222, 223, 224, 226, 228, 231, 233; *see also jawr*, oppression, *ẓulm*
innovation, 9, 30, 104, 110, 234; *see also bidᶜa*
innovator, 232
intelligent person(s), persons of rational intelligence, 10, 11, 21, 22, 90, 111, 112, 119, 122, 128, 131, 174, 192, 232, 245; *see also ahl al-ᶜaql*, *ahl al-ᶜuqūl*, *ᶜāqil*, *ᶜuqalāʾ*
iqṭāᶜ, 167, 168, 193
iqtibās, 36
iṣābat al-ḥaqq, 107, 108
Isḥāq b. Aḥmad, 213, 236
ᶜishq, 104, 155, 156, 298n
iṣlāḥ, 137, 145; *see also* improve, improvement
ism (pl. *asmāʾ*), 67, 77, 78, 79, 115, 150, 151, 202
al-asmāʾ al-ḥusnā, 150
ᶜiṣma (pl. *ᶜiṣam*), 76, 175
Ismāᶜīl b. Aḥmad, 41, 58, 178, 182
Ismaᶜili, Ismaᶜiliyya, 76, 106, 109, 247, 248, 289n
al-Iṣṭakhrī, 167, 236
istidlāl, 96, 108, 185
istikhfāf, 105
istikhrāj, 96, 135
iṣṭināᶜ, 140, 165
istiqāmat al-ṭarīqa, 122, 126
istiṣlāḥ, 33, 189, 222; *see also iṣlāḥ*, *maṣlaḥa*, *ṣalāḥ*
iᶜtiqād, 32, 80, 81, 83, 105, 106; *see also* conviction
ᶜiyān, 81

Jacob, 118
Jaᶜfar b. Yaḥyā al-Barmakī, 129
jāhiliyya, 77
al-Jāḥiẓ, 45, 59, 67, 74, 106, 123, 124, 125, 133, 134, 143, 250
al-Akhlāq al-maḥmūda wa-l-madhmūma, 73, 133
al-Maᶜāsh wa-l-maᶜād, 73, 123, 133–4
jalsa, 74; *see also majlis*, *mujālasa*
jamāᶜa, 11, 12, 148, 199, 235, 241
Jāvīdān khirad, 65, 250
jawr, 93, 198; *see also ẓulm*
al-Jayhānī, 37, 99, 274n
jaysh (pl. *juyūsh*), 175, 181, 182, 183, 186
Jesus, 177
jihād, 31, 32, 84, 164, 165, 174, 175, 222
jīl (pl. *jiyal*), 77, 115, 148
jins, 90, 128, 148, 203
jirāyāt, 166
jizya, 188, 189, 207; *see also* poll-tax
jocularity, 115
Joseph, 118
jottings, 36
judge, 39, 100, 134, 167, 181, 184, 186, 202, 214, 215, 216, 218, 227; *see also ḥākim*, *qāḍī*
julūs, 230
jumhūr, 234
jund (pl. *junūd*), 13, 141, 145, 175, 190, 202, 204
jurisconsult, 100; *see also muftī*
jurisprudence, 18, 22, 29, 91, 99, 101, 109, 138, 159, 214; *see also fiqh*
jurist, 19, 25, 29, 33, 76, 100, 103, 156, 201, 202, 244; *see also faqīh*
justice, 8, 23, 26, 32, 50, 51, 75, 78, 83, 85, 88, 112, 113, 116, 126, 127, 131, 169, 170, 173, 180, 182, 187, 188, 189, 191, 197, 198, 199, 200, 201, 203, 204, 205, 207, 208, 209, 211, 213, 214, 215, 216, 221, 223, 225, 226, 228, 230, 231, 239, 244
circle of ~, 50–1, 188, 189
see also ᶜadl

Ka^c^ba, 129
al-Ka^c^bī, Abū l-Qāsim, 33, 75, 76, 78, 80, 81, 82, 83, 84, 85, 87, 96, 98, 108, 123, 152, 160, 176, 177, 213, 246, 248
  Kayfiyyat al-istidlāl bi-l-shāhid ^c^alā l-ghā^ɔ^ib, 96
  Maqālāt, 76
  Qabūl al-akhbār, 33
  Tafsīr, 33
kabīra (pl. *kabā^ɔ^ir*), 78, 79, 84, 130, 164, 171, 179
kafā^ɔ^a, 149; *see also* marriage, equality in ~
kalām, 82, 91, 92, 95, 101
  ^c^ilm al-kalām, 91, 92, 97
Kalīla wa-Dimna, 3, 8, 10, 20, 36, 38, 39–40, 43, 49, 52, 60–5, 67, 68, 69, 157, 161
karāma (pl. *karāmāt*), 207
karma, 63
Kārnāmak i Artaxšēr i Pāpakān, 158, 160
Karrāmiyya, 74, 125
Kārwand, 59
kātib (pl. *kuttāb*), 96, 145, 181, 182, 183, 184, 186, 270n
  ~ *al-rasā^ɔ^il*, 182, 183; *see also* secretary
Kayānids, 40
Kaykā^ɔ^ūs, 5, 161, 162
  Qābūsnāmeh, 5, 161, 162
khabar (pl. *akhbār*), 6, 25, 27, 33, 35, 81, 90, 97, 98, 99, 115, 117, 129, 130, 135, 136, 155, 156, 181, 183, 191, 193
khadam, 13, 14, 16, 140, 144, 145, 146, 148, 163, 164, 169, 170, 171, 174, 180, 181, 184, 202, 204, 248
khalīfa (pl. *khulafā^ɔ^*)
  caliph, 14, 17, 97, 99, 156
  deputy, 181, 182, 183, 190, 214, 244
khamriyya, 156
kharāj, 50, 182, 188, 201; *see also* land-tax
Kharijites, 79, 94
khaṣm, 109
khāṣṣa, khāṣṣ, khawāṣṣ, 13, 22, 23, 56, 73, 87, 88, 95, 120, 121, 122, 139, 140, 141, 142, 145, 146, 147, 148, 160, 162, 163, 166, 167, 168, 169, 170, 171, 172, 173, 174, 175, 176, 177, 178, 179, 180, 181, 182, 184, 185, 189, 195, 196, 202, 203, 205, 209, 210, 224, 225, 229, 230, 231, 232, 234, 249
al-Khaṭṭābī, Ḥamd b. Muḥammad, 31, 32, 263n
  al-^c^Uzla, 32
Khawla, 150
khidma, 20, 140, 146, 165, 169, 192, 193, 219, 247
khirad, 17
Khudaynāmeh, 9, 39, 50, 58, 61
Khurasan, 5, 68, 76, 167, 207, 240, 248, 301n
khurūj, 32; *see also* rebellion, revolt
Khusraw Parvīz, 12, 16, 20, 51, 52, 56, 57, 125, 272n, 273n
khuṭba, 5, 158, 206, 237; *see also* oration
Khwarazm, 45, 66
al-Khwārazmī, 39, 73, 89, 147, 153, 167, 168, 181, 182, 183
  Mafātīḥ al-^c^ulūm, 39, 147, 153, 168
kidhb, 39, 119
al-Kindī, 7, 37, 66, 70, 82, 88, 91, 102, 108, 113, 114
  'On Definitions', 113
Kindian tradition, 7, 41, 68, 73, 74, 91, 92, 113, 135, 205
kindness, 120, 127, 150, 163, 170, 172, 180, 189, 192, 200, 201, 218, 219, 227, 234, 235, 241, 243, 244; *see also iḥsān*
Kirman, 237
Kisrā, 51, 56
Kisrā Anūshīrvān, 51, 226
kitāb (pl. *kutub*), 3, 7, 17, 24, 36, 48, 49, 51, 52, 54, 55, 56, 61, 64, 65, 67, 69, 75, 103, 154, 156, 194, 221, 223, 238, 250
  kitāb dīnī, 75, 154
Kitāb Ādāb mulūk al-hind, 68
Kitāb Bilawhar wa-Būdhāṣaf, 69
Kitāb al-Budd, 69
Kitāb Būdhāṣaf al-mufrad, 69
kitāb (*kutub*) *lil-hind*, 64, 67, 277n
kitāb al-rusūm, 53
Kitāb al-Sa^c^āda wa-l-is^c^ād, 9, 50, 56, 209
Kitāb al-Tāj, 3, 20, 45, 46, 48, 52, 54, 55–8, 75, 160, 171, 226
knowledge, 11, 22, 23, 24, 37, 40, 44, 52, 53, 56, 57, 59, 60, 61, 64, 74, 79, 80, 81, 82, 83, 84, 88, 89, 90, 91, 92, 93, 94, 95, 97, 98, 99, 101, 102, 103, 104, 106, 107, 108, 112, 114, 115, 116, 117, 120, 123, 126, 136, 138, 152, 155, 156, 157, 158, 159, 171, 173, 175, 182, 186, 189, 201, 204, 214, 215, 218, 231, 232, 238, 239, 244; *see also ^c^ilm, ma^c^rifa*
Kufa, 45, 216, 223
kufr, 77, 78, 92, 106, 179
kunya, 150, 297n

la^c^b, 133; *see also lahw wa-la^c^b*
Labīd, 157
lahw al-ḥadīth, 64

lahw wa-la^c^b, 105, 161, 225, 232
land-tax, 182, 188, 189, 201, 210; *see also kharāj*
language, 36, 37, 43, 67, 70, 79, 91, 92, 96, 108, 113, 115, 137, 141, 153, 154, 155, 159, 164, 186, 250, 276n, 296n
  instruction in Arabic ~, 92, 153, 155–6, 157, 250
Lecomte, G., 56
Līlī b. Nuᶜmān, 236
lineage, 42, 148, 218, 287n
  intellectual ~, 123
  nobility of ~, 148, 149, 305n
  pollution of ~, 148, 149
love, 11, 13, 16, 28, 39, 87, 88, 104, 106, 108, 112, 117, 121, 122, 128, 150, 155, 156, 170, 179, 204, 206, 219, 227, 234, 243, 249, 257n; *see also ᶜishq, maḥabba*
love stories, 39, 156
lovers, 156
loyalty, 118, 121, 146, 168, 171, 175, 180, 185, 197, 206, 207, 219, 221, 243; *see also wafāʾ*
lugha, 114, 115, 153, 159, 276n; *see also* language
Luqmān, 17, 121, 127
luṭf, 179, 180

maᶜād, 5, 62, 73, 75
maᶜāsh, 73, 75
al-Madāʾin, 226
al-Madāʾinī, 36
maḍarra (pl. *maḍārr*), 19, 20, 33, 220; *see also ḍarar*
mādda, 187, 204, 205
madḥ see praise
madhhab (pl. *madhāhib*), 12, 22, 91, 94, 95, 97, 99, 105, 106, 107, 109, 110, 111, 122, 171, 172, 234
mafsada (pl. *mafāsid*), 33
maghāzī, 91, 97, 156
mahāba, 76, 88, 170
maḥabba, 13, 170, 227; *see also* love
maḥfil (pl. *maḥāfil*), 93, 157, 234; *see also majlis*
maḥjūb, 20, 21, 94, 258n; *see also ḥijāb*
Maḥmūd of Ghazna, 5, 39, 162
Maḥmūd al-Warrāq, 231
majlis (pl. *majālis*), 19, 29, 30, 32, 54, 55, 93, 103, 104, 106, 159, 216, 224, 228, 234
majlis al-ᶜiẓa, 30
Majūs, 39
Mākān b. Kākī, 236, 237
mamlaka (pl. *mamālik*), 28, 95, 110, 118, 170, 175, 181, 182, 202, 203, 204, 229, 233, 241, 244, 245
mamlakeh-yi khāṣṣ, 182
mamlūk (pl. *mamālīk*), 145, 146
al-Maʾmūn, 5, 35, 76, 98, 227, 228
maᶜnā (pl. *maᶜānī*), 47, 79, 91, 107, 115, 178, 194, 276n, 282n
manfaᶜa (pl. *manāfiᶜ*), 19, 20, 33, 220; *see also nafᶜ*, usefulness, utility
manly virtue, 8, 121, 133, 222, 235; *see also muruwwa*
manshūrāt, 104
al-Manṣūr, 25, 26, 35, 255n, 261n
Manṣūr b. Aḥmad, 236
Manṣūr b. Isḥāq, 236
Manṣūr b. Nūḥ, 160, 167
al-manzila bayn al-manzilatayn, 75, 78, 301n
maqāla (pl. *maqālāt*), 76, 91, 109, 110, 234; *see also* doctrine
Mardāvīj b. Ziyār, 237
maᶜrifa, 22, 79, 80, 81, 82, 90, 91, 99, 112, 114, 120, 123, 204, 232, 282n
  maᶜrifat Allāh, 79, 80, 81, 82, 90, 91, 112, 114
  maᶜrifat al-milla, 91
  see also knowledge
marriage, 100, 146, 148, 149, 152
  equality in ~, 148, 149
Marv, 45, 266n
marzubān (pl. *marāziba*), 51
mashaqqa, 108
mashāyikh, 191; *see also* elders
mashāyikh Samarqand, 82, 289n
mashriq, 18
maᶜshūq, 104; *see also* beloved
maṣlaḥa (pl. *maṣāliḥ*), 12, 33, 59, 75, 114, 205, 241, 250, 264n, 280n; *see also ṣalāḥ*
Masrūr al-Khādim, 293n
al-Masᶜūdī, 46, 49, 53
al-Māturīdī, 41, 76, 81, 82, 85, 87, 89, 108, 114
  Radd al-Kaᶜbī fī waᶜīd al-fussāq, 85; *see also Pandnāmeh-yi Māturīdī*
Māturīdī, Māturīdiyya, 41, 80, 81, 83, 89, 102, 108
maᶜūna, 13, 130, 131, 167, 179
mawᶜiẓa (pl. *mawāᶜiẓ*), 11, 13, 14, 19, 44, 62, 91, 102, 251, 253n
ᶜilm al-mawāᶜiẓ, 91, 101, 288n; *see also waᶜẓ*
al-Maydānī, 29, 126
Maysarī, Ḥakīm, 42
maysir, 84, 177, 210
maẓālim, 58, 100, 101, 157, 158, 214, 223, 227, 231; *see also* grievance(s)

Mecca, 220, 221
medicine, 102, 152–3
Medina, 129
memory, 11, 13, 29, 59, 60, 62, 70, 92, 130, 131, 137, 155, 156, 161, 227; *see also* remembrance
merchant, 157, 218, 220
mercy, 80, 130, 131, 133, 144, 179, 191, 197, 198, 199, 203, 217, 227, 242; *see also* compassion
merit, 77, 115, 116, 132, 168, 169, 218, 219, 232, 243
mihna, 22
miḥna, 213
Mihragan (Mihrajan), 48, 58, 224
milla (pl. *milal*), 22, 77, 85, 91, 93, 94, 95, 97, 104, 105, 110, 118, 121, 136, 137, 138, 148, 149, 151, 153, 154, 187, 203, 204, 207, 208, 236
millī, 88, 89
minimalism, minimalist, 235, 247; *see also* sum
miracle, 97, 207
mirror, 24
mirrors for princes, 3, 4, 6–7, 74, 103, 248, 248–9, 250, 251, 252
Miskawayh, 65, 127, 139, 156
mizāj, 151, 152
mōbadh, 39, 54, 224, 225
mōbadhān mōbadh, 39, 224
moderation, 127, 128, 166
Moses, 176
Mosul, 61, 68
mother, 148, 151, 152, 158
Mottahedeh, R. P., 165
al-muʾallafa qulūbuhum, 220, 221, 239
Muʿāwiya b. Abī Sufyān, 35, 57, 94, 217, 221, 229
muʿāyana, 88
al-Mubashshir b. Fātik, 65, 66
muftī, 100
Muḥammad b. al-Ḥanafiyya, 150
Muḥammad b. al-Ḥusayn b. Mutt, 236
Muḥammad b. Ilyās, 237
Muḥammad b. ʿAbdallāh *see* al-Nafs al-Zakiyya
Muḥammad b. Zayd al-Dāʿī, 76
Muḥammadī, M., 55
muḥtasib, 182
mujālasa (pl. *mujālasāt*), 19, 103, 105
muʿjiza (pl. *muʿjizāt*), 97
mujrim, 117; *see also* criminal
mulhid (pl. *malāḥida*, *mulḥidūn*), 95
mulūk al-ʿajam, 24, 54, 56, 57, 154
muʾmin (pl. *muʾminūn*), 77, 79, 83
munāfiq (pl. *munāfiqūn*), 240
munāẓara, 96, 106, 157, 234; *see also* debate, disputation
Muntakhab Ṣiwān al-ḥikma, 66
al-Murādī, Abū l-Ḥusayn Muḥammad, 160
Murjiʾa, 79, 80, 83
muruwwa (pl. *murūʾāt*), 9, 41, 133, 222, 235, 266n; *see also* manly virtue
al-Muṣʿabī, 106, 289n
mushāhada, 80, 81, 88, 110
mushrif, 183, 191, 193
mushrik, 240
musicians, 103, 106
al-Mustaḍīʿ, 251
mustawfī, 182
muṭālaʿa, 104
mutanabbiʾ, 12, 111; *see also* pseudo-prophet
mutaqārib, 42
al-Mutawakkil, 45
Muʿtazila, 25, 26, 28, 41, 73, 75, 76, 78, 79, 80, 81, 82, 83, 84, 86, 87, 90, 92, 94, 96, 101, 102, 108, 109, 113, 114, 131, 134, 137, 143, 163, 165, 166, 167, 178, 180, 185, 199, 210, 239, 249, 250
Baghdadi ~, 75, 82, 87, 123, 176, 250
Basran ~, 79, 82, 108
muṭīʿ, 77; *see also ṭāʿa*

al-Naḍr b. al-Ḥārith b. Kalada, 64–5, 157
nafʿ, 20, 33, 89, 90, 92; *see also manfaʿa*, usefulness, utility
nafs (pl. *anfus*), 8, 9, 13, 73, 82, 100, 108, 113, 116, 121, 132, 133, 159, 198
al-Nafs al-Zakiyya, 26
name(s) *see ism*, *kunya*
naqīb (pl. *nuqabāʾ*), 181, 183
naqīb al-nuqabāʾ, 183
narrative, 6, 25, 27, 30, 31, 35, 39, 40, 43, 44, 46, 57, 58, 59, 61, 63, 69, 90, 129, 130, 138, 154, 155, 156, 160, 173, 196, 201, 225, 228, 252; *see also asmār*, fable, *khabar*, story, tale
Narshakhī, 147, 181, 182
Nasaf, 207
al-Nasafī, Abū l-Muʿīn, 89, 108, 114
nāṣiḥ, 23, 232; *see also* counsellor
naṣīḥa (pl. *naṣāʾiḥ*), 5, 8, 9, 11–12, 13, 15, 16, 18, 19, 21, 24, 28–34, 42, 44, 61, 119, 175, 207, 215
nāsik (pl. *nussāk*), 64, 69, 111, 218, 232, 244; *see also* ascetic

Naṣr I b. Aḥmad, 183
Naṣr II b. Aḥmad, 21, 38, 76, 105, 106, 111, 147, 160, 181, 182, 193, 213, 219, 236, 237, 239, 243
Naṣr b. Muḥammad b. Mutt, 237
Naṣr b. Sayyār, 240
Naṣr Allāh Munshī, 61
natural characteristics, natural qualities, 24, 152
nature, 11, 14, 28, 79, 114, 122, 123, 151, 152, 153, 161, 164, 166, 192, 203, 232, 238, 250; *see also ṭabīʿa*
nawāfil, 164, 166
Nawruz, 48, 58, 224
naẓar, 57, 80, 81, 96, 100, 101, 103, 107, 108, 157
naẓarī, 80
nāzila (pl. *nawāzil*), 100
al-Naẓẓām, 82, 123, 250
network, 142, 145, 243
niḥla (pl. *niḥal*), 77, 91, 115, 148
niʿma (pl. *niʿam*), 120, 122, 132, 133, 146, 191, 232
Nishapur, 182, 237
nīti, 66
nītiśāstra, 66
Niẓām al-Mulk, 58, 111, 166, 168, 168–9, 193, 208, 251
  Siyar al-mulūk of ~, 58, 251
Nūḥ b. Asad, 183
Nūḥ b. Manṣūr, 42
Nūḥ b. Naṣr, 42
nuṣḥ, 23, 31; *see also naṣīḥa*

oath, 100, 172, 216, 217, 223
obedience, 12, 32, 63, 77, 78, 84, 93, 120, 140, 165, 166, 168, 180, 203, 204, 207, 208, 212, 218, 219, 236, 238, 239, 240, 257n, 270n, 275n; *see also ṭāʿa*
obscenity, 84, 119, 121, 159
obstinacy, 164, 234, 235, 238; *see also ʿinād, ʿunūd*
oppression, 84, 93, 188, 198, 222, 226, 230; *see also jawr, ẓulm*
optimal *see (al-)aṣlaḥ*
oration, 91, 158; *see also khuṭba*
ordinances, 23, 85, 90, 95, 99, 100, 137, 142, 169, 186, 233, 235; *see also aḥkām*
Oxus, 73, 248

Pacha, A. Z., 58
pahlavān, 39
Pali, 60
Pañcatantra, 40, 61
pand, 42
Pandnāmeh-yi Māturīdī, 41
Pandnāmeh of Sebüktigin, 5, 168, 169, 192
panaegyric, 134
panaegyrist, 106, 133
parallelism, 5
partiality, 85, 169, 171, 174, 208, 211, 212, 214, 216, 225
passion(s), 14, 19, 21, 28, 33, 50, 114, 121, 214
patience, 8, 9, 122, 123, 165, 228, 242, 243; *see also ṣabr*
penalties, stipulated *see ḥadd*
Persepolis *see* Takht-i Jamshīd
Persian(s), 23, 24, 37, 40, 42, 44, 48, 49, 51, 53, 54, 56, 57, 58, 59, 65, 73, 114, 154, 158, 161, 206, 226, 229; *see also al-furs*
  Middle ~, 4, 8, 9, 10, 28, 29, 36, 37, 38, 40, 44, 50, 53, 55, 58, 59, 60, 61, 66, 146, 160
  New ~, 4, 5, 36, 37, 38, 39, 40, 41, 44, 45, 49, 58, 59, 60, 61, 73, 106, 129, 148, 154, 161, 162, 250
philosopher, 15, 16, 17, 24, 27, 37, 43, 44, 65, 80, 88, 103, 105, 108, 111, 115, 118, 127, 149, 174, 226, 257n, 285n; *see also faylasūf, ḥakīm*
philosophy, 73, 92, 108, 113, 115, 135, 138, 152
  definition of ~, 74, 113
physical education, physical training, 116, 158, 160
Pīshdādīyān, 40
Plato, Platonic, 44, 77, 104, 113, 127, 140, 268n, 311n
pleasure, 10, 13, 20, 28, 62, 63, 64, 105, 106, 128, 131, 132, 174
Pledge of Good Pleasure, 176
poet(s), 38, 42, 77, 104, 105, 106, 132, 151, 157, 160, 231, 240, 241, 242
poetry, 6, 24, 37, 38, 39, 41, 60, 77, 105, 106, 155, 156, 157, 159, 192, 196, 250
poll-tax, 188, 189, 207; *see also jizya*
polo, 53, 160–1
power, 3, 4, 6, 20, 23, 26, 27, 30, 31, 32, 34, 42, 80, 82, 99, 113, 116, 117, 118, 120, 121, 129, 132, 134, 137, 138, 146, 147, 167, 170, 177, 190, 195, 202, 208, 209, 218, 220, 222, 230, 232, 233, 235, 236, 237, 238, 244, 248, 250; *see also shawka, sulṭān*
praise, 11, 13, 15, 19, 22, 24, 73, 77, 78, 79, 86, 89, 115, 116, 117, 118, 119, 122, 126, 128, 130, 131, 132, 133, 134, 136, 163, 179, 180, 198, 206, 220, 225, 230, 245

praiseworthy, 22, 26, 28, 62, 73, 88, 99, 100, 123, 126, 131, 132, 133, 134, 155, 161, 164, 174, 226, 227
prayer(s), 5, 84, 123, 124, 164, 177, 199, 200, 206, 207, 228
funeral ~, 101
public ~, 5, 13, 206, 207, 213, 248
ritual ~, 84, 100, 123, 124, 164, 199, 200
congregational ~, 206
festival ~, 207
preacher, 19, 29, 30, 68, 251; *see also wāᶜiẓ*
prisoner(s), 22, 212, 213, 250
promise, 14, 119, 120, 197, 204, 223
promise and threat, 75, 83, 131, 173, 223, 238, 239
prose, 4, 6, 8, 38, 39, 43, 45, 61, 265n
prosody, 155
proverb, 29, 126, 221
proximity, 16, 86, 129, 139, 140, 146, 163, 168, 203, 219, 249
Pseudo-Callisthenes, 44
pseudo-prophet, 12, 16, 111; *see also mutanabbiʾ*
punishment, 30, 75, 77, 78, 79, 83, 84, 85, 117, 119, 121, 131, 142, 143, 144, 164, 170, 171, 172, 173, 174, 180, 191, 195, 197, 212, 212, 213, 223, 224, 241, 243
puruṣārthas, 62

qaḍāʾ, 174, 182, 192, 216, 232
wallā qaḍāʾ, 193
qāḍī (pl. *quḍāt*), 100, 167, 184, 186, 214, 216, 223, 224; *see also* judge
qāḍī l-quḍāt, 227
Qaḥṭaba b. Ḥumayd, 227
qāʾid (pl. *quwwād*), 13, 145, 167, 190
Qaratigin, 236
Qarmaṭī, 109, 213
al-Qāsim b. ᶜAbd al-Raḥmān, 200
qaṣaṣ, 30
Qays b. ᶜĀṣim al-Minqarī, 220
Qayṣar, 51
qiṣāṣ, 223; *see also* retribution
qisṭ, 85, 133, 197, 198, 200; *see also* equity
Qudāma b. Jaᶜfar, 139
qudra, 78, 82, 84, 116, 123, 202; *see also* capacity, power
Quraysh, 177, 203, 220
quṭb al-siyāsa, 93
Qutham b. Jaᶜfar b. Sulaymān, 129

al-Rabīᶜ b. Ziyād al-Ḥārithī, 41
rāᶜī (pl. *ruᶜāt*), 12, 167, 201, 202, 203, 232
raʾīs (pl. *ruʾasāʾ*), 135, 190
al-Raʾīs al-Nasafī, Saᶜīd b. Ibrāhīm, 213
raᶜiyya (pl. *raᶜāyā*), 12, 13, 48, 100, 137, 144, 157, 162, 167, 187, 200, 201, 202, 203, 204, 206, 207, 214, 215, 223, 224, 229, 231, 232, 244
Ramadan, 142
Rāshidūn (Rightly Guided Caliphs), 14, 17, 35, 57, 75, 97, 176, 201, 215
rasm (pl. *rusūm*), 24, 58, 75, 186, 188, 233; *see also kitāb al-rusūm*
raʾs māl, 204
rāwī (pl. *ruwāt*), 136, 159
raʾy (pl. *ārāʾ*), 9, 17, 18, 23, 33, 54, 96, 100, 114, 123, 234
ᶜilm al-raʾy, 18
rayb, 100, 159; *see also* doubt, *shubha*
al-Rayḥānī, ᶜAlī b. ᶜUbayda, 69
al-Rāzī, Muḥammad b. Zakariyyāʾ, 135
rebellion, 26, 31, 32, 93, 213, 219, 235, 236, 237, 247, 248; *see also khurūj*, revolt
rebels, 210, 211, 236, 243
rebuke, 31, 115, 133, 178; *see also* blame, censure
remembrance, 7, 28, 130, 131, 163, 230; *see also* memory
renunciant(s), 19, 25, 29, 81, 207, 248; *see also zāhid*
renunciation, 64, 86; *see also zuhd*
repentance, 85, 117, 118, 130, 131, 165, 213
reputation, 26, 40, 42, 50, 62, 63, 85, 88, 103, 119, 131, 132, 134, 137, 161, 170, 173, 174, 199, 204, 207, 226
repute, 63, 228
resolve, 123, 124, 125, 126, 127, 226, 238; *see also ḥazm*
retinue, 22, 140, 145, 163, 222; *see also ḥāshiya*
retribution, 213, 221, 223
revolt, 93, 95, 236, 237, 239, 248; *see also khurūj*, rebellion
reward, 12, 28, 30, 75, 78, 79, 83, 86, 87, 91, 103, 130, 143, 149, 168, 171, 173, 175, 179, 180, 204, 217, 220, 223, 225, 230, 232, 245
riʾāsa see riyāsa
ribāṭ, 175
riḍwān, 206
Rightly Guided Caliphs *see* Rāshidūn
Rigistān, 147, 182
risāla (pl. *rasāʾil*), 66, 153, 182, 183
riyāḍa, 73, 142
riyāḍat al-nafs, 73

riyāsa, *ri°āsa* (pl. *riyāsāt*, *ri°āsāt*), 54, 244, 247, 262n, 287n
rizq, 167, 192, 297n; *see also arzāq*
Rowson, E. K., 77
Rūdakī, 38, 39, 42, 60, 61, 106, 147, 265n
rūm, 65
Rustam, 39, 40, 41, 299n
Rustam b. Mihr-Hurmuzd al-Majūsī, 41

sa°āda, 92, 270n
ṣabr, 8, 9, 116, 122; *see also* patience
Sāb.t.r.m, 36, 65, 66, 67, 104
ṣadaqa (pl. *ṣadaqāt*), 100, 188, 189, 210, 211
al-Ṣafadī, 7
Saffarids, 160, 213
sage, 5, 7, 12, 14, 15, 17, 24, 36, 40, 42, 53, 61, 77, 121, 122, 131, 144, 161, 196, 223, 245; *see also ḥakīm*
ṣaghīra (pl. *ṣaghā°ir*), 130, 164, 170
ṣaḥāba, 9
ṣāḥib barīd, 167
ṣāḥib ḥaras, 181, 183
ṣāḥib shurat, 181, 182, 183
Sa°īd b. Ibrāhīm *see* al-Ra°īs al-Nasafī
ṣalāḥ, 12, 20, 24, 59, 86, 93, 110, 115, 137, 144, 145, 149, 167, 170, 204, 222, 250; *see also maṣlaḥa*
salaries *see waẓā°if*
Samarqand, 30, 81, 82, 87, 114, 125, 147, 182, 183, 236, 237
al-Samarqandī, Abū l-Layth, 30, 41, 82, 102, 143, 153, 154, 163, 175
Bustān al-°ārifīn, 153
Tanbīh al-ghāfilīn, 175
ṣāni° (pl. *ṣunnā°*), 140, 141, 165, 204, 205, 218; *see also* craftsman
ṣanī°a, 118, 120, 140, 170, 227, 231
Sanskrit, 40, 60, 66
al-Sarakhsī, 7
Ādāb al-mulūk, 7
al-Siyāsa al-kabīr, 7
al-Siyāsa al-ṣaghīr, 7
Zād al-musāfir wa-khidmat al-mulūk, 7
Sasanian(s), 9, 16, 20, 35, 38, 39, 40, 45, 46, 48, 49, 50, 52, 54, 55, 56, 57, 58, 60, 61, 67, 69, 70, 75, 125, 126, 160, 189, 196, 224
satire, 156
al-Sawād al-a°ẓam, 125
Sayf al-Dīn Ghāzī, 61
Schoeler, G., 36, 45
scholar(s), 15, 19, 21, 24, 25, 30, 31, 46, 67, 69, 82, 91, 101, 103, 104, 105, 114, 136, 137, 202, 207, 213, 218, 248, 251, 286n; *see also* °ulamā°
Sebüktigin, 5, 162, 168, 169
Pandnāmeh of ~ *see Pandnāmeh* of Sebüktigin
secret, 57, 67, 118, 119, 173, 175, 184, 217, 229, 236
secretary, 22, 69, 76, 96, 145, 158, 161, 181, 182, 183, 186; *see also kātib*
Secretum secretorum, 4
session, 19, 101, 103, 105, 158, 226, 227, 228; *see also* assembly, *majlis*
shāhnāmeh, 38, 39, 40, 59, 99, 277n
~ of Abū Manṣūr, 40
Older Preface to ~, 38, 40
Shāhnāmeh of Firdawsī, 39, 42, 53, 61
al-Shahrazūrī, 66
Rawḍat al-afrāḥ wa-nuzhat al-arwāḥ, 66
shahwa (pl. *shahawāt*), 19, 62, 123; *see also* desire
Shaked, Sh., 36, 47
shame, 121, 222, 235
Shānāq, 66
Shāpūr, 24, 35, 46, 47, 49, 57, 125, 189, 271n
Testament of ~ *see °Ahd Sābūr*
Shaqīq al-Balkhī, 81
sharī°a (pl. sharā°i°), 90, 91, 97, 99, 105, 118, 121, 137, 138, 148, 153, 164, 187, 208, 209, 233, 235, 264n
umm al- ~, 235
ẓāhir (*ẓawāhir*) *al-* ~, 137, 209
shawka, 235; *see also* power
Shi°a, 94
Shīrūya (Shīrawayh), 52, 56
shubha, 94, 135; *see also* doubt, *rayb*
Shuhayd-i Balkhī, 42, 289n
Shurayḥ b. al-Ḥārith b. Qays, 223
shurṭa see ṣāḥib shuraṭ
shu°ūbī, *shu°ūbiyya*, 37, 99
ṣidq, 39, 119, 132, 133, 156
ṣifa (pl. *ṣifāt*), 79, 82, 150, 169
ṣifāt al-dhāt, 82
ṣifāt al-fi°l, 82
Siffin, Battle of, 94
sifla, 222
Sīmjūr, 236
sin, 23, 78, 79, 80, 84, 85, 117, 118, 130, 135, 164, 165, 171, 172, 175, 179, 205, 223, 224; *see also kabīra*, *ṣaghīra*
ṣinā°a, 22, 89, 90, 91, 141, 155, 204, 205; *see also* craft
Sind, 109

Sindbād
Book of ~, 38, 39, 156
Kitāb ~, 156
Sindbādnāmeh, 38, 265n
singer(s), 103, 104, 106
sinner, 75, 85, 117, 163, 171, 172, 212
sīra, 12, 55, 56, 85, 126, 136, 200, 245; *see also* *siyar*
Sirr al-asrār, 3, 43, 69
Sistan, 31, 41, 266n
Sistani cycle, 39, 40
Ṣiwān al-ḥikma, 66
siyar, 9, 14, 17, 46, 50, 56, 57, 59, 67, 87, 97, 112, 135, 137, 156, 224; *see also sīra*
Siyar al-ᶜajam, 48, 58, 59
Siyar al-mulūk, 58, 59, 251
siyāsa (pl. *siyāsāt*), 7, 57, 68, 73, 88, 89, 91, 93, 96, 99, 100, 112, 139, 142, 157, 195, 197, 204, 220, 241, 245
siyāsat al-ᶜāmma, 73, 197–245
al-siyāsa al-ḥikmiyya al-milliyya, 88
siyāsat al-hind, 68, 69
siyāsat al-khāṣṣa, 73
siyāsat al-nafs, 73–138
al-Siyāsa al-ᶜāmmiyya, 43, 44
Siyāsat al-mulūk, 253n, 264n
Sogdia (Sughd), Sogdian, 165, 237
spies, 175, 191, 229, 230
stipend(s), 166, 167, 193, 199, 200; *see also* *arzāq*
story (stories), 37, 39, 40, 41, 42, 51, 61, 62, 64–5, 69, 118, 121, 154, 156, 157, 299n
Š.t.p.r.m, 67
study, 37, 93, 96, 99, 103, 104, 108, 153, 288n
Sufyān al-Thawrī, 25, 33, 260n
sukūn al-nafs, 108, 289n
Sulaymān b. ᶜAbd al-Malik, 179
sulṭān, 4, 6, 12, 31, 33, 48, 104, 134, 147, 190, 208, 212, 218, 223, 230, 231, 232, 244; *see also* power
sum, 31, 90, 103, 127; *see also* minimal, minimalism
sunna (pl. *sunan*), 9, 14, 17, 18, 29, 31, 35, 75, 85, 86, 87, 91, 93, 107, 108, 118, 122, 124, 135, 149, 153, 175, 177, 200, 208, 214, 215, 216, 223
sūqa, 132, 244
Syria, 30, 68, 207
Syriac, 61, 67

ṭāᶜa, 11, 12, 78, 93, 166, 168, 203, 207; *see also* obedience
taᵓaddub, 86, 245
taᶜaṣṣub, 59, 99, 107, 212, 213, 287n
~ *baladī*, 287n
~ *malakī*, 99
~ *nasabī*, 99, 287n
~ *al-qarāmiṭa*, 213
ṭabaqa (pl. *ṭabaqāt*), 66, 103, 115, 122, 145, 151, 229, 287n
ṭabaqāt al-nās, 218, 219
al-Ṭabarī, 38
History of ~, 38
Tafsīr, 38
Tabaristan, 5, 45, 76, 236
tabiᶜa, 63
ṭabīᶜa (pl. *ṭabāᵓiᶜ*), 11, 122, 123, 152, 203, 268n
tadabbur, 106, 131, 238
tadbīr, 66, 73, 128, 142, 185, 238, 241, 274n
taᵓdīb, 142, 146, 212, 234
tadhkīr, 30, 101, 263n
tafakkur, 80, 81, 106, 238
tafḍīl, 137, 139, 141, 176, 181, 195
tafrīṭ, 126
tafsīr, 97, 135, 157
al-Taghlibī, 20, 46, 48, 52, 54, 55, 56, 57, 58, 75, 160, 171
al-Ṭaḥāwī, 18
Bayān mushkil al-ḥadīth, 18
Maᶜānī l-āthār, 18
Ṭāhir b. al-Ḥusayn, 5, 6
Tahirids, 5
Takht-i Jamshīd, 38
taklīf, 113, 114, 143
tale(s), 40, 56, 59, 65, 67, 157, 276n; *see also* *asmār*, stories
Ṭalḥa, 94
taᶜlīm al-Qurᵓān, 153
ṭamaᶜ (pl. *aṭmāᶜ*), 167, 301n
Tamīm, 220
Tamīm al-Dārī, 30
Tansar, Letter of, 45, 66
taqiyy, 77, 79, 159
taqlīd, 14, 81, 101, 106, 108, 234
taqrīb, 134, 139, 163, 195, 218, 219, 232, 234, 243
taqwā, 5, 41, 63, 76–88, 91, 112, 137, 138, 159, 198, 281n
Ṭarafa b. al-ᶜAbd, 105
tasābuq, 218
tashjīr, 8
taswiya, 169
tawāḍuᶜ, 121, 127; *see also* humility

tawakkul, 123, 124, 125, 128
tawba see repentance
tawfiq, 130, 131, 179, 180
tawḥīd, 12, 41, 75, 82, 90, 91, 155, 164, 165
al-Tawḥīdī, Abū Ḥayyān, 37
taʾwīl (pl. *taʿwīlāt*), 15, 100, 101
tax, taxation, 21, 167, 183, 186, 188, 189, 192, 201, 207, 208, 210, 211, 250; *see also jizya, kharāj*, land-tax, poll-tax
teacher, 27, 44, 142, 143, 155, 158–60, 163
testament, 4, 5, 6, 23, 24, 35, 42, 44–5, 46, 47, 50, 53, 58, 65, 66, 104, 115, 140, 144, 221, 223, 231
- of an Indian king, 35–6, 65–8, 69, 104, 115, 200, 201, 223, 231; *see also ʿahd, ʿAhd Ardashīr, ʿAhd Sābūr, waṣiyya*
al-Thaʿālibī, 50, 55, 111, 149, 160, 251
Ādāb al-mulūk, 149, 251
Ghurar al-siyar, 50
ṭibāʿ, 24, 123; *see also* natural characteristics, nature
al-Tirmidhī, al-Ḥakīm, 18, 73
Kitāb al-Riyāḍa wa-adab al-nafs, 73
al-Tirmidhī, Abū ʿĪsā, 29
al-Jāmiʿ al-ṣaḥīḥ, 29
Transoxiana, 207, 262n
Tukharistan, 59, 60
al-Ṭurṭūshī, 25
Tus, 39, 40, 59
Ṭūsī, Naṣīr al-Dīn, 139, 156, 299n

ʿulamāʾ, 15, 19, 103, 104, 105, 128, 136, 142, 143, 144, 156, 191, 214, 215, 218; *see also* scholar(s)
al-ʿulūm al-ḥikmiyya, 89
al-ʿulūm al-milliyya, 89
ʿUmar b. al-Khaṭṭāb, 30, 35, 57, 104, 127, 136, 176, 199, 200, 201, 215, 216, 217, 221, 223, 229
Umayyad(s), 5, 35, 36, 41, 46, 55, 157, 179, 217, 240, 241, 243
umma (pl. *umam*), 12, 14, 73, 85, 98, 107, 136, 144
unbelief, 75, 77, 78, 92, 105, 106, 117, 118, 179; *see also kufr*
ʿunūd, 118, 238; *see also ʿinād*, obstinacy
ʿuqalāʾ, 11, 15, 105; *see also ahl al-ʿaql, ahl al-ʿuqūl, ʿāqil*, intelligent person(s)
usefulness, 89, 90, 115, 131; *see also manfaʿa, nafʿ*, utility
ʿushr, 188, 189, 306n; *see also* tax
al-uṣūl al-khamsa, 75, 80; *see also* five principles
ʿUthmān, 216, 223
utility, 20, 33, 90, 93; *see also manfaʿa, nafʿ*, usefulness

vakīl-i khāṣṣ, 184
vice, 23, 86, 128, 134, 135, 138
virtue, 18, 22, 31, 33, 47, 59, 74, 76, 77, 86, 88, 89, 97, 99, 100, 105, 110, 116, 120, 122, 123, 124, 126, 127, 128, 132, 134, 135, 136, 137, 138, 144, 148, 154, 155, 156, 157, 159, 163, 172, 185, 186, 189, 198, 202, 227, 228, 230, 245; *see also faḍīla*, manly virtue
virtuous, 6, 8, 11, 76, 77, 87, 88, 102, 103, 104, 105, 106, 110, 111, 116, 118, 121, 130, 131, 132, 133, 136, 145, 155, 159, 163, 173, 190, 231, 232, 234, 249; *see also fāḍil*
vizier, 20, 21, 22, 23, 36, 37, 38, 39, 42, 50, 61, 64, 66, 76, 89, 96, 97, 99, 106, 145, 146, 181, 182, 199, 200, 213, 228, 230, 231; *see also wazīr*
vizierate, 169, 176
Vushmgīr b. Ziyār, 237

al-waʿd wa-l-waʿīd, 75
wafāʾ, 119, 120, 133, 175, 203, 204, 219, 247
wāʿiẓ (pl. *wuʿʿāẓ*), 19, 29, 30, 251; *see also* preacher
wakīl (pl. *wukalāʾ*), 181, 183, 184, 186
wālī (pl. *wulāt*), 7, 19, 167, 186, 199, 229, 231, 257n
waqf (pl. *awqāf*), 101, 182, 183
al-Wāqidī, 36, 48, 53
Wāṣil b. ʿAṭāʾ, 26, 261n
waṣiyya (pl. *waṣāyā*), 4, 5, 6, 9, 65, 66, 77, 214; *see also ʿahd*, testament
Waṣiyyat Arisṭāṭālīs ilā l-Iskandar, 65, 66, 68
waʿz, 30, 242, 263n; *see also mawʿiẓa*
waẓāʾif, 105, 166, 210
wazīr (pl. *wuzarāʾ*), 22, 96, 98, 99, 145, 146, 181, 182
wuzarāʾ al-sūʾ, 64
see also vizier
wet-nurse, 151, 152, 158, 165
wilāya (pl. *wilāyāt*), 28, 170, 181, 192, 193, 244
wine, 84, 106, 156, 177, 210
wisdom, 3, 4, 8, 10, 15, 16, 17, 24, 27, 30, 34, 35, 37, 39, 40, 41, 42, 44, 49, 53, 58, 60, 61, 62, 65, 66, 68, 70, 74, 101, 112, 113, 114, 115, 116, 128, 135, 136, 155, 156, 157, 178, 180, 189, 192, 196, 209, 241, 145, 250, 252; *see also ḥikma*

xrad, 17

Yaḥyā b. Aḥmad b. Ismāᶜīl, 236, 237
Yaḥyā b. Aḥmad b. Asad, 182
Yaḥyā b. Aktham, 227, 228
Yaḥyā b. Khālid al-Barmakī, 36, 66
Yānis al-Khādim, 7
al-Yaᶜqūbī, 3
Yāqūt, 7
Yazdagird, 57, 125
Yazdagird 'the Sinner', 225, 312n
Yazīd b. Abī Sufyān, 221

Zabul, 39, 40
Ẓafarnāmeh, 42, 267n
zāhid (pl. *zuhhād*), 19, 29; *see also* renunciant(s)
zaᶜīm (pl. *zuᶜamāᵓ*), 68
zakāt (pl. *zakawāt*), 100, 188, 189, 207, 211
  zakāt al-fiṭr, 142
Zakeri, M., 69
Zāl, 39, 40
Zayd b. Thābit, 223
Zaydī, Zaydiyya, 177
zindīq (pl. *zanādiqa*), 95, 286n
Ziyād b. Abīhī, 57, 229
ziyāda, 168, 169; *see also* increase
Zoroastrian, Zoroastrianism, 17, 39
al-Zubayr, 94
zuhd, 29, 136, 155
zuhdiyyāt, 156
ẓulm, 93, 169, 198, 218, 222, 224, 231; *see also* injustice